THE WAITE GROUP®

OBJECT-ORIENTED PROGRAMMING IN MICROSOFT C++

ROBERT LAFORE

Galgotia Publications pvt. ltd.
5, Ansari Road, Daryaganj, New Delhi-110002

Robert Lafore
The Waite Group®
Object Oriented Programming in Microsoft C++ – 2000

© 1992 The Waite Group, Inc.

AUTHORIZED EDITION FOR SALE IN INDIA ONLY

ISBN : 81-85623-105-8

First published in India-1995   Reprinted – 2000

Printed at : Cambridge Printing Works, B-85,
Naraina Industrial Area, Phase-II, New Delhi - 28.

TABLE OF CONTENTS

Introduction   xix

A Note To Teachers   xxii

Chapter 1: The Big Picture   1

Chapter 2: Using Microsoft C++   19

Chapter 3: C++ Programming Basics   35

Chapter 4: Loops and Decisions   77

Chapter 5: Structures   129

Chapter 6: Functions   159

Chapter 7: Objects and Classes   205

Chapter 8: Arrays   241

Chapter 9: Operator Overloading   283

Chapter 10: Inheritance   323

Chapter 11: Microsoft C++ Graphics   371

Chapter 12: Pointers   415

Chapter 13: Virtual Functions and Other
            Subtleties   467

Chapter 14: Files and Streams   521

Chapter 15: Larger Programs   553

Chapter 16: Microsoft Foundation Classes   595

Chapter 17: Just for Fun   647

Appendix A: ASCII Table   679

Appendix B: Microsoft C++ Keywords   683

Appendix C: Using the Project Feature   685

Appendix D: Answers to Questions and Exercises   689

Appendix E: Bibliography   741

Index   743

Contents

INTRODUCTION XIX

Advantages of OOP xix
Languages and Development Platforms xix
What This Book Does xix
New Concepts xix
The Gradual Approach xx
What You Need to Know to Use This Book xx
Hardware and Software xx
Go For It xxi

A NOTE TO TEACHERS XXII

Treat C++ as a Separate Language xxii
Optimize Organization for OOP xxii
Substitute Superior C++ Features xxiii
Minimize Irrelevant Capabilities xxiii

CHAPTER 1: THE BIG PICTURE 1

Why Do We Need Object-Oriented Programming? 3
Procedural Languages 3
The Object-Oriented Approach 7
Characteristics of Object-Oriented Languages 9
Objects 9
Classes 11
Inheritance 12
Reusability 13
Creating New Data Types 14
Polymorphism and Overloading 14
C++ and C 14
Laying the Groundwork 15
Summary 16
Questions 16

CHAPTER 2: USING MICROSOFT C/C++ 19

Setting Up Microsoft C/C++ 21
If Windows Is Installed 21

If Windows Is Not Installed   22

Running the Programmer's WorkBench   22

Your First Program   23

Using the PWB Editor   23

Saving Your Program   24

Compiling and Linking   24

Running Your Program   27

Loading an Existing Source File   27

Errors   28

Compiler Errors   28

Linker Errors   29

Run-Time Errors   30

Conceptual Errors: Debugging   30

Conceptual Errors: The Browser   30

Compiler Warning Level   32

What to Read   32

Summary   33

CHAPTER 3: C++ PROGRAMMING BASICS   35

Basic Program Construction   37

Functions   37

Program Statements   38

White Space   39

Output Using cout   40

String Constants   40

Preprocessor Directives   41

The #include Directive   41

Header Files   42

Comments   42

Comment Syntax   42

When to Use Comments   43

Alternative Comment Syntax   43

Integer Variables   43

Defining Integer Variables   44

Declarations and Definitions   45

Variable Names   45

Assignment Statements   46

Integer Constants   46

Output Variations   46

Character Variables   47

Character Constants   47

Initialization 48
Escape Sequences 48
Input with c i n 50
Variables Defined at Point of Use 50
Cascading << 51
Expressions 51
Precedence 52
Type float 52
Floating-Point Constants 53
The const Qualifier 54
The #define Directive 54
Manipulators 54
The endl Manipulator 54
The setw manipulator 54
Type long 56
Cascading the Insertion Operator 56
Multiple Definitions 57
The IOMANIP.H Header File 57
Variable Type Summary 58
unsigned Data Types 59
Type Conversion 61
Automatic Conversions 61
Casts 62
Arithmetic Operators 64
The Remainder Operator 64
Arithmetic Assignment Operators 65
Increment Operators 67
Library Functions 69
Header Files 70
Library Files 70
Header Files and Library Files 70
Two Ways to Use #include 72
Summary 72
Questions 73
Exercises 75

CHAPTER 4: LOOPS AND DECISIONS 77
Relational Operators 79
Loops 81
The for Loop 81

for Loop Variations   86
The while Loop   87
Precedence: Arithmetic and Relational Operators   91
The do Loop   92
When to Use which Loop   93
Decisions   94
The if Statement   95
The if...else Statement   99
The else...if Construction   107
The switch Statement   108
The Conditional Operator   112
Logical Operators   115
The Logical AND Operator   115
The Logical OR Operator   117
The Logical NOT Operator   117
Precedence Summary   118
Other Control Statements   119
The break Statement   119
The continue Statement   122
The goto Statement   123
Summary   123
Questions   124
Exercises   126

CHAPTER 5: STRUCTURES   129

Structures   131
A Simple Structure   131
Specifying the Structure   132
Defining a Structure Variable   134
Accessing Structure Members   135
Other Structure Features   137
A Measurement Example   139
Structures within Structures   141
A Card Game Example   145
Structures and Classes   147
Enumerated Data Types   148
Days of the Week   148
Inventing a Boolean Type   151
Organizing the Cards   152
Specifying Integer Values   154

Not Perfect   154
Other Examples   155
Summary   155
Questions   156
Exercises   157

CHAPTER 6: FUNCTIONS   159

Simple Functions   161
The Function Declaration   162
Calling the Function   163
The Function Definition   164
Comparison with Library Functions   164
Eliminating the Declaration   164
Passing Arguments to Functions   167
Passing Constants   167
Passing Variables   168
Passing by Value   169
Passing Structure Variables   170
Names in the Declaration   173
Returning Values from Functions   173
The return Statement   174
Returning Structures Variables   177
Reference Arguments   178
Passing Simple Data Types by Reference   179
A More Complex Pass by Reference   182
Passing Structures by Reference   183
Notes on Passing by Reference   184
Overloaded Functions   185
Different Numbers of Arguments   185
Different Kinds of Arguments   187
Inline Functions   189
Default Arguments   191
Variables and Storage Classes   193
Automatic Variables   193
External Variables   195
Static Variables   197
Storage   198
Returning by Reference   199
Summary   200

Questions   201
Exercises   203

CHAPTER 7: OBJECTS AND CLASSES   205

A Simple Class   207
    Classes and Objects   208
    Specifying the Class   209
    Using the Class   212
C++ Objects as Physical Objects   214
C++ Objects as Data Types   215
Constructors   216
    A Counter Example   217
    Destructors   219
Objects as Function Arguments   220
    Overloaded Constructors   221
    Member Functions Defined Outside the Class   222
    Objects as Arguments   223
Returning Objects from Functions   225
A Card Game Example   228
Structures and Classes   231
Classes, Objects, and Memory   232
Static Class Data   233
What Does It All Mean?   236
Summary   237
Questions   237
Exercises   239

CHAPTER 8: ARRAYS   241

Array Fundamentals   243
    Defining Arrays   244
    Array Elements   245
    Accessing Array Elements   246
    Averaging Array Elements   246
    Initializing Arrays   247
    Multidimensional Arrays   248
    Passing Arrays to Functions   253
    Arrays of Structures   255
Arrays as Class Member Data   256

Arrays of Objects   260
    Arrays of English Distances   260
    Arrays of Cards   263
Strings   267
    String Variables   267
    Avoiding Buffer Overflow   268
    String Constants   269
    Reading Embedded Blanks   270
    Reading Multiple Lines   270
    Copying a String the Hard Way   271
    Copying a String the Easy Way   272
    Arrays of Strings   273
    Strings as Class Members   274
    A User-Defined String Type   276
Summary   278
Questions   278
Exercises   280

CHAPTER 8: OPERATOR OVERLOADING   283
Overloading Unary Operators   286
    The operator Keyword   287
    Operator Arguments   287
    Operator Return Values   288
    Nameless Temporary Objects   289
    Postfix Notation   291
Overloading Binary Operators   292
    Arithmetic Operators   292
    Adding Polar Coordinates   295
    Concatenating Strings   300
    Multiple Overloading   302
    Comparison Operators   302
    Arithmetic Assignment Operators   305
Data Conversion   307
    Conversions between Basic Types   308
    Conversions between Objects and Basic Types   308
    Conversions between Objects of Different Classes   313
    Conversions: When to Use What   317
Pitfalls of Operator Overloading and Conversion   318
    Use Similar Meanings   318

Use Similar Syntax   318
Show Restraint   319
Avoid Ambiguity   319
Not All Operators Can Be Overloaded   319
Summary   319
Questions   320
Exercises   322

CHAPTER 10: INHERITANCE   323

Derived Class and Base Class   325
Specifying the Derived Class   328
Accessing Base Class Members   328
The protected Access Specifier   330
Derived Class Constructors   332
Overriding Member Functions   334
Which Function Is Used?   336
Scope Resolution with Overridden Functions   336
Inheritance in the English Distance Class   337
Operation of ENGLEN   338
Constructions in DistSign   339
Member Functions in DistSign   339
Abetting Inheritance   340
Class Hierarchies   340
"Abstract" Base Class   344
Constructors and Member Functions   344
Public and Private Inheritance   344
Access Combinations   345
Classes and Structures   346
Access Specifiers: When to Use What   346
Levels of Inheritance   347
Multiple Inheritance   350
Member Functions in Multiple Inheritance   351
Constructors in Multiple Inheritance   356
Ambiguity in Multiple Inheritance   360
Containership: Classes within Classes   361
Inheritance and Program Development   365
Summary   366
Questions   367
Exercises   368

CHAPTER 11: MICROSOFT C++ GRAPHICS 371

Text-Mode Graphics Functions 374
    Developing Graphics Programs 374
    The _settextwindow() Function 374
    Using Text-Mode Functions 375
    The _outtext() Function 376
    The _clearscreen() Function 377
    A Fancier box Class 377
Graphics-Mode Graphics Functions 383
    The _setvideomode() Function 385
    The _ellipse() Function 385
    Ending a Graphics Program 386
Colors 386
    The _setcolor() Function 388
    The _floodfill() Function 388
Rectangles and Lines 389
    The _rectangle() Function 390
    The _moveto() Function 391
    The _lineto() Function 391
Shapes and Inheritance 391
    The shape Class 393
    Polygons 394
    Program Design 395
Motion 396
    Class Hierarchy in SLOT 402
    Operation of SLOT 402
    Delaying the Program 403
    Thinking about Classes 403
Text in Graphics Mode 404
    A Graphics String Class 404
    Microsoft C++ Text Graphics Functions 407
    Redefining a Function Set 410
    Extending the Gstring Class 410
Summary 411
Questions 411
Exercises 412

CHAPTER 12: POINTERS 415

Addresses and Pointers 418
    The Address of Operator & 419

Pointer Variables   420
Accessing the Variable Pointed To   422
Pointer to **void**   425
Pointers and Arrays   426
Pointer Constants and Pointer Variables   428
Pointers and Functions   429
Passing Simple Variables   429
Passing Arrays   432
Sorting Array Elements   433
Pointers and Strings   437
Pointers to String Constants   438
Strings as Function Arguments   438
Copying a String Using Pointers   440
Library String Functions   440
Arrays of Pointers to Strings   441
Memory Management: **new** and **delete**   442
The **new** Operator   444
The **delete** Operator   446
A String Class Using **new**   446
Pointers to Objects   448
Referring to Members   449
Another Approach to **new**   449
An Array of Pointers to Objects   450
A Linked List Example   452
A Chain of Pointers   452
Adding an Item to the List   454
Displaying the List Contents   455
Self-Containing Classes   456
Augmenting LINKLIST   456
Pointers to Pointers   457
Sorting Pointers   459
The **person**** Data Type   459
Comparing Strings   459
Debugging Pointers   461
Summary   462
Questions   463
Exercises   465

CHAPTER 13: VIRTUAL FUNCTIONS AND OTHER SUBTLETIES   467

Virtual Functions   469
Normal Member Functions Accessed with Pointers   470

Virtual Member Functions Accessed with Pointers   471
Late Binding   473
Virtual Functions and the `employee` Class   474
Pure Virtual Functions   478
Virtual Functions and the `person` Class   479
Virtual Functions in a Graphics Example   483
Abstract Classes   485
Virtual Base Classes   486
Friend Functions   487
Friends as Bridges   488
Breaching the Walls   489
English Distance Example   489
`friend`s for Functional Notation   492
`friend` Classes   494
Static Functions   495
Accessing `static` Functions   496
Numbering the Objects   497
Investigating Destructors   498
Assignment and Copy-Initialization   498
Overloading the Assignment Operator   499
The Copy Constructor   501
A Memory-Efficient String Class   504
The `this` Pointer   510
Accessing Member Data with `this`   511
Using `this` for Returning Values   512
Revised STRIMEM Program   513
Summary   515
Questions   516
Exercises   518

CHAPTER 14: FILES AND STREAMS   521

Streams   523
The Stream Class Hierarchy   523
Stream Classes   524
Header Files   525
String I/O   526
Writing Strings   526
Reading Strings   526
Detecting End-of-File   527
Character I/O   527

Object I/O 528
    Writing an Object to Disk 528
    Binary versus Text Files 529
    Reading an Object from Disk 530
    Compatible Data Structures 530
I/O with Multiple Objects 531
    The fstream Class 533
    The open() Function 533
File Pointers 534
    Specifying the Position 534
    Specifying the Offset 534
    The tellg() Function 537
Disk I/O with Member Functions 537
    Closing Files 540
    Other Data Structures 540
Error Handling 540
Redirection 542
    ios Flags 543
    Using REDIR 543
    Redirecting Output 543
    Redirecting Input 544
    Redirecting Input and Output 545
    The cerr and clog Objects 545
Command-Line Arguments 545
Printer Output 547
Overloading the Extraction and Insertion Operators 548
Summary 550
Questions 551
Exercises 552

CHAPTER 15: LARGER PROGRAMS 553
Reasons for Multi-File Programs 555
    Class Libraries 555
    Components of a Class Library 556
    Other Reasons for Multi-File Programs 557
A Pocket Calculator: The CALC Program 558
    Using the Calculator 558
    Files in the CALC Program 559
    Class Declarations 563
    The Base Class Window 563

The **Border** Class 565
The **Button** Class 566
The Output Window 567
The CALC_APP.CPP File 567
Not a Standalone File 571
Not the Windows Approach 571
A Very Long Number Class 571
Numbers as Strings 572
The Class Specifier 572
The Member Functions 573
The Application Program 577
A Water-Distribution System 577
Components of a Water System 579
Flow, Pressure, and Back Pressure 579
Component Input and Ouput 580
Making Connections 581
Simplifying Assumptions 581
Program Design 582
Programming the Connections 586
Base and Derived Classes 587
The **Component** Base Class 587
The *Flows-Into* Operator 587
Derived Classes 588
The PIPE_APP.CPP File 589
Summary 593
Questions 593
Projects 594

CHAPTER 16: MICROSOFT FOUNDATION CLASSES 595

Programming Environment 597
Library File 597
Header Files 598
Strings 599
Time and Date 601
Files 602
The **CFile** Class 603
The **CStdioFile** Class 605
The Data-Structure Classes 606
Header File 607
Array Classes 607

xvi

Lists   611
Maps   619
Exceptions   624
Exception Syntax   625
Memory Exceptions   627
File Exceptions   628
Throwing Your Own Exceptions   629
Throwing Specific Exceptions   631
Exception Note   633
Serialization   633
Debugging   636
Preparation   637
TRACE and ASSERT   637
Summary   643
Questions   643
Exercises   645

CHAPTER 17: JUST FOR FUN   647

Fractal Flowers   649
Fractal Fundamentals   649
Constants   654
Clusters   654
Polar Coordinates   654
Recursion   655
Conway's Game of Life   656
Rules of Life   656
Running LIFE   658
Architecture of LIFE   658
The main() Function   662
A Tic-Tac-Toe Program   663
The Position Class   670
Member Functions of Position   670
Evaluating a Position   674
The main() Function   675
Further Thoughts   675
Summary   675
Questions and Exercises   676

APPENDIX A: ASCII TABLE   679

APPENDIX B: MICROSOFT C++ KEYWORDS   683

APPENDIX C: USING THE PROJECT FEATURE 685

A Group of Files 685
Adding Files 686
Environmental Variables 686
Saving the Project List 687
Automatic Version Control 687

APPENDIX D: ANSWERS TO QUESTIONS AND EXERCISES 689

APPENDIX E: BIBLIOGRAPHY 741

INDEX 743

INTRODUCTION

Object-oriented programming (OOP) is the most dramatic innovation in software development in the last decade. It ranks in importance with the development of the first higher-level languages at the dawn of the computer age. Sooner or later every programmer will be affected by the object-oriented approach to program design.

ADVANTAGES OF OOP

Why is everyone so excited about OOP? The chief problem with computer programs is complexity. Large programs are probably the most complicated entities ever created by humans. Because of this complexity, programs are prone to error, and software errors can be expensive and even life-threatening. Object-oriented programming offers a new and powerful way to cope with this complexity. Its goal is clearer, more reliable, more easily maintained programs.

LANGUAGES AND DEVELOPMENT PLATFORMS

Of the object-oriented programming languages, C++ is by far the most popular; and, if you want to learn C++, Microsoft C/C++ offers one of the most powerful and easy-to-use development platforms on the market. This product provides a complete, easy-to-use development environment. It is also among the best platforms for professional software developers.

WHAT THIS BOOK DOES

This book teaches object-oriented programming with the C++ programming language, using Microsoft C/C++. It is suitable for professional programmers, students, and kitchen-table enthusiasts.

New Concepts

OOP involves concepts that are new to programmers of traditional languages such as Pascal, Basic, and C. These ideas, such as data hiding, encapsulation, and polymorphism, lie at the heart of object-oriented programming. But it's easy to lose sight of these concepts when discussing the specifics of an object-oriented language. Many books tend to overwhelm the reader with the details of language features, while ignoring the reason these features exist. This book attempts to keep an eye on the big picture and relate the details to the larger concepts.

The Gradual Approach

We take a gradual approach in this book, starting with very simple programming examples and working up to full-fledged object-oriented applications. We will introduce new concepts slowly so that you will have time to digest one idea before going on to the next. We will use figures whenever possible to help clarify new ideas. Questions and programming exercises at the end of each chapter (with answers in the back of the book) enhance the book's usefulness in the classroom.

What You Need to Know to Use This Book

To use this book, you should have some experience with at least one computer language, such as Pascal, BASIC, or FORTRAN. Thus we will assume that you know what variables are, and that you are familiar with basic programming constructions such as loops and decisions.

You do *not* need to know the C language to use this book. Many books on C++ assume that you already know C, but this one does not. It teaches C++ from the ground up. If you *do* know C, it won't hurt, but you may be surprised at how little overlap there is between C and C++.

We assume you have some experience with MS-DOS (the operating system for IBM PCs and compatibles). You should know how to list, copy, and delete files, and how to move around in the directory structure and perform other DOS-related activities.

Since this book uses the Programmer's Workbench, a character-based graphics user interface provided by Microsoft C/C++, we also assume you are familiar with on-screen windows and menus, and know how to use a mouse.

Hardware and Software

Here's the hardware and software you need to use this book.

The hardware requirements for Microsoft C/C++ are moderately severe, but any system that runs Windows 3.x comfortably will probably handle Microsoft C/C++. You need a computer with an 80386 or better processor and 4 megabytes or more of RAM. You will also need something like 25 megabytes of free disk space on your hard disk; maybe less if you work at cutting out everything but the essentials. It's difficult to make the system work with a 40-megabyte hard disk even if there isn't much else on it; so an 80-megabyte disk is the practical minimum.

Most of the examples in this book are character-based, so you don't absolutely need a graphics display system. However, all of Chapter 11 (on graphics) and several other examples use graphics output, so it's preferable to have a graphics display such as EGA, VGA, or better. You'll need a mouse to operate the Programmer's WorkBench (in theory, all user input to the PWB can be made from the keyboard, but this approach is more cumbersome). A printer is very nice, but not absolutely necessary.

The most essential software for this book is of course the Microsoft C/C++ development system itself, available from Microsoft Corporation in Redmond, Washington. You should be running MS-DOS version 3.3 or later. You also need a DPMI (DOS Protected Mode Interface) server, since Microsoft C/C++ operates in protected mode. The server can be either Windows or 386MAX, which is bundled with Microsoft C/C++. If Windows is already installed on your system, it's easiest to use it as the server; but if you don't want to use Windows, or can't fit it on your hard disk, then you can use 386MAX, which occupies less than 2 megabytes of disk space.

We'll discuss software installation in Chapter 2.

Go For It!

You may have heard that C++ is difficult to learn. It's true that it might be a little more challenging than BASIC, but it's really quite similar to other languages, with two or three "grand ideas" thrown in. These new ideas are fascinating in themselves, and we think you'll have fun learning about them. They are also becoming part of the programming culture; they're something you should know a little bit about, like evolution and psychoanalysis. We hope this book will help you enjoy learning about these new ideas, at the same time it teaches you the details of programming in C++.

A NOTE TO TEACHERS

Teachers, and others who already know C, may be interested in some details of the approach we use in this book and how it's organized.

TREAT C++ AS A SEPARATE LANGUAGE

We should emphasize that C and C++ are entirely separate languages. It's true that their syntax is similar; C is actually a subset of C++. But the similarity is largely a historical accident. In fact, the basic approach in a C++ program is radically different from that in a C program.

We think that C++ is the language of the future—that it will become increasingly important in the years ahead and that it may soon surpass C as the most popular language for serious programmers. Thus we don't believe it is necessary or advantageous to teach C before teaching C++. Students who don't know C are saved the time and trouble of learning C and then learning C++, an inefficient approach. Students who already know C may be able to skim parts of some chapters, but they will find that a remarkable percentage of the material is new.

Optimize Organization for OOP

We could have begun the book by teaching the procedural concepts common to C and C++, and moved on to the new OOP concepts once the procedural approach had been digested. That seemed counterproductive, however, since one of our goals is to begin true object-oriented programming as quickly as possible. Accordingly, we provide a minimum of procedural groundwork before getting to objects in Chapter 7. Even the initial chapters are heavily steeped in C++, as opposed to C, usage.

We introduce some concepts earlier than is traditional in books on C. For example, structures are a key feature for understanding C++, since classes are syntactically an extension of structures. For this reason we introduce structures in Chapter 5, so that they will be familiar when we discuss classes.

Some concepts, such as pointers, are introduced later than in traditional C books. It's not necessary to understand pointers to follow the essentials of OOP, and pointers are usually a stumbling block for C and C++ students. Therefore, we defer a discussion of pointers until the main concepts of OOP have been thoroughly digested.

Substitute Superior C++ Features

Some features of C have been superseded by new approaches in C++. For instance, the `printf()` and `scanf()` functions, input/output workhorses in C, are seldom used in C++ because `cout` and `cin` do a better job. Consequently, we leave out detailed descriptions of `printf()` and `scanf()`. Similarly, `#define` constants and macros in C have been largely superseded by the `const` qualifier and `inline` functions in C++, and need to be mentioned only briefly.

Minimize Irrelevant Capabilities

Since the focus in this book is on object-oriented programming, we can leave out some features of C that are seldom used and are not particularly relevant to OOP. For instance, it isn't necessary to understand the C bit-wise operators (used to operate on individual bits), to learn object-oriented programming. These and a few other features can be dropped from our discussion, or mentioned only briefly, with no loss in understanding of the major features of C++.

The result is a book that focuses on the fundamentals of OOP, moving the reader gently but briskly toward an understanding of new concepts and their application to real programming problems.

Dear Reader:

Thank you for considering the purchase of *The Waite Group's Object-Oriented Programming in Microsoft C++*. Readers have come to know products from The Waite Group for the care and quality we put in them. Let me tell you a little about our group and how we make our books.

It started in 1976 when I could not find a computer book that really taught me anything. The books that were available talked down to people, lacked illustrations and examples, were poorly laid out, and were written as if you already understood all the terminology. So I set out to write a good book about microcomputers. This was to be a special book—very graphic, with a friendly and casual style, and filled with examples. The result was an instant best-seller.

Over the years, I developed this approach into a "formula" (nothing really secret here, just a lot of hard work—I am a crazy man about technical accuracy and high-quality illustrations). I began to find writers who wanted to write books in this way. This led to co-authoring and then to multiple-author books and many more titles (over 70 titles currently on the market). As The Waite Group author base grew, I trained a group of editors to manage our products. We now have a team devoted to putting together the best possible book package and maintaining the high standard of our existing books.

WAITE
GROUP
PRESS™

We are most proud of this particular book, *Object-Oriented Programming in Microsoft C++*. The author, Robert Lafore, also wrote *Object-Oriented Programming in Turbo C++*, *Turbo C Programming for the PC*, and *C Programming Using Turbo C++*, known as clear, accessible C tutorials using Borland's low-end compilers. This new title on C++ specifically focuses on object-oriented programming, and takes the approach that C++ is a standalone language, and therefore you don't have to know C to use this book. Lafore is one of The Waite Group's most popular authors; many of you have requested this particular title.

We hope you enjoy this and all the other books upcoming from Waite Group Press. If you wish to be on our mailing list, or if you have any comments to tell us after you have purchased and read the book, please fill out and send in the detachable postpaid card.

Mitchell Waite

Mitchell Waite
President

200 Tamal Plaza   Corte Madera   California   94925   415-924-2575   Fax 415-924-2576

This book is dedicated to GGL and her indomitable spirit.

ACKNOWLEDGMENTS

My primary thanks go to Mitch Waite, who pored over every inch of the manuscript with painstaking attention to detail and made a semi-infinite number of helpful suggestions. Bill McCarty of Azusa Pacific University reviewed the content of the manuscript and its suitability for classroom use, suggested many excellent improvements, and attempted to correct my dyslexic spelling. Scott Calamar of The Waite Group dealt with the myriad organizational aspects of writing and producing this book; his competence and unfailing food humor were important ingredients in its completion. I would also like to acknowledge Paul Mitchell of Microsoft for checking the Microsoft Foundation Class material and offering his valuable insights, and George Leach and Harry Henderson for their reviews and suggestions. Thanks to John Crudo of The Waite Group for shepherding the book into production, and to Julianne Ososke of The Waite Group for gracefully coordinating its trouble-free production. I also wish to extend my gratitude to Juan Vargas for his innovative graphic design, and to Frances Hasegawa for her beautiful and effective art.

ABOUT THE AUTHOR

Robert Lafore has been writing books about computer programming since 1982. His best-selling titles include *Assembly Language Programming for the IBM PC and XT*, *C Programming Using Turbo C++*, *Microsoft C Programming for the PC*, and *Object-Oriented Programming in Turbo C++*. Mr. Lafore holds degrees in mathematics and electrical engineering, and has been active in programming since the days of the PDP-5, when 4K of main memory was considered luxurious. His interests include hiking, windsurfing, and recreational mathematics.

THE BIG PICTURE

WHY WE NEED OBJECT-ORIENTED PROGRAMMING

PROCEDURAL VERSUS OBJECT-ORIENTED LANGUAGES

FEATURES OF OBJECT-ORIENTED LANGUAGES

INTRODUCTION TO CLASSES AND OBJECTS

INTRODUCTION TO INHERITANCE

C++ AND C

This book teaches you how to program in C++, a computer language that supports *object-oriented programming* (OOP). Why do we need OOP? What does it do that traditional languages like C, Pascal, and BASIC, don't? What are the principles behind OOP? Two key concepts in OOP are *objects* and *classes*. What do these terms mean? What is the relationship between C++ and the older C language?

This chapter explores these questions and provides an overview of the features to be discussed in the balance of the book. What we say here will necessarily be rather general (although mercifully brief). If you find the discussion somewhat abstract, don't worry. The concepts we mention here will come into focus as we demonstrate them in detail in subsequent chapters.

WHY DO WE NEED OBJECT-ORIENTED PROGRAMMING?

Object-oriented programming was developed because limitations were discovered in earlier approaches to programming. To appreciate what OOP does, we need to understand what these limitations are and how they arose from traditional programming languages.

PROCEDURAL LANGUAGES

Pascal, C, BASIC, FORTRAN, and similar languages are *procedural* languages. That is, each statement in the language tells the computer to *do* something: Get some input, add these numbers, divide by 6, display that output. A program in a procedural language is a *list of instructions*.

For very small programs, no other organizing principle (often called a *paradigm*) is needed. The programmer creates the list of instructions, and the computer carries them out.

Division Into Functions

When programs become larger, a single list of instructions becomes unwieldy. Few programmers can comprehend a program of more than a few hundred statements unless it is broken down into smaller units. For this reason the *function* was adopted as a way to make programs more comprehensible to their human creators. (The term *function* is used in C++ and C. In other languages the same concept may be referred to as a *subroutine*, a *subprogram*, or a *procedure*.) A program is divided into functions, and (ideally, at least) each function has a clearly defined purpose and a clearly defined interface to the other functions in the program.

The idea of breaking a program into functions can be further extended by grouping a number of functions together into a larger entity called a *module*, but the principle is similar: a grouping of components that carry out specific tasks.

Dividing a program into functions and modules is one of the cornerstones of *structured programming*, the somewhat loosely defined discipline that has influenced programming organization for more than a decade.

Problems with Structured Programming

As programs grow ever larger and more complex, even the structured programming approach begins to show signs of strain. You may have heard about, or been involved in, horror stories of program development. The project is too complex, the schedule slips, more programmers are added, complexity increases, costs skyrocket, the schedule slips further, and disaster ensues. (See *The Mythical Man-Month*, by Frederick P. Brooks, Jr., Addison-Wesley, 1982, for a vivid description of this process.)

Analyzing the reasons for these failures reveals that there are weaknesses in the procedural paradigm itself. No matter how well the structured programming approach is implemented, large programs become excessively complex.

What are the reasons for this failure of procedural languages? One of the most crucial is the role played by data.

Data Undervalued

In a procedural language, the emphasis is on *doing* things—*read the keyboard, invert the vector, check for errors*, and so on. The subdivision of a program into functions continues this emphasis. Functions *do* things, just as single program statements do. What they do may be more complex or abstract, but the emphasis is still on the action.

What happens to the data in this paradigm? Data is, after all, the reason for a program's existence. The important part of an inventory program isn't a function that displays the data, or a function that checks for correct input; it's the inventory data itself. Yet data is given second-class status in the organization of procedural languages.

For example, in an inventory program, the data that makes up the inventory is probably read from a disk file into memory, where it is treated as a global variable. By *global* we mean that the variables that constitute the data are declared outside of any function, so they are accessible to all functions. These functions perform various operations on the data. They read it, analyze it, update it, rearrange it, display it, write it back to the disk, and so on.

We should note that most languages, such as Pascal and C, also support *local* variables, which are hidden within a single function. But local variables are not useful for important data that must be accessed by many different functions. Figure 1-1 shows the relationship between global and local variables.

Now suppose a new programmer is hired to write a function to analyze this inventory data in a certain way. Unfamiliar with the subtleties of the program, the programmer creates a function that accidentally corrupts the data. This is easy to do, because every function has complete access to the data. It's like leaving your personal papers in the lobby of your apartment building: anyone can change or destroy them. In the same way, global data can be corrupted by functions that have no business changing it.

In addition, since many functions access the same data, the way the data is stored becomes critical. The arrangement of the data can't be changed without modifying all the functions that access it. If you add new data, for example, you'll need to modify all the functions that access the data so that they can also access these new items. It will be hard to find all such functions, and even harder to modify all of them correctly. It's similar to what happens when your local supermarket moves the bread from aisle 4 to aisle 12. Everyone who patronizes the supermarket must figure out where the bread has gone, and adjust their shopping habits accordingly. The relationship of functions and data in procedural programs is shown in Figure 1-2.

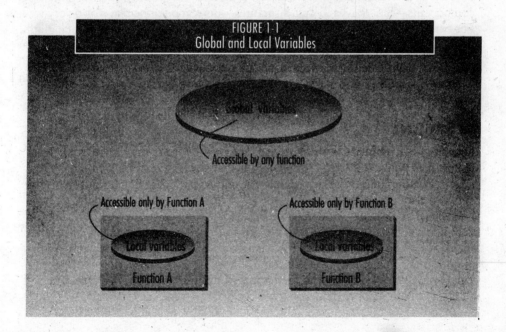

FIGURE 1-1
Global and Local Variables

Global Variables

Accessible by any function

Accessible only by Function A

Accessible only by Function B

Local Variables

Local Variables

Function A

Function B

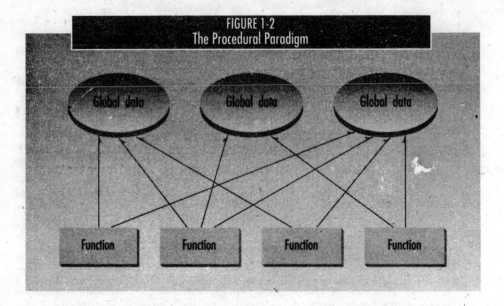

FIGURE 1-2
The Procedural Paradigm

What is needed is a way to restrict access to the data, to *hide* it from all but a few critical functions. This will protect the data, simplify maintenance, and offer other benefits as well (as we'll see).

Relationship to the Real World

Procedural programs are often difficult to design. The problem is that their chief components—functions and data structures—don't model the real world very well. For example, suppose you are writing a program to create the elements of a graphics user interface: menus, windows, and so on. Quick now, what functions will you need? What data structures? The answers are not obvious, to say the least. It would be better if windows and menus corresponded more closely to actual program elements.

New Data Types

There are other problems with traditional languages. One is the difficulty of creating new data types. Computer languages typically have several built-in data types: integers, floating-point numbers, characters, and so on. What if you want to invent your own data type? Perhaps you want to work with complex numbers, or two-dimensional coordinates, or dates—quantities the built-in data types don't handle easily. Being able to create your own types is called *extensibility*; you can extend the capabilities of the language. Traditional languages are not usually extensible. Without unnatural convolutions, you can't bundle together both X and Y coordinates into a single variable called *Point*, and then add and subtract values of this type. The result is that traditional programs are more complex to write and maintain.

THE OBJECT-ORIENTED APPROACH

The fundamental idea behind object-oriented languages is to combine into a single unit both *data* and *the functions that operate on that data*. Such a unit is called an *object*.

An object's functions, called *member functions* in C++, typically provide the only way to access its data. If you want to read a data item in an object, you call a member function in the object. It will read the item and return the value to you. You can't access the data directly. The data is *hidden*, so it is safe from accidental alteration. Data and its functions are said to be *encapsulated* into a single entity. *Data encapsulation* and *data hiding* are key terms in the description of object-oriented languages.

If you want to modify the data in an object, you know exactly what functions interact with it: the member functions in the object. No other functions can access the data. This simplifies writing, debugging, and maintaining the program.

A C++ program typically consists of a number of objects, which communicate with each other by calling one another's member functions. The organization of a C++ program is shown in Figure 1-3.

We should mention that what are called *member functions* in C++ are called *methods* in some other object-oriented (OO) languages (such as Smalltalk, one of the first OO languages). Also, data items are referred to as *instance variables*. Calling an object's member function is referred to as *sending a message* to the object. These terms are sometimes used in C++.

An Analogy

You might want to think of objects as departments—such as sales, accounting, personnel, and so on—in a company. Departments provide an important approach to corporate organization. In most companies (except very small ones), people don't work on personnel problems one day, payroll the next, and then go out in the field as salespeople the week after. Each department has its own personnel, with clearly assigned duties. It also has its own data: payroll, sales figures, personnel records, inventory, or whatever, depending on the department.

The people in each department control and operate on that department's data. Dividing the company into departments makes it easier to comprehend and control the company's activities, and helps maintain the integrity of the information used by the company. The payroll department, for instance, is responsible for the payroll data. If you are from the sales department, and you need to know the total of all the salaries paid in the southern region in July, you don't just walk into the payroll department and start rummaging through file cabinets. You send a memo to the appropriate person in the department, and then you wait for that person to access the data and send you a reply with the information you want. This ensures that the data is accessed accurately and that it is not corrupted by inept outsiders. This view of

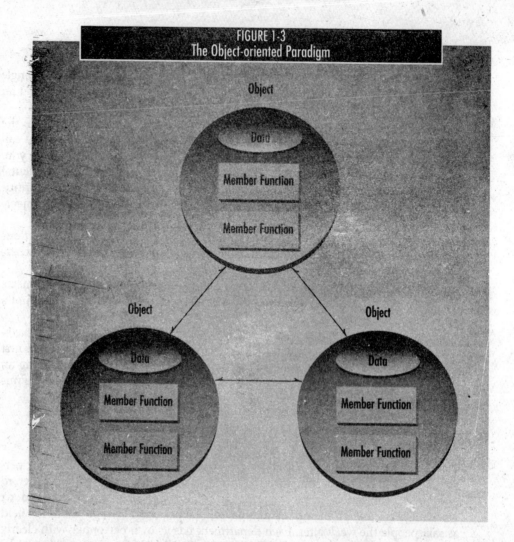

FIGURE 1-3
The Object-oriented Paradigm

corporate organization is shown in Figure 1-4. In the same way, objects provide an approach to program organization, while helping to maintain the integrity of the program's data.

OOP: An Approach to Organization

Keep in mind that object-oriented programming is not primarily concerned with the details of program operation. Instead, it deals with the overall organization of the program. Most individual program statements in C++ are similar to statements in procedural languages, and many are identical to statements in C. Indeed, an entire member function in a C++ program may be very similar to a procedural function in C. It is only when you look at the larger context that you can determine whether a statement or a function is part of a procedural C program or an object-oriented C++ program.

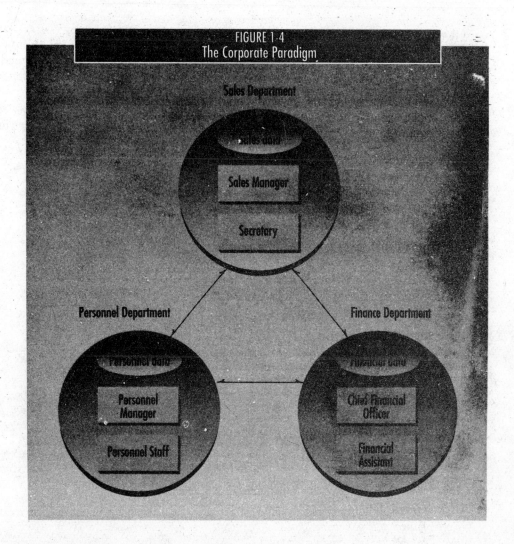

FIGURE 1-4
The Corporate Paradigm

CHARACTERISTICS OF OBJECT-ORIENTED LANGUAGES

Let's briefly examine a few of the major elements of object-oriented languages in general and C++ in particular.

OBJECTS

When you approach a programming problem in an object-oriented language, you no longer ask how the problem will be divided into functions, but how it will be divided into objects. Thinking in terms of objects, rather than functions, has a surprisingly helpful effect on how easily programs can be designed. This results from the close match between objects in the programming sense and objects in the real world.

What kinds of things become objects in object-oriented programs? The answer to this is limited only by your imagination, but here are some typical categories to start you thinking:

- **Physical objects**
  Automobiles in a traffic-flow simulation
  Electrical components in a circuit-design program
  Countries in an economics model
  Aircraft in an air-traffic-control system

- **Elements of the computer-user environment**
  Windows
  Menus
  Graphics objects (lines, rectangles, circles)
  The mouse and the keyboard

- **Programming Constructs**
  Customized arrays
  Stacks
  Linked lists
  Binary trees

- **Collections of data**
  An inventory
  A personnel file
  A dictionary
  A table of the latitudes and longitudes of world cities

- **User-defined data types**
  Time
  Angles
  Complex numbers
  Points on the plane

- **Components in computer games**
  Ghosts in a maze game
  Positions in a board game (chess, checkers)
  Animals in an ecological simulation
  Opponents and friends in adventure games

The match between programming objects and real-world objects is the happy result of combining data and functions: The resulting objects offer a revolution in program design. No such close match between programming constructs and the items being modeled exists in a procedural language.

CLASSES

In OOP we say that objects are *members of classes*. What does this mean? Let's look at an analogy. Almost all computer languages have built-in data types. For instance, a data type `int`, meaning *integer*, is predefined in C++ (as we'll see in Chapter 3). You can declare as many variables of type `int` as you need in your program:

```
int day;
int count;
int divisor;
int answer;
```

In a similar way, you can define many objects of the same *class*, as shown in Figure 1-5. A class serves as a plan, or blueprint. It specifies what data and what

FIGURE 1-5
A Class and Its Objects

functions will be included in objects of that class. Defining the class doesn't create any objects, just as the mere existence of a type int doesn't create any variables.

A class is thus a collection of similar objects. This fits our nontechnical understanding of the word *class*. Prince, Sting, and Madonna are members of the class of rock musicians. There is no one person called "rock musician," but specific people with specific names are members of this class if they possess certain characteristics.

INHERITANCE

The idea of classes leads to the idea of *inheritance*. In our daily lives, we use the concept of classes being divided into subclasses. We know that the class of animals is divided into mammals, amphibians, insects, birds, and so on. The class of vehicles is divided into cars, trucks, buses, and motorcycles.

The principle in this sort of division is that each subclass shares common characteristics with the class from which it's derived. Cars, trucks, buses, and motorcycles all have wheels and a motor; these are the defining characteristics of vehicles. In addition to the characteristics shared with other members of the class, each subclass also has its own particular characteristics: buses, for instance, have seats for many people, while trucks have space for hauling heavy loads.

This idea is shown in Figure 1-6. Notice in the figure that features A and B, which are part of the base class, are common to all the derived classes, but that each derived class also has features of its own.

In a similar way, an OOP class can be divided into subclasses. In C++ the original class is called the *base class*; other classes can be defined that share its characteristics, but add their own as well. These are called *derived classes*.

Don't confuse the relation of objects to classes, on the one hand, with the relation of a base class to derived classes, on the other. Objects, which exist in the computer's memory, embody the exact characteristics of their class, which serves as a design. Derived classes inherit some characteristics from their base class, but add new ones of their own.

Inheritance is somewhat analogous to using functions to simplify a traditional procedural program. If we find that three different sections of a procedural program do almost exactly the same thing, we recognize an opportunity to extract the common elements of these three sections and put them into a single function. The three sections of the program can call the function to execute the common actions, and they can perform their own individual processing as well. Similarly, a base class contains elements common to a group of derived classes. As functions do in a procedural program, inheritance shortens an object-oriented program and clarifies the relationship among program elements.

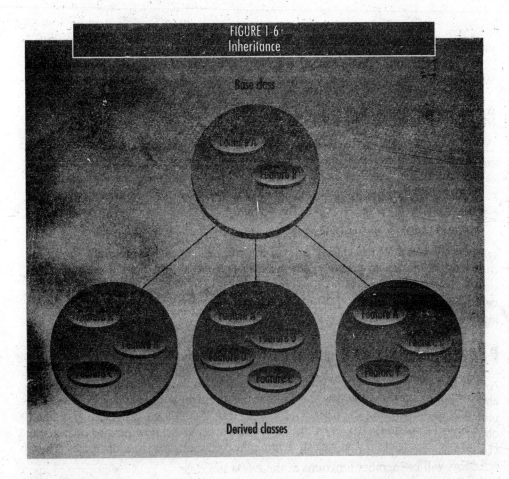

FIGURE 1-6
Inheritance

REUSABILITY

Once a class has been written, created, and debugged, it can be distributed to other programmers for use in their own programs. This is called *reusability*. It is similar to the way a library of functions in a procedural language can be incorporated into different programs.

However, in OOP, the concept of inheritance provides an important extension to the idea of reusability. A programmer can take an existing class, and without modifying it, add additional features and capabilities to it. This is done by deriving a new class from the existing one. The new class will inherit the capabilities of the old one but is free to add new features of its own.

For example, you might have written (or purchased from someone else) a class that creates a menu system, such as that used in the Programmer's WorkBench. This class works fine, and you don't want to change it, but you want to add the capability to make some menu entries flash on and off. To do this, you simply create a new class that inherits all the capabilities of the existing one but adds flashing menu entries.

The ease with which existing software can be reused is a major benefit of OOP. We'll have more to say about this in Chapters 10 and 15.

CREATING NEW DATA TYPES

One of the benefits of objects is that they give the programmer a convenient way to construct new data types. Suppose you work with two-dimensional positions (such as X and Y coordinates, or latitude and longitude) in your program. You would like to express operations on these positional values with normal arithmetic operations, such as

```
position1 = position2 + origin;
```

where the variables position1, position2 and origin each represent a *pair* of independent numerical quantities. By creating a class that incorporates these two values, and declaring position1, position2 and origin to be objects of this class, we can, in effect, create a new data type. Many features of C++ are intended to facilitate the creation of new data types in this manner.

POLYMORPHISM AND OVERLOADING

Note that the = (equal) and + (plus) operators, used in the position arithmetic shown above, don't act the same way they do in operations on built-in types like int. The objects position1 and so on are not predefined in C++, but are programmer-defined objects of class Position. How do the = and + operators know how to operate on objects? The answer is that we can define new operations for these operators. These operators will be member functions of the Position class.

Using operators or functions in different ways, depending on what they are operating on, is called *polymorphism* (one thing with several distinct forms). When an existing operator, such as + or =, is given the capability to operate on a new data type, it is said to be *overloaded*. Overloading is a kind of polymorphism; it is also an important feature of OOP.

C++ AND C

C++ is derived from the C language. Strictly speaking, it is a superset of C: Almost every correct statement in C is also a correct statement in C++, although the reverse is not true. The most important elements added to C to create C++ are concerned with classes, objects, and object-oriented programming. (C++ was originally called "C with classes"). However, C++ has many other new features as well, including an improved approach to I/O and a new way to write comments. Figure 1-7 shows the relationship of C and C++.

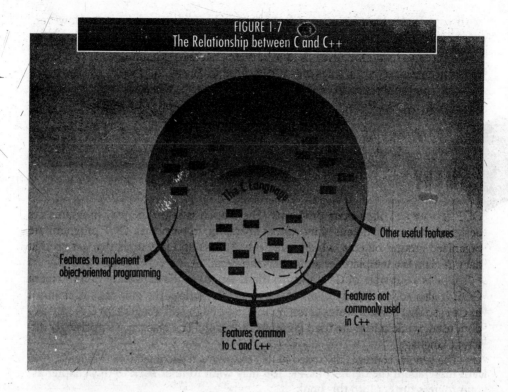

FIGURE 1-7
The Relationship between C and C++

Other useful features

Features to implement
object-oriented programming

The C Language

Features not
commonly used
in C++

Features common
to C and C++

In fact, the practical differences between C and C++ are larger than you migh think. Although you *can* write a program in C++ that looks like a program in C, hardly anyone does: C++ programmers not only make use of the new features of C++; they also emphasize the traditional C features in different proportions than do C programmers.

If you already know C, you will have a head start in learning C++ (although you may also have some bad habits to unlearn), but much of the material will be new.

LAYING THE GROUNDWORK

Our goal is to help you begin writing OOP programs as soon as possible. However, as we noted, much of C++ is inherited from C, so while the overall structure of a C++ program may be OOP, down in the trenches you need to know some old-fashioned procedural fundamentals. Chapters 3 through 6 of this book therefore deal with the "traditional" aspects of C++, many of which are also found in C. You will learn about variables and I/O, about control structures like loops and decisions, and about functions themselves. You will also learn about structures in general, since the same syntax that's used for structures is used for classes.

If you already know C, you might be tempted to skip these chapters. However, you will find that there are many differences, some obvious and some rather subtle, between C and C++. Our advice is to read these chapters, skimming what you know, and concentrating on the ways C++ differs from C.

The specific discussion of OOP starts in Chapter 7, when we begin to explore objects and classes. From then on the examples will be object-oriented.

MARY

OOP is a way of organizing programs. The emphasis is on the way programs are designed, not on the details of individual operators. In particular, OOP programs are organized around objects, which contain both data and functions that act on that data. A class is a template for a number of objects.

C++ is a superset of C. It adds to the C language the capability to implement OOP. It also adds a variety of other features. In addition, the emphasis is changed in C++, so that some features common to C, although still available in C++, are seldom used, while others are used far more frequently. The result is a surprisingly different language.

The general concepts discussed in this chapter will become more concrete as you learn more about the details of C++. You may want to refer back to this chapter as you progress further into this book.

STIONS

1. Pascal, BASIC, and C are p_____ languages, while C++ is an
   o_____ language.
2. A widget is to the blueprint for a widget as an object is to
   a. a member function
   b. a class
   c. an operator
   d. a data item
3. The two major components of an object are _____ and functions
   that _____.
4. In C++, a function contained within a class is called
   a. a member function
   b. an operator
   c. a class function
   d. a method

5. Protecting data from access by unauthorized functions is called
_____.

6. Which of the following are good reasons to use an object-oriented language?
   a. You can define your own data types.
   b. Program statements are simpler than in procedural languages.
   c. An OO program can be taught to correct its own errors.
   d. It's easier to conceptualize an OO program.

7. _____ model entities in the real world more closely than do functions.

8. True or false: A C++ program is similar to a C program except for the details of coding.

9. Bundling data and functions together is called _____.

10. When a language has the capability to produce new data types, it is said to be
    a. reprehensible
    b. encapsulated
    c. overloaded
    d. extensible

11. True or false: You can easily tell, from any two lines of code, whether a program is written in C or C++.

12. The ability of a function or operator to act in different ways on different data types is called _____.

13. A normal C++ operator that acts in special ways on newly defined data types is said to be
    a. glorified
    b. encapsulated
    c. classified
    d. overloaded

14. Memorizing the new terms used in C++ is
    a. critically important
    b. something you can return to later
    c. the key to wealth and success
    d. completely irrelevent

CHAPTER 2

USING MICROSOFT C/C++

SETTING UP MICROSOFT C/C++

YOUR FIRST PROGRAM

USING THE PROGRAMMER'S WORKBENCH

EDITING, COMPILING, AND LINKING

Microsoft C/C++ provides a powerful environment for the most sophisticated program development. It will handle source code in C or C++, and create applications for Windows or DOS. This product, in its previous C-language versions, became the standard for professional software development. Now it has been expanded to work with C++ as well. It has also been made very easy to use. The Programmer's WorkBench (PWB) is an integrated development environment that allows you to create, edit, compile, link, and execute your program from a convenient screen display. It's fast and friendly.

In this chapter we'll discuss how to set up Microsoft C/C++ to handle C++ in general and the examples in this book in particular. We'll also introduce you to your first C++ program.

SETTING UP MICROSOFT C/C++

The SETUP program provided with Microsoft C/C++ makes it easy to create the necessary directories, load the files from the distribution disks, and modify your programming environment so you can develop C++ programs. However, there are several options to consider.

Microsoft C/C++ contains many features to aid in developing programs to run in the Microsoft Windows environment. However, this book does not deal with Windows programming; all the example programs are for MS-DOS. Thus you can save space on your hard disk by installing only the MS-DOS development capability. There are two possibilites here: either you have Windows installed in your system, or you don't.

IF WINDOWS IS INSTALLED

If Windows 3.0 or later is installed in your system, start from the DOS prompt and execute the CSETUP program on Disk 1 (instead of SETUP). This will invoke an MS-DOS installation program, and automatically exclude all the Windows-specific files.

The CSETUP program will prompt you to insert the distribution disks. (This will take awhile, so have a good book handy.)

Alternatively, you can run the SETUP program directly from Windows. To do this, select Run from the File menu in the Program Manager, and type a:setup (or b:setup). When SETUP runs, select Custom Installation. When the Custom Installation: C/C++ File Groups window appears, click on the Target button and select the MS-DOS radio button (instead of the Both MS-DOS and Windows button). Then continue normal installation, following the prompts.

In either case you'll need to choose all the file groups shown in the Custom Installation window: the C/C++ Compiler, Run-Time Libraries, Microsoft Foundation Classes, Programmer's WorkBench, CodeView Debugger, Sample Source Code, Online Help, and MS-DOS Graphics Libraries. For this book you don't absolutely need CodeView, or the sample source code, but you might find them handy. The foundation classes alone take more than 6 megabytes of disk space, but are necessary for the programs in Chapter 16.

You need only use the Small memory model for the programs in this book, but the SETUP program installs both Small and Medium libraries as the default. If you want to conserve disk space, you can specify only the Small model. To specify memory models in the Windows version of the SETUP program, click on the Libraries button in the Custom Installation window, and click the appropriate check boxes.

The SETUP program creates a Windows group icon and places the PWB icon inside it. Once Microsoft C/C++ is installed, you can invoke the Programmer's WorkBench by double-clicking on this icon.

If Windows Is Not Installed

If Windows isn't installed, you can invoke the normal SETUP program (which will in turn call CSETUP when it finds Windows is unavailable). However, you must also install a separate server program. Microsoft C/C++ runs in protected mode, so it requires support for DOS Protected Mode Interface (DPMI) services. Windows can provide these services, but without Windows you'll need another program. Microsoft bundles 386MAX from Qualitas Software, which includes this capability (among others). For maximum efficiency, Microsoft recommends installing C/C++ before you install 386MAX, but both ways work. Other products also supply DPMI services; if you have one, you may not need 386MAX or Windows.

Running the Programmer's WorkBench

To run PWB, first switch to the directory where you want to do your program development, for example, C:\MYPROGS\. Then invoke PWB from the DOS command line:

```
C>pwb
```

This should bring up the initial PWB screen, which is largely a blank area with a menu on the top line and some help information on the bottom.

If you're running Windows, you can start PWB by double-clicking on the Programmer's WorkBench icon in the Microsoft C/C++ group.

In either case the result is a character-based display. In Windows the PWB is running in a DOS box, and making use of Windows DPMI services. So whether you're running PWB from Windows or DOS, it appears to be a straight DOS application. In Windows, of course, as with any program running in the DOS box, you can switch to any other WIndows session with (CTRL)-(ESC) or (ALT)-(ESC).

YOUR FIRST PROGRAM

We're going to begin our exploration of the PWB with a simple program called FIRST. Here's what this program looks like:

```
#include <iostream.h>

void main()
{
    cout << "Every age has a language of its own";
}
```

USING THE PWB EDITOR

To type in this program, select New from the File menu. A window will open; it will be in color if you have a color monitor. At the top of the window is the file name UNTITLED.001. Type the program shown above into this window. Don't worry about the meaning of the program lines. We're interested here in how to turn the program into an executable file. However, you should make sure that the program is typed in correctly. Note especially the use of lowercase letters, the paired braces { and }, and the semicolon at the end of the long line. Spell void, main, and cout correctly. Don't forget the quote marks around the phrase "Every age has a language of its own" (attributed to the the nineteenth-century English travel writer Augustus Hare). When you have typed in this source file, your screen should resemble Figure 2-1.

There aren't many surprises in using the PWB editor for simple tasks. What you type appears on the screen. Pressing the (ENTER) key takes you down to the next line. You can move the cursor with the mouse or the arrow keys. Table 2-1 provides a list of the more useful cursor commands:

You can also cut and paste using the mouse and the Edit menu, and search or search-and-replace using the Search menu. The Microsoft *Environment and Tools* book, and the Help menu, provide a complete description of the PWB editor's capabilities.

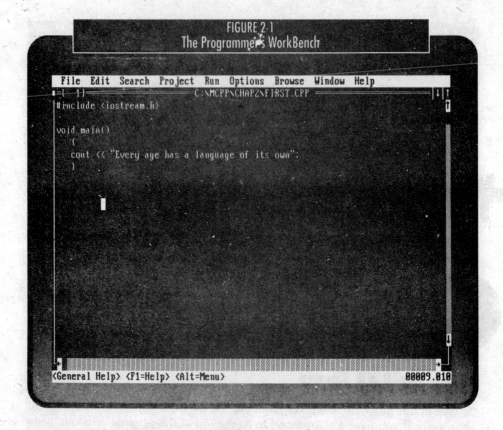

FIGURE 2-1
The Programmer's WorkBench

```
 File  Edit  Search  Project  Run  Options  Browse  Window  Help
[ ]                       C:\MCPP\CHAP2\FIRST.CPP
#include <iostream.h>

void main()
{
    cout << "Every age has a language of its own";
}




<General Help> <F1=Help> <Alt=Menu>                      00009.010
```

SAVING YOUR PROGRAM

After you've typed in your program, you'll want to save it to the hard disk. Select Save As from the File menu. When the Save As dialog box appears, fill in the name of the program, using the .CPP file extension. All C++ programs use this same file extension. We'll call this program FIRST, so type **first.cpp**. Then press (ENTER) or click on the OK button. The file will be saved under this name. You'll see the new name appear at the top of the text window. (Don't use the .C file extension. If you do, the PWB will invoke the C compiler rather than the C++ compiler, and errors will be generated.)

COMPILING AND LINKING

You're probably already familiar with compiled languages, but if you're not, the process of transforming your source file into a form acceptable to the computer may seem a little obscure.

TABLE 2-1
Some Useful Cursor Commands

Keyboard key	Action
↑	Cursor up one line
↓	Cursor down one line
→	Cursor right one line
←	Cursor left one line
CTRL-↑	Window up one line
CTRL-↓	Window down one line
CTRL-→	Cursor right one word
CTRL-←	Cursor left one word
HOME	Cursor to start of line
END	Cursor to end of line
PGUP	Scroll one screen up
PGDN	Scroll one screen down
ENTER	Insert line, go to next line
BACKSPACE	Delete character to left of cursor
DEL	Delete character under cursor
INS	Toggle insert/write-over
CTRL-HOME	Cursor to beginning of file
CTRL-END	Cursor to end of file

Remember that the source file is simply a text file, like one generated by a word processor. The microprocessor in your computer can't read it. Two steps are necessary to transform the source file into machine-readable form: *compiling* and *linking*.

Compiling is a translation process that transforms your text file into machine-readable form. The compiler generates an *object file* with the .OBJ extension, in this case FIRST.OBJ. However, the .OBJ file does not contain various library routines necessary for input/output and other purposes. You need to link these routines to your program. (In a multi-file project, the linker also combines the object files generated from your source files.) Figure 2-2 shows the relationship between compiling and linking.

FIGURE 2-2
Compiling and Linking

Source file

Possible other source files

Compiler

Compiler

Object file

Library file

Possible other object files

Linker

Executable file

Fortunately, the PWB makes it easy for you to compile and link your program. You need only select Build from the Project menu. The Build selection first causes the source file to be compiled into an object file, and then links this object file with the necessary library files. The library files are selected automatically on the basis of settings in the Options menu. For example, you can change the memory model using the Memory Model box in the C++ Compiler Options submenu of the Langage

Options submenu on the Options menu (or, more succinctly, Options/Language Options/C++ Compiler Options/Memory Model). However, the default settings already provide the Small memory model; so for the programs in this book (at least for now), you don't need to change any settings with the Options menu.

When the build operation is complete, a box will appear on your screen. If you have typed in the program correctly, and if your system is set up correctly, the box will say Build Operation Complete, 0 Errors/Warnings. (See the section Errors, below, if something else happens.)

The compiling and linking process we've described here works for the majority of programs in this book. For some programs, however, such as graphics programs and those that use the Microsoft Foundation classes, you need a fancier approach to building your program. Appendix C explains how to use the Project feature to combine non-standard library files and multiple-object files.

Running Your program

If the Build Operation Complete box is on the screen, you can run your program by clicking on the Run Program button. Otherwise, you can select the Execute item from the Run menu. The output might look something like this:

```
C>pwb
Every age has a language of its own.
Strike any key when ready . . .
```

The output appears on a separate screen, which is the regular MS-DOS (or DOS box) screen. The first line of the output shown here is your typed input when you invoked the PWB (there may be other lines you typed before this). The middle line is the output from FIRST.CPP, and the last line is a standard prompt, always displayed by the PWB when a program terminates. When you press a key, you'll find yourself back in the PWB.

You can also execute your program directly from DOS or the DOS box in Windows. Just move to the directory where you built the program, and enter the name FIRST at the DOS prompt. If you examine the directory where you started the PWB, you'll see there are now three new files: the source file FIRST.CPP, the object file FIRST.OBJ, and FIRST.EXE, which is a standalone executable that can be transferred to other computers. There will be other files with different extensions, such as .SBR and .BSC. The PWB uses these files for its own internal bookkeeping; you can ignore them (and erase them when you've finished working on a particular program).

Loading an Existing Source File

If you want to load a source file you've already written, select Open from the File menu. When the Open File box appears, select the file name from the File List box or type in the name of the file in the File Name field. (Don't try to open a .OBJ or

.EXE file this way.) To close a file, select Close from the File menu. This will remove it from the screen. You can have more than one file open at once in separate windows, but only the top window will be active—that is, responsive to commands like Build. A file with the .BAK extension saves the previous version of a source file when you start an editing session on an existing file.

Errors

When you build your program, or when you run it, you may encounter an unexpected or disappointing result. There are four major kinds of errors: compiler errors, linker errors, run-time errors, and conceptual errors. Compiler and linker errors are reported on the PWB screen. Run-time errors are reported on the output screen. Two tools are available to help track down conceptual errors: a debugger called CodeView, and the class Browser. Let's look at these four categories.

Compiler Errors

Compiler errors occur when the compiler attemps to parse (analyze) your source code. Simple typographic errors can cause a compiler error. For example, if you forget to put a close-quote symbol at the end of the phrase "Every age has a language of its own," the Build Operation Complete box will say "3 Errors/Warnings," as shown in Figure 2-3.

To see what these errors are, click on the View Results button in the Build Operation Complete box. You'll see the following three lines:

```
first.cpp(5) : error C2001: newline in constant
first.cpp(6) : error C2143: syntax error : missing ';' before '}'
NMAKE : fatal error U1007: 'CL' : return code '2'
```

The first two errors are generated by the compiler, as indicated by the C before the error numbers 2001 and 2143. The numbers in parentheses, 5 and 6, are the line number in the source file where the compiler found the errors. The "newline in constant" error occurs when you break text within quotes (called a *string constant*, as we'll see later) into two lines. The "syntax error" occurs because every program line must end with a semicolon, but without the close quote the semicolon is interpreted as part of the string and not recognized as a line terminator. When the compiler gets to the closing brace, it realizes there's no semicolon for the previous line, and generates the error.

The PWB calls different executable files to carry out different operations. The executable that handles building your program is NMAKE, and the executable that handles compiling is CL. Since CL found errors when compiling, it returns an error code to NMAKE, which then places the third error on the screen. This is U1007,

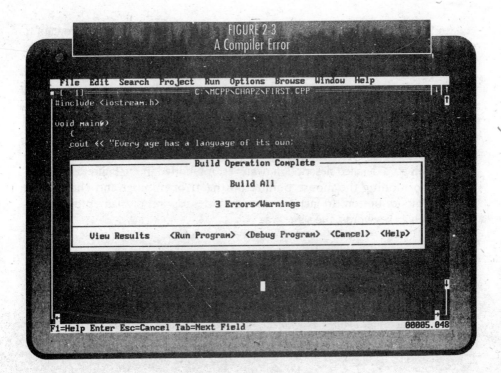

FIGURE 2-3
A Compiler Error

where the U indicates an NMAKE program error. Thus fixing the compiler errors will automatically cure the NMAKE error.

You can return to your source file by selecting the file name at the bottom of the Window menu. With your source file on the screen you can step through all the errors by repeatedly selecting Next Error from the Project menu. You can see the list or errors at any time by selecting Build Results from the Window menu. If you put the mouse pointer on an error line in this window, you can go directly to the offending program line in the text window by selecting Goto Error from the Project menu.

LINKER ERRORS

The most common linker error occurs when the linker can't find a function or other program element referred to in a source file. To see an example of this, first put the close quote back in the FIRST program so there will be no compiler error. (The build process stops if there is a compiler error, so you must fix all the compiler errors before you find out about linker errors.) Now change the name `main()` in the program to something else, say `maid()`. When you build the program again, you'll see the error

```
SLIBCE.LIB(crt0.asm) : error L2029: '_main' : unresolved external
```

This error is generated by the linker, as indicated by the L in the error number L2029. Every C++ program must have a function called `main()`. The library file SLIBCE.LIB includes a routine that calls this function, but the linker could not find `main()`, so it produced the error. A common cause of linker errors is misspelling function names.

You can get a detailed description of any error reported in the Build Results window by positioning the mouse pointer on the error number and clicking the *righthand* mouse button. In fact, you can get a description of many program elements, such as keywords, the same way.

RUN-TIME ERRORS

Sometimes an error occurs that the system does not detect until the program is running. Such errors are comparatively rare. They include division by 0, stack overflow, and the dreaded *null pointer assignment*. We'll have more to say about run-time errors later on.

CONCEPTUAL ERRORS: DEBUGGING

Of course many errors occur because you make a mistake in conceptualizing the program. Microsoft C/C++ includes a debugger called CodeView that helps track down such errors. We won't discuss this debugger in detail, but the mention of a few highlights will alert you to CodeView's existence, so that later, when you start to experiment with more complex programs, you'll know where to start when they act in some unexpected way.

Building with Debug Options

To use the debugger, you need to build a different version of your program than you would normally. To do this select Build Options from the Options menu, and click on the Use Debug Options button, then click on OK. Now rebuild your program. To start a debugging session, click on Debug Program in the Build Operation Complete box, or select Debug from the Run menu. There will be a pause as the PWB loads the debugger. Then you'll see three windows appear, the middle one containing the program listing.

Some of the most useful things you can do with a debugger are single-stepping through the program, examining the value of program variables, and setting breakpoints.

Single-Stepping

To single-step through the program, press the (F10) key. You'll see the highlight appear and move from statement to statement as you continue pressing. (Note that (F10) steps *over* function calls. To trace *into* functions, press (F8) instead.)

Watching Variables

The topmost of the three windows, called Locals, shows the values of local variables (those in the current function). You can watch these variables change as you step through the program. However, external variables aren't shown here. To see external variables, select Add Watch from the Data menu, and fill in the name of the variable in the dialog box. A window called Watch will appear that displays the values of these variables.

Breakpoints

A breakpoint stops your program's execution at a certain point. You run your program full-speed up to that point, then you find yourself in the debugger. At this point you can examine variables, single-step additional statements, and so on. Breakpoints are useful when you want to execute many statements, say those in a loop, before stopping for a detailed look at what's happening.

To set a breakpoint, position the mouse pointer on the statement where you want the program to stop. Then select Set Breakpoint from the Data menu. Click on OK in the resulting dialog box (or select one of the other numerous options). The line you selected will be highlighted. Now when you run your program, control will stop at this line.

Other Commands

To run a program full-speed, press the (F5) key. This will execute the program to the end, or to the next breakpoint.

To see the output of a program, press the (F4) key. This brings up an output screen. Press (F4) again to return to the CodeView screen.

If your program has not terminated but you want to run it again from the beginning, select Restart from the Run menu.

To exit the debugger, select Exit from the File menu. This will return you to the normal PWB. Don't forget to select Use Release Options from the Build Options item in the Options menu when you've finished your debugging session.

CONCEPTUAL ERRORS: THE BROWSER

The CodeView debugger works on a rather detailed level, looking at individual program statements and variables. In C++ there are (as we noted in the last chapter) larger program units called classes. A feature called the Browser, which is built into the PWB (unlike CodeView), lets you interact with classes and their relationship with each other (among other things).

To use the Browser you must click on the Generate Browse Information check box in the Browse Options selection from the Options menu. Then build your program again. Now the items in the Browse menu are active. If you have a large program with many classes, the Browser will help you keep track of them. For instance, you can select Display Tree from the Browse menu, and then enter the name of a particular source file, to see a diagram showing the relationships between the classes. Or if you position the cursor on a class name, you can view a definition of the class by selecting Goto Definition from the Browse menu. You can begin to experiment with these features after we encounter classes in Chapter 7.

COMPILER WARNING LEVEL

The compiler generates both errors and warnings. Errors are severe problems that make it impossible to compile a part of your code. Warnings indicate potential problems, along the lines of, "Do you really mean this?" You can adjust the compiler to report different levels of warnings. At level 0 it doesn't report warnings at all. At level 1 it reports only the most obvious warnings, while at level 4 it reports everything that looks the least little bit out of line.

You can change the warning level by selecting the Warning Level box in the C++ Compiler Options submenu of the Language Options submenu in the Options menu. We recommend you set the warning level to 3. You need all the help you can get in compiling your programs, but level 4 is sometimes excessively picky.

WHAT TO READ

Several of the publications that accompany Microsoft C/C++ are important for C++ programmers. Here's a brief description.

The *Getting Started* booklet shows you how to configure your system and install Microsoft C/C++.

The *Environments and Tools* manual describes the Programmer's WorkBench, the CodeView debugger, and the class Browser, among other topics.

The *C++ Tutorial* booklet is full of useful information, but covers C++ rather briskly. You might want to read it after you read this book.

The *C++ Language Reference* book is a technical description of the C++ language. Again, you may find it useful after you have digested this book.

The *Run-Time Libraries Reference* provides descriptions of library functions that can be called from C as well as C++. These functions perform data conversions, manipulate strings, do advanced math, display graphics, handle some kinds of I/O, and so on. We'll encounter many of these functions as we go along, so this is an important reference to keep handy.

The *Class Libraries User's Guide* includes a tutorial on the Microsoft Foundation classes, which we'll discuss in Chapter 16. This tutorial is fairly complex, so you will probably want to read Chapter 16 before getting into it. There is also a discussion of stream classes, which we'll explore in Chapter 14.

The *Class Libraries Reference* will be useful when we get to Chapter 16, on the Microsoft Foundation classes. This reference also contains a description of the stream class library, which we'll discuss in Chapter 14.

Finally, don't forget the *Comprehensive Index and Errors Reference*. This is a good place to look something up when you don't have any idea where it might be found. It also provides a description of all the error messages generated by the compiler, the linker, and various other utilities. (Many of these descriptions are available from online help, as mentioned earlier.)

The bibliography at the back of this book contains other books that you may want to look at.

SUMMARY

In this chapter you've learned a few details about installing Microsoft C/C++ in your computer, and how to run the Programmer's WorkBench, which centralizes the edit-compile-link-debug operations. You've written your first simple program, and (hopefully) seen that it works. You've also learned something about errors, and about the tools available for tracking them down.

In the next chapter, we'll begin our exploration of C++ itself.

C++ PROGRAMMING

C++ PROGRAM STRUCTURE

VARIABLES

INPUT/OUTPUT WITH cout AND cin

ARITHMETIC OPERATORS

ASSIGNMENT AND INCREMENT OPERATORS

In any language there are some fundamentals you need to know before you can write even the most elementary programs. This chapter introduces three such fundamentals: basic program construction, variables, and input/output (I/O). It also touches on a variety of other language features, including comments, arithmetic operators, the increment operator, data conversion, and library functions.

Most of these topics are not conceptually difficult, but you may find that the style in C++ is a little austere compared with, say, BASIC and Pascal. Before you learn what it's all about, a C++ program may remind you more of a mathematics formula than of a computer program. Don't worry about this. You'll find that as you gain familiarity with C++ it starts to look less forbidding, while simultaneously other languages begin to seem unnecessarily fancy and verbose.

BASIC PROGRAM CONSTRUCTION

Let's look more closely at the FIRST program introduced in Chapter 2. Here it is again:

```
#include <iostream.h>

void main()
    {
    cout << "Every age has a language of its own";
    }
```

Despite its small size, this program demonstrates a great deal about the construction of C++ programs. Let's examine it in detail.

FUNCTIONS

Functions are one of the fundamental building blocks of C++. The FIRST program consists almost entirely of a single function called **main()**. The only part of this program that is not part of the function is the first line—the one that starts with **#include**. (We'll see what this line does in a moment.)

We noted in Chapter 1 that a function can be part of a class, in which case it is called a *member* function. However, functions can also exist independent of classes. We are not yet ready to talk about classes, so we will show functions that are separate standalone entities, as `main()` is here.

Function Name

The parentheses following the word `main` are the distinguishing feature of a function. Without the parentheses the compiler would think that `main` referred to a variable or to some other program element. When we discuss functions in the text, we'll follow the same convention that C++ uses: We'll put parentheses following the function name. Later on we'll see that the parentheses aren't always empty. They're used to hold function *arguments*: values passed from the calling program to the function.

The word `void` preceding the function name indicates that this particular function does not have a return value. Don't worry about this now; we'll learn about return values and type `void` in Chapter 6.

Braces and the Function Body

The *body* of a function is surrounded by braces (sometimes called *curly brackets*). These braces play the same role as the `BEGIN` and `END` keywords in Pascal and BASIC: They surround or *delimit* a block of program statements. Every function must use this pair of braces. In this example there is only one statement within the braces: the line starting with `cout`. However, a function body can consist of many statements.

Always Start with main()

When you run a C++ program, the first statement executed will be at the beginning of a function called `main()`. The program may consist of many functions, classes, and other program elements, but on startup control always goes to `main()`. If there is no function called `main()` in your program, the linker will signal an error.

In most C++ programs, as we'll see later, `main()` calls member functions in various objects to carry out the program's real work. The `main()` function may also contain calls to other stand-alone functions. This is shown in Figure 3-1.

PROGRAM STATEMENTS

The program statement is the fundamental unit of C++ programming. There's only one statement in the FIRST program: the line

```
cout << "Every age has a language of its own";
```

This statement tells the computer to display the quoted phrase. Most statements tell the computer to do something. In this respect, statements in C++ are similar to statements in other languages. In fact, as we've noted, the majority of statements in C++ are identical to statements in C.

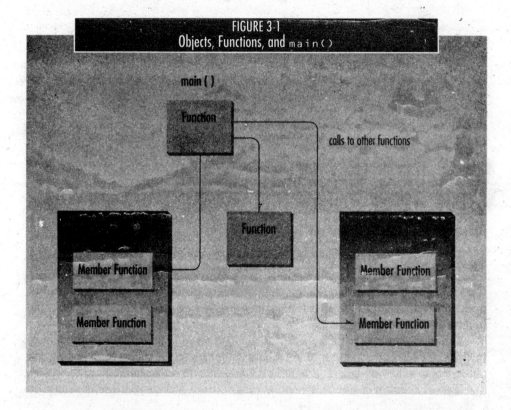

FIGURE 3-1
Objects, Functions, and main()

A semicolon signals the end of the statement. This is a crucial part of the syntax but easy to forget. In some languages (like BASIC), the end of a statement is signaled by the end of the line, but that's not true in C++. If you leave out the semicolon, the compiler will signal an error.

WHITE SPACE

Actually, the C++ compiler ignores white space almost completely. *White space* is defined as spaces, carriage returns, linefeeds, tabs, vertical tabs, and formfeeds. These characters are invisible to the compiler. You can put several statements on one line, separated by any number of spaces or tabs, or you can run a statement over two or more lines. It's all the same to the compiler. Thus the FIRST.CPP program could be written this way:

```
#include <iostream.h>

void main () { cout
<<
"Every age has a language of its own"
}
```

We don't recommend this syntax—it's nonstandard and hard to read—but it does compile correctly.

There are several exceptions to the rule that white space is invisible to the compiler. The first line of the program, starting with #include, is a *preprocessor directive*, which must be written on one line. Also, string constants, such as "Every age has a language of its own", cannot be broken into separate lines (although inserting a backslash \ at the break does permit multiline constructions in these circumstances).

OUTPUT USING cout

As you have seen, the statement

```
cout << "Every age has a language of its own";
```

causes the phrase in quotation marks to be displayed on the screen. How does this work? A complete description of this statement requires an understanding of objects, operator overloading, and other topics we won't discuss until later in the book, but here's a brief preview:

The identifier cout (pronounced "C out") is actually an *object*. It is predefined in Turbo C++ to correspond to the *standard output stream*. A *stream* is an abstraction that refers to a flow of data. The standard output stream normally flows to the screen display—although it can be redirected to other output devices. We'll discuss streams (and redirection) in Chapter 14.

The operator << is called the *insertion* or *put to* operator. It directs the contents of the variable on its right to the object on its left. In FIRST it directs the string constant "Every age has a language of its own" to cout, which sends it to the display.

(If you know C, you'll recognize << as the *left-shift* bit-wise operator and wonder how it can also be used to direct output. In C++, operators can be *overloaded*; That is, they can perform different activities, depending on the context. We'll learn about overloading in Chapter 9.)

Although the concepts behind the use of cout and << may be obscure at this point, using them is easy. They'll appear in almost every example program. Figure 3-2 shows the result of using cout and the insertion operator <<.

STRING CONSTANTS

The phrase in quotation marks, "Every age has a language of its own", is an example of a *string constant*. As you probably know, a constant, unlike a variable, cannot be given new values as the program runs. Its value is set when the program is written, and it retains this value throughout the program's existence.

FIGURE 3-2
Output with cout

type **char** to hold string variables. On the other hand, C++ recognizes string constants, surrounded by quotation marks as shown. We'll learn more about strings in Chapter 8.

PREPROCESSOR DIRECTIVES

The first line of the FIRST program,

```
#include <iostream.h>
```

might look like a program statement, but it's not. It isn't part of a function body and doesn't end with a semicolon, as program statements must. Instead, it starts with a number sign (#). It's called a *preprocessor directive*. Recall that program statements are instructions to the computer. A preprocessor directive, on the other hand, is an instruction to the compiler itself. A part of the compiler called the *preprocessor* deals with these directives before it begins the real compilation process.

THE #include DIRECTIVE

The preprocessor directive #include tells the compiler to insert another file into your source file. In effect, the #include directive is replaced by the contents of the file indicated. Using an #include directive to insert another file into your source file is similar to pasting a block of text into a document with your word processor.

HEADER FILES

In the FIRST example, the preprocessor directive #include tells the compiler to add the source file IOSTREAM.H to the FIRST.CPP source file before compiling. Why do this? IOSTREAM.H is an example of a *header file* (sometimes called an *include file*). It contains declarations that are needed by the cout identifier and the << operator. Without these declarations, the compiler won't recognize cout and will think << is being used incorrectly. (In C header files are often optional; in C++ they're always necessary.)

If you want to see what's in IOSTREAM.H, you can go to the C700\INCLUDE directory and use the DOS TYPE command (or the PWB editor) to examine the file. The contents won't make much sense at this point, but you will at least prove to yourself that IOSTREAM.H is a source file, written in normal ASCII characters.

We'll return to the topic of header files at the end of this chapter, when we introduce library functions.

#include is only one of many preprocessor directives, all of which can be identified by the initial # sign. The use of preprocessor directives is not as common in C++ as it is in C, but we'll look at a few additional examples as we go along.

COMMENTS

Comments are an important part of any program. They help the person writing a program, and anyone else who must read the source file, to understand what's going on. The compiler ignores comments, so they do not add to the file size or execution time of the executable program.

COMMENT SYNTAX

Let's rewrite our FIRST program, incorporating comments into our source file:

```
// comments.cpp
// demonstrates comments
#include <iostream.h>              // preprocessor directive

d main()                          // function name
{                                 // start function body
  cout << "Every age has a language of its own";  // statement
}                                 // end function body
```

Comments start with a double slash symbol (//) and terminate at the end of the line. (This is one of the exceptions to the rule that the compiler ignores white space.) A comment can start at the beginning of the line or on the same line following a program statement. Both possibilities are shown in the example.

WHEN TO USE COMMENTS

Comments are almost always a good thing. Most programmers don't use enough of them. If you're tempted to leave out comments, remember that not everyone is as smart as you; they may need more explanation than you do about what your program is doing. Also, you may not be as smart next month, when you've forgotten key details of your program's operation, as you are today.

Use comments to explain to the person looking at the listing what you're trying to do. The details are in the program statements themselves, so the comments should concentrate on the big picture, clarifying your reasons for using a certain statement.

ALTERNATIVE COMMENT SYNTAX

There's a second comment style available in C++:

```
/* this is an old-style comment */
```

This type of comment (the only comment available in C) begins with the /* character pair and ends with */ (not with the end of the line). These symbols are harder to type (since / is lowercase while * is uppercase) and take up more space on the line, so this style is not generally used in C++. However, it has advantages in special situations. You can write a multiline comment with only two comment symbols:

```
/* this
is a
potentially
very long
multiline
comment
*/
```

This is a good approach to making a comment out of a large text passage, since it saves inserting the // symbol on every line.

You can also insert a /* */ comment anywhere within the text of a program line:

```
func1()
   {  /* empty function body */  }
```

If you attempt to use the // style comment in this case, the closing brace won't be visible to the compiler—since a // style comment runs to the end of the line—and the code won't compile correctly.

INTEGER VARIABLES

Variables are the most fundamental part of any language. A variable is a symbolic name that can be given a variety of values. Variables are stored in particular places in the computer's memory. When a variable is given a value, that value is actually placed in the memory space occupied by the variable. Most popular languages use the same general variable types, such as integers, floating-point numbers, and characters, so you are probably already familiar with the ideas behind them.

Integer variables represent integer numbers like 1; 30,000; and −27. Such numbers are used for counting discrete numbers of objects. Unlike floating-point numbers, integers have no fractional part; you can express the idea of *four* using integers, but not *four and one-half*.

DEFINING INTEGER VARIABLES

Integer variables exist in several sizes, but the most commonly used is type `int`. This type requires 2 bytes of storage (in MS-DOS computers) and holds numbers in the range −32,768 to 32,767. Figure 3-3 shows an integer variable in memory.

(While type `int` occupies 2 bytes in MS-DOS computers, it may occupy 4 bytes on some other computers, such as some mainframes.

Here's a program that defines and uses several variables of type `int`:

```
// intvars.cpp
// demonstrates integer variables
#include <iostream.h>

d main()
    {
    int var1;                    // define var1
    int var2;                    // define var2

    var1 = 20;                   // assign value to var1
    var2 = var1 + 10;            // assign value to var2
    cout << "var1+10 is ";       // output text
    cout << var2;                // output value of var2
    }
```

Type this program into the PWB, compile and link it, and then run it. The statements

```
int var1;
int var2;
```

define two integer variables, `var1` and `var2`. The keyword `int` signals the type of variable. These statements, which are called *definitions*, must terminate with a semicolon, like other program statements.

You must define a variable before using it. However, you can place variable definitions anywhere in a program. It's not necessary to define variables before the first executable statement (as you must do in C).

FIGURE 3-3
Variable of Type int in Memory

DECLARATIONS AND DEFINITIONS

Let's digress for a moment to note a subtle distinction between the terms *definition* and *declaration* as applied to variables.

A *declaration* introduces a variable's name (such as var1) into a program and specifies its type. If a declaration also sets aside memory for the variable, it is called a *definition*. The statements

```
int var1;
int var2;
```

in the INTVARS program are definitions because they set aside memory for var1 and var2. We'll be concerned mostly with declarations that are also definitions; but in Chapter 15, when we discuss multifile programs, we'll see examples of declarations that are not definitions.

VARIABLE NAMES

The program INTVARS uses variables named var1 and var2. What are the rules for naming variables? You can use upper- and lowercase letters, and the digits from 1 to 9. You can also use the underscore (_). The first character must be a letter or underscore. Names can be as long as you like, but only the first 32 characters will be recognized. The compiler distinguishes between upper- and lowercase letters, so Var is not the same as var or VAR. (These same naming rules are used in C.)

You can't use a C++ *keyword* as a variable name. A keyword is the identifier for a language feature, like `int`, `class`, `if`, `while`, and so on. A complete list of keywords can be found in Appendix B and in Microsoft's documentation.

Many C++ programmers follow the convention of using all lowercase letters for variable names. Other programmers use a mixture of upper- and lowercase, as in `IntVar` or `dataCount`. Names in all uppercase are generally reserved for constants (see the discussion of `const` that follows).

These same conventions apply to naming other program elements such as classes and functions.

ASSIGNMENT STATEMENTS

The statements

```
var1 = 20;
var2 = var1 + 10;
```

assign values to the two variables. The equal sign =, as you might guess, causes the value on the right to be assigned to the variable on the left. The = in C++ is equivalent to the := in Pascal or the = in BASIC. In the first line shown here, `var1`, which previously had no value, is given the value 20.

INTEGER CONSTANTS

The number 20 is an *integer constant*. Constants don't change during the course of the program. An integer constant consists of numerical digits, as shown. There can be no decimal point in an integer constant, and it must lie within the range of integers.

In the second program line shown here, the plus sign + adds the value of `var1` and 10, in which 10 is another constant. The result of this addition is then assigned to `var2`.

OUTPUT VARIATIONS

The statement

```
cout << "var1+10 is ";
```

displays a string constant, as we've seen before. The next statement,

```
cout << var2;
```

displays the value of the variable `var2`. As you can see when you run the program, the output is

```
var1+10 is 30
```

Note that `cout` and the `<<` operator know how to treat an integer and a string differently. If we send them a string, they print it as text. If we send them an integer, they print it as a number. This may seem obvious, but it is another example of operator overloading, a key feature of C++. (C programmers will remember that such functions as `printf()` need to be told not only the *variable* to be displayed, but the *type* of the variable as well, which makes the syntax far less intuitive.)

CHARACTER VARIABLES

We've seen one kind of integer variable, type `int`. Another integer variable is type `char`. This type stores integers that range in value from –128 to 127. Variables of this type occupy only 1 byte of memory. Character variables are sometimes used to store numbers that confine themselves to this limited range, but they are more commonly used to store ASCII characters.

As you probably know, the ASCII character set is a way of representing characters such as 'a', 'B', '$', '3', and so on, as numbers. These numbers range from 0 to 127. (Most MS-DOS computers extend this range to 255 to accommodate various foreign-language and graphics characters.) Appendix A shows the ASCII character set.

CHARACTER CONSTANTS

Character constants use single quotation marks around a character, as shown in the previous paragraph. (Note that this differs from string constants, which use double quotation marks.) When the C++ compiler encounters such a character constant, it translates it into the corresponding ASCII code and stores that number in the program. The constant 'a' appearing in a program, for example, will be stored as 97, as shown in Figure 3-4.

Character variables can be assigned character constants as values. The following program shows some examples of character constants and variables:

```
// charvars.cpp
// demonstrates character variables
#include <iostream.h>          // for cout, etc.
void main()
    {
    char charvar1 = 'A';       // define char variable as character
    char charvar2 = '\t';      // define char variable as tab

    cout << charvar1;          // display character
    cout << charvar2;          // display character
    charvar1 = 'B';            // set char variable to char constant
    cout << charvar1;          // display character
    cout << '\n';              // display newline character
    }
```

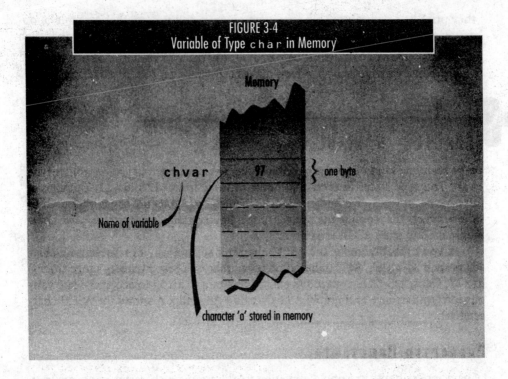

FIGURE 3-4
Variable of Type char in Memory

Memory

chvar — 97 } one byte

Name of variable

character 'a' stored in memory

INITIALIZATION

Variables can be initialized at the same time they are defined. In this program two variables of type char—charvar1 and charvar2—are initialized to the character constants 'A' and '\t'.

ESCAPE SEQUENCES

This second character constant, '\t', is an odd one. It is called an *escape sequence*, since the backslash causes an "escape" from the normal way characters are interpreted. In this case the t is interpreted not as the character 't' but as the tab character. (In Microsoft C/C++ a tab causes printing to continue eight spaces to the right.)

Another character constant, '\n', is sent directly to cout in the last line of the program. This is the escape sequence for the newline character. This character causes both a carriage return and linefeed, so that the next character to be printed appears at the beginning of the next line down. This is by far the most frequently used escape sequence.

Escape sequences can be used in both character and string constants. Table 3-1 shows a list of common escape sequences.

Since the backslash, the single quotation marks, and the double quotation marks all have specialized meanings when used in constants, they must be represented by escape sequences. Here's an example of a quoted phrase in a string constant:

```
cout << "\"Run, Spot, run,\" she said.";
```

Sometimes you need to represent a character constant that doesn't appear on the keyboard, such as the graphics characters above ASCII code 127. To do this, you can use the '\xdd' representation, where each d stands for a hexadecimal digit. If you want to print a solid rectangle, for example, you'll find such a character listed as decimal number 178, which is hexadecimal number B2 in the ASCII table. This character would be represented by the character constant '\xB2'. We'll see some examples of this later.

The CHARVARS program prints the value of **charvar1** ('A') and the value of **charvar2** (a tab). It then sets **charvar1** to a new value ('B'), prints that, and finally prints the newline. The output looks like this:

A   B

TABLE 3-1 Common Escape Sequences	
\a	Bell (beep)
\f	Formfeed
\r	Return
\\	Backslash
\"	Double quotation marks

49

INPUT WITH cin

Now that we've seen some variable types in use, let's see how a program accomplishes input. The next example program asks the user for a temperature in degrees Fahrenheit, converts it to Celsius, and displays the result.

```
// fahren.cpp
// demonstrates cin, newline
#include <iostream.h>

void main()
    {
    int ftemp;

    cout << "Enter temperature in fahrenheit: ";
    cin >> ftemp;
    int ctemp = (ftemp-32) * 5 / 9;
    cout << "Equivalent in Celsius is: " << ctemp << '\n';
    }
```

The statement

```
cin >> ftemp;
```

causes the program to wait for the user to type in a number. The resulting number is placed in the variable `ftemp`. The keyword `cin` (pronounced "C in") is an object, predefined in C++ to correspond to the standard input stream. This stream represents data coming from the keyboard (unless it has been redirected). The `>>` is the *extraction* or *get from* operator. It takes the value from the stream object on its left and places it in the variable on its right.

Here's some sample interaction with the program:

```
Enter temperature in fahrenheit: 212
Equivalent in Celsius is: 100
```

Figure 3-5 shows input using `cin` and the extraction operator `>>`.

VARIABLES DEFINED AT POINT OF USE

The FAHREN program has several new wrinkles besides its input capability. Look closely at the listing. Where is the variable `ctemp` defined? Not at the beginning of the program, but in the next-to-the-last line, where it's used to store the result of the arithmetic operation. As we noted earlier, you can define variables throughout a program, not just at the beginning. (Many languages, including C, require all variables to be defined before the first executable statement.)

Defining variables where they are used can make the listing easier to understand, since you don't need to refer repeatedly to the start of the listing to find the variable

FIGURE 3-5
Input with `cin`

Variable

definitions. However, the practice should be used with discretion. Variables that are used in many places in a function are probably better defined at the start of the function.

CASCADING <<

The insertion operator `<<` is used repeatedly in the second `cout` statement in FAHREN. This is perfectly legal. The program first sends the phrase *Equivalent in centigrade is:* to `cout`, then it sends the value of `ctemp`, and finally the newline character '\n'.

The extraction operator `>>` can be cascaded with `cin` in the same way, allowing the user to enter a series of values. However, this capability is not used so often, since it eliminates the opportunity to prompt the user between inputs.

EXPRESSIONS

Any arrangement of variables and operators that specifies a computation is called an *expression*. Thus `alpha+12` and `(alpha-37)*beta/2` are expressions. When the computations specified in the expression are performed, the result is usually a value. Thus if `alpha` is 7, the first expression shown has the value 19.

Parts of expressions may also be expressions. In the second example, `alpha-37` and `beta/2` are expressions. Even single variables and constants, like `alpha` and 37, are considered to be expressions.

Note that expressions aren't the same as statements. Statements tell the compiler to do something and terminate with a semicolon, while expressions specify a computation. There can be several expressions in a statement.

PRECEDENCE

Note the parentheses in the expression

```
(ftemp-32) * 5 / 9
```

Without the parentheses, the multiplication would be carried out first, since * has higher priority than -. With the parentheses, the subtraction is done first, then the multiplication, since all operations inside parentheses are carried out first. Precedence and parentheses are normally applied this same way in algebra and in other computer languages, so their use probably seems quite natural. However, precedence is an important topic in C++. We'll return to it later when we introduce different kinds of operators.

TYPE float

We've talked about type int and type char, both of which represent numbers as integers—that is, numbers without a fractional part. Now let's examine a different way of storing numbers: as *floating-point* variables.

Floating-point variables represent numbers with a decimal place—like 3.1415927, 0.0000625, and −10.2. They have both an integer part, to the left of the decimal point, and a fractional part, to the right. Floating-point variables represent *real numbers*, which are used for measurable quantities like distance, area, temperature, and so on, and typically have a fractional part.

There are three kinds of floating-point variables in C++: type float, type double, and type long double. Let's look at the smallest of these, type float.

Type float stores numbers in the range 3.4×10^{-38} to 3.4×10^{38}, with a precision of seven digits. It occupies 4 bytes in memory, as shown in Figure 3-6.

The following example program prompts the user to type in a floating-point number representing the radius of a circle. It then calculates and displays the circle's area.

```
// circarea.cpp
// demonstrates floating point variables
#include <iostream.h>                      // for cout, etc.

d main()
{
float rad;                              // variable of type float
const float PI = 3.14159;               // type const float

cout << "Enter radius of circle: ";     // prompt
cin >> rad;                             // get radius
float area = PI * rad * rad;            // find area
cout << "Area is " << area << endl;     // display answer
}
```

FIGURE 3-6
Variable of Type f l o a t in Memory

Here's a sample interaction with the program:

```
Enter radius of circle: 0.5
Area is 0.785398
```

This is the area in square feet of a 12-inch LP record (which has a radius of 0.5 feet). At one time this was an important quantity for manufacturers of vinyl.

FLOATING-POINT CONSTANTS

The number 3.14159 in CIRCAREA is an example of a *floating-point constant*. The decimal point signals that it is a floating-point constant, and not an integer. This number is written in normal decimal notation.

You can also write floating-point constants using exponential notation. For example, the number 1234.56 would be written 1.23456E3 in exponential notation. This is the same as 1.23456 times 10^3. The number following the E is called the *exponent*. It indicates how many places the decimal point must be moved to change the number to ordinary decimal notation.

The exponent can be positive or negative. The exponential number 6.35239E–5 is equivalent to 0.0000635239 in decimal notation. This is the same as 6.35239 times 10^{-5}.

THE const QUALIFIER

Besides demonstrating variables of type float, the CIRCAREA example also introduces the qualifier const. The keyword const (for *constant*) precedes the data type of a variable. It specifies that the value of a variable *will not change* throughout the program. Any attempt to alter the value of a variable defined with this qualifier will elicit an error message from the compiler.

The qualifier const ensures that your program does not inadvertently alter a variable that you intended to be a constant, such as the value of PI in CIRCAREA. It also reminds anyone reading the listing that the variable is not intended to change. Variables with this qualifier are sometimes named in all uppercase, as a reminder that they are constants.

THE #define DIRECTIVE

Although the construction is not popular in C++, we should note that you can also specify constants using the preprocessor directive #define. This directive sets up an equivalence between an identifier and a text phrase. For example, the line

```
#define PI 3.14159
```

appearing at the beginning of your program specifies that the identifier PI will be replaced by the text 3.14159 throughout program. This construction has long been popular in C. However, you can't specify the data type of the constant using #define, which can lead to program bugs; so even in C #define is being superseded by const used with normal variables.

ANIPULATORS

Manipulators are operators used with the insertion operator << to modify—or manipulate—the way data is displayed. We'll look at two of the most common here: endl and setw.

THE endl MANIPULATOR

The last cout statement in the CIRCAREA program ends with an unfamiliar word: endl. This is a manipulator that causes a linefeed to be inserted into the stream. It has the same effect as sending the single '\n' character, but is perhaps somewhat clearer.

THE setw MANIPULATOR

You can think of each value displayed by cout as occupying a *field*: an imaginary box with a certain width. The default field is just wide enough to hold the value.

That is, the integer 567 will occupy a field three characters wide, and the string "pajamas" will occupy a field seven characters wide. However, in certain situations this may not lead to optimal results. Here's an example. The WIDTH1 program prints the names of three cities in one column, and their populations in another.

```
// width1.cpp
// demonstrates need for setw manipulator
#include <iostream.h>

void main()
{
    long pop1=2425785, pop2=47, pop3=9761;

    cout << "LOCATION " << "POP." << endl
         << "Portcity " << pop1 << endl
         << "Hightown " << pop2 << endl
         << "Lowville " << pop3 << endl;
}
```

Here's the output from this program:

```
LOCATION POP.
Portcity 2425785
Hightown 47
Lowville 9761
```

Unfortunately, the output of WIDTH1 is not ideal. It's hard to compare the numbers; it would be better if they lined up to the right. Also, we had to insert spaces into the names of the cities to separate them from the numbers. This is an inconvenience.

Here's a variation of this program, WIDTH2, that uses the setw manipulator to eliminate these problems by specifying field widths for the names and the numbers:

```
// width2.cpp
// demonstrates setw manipulator
#include <iostream.h>
#include <iomanip.h>        // for setw

void main()
{
    long pop1=2425785, pop2=47, pop3=9761;

    cout << setw(8) << "LOCATION" << setw(12)
                                  << "POPULATION" << endl
         << setw(8) << "Portcity" << setw(12) << pop1 << endl
         << setw(8) << "Hightown" << setw(12) << pop2 << endl
         << setw(8) << "Lowville" << setw(12) << pop3 << endl;
}
```

The setw manipulator causes the number (or string) that follows it in the stream to be printed within a field n characters wide, where n is the argument to setw(n). The value is right-justified within the field. Figure 3-7 shows how this looks.

Here's the output of WIDTH2:

```
LOCATION  POPULATION
Portcity     2425785
Hightown          47
Lowville        9761
```

TYPE Long

Besides the use of setw, there are several new aspects to the WIDTH1 and WIDTH2 programs. First, we've used a new data type: long. This is the third of the integer types, after char and int. Type long can also be written as long int; these mean the same thing. Type long can hold integers in the range −2,147,483,648 to 2,147,483,647. It's used when type int is too small for the values being stored. In WIDTH1 and WIDTH2 the population figures exceed the upper limit of type int—32,767—so type long must be used. Variables of type long occupy four bytes of memory (twice as much as type int), as shown in Figure 3-8.

If you want to create a constant of type long, use the letter L following the numerical value, as in

```
longvar = 7678L; // assigns long constant 7678 to longvar
```

If a constant's value is greater than 65,535, it is interpreted as type long whether you use the L or not.

CASCADING THE INSERTION OPERATOR

Note that there's only one cout statement in WIDTH1 and WIDTH2, although it's written on multiple lines. In doing this, we take advantage of the fact that the

FIGURE 3-7
Field Widths and setw

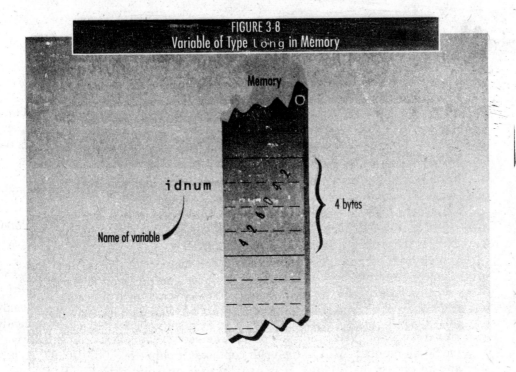

FIGURE 3-8
Variable of Type Long in Memory

Memory

idnum

Name of variable

4 bytes

compiler ignores white space, and that the insertion operator can be cascaded. The effect is the same as using four separate statements, each beginning with `cout`.

MULTIPLE DEFINITIONS

We've initialized the variables `pop1`, `pop2`, and `pop3` to specific values at the same time we defined them. This is similar to the way we initialized `char` variables in the CHARVARS example. Here, however, we've defined and initialized all three variables on one line, using the same `long` keyword and separating the variable names with commas. This saves space where a number of variables are all the same type.

THE IOMANIP.H HEADER FILE

The declarations for the manipulators are not in the usual IOSTREAM.H header file, but in a separate header file called IOMANIP.H. When you use these manipulators you must `#include` this header file in your program, as we do in the WIDTH2 example.

VARIABLE TYPE SUMMARY

Our program examples so far have covered four data types—int, char, float, and long. There are three others we haven't seen yet: short, double, and long double. Let's pause now to summarize these data types. Table 3-2 shows the keyword used to define the type, the numerical range the type can accommodate, the digits of precision (in the case of floating-point numbers), and the bytes of memory occupied in the MS-DOS environment.

There are four integer types: char, int, short, and long; and three floating-point types: float, double, and long double.

In the current MS-DOS environment, short is identical to int, so it is seldom used except in certain Microsoft library functions. However, on some computer systems, such as those using a 32-bit word length, short is smaller than int.

Type double occupies 8 bytes, twice as much memory as type float, and stores floating-point numbers with much larger range and precision. It stands for *double-precision floating point*. It's used when type float is too small or insufficiently precise. Floating-point type long double occupies 10 bytes, and has only slightly greater range and precision than type double. However, it offers compatibility with the 80-bit numbers used in the math coprocessor chip (the 8087, 80287, 80387, and so on, or the 80486). It is usually used in conjunction with the math coprocessor. Figure 3-9 shows types double and long double.

Remember that integer type long extracts a performance penalty compared with type int. It is slower in arithmetic operations, and it occupies more memory, making your program larger. Similarly, the floating-point types double and long double

TABLE 3-2 Basic C++ Variable Types				
Keyword	Numerical range: low	high	Digits of precision	Bytes of memory
char	−128	127	n/a	1
int (and short)	−32,768	32,767	n/a	2
long	−2,147,483,648	2,147,483,647	n/a	4
float	3.4×10^{-38}	3.4×10^{38}	7	4
double	1.7×10^{-308}	1.7×10^{308}	15	8
long double	3.4×10^{-4932}	1.1×10^{4932}	19	10

are slower and larger than type `float`. You should use the smallest variable type that stores the values you're using in your program.

unsigned DATA TYPES

By eliminating the sign of the character and integer types, you can change their range to start at 0 and include only positive numbers. This allows them to represent numbers twice as big as the signed type. Table 3-3 shows the unsigned versions.

The `unsigned` types are used when the quantities represented are always positive—such as when representing a count of something—or when the positive range of the signed types is not quite long enough.

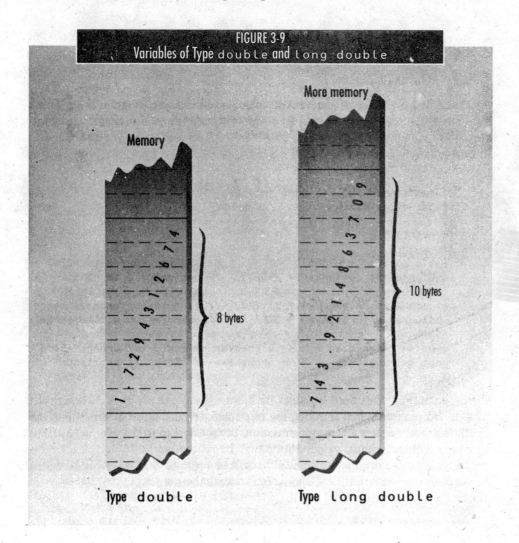

FIGURE 3-9
Variables of Type `double` and `long double`

Keyword	Numerical range: low	high	Bytes of memory
unsigned char	0	255	1
unsigned int	0	65,535	2
unsigned long	0	4,294,967,295	4

TABLE 3-3
Unsigned Integer Types

To change an integer type to an unsigned type, precede the data type keyword with the keyword `unsigned`. For example, an unsigned variable of type `char` would be defined as

```
unsigned char ucharvar;
```

Exceeding the range of signed types can lead to obscure program bugs. These bugs can sometimes be eliminated by using unsigned types. For example, the following program stores the constant 25000 both as an `int` in `signedVar`, and as an `unsigned int` in `unsignVar`.

```
// signtest.cpp
// tests signed and unsigned integers
#include <iostream.h>

void main()
    {
    int signedVar = 25000;           // signed: -32768 to 32767
    unsigned int unsignVar = 25000;  // unsigned: 0 to 65535

    signedVar = (signedVar * 2) / 3; // calculation exceeds range
    unsignVar = (unsignVar * 2) / 3; // calculation within range

    cout << "signedVar = " << signedVar << endl;  // wrong: -5178
    cout << "unsignVar = " << unsignVar << endl;  // ok: 16666
    }
```

The program multiplies both variables by 2, then divides them by 3. Although the result is 2/3 of the original number, the intermediate calculation is larger than the original number. This is a common situation, but it can lead to trouble. In SIGNTEST we expect that the original value, 25000, will be restored to both variables. Unfortunately, in `signedVar` the multiplication created a result—50,000—that exceeded the range of the variable (-32768 to 32767). Here's the output:

```
signedVar = -5178
unsignVar = 16666
```

The signed variable now displays an incorrect answer, while the unsigned variable, which is large enough to hold the intermediate result of the multiplication, records the result correctly. The moral is this: Be careful that all values generated in your program are within the range of the variables that hold them. (The results may be different on non-MS-DOS computers, which may use more bytes for type int.)

TYPE CONVERSION

C++, like C, is more forgiving than some languages in the way it treats expression involving several different data types. As an example, consider the MIXED program:

```
// mixed.cpp
// shows mixed expressions
#include <iostream.h>

void main()
{
    int count = 7;
    float avgWeight = 155.5;

    double totalWeight = count * avgWeight;
    cout << "totalWeight=" << totalWeight << endl;
}
```

Here a variable of type int is multiplied by a variable of type float to yield a result of type double. This program compiles without error, the compiler considers it normal that you want to multiply (or perform any other arithmetic operation on) numbers of different types. (However, you may get a warning message, depending on the warning level you set from the Options menu.)

Not all languages are this relaxed. Some don't permit mixed expressions, and would flag as an error the line that performs the arithmetic in MIXED. Such languages assume that when you mix types you're making a mistake, and they try to save you from yourself. C++ and C, however, assume that you must have a good reason for doing what you're doing, and they help to carry out your intentions. This is one reason for the popularity of C++ and C. They give you more freedom.

AUTOMATIC CONVERSIONS

Let's consider what happens when the compiler confronts such mixed-type expressions as that in MIXED. Types are considered "higher" or "lower," based roughly on the order shown in Table 3-4.

When two operands of different types are encountered in the same expression, the lower-type variable is converted to the type of the higher-type variable. Thus in

Data type	Order
long double	(highest)
double	
float	
long	
int	
char	(lowest)

TABLE 3-4
Order of Data Types.

MIXED the `int` value of `count` is converted to type `float` and stored in a temporary variable before being multiplied by the `float` variable `avgWeight`. The result (still of type `float`) is then converted to `double` so that it can be assigned to the `double` variable `totalWeight`. This process is shown in Figure 3-10.

These conversions take place invisibly, and ordinarily you don't need to think too much about them; C++ automatically does what you want. However, when we start to use objects, we will in effect be defining our own data types. We may want to use these new data types in mixed expressions, just as we use normal variables in mixed expressions. When this is the case, we must be careful to create our own conversion routines to change objects of one type into objects of another. The compiler won't do it for us, as it does here with the built-in data types.

CASTS

In C++ the term *casts* applies to data conversions specified by the programmer, as opposed to the automatic data conversions we just described. What are casts for? Sometimes a programmer needs to convert a value from one type to another in a situation where the compiler will not do it automatically. Recall that in the SIGNTEST example an intermediate result exceeded the capacity of the variable type, resulting in an erroneous result. We fixed the problem by using `unsigned int` instead of `int`. This worked because the intermediate result—50,000—would fit in the range of the unsigned variable.

But suppose an intermediate result won't fit the unsigned type either. In such a case, we might be able to solve the problem by using a cast. Here's an example:

```
// cast.cpp
// tests signed and unsigned integers
#include <iostream.h>

void main()
    {
```

```
    int intVar = 25000;              // signed: -32768 to 32767
    intVar = (intVar * 10) / 10;     // result too large
    cout << "intVar = " << intVar << endl;   // wrong answer

    intVar = 25000;
    intVar = ( long(intVar) * 10) / 10;      // cast to long
    cout << "intVar = " << intVar << endl;   // right answer
    }
```

When we multiply the variable intVar by 10, the result—250,000—is far too large to fit in a variable of type int, or unsigned int. This leads to the wrong answer, as shown in the first part of the program.

We could redefine the data type of the variables to be long; this provides plenty of room, since this type holds numbers up to 2,147,483,647. But suppose that for some reason, such as keeping the program small, we don't want to change the variables to type long. In this case there's another solution: We can cast intVar

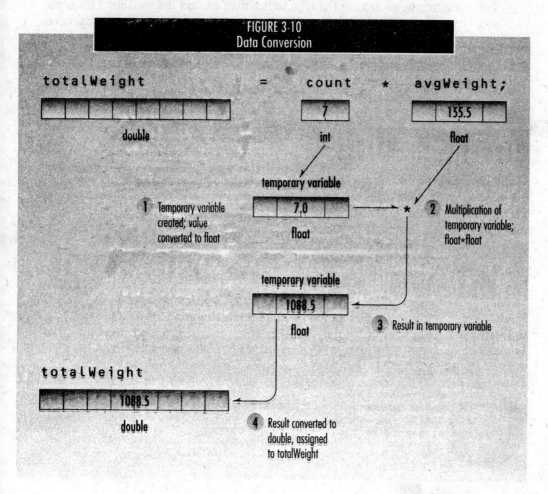

FIGURE 3-10
Data Conversion

to type long before multiplying. This is sometimes called *coercion*; the data is *coerced* into becoming another type. The expression

```
long(intVar)
```

casts intVar to type long. It generates a temporary variable of type long with the same value as intVar. It is this temporary variable that is multiplied by 10. Since it is type long, the result fits. This result is then divided by 10 and assigned to the normal int variable intVar. Here's the program's output:

```
intVar = -1214
intVar = 25000
```

The first answer, without the cast, is wrong; but in the second answer, the cast produces the correct result.

You can use another syntax for casts. You can say

```
(long)intVar
```

with the parentheses around the type rather than around the variable. This is the only syntax acceptable in C, but in C++ the first approach (called "functional notation") is preferred, because it is similar to the way other parts of C++, such as functions, are written. (Occassionally, however, you may find situations where the preferred approach doesn't work.)

ARITHMETIC OPERATORS

As you have probably gathered by this time, C++ uses the four normal arithmetic operators +, -, *, and / for addition, subtraction, multiplication, and division. These operators work on all the data types, both integer and floating-point. They are used in much the same way as in other languages, and are closely analogous to their use in algebra. However, there are some other arithmetic operators whose use is not so obvious.

THE REMAINDER OPERATOR

There is a fifth arithmetic operator that works only with integer variables (types char, int and long). It's called the *remainder* operator, and is represented by %, the percent symbol. This operator (also called the *modulus* operator) finds the remainder when one number is divided by another. The REMAIND program demonstrates the effect.

```
// remaind.cpp
// demonstrates remainder operator
#include <iostream.h>

void main()
    {
```

```
cout <<  6 % 8 << endl      // 6
     <<  7 % 8 << endl      // 7
     <<  8 % 8 << endl      // 0
     <<  9 % 8 << endl      // 1
     << 10 % 8 << endl;     // 2
}
```

Here the numbers 6 through 10 are divided by 8, using the remainder operator. The answers are 6, 7, 0, 1, and 2—the remainders of these divisions. The remainder operator is used in a wide variety of situations. We'll show examples as we go along.

A note about precedence: In the expression

```
cout << 6 % 8
```

the remainder operator is evaluated first because it has higher precedence than the << operator. If it did not, we would need to put parentheses around (6 % 8) to ensure it was evaluated before being acted on by <<.

ARITHMETIC ASSIGNMENT OPERATORS

C++ offers several ways to shorten and clarify your code. One of these is the *arithmetic assignment operator*. While not a key feature of the language, this operator is commonly used, and it helps to give C++ listings their distinctive appearance.

The following kind of statement is common in most languages:

```
total = total + item;  // adds "item" to "total"
```

In this situation you add something to an existing value (or you perform some other arithmetic operation on it). But the syntax of this statement offends those for whom brevity is important, because the name total appears twice. So C++ offers a condensed approach: the arithmetic assignment operator, which combines an arithmetic operator and an assignment operator, and eliminates the repeated operand. Here's a statement that has exactly the same effect as the one above:

```
total += item;   // adds "item" to "total"
```

Figure 3-11 emphasizes the equivalence of the two forms.

There are arithmetic assignment operators corresponding to all the arithmetic operations: +=, -=, *=, /=, and %= (and some other operators as well). The following example shows the arithmetic assignment operators in use:

```
// assign.cpp
// demonstrates arithmetic assignment operators
#include <iostream.h>

d main()
{
int ans = 27;
ans += 10;                  // same as: ans = ans + 10;
```

```
cout << endl << ans;
ans -= 7;                    // same as: ans = ans - 7;
cout << endl << ans;
ans *= 2;                    // same as: ans = ans * 2;
cout << endl << ans;
ans /= 3;                    // same as: ans = ans / 3;
cout << endl << ans;
ans %= 3;                    // same as: ans = ans % 3;
cout << endl << ans;
}
```

Here's the output from this program:

```
37
30
60
20
2
```

You don't need to use arithmetic assignment operators in your code, but they are a common feature of the language; they'll appear in numerous examples in this book.

FIGURE 3-11
Arithmetic Assignment Operator

INCREMENT OPERATORS

Here's an even more specialized operator. You often need to add 1 to the value of an existing variable. You can do this the "normal" way:

```
count = count + 1;   // adds 1 to "count"
```

Or you can use an arithmetic assignment operator:

```
count += 1;   // adds 1 to "count"
```

But there's an even more condensed approach:

```
++count;   // adds 1 to "count"
```

The **++** operator *increments* (adds 1 to) its argument.

Prefix and Postfix

As if this weren't weird enough, the increment operator can be used in two ways: as a *prefix*, meaning that the operator precedes the variable; and as a *postfix*, meaning that the operator follows the variable. What's the difference? Often a variable is incremented within a statement that performs some other operation on it. For example,

```
totalWeight = avgWeight * ++count;
```

The question here is, is the multiplication performed before or after `count` is incremented? In this case `count` is incremented first. How do we know that? Because *prefix* notation is used: **++count**. If we had used postfix notation, **count++**, the multiplication would have been performed first, then `count` would have been incremented. This is shown in Figure 3-12.

Here's an example that shows both the prefix and postfix versions of the increment operator:

```
// increm.cpp
// demonstrates the increment operator
#include <iostream.h>

void main()
    {
    int count = 10;

    cout << "count=" << count << endl;     // displays 10
    cout << "count=" << ++count << endl;   // displays 11 (prefix)
    cout << "count=" << count << endl;     // displays 11
    cout << "count=" << count++ << endl;   // displays 11 (postfix)
    cout << "count=" << count << endl;     // displays 12
    }
```

FIGURE 3-12
The Increment Operator

Here's the program's output:

```
count=10
count=11
count=11
count=11
count=12
```

The first time **count** is incremented, the prefix **++** operator is used. This causes the increment to happen at the beginning of the statement evaluation, before the output operation has been carried out. When the value of the expression **++count** is displayed, it has already been incremented, and **<<** sees the value 11. The second time **count** is incremented, the postfix **++** operator is used. When the expression `count++` is displayed, it retains its unincremented value of 11. Following the completion of this statement, the increment takes effect, so that in the last statement of the program we see that `count` has acquired the value 12.

The Decrement (−−) Operator

The decrement operator, `--`, behaves very much like the increment operator, except that it subtracts 1 from its operand. It can also be used in both prefix and postfix forms.

LIBRARY FUNCTIONS

Many activities in C++ are carried out by *library functions*. These functions perform file access, mathematical computations, graphics, memory management, and data conversion, among other things. We don't want to dig too deeply into library functions before we explain how functions work (see Chapter 6), but you can use simple library functions without a thorough understanding of their operation. Here's a preview.

The next example, SQRT, uses the library function `sqrt()` to calculate the square root of a number entered by the user:

```
// sqrt.cpp
// demonstrates sqrt() library function
#include <iostream.h>              // for cout, etc.
#include <math.h>                  // for sqrt()
void main()
    {
    double number, answer;        // sqrt() requires type double
    cout << "Enter a number: ";
    cin >> number;                // get the number
    answer = sqrt(number);        // find square root
    cout << "Square root is "
         << answer << endl;       // display it
    }
```

The program first obtains a number from the user. This number is then used as an *argument* to the `sqrt()` function, in the statement

```
answer = sqrt(number);
```

An argument is the input to the function; it is placed inside the parentheses following the function name. The function then processes the argument and *returns* a value; this is the output from the function. In this case the return value is the square root of the original number. *Returning a value* means that the function expression takes on this value, which can then be assigned to another variable—in this case `answer`. The program then displays this value. Here's some output from the program:

```
Enter a number: 1000
Square root is 31.622777
```

Multiplying 31.62777 by itself on your pocket calculator will verify that this answer is pretty close.

The arguments to a function, and their return values, must be the correct data type. You can find what these data types are by looking at the description of the library function in the Microsoft *Run-Time Library Reference*, which describes each of the hundreds of library functions. For `sqrt()` the description specifies both an argument and a return value of type `double`, so we use variables of this type in the program.

HEADER FILES

As with `cout` and other such objects, you must `#include` a header file that contains various declarations describing any library functions you use. In the documentation for the `sqrt()` function, you'll see that the specified header file is MATH.H. In SQRT the preprocessor directive

```
#include <math.h>
```

takes care of incorporating this header file into our source file.

If you don't include the appropriate header file when you use a library function, you'll get an error message from the compiler.

LIBRARY FILES

We mentioned earlier that a file containing library functions and objects will usually be linked to your program to create an executable file. This is true for all the programs in this chapter, since they use `cout` and other objects. If you're using the Small memory model, this library file is called SLIBCE.LIB (where the S indicates *Small*). The `sqrt()` function is also found in this file. It is extracted from the file automatically by the linker, and the proper connections are made so that it can be called (that is, invoked or accessed) from the SQRT program.

HEADER FILES AND LIBRARY FILES

The relationship between library files and header files can be confusing, so let's review it. To use a library function like `sqrt()`, you must link the library file SLIBCE.LIB to your program. The appropriate functions from the library file are then connected to your program by the linker.

However, that's not the end of the story. The functions in your source file need to know the names and types of the functions and other elements in the library file. They are given this information in a header file. Each header file contains information for a particular group of functions. The functions themselves are in SLIBCE.LIB, but the information about them is scattered throughout a number of header files. The IOSTREAM.H header file contains information for various I/O functions and objects, including **cout**, while the MATH.H header file contains information for mathematics functions like **sqrt()**. If you were using memory management functions, you would include MEMORY.H, while string functions would require STRING.H, and so on.

Figure 3-13 shows the relationship of header files and library files to the other files used in program development.

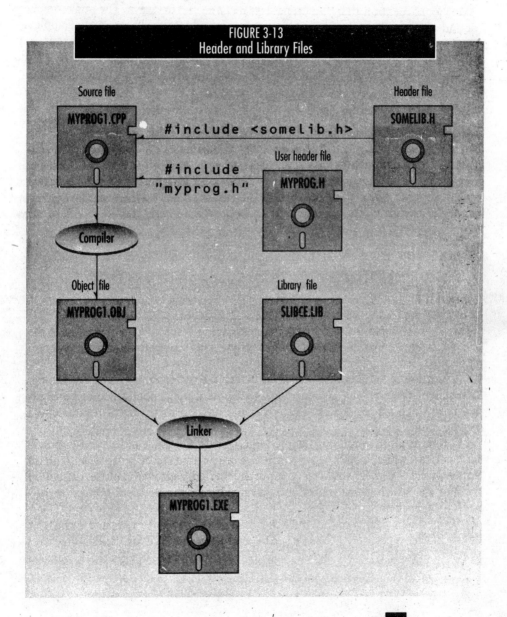

FIGURE 3-13
Header and Library Files

The use of header files is common in C++. Whenever you use a library function or a predefined object or operator, you will need to use a header file that contains appropriate declarations.

Two Ways to Use #include

We should mention that you can use `#include` in two ways. The angle brackets < and > surrounding the filenames IOSTREAM.H and MATH.H in the SQRT example indicate that the compiler should begin searching for these files in the standard INCLUDE directory. This directory holds the header files supplied by Microsoft for the system.

Instead of angle brackets around the filename, you can also use quotation marks, as in

```
#include "myheader.h"
```

Quotation marks instruct the compiler to begin its search for the header file in the *current* directory; this is usually the directory that contains the source file. You normally use quotation marks for header files you write yourself (a situation we'll explore in Chapter 15, on larger programs). Either quotation marks or angle brackets work in any case, but making the appropriate choice speeds up the compilation process slightly by giving the compiler a hint about where to find the file.

Summary

In this chapter we've learned that a major building block of C++ programs is the *function*. A function named `main()` is always the first one executed when a program is executed.

A function is composed of *statements*, which tell the computer to do something. Each statement ends with a semicolon. A statement may contain one or more *expressions*, which are sequences of variables and operators that usually evaluate to a specific value.

Output is most commonly handled in C++ with the `cout` object and `<<` insertion operator, which together cause variables or constants to be sent to the standard output device—usually the screen. Input is handled with `cin` and the extraction operator `>>`, which cause values to be received from the standard input device—usually the keyboard.

Seven major data types are built into C++: `char`, `short`, `int`, and `long int` are the integer types; and `float`, `double`, and `long double` are the floating-point types. All of these types are signed. Unsigned versions of the integer types, signaled by the keyword **unsigned**, hold numbers twice as large. The **const** keyword stipulates that a variable's value will not change in the course of a program.

A variable is converted from one type to another in mixed expressions (those involving different data types) and by casting, which allows the programmer to specify a conversion.

C++ employs the usual arithmetic operators **+**, **-**, *****, and **/**. In addition, the remainder operator, **%**, returns the remainder of integer division.

The arithmetic assignment operators **+=**, **-=**, and so on, perform an arithmetic operation and an assignment simultaneously. The increment and decrement operators **++** and **--** increase or decrease a variable by 1.

Preprocessor directives consist of instructions to the compiler, rather than to the computer. The **#include** directive tells the compiler to insert another file into the present source file, and the **#define** directive tells it to substitute one thing for another.

If you use a library function in your program, the code for the function is in a library file, which is automatically linked to your program. A header file containing the function's declaration must be inserted into your source file with an **#include** statement.

QUESTIONS

1. Dividing a program into functions
   a. is the key to object-oriented programming
   b. makes the program easier to conceptualize
   c. may reduce the size of the program
   d. makes the program run faster

2. A function name must be followed by _____.

3. A function body is delimited by _____.

4. Why is the **main()** function special?

5. A C++ instruction that tells the computer to do something is called a _____.

6. Write an example of a normal C++ comment and an example of an old-fashioned **/*** comment.

7. An expression
   a. usually evaluates to a numerical value
   b. indicates the emotional state of the program
   c. always occurs outside a function
   d. may be part of a statement

8. Specify how many bytes are occupied by the following data types in Microsoft C/C++:
   a. Type `int`
   b. Type `long double`
   c. Type `float`
   d. Type `long`

9. True or false: A variable of type `char` can hold the value 301.

10 What kind of program elements are the following?
   a. `12`
   b. `'a'`
   c. `4.28915`
   d. `JungleJim`
   e. `JungleJim()`

11. Write statements that display on the screen
   a. the character 'x'
   b. the name *Jim*
   c. the number 509

12. True or false: In an assignment statement, the value on the left of the equals sign is always equal to the value on the right.

13. Write a statement that displays the variable `george` in a field ten characters wide.

14. What header file must you `#include` with your source file to use `cout` and `cin`?

15. Write a statement that gets a numerical value from the keyboard and places it in the variable `temp`.

16. What header file must you `#include` with your program to use `setw`?

17. Three exceptions to the rule that the compiler ignores white space are _____, _____, and _____.

18. True or false: It's perfectly all right to use variables of different data types in the same arithmetic expression.

19. The expression `11%3` evaluates to _____.

20. An arithmetic assignment operator combines the effect of what two operators?

21. Write a statement that uses an arithmetic assignment operator to increase the value of the variable `temp` by 23. Write the same statement without the arithmetic assignment operator.

22. The increment operator increases the value of a variable by how much?

23. Assuming `var1` starts with the value 20, what will the following code fragment print out?

```
cout << var1--;
cout << ++var1;
```

24. In the examples we've seen so far, header files have been used for what purpose?
25. If you use the Small memory model, what library file must be linked to your program to provide standard library functions?

EXERCISES

1. Assuming there are 7.481 gallons in a cubic foot, write a program that asks the user to enter a number of gallons, and then displays the equivalent in cubic feet.
2. Write a program that generates the following table:

```
1990        135
1991       7290
1992      11300
1993      16200
```

Use a single **cout** statement for all output.
3. Write a program that generates the following output:

```
10
20
19
```

Use an integer constant for the 10, an arithmetic assignment operator to generate the 20, and a decrement operator to generate the 19.

LOOPS AND DECISIONS

RELATIONAL OPERATORS

for, while, AND do LOOPS

if AND if...else STATEMENTS

THE switch STATEMENT

THE CONDITIONAL OPERATOR

LOGICAL OPERATORS

Not many programs execute all their statements in strict order from beginning to end. Most programs (like many humans) decide what to do in response to changing circumstances. The flow of control jumps from one part of the program to another, depending on calculations performed in the program. Program statements that cause such jumps are called *control statements*. There are two major categories: loops and decisions.

How many times a loop is executed, or whether a decision results in the execution of a section of code, depends on whether certain expressions are true or false. These expressions typically involve a kind of operator called a *relational operator*, which compares two values. Since the operation of loops and decisions is so closely involved with these operators, we'll examine them first.

RELATIONAL OPERATORS

A relational operator compares two values. The values can be any built-in C++ data type, such as `char`, `int`, and `float`, or—as we'll see later—they can be user-defined classes. The comparison involves such relationships as *equal to*, *less than*, *greater than*, and so on. The result of the comparison is true or false; for example, either two values are equal (true), or they're not (false).

Our first program, RELAT, demonstrates relational operators in a comparison of integer variables and constants.

```
// relat.cpp
// demonstrates relational operators
#include <iostream.h>

d main()
    {
    int numb;

    cout << "Enter a number: ";
    cin >> numb;
```

```
cout << "numb<10   is " << (numb < 10)   << endl;
cout << "numb>10   is " << (numb > 10)   << endl;
cout << "numb==10 is " << (numb == 10) << endl;
}
```

This program performs three kinds of comparisons between 10 and a number entered by the user. Here's the output when the user enters 20:

```
Enter a number: 20
numb<10   is 0
numb>10   is 1
numb==10 is 0
```

The first expression is true if `numb` is less than 10. The second expression is true if `numb` is greater than 10, and the third is true if `numb` is equal to 10. As you can see from the output, the C++ compiler considers that a true expression has the value 1, while a false expression has the value 0. Some languages have special Boolean variables to represent true and false values, but C++ does not. It uses the integer values 0 and 1 instead.

Here's the complete list of C++ relational operators:

Operator	Meaning
>	Greater than
<	Less than
==	Equal to
!=	Not equal to
>=	Greater than or equal to
<=	Less than or equal to

Now let's look at some expressions that use relational operators, and also look at the value of each expression. The first two lines are assignment statements that set the values of the variables `harry` and `jane`. You might want to hide the comments with your old Jose Canseco baseball card and see if you can predict which expressions evaluate to true and which to false.

```
jane = 44;           // assignment statement
harry = 12;          // assignment statement
(jane == harry)      // false
(harry <= 12)        // true
(jane > harry)       // true
(jane >= 44)         // true
(harry != 12)        // false
(7 < harry)          // true
(0)                  // false (by definition)
(44)                 // true (since it's not 0)
```

Note that the equals operator, ==, uses two equals signs. A common mistake is to use a single equals sign—the assignment operator—as a relational operator. This is a nasty bug, since the compiler won't notice anything wrong. However, your program won't do what you want.

Although C++ generates a 1 to indicate true, it assumes that any value other than 0 (such as –7 or 44) is true; only 0 is false. Thus the last expression in the list is true.

Now let's see how these operators are used in typical situations. We'll examine loops first, then decisions.

LOOPS

Loops cause a section of your program to be repeated a certain number of times. The repetition continues while a condition is true. When the condition becomes false, the loop ends and control passes to the statements following the loop.

There are three kinds of loops in C++: the for loop, the while loop, and the do loop.

THE for LOOP

The for loop is (for many people, anyway) the easiest to understand of the C++ loops. All its loop-control elements are gathered in one place, while in the other loop constructions they are scattered about the program, which can make it harder to unravel how these loops work. Also, the for loop is a key concept in other languages; for a long time it was the *only* loop construction available in BASIC, for example.

The for loop executes a section of code a fixed number of times. It's usually (although not always) used when you know, before entering the loop, how many times you want to execute the code.

Here's an example, FORDEMO, that displays the squares of the numbers from 0 to 14:

```
// fordemo.cpp
// demonstrates simple FOR loop
#include <iostream.h>

void main()
   {
   int j;                       // define a loop variable

   for(j=0; j<15; ++j)          // loop from 0 to 14,
      cout << j * j << " ";     // displaying the square of j
   }
```

Here's the output:

```
0  1  4  9  16  25  36  49  64  81  100  121  144  169  196
```

How does this work? The for statement controls the loop. It consists of the keyword for, followed by parentheses that contain three expressions separated by semicolons:

```
for(j=0; j<15; ++j)
```

These three expressions are the *initialization expression*, the *test expression*, and the *increment expression*, as shown in Figure 4-1.

These three expressions usually (but not always) involve the same variable, which we can call the *loop variable*. In the FORDEMO example the loop variable is j. It's defined before the loop begins.

The *body* of the loop is the code to be executed each time through the loop. Repeating this code is the *raison d'être* for the loop. In this example the loop body consists of a single statement:

```
cout << j * j << "  ";
```

This statement prints out the square of j, followed by two spaces. The square is found by multiplying j by itself. As the loop executes, j goes through the sequence 0, 1, 2, 3, and so on up to 14; so the squares of these numbers are displayed—0, 1, 4, 9, up to 196.

Note that the for statement is not followed by a semicolon. That's because the for statement and the loop body are *together* considered to be a program statement.

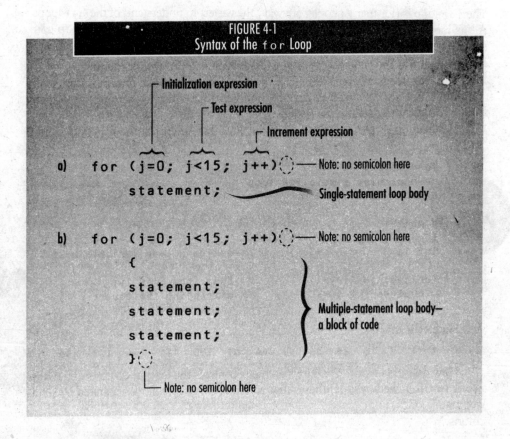

FIGURE 4-1
Syntax of the for Loop

This is an important detail. If you put a semicolon after the for statement, the compiler will think there is no loop body, and the program will do things you don't expect.

Let's see how the three expressions in the for statement control the loop.

The Initialization Expression

The initialization expression is executed only once, when the loop first starts. It gives the loop variable an initial value. In the FORDEMO example it sets j to 0.

The Test Expression

The test expression usually involves a relational operator. It is evaluated each time through the loop, just before the body of the loop is executed. It determines whether the loop will be executed again. If the test expression is true, the loop is executed one more time. If it's false, the loop ends, and control passes to the statements following the loop. In the FORDEMO example there are no statements following the loop, so the program ends when the test expression becomes false.

The Increment Expression

The increment expression changes the value of the loop variable, often by incrementing it. It is always executed at the end of the loop, after the loop body has been executed. Here the increment operator ++ adds 1 to j each time through the loop. Figure 4-2 shows a flowchart of a for loop's operation.

How Many Times?

The loop in the FOR example executes exactly 15 times. The first time, j is 0. This is ensured in the initialization expression. The last time through the loop, j is 14. This is determined by the test expression j<15. When j becomes 15, the loop terminates; the loop body is not executed when j has this value. The arrangement shown is commonly used to do something a fixed number of times: start at 0, use a test expression with the less-than operator and a value equal to the desired number of iterations, and increment the loop variable after each iteration.

Here's another for loop example:

```
for(count=0; count<100; count++)
    // loop body
```

How many times will the loop body be repeated here? Exactly 100 times, with count going from 0 to 99.

Multiple Statements in Loop Body

Of course you may want to execute more than one statement in the loop body. Multiple statements are delimited by braces, just as functions are. Note that there is no semicolon following the final brace of the loop body, although there are semicolons

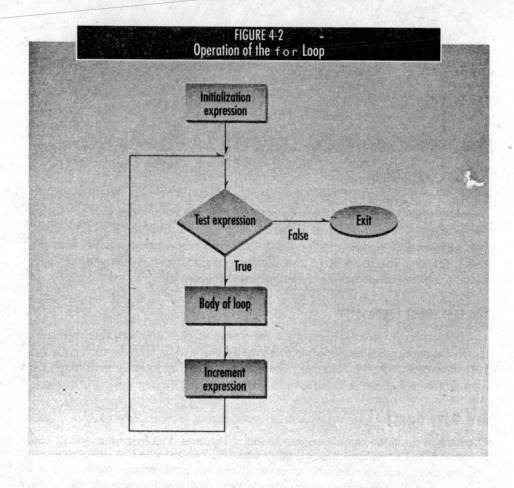

FIGURE 4-2
Operation of the for Loop

following the individual statements in the loop body. See Figure 4-1-b for the syntax of a multistatement for loop.

The next example, CUBELIST, uses three statements in the loop body. It prints out the cubes of the numbers from 1 to 10, using a two-column format.

```cpp
// cubelist.cpp
// lists cubes from 1 to 10
#include <iostream.h>
#include <iomanip.h>                    // for setw

void main()
   {
   int numb;                           // define loop variable

   for(numb=1; numb<=10; numb++)       // loop from 1 to 10
      {
```

```
    cout << setw(4) << numb;          // display 1st column
    int cube = numb*numb*numb;        // calculate cube
    cout << setw(6) << cube << endl;  // display 2nd column
    }
}
```

Here's the output from the program:

```
 1     1
 2     8
 3    27
 4    64
 5   125
 6   216
 7   343
 8   512
 9   729
10  1000
```

We've made another change in the program, to show there's nothing immutable about the format used in the last example. The loop variable is initialized to 1, not to 0. It also ends at 10, not at 9, by virtue of <=, the less-than-or-equal-to operator. The effect is that the loop body is executed 10 times, with the loop variable running from 1 to 10 (not from 0 to 9).

Blocks and Variable Visibility

The loop body, which consists of braces delimiting several statements, is called a block of code. One important aspect of a block is that a variable defined inside the block is not visible outside it. In CUBELIST we define the variable cube inside the block, in the statement

```
int cube = numb*numb*numb;
```

You can't access this variable outside the block; it's only visible within the braces. Thus if you placed the statement

```
cube = 10;
```

after the loop body, the compiler would signal an error because the variable cube would be undefined outside the loop.

One advantage of restricting the visibility of variables is that the same variable name can be used within different blocks in the same program. We'll see examples later. (Defining variables inside a block, as we did in CUBELIST, is common in C++ but is not popular in C.)

Indentation and Loop Style

Good programming style dictates that the loop body be indented—that is, shifted right, relative to the loop statement (and to the rest of the program). In the FOR example, one line is indented; and in CUBELIST the entire block, including the braces, is indented. This indentation is an important visual aid to the programmer: It makes it easy to see where the loop body begins and ends. The compiler doesn't care whether you indent or not (at least there's no way to tell if it cares).

There is a common variation on the style we use for loops in this book. We show the braces aligned vertically, but some programmers prefer to place the opening brace just after the loop statement, like this:

```
for(numb=1; numb<=10; numb++)  {
    cout << setw(4) << numb;
    int cube = numb*numb*numb;
    cout << setw(6) << cube << endl;
    }
```

This saves a line in the listing but makes it more difficult to read, since the opening brace is harder to see and harder to match with the corresponding closing brace.

for LOOP VARIATIONS

The increment expression doesn't need to increment the loop variable; it can perform any operation it likes. In the next example it *decrements* the loop variable. This program, FACTOR, asks the user to type in a number, and then calculates the factorial of this number. (The factorial is calculated by multiplying the original number by all the positive integers smaller than itself. Thus the factorial of 5 is 5*4*3*2*1, or 120.)

```
// factor.cpp
// calculates factorials, demonstrates FOR loop
#include <iostream.h>

void main()
    {
    unsigned int numb;
    unsigned long fact=1;                // long for larger numbers

    cout << "\nEnter a number: ";
    cin >> numb;                         // get number

    for(int j=numb; j>0; j--)            // multiply 1 by
        fact *= j;                       // numb, numb-1, ..., 2, 1
    cout << "Factorial is " << fact;     // result is factorial
    }
```

In this example the initialization expression sets j to the value entered by the user. The test expression causes the loop to execute as long as j is greater than 0. The increment expression decrements j after each iteration.

We've used type `unsigned long` for the factorial, since the factorials even of small numbers are very large, as can be seen in the following output:

```
Enter a number: 10
Factorial is 3628800
```

Even using type `unsigned long`, the largest number you can use for input is 12.

Variables Defined in for Statements

There's another wrinkle in this program: The loop variable `j` is defined inside the `for` statement:

```
for(int j=numb; j>0; j--)
```

This is a common construction in C++. It defines the variable as close as possible to its point of use in the listing. Variables defined in the loop statement this way are visible from the point of definition onward in the listing (unlike variables defined within a block, which are visible only within the block).

Multiple Initialization and Test Expressions

You can put more than one expression in the initialization part of the `for` statement, separating the different expressions by commas. You can also have more than one increment expression, although you can have only one test expression. Here's an example:

```
for( j=0, alpha=100; j<50; j++, beta-- )
   {
   // body of loop
   }
```

This example has a normal loop variable `j`, but it also initializes another variable, `alpha`, and increments a third, `beta`. The variables `alpha` and `beta` don't need to have anything to do with each other, or with `j`. Multiple initialization expressions and multiple increment expressions are separated by commas.

We'll avoid using such multiple expressions. While this approach can make the listing more concise, it also tends to decrease its readability. It's always possible to use standalone statements to achieve the same effect.

THE while LOOP

The `for` loop does something a fixed number of times. What happens if you don't know how many times you want to do something before you start the loop? In this case a different kind of loop may be used: the `while` loop.

In the next example, ENDON0, we ask the user to enter a series of numbers. When the number entered is 0, the loop terminates. Notice that there's no way for the program to know in advance how many numbers will be typed before the 0 appears; that's up to the user.

```
// endon0.cpp
// demonstrates WHILE loop
#include <iostream.h>

void main()
   {
   int n = 99;         // make sure n isn't initialized to 0

   while( n != 0 )     // loop until n is 0
      cin >> n;        // read a number into n
   }
```

Here's some sample output. The user enters numbers, and the loop continues until 0 is entered, at which point the program terminates.

```
1
27
33
144
9
0
```

The `while` loop looks like a simplified version of the `for` loop. It contains a test expression but no initialization or increment expressions. Figure 4-3 shows the syntax of the `while` loop.

As long as the test expression is true, the loop continues to be executed. In ENDON0, the text expression

```
n != 0
```

is true until the user enters 0.

Figure 4-4 shows the operation of a `while` loop. The simplicity of the `while` loop is a bit illusory. Although there is no initialization expression, the loop variable (n in ENDON0) must be initialized before the loop begins. The loop body must also contain some statement that changes the value of the loop variable; otherwise the loop would never end. In ENDON0 it's `cin>>n;`.

Multiple Statements in while Loop

The next example, WHILE4, uses multiple statements in a `while` loop. It's a variation of the CUBELIST program shown earlier with a `for` loop, but it calculates the fourth power, instead of the cube, of a series of integers. Let's assume that in this

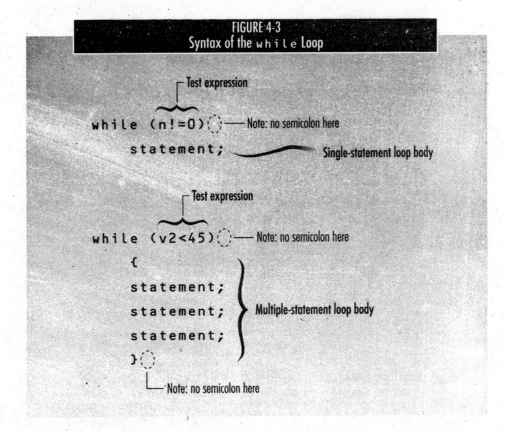

FIGURE 4-3
Syntax of the while Loop

program it's important to put the results in a column 4 digits wide. To ensure that the results fit this column width, we must stop the loop before the results become larger than 9999. Without prior calculation we don't know what number will generate a result of this size, so we let the program figure it out. The test expression in the while statement terminates the program before the powers become too large.

```cpp
// while4.cpp
// prints numbers raised to fourth power
#include <iostream.h>
#include <iomanip.h>                // for setw

void main()
    {
    int pow=1;                      // power initially 1
    int numb=1;                     // numb goes from 1 to ???

    while( pow<9999 )               // loop while power < 4 digits
        {
```

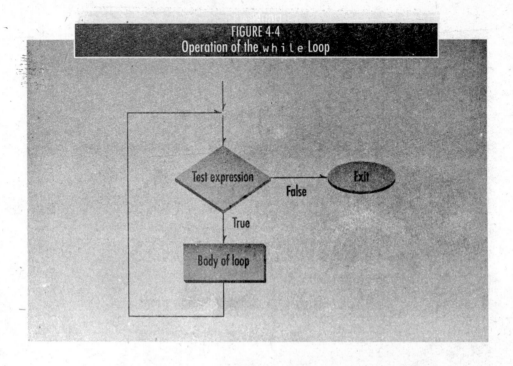

FIGURE 4-4
Operation of the `while` **Loop**

```
cout << setw(2) << numb;            // display number
cout << setw(5) << pow << endl;     // display fourth power
++numb;                             // get ready for next power
pow = numb*numb*numb*numb;          // calculate fourth power
   }
}
```

To find the fourth power of `numb`, we simply multiply it by itself four times. Each time through the loop we increment `numb`. But we don't use `numb` in the test expression in `while`; instead, the resulting value of `pow` determines when to terminate the loop. Here's the output:

```
1    1
2    16
3    81
4    256
5    625
6 1296
7 2401
8 4096
9 6561
```

The next number would be 10,000—too wide for our four-digit column; but by this time the loop has terminated.

PRECEDENCE: ARITHMETIC AND RELATIONAL OPERATORS

The next program touches on the question of operator precedence. It generates the famous sequence of numbers called *the Fibonacci series*. Here are the first few terms of the series:

> 1   1   2   3   5   8   13   21   34   55

Each term is found by adding the two previous ones: 1+1 is 2, 1+2 is 3, 2+3 is 5, 3+5 is 8, and so on. The Fibonacci series has applications in amazingly diverse fields, from sorting methods in computer science to the number of spirals in sunflowers.

One of the most interesting aspects of the Fibonacci series is its relation to the *golden ratio*. The golden ratio is supposed to be the ideal proportion in architecture and art, and was used in the design of ancient Greek temples. As the Fibonacci series is carried out further and further, the ratio of the last two terms approaches closer and closer to the golden ratio. Here's the listing for FIBO.CPP:

```
// fibo.cpp
// demonstrates WHILE loops using fibonacci series
#include <iostream.h>

void main()
   {                                 // largest unsigned long
   const unsigned long limit = 4294967295;
   unsigned long next=0;             // next-to-last term
   unsigned long last=1;             // last term

   while( next < limit / 2 )         // don't let results get too big
      {
      cout << last << " ";           // display last term
      long sum = next + last;        // add last two terms
      next = last;                   // variables move forward
      last = sum;                    //   in the series
      }
   }
```

Here's the output:

```
1  1  2  3  5  8  13  21  34  55  89  144  233  377  610  987
1597  2584  4181  6765  10946  17711  28657  46368  75025  121393
196418  317811  514229  832040  1346269  2178309  3524578
5702887  9227465  14930352  24157817  39088169  63245986
102334155  165580141  267914296  433494437  701408733  1134903170
1836311903  2971215073
```

For you temple builders, the ratio of the last two terms gives an approximation of the golden ratio as 0.618033988—close enough for government work.

The FIBO program uses type **unsigned long**, the type that holds the largest positive integers. The test expression in the **while** statement terminates the loop before the numbers exceed the limit of this type. We define this limit as a **const** type, since it doesn't change. We must stop when **next** becomes larger than half the limit, otherwise **sum** would exceed the limit.

The test expression uses two operators:

```
(next < limit / 2)
```

Our intention is to compare **next** with the result of **limit/2**. That is, we want the division to be performed before the comparison. We could put parentheses around the division, to ensure that it's performed first:

```
(next < (limit/2) )
```

But we don't need the parentheses. Why not? Because arithmetic operators have a higher precedence than relational operators. This guarantees that **limit/2** will be evaluated before the comparison is made, even without the parentheses. We'll summarize the precedence situation later in this chapter, when we look at logical operators.

THE do LOOP

In a **while** loop, the test expression is evaluated at the *beginning* of the loop. If the test expression is false when the loop is entered, the loop body won't be executed at all. In some situations this is what you want. But sometimes you want to guarantee that the loop body is executed at least once, no matter what the initial state of the test expression. When this is the case you should use the **do** loop, which places the test expression at the *end* of the loop.

Our example, DIVDO, invites the user to enter two numbers: a dividend (the top number in a division) and a divisor (the bottom number). It then calculates the quotient (the answer) and the remainder, using the **/** and **%** operators, and prints out the result.

```
// divdo.cpp
// demonstrates DO loop
#include <iostream.h>

void main()
   {
   long dividend, divisor;
   char ch;

   do                                    // start of do loop
      {                                  // do some processing
      cout << "Enter dividend: "; cin >> dividend;
```

```
cout << "Enter divisor: ";  cin >> divisor;
cout << "Quotient is " << dividend / divisor;
cout << ", remainder is " << dividend % divisor;

cout << "\nDo another? (y/n): ";  // do it again?
cin >> ch;
}
while( ch != 'n' );                    // loop condition
}
```

Most of this program resides within the **do** loop. First, the keyword **do** marks the beginning of the loop. Then, as with the other loops, braces delimit the body of the loop. Finally, a **while** statement provides the test expression and terminates the loop. This **while** statement looks much like the one in a **while** loop, except for its position at the end of the loop, and the fact that it ends with a semicolon (which is easy to forget!). The syntax of the **do** loop is shown in Figure 4-5.

Following each computation, DIVDO asks if the user wants to do another. If so, the user enters a 'y' character, and the test expression

```
ch != 'n'
```

remains true. If the user enters '**n**', the test expression becomes false and the loop terminates. Figure 4-6 flowcharts the operation of the **do** loop. Here's an example of **divdo's** output:

```
Enter dividend: 11
Enter divisor: 3
Quotient is 3, remainder is 2
Do another? (y/n): y
Enter dividend: 222
Enter divisor: 17
Quotient is 13, remainder is 1
Do another? (y/n): n
```

WHEN TO USE WHICH LOOP

We've made some general statements about how loops are used. The **for** loop is appropriate when you know in advance how many times the loop will be executed. The **while** and **do** loops are used when you don't know in advance when the loop will terminate; the **while** when you may not want to execute the loop body even once, and the **do** loop when you're sure you want to execute the loop body at least once.

These criteria are somewhat arbitrary. Which loop type to use is more a matter of style than of hard-and-fast rules. You can actually make any of the loop types work in almost any situation. You should choose the type that makes your program the clearest and easiest to follow.

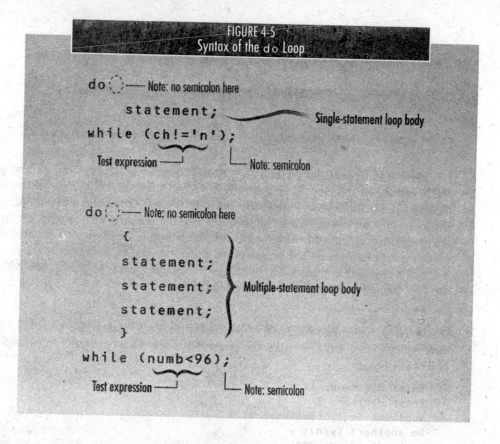

FIGURE 4-5
Syntax of the do Loop

The decisions in a loop always relate to the same question: Should we do this (the loop body) again? As humans we would find it boring to be so limited in our decision-making processes. We need to decide, not only whether to go to work again today (continuing the loop), but also whether to buy a red shirt or a green one (or no shirt at all), whether to take a vacation, and if so, in the mountains or by the sea.

Programs also need to make these one-time decisions. In a program a decision causes a one-time jump to a different part of the program, depending on the value of an expression. Decisions can be made in C++ in several ways. The most important is with the if...else statement, which chooses between two alternatives. This statement can be used without the else, as a simple if statement. Another decision statement, switch, creates branches for multiple alternative sections of code, depending on the value of a single variable. Finally the *conditional operator* is used in specialized situations. We'll examine each of these constructions.

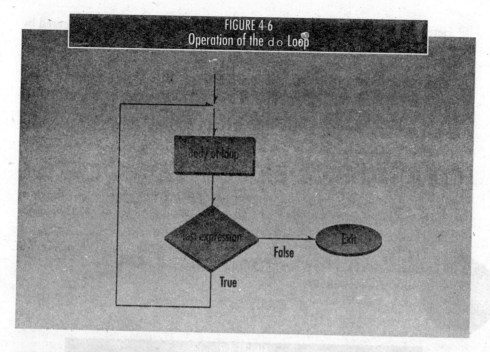

FIGURE 4-6
Operation of the do Loop

THE if STATEMENT

The if statement is the simplest of the decision statements. Our next program, IFDEMO, provides an example.

```
// ifdemo.cpp
// demonstrates IF statement
#include <iostream.h>

void main()
{
int x;

cout << "Enter a number: ";
cin >> x;
if( x > 100 )
    cout << "That number is greater than 100\n";
}
```

The if keyword is followed by a test expression in parentheses. The syntax of the if is shown in Figure 4-7. As you can see, the syntax of if is very much like that of while. The difference is that the statements following the if are executed only once if the test expression is true; the statements following while are executed repeatedly until the test expression becomes false. Figure 4-8 shows the operation of the if statement.

Here's an example of the IFDEMO program's output when the number entered by the user is greater than 100:

```
C>if
Enter a number: 2000
That number is greater than 100
C>
```

If the number entered is not greater than 100, the program will terminate without printing anything.

Multiple Statements in the if Body

As in loops, the code in an if body can consist of a single statement—as shown in the IFDEMO example—or of a block of statements delimited by braces. This variation on IFDEMO, called IF2, shows how that looks:

```
// if2.cpp
// demonstrates IF with multiline body
#include <iostream.h>
```

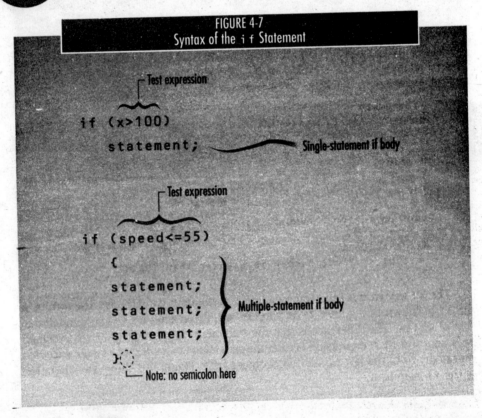

FIGURE 4-7
Syntax of the if Statement

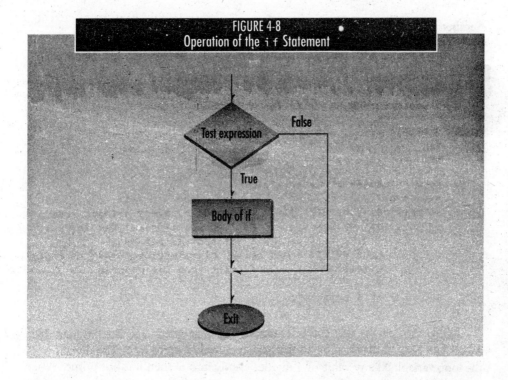

FIGURE 4-8
Operation of the if Statement

```
void main()
    {
    int x;

    cout << "Enter a number: ";
    cin >> x;
    if( x > 100 )
        {
        cout << "The number " << x;
        cout << " is greater than 100\n";
        }
    }
```

Here's some output from IF2:

```
Enter a number: 12345
The number 12345 is greater than 100
```

Nesting ifs Inside Loops

The loop and decision structures we've seen so far can be nested inside one another. You can nest ifs inside loops, loops inside ifs, ifs inside ifs, and so on. Here's an example, PRIME, that nests an if within a for loop. This example tells you if a number you enter is a prime number. (Prime numbers are integers divisible only by themselves and 1. The first few primes are 2, 3, 5, 7, 11, 13, 17, and so on.)

```cpp
// prime.cpp
// demonstrates IF statement with prime numbers
#include <iostream.h>
#include <process.h>      // for exit()

void main()
   {
   unsigned long n, j;

   cout << "Enter a number: ";
   cin >> n;                      // get number to test
      for(j=2; j <= n/2; j++)     // divide by every integer from
         if(n%j == 0)             // 2 on up; if remainder is 0,
            {                     // it's divisible by j
            cout << "It's not prime; divisible by " << j << endl;
            exit(0);              // exit from the program
            }
   cout << "It's prime\n";
   }
```

In this example the user enters a number that is assigned to n. The program then uses a for loop to divide n by all the numbers from 2 up to n/2. The divisor is j, the loop variable. If any value of j divides evenly into n, then n is not prime. When a number divides evenly into another, the remainder is 0; so we use the remainder operator % in the if statement to test for this condition with each value of j. If the number is not prime, we tell the user and we exit from the program.

Here's some output:

```
C>prime
Enter a number: 13
It's prime
C>prime
Enter a number: 22229
It's prime
C>prime
Enter a number: 22231
It's not prime; divisible by 11
```

(Beware: If you enter a number that is substantially larger than those shown, and it happens to be prime, the program will take a long time to execute.)

Notice that there are no braces around the loop body. This is because the if statement and the statements in its body, are considered to be a single statement.

Library Function exit()

When PRIME discovers that a number is not prime, it exits immediately, since there's no use proving more than once that a number isn't prime. This is accomplished with the library function `exit()`. This function causes the program to terminate, no matter where it is in the listing. It has no return value. Its single argument, 0 in our example, is returned to the operating system when the program exits. (This value is useful in batch files, where you can use the ERRORLEVEL value to query the return value provided by `exit()`. The value 0 is normally used for a successful termination; other numbers indicate errors.)

THE if...else STATEMENT

The `if` statement lets you do something if a condition is true. If it isn't true, nothing happens. But suppose we want to do one thing if a condition is true, and do something else if it's false. That's where the `if...else` statement comes in. It consists of an `if` statement, followed by a statement or block of statements, followed by the keyword `else`, followed by *another* statement or block of statements. The syntax is shown in Figure 4-9.

Here's a variation of our IF example, with an `else` added to the `if`:

```
// ifelse.cpp
// demonstrates IF...ELSE statememt
#include <iostream.h>

void main()
    {
    int x;

    cout << "\nEnter a number: ";
    cin >> x;
    if( x > 100 )
        cout << "That number is greater than 100\n";
    else
        cout << "That number is not greater than 100\n";
    }
```

If the test expression in the `if` statement is true, the program prints one message; if it isn't, it prints the other.

Here's some output:

```
C>ifelse
Enter a number: 300
That number is greater than 100
C>ifelse
Enter a number: 3
That number is not greater than 100
C>
```

The operation of the `if...else` statement is shown in Figure 4-10.

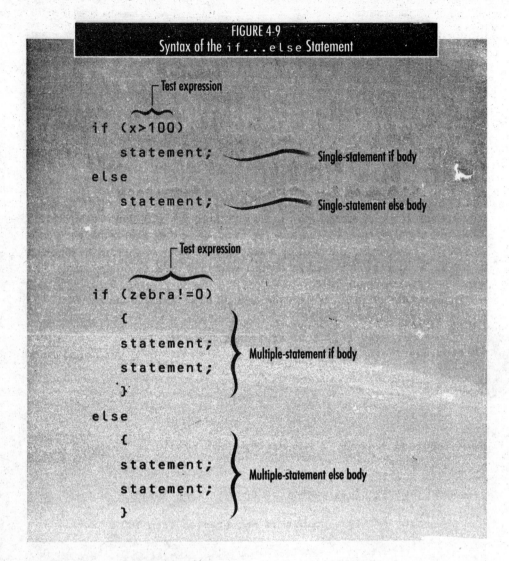

FIGURE 4-9
Syntax of the if...else Statement

Test expression

```
if (x>100)
    statement;          Single-statement if body
else
    statement;          Single-statement else body
```

Test expression

```
if (zebra!=0)
    {
    statement;
    statement;          Multiple-statement if body
    }
else
    {
    statement;
    statement;          Multiple-statement else body
    }
```

The getche() Library Function

Our next example shows an **if...else** statement embedded in a **while** loop. It also introduces a new library function: **getche()**. This program, CHCOUNT, counts the number of words and the number of characters in a phrase typed in by the user.

```
// chcount.cpp
// counts characters and words typed in
#include <iostream.h>
#include <conio.h>          // for getche()

void main()
    {
```

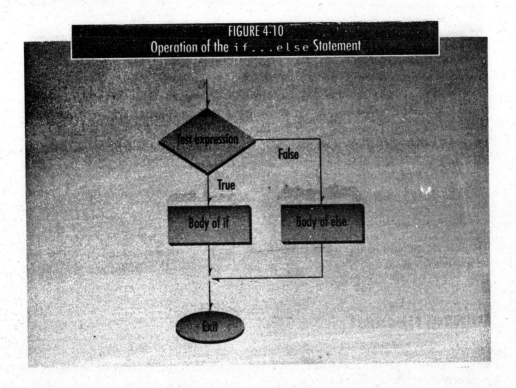

FIGURE 4-10
Operation of the if...else Statement

```
int chcount=0;              // counts non-space characters
int wdcount=1;              // counts spaces between words
char ch = 'a';              // ensure it isn't '\r'

while( ch != '\r' )         // loop until Enter typed
    {
    ch = getche();          // read one character
    if( ch==' ' )           // if it's a space
        wdcount++;          // count a word
    else                    // otherwise,
        chcount++;          // count a character
    }                       // display results
cout << "\nWords=" << wdcount << endl
     << "Letters=" << chcount-1 << endl;
}
```

So far we've used only cin and >> for input. That approach requires that the user always presses the (ENTER) key to inform the program that the input is complete. This is true even for single characters: The user must type the character, then press (ENTER). However, as in the present example, a program often needs to process each character typed by the user without waiting for an Enter. The getche() library function performs this service. It returns each character typed, as soon as it's typed. It takes no arguments, and requires the CONIO.H header file. In CHCOUNT the value of the character returned from `getche()` is assigned to `ch`. (The `getche()` function echoes the character to the screen. That's why there's an `e` in `getche`. Another function, `getch()`, is similar to `getche()` but doesn't echo the character to the screen.)

The `if...else` statement causes the word count `wdcount` to be incremented if the character is a space, and the character count `chcount` to be incremented if the character is anything *but* a space. Thus anything that *isn't* a space is assumed to count as a character. (Note that this program is fairly naïve; it will be fooled by multiple spaces between words.)

Here's some sample interaction with CHCOUNT:

```
For while and do
Words=4
Letters=13
```

The test expression in the `while` statement checks to see if `ch` is the '\r' character, which is the character received from the keyboard when the (ENTER) key is pressed. If so, the loop and the program terminate.

Assignment Expressions

The CHCOUNT.CPP program can be rewritten to save a line of code and demonstrate some important points about assignment expressions and precedence. The result is a construction that looks rather peculiar but is commonly used in C++ (and in C).

Here's the rewritten version, called CHCNT2:

```
// chcnt2.cpp
// counts characters and words typed in
#include <iostream.h>
#include <conio.h>                    // for getche()

void main()
    {
    int chcount=0;
    int wdcount=1;                    // space between two words
    char ch;

    while( (ch=getche()) != '\r' )    // loop until Enter typed
        {
        if( ch==' ' )                 // if it's a space
            wdcount++;                // count a word
        else                          // otherwise,
            chcount++;                // count a character
        }                             // display results
    cout << "\nWords=" << wdcount << endl
         << "Letters=" << chcount-1 << endl;
```

The value returned by `getche()` is assigned to `ch` as before, but this entire assignment expression has been moved inside the test expression for `while`. The assignment expression is compared with '\r' to see if the loop should terminate. This works because the entire assignment expression takes on the value used in the assignment. That is, if `getche()` returns 'a', then not only does `ch` take on the value 'a', but the expression

```
(ch=getche())
```

also takes on the value 'a'. This is then compared with '\r'.

The fact that assignment expressions have a value is also used in statements such as

```
x = y = z = 0;
```

This is perfectly legal in C++. First, `z` takes on the value 0, then `z = 0` takes on the value 0, which is assigned to `y`. Then the expression `y = z = 0` likewise takes on the value 0, which is assigned to `x`.

The parentheses around the assignment expression in

```
(ch=getche())
```

are necessary because the assignment operator `=` has a lower precedence than the relational operator `!=`. Without the parentheses the expression would be evaluated as

```
while( ch = (getche() != '\r') )    // not what we want
```

which would assign a true or false value to `ch`; not what we want.

The `while` statement in CHCNT2 provides a lot of power in a small space. It is not only a test expression (checking `ch` to see if it's '\r'); it also gets a character from the keyboard and assigns it to `ch`. It's also not easy to unravel the first time you see it.

Nested if...else Statements

Remember adventure games? You move your "character" around an imaginary landscape, and discover castles, sorcerers, treasure, and so on. This program, ADIFELSE, models a small part of an adventure game.

```
// adifelse.cpp
// demonstrates IF...ELSE with adventure program
#include <iostream.h>
#include <conio.h>       // for getche()

void main()
    {
    char dir='a';
    int x=10, y=10;
```

```
        cout << "Enter x to exit\n";
        while( dir != 'x' )                // until x is entered
          {
          cout << "\nYour location is " << x << ", " << y;
          cout << "\nEnter direction (n, s, e, w): " << flush;
          dir = getche();          // get character
          if( dir=='n')            // go north
            y--;
          else
            if( dir=='s' )         // go south
              y++;
            else
              if( dir=='e' )       // go east
                x++;
              else
                if( dir=='w' )     // go west
                  x--;
          } // end while
        } // end main
```

When the game starts, you find yourself on a barren moor. You can go one "unit" north, south, east, or west, while the program keeps track of where you are, and reports your position, which starts at coordinates 10,10. Unfortunately, nothing exciting happens to your character, no matter where you go; the moor stretches on almost limitlessly in all directions, as shown in Figure 4-11. We'll try to provide a little more excitement to this game later on.

Here's some sample interaction with ADIFELSE:

```
Your location is 10, 10
Enter direction (n, s, e, w): n
Your location is 10, 9
Enter direction (n, s, e, w): e
Your location is 11, 9
Enter direction (n, s, e, w):
```

You can press the ⓧ key to exit from the program.

This program may not cause a sensation in the video arcades, but it does demonstrate one way to handle multiple branches. It uses an if statement nested inside an if...else statement, which is nested inside another if...else statement, which is nested inside yet another if...else statement. If the first test condition is false, the second one is examined, and so on until all four have been checked. If any one proves true, the appropriate action is taken—changing the x or y coordinate—and the program exits from all the nested decisions. Such a nested group of if...else statements is called a *decision tree*.

Flushing the Streams

Due to a peculiarity in the way the getche() library function interacts with the C++ streams, it's necessary to flush the streams before using getche(). You flush the

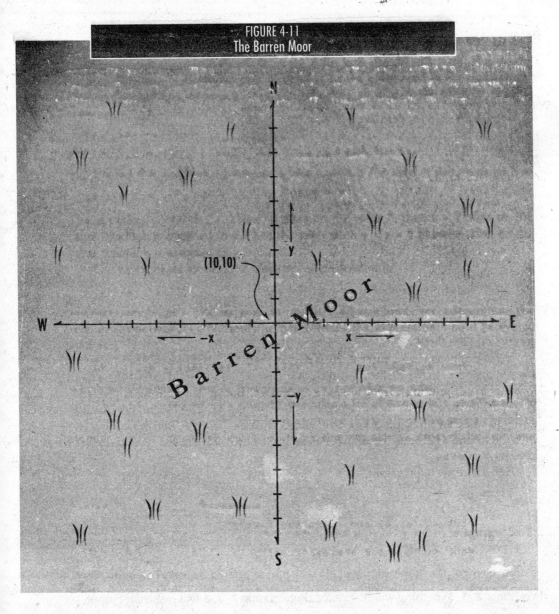

FIGURE 4-11
The Barren Moor

streams by sending the manipulator `flush` as the last item to the insertion operator. In the ADIFELSE program, it looks like this:

```
cout << "\nEnter direction (n, s, e, w): " << flush;
```

If you don't flush the streams, `getche()` won't respond to input until you
press the (ENTER) key, which defeats the purpose of using it. The `endl` manipulator also flushes the streams, but it also causes a newline, which is not what we
want in this case.

Matching the else

There's a potential problem in nested if...else statements: You can inadvertently match an else with the wrong if. BADELSE provides an example:

```
// badelse.cpp
// demonstrates ELSE matched with wrong IF
#include <iostream.h>

void main()
    {
    int a, b, c;
    cout << "Enter a, b, and c:\n";
    cin >> a >> b >> c;

    if( a==b )
        if( b==c )
            cout << "a, b, and c are the same";
    else
        cout << "a and b are different";
    }
```

We've used multiple values with a single cin. Press (ENTER) following each value you type in; the three values will be assigned to a, b, and c.

What happens if you enter 2, then 3, and then 3? Variable a is 2, and b is 3. They're different, so the first test expression is false, and you would expect the else to be invoked, printing a and b are different. But in fact nothing is printed. Why not? Because the else is matched with the wrong if. The indentation would lead you to believe that the else is matched with the first if, but in fact it goes with the second if. Here's the rule: An else is matched with the last if that doesn't have its own else.

Here's a corrected version:

```
if(a==b)
    if(b==c)
        cout << "a, b, and c are the same";
    else
        cout << "b and c are different";
```

We changed the indentation and also the phrase printed by the else body. Now if you enter 2, 3, 3, nothing will be printed. But entering 2, 2, 3 will cause the output

```
b and c are different
```

If you really want to pair an else with an earlier if, you can use braces around the inner if:

```
if(a==b)
    {
    if(b==c)
        cout << "a, b, and c are the same";
```

```
        }
    else
        cout << "a and b are different";
```

Here the else is paired with the first if, as the indentation indicates. The braces make the material within them invisible to the following else.

THE else...if CONSTRUCTION

The nested if...else statements in the ADIFELSE program look clumsy and can be hard—for humans—to interpret, especially if they are nested more deeply than shown. However there's another approach to writing the same statements. We need only reformat the program, obtaining the next example, ADELSEIF.

```
// adelseif.cpp
// demonstrates ELSE...IF with adventure program
#include <iostream.h>
#include <conio.h>          // for getche()

void main()
    {
    char dir='a';
    int x=10, y=10;

    cout << "Type x to exit\n";
    while( dir != 'x' )              // until x is entered
        {
        cout << "\nYour location is " << x << ", " << y;
        cout << "\nEnter direction (n, s, e, w): " << flush;
        dir = getche();             // get character
        if( dir=='n')               // go north
            y--;
        else if( dir=='s' )         // go south
            y++;
        else if( dir=='e' )         // go east
            x++;
        else if( dir=='w' )         // go west
            x--;
        } // end while
    } // end main
```

The compiler sees this as identical to ADIFELSE, but we've rearranged the ifs so that they directly follow the elses. The result looks almost like a new keyword: else if. The program goes down the ladder of else...ifs until one of the test expressions is true. It then executes the following statement and exits from the ladder. This format is clearer and easier to follow than the if...else approach.

THE switch STATEMENT

If you have a large decision tree, and all the decisions depend on the value of the same variable, you will probably want to consider a switch statement instead of a series of if...else or else if constructions. Here's a simple example called PLAT-TERS that will appeal to nostalgia buffs:

```
// platters.cpp
// demonstrates SWITCH statement
#include <iostream.h>

void main()
   {
   int speed;                            // turntable speed

   cout << "\nEnter 33, 45, or 78: ";
   cin >> speed;                         // user enters speed
   switch(speed)                         // selection based on speed
      {
      case 33:                           // user entered 33
         cout << "LP album\n";
         break;
      case 45:                           // user entered 45
         cout << "Single selection\n";
         break;
      case 78:                           // user entered 78
         cout << "Obsolete format\n";
         break;
      }
   }
```

This program prints one of three possible messages, depending on whether the user inputs the number 33, 45, or 78. The keyword switch is followed by a *switch variable* in parentheses:

```
switch(speed)
```

Braces then delimit a number of case statements. Each case keyword is followed by a constant, which is not in parentheses but is followed by a colon:

```
case 33:
```

The data type of the case constants should match that of the switch variable. Figure 4-12 shows the syntax of the switch statement.

Before entering the switch, the program should assign a value to the switch variable. This value will usually match a constant in one of the case statements. When this is the case (pun intended!), the statements immediately following the keyword case will be executed, until a break is reached.

Here's an example of platter's output:

```
Enter 33, 45, or 78: 45
Single selection
```

The break Statement

PLATTERS has a `break` statement at the end of each `case` section. The `break` keyword causes the entire `switch` statement to exit. Control goes to the first statement following the end of the `switch` construction, which in PLATTERS is the end of the program. Don't forget the `break`; without it, control passes down (or "falls through") to the statements for the next `case`, which is usually not what you want (although sometimes it's useful).

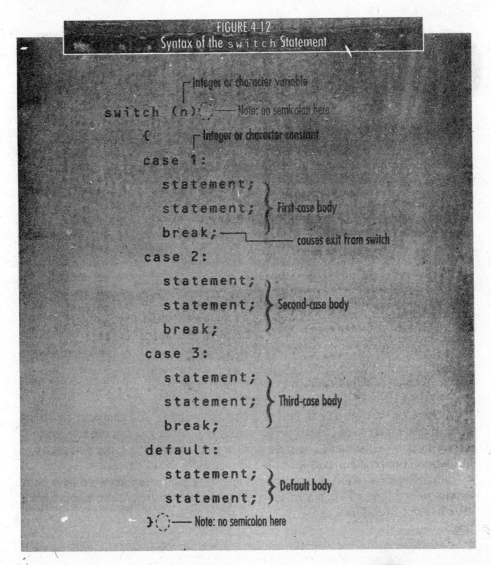

FIGURE 4-12
Syntax of the `switch` Statement

If the value of the switch variable doesn't match any of the `case` constants, then control passes to the end of the switch without doing anything. The operation of the `switch` statement is shown in Figure 4-13. The `break` keyword is also used to escape from loops; we'll discuss this soon.

switch Statement with Character Variables

The PLATTERS example showed a `switch` statement based on a variable of type `int`. You can also use type `char`. Here's our ADELSEIF program rewritten as ADSWITCH:

```
// adswitch.cpp
// demonstrates SWITCH with adventure program
#include <iostream.h>
#include <conio.h>          // for getche()

void main()
    {
    char dir='a';
    int x=10, y=10;

    while( dir != 'x' )
        {
        cout << "\nYour location is " << x << ", " << y;
        cout << "\nEnter direction (n, s, e, w): " << flush;
        dir = getche();                          // get character
        switch(dir)                              // switch on it
            {
            case 'n':  y--; break;               // go north
            case 's':  y++; break;               // go south
            case 'e':  x++; break;               // go east
            case 'w':  x--; break;               // go west
            case 'x':  cout << "\nExiting"; break; // exit
            default:   cout << "\nTry again";    // unknown char
            }  // end switch
        }  // end while
    }  // end main
```

A character variable `dir` is used as the switch variable, and character constants 'n', 's', and so on are used as the case constants. (Note that you can use integers and characters as switch variables, as shown in the last two examples, but you can't use floating-point numbers.)

Since they are so short, the statements following each `case` keyword have been written on one line, which makes for a more compact listing. We've also added a `case` to print an exit message when the (x) key is pressed.

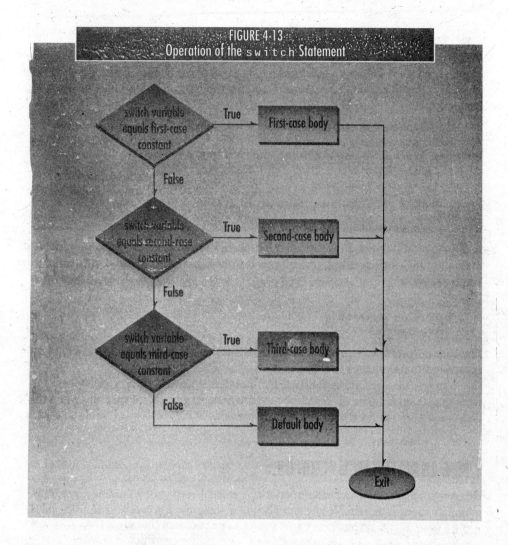

FIGURE 4-13
Operation of the switch Statement

The default Keyword

In the ADSWITCH program, where you expect to see the last `case` at the bottom of the `switch` construction, you'll instead see the keyword `default`. This keyword gives the `switch` construction a way to take an action if the value of the loop variable doesn't match any of the `case` constants. Here we use it to print *Try again* if the user types an unknown character. No `break` is necessary after `default`, since we're at the end of the `switch` anyway.

A `switch` statement is a common approach to *parsing* (figuring out) input entered by the user. Each of the possible characters is represented by a `case`.

switch VERSUS if...else

When do you use a series of if...else (or else...if) statements, and when do you use a switch statement? In an if...else construction, you can use a series of expressions that involve unrelated variables and that are as complex as you like. For example:

```
if( SteamPressure*Factor > 56 )
    // statements
else if( VoltageIn + VoltageOut < 23000)
    // statements
else if( day==Thursday )
    // statements
else
    // statements
```

In a switch statement, however, all the branches are selected by the same variable; the only thing distinguishing one branch from another is the value of this variable. You can't say

```
case a<3:
    // do something
break;
```

The case constant must be an integer or character constant, like 3 or 'a', or an expression that evaluates to a constant, like 'a'+32.

When these conditions are met, the switch statement is very clean—easy to write and to understand. It should be used whenever possible, especially when the decision tree has more than a few possibilities.

THE CONDITIONAL OPERATOR

Here's a strange sort of decision operator. It exists because of a common programming situation: A variable is given one value if something is true and another value if it's false. For example, here's an if...else statement that gives the variable min the value of alpha or the value of beta, depending on which is smaller.

```
if( alpha < beta )
    min = alpha;
else
    min = beta;
```

This sort of construction is so common that the designers of C++ (actually the designers of C, long ago) invented a compressed way to express it: the *conditional operator*. This operator consists of two symbols, which operate on three operands. It's the only such operator in C++; other operators operate on one or two operands. Here's the equivalent of the same program fragment, using a conditional operator:

```
min = (alpha<beta) ? alpha : beta;
```

The part of this statement to the right of the equals sign is called the *conditional expression:*

```
(alpha<beta) ? alpha : beta    // conditional expression
```

The question mark and the colon make up the conditional operator. The expression before the question mark,

```
(alpha<beta)
```

is the test expression. It and `alpha` and `beta` are the three operands.

If the test expression is true, then the entire conditional expression takes on the value of the operand following the question mark: `alpha` in this example. If the test expression is false, the conditional expression takes on the value of the operand following the colon: `beta`. The parentheses around the test expression aren't needed for the compiler, but they're customary; they make the statement easier to read (and it needs all the help it can get). Figure 4-14 shows the syntax of the conditional statement, and Figure 4-15 shows its operation.

The conditional expression can be assigned to another variable, or used anywhere a value can be. In this example it's assigned to the variable `min`.

Here's another example: a statement that uses a conditional operator to find the absolute value of a variable n. (The absolute value of a number is the number with any negative sign removed, so it's always positive.)

```
absvalue = n<0 ? -n : n;
```

If n is less than 0, the expression becomes -n, a positive number. If n is not less than 0, the expression remains n. The result is the absolute value of n, which is assigned to `absvalue`.

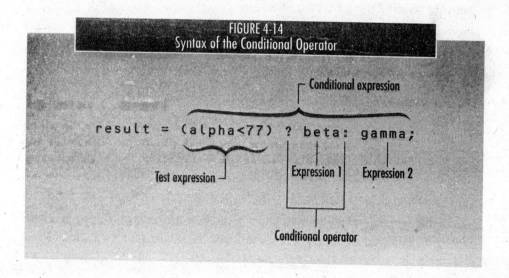

FIGURE 4-14
Syntax of the Conditional Operator

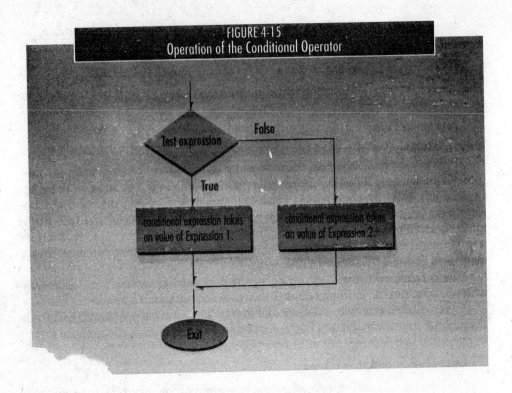

FIGURE 4-15
Operation of the Conditional Operator

Here's a program, CONDI.CPP, that uses the conditional operator to print an x every eight spaces in a line of text. You might use this to see where the tab stops are on your screen.

```cpp
// condi.cpp
// prints 'x' every 8 columns
// demonstrates conditional operator
#include <iostream.h>

void main()
    {
    for(int j=0; j<80; j++)           // for every column,
        {                              // ch is 'x' if column is
        char ch = (j%8) ? ' ' : 'x';   // multiple of 8, and
        cout << ch;                    // ' ' (space) otherwise
        }
    }
```

Some of the right side of the output is lost because of the page width, but you can probably imagine it:

    x   x   x   x   x   x   x   x   x

As j cycles through the numbers from 0 to 7, the remainder operator causes the expression (j % 8) to become false—that is, 0—only when j is a multiple of 8. So the conditional expression

```
(j%8) ? ' ' : 'x'
```

has the value ' ' when j is not a multiple of 8, and the value 'x' when it is.

You may think this is terse, but we could have combined the two statements in the loop body into one, eliminating the ch variable:

```
cout << ( (j%8) ? ' ' : 'x' );
```

Hotshot C++ (and C) programmers love this sort of thing—getting a lot of bang from very little code. But you don't need to strive for concise code if you don't want to. Sometimes it becomes so obscure it's not worth the effort. Even using the conditional operator is optional: An if...else statement and a few extra program lines will accomplish the same thing.

Logical Operators

So far we've seen two families of operators (besides the oddball conditional operator). First are the arithmetic operators +, -, *, /, and %. Second are the relational operators <, >, <=, >=, ==, and !=.

Let's examine a third family of operators, called *logical operators*. These operators allow you to logically combine Boolean (true/false) values. For example, *Today is a weekday* has a Boolean value, since it's either true or false. Another Boolean expression is *Maria took the car*. We can connect these expressions logically: *If today is a weekday, and Maria took the car, then I'll have to take the bus.* The logical connection here is the word *and*, which provides a true or false value to the combination of the two phrases. Only if they are both true will I have to take the bus.

The Logical AND Operator

Let's see how logical operators combine Boolean expressions in C++. Here's an example, ADVENAND.CPP, that uses a logical operator to spruce up the adventure game from the ADSWITCH example. We'll bury some treasure at coordinates (7,11) and see if the player can find it.

```
// advenand.cpp
// demonstrates AND logical operator
#include <iostream.h>
#include <conio.h>            // for getche()
#include <process.h>         // for exit()
void main()
    {
```

```
char dir='a';
int x=10, y=10;

while( dir != 'x' )
   {
   cout << "\nYour location is " << x << ", " << y;
   cout << "\nEnter direction (n, s, e, w): " << flush;
   dir = getche();            // get direction
   switch(dir)
      {
      case 'n': y--; break;    // update coordinates
      case 's': y++; break;
      case 'e': x++; break;
      case 'w': x--; break;
      }
   if( x==7 && y==11 )          // if x is 7 and y is 11
      {
      cout << "\nYou found the treasure!\n";
      exit(0);                  // exit from program
      }
   } // end switch
} // end main
```

The key to this program is the if statement

```
if( x==7 && y==11 )
```

The test expression will be true only if *both* x is 7 *and* y is 11. The logical AND operator && joins the two relational expressions to achieve this result.

Notice that parentheses are not necessary around the relational expressions:

```
( (x==7) && (y==11) )    // inner parentheses not necessary
```

This is because the relational operators have higher precedence than the logical operators.

Here's some interaction as the user arrives at these coordinates:

```
Your location is 7, 10
Enter direction (n, s, e, w): s
You found the treasure!
```

There are three logical operators in C++:

Operator	Effect
&&	Logical AND
||	Logical OR
!	Logical NOT

Let's look at examples of the || and ! operators.

THE LOGICAL OR OPERATOR

Suppose in the adventure game you decide there will be dragons if the user goes too far east or too far west. Here's an example, ADVENOR, that uses the logical OR operator to implement this frightening impediment to free adventuring. It's a variation on the ADVENAND program.

```
// advenor.cpp
// demonstrates OR logical operator
#include <iostream.h>
#include <conio.h>              // for getche()
#include <process.h>           // for exit()
void main()
    {
    char dir='a';
    int x=10, y=10;

    while( dir != 'x' )
        {
        cout << "\n\nYour location is " << x << ", " << y;

        if( x<5 || x>15 )             // if x west of 5 OR east of 15
            cout << "\nBeware: dragons lurk here";

        cout << "\nEnter direction (n, s, e, w): " << flush;
        dir = getche();              // get direction
        switch(dir)
            {
            case 'n': y--; break;    // update coordinates
            case 's': y++; break;
            case 'e': x++; break;
            case 'w': x--; break;
            }
        } // end while
    } // end main
```

The expression

```
x<5 || x>15
```

is true whenever *either* x is less than 5 (the player is too far west), or x is greater than 15 (the player is too far east). Again, the || operator has lower precedence than the relational operators < and >, so no parentheses are needed in this expression.

THE LOGICAL NOT OPERATOR

The logical NOT operator ! is a unary operator—that is, it takes only one operand. (Almost all the operators we've seen thus far are binary operands; they take two operands. The conditional operator is the only ternary operator in C++.) The effect of the ! is that the logical value of its operand is reversed: If something is true, ! makes it false; if it is false, ! makes it true.

For example, (x==7) is true if x is equal to 7, but !(x==7) is true if x is *not* equal to 7. (In this situation you could use the relational *not equals* operator, x != 7, to achieve the same effect.)

A True/False Value for Every Integer Variable

We may have given you the impression that for an expression to have a true/false value, it must involve a relational operator. But in fact, every integer expression has a true/false value, even if it is only a single variable. The expression x is true whenever x is not 0, and false when x is 0. Applying the ! operator to this situation, we can see that the !x is true whenever x is 0, since it reverses the truth value of x.

Let's put these ideas to work. Imagine in your adventure game that you wanted to place a mushroom on all the locations where both x and y are a multiple of 7. (As you probably know, mushrooms, when consumed by the player, confer magical powers.) The remainder when x is divided by 7, which can be calculated by x%7, is 0 only when x is a multiple of 7. So to specify the mushroom locations, we can write

```
if( x%7==0 && y%7==0 )
    cout << "There's a mushroom here.\n";
```

However, remembering that expressions are true or false even if they don't involve relational operators, you can use the ! operator to provide a more concise format:

```
if( !(x%7) && !(y%7) )    // if not x%7 and not y%7
```

This has exactly the same effect.

We've said that the logical operators && and || have lower precedence than the relational operators. Why then do we need parentheses around x%7 and y%7? Because, even though it is a logical operator, ! is a unary operator, which has higher precedence than relational operators.

PRECEDENCE SUMMARY

Lets summarize the precedence situation for the operators we've seen so far. The operators higher on the list have higher precedence than those lower down. Operators with higher precedence are evaluated before those with lower precedence. Operators on the same row have equal precedence. You can force an expression to be evaluated first by placing parentheses around it.

Operator type	Operators
Unary	!, ++, --, -
Arithmetic	
Multiplicative	*, /, %
Additive	+, -
Relational	
inequality	<, >, <=, >=
equality	==, !=
Logical	
and	&&
or	||
Conditional	?:
Assignment	=, +=, -=, *=, /=, %=

OTHER CONTROL STATEMENTS

There are several other control statements in C++. We've already seen one, break, used in switch statements, but it can be used other places as well. Another statement, continue, is used only in loops, and a third, goto, should be avoided. Let's look at these statements in turn.

THE break STATEMENT

The break statement causes an exit from a loop, just as it does from a switch statement. The next statement after the break is executed is the statement following the loop. Figure 4-16 shows the operation of the break statement.

To demonstrate break, here's a program, SHOWPRIM, that displays the distribution of prime numbers in graphical form:

```
// showprim.cpp
// displays prime number distribution
#include <iostream.h>
#include <conio.h>                          // for getch()

void main()
    {
    const unsigned char WHITE = 219;    // solid color (primes)
    const unsigned char GRAY  = 176;    // gray (non-primes)
    unsigned char ch;
                                        // for each screen position
    for(int count=0; count<80*25-1; count++)
        {
```

```
ch = WHITE;                    // assume it's prime
for(int j=2; j<count; j++)     // divide by every integer from
   if(count%j == 0)            // 2 on up; if remainder is 0,
      {
      ch = GRAY;               // it's not prime
      break;                   // break out of inner loop
      }
   cout << ch;                 // display the character
   }
cout << flush;                 // flush buffers
getch();                       // freeze screen until keypress
}                              // end main
```

In effect every position on the screen is numbered, from 0 to 1999 (which is 80*25–1). If the number at a particular position is prime, the position is colored white (or whatever color your monitor displays); if it's not prime, it's colored gray.

Figure 4-17 shows the display. Strictly speaking, 0 is not considered a prime, but it's shown as white to avoid complicating the program. Think of the columns across the top as being numbered from 0 to 79. Notice that no primes appear in even-numbered columns, since they're all divisible by 2. Is there a pattern to the other numbers? The mathematics world will be very excited if you find a pattern that allows you to predict whether any given number is prime. Type any character to terminate the program.

When the inner for loop determines that a number is not prime, it sets the character ch to GRAY, and then executes break to escape from the inner loop. (We

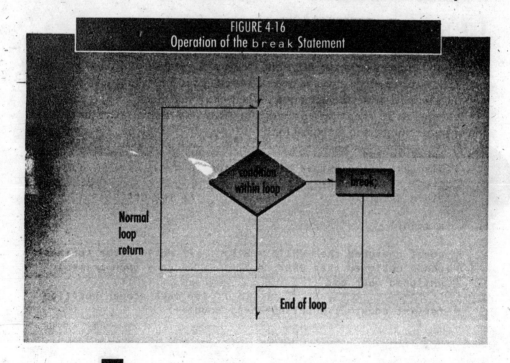

FIGURE 4-16
Operation of the break Statement

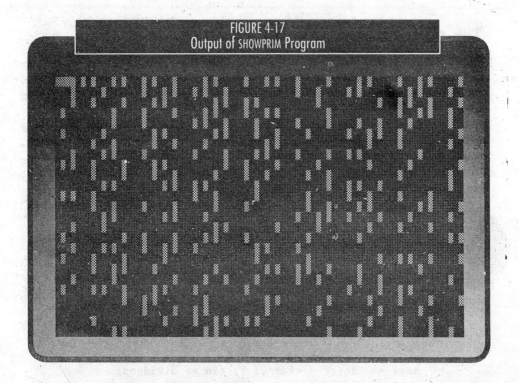

FIGURE 4-17
Output of SHOWPRIM Program

don't want to exit from the entire program, as in the PRIME example, since we have a whole series of numbers to work on.)

Notice that break only takes you out of the *innermost* loop. This is true no matter what constructions are nested inside each other: break only takes you out of the construction in which it's embedded. If there were a switch within a loop, a break in the switch would only take you out of the switch, not out of the loop.

The last cout statement prints the character, and then the loop continues, testing the next number for primeness.

IBM Extended Character Set

This program uses two characters from the *extended IBM character set*, the characters represented by the numbers from 128 to 255, as shown in Appendix A. The value 219 represents a solid-colored block (white on a black-and-white monitor), while 176 represents a gray block.

The SHOWPRIM example uses getche() in the last line, to keep the DOS prompt from scrolling the screen up when the program terminates. It freezes the screen until you press a key.

We use type unsigned char for the character variables in SHOWPRIM, since it goes up to 255. Type char only goes up to 127.

THE continue STATEMENT

The break statement takes you out of the bottom of a loop. Sometimes, however, you want to go back to the top of the loop when something unexpected happens. Executing continue has this effect. Figure 4-18 shows the operation of continue.

Here's a variation on the DIVDO example. This program, which we saw earlier in this chapter, does division, but it has a fatal flaw: If the user inputs 0 as the divisor, the program undergoes catastrophic failure and terminates with the run-time error message *integer divide by 0*. The revised version of the program, DIVDO2, deals with this situation more gracefully.

```cpp
// divdo2.cpp
// demonstrates CONTINUE statement
#include <iostream.h>

d main()
   {
   long dividend, divisor;
   char ch;

   do
      {
      cout << "Enter dividend: "; cin >> dividend;
      cout << "Enter divisor: ";  cin >> divisor;
      if( divisor == 0 )                  // if attempt to
         {                                // divide by 0,
         cout << "Illegal divisor\n";     // display message
         continue;                        // go to top of loop
         }
      cout << "Quotient is " << dividend / divisor;
      cout << ", remainder is " << dividend % divisor;

      cout << "\nDo another? (y/n): ";
      cin >> ch;
      }
   while( ch != 'n' );
   }
```

If the user inputs 0 for the divisor, the program prints an error message and, using continue, returns to the top of the loop to issue the prompts again. Here's some sample output:

```
Enter dividend: 10
Enter divisor: 0
Illegal divisor
Enter dividend:
```

A break statement in this situation would cause an exit from the do loop and the program, an unnecessarily harsh response.

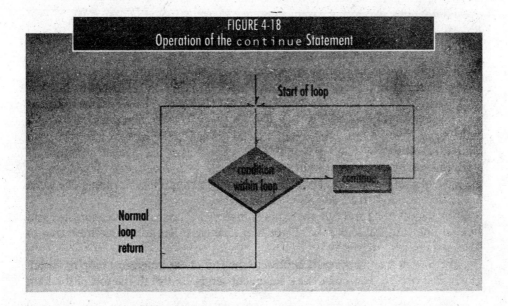

FIGURE 4-18
Operation of the `continue` Statement

THE goto STATEMENT

We'll mention the `goto` statement here for the sake of completeness—not because it's a good idea to use it. If you've had any exposure to structured programming principles, you know that `goto`'s can quickly lead to "spaghetti" code that is difficult to understand and debug. There is almost never any need to use `goto`, as is demonstrated by its absence in the program examples in this book.

With that lecture out of the way, here's the syntax. You insert a *label* in your code at the desired destination for the `goto`. The label is always terminated by a colon. The keyword `goto`, followed by this label name, then takes you to the label. The following code fragment demonstrates this approach:

```
goto SystemCrash;
// other statements
SystemCrash:
// control will begin here following goto
```

SUMMARY

Relational operators compare two values to see if they're equal, if one is larger than the other, and so on. The result is a logical or Boolean value, which is true or false. False is indicated by 0, and true by any other number.

There are three kinds of loops in C++. The `for` loop is most often used when you know in advance how many times you want to execute the loop. The `while` loop and do loops are used when the condition causing the loop to terminate arises within the loop, with the while loop not necessarily executing at all, and the do loop always executing at least once.

A loop body can be a single statement, or a block of multiple statements delimited by braces. A variable defined within a block is visible only within that block.

There are four kinds of decision-making statements. The if statement does something if a test expression is true. The if...else statement does one thing if the test expression is true, and another thing if it isn't. The else if construction is a way of rewriting a ladder of nested if...else statements to make it more readable. The switch statement branches to multiple sections of code, depending on the value of a single variable. The conditional operater simplifies returning one value if a test expression is true, and another if it's false.

The logical AND and OR operators combine two Boolean expressions to yield another one, and the logical NOT operator changes a Boolean value from true to false, or from false to true.

The break statement sends control to the end of the innermost loop or switch in which it occurs. The continue statement sends control to the top of the loop in which it occurs. The goto statement sends control to a label.

Precedence specifies which kinds of operations will be carried out first. The order is unary, arithmetic, relational, logical, conditional, assignment.

ESTIONS

1. A relational operator
   a. assigns one operand to another
   b. yields a Boolean result
   c. compares two operands
   d. logically combines two operands

2. Write an expression that uses a relational operator to return true if the variable george is not equal to sally.

3. Is −1 true or false?

4. Name and describe the usual purpose of three expressions in a for statement.

5. In a for loop with a multistatement loop body, semicolons should appear following
   a. the for statement itself
   b. the closing brace in a multistatement loop body
   c. each statement within the loop body
   d. the test expression

6. True or false: The increment expression in a for loop can decrement the loop variable.

7. Write a `for` loop that displays the numbers from 100 to 110. Thank you.

8. A block of code is delimited by _____.

9. A variable defined within a block is visible
   a. from the point of definition onward in the program
   b. from the point of definition onward in the function
   c. from the point of definition onward in the block
   d. throughout the function

10. Write a `while` loop that displays the numbers from 100 to 110.

11. True or false: Relational operators have a higher precedence than arithmetic operators.

12. How many times is the loop body executed in a `do` loop?

13. Write a `do` loop that displays the numbers from 100 to 110.

14. Write an `if` statement that prints `Yes` if a variable `age` is greater than 21.

15. The library function `exit()` causes an exit from
    a. the loop in which it occurs
    b. the block in which it occurs
    c. the function in which it occurs
    d. the program in which it occurs

16. Write an `if...else` statement that displays *Yes* if a variable `age` is greater than 21, and displays *No* otherwise.

17. The `getche()` library function
    a. returns a character when any key is pressed
    b. returns a character when (ENTER) is pressed
    c. displays a character on the screen when any key is pressed
    d. does not display a character on the screen

18. What is the character obtained from `cin` when the user presses the (ENTER) key?

19. An `else` always matches the _____ `if`, unless the `if` is
    _____.

20. The `else if` construction is obtained from `if...else` by
    _____.

21. Write a `switch` statement that prints `Yes` if a variable `ch` is 'y', prints `No` if `ch` is 'n', and prints `Unknown response` otherwise.

22. Write a statement that uses a conditional operator to set `ticket` to 1 if `speed` is greater than 55, and to 0 otherwise.

23. The `&&` and `||` operators
    a. compare two numeric values
    b. combine two numeric values
    c. compare two Boolean values
    d. combine two Boolean values

24. Write an expression involving a logical operator that is true if `limit` is 55 and `speed` is greater than 55.

25. Arrange in order of precedence (highest first) the following kinds of operators: logical, unary, arithmetic, assignment, relational, conditional.

26. The **break** statement causes an exit
    a. only from the innermost loop
    b. only from the innermost switch
    c. from all loops and switches
    d. from the innermost loop or switch

27. Executing the **continue** operator from within a loop causes control to go to
    _____.

28. The **goto** statement causes control to go to
    a. an operator
    b. a label
    c. a variable
    d. a function

ERCISES

1. Assume you want to generate a table of multiples of any given number. Write a program that allows the user to enter the number, and then generates the table, formatting it into ten columns and 20 lines. Interaction with the program should look like this (only the first three lines are shown):

```
Enter a number: 7
    7    14    21    28    35    42    49    56    63    70
   77    84    91    98   105   112   119   126   133   140
  147   154   161   168   175   182   189   196   203   210
```

2. Write a temperature-conversion program that gives the user the option of converting Fahrenheit to Celsius or Celsius to Fahrenheit. Then carry out the conversion. Use floating-point numbers. Interaction with the program might look like this:

```
Type 1 to convert Fahrenheit to Celsius,
    2 to convert Celsius to Fahrenheit: 1
Enter temperature in Fahrenheit: 70
In Celsius that's 21.111111
```

3. Operators such as >>, which read input from the keyboard, must be able to convert a series of digits into a number. Write a program that does the same thing. It should allow the user to type up to six digits, and then display the resulting number as a type **long** integer. The digits should be read individually, as characters, using **getche()**. Constructing the number involves multiplying the existing value by 10 and then adding the new digit. (Hint: Subtract 48 or

'0' to go from ASCII to a numerical digit.) Don't forget that you may need to clear the input stream to get ready for getche() like this:

```
cout << "\nEnter a number: " << flush;
```

Here's some sample interaction:

```
Enter a number: 123456
Number is: 123456
```

4. Create the equivalent of a four-function calculator. The program should request the user to enter a number, an operator, and another number. It should then carry out the specified arithmetical operation: adding, subtracting, multiplying, or dividing the two numbers. (It should use a switch statement to select the operation.) Finally it should display the result.

When it finishes the calculation, the program should ask if the user wants to do another calculation. The response can be 'y' or 'n'. Some sample interaction with the program might look like this:

```
Enter first number, operator, second number: 10 / 3
Answer = 3.333333
Do another (y/n)? y
Enter first number, operator, second number: 12 + 100
Answer = 112
Do another (y/n)? n
```

CHAPTER 5

5

STRUCTURES

STRUCTURE SPECIFIERS AND DEFINITIONS

ACCESSING STRUCTURE MEMBERS

NESTED STRUCTURES

STRUCTURES AS OBJECTS AND DATA TYPES

ENUMERATED DATA TYPES

We've seen variables of simple data types, such as **float**, **char**, and **int**. Variables of such types represent one item of information: a height, an amount, a count, and so on. But just as eggs are organized into cartons, employees into departments, and soldiers into platoons and regiments, it's often convenient to organize simple variables into more complex entities. The C++ construction called the *structure* is one way to do this.

The first part of this chapter is devoted to structures. In the second part we'll look at a related topic: the enumerated data type.

STRUCTURES

A structure is a collection of simple variables. The variables in a structure can be of different types: Some can be **int**, some can be **float**, and so on. (This is unlike the array, which we'll meet later, in which all the variables must be the same type.) The data items in a structure are called the *members* of the structure.

In books on C programming, structures are often considered an advanced feature and are introduced toward the end of the book. However, for C++ programmers, structures are one of the two important building blocks in the understanding of objects and classes. In fact, the syntax of a structure is almost identical to that of a class. A structure (as typically used) is a collection of data, while a class is a collection of both data and functions. So by learning about structures we'll be paving the way for an understanding of classes and objects. Structures in C++ (and C) serve a similar purpose to *records* in BASIC and Pascal.

A SIMPLE STRUCTURE

Let's start off with a structure that contains three variables: two integers and a floating-point number. This structure represents an item in a widget company's parts inventory. It is a template for information about a single widget part. The company makes several kinds of widgets, so the widget model number is the first member of the structure. The number of the part itself is the next member, and the final member is the part's cost. (Those of you who consider part numbers unexciting need to open your eyes to the romance of commerce.)

The program PARTS specifies the structure `part`, defines a structure variable of that type called `part1`, assigns values to its members, and then displays these values.

```
// parts.cpp
// uses parts inventory to demonstrate structures
#include <iostream.h>

struct part              // specify a structure
   {
   int modelnumber;      // ID number of widget
   int partnumber;       // ID number of widget part
   float cost;           // cost of part
   };

void main()
   {
   part part1;                        // define a structure variable

   part1.modelnumber = 6244;  // give values to structure members
   part1.partnumber = 373;
   part1.cost = 217.55;
                                      // display structure members
   cout << "\nModel "  << part1.modelnumber;
   cout << ", part "   << part1.partnumber;
   cout << ", costs $" << part1.cost;
   }
```

The program's output looks like this:

```
Model 6244, part 373, costs $217.55
```

The PARTS program has three main aspects: specifying the structure, defining a structure variable, and accessing the members of the structure. Let's look at each of these.

SPECIFYING THE STRUCTURE

The structure *specifier* tells how the structure is organized: It specifies what members the structure will have. Here it is:

```
struct part
   {
   int modelnumber;
   int partnumber;
   float cost;
   };
```

This construction is often called a structure *declaration*. However, the word *declaration* is also used in another sense—as we'll see later—so for clarity we'll use the word *specifier*.

Syntax of the Structure Specifier

The keyword `struct` introduces the specifier. Next comes the *structure name* or *tag*, which is `part`. The declarations of the structure members—`modelnumber`, `partnumber`, and `cost`—are enclosed in braces. A semicolon follows the closing brace, terminating the entire structure. Note that this use of the semicolon for structures is unlike the usage for a block of code. As we've seen, blocks of code, which are used in loops, decisions, and functions, are also delimited by braces. However, they don't use a semicolon following the final brace. Figure 5-1 shows the syntax of the structure specifier.

Use of the Structure Specifier

The specifier serves as a blueprint for the creation of variables of type `part`. The specifier does not itself define any variables; that is, it does not set aside any space in memory. It's merely a specification for how such structure variables will look when they are defined. This is shown in Figure 5-2.

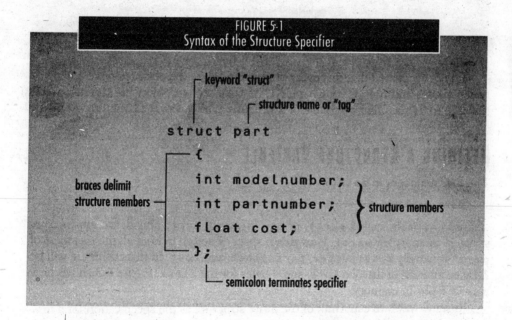

FIGURE 5-1
Syntax of the Structure Specifier

FIGURE 5-2
Structures and Structure Variables

Structure specifier for Foo

Foo 1

Foo 2

Foo 3

Variables of type Foo

It's not accidental that this description sounds like the distinction we noted between classes and objects, in Chapter 1. As we'll see, an object has the same relationship to its class that a variable of a structure type has to the structure specifier.

DEFINING A STRUCTURE VARIABLE

The first statement in `main()`,

```
part part1;
```

defines a variable, called `part1`, of type structure `part`. This definition reserves space in memory for `part1`. How much space? Enough to hold all the members of `part1`—namely `modelnumber`, `partnumber`, and `cost`. In this case there will be 2 bytes for each of the two `int`'s, and 4 bytes for the `float`. Figure 5-3 shows how `part1` looks in memory.

In some ways we can think of the `part` structure as the specification for a new data type. This will become clearer as we go along, but notice that the format for

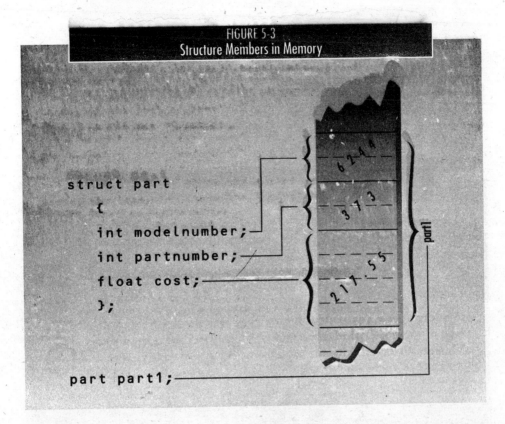

FIGURE 5-3
Structure Members in Memory

```
struct part
    {
    int modelnumber;
    int partnumber;
    float cost;
    };

part part1;
```

defining a structure variable is the same as that for defining a built-in data type such as int:

```
part part1;
int var1;
```

This similarity is not accidental. One of the aims of C++ is to make the syntax and the operation of user-defined data types as similar as possible to that of built-in data types. (In C you need to include the keyword **struct** in structure definitions, as in **struct part part1;**. In C++ the keyword is not necessary.)

ACCESSING STRUCTURE MEMBERS

Once a structure variable has been defined, its members can be accessed using something called the *dot operator*. Here's how the first member is given a value:

```
part1.modelnumber = 6244;
```

The structure member is written in three parts: the name of the structure variable (**part1**); the dot operator, which consists of a period (**.**); and the member name (**modelnumber**). This means "the **modelnumber** member *of* **part1**."

Remember that the first component of an expression involving the dot operator is the name of the specific structure variable (`part1` in this case), not the name of the structure specifier (`part`). The variable name must be used to distinguish one variable from another when there is more than one, such as `part1`, `part2`, and so on, as shown in Figure 5-4.

Structure members are treated just like other variables. In the statement `part1.modelnumber = 6244;`, the member is given the value 6244 using a normal

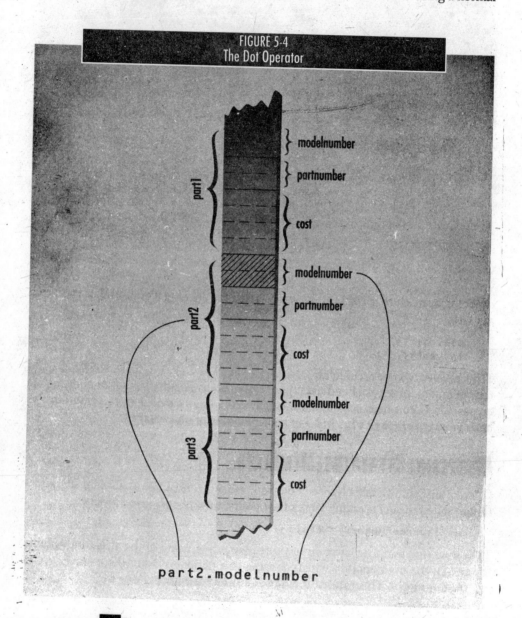

FIGURE 5-4
The Dot Operator

part1 — modelnumber, partnumber, cost

part2 — modelnumber, partnumber, cost

part3 — modelnumber, partnumber, cost

`part2.modelnumber`

assignment operator. The program also shows members used in `cout` statements such as:

```
cout << "\nModel " << part1.modelnumber;
```

These statements output the values of the structure members.

OTHER STRUCTURE FEATURES

Structures are surprisingly versatile. Let's look at some additional features of structure syntax and usage.

Combining Specifier and Definition

In the PARTS example we showed the structure specifier and the definition as two separate statements. These two statements can also be combined into a single statement, as shown in the next example, PARTSCOM:

```
// partscom.cpp
// uses parts inventory to demonstrate structures
#include <iostream.h>

uct                    // no tag needed
    {
    int modelnumber;   // ID number of widget
    int partnumber;    // ID number of widget part
    float cost;        // cost of part
    } part1;           // definition goes here

void main()
    {
    part1.modelnumber = 6244;  // give values to structure members
    part1.partnumber = 373;
    part1.cost = 217.55;
                               // display structure members
    cout << "\nModel "  << part1.modelnumber;
    cout << ", part "   << part1.partnumber;
    cout << ", costs $" << part1.cost;
    }
```

In this program there is no separate statement for the structure definition:

```
part part1;
```

Instead, the variable name `part1` is placed at the end of the specifier:

```
struct
    {
    int modelnumber;
    int partnumber;
    float cost;
    } part1;
```

Notice that the tag name in the structure specifier can be removed, as we show here, if no more variables of this structure type will be defined.

Merging the structure specification and definition this way is a shorthand approach that can save a few program lines. Generally, it is less clear and less flexible than using separate specifiers and definitions.

Initializing Structure Members

The next example shows how structure members can be initialized when the structure is defined. It also demonstrates that you can have more than one variable of a given structure type (we hope you suspected this all along).

Here's the listing for PARTINIT:

```
// partinit.cpp
// shows initialization of structure variables
#include <iostream.h>

struct part              // specify a structure
   {
   int modelnumber;      // ID number of widget
   int partnumber;       // ID number of widget part
   float cost;           // cost of part
   };

void main()
   {
   part part1 = { 6244, 373, 217.55 };  // initialize variable
   part part2;                          // define variable
                             // display first variable
   cout << "\nModel ".  << part1.modelnumber;
   cout << ", part "    << part1.partnumber;
   cout << ", costs $"  << part1.cost;

   part2 = part1;            // assign first variable to second
                             // display second variable
   cout << "\nModel "   << part2.modelnumber;
   cout << ", part "    << part2.partnumber;
   cout << ", costs $"  << part2.cost;
   }
```

This program defines two variables of type part: part1 and part2. It initializes part1, prints out the values of its members, assigns part1 to part2, and prints out its members.

Here's the output:

```
Model 6244, part 373, costs $217.55
Model 6244, part 373, costs $217.55
```

Not surprisingly, the same output is repeated, since one variable is made equal to the other.

Initializing Structure Variables

The part1 structure variable's members are initialized when the variable is defined:

```
part part1 = { 6244, 373, 217.55 };
```

The values to be assigned to the structure members are surrounded by braces and separated by commas. The first value in the list is assigned to the first member, the second to the second member, and so on.

Structure Variables in Assignment Statements

As can be seen in PARTINIT, one structure variable can be assigned to another:

```
part2 = part1;
```

The value of each member of part1 is assigned to the corresponding member of part2. Since a large structure can have dozens of members, such an assignment statement can require the computer to do a considerable amount of work.

Note that one structure variable can be assigned to another only when they are of the same structure type. If you try to assign a variable of one structure type to a variable of another type, the compiler will complain.

A MEASUREMENT EXAMPLE

Let's see how a structure can be used to group a different kind of information. If you've ever looked at an architectural drawing, you know that (at least in the United States) distances are measured in feet and inches. The length of a living room, for example, might be given as 12'–8", meaning 12 feet 8 inches. The dash isn't a negative sign; it merely separates the feet from the inches. This is part of the English system of measurement. (We'll make no judgment here on the merits of English versus metric.) Figure 5-5 shows typical length measurements in the English system.

Suppose you want to create a drawing or architectural program that uses the English system. It will be convenient to store distances as two numbers, representing feet and inches. The next example, ENGLSTRC, gives an idea how this could be done using a structure. This program will show how two measurements of type Distance can be added together.

```
// englstrc.cpp
// demonstrates structures using English measurements
#include <iostream.h>

struct Distance                    // English distance
    {
    int feet;
    float inches;
    };

void main()
    {
```

```
Distance d1, d3;              // define two lengths
Distance d2 = { 11, 6.25 }; // define & initialize one length

                             // get length d1 from user
cout << "\nEnter feet: ";  cin >> d1.feet;
cout << "Enter inches: ";  cin >> d1.inches;

                             // add lengths d1 and d2 to get d3
d3.inches = d1.inches + d2.inches;  // add the inches
d3.feet = 0;                         // (for possible carry)
if(d3.inches >= 12.0)               // if total exceeds 12.0,
   {                                // then decrease inches
   d3.inches -= 12.0;               // by 12.0 and
   d3.feet++;                       // increase feet
   }                                // by 1
d3.feet += d1.feet + d2.feet;       // add the feet

                             // display all lengths
cout << d1.feet << "\'-" << d1.inches << "\" + ";
cout << d2.feet << "\'-" << d2.inches << "\" = ";
cout << d3.feet << "\'-" << d3.inches << "\"\n";
}
```

FIGURE 5-5
Measurements in the English System

140

Here the structure Distance has two members: feet and inches. The inches variable may have a fractional part, so we'll use type float for it. Feet are always integers, so we'll use type int for them.

We define two such distances, d1 and d3, without initializing them, while we initialize another, d2, to 11'–6.25". The program asks the user to enter a distance in feet and inches, and assigns this distance to d1. (The inches value should be smaller than 12.0.) It then adds the distance d1 to d2, obtaining the total distance d3. Finally the program displays the two initial distances and the newly calculated total distance. Here's some output:

```
Enter feet: 10
Enter inches: 6.75
10'-6.75" + 11'-6.25" = 22'-1"
```

Notice that we can't add the two distances with a program statement like

```
d3 = d1 + d2;   // can't do this in ENGLSTRC
```

Why not? Because there is no routine built into C++ that knows how to add variables of type Distance. The + operator works with built-in types like float, but not with types we define ourselves, like Distance. (However, one of the benefits of using classes, as we'll see, is the ability to add and perform other operations on user-defined data types.)

STRUCTURES WITHIN STRUCTURES

You can nest structures within other structures. Here's a variation on the ENGLSTRC program that shows how this looks. In this program we want to create a data structure that stores the dimensions of a typical room: its length and width. Since we're working with English distances, we'll use two variables of type Distance as the length and width variables, like this:

```
struct Room
   {
   Distance length;
   Distance width;
   }
```

Here's a program, ENGLAREA, that uses the Room structure to represent a room.

```
// englarea.cpp
// demonstrates nested structures
#include <iostream.h>

struct Distance              // English distance
   {
   int feet;
   float inches;
   };
```

```
struct Room                        // rectangular area
   {
   Distance length;                // length of rectangle
   Distance width;                 // width of rectangle
   };

void main()
   {
   Room dining;                              // define a room

   dining.length.feet = 13;         // assign values to room
   dining.length.inches = 6.5;
   dining.width.feet = 10;
   dining.width.inches = 0.0;

                                    // convert length & width
   float l = dining.length.feet + dining.length.inches/12;
   float w = dining.width.feet  + dining.width.inches/12;
                                    // find area and display it
   cout << "\nDining room area is " << l * w
        << " square feet" ;
   }
```

This program defines a single variable—dining—of type Room, in the line

```
Room dining;  // variable dining of type Room
```

It then assigns values to the various members of this structure.

Accessing Nested Structure Members

Because one structure is nested inside another, we must apply the dot operator twice to access the structure members:

```
dining.length.feet = 13;
```

In this statement dining is the name of the structure variable, as before; length is the name of a member in the outer structure (Room); and feet is the name of a member of the inner structure (Distance). The statement means "take the feet member of the length member of the variable dining and assign it the value 13." Figure 5-6 shows how this works.

Once values have been assigned to members of dining, the program calculates the floor area of the room, as shown in Figure 5-7.

To find the area, the program converts the length and width from variables of type Distance to variables of type float, l, and w, representing distances in feet. The values of l and w are found by adding the feet member of Distance to the inches member divided by 12. The feet member is converted to type float automatically before the addition is performed, and the result is type float. The l and w variables are then multiplied together to obtain the area.

FIGURE 5-6
Dot Operator and Nested Structures

```
dining.length.feet = 13;
```

User-Defined Type Conversions

Note that the program converts two distances of type **Distance** to two distances of type **float**: the variables **l** and **w**. In effect it also converts the room's area, which is stored as four separate variables in a structure of type **Room**, to a single floating-point number representing the area in square feet. Here's the output:

```
Dining room area is 135.417 square feet
```

Converting a value of one type to a value of another is an important aspect of programs that employ user-defined data types.

FIGURE 5-7
Area in Feet and Inches

Initializing Nested Structures

How do you initialize a structure variable that itself contains structures? The following statement initializes the variable `dining` to the same values it is given in the ENGLAREA program:

```
Room dining = { {13, 6.5}, {10, 0.0} };
```

Each structure of type `Distance`, which is embedded in `Room`, is initialized separately. Remember that this involves surrounding the values with braces and separating them with commas. The first `Distance` is initialized to

```
{13, 6.5}
```

and the second to

```
{10, 0.0}
```

These two `Distance` values are then used to initialize the `Room` variable, again surrounding them with braces and separating them by commas.

Depth of Nesting

In theory, structures can be nested to any depth. In a program that designs apartment buildings, you might find yourself with statements like

```
apartment1.laundry_room.washing_machine.width.feet
```

A CARD GAME EXAMPLE

Let's examine a different kind of example. This one uses a structure to model a playing card. The program imitates a game played by cardsharps (professional gamblers) at carnivals. The cardsharp shows you three cards, then places them face down on the table and interchanges their positions several times. If you can guess correctly where a particular card is, you win. Everything is in plain sight, yet the cardsharp switches the cards so rapidly and confusingly that the player (the "mark") almost always loses track of the card and loses the game (which is, of course, played for money).

Here's the structure the program uses to represent a playing card:

```
struct card
    {
    int number;
    int suit;
    }
```

This structure uses separate members to hold the number of the card and the suit. The number runs from 2 to 14, where 11, 12, 13, and 14 represent the jack, queen, king, and ace, respectively (this is the order used in poker). The suit runs from 0 to 3, where these four numbers represent clubs, diamonds, hearts, and spades.

Here's the listing for CARDS:

```
// cards.cpp
// demonstrates structures using playing cards
#include <iostream.h>

const int clubs = 0;
const int diamonds = 1;
const int hearts = 2;
const int spades = 3;

const int jack = 11;
const int queen = 12;
const int king = 13;
const int ace = 14;

struct card
    {
    int number;    // 2 to 10, jack, queen, king, ace
    int suit;      // clubs, diamonds, hearts, spades
    };

void main()
    {
    card temp, chosen, prize;          // define cards
    int position;
```

```
card card1 = { 7, clubs };                    // initialize card1
cout << "Card 1 is the 7 of clubs\n";

card card2 = { jack, hearts };                // initialize card2
cout << "Card 2 is the jack of hearts\n";

card card3 = { ace, spades };                 // initialize card3
cout << "Card 3 is the ace of spades\n";

prize = card3;                 // copy this card, to remember it

cout << "I'm swapping card 1 and card 3\n";
temp = card3; card3 = card1; card1 = temp;

cout << "I'm swapping card 2 and card 3\n";
temp = card3; card3 = card2; card2 = temp;

cout << "I'm swapping card 1 and card 2\n";
temp = card2; card2 = card1; card1 = temp;

cout << "Now, where (1, 2, or 3) is the ace of spades? ";
cin >> position;

switch (position)
    {
    case 1: chosen = card1; break;
    case 2: chosen = card2; break;
    case 3: chosen = card3; break;
    }
if(chosen.number == prize.number &&            // compare cards
                    chosen.suit == prize.suit)
    cout << "That's right!  You win!\n";
else
    cout << "Sorry. You lose.\n";
}
```

Here's some sample interaction with the program:

```
Card 1 is the 7 of clubs
Card 2 is the jack of hearts
Card 3 is the ace of spades
I'm swapping card 1 and card 3
I'm swapping card 2 and card 3
I'm swapping card 1 and card 2
Now, where (1, 2, or 3) is the ace of spades? 3
Sorry. You lose.
```

In this case the hapless mark chose the wrong card (the right answer is 2).

The program begins by defining a number of variables of type `const` for the face card and suit values. (Not all these variables are used in the program; they're included for completeness.) Next the `card` structure is specified. The program then defines three uninitialized variables of type `card`: `temp`, `chosen`, and `prize`. It also defines three cards—`card1`, `card2`, and `card3`—which it initializes to three arbitrary card values. It prints out the values of these cards for the user's information. It then sets a card variable, `prize`, to one of these card values as a way of remembering it. This card is the one whose location the player will be asked to guess at the end of the game.

Next the program rearranges the cards. It swaps the first and third cards, the second and third cards, and the first and second cards. Each time it tells the user what it's doing. (If you find the program too easy, you can add more such statements to further shuffle the cards. Flashing the statements on the screen for a limited time would also increase the challenge.)

Finally the program asks the player what position a particular card is in. It sets a card variable, `chosen`, to the card in this position, and then compares `chosen` with the `prize` card. If they match, it's a win for the player; if not, it's a loss.

Notice how easy swapping cards is:

```
temp = card3;   card3 = card1;   card1 = temp;
```

Although the cards represent structures, they can be moved around very naturally, thanks to the ability of the assignment operator = to work with structures.

Unfortunately, just as structures can't be added, they also can't be compared. You can't say

```
if( chosen == prize )                        // not legal yet
```

because there's no routine built into the == operator that knows about the `card` structure. But, as with addition, this problem can be solved with operator overloading, as we'll see later.

STRUCTURES AND CLASSES

We must confess to having misled you slightly on the capabilities of structures. It's true that structures are usually used to hold data only, and classes are used to hold both data and functions. However, in C++, structures can in fact hold both data and functions. (In C they can hold only data.) The syntactical distinction between structures and classes in C++ is minimal, so they can in theory be used interchangeably. But most C++ programmers use structures as we have in this chapter, exclusively for data. Classes are usually used to hold both data and functions, as we'll see in Chapter 7.

ENUMERATED DATA TYPES

As we've seen, structures can be looked at as a way to provide user-defined data types. Another approach to defining your own data type is the *enumerated data type*. This feature of C++ is somewhat less crucial than structures. You can write perfectly good object-oriented programs in C++ without knowing anything about enumerated data types. However, they are very much in the spirit of C++, in that, by allowing you to define your own data types, they can simplify and clarify your programming. C++ programmers use enumerated types frequently. (C programmers use them less often.) Enumerated types also exist in Pascal.

DAYS OF THE WEEK

Enumerated types work when you know in advance a finite (usually short) list of values that a data type can take on. Here's an example program, DAYENUM, that uses an enumerated data type for the days of the week:

```
// dayenum.cpp
// demonstrates enum types
#include <iostream.h>
                                // specify enum type
    days_of_week { Sun, Mon, Tue, Wed, Thu, Fri, Sat };

void main()
    {
    days_of_week day1, day2;    // define variables
                                // of type days_of_week
    day1 = Mon;                 // give values to
    day2 = Thu;                 // variables

    int diff = day2 - day1;     // can do integer arithmetic
    cout << "Days between = " << diff << endl;

    if(day1 < day2)             // can do comparisons
        cout << "day1 comes before day2\n";
    }
```

An **enum** specifier defines the set of all names that will be permissible values of the type. These permissible values are called *members*. The **enum** type **days_of_week** has seven members: **Sun**, **Mon**, **Tue**, and so on, up to **Sat**. Figure 5-8 shows the syntax of an **enum** specifier.

Enumerated means that all the values are listed. This is unlike the specification of an **int**, for example, which is given in terms of a range of possible values. In an **enum** you must give a specific name to every possible value. Figure 5-9 shows the difference between an **int** and an **enum**.

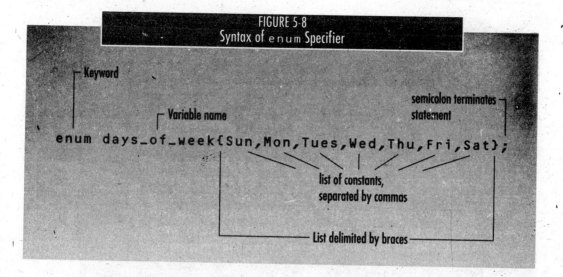

FIGURE 5-8
Syntax of enum Specifier

Once you've specified the data type `days_of_week` as shown, you can **define** variables of this type. DAYENUM has two such variables, `day1` and `day2`, defined in the statement

```
days_of_week  day1, day2;
```

(In C you must use the keyword `enum` before the type name, as in

```
enum days_of_week day1, day2;
```

In C++ this isn't necessary.)

Variables of an enumerated type, like `day1` and `day2`, can be given any of the values listed in the `enum` specifier. In the example we give them the values `Mon` and `Thu`. You can't use values that weren't listed in the specifier. Such statements as

```
day1 = halloween;
```

are illegal.

You can use the standard arithmetic operators on `enum` types. In the program we subtract two values. You can also use the comparison operators, as we show. Here's the program's output:

```
Days between = 3
day1 comes before day2
```

The use of arithmetic and relational operators doesn't make much sense with some `enum` types. For example, if you have the specifier

```
enum pets { cat, dog, hamster, canary, ocelot };
```

then it may not be clear what expressions like `dog + canary` or `(cat < hamster)` mean.

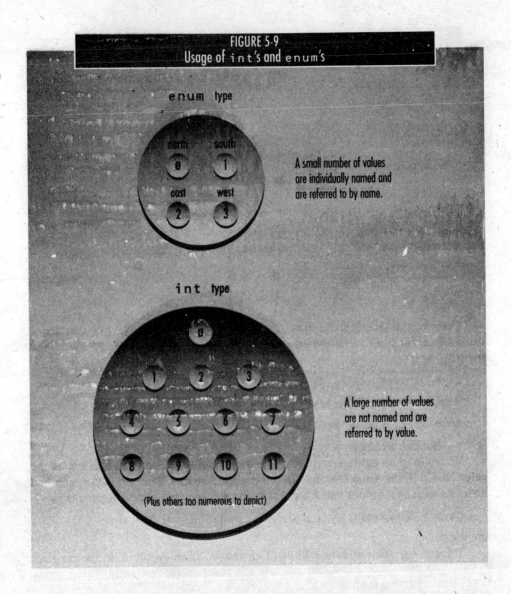

FIGURE 5-9
Usage of `int`'s and `enum`'s

enum type

north   south
  0   1

east   west
  2   3

A small number of values
are individually named and
are referred to by name.

int type

              0

      1   2   3

  4   5   6   7

  8   9   10   11

(Plus others too numerous to depict)

A large number of values
are not named and are
referred to by value.

Enumerated data types are treated internally as integers. (This explains why you can perform arithmetic and relational opertions on them.) Ordinarily the first name in the list is given the value 0, the next name is given the value 1, and so on. In the DAYENUM example the values `Sun` through `Sat` are stored as the integer values 0 through 6.

Arithmetic operations on `enum` types take place on the integer values. However, although the compiler knows that your `enum` variables are really integers, you must be careful of trying to take advantage of this fact. If you say

```
day1 = 5;
```

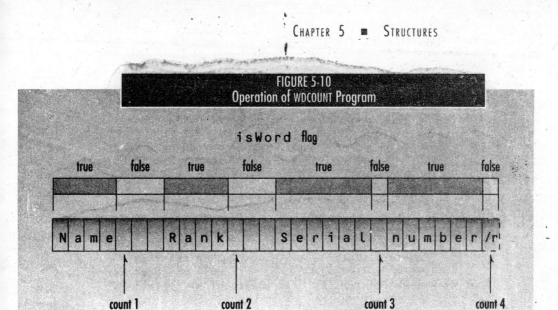

FIGURE 5-10
Operation of WDCOUNT Program

the compiler will issue a warning (although it will compile). It's better to forget—whenever possible—that **enum**'s are really integers.

INVENTING A BOOLEAN TYPE

We noted in the last chapter that there is no Boolean (false or true) data type in C++; the integer values 0 and 1 are used instead. However, it is easy to invent your own Boolean type using **enum**.

Our next example counts the words in a phrase typed in by the user. Unlike the earlier CHCOUNT example, however, it doesn't simply count spaces to determine the number of words. Instead it counts the places where a string of nonspace characters changes to a space, as shown in Figure 5-10.

This way you don't get a false count if you type multiple spaces between words. (It still doesn't handle tabs and other whitespace characters.) Here's the listing for WDCOUNT:

```
// wdcount.cpp
// demonstrates enums, counts words in phrase
#include <iostream.h>
#include <conio.h>                  // for getche()

enum boolean { false, true };      // false=0, true=1

void main()
   {
   boolean isWord = false;        // true when in a word,
                                  // false when in whitespace
   char ch = 'a';                 // character read from keyboard
   int wordcount = 0;             // number of words read
```

```
do
   {
   ch = getche();                    // get character
   if(ch==' ' || ch=='\r')           // if white space,
      {
      if( isWord )                   // and doing a word,
         {                           // then it's end of word
         wordcount++;                // count the word
         isWord = false;             // reset flag
         }
      }                              // otherwise, it's
   else                              // normal character
      if( !isWord )                  // if start of word,
         isWord = true;              // then set flag
   } while( ch != '\r' );            // quit on Enter key
   cout << "\n--Word count is " << wordcount << "--\n";
   }
```

The program cycles in a **do** loop, reading characters from the keyboard. It passes over (nonspace) characters until it finds a space. At this point it counts a word. Then it passes over spaces until it finds a character, and again counts characters until it finds a space. Doing this requires the program to remember whether it's in the middle of a word, or in the middle of a string of spaces. It remembers this with the variable **isWord**. This variable is defined to be of type **boolean**. This type is specified in the statement

```
enum boolean { false, true };
```

Variables of type **boolean** have only two possible values: *false* and *true*. Notice that the list starts with *false*, so this value will be given the value 0—the value of false used in comparisons.

The **isWord** variable is set to **false** when the program starts. When the program encounters the first nonspace character, it sets **isWord** to **true** to indicate that it's in the middle of a word. It keeps this value until the next space is found, at which point it's set back to **false**. Notice that, since **isWord** is either true or false, we can use the expression

```
if( isWord )
```

This will be true if **isWord** is true (1), and false if **isWord** is false (0).

Note also that we need an extra set of braces around the second **if** statement in the program, so that the **else** will match with the first **if**.

This specification of a Boolean data type is commonly used in C++ programming when flags and similar variables must be defined.

ORGANIZING THE CARDS

Here's another example of **enum** types. Remember that in the CARDS program earlier in this chapter we defined a group of constants of type **const int** to represent a card's suits:

```
const int clubs = 0;
const int diamonds = 1;
const int hearts = 2;
const int spades = 3;
```

This sort of list is somewhat clumsy. Let's revise the CARDS program to use enumerated data types instead. Here's the listing for CARDENUM:

```
// cardenum.cpp
// demonstrates the enumerated data type
#include <iostream.h>

const int jack = 11;    // 2 through 10 are unnamed integers
const int queen = 12;
const int king = 13;
const int ace = 14;

enum Suit { clubs, diamonds, hearts, spades };

struct card
   {
   int number;          // 2 to 10, jack, queen, king, ace
   Suit suit;           // clubs, diamonds, hearts, spades
   };

void main()
   {
   card temp, chosen, prize;              // define cards
   int position;

   card card1 = { 7, clubs };             // initialize card1
   cout << "Card 1 is the seven of clubs\n";

   card card2 = { jack, hearts };         // initialize card2
   cout << "Card 2 is the jack of hearts\n";

   card card3 = { ace, spades };          // initialize card3
   cout << "Card 3 is the ace of spades\n";

   prize = card3;              // copy this card, to remember it

   cout << "I'm swapping card 1 and card 3\n";
   temp = card3; card3 = card1; card1 = temp;

   cout << "I'm swapping card 2 and card 3\n";
   temp = card3; card3 = card2; card2 = temp;

   cout << "I'm swapping card 1 and card 2\n";
   temp = card2; card2 = card1; card1 = temp;

   cout << "Now, where (1, 2, or 3) is the ace of spades? ";
   cin >> position;
```

```
switch (position)
  {
  case 1: chosen = card1; break;
  case 2: chosen = card2; break;
  case 3: chosen = card3; break;
  }
if(chosen.number == prize.number &&            // compare cards
                chosen.suit == prize.suit)
  cout << "That's right!  You win!\n";
else
  cout << "Sorry.  You lose.\n";
}
```

Here the set of definitions for suits used in CARDS has been replaced by an **enum** specifier:

```
enum Suit { clubs, diamonds, hearts, spades };
```

This is a cleaner approach than using **const** variables. We know exactly what the possible values of the suit are; attempts to use other values, as in

```
card1.suit = 5;
```

result in warnings from the compiler.

SPECIFYING INTEGER VALUES

We said that in an **enum** specifier the first name was given the integer value 0, the second the value 1, and so on. This ordering can be altered by using an equals sign to specify a starting point other than 0. For example, if you want the suits to start with 1 instead of 0, you can say

```
enum Suit { clubs=1, diamonds, hearts, spades };
```

Subsequent names are given values starting at this point, so **diamonds** is 2, **hearts** is 3, and **spades** is 4.

NOT PERFECT

One annoying aspect of **enum** types is that they are not recognized by C+ Input/Output statements. As an example, what do you think the following code fragment will cause to be displayed?

```
enum direction { north, south, east, west };
direction dir1 = south;
cout << dir1;
```

Would you guess the output will be **south**? That would be nice, but C++ I/O treats variables of **enum** types as integers, so the output will be **1**.

OTHER EXAMPLES

Here are some other examples of enumerated data specifiers, to give you a feeling for possible uses of this feature:

```
enum months { Jan, Feb, Mar, Apr, May, Jun,
              Jul, Aug, Sep, Oct, Nov, Dec };

enum lightswitch { off, on };

enum meridian { am, pm };

enum chess { pawn, knight, bishop, rook, queen, king };

enum coins { penny, nickel, dime, quarter, half-dollar, dollar }
```

We'll see other examples in future programs.

SUMMARY

We've covered two topics in this chapter: structures and the enumerated data type. Structures are an important component of C++, since their syntax is the same as that used in classes. In fact, classes are nothing more than structures that include functions. Structures are typically used to group several data items together to form a single entity. A structure specifier lists the variables that make up the structure. Definitions then set aside memory for structure variables. Structure variables are treated as indivisible units in some situations (such as setting one structure variable equal to another), but in other situations their members are accessed individually (often using the dot operator).

The enumerated data type is a programmer-defined type that is limited to a fixed list of values. A specifier gives the type a name and specifies the permissible values. Definitions then create variables of this type. Internally the compiler treats enumerated variables as integers.

Structures should not be confused with enumerated data types. Structures are a powerful and flexible way of grouping a diverse collection of data into a single entity. An enumerated data type allows the definition of variables that can take on a fixed set of values that are listed (enumerated) in the type's specifier.

QUESTIONS

1. A structure brings together a group of
   a. items of the same data type
   b. related data items
   c. integers with user-defined names
   d. variables

2. True or false: A structure and a class use similar syntax.

3. The closing brace of a structure is followed by a _____.

4. Write a structure specification that includes three variables—all of type int—called hrs, mins, and secs. Call this structure time.

5. True or false: A structure specifier creates space in memory for a variable.

6. When accessing a structure member, the identifier to the left of the dot operator is the name of
   a. a structure member
   b. a structure tag
   c. a structure variable
   d. the keyword struct

7. Write a statement that sets the hrs member of the time2 structure variable equal to 11.

8. If you have three variables defined to be of type struct time, and this structure contains three int members, how many bytes of memory do the variables use together?

9. Write a definition that initializes the members of time1—which is a variable of type struct time, as defined in question 4—to hrs = 11, mins = 10, secs = 59.

10. True or false: You can assign one structure variable to another, provided they are of the same type.

11. Write a statement that sets the variable temp equal to the paw member of the dogs member of the fido variable.

12. An enumerated data type brings together a group of
    a. items of different data types
    b. related data variables
    c. integers with user-defined names
    d. constant values

13. Write a statement that declares an enumerated data type called players with the values B1, B2, SS, B3, RF, CF, LF, P, and C.

14. Assuming the enum type team as declared in Question 13, define two variables joe and tom, and assign them the values LF and P, respectively.

15. Assuming the statements of questions 13 and 14, state whether each of the following statements is legal:

    a. joe = QB;
    b. tom = SS;
    c. LF = tom;
    d. difference = joe - tom;

16. The first three members of an enum type are normally represented by the values _____; _____, and _____.

17. Write a statement that declares an enumerated data type called speeds with the values obsolete, single, and album. Give these three names the integer values 78, 45, and 33.

18. State the reason why

    ```
    enum boolean{ false, true };
    ```

    is better than

    ```
    enum boolean{ true, false };
    ```

EXERCISES

1. A phone number, such as (212) 767-8900, can be thought of as having three parts: the area code (212), the exchange (767), and the number (8900). Write a program that uses a structure to store these three parts of a phone number separately. Call the structure phone. Create two structure variables of type phone. Initialize one, and have the user input a number for the other one. Then display both numbers. The interchange might look like this:

    ```
    Enter your area code, exchange, and number: 415 555 1212
    My number is (212) 767-8900
    Your number is (415) 555-1212
    ```

2. A point on the two-dimensional plane can be represented by two numbers: an X coordinate and a Y coordinate. For example, (4,5) represents a point 4 units to the right of the origin along the X axis, and 5 units up the Y axis. The sum of two points can be defined as a new point whose X coordinate is the sum of the X coordinates of the two points, and whose Y coordinate is the sum of their Y coordinates.

    Write a program that uses a structure called point to model a point. Define three points, and have the user input values to two of them. Then set the third point equal to the sum of the other two, and display the value of the new point. Interaction with the program might look like this:

```
Enter coordinates for p1: 3 4
Enter coordinates for p2: 5 7
Coordinates of p1+p2 are: 8, 11
```

3. Create a structure called `Volume` that uses three variables of type `Distance` (from the ENGLSTRC example) to model the volume of a room. Initialize a variable of type `Volume` to specific dimensions, then calculate the volume it represents, and print out the result. To calculate the volume, convert each dimension from a `Distance` variable to a variable of type `float` representing feet and fractions of a foot, and then multiply the resulting three numbers.

CHAPTER 6

FUNCTIONS

FUNCTION DEFINITIONS AND DECLARATIONS

ARGUMENTS AND RETURN VALUES

REFERENCE ARGUMENTS

OVERLOADED FUNCTIONS

DEFAULT ARGUMENTS

STORAGE CLASSES

A function groups a number of program statements into a unit and gives it a name. This unit can then be invoked from other parts of the program.

The most important reason to use functions is to aid in the conceptual organization of a program. Dividing a program into functions is, as we discussed in Chapter 1, one of the major principles of structured programming. (However, as we also noted, object-oriented programming provides other, more powerful ways to organize programs.)

Another reason to use functions (and the reason they were invented, long ago) is to reduce program size. Any sequence of instructions that appears in a program more than once is a candidate for being made into a function. The function's code is stored in only one place in memory, even though the function is executed many times in the course of the program. Figure 6-1 shows how a function is invoked from different sections of a program.

Functions in C++ (and C) serve the same purpose as subprograms and procedures in BASIC, and procedures and functions in Pascal.

SIMPLE FUNCTIONS

Our first example demonstrates a simple function whose purpose is to print a line of 45 asterisks. The example program generates a table, and lines of asterisks are used to make the table more readable. Here's the listing for TABLE:

```cpp
// table.cpp
// demonstrates simple function
#include <iostream.h>

void starline();                          // function declaration
                                          //    (prototype)
void main()
    {
    starline();                           // call to function
```

```
cout << "Data type    Range" << endl;
starline();                              // call to function
cout << "char          -128 to 127" << endl
     << "int           -32,768 to 32,767" << endl
     << "double        -2,147,483,648 to 2,147,483,647" << endl;
starline();                              // call to function
}

// starline()
// function definition
void starline()                          // function declarator
   {
   for(int j=0; j<45; j++)
      cout << '*';                        // function body
   cout << endl;
   }
```

The output from the program looks like this:

```
*********************************************
Data type    Range
*********************************************
char         -128 to 127
int          -32,768 to 32,767
double       -2,147,483,648 to 2,147,483,647
*********************************************
```

The program consists of two functions: `main()` and `starline()`. You've already seen many programs that use `main()` alone. What other components are necessary to add a function to the program? There are three: the function declaration, the calls to the function, and the function definition.

THE FUNCTION DECLARATION

Just as you can't use a variable without first telling the compiler what it is, you also can't use a function without telling the compiler about it. The most common approach is to *declare* the function at the beginning of the program. In the TABLE program the function `starline()` is declared in the line

```
void starline();
```

The declaration tells the compiler that at some later point we plan to present a function called *starline*. The keyword `void` specifies that the function has no return value, and the empty parentheses indicate that it takes no arguments. (You can also use the keyword `void` in parentheses to indicate that the function takes no arguments, as is often done in C, but leaving them empty is the more common practice in C++.) We'll have more to say about arguments and return values soon.

Notice that the function declaration is terminated with a semicolon. It is a complete statement in itself.

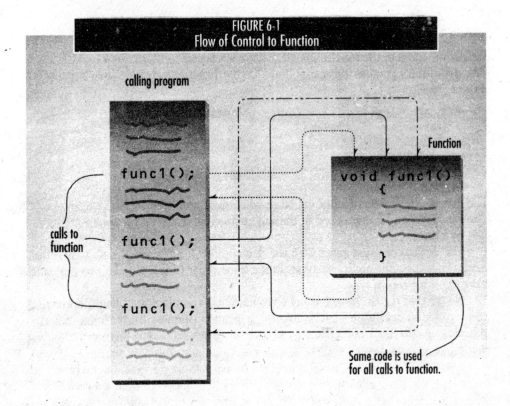

FIGURE 6-1
Flow of Control to Function

calling program

calls to function

func1();

func1();

func1();

Function

void func1()
{

}

Same code is used
for all calls to function.

Function declarations are also called *prototypes*, since they provide a model or blueprint for the function. They tell the compiler, "a function that looks like this is coming up later in the program, so it's all right if you see references to it before you see the function itself."

CALLING THE FUNCTION

The function is *called* (or invoked, or executed) three times from `main()`. Each of the three calls looks like this:

```
starline();
```

This is all we need to call the function: the function name, followed by parentheses. The syntax of the call is very similar to that of the declaration, except that the return type is not used. The call is terminated by a semicolon. Executing the call statement causes the function to execute; that is, control is transferred to the function, the statements in the function definition (which we'll examine in a moment) are executed, and then control returns to the statement following the function call.

The Function Definition

Finally we come to the function itself, which is referred to as the function *definition*. The definition contains the actual code for the function. Here's the definition for starline():

```
void starline()                   // declarator
   {
   for(int j=0; j<45; j++)        // function body
      cout << '*';
   cout << endl;
   }
```

The definition consists of a line called the *declarator*, followed by the function body. The function body is composed of the statements that make up the function, delimited by braces.

The declarator must agree with the declaration: It must use the same function name, have the same argument types in the same order (if there are arguments), and have the same return type.

Notice that the declarator is *not* terminated by a semicolon. As with loops, the entire function definition—including the declarator, opening brace, function body, and closing brace—is considered to be one program statement. Figure 6-2 shows the syntax of the function declaration, function call, and function definition.

When the function is called, control is transferred to the first statement in the function body. The other statements in the function body are then executed, and when the closing brace is encountered, control returns to the calling program.

Table 6-1 summarizes the different function components.

Comparison with Library Functions

We've already seen some library functions in use. We have embedded calls to library functions, such as

```
ch = getche();
```

in our program code. Where are the declaration and definition for this library function? The declaration is in the header file specified at the beginning of the program (CONIO.H, for getche()). The definition (compiled into executable code) is in the library file SLIBCE.LIB (or a similar file). When we use a library function we don't need to write the declaration or definition.

But when we write our own functions, the declaration and definition are part of our source file, as we've shown in the TABLE example. (Things get more complicated in multifile programs, as we'll discuss in Chapter 15.)

Eliminating the Declaration

We should note that you can eliminate the function declaration if the function definition (the function itself) appears in the listing before the first call to the function.

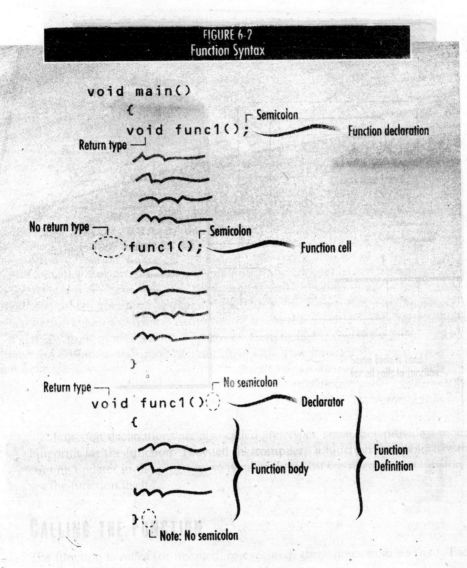

FIGURE 6-2
Function Syntax

For example, we could rewrite TABLE to produce TABLE2, in which the function definition appears first:

```
// table2.cpp
// demonstrates function definition preceding function calls
#include <iostream.h>                    // no function declaration

// starline()                            // function definition
void starline()
   {
```

```
     for(int j=0; j<45; j++)
        cout << '*';
     cout << endl;
     }


void main()                            // main follows function
   {
   starline();                         // call to function
   cout << "Data type    Range" << endl;
   starline();                         // call to function
   cout << "char         -128 to 127" << endl
        << "int          -32,768 to 32,767" << endl
        << "double       -2,147,483,648 to 2,147,483,647" << endl;
   starline();                         // call to function
   }
```

This approach is simpler for short programs, in that it removes the declaration, but it is less flexible. To use this technique when there are more than a few functions, the programmer must give considerable thought to arranging the functions so that each one appears before it is called by any other. Sometimes this is impossible. Also, many programmers prefer to place main() first in the listing, since it is where execution begins. In general we'll stick with the first approach, using declarations and starting the listing with main().

TABLE 6-1 Function Components		
Component	Purpose	Example
Declaration (prototype)	Specifies function name, argument types, and return value. Alerts compiler (and programmer) that function is coming up later.	`void func();`
Call	Causes the function to be executed.	`func();`
Definition	The function itself. Contains the lines of code that constitute the function.	`void func()` `{` `// lines of code` `}`
Declarator	First line of definition.	`void func()`

Passing Arguments to Functions

An argument is a piece of data (an `int` value, for example) passed from a program to the function. Arguments allow a function to operate with different values, or even to do different things, depending on the requirements of the program calling it.

Passing Constants

As an example, let's suppose we decide that the `starline()` function in the last example is too rigid. Instead of a function that always prints 45 asterisks, we want a function that will print any character any number of times.

Here's a program, TABLEARG, that incorporates just such a function. We use arguments to pass the character to be printed and the number of times to print it.

```
// tablearg.cpp
// demonstrates function arguments
#include <iostream.h>

void repchar(char, int);                    // function declaration

void main()
   {
   repchar('-', 43);                        // call to function
   cout << "Data type    Range" << endl;
   repchar('=', 23);                        // call to function
   cout << "char         -128 to 127" << endl
        << "int          -32,768 to 32,767" << endl
        << "double       -2,147,483,648 to 2,147,483,647" << endl;
   repchar('-', 43);                        // call to function
   }

// repchar()
// function definition
void repchar(char ch, int n)                // function declarator
   {
   for(int j=0; j<n; j++)                    // function body
      cout << ch;
   cout << endl;
   }
```

The new function is called `repchar()`. Its declaration looks like this:

```
void repchar(char, int);    // declaration specifies data types
```

The items in the parentheses are the data types of the arguments that will be sent to `repchar()`: `char` and `int`.

In the function call, specific values—constants in this case—are inserted in the appropriate place in the parentheses:

```
repchar('-', 43);    // function call specifies actual values
```

This statement instructs `repchar()` to print a line of 43 dashes. The values supplied in the call must be of the types specified in the declaration: the first argument, the '—' character, must be of type `char`; and the second argument, the number 43, must be of type `int`. The types in the declaration and the definition must also agree.

The next call to `repchar()`,

```
repchar('=', 23);
```

tells it to print a line of 23 equal signs. The third call again prints 43 dashes. Here's the output from TABLEARG:

```
------------------------------------------
Data type    Range
========================
char         -128 to 127
int          -32,768 to 32,767
double       -2,147,483,648 to 2,147,483,647
------------------------------------------
```

The calling program supplies arguments, such as '—' and 43, to the function. The variables used within the function to hold the argument values are called *parameters*; in `repchar()` they are `ch` and `n`. (We should note that many programmers use the terms *argument* and *parameter* interchangeably.) The declarator in the function definition specifies both the data types and the names of the parameters:

```
void repchar(char ch, int n)   // declarator specifies parameter
                               // names and data types
```

These parameter names, `ch` and `n`, are used in the function as if they were normal variables. Placing them in the declarator is equivalent to defining them with statements like

```
char ch;
int n;
```

When the function is called, its parameters are automatically initialized to the values passed by the calling program.

PASSING VARIABLES

In the TABLEARG example the arguments were constants: '—', 43, and so on. Let's look at an example where variables, instead of constants, are passed as arguments. This program, VARARG, incorporates the same `repchar()` function as did TABLEARG, but lets the user specify the character and the number of times it should be repeated.

```
// vararg.cpp
// demonstrates variable arguments
#include <iostream.h>

void repchar(char, int);                        // function declaration

void main()
    {
    char chin;
    int nin;

    cout << "Enter a character: ";
    cin >> chin;
    cout << "Enter number of times to repeat it: ";
    cin >> nin;
    repchar(chin, nin);
    }

// repchar()
// function definition
void repchar(char ch, int n)                    // function declarator
    {
    for(int j=0; j<n; j++)                      // function body
        cout << ch;
    cout << endl;
    }
```

Here's some sample interaction with VARARG:

```
Enter a character: +
Enter number of times to repeat it: 20
++++++++++++++++++++
```

Here `chin` and `nin` in `main()` are used as arguments to `repchar()`:

```
repchar(chin, nin);   // function call
```

The data types of variables used as arguments must match those specified in the function declaration and definition, just as they must for constants. That is, `chin` must be a `char`, and `nin` must be an `int`.

PASSING BY VALUE

In VARARG the particular values possessed by `chin` and `nin` when the function call is executed will be passed to the function. As it did when constants were passed to it, the function creates new variables to hold the values of these variable arguments. The function gives these new variables the names and data types of the parameters specified in the declarator: `ch` of type `char` and `n` of type `int`. It initializes these parameters to the values passed. They are then accessed like other variables by statements in the function body.

Passing arguments in this way, where the function creates copies of the arguments passed to it, is called *passing by value*. We'll explore another approach, passing by reference, later in this chapter. Figure 6-3 shows how new variables are created in the function when arguments are passed by value.

PASSING STRUCTURE VARIABLES

Entire structures can be passed as arguments to functions. The next example features a function that uses an argument of type **Distance**, the same structure type we saw in several programs in Chapter 5. Here's the listing for ENGLDISP:

```cpp
// engldisp.cpp
// demonstrates passing structure as argument
#include <iostream.h>

struct Distance                      // English distance
   {
   int feet;
   float inches;
   };

void engldisp( Distance );          // declaration

void main()
   {
   Distance d1, d2;                 // define two lengths

                                    // get length d1 from user
   cout << "\nEnter feet: ";  cin >> d1.feet;
   cout << "Enter inches: ";  cin >> d1.inches;

                                    // get length d2 from user
   cout << "\nEnter feet: ";  cin >> d2.feet;
   cout << "Enter inches: ";  cin >> d2.inches;

   cout << "\nd1 = ";
   engldisp(d1);                    // display length 1
   cout << "\nd2 = ";
   engldisp(d2);                    // display length 2
   }

// engldisp()
// display structure of type Distance in feet and inches
void engldisp( Distance dd )    // parameter dd of type Distance
   {
   cout << dd.feet << "\'-" << dd.inches << "\"";
   }
```

The **main()** part of this program accepts two distances in feet-and-inches format from the user, and places these values in two structures, **d1** and **d2**. It

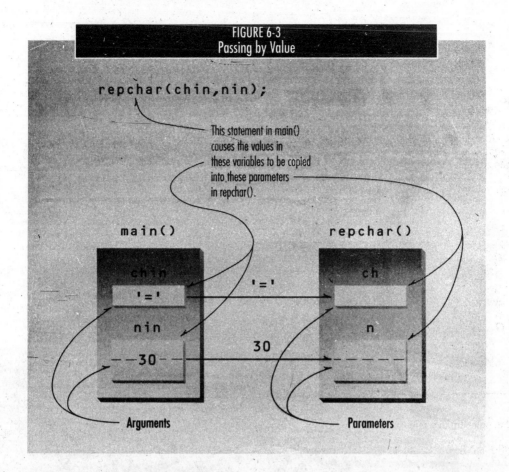

FIGURE 6-3
Passing by Value

then calls a function, `engldisp()`, that takes a `Distance` structure variable as an argument. The purpose of the function is to display the distance passed to it in the standard format, such as 10'–2.25". Here's some sample interaction with the program:

```
Enter feet: 6
Enter inches: 4

Enter feet: 5
Enter inches: 4.25

d1 = 6'-4"
d2 = 5'-4.25"
```

The function declaration and the function calls in `main()`, and the declarator in the function body, treat the structure variables just as they would any other variable used as an argument; this one just happens to be type `Distance`, rather than a basic type like `char` or `int`.

In `main()` there are two calls to the function `engldisp()`. The first passes the structure `d1`; the second passes `d2`. The function `engldisp()` uses a parameter that is a structure of type `Distance`, which it names `dd`. As with simple variables, this structure variable is automatically initialized to the value of the structure passed from `main()`. Statements in `engldisp()` can then access the members of `dd` in the usual way, with the expressions `dd.feet` and `dd.inches`. Figure 6-4 shows a structure being passed as an argument to a function.

As with simple variables, the structure parameter `dd` in `engldisp()` is not the same as the arguments passed to it (`d1` and `d2`). Thus `engldisp()` could (although it doesn't do so here) modify `dd` without affecting `d1` and `d2`. That is, if `engldisp()` contained statments like

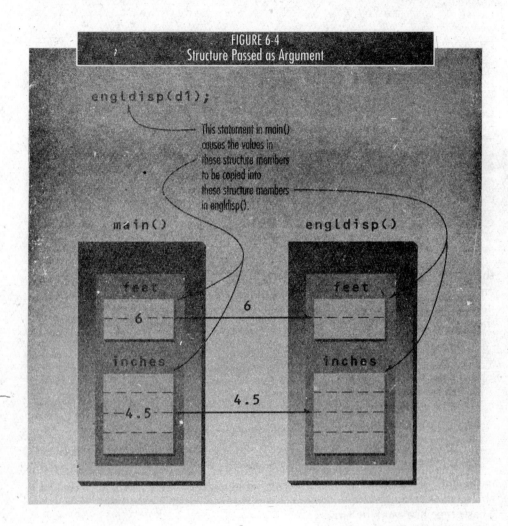

FIGURE 6-4
Structure Passed as Argument

```
    dd.feet = 2;
    dd.inches = 3.25;
```

this would have no effect on **d1** or **d2** in **main()**.

NAMES IN THE DECLARATION

Here's a way to increase the clarity of your function declarations. The idea is to insert meaningful names in the declaration, along with the data types. For example, suppose you were using a function that displayed a point on the screen. You could use a declaration with only data types:

```
void display_point(int, int);  // declaration
```

but a better approach is

```
void display_point(int horiz, int vert);  // declaration
```

These two declarations mean exactly the same thing to the compiler. However, the first approach, with **(int, int)**, doesn't contain any hint about which argument is for the vertical and which is for the horizontal coordinate. The advantage of the second approach is clarity for the programmer: Anyone seeing this declaration is more likely to use the correct arguments when calling the function.

Note that the names in the declaration have no effect on the names you use when calling the function. You are perfectly free to use any argument names you want:

```
display_point(x, y);  // function call
```

We'll use this name-plus-data-type approach when it seems to make the listing clearer.

RETURNING VALUES FROM FUNCTIONS

When a function completes its execution it can return a single value to the calling program. Usually this return value consists of an answer to the problem the function has solved. The next example demonstrates a function that returns a weight in kilograms, after being given a weight in pounds. Here's the listing for CONVERT:

```
// convert.cpp
// demonstrates return values, converts pounds to kg
#include <iostream.h>

float lbstokg(float);

void main()
    {
    float lbs, kgs;
```

```
    cout << "\nEnter your weight in pounds: ";
    cin >> lbs;
    kgs = lbstokg(lbs);
    cout << "Your weight in kilograms is " << kgs;
    }

// lbstokg()
// converts pounds to kilograms
float lbstokg(float pounds)
    {
    float kilograms =  0.453592 * pounds;
    return kilograms;
    }
```

Here's some sample interaction with this program:

```
Enter your weight in pounds: 182
Your weight in kilograms is 82.5537
```

When a function returns a value, the data type of this value must be specified. The function declaration does this by placing the data type, **float** in this case, before the function name in the declaration and the definition. Functions in earlier program examples returned no value, so the return type was **void**. In the CONVERT program the function **lbstokg()** (*pounds to kilograms*, where **lbs** means pounds) returns type **float**, so the declaration is

```
float lbstokg(float);
```

The first **float** specifies the return type. The **float** in parentheses specifies that an argument to be passed to **lbstokg()** is also of type **float**.

When a function returns a value, the call to the function

```
lbstokg(lbs)
```

is considered to be an expression that takes on the value returned by the function. We can treat this expression like any other variable; in this case we use it in an assignment statement:

```
kgs = lbstokg(lbs);
```

This causes the variable **kgs** to be assigned the value returned by **lbstokg()**.

THE return STATEMENT

The function **lbstokg()** is passed an argument representing a weight in pounds, which it stores in the parameter **pounds**. It calculates the corresponding weight in kilograms by multiplying this pounds value by a constant; the result is stored in the variable **kilograms**. The value of this variable is then returned to the calling program using a **return** statement:

```
    return kilograms;
```

Notice that both `main()` and `lbstokg()` have a place to store the kilogram variable: `kgs` in `main()`, and `kilograms` in `lbstokg()`. When the function returns, the value in kilograms is copied into `kgs`. The calling program does not access the `kilograms` variable in the function; only the value is returned. This process is shown in Figure 6-5.

While many arguments may be sent to a function, only one argument may be returned from it. This is a limitation when you need to return more information. However, there are other approaches to returning multiple variables from functions. One is to pass arguments by reference, which we'll look at later in this chapter.

You should always include a function's return type in the function declaration. If the function doesn't return anything, use the keyword `void` to indicate this fact. If you don't use a return type in the declaration, the compiler will assume that the function returns an `int` value. For example, the declaration

```
somefunc();    // declaration -- assumes return type is int
```

tells the compiler that `somefunc()` has a return type of `int`.

The reason for this is historical, based on usage in early versions of C. In practice you shouldn't take advantage of this default type. Always specify the return type explicitly, even if it's `int`. This keeps the listing consistent and readable.

FIGURE 6-5
Returning a Value

Eliminating Unnecessary Variables

The CONVERT program contains several variables that were used in the interest of clarity but are not really necessary. A variation of this program, CONVERT2, shows how expressions can often be used in place of variables:

```
// convert2.cpp
// eliminates unnecessary variables
#include <iostream.h>

float lbstokg(float);

void main()
    {
    float lbs;

    cout << "\nEnter your weight in pounds: ";
    cin >> lbs;
    cout << "Your weight in kilograms is " << lbstokg(lbs);
    }

// lbstokg()
// converts pounds to kilograms
float lbstokg(float pounds)
    {
    return 0.453592 * pounds;
    }
```

In `main()` the variable `kgs` from the CONVERT program has been eliminated. Instead the expression `lbstokg(lbs)` is inserted directly into the `cout` statement:

```
cout << "Your weight in kilograms is " << lbstokg(lbs);
```

Also in the `lbstokg()` function the variable `kilograms` is no longer with us. The expression `0.453592*pounds` is inserted directly into the `return` statement:

```
return 0.453592 * pounds;
```

The calculation is carried out, and the resulting value is returned to the calling program, just as the value of a variable would be.

For clarity, programmers often put parentheses around the expression used in a `return` statement:

```
return (0.453592 * pounds);
```

Even when not required by the compiler, extra parentheses in an expression don't do any harm, and they may help make the listing easier for us poor humans to read.

Experienced C++ (and C) programmers will probably prefer the concise form of CONVERT2 to the more verbose CONVERT. However, CONVERT2 is not so easy to understand, especially for the nonexpert. The brevity-versus-clarity issue is a question of style, depending on your personal preference, and on the expectations of others who will be reading your listing.

RETURNING STRUCTURE VARIABLES

We've seen that structures can be used as arguments to functions. You can also use them as return values. Here's a program, RETSTRC, that incorporates a function that adds variables of type structure **Distance** and returns a value of this same type.

```
// retstrc.cpp
// demonstrates returning a structure
#include <iostream.h>

struct Distance                         // English distance
    {
    int feet;
    float inches;
    };

Distance addengl(Distance, Distance);   // declarations
void engldisp(Distance);

void main()
    {
    Distance d1, d2, d3;                // define three lengths
                                        // get length d1 from user
    cout << "\nEnter feet: ";  cin >> d1.feet;
    cout << "Enter inches: ";  cin >> d1.inches;
                                        // get length d2 from user
    cout << "\nEnter feet: ";  cin >> d2.feet;
    cout << "Enter inches: ";  cin >> d2.inches;

    d3 = addengl(d1, d2);               // d3 is sum of d1 and d2

    engldisp(d1); cout << " + ";  // display all lengths
    engldisp(d2); cout << " = ";
    engldisp(d3); cout << "\n";
    }

// addengl()
// adds two structures of type Distance, returns sum
Distance addengl( Distance dd1, Distance dd2 )
    {
    Distance dd3;        // define a new structure for sum

    dd3.inches = dd1.inches + dd2.inches;  // add the inches
    dd3.feet = 0;                          // (for possible carry)
    if(dd3.inches >= 12.0)                 // if inches >= 12.0,
        {                                  // then decrease inches
        dd3.inches -= 12.0;                // by 12.0 and
        dd3.feet++;                        // increase feet
        }                                  // by 1
```

```
    dd3.feet += dd1.feet + dd2.feet;        // add the feet
    return dd3;                              // return structure
}

// engldisp()
// display structure of type Distance in feet and inches
void engldisp( Distance dd )
    {
    cout << dd.feet << "\'-" << dd.inches << "\"";
    }
```

The program asks the user for two lengths, in feet-and-inches format, adds them together by calling the function `addengl()`, and displays the results using the `engldisp()` function introduced in the ENGLDISP program. Here's some output from the program:

```
Enter feet: 4
Enter inches: 5.5

Enter feet: 5
Enter inches: 6.5

4'-5.5" + 5'-6.5" = 10'-0"
```

The `main()` part of the program adds the two lengths, each represented by a structure of type `Distance`, by calling the function `addEngl`:

```
d3 = addengl(d1, d2);
```

This function returns the sum of `d1` and `d2`, and the result is assigned to the structure `d3`.

Internally the `addengl()` function must create a new variable of type `Distance` to hold the results of its calculation. It can't simply return an expression, as in

```
return dd1+dd2;    // doesn't make sense
```

because the process of adding the two structures actually takes several steps: The inches are added separately from the feet. Instead the values of the individual members of `d3` are calculated, and then `d3` is returned to the calling program with the statement

```
return d3;
```

Besides showing how structures are used as return values, this program also shows two functions (three if you count `main()`) used in the same program. You can arrange the functions in any order. The only rule is that the function declarations must appear in the listing before any calls are made to the functions.

REFERENCE ARGUMENTS

A reference provides an alias—a different name—for a variable. By far the most important use for references is in passing arguments to functions.

We've seen examples of function arguments passed by value. When arguments are passed by value, the called function creates a new variable of the same type as the argument and copies the argument's value into it. As we noted, the function does not have access to the original variable in the calling program, only to the copy it created. Passing arguments by value is useful when the function does not need to modify the original variable in the calling program. In fact, it offers insurance that the function cannot harm the original variable.

Passing arguments by reference uses a different mechanism. Instead of a value being passed to the function, a reference to the original variable, in the calling program, is passed.

The primary advantage of passing by reference is that the function can access the actual variables in the calling program. Among other benefits this provides a mechanism for passing more than one value from the function back to the calling program.

PASSING SIMPLE DATA TYPES BY REFERENCE

The next example, REF, shows a simple variable passed by reference:

```
// ref.cpp
// demonstrates passing by reference
#include <iostream.h>

void main()
    {
    void intfrac(float, float&, float&);      // prototype
    float number, intpart, fracpart;          // float variables
    do
        {
        cout << "\nEnter a real number: ";    // number from user
        cin >> number;
        intfrac(number, intpart, fracpart);   // find int and frac
        cout << "Integer part is " << intpart // print them
            << ", fraction part is " << fracpart;
        } while( number != 0 );               // exit loop on 0
    }

// intfrac()
// finds integer and fractional parts of real number
void intfrac(float n, float& intp, float& fracp)
    {
    intp = float( long(n) );  // convert to int, back to float
    fracp = n - intp;         // subtract integer part
    }
```

The main() part of this program asks the user to enter a number of type float. The program will separate this number into an integer and a fractional part. That is, if the user's number is 12.456, the program should report that the integer part is 12.0 and the fractional part is 0.456. To find these values, main() calls the function intfrac(). Here's some sample interaction:

```
Enter a real number: 99.44
Integer part is 99, fractional part is 0.44
```

The `intfrac()` function finds the integer part by converting the number (which was passed to the parameter n) into a variable of type `long int` with a cast, using the expression

```
long(n)
```

This effectively chops off the fractional part of the number, since integers (of course) store only the integer part. The result is then converted back to type `float` with another cast:

```
float( long(n) )
```

The fractional part is simply the original number less the integer part. (We should note that a library function, `fmod()`, performs a similar operation on type `double`.)

The `intfrac()` function can find the integer and fractional parts, but how does it pass them back to `main()`? It could use a `return` statement to return one value but not both. The problem is solved using reference arguments. Here's the declarator for the function:

```
void intfrac(float n, float& intp, float& fracp)
```

Reference arguments are indicated by the ampersand (`&`) following the data type of the argument:

```
float& intp
```

The `&` indicates that `intp` is an alias—another name—for whatever variable is passed as an argument. In other words, when you use the name `intp` in the `intfrac()` function, you are really referring to `intpart` in `main()`. The `&` can be taken to mean *reference to*, so

```
float& intp
```

means `intp` is *a reference to the* `float` *variable passed to it*. Similarly, `fracp` is an alias for—or a reference to—`fracpart`.

The function declaration echoes the usage of the ampersand in the definition:

```
void intfrac(float, float&, float&);    // ampersands
```

As in the definition, the ampersand follows those arguments that are passed by reference.

The ampersand is *not* used in the function call:

```
intfrac(number, intpart, fracpart);     // no ampersands
```

From the function call alone there's no way to tell whether an argument will be passed by reference or by value.

While `intpart` and `fracpart` are passed by reference, the variable `number` is passed by value. `intp` and `intpart` are different names for the same place in memory, as are `fracp` and `fracpart`. On the other hand, since it is passed by value, the parameter n in intfrac() is a separate variable into which the value of **number** is copied. It can be passed by value because the intfrac() function doesn't need to modify **number**. Figure 6-6 shows how reference arguments work.

(C programmers should not confuse the ampersand that is used to mean *reference to* with the same symbol used to mean *address of*. These are different usages. We'll discuss the *address of* meaning of **&** when we talk about pointers in Chapter 12.)

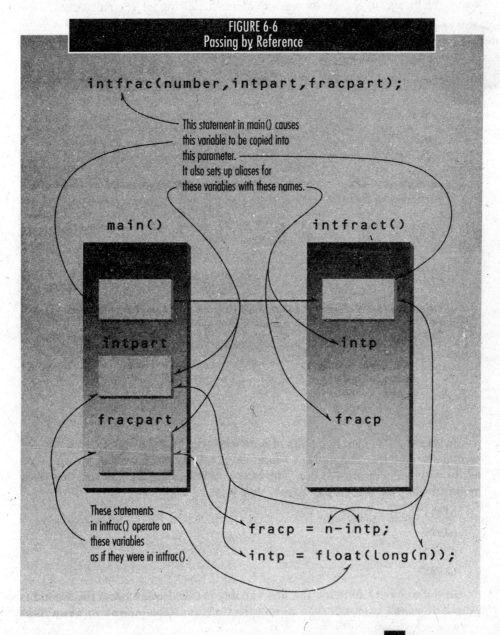

FIGURE 6-6
Passing by Reference

intfrac(number,intpart,fracpart);

This statement in main() causes this variable to be copied into this parameter.
It also sets up aliases for these variables with these names.

main()

intfract()

intpart

intp

fracpart

fracp

These statements in intfrac() operate on these variables as if they were in intfrac().

fracp = n-intp;

intp = float(long(n));

A MORE COMPLEX PASS BY REFERENCE

Here's a somewhat more complex example of passing simple arguments by reference. Suppose you have pairs of numbers in your program, and you want to be sure that the smaller one always precedes the larger one. To do this you call a function, order(), which checks two numbers passed to it by reference and swaps the originals if the first is larger than the second. Here's the listing for REFORDER.CPP:

```cpp
// reorder.cpp
// orders two arguments passed by reference
#include <iostream.h>

void main()
    {
    void order(int&, int&);           // prototype

    int n1=99, n2=11;                 // this pair not ordered
    int n3=22, n4=88;                 // this pair ordered

    order(n1, n2);                    // order each pair of numbers
    order(n3, n4);

    cout << endl << "n1=" << n1;      // print out all numbers
    cout << endl << "n2=" << n2;
    cout << endl << "n3=" << n3;
    cout << endl << "n4=" << n4;
    }

void order(int& numb1, int& numb2)    // orders two numbers
    {
    if(numb1 > numb2)                 // if 1st larger than 2nd,
        {
        int temp = numb1;             // swap them
        numb1 = numb2;
        numb2 = temp;
        }
    }
```

In main() there are two pairs of numbers—the first pair not ordered and the second pair ordered. The order() function is called once for each pair, and then all the numbers are printed out. The output reveals that the first pair has been swapped while the second pair hasn't. Here it is:

```
n1=11

n2=99

n3=22

n4=88
```

In the order() function the first variable is called numb1 and the second is numb2. If numb1 is greater than numb2 the function stores numb1 in temp, puts numb2 in numb1, and finally puts temp back in numb2. Remember that numb1 and numb2 are simply different names for whatever arguments were passed: in this case n1 and n2 on the first call to the function, and n2 and n3 on the second call. The effect is to check the ordering of the original arguments in the calling program and swap them if necessary.

Using reference arguments in this way is a sort of remote-control operation. The calling program tells the function what variables in the calling program to operate on, and the function modifies these variables without ever knowing their real names. It's as if you called the housepainters and then sat back and watched as your dining room walls mysteriously changed color.

PASSING STRUCTURES BY REFERENCE

You can pass structures by reference just as you can simple data types. Here's a program, REFERST, that performs scale conversions on values of type Distance. A scale conversion involves multiplying a group of distances by a factor. If a distance is 6'–8", and a scale factor is 0.5, the new distance is 3'–4". Such a conversion might be applied to all the dimensions of a building to make the building shrink but remain in proportion.

```
// referst.cpp
// demonstrates passing structure by reference
#include <iostream.h>

struct Distance                        // English distance
    {
    int feet;
    float inches;
    };

void scale( Distance&, float );        // function
void engldisp( Distance );             // declarations

void main()
    {
    Distance d1 = { 12, 6.5 };         // initialize d1 and d2
    Distance d2 = { 10, 5.5 };

    cout << "\nd1 = "; engldisp(d1);    // display old d1 and d2
    cout << "\nd2 = "; engldisp(d2);

    scale(d1, 0.5);                     // scale d1 and d2
    scale(d2, 0.25);

    cout << "\nd1 = "; engldisp(d1);    // display new d1 and d2
    cout << "\nd2 = "; engldisp(d2);
    }
```

```
// scale()
// scales value of type Distance by factor
void scale( Distance& dd, float factor)
   {
   float inches = (dd.feet*12 + dd.inches) * factor;
   dd.feet = inches / 12;
   dd.inches = inches - dd.feet * 12;
   }


// engldisp()
// display structure of type Distance in feet and inches
void engldisp( Distance dd )   // parameter dd of type Distance
   {
   cout << dd.feet << "\'-" << dd.inches << "\"";
   }
```

REFERST intializes two **Distance** variables—**d1** and **d2**—to specific values, and displays them. Then it calls the **scale()** function to multipy **d1** by 0.5 and **d2** by 0.25. Finally it displays the resulting values of the distances. Here's the program's output:

```
d1 = 12'-6.5"
d2 = 10'-5.5"
d1 = 6'-3.25"
d2 = 2'-7.375"
```

Here are the two calls to the function **scale()**:

```
scale(d1, 0.5);
scale(d2, 0.25);
```

The first call causes **d1** to be multiplied by 0.5, the second causes **d2** to be multiplied by 0.25. Notice that these changes take place directly to **d1** and **d2**. The function doesn't return anything; the operation is performed directly on the **Distance** argument, which is passed by reference to **scale**. (Since only one value is changed in the calling program, you could rewrite the function to pass the argument by value and return the scaled value. Calling the function would look like this:

```
d1 = scale(d1, 0.5);
```

However, this is inelegant and unnecessarily verbose.)

NOTES ON PASSING BY REFERENCE

Passing arguments by reference is also possible in Pascal and BASIC. References don't exist in C, where pointers serve a somewhat similar purpose, although often less conveniently. Reference arguments were introduced into C++ to provide flexibility in a variety of situations involving objects as well as simple variables.

The third way to pass arguments to functions, besides by value and by reference, is to use pointers. We'll explore this when we discuss pointers in Chapter 12.

OVERLOADED FUNCTIONS

An overloaded function appears to perform different activities depending on the kind of data sent to it. Overloading is like the joke about the famous scientist who insisted that the thermos bottle was the greatest invention of all time. Why? "It's a miracle device," he said. "It keeps hot things hot, but cold things it keeps cold. How does it know?"

It may seem equally mysterious how an overloaded function knows what to do. It performs one operation on one kind of data but another operation on a different kind. Let's clarify matters with some examples.

DIFFERENT NUMBERS OF ARGUMENTS

Recall the `starline()` function in the TABLE example, and the `repchar()` function from the TABLEARG example, both shown earlier in this chapter. The `starline()` function printed a line using 45 asterisks, while `repchar()` used a character and a line length that were both specified when the function was called. We might imagine a third function, `charline()`, that always prints 45 characters but that allows the calling program to specify the character to be printed. These three functions—`starline()`, `repchar()`, and `charline()`—perform similar activities but have different names. For programmers using these functions, that means three names to remember and three places to look them up if they are listed alphabetically in an application's *Library Reference* documentation.

It would be far more convenient to use the same name for all three functions, even though they each have different arguments. Here's a program, OVERLOAD, that makes this possible:

```
// overload.cpp
// demonstrates function overloading
#include <iostream.h>

void repchar();
void repchar(char);
void repchar(char, int);

void main()
    {
    repchar();
    repchar('=');
    repchar('+', 30);
    }

// repchar()
// displays 45 asterisks
```

```
void repchar()
   {
   for(int j=0; j<45; j++)    // always loops 45 times
      cout << '*';            // always prints asterisk
   cout << endl;
   }

// repchar()
// displays 45 copies of specified character
void repchar(char ch)
   {
   for(int j=0; j<45; j++)    // always loops 45 times
      cout << ch;            // prints specified character
   cout << endl;
   }

// repchar()
// displays specified number of copies of specified character
void repchar(char ch, int n)
   {
   for(int j=0; j<n; j++)     // loops n times
      cout << ch;            // prints specified character
   cout << endl;
   }
```

This program prints out three lines of characters. Here's the output:

```
*********************************************
=============================================
+++++++++++++++++++++++++++++++
```

The first two lines are 45 characters long, and the third is 30.

The program contains three functions with the same name. There are three declarations, three function calls, and three function definitions. What keeps the compiler from becoming hopelessly confused? It uses the number of arguments, and their data types, to distinguish one function from another. In other words, the declaration

```
void repchar();
```

which takes no arguments, describes an entirely different function than does the declaration

```
void repchar(char);
```

which takes one argument of type `char`, or the declaration

```
void repchar(char, int);
```

which takes one argument of type `char` and another of type `int`.

The compiler, seeing several functions with the same name but different numbers of arguments, could decide the programmer had made a mistake (which is what it would do in C). Instead, it very tolerantly sets up a separate function for every such

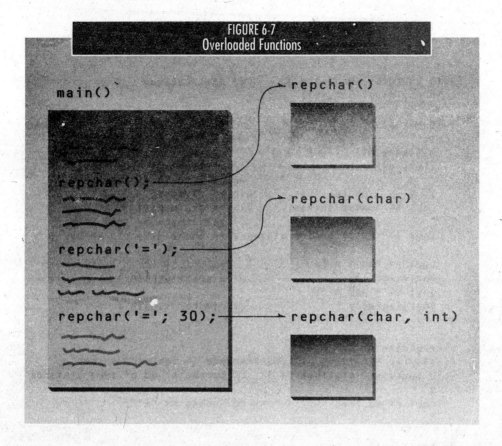

FIGURE 6-7
Overloaded Functions

definition. Which one of these functions will be called depends on the number of arguments supplied in the call. Figure 6-7 shows this process.

DIFFERENT KINDS OF ARGUMENTS

In the OVERLOAD example, we created several functions with the same name but different numbers of arguments. The compiler can also distinguish between overloaded functions with the same number of arguments, provided their type is different. Here's a program, OVERENGL, that uses an overloaded function to display a quantity in feet-and-inches format. The single argument to the function can be either a structure of type `Distance` (as used in the ENGLDISP example) or a simple variable of type `float`. Different functions are used depending on the type of argument.

```
// overengl.cpp
// demonstrates overloaded functions
#include <iostream.h>

struct Distance                      // English distance
   {
```

```
      int feet;
      float inches;
      };

void engldisp( Distance );        // declarations
void engldisp( float );

void main()
    {
    Distance d1;                  // distance of type Distance
    float d2;                     // distance of type float
                                  // get length d1 from user
    cout << "\nEnter feet: ";  cin >> d1.feet;
    cout << "Enter inches: ";  cin >> d1.inches;
                                  // get length d2 from user
    cout << "Enter entire distance in inches: "; cin >> d2;

    cout << "\nd1 = ";
    engldisp(d1);                 // display length 1
    cout << "\nd2 = ";
    engldisp(d2);                 // display length 2
}

// engldisp()
// display structure of type Distance in feet and inches
void engldisp( Distance dd )   // parameter dd of type Distance
    {
    cout << dd.feet << "\'-" << dd.inches << "\"";
    }

// engldisp()
// display variable of type float in feet and inches
void engldisp( float dd )        // parameter dd of type float
    {
    int feet = dd / 12;
    float inches = dd - feet*12;
    cout << feet << "\'-" << inches << "\"";
    }
```

The user is invited to enter two distances, the first with separate feet and inches inputs, the second with a single large number for inches (109.5 inches, for example, instead of 9'-1.5"). The program calls the overloaded function engldisp() to display a value of type Distance for the first distance and of type float for the second. Here's a sample interaction with the program:

```
Enter feet: 5
Enter inches: 10.5
Enter entire distance in inches: 76.5
d1 = 5'-10.5"
d2 = 6'-4.5"
```

Notice that, while the different versions of `engldisp()` do similar things, the code is quite different. The version that accepts the all-inches input has to convert to feet and inches before displaying the result.

Overloaded functions can simplify the programmer's life by reducing the number of function names to be remembered. As an example of the complexity that arises when overloading is not used, consider the Mirosoft C/C++ library routines for finding the absolute value of a number. Because these routines must work with C (which does not allow overloading) as well as with C++, there must be separate versions of the absolute value routine for each data type. There are four of them: `abs()` for type `int`, `cabs()` for complex numbers, `fabs()` for type double, and `labs()` for type `long int`. In C++ a single name, `abs()`, would suffice for all these data types.

As we'll see later, overloaded functions are also useful for handling different types of objects.

INLINE FUNCTIONS

We mentioned that functions save memory space because all the calls to the function cause the same code to be executed; the function body need not be duplicated in memory. When the compiler sees a function call, it normally generates a jump to the function. At the end of the function it jumps back to the instruction following the call, as we showed in Figure 6-1.

While this sequence of events may save memory space, it takes some extra time. There must be an instruction for the jump to the function (actually the assembly-language instruction CALL), instructions for saving registers, instructions for pushing arguments onto the stack in the calling program and removing them from the stack in the function (if there are arguments), instructions for restoring registers, and an instruction to return to the calling program. The return value (if any) must also be dealt with. All these instructions slow down the program.

To save execution time in short functions, you may elect to put the code in the function body directly in line with the code in the calling program. That is, each time there's a function call in the source file, the actual code from the function is inserted, instead of a jump to the function. The difference between a function and inline code is shown in Figure 6-8.

Long sections of repeated code are generally better off as normal functions: The saving in memory space is worth the comparatively small sacrifice in execution speed. But making a short section of code into a function may result in little saving in memory space, while imposing just as much time penalty as a larger function. In fact, if a function is very short, the instructions necessary to call it may even take up as much space as the instructions within the function body, so that there is not only a time penalty but a space penalty as well.

In such cases you could simply repeat the necessary code in your program, inserting the same group of statements wherever it was needed. The trouble with

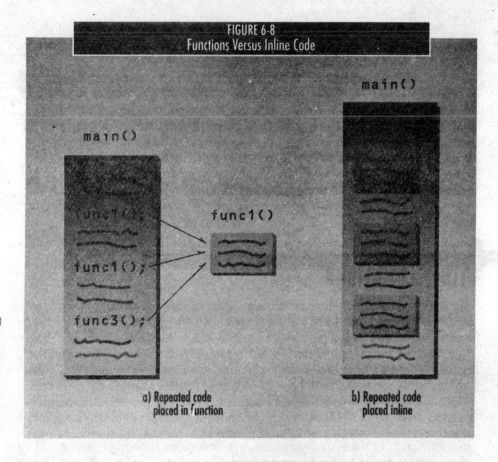

FIGURE 6-8
Functions Versus Inline Code

main()

func1();

func1();

func3();

func1()

main()

a) Repeated code
placed in function

b) Repeated code
placed inline

repeatedly inserting the same code is that you lose the benefits of program organization and clarity that come with using functions. The program may run faster and take less space, but the listing is longer and more complex.

The solution to this quandary is the *inline function*. This kind of function is written like a normal function in the source file but compiles into inline code instead of into a function. The source file remains well organized and easy to read, since the function is shown as a separate entity. However, when the program is compiled, the function body is actually inserted into the program wherever a function call occurs.

Functions that are very short, say one or two statements, are candidates to be inlined. Here's INLINE, a variation on the CONVERT2 program. It inlines the lbstokg() function.

```
// inline.cpp
// demonstrates inline functions
#include <iostream.h>

// lbstokg()                          // definition of
// converts pounds to kilograms      // inline function
```

```
inline float lbstokg(float pounds)    // (must precede calls
   {                                   // to it)
   return 0.453592 * pounds;
   }

void main()                           // main() must follow any
   {                                   // inline definitions
   float lbs;

   cout << "\nEnter your weight in pounds: ";
   cin >> lbs;
   cout << "Your weight in kilograms is " << lbstokg(lbs);
   }
```

It's easy to make a function inline: All you need is the keyword `inline` in the function definition:

```
inline float lgstokg(float pounds)
```

However, there are some subtleties to using inline functions. The compiler must have seen the function definition (not just the declaration) before it gets to the first function call. This is because it must insert the actual code into the program, not just instructions to call the function. In INLINE we must place the definition of `lbstokg()` before `main()`. When you do this the function declaration is unnecessary and can be eliminated.

You should be aware that the `inline` keyword is actually just a *request* to the compiler. Sometimes the compiler will ignore the request and compile the function as a normal function. It might decide the function is too long to be inline, for instance.

(C programmers should note that inline functions largely take the place of `#define` macros in C. They serve the same purpose but provide better type checking and do not need special care with parentheses as macros do.)

DEFAULT ARGUMENTS

Surprisingly, a function can be called without specifying all its arguments. This won't work on just any function: The function declaration must provide default values for those arguments that are not specified.

Here's an example, a variation on the OVERLOAD program, that demonstrates this effect. In OVERLOAD we used three different functions with the same name to handle different numbers of arguments. The present example, MISSARG, achieves the same effect in a different way.

```
// missarg.cpp
// demonstrates missing and default arguments
#include <iostream.h>

   repchar(char='*', int=45);    // prototype with
                                 // default arguments
```

```
void main()
  {
  repchar();          // prints 45 asterisks
  repchar('=');       // prints 45 equal signs
  repchar('+', 30);   // prints 30 plus signs
  }

// repchar()
// displays line of characters
void repchar(char ch, int n)   // defaults supplied if necessary
  {
  for(int j=0; j<n; j++)   // loops n times
     cout << ch;           // prints ch
  cout << endl;
  }
```

In this program the function repchar() takes two arguments. It's called three times from main(). The first time it's called with no arguments, the second time with one, and the third time with two. Why do the first two calls work? Because the called function provides *default arguments*, which will be used if the calling program doesn't supply them. The default arguments are specified in the prototype to repchar():

```
void repchar(char='*', int=45);  // prototype (declaration)
```

The default argument follows an equals sign, which is placed directly after the type name. You can also use variable names, as in

```
void repchar(char reptChar='*', int numberReps=45);
```

If one argument is missing when the function is called, it is assumed to be the last argument. The repchar() function assigns the value of the single argument to the ch parameter and uses the default value 45 for the n parameter.

If both arguments are missing, the function assigns the default value '*' to ch and the default value 45 to n. Thus the three calls to the function all work, even though each has a different number of arguments.

Remember that missing arguments must be the trailing arguments—those at the end of the argument list. You can leave out the last three arguments, but you can't leave out the next-to-last and then put in the last. This is reasonable; how would the compiler know which arguments you meant, if you left out some in the middle? (Missing arguments could have been indicated with commas, but commas are notoriously subject to misprints, so the designers of C++ ignored this possibility.) Not surprisingly, the compiler will flag an error if you leave out arguments for which the function you're calling does not provide default values.

Default arguments are useful if you just don't want to go to the trouble of writing arguments that, for example, almost always have the same value. They are also useful in cases where, after a program is written, the programmer decides to increase the capability of a function by adding another argument. Using default arguments means that the existing function calls can continue to use the old number of arguments, while new function calls can use more.

VARIABLES AND STORAGE CLASSES

Now that we know about functions, we can explore a feature of C++ that's related to the interaction of variables and functions: the `storage class`. The storage class of a variable determines which parts of the program can access it and how long it stays in existence. We'll look at variables with three storage classes—automatic, external, and static.

AUTOMATIC VARIABLES

So far all the variables we've used in example programs have been defined inside the function in which they are used. That is, the definition occurs inside the braces that delimit the function body:

```
void somefunc()
   {
   int somevar;          // variables defined within
   float othervar;       // the function body
   // other statements
   }
```

Variables may be defined inside `main()` or inside other functions; the effect is the same, since `main()` is a function. Variables defined within a function body are called *automatic variables*. Actually, a keyword, `auto`, can be used to specify an automatic variable. You would say

```
void somefunc()
   {
   auto int somevar;          // same as int somevar
   auto float othervar;       // same as float othervar
   // other statements
   }
```

However, since this is the default, there is seldom any need to use the `auto` keyword. Variables defined within a function are automatic automatically.

Let's look at the two important characteristics of automatic variables—lifetime and visibility.

Lifetime

An automatic variable is not created until the function in which it is defined is called. (More accurately, we can say that variables defined within any block of code are not created until the block is executed.) In the program fragment just given, the variables somevar and othervar don't exist until the somefunc() function is called. That is, there is no place in memory where their values are stored; they are undefined. When control is transferred to somefunc(), the variables are created and memory space is set aside for them. Later, when somefunc() exits and control is returned to the calling program, the variables are destroyed and their values are lost. The name *automatic* is used because the variables are automatically created when a function is called and automatically destroyed when it returns.

The time period between the creation and destruction of a variable is called its *lifetime* (or sometimes its *duration*). The lifetime of an automatic variable coincides with the time when the function in which it is defined is executing.

The idea behind limiting the lifetime of variables is to save memory space. If a function is not executing, the variables it uses during execution are presumably not needed. Removing them frees up memory that can then be used by other functions.

Visibility

A variable's *visibility* describes where within a program it can be accessed. It can be referred to in statements in some parts of the program; in others, attempts to access it lead to an *unknown variable* error message. The word *scope* is also used to describe visibility. The scope of a variable is that part of the program where the variable is visible.

Automatic variables are only visible, meaning they can only be accessed, within the function in which they are defined. Suppose you have two functions in a program:

```
void somefunc()
   {
   int somevar;      // automatic variables
   float othervar;

   somevar = 10;     // ok
   othervar = 11;    // ok
   nextvar = 12;     // illegal: not visible in somefunc()
   }

void otherfunc()
   {
   int nextvar;      // automatic variable

   somevar = 20;     // illegal: not visible in otherfunc()
   othervar = 21;    // illegal: not visible in otherfunc()
   nextvar = 22;     // ok
   }
```

The variable nextvar is invisible in function somefunc(), and the variables somevar and othervar are invisible in otherfunc().

Limiting the visibility of variables helps to organize and modularize the program. You can be confident that the variables in one function are safe from accidental alteration by other functions, because the other functions can't see them. This is an important part of structured programming, the methodology for organizing old-fashioned procedural programs. Limiting visibility is also an important part of object-oriented programming.

In the case of automatic variables, lifetime and visibility coincide: These variables exist only while the function in which they are defined is executing, and are only visible within this function. For some storage classes, however, lifetime and visibility are not the same.

Initialization

When an automatic variable is created, the compiler does not try to initialize it. Thus it will start off with an arbitrary value, which may be 0 but probably will be something else. If you want it initialized, you must do it explicitly, as in

```
int n = 33;
```

then it will start off with this value.

Automatic variables are sometimes called *local* variables, since they are visible only locally, in the function where they are defined.

EXTERNAL VARIABLES

The next major storage class is *external*. While automatic variables are defined within functions, external variables are defined outside of any function. External variables are also called *global* variables, since they are known by all the functions in a program.

Here's a program, EXTERN, in which three functions all access an external variable.

```cpp
// extern.cpp
// demonstrates external variables
#include <iostream.h>

   exint = 99;                // external variable

void getanint();             // function declarations
void putanint();

void main()
   {
   while( exint != 0 )        // main() accesses exint
      {                       // (enter 0 to terminate program)
      getanint();
      putanint();
      }
   }

void getanint()              // getanint() accesses exint
   {
```

```
    cin >> exint;
    }

void putanint()             // putanint() accesses exint
    {
    cout << exint << endl;
    }
```

One function in EXTERN, `getanint()`, reads numbers from the keyboard. A second function, `putanint()`, echoes the numbers to the screen. The effect is that each number is displayed twice:

```
123
123
```

The significant thing about this program is that the variable `exint` is not defined in any of the functions. Instead it is defined at the beginning of the file, before the first function. It is an external variable. Any function that follows the definition of `exint` in the listing can access it—in this case all the functions in EXTERN: `main()`, `getanint()`, and `putanint()`. Thus the visibility of `exint` is the entire source file.

Role of External Variables

The external storage class is used when a variable must be accessible to more than one function in a program. In procedural programs external variables are often the most important variables in the program. However, as we noted in Chapter 1, external variables create organizational problems for the very reason that they can be accessed by any function. The wrong functions may access them, or functions may access them incorrectly. In an object-oriented program there is less necessity for external variables.

Initialization

If an external variable is initialized by the program, as in

```
int exvar = 199;
```

this initialization takes place when the file is first loaded but not thereafter. If an external variable is not initialized explicitly by the program—for example, if it is defined as

```
int exvar;
```

—then it is initialized automatically to 0 when it is created. (This is unlike automatic variables, which are not initialized and probably contain random or "garbage" values when they are created.)

Lifetime and Visibility

External variables exist for the life of the program. That is, memory space is set aside for them when the program begins, and continues in existence until the program ends.

External variables are visible in the file in which they are defined, starting at the point where they are defined. If `ch` were defined following `main()` but before `getachar()`, it would be visible in `getachar()` and `putachar()`, but not in `main()`.

STATIC VARIABLES

We'll touch on another storage class: *static*. Here we'll be concerned with static automatic variables. There are static external variables, but they are meaningful only in multifile programs, which we don't examine until Chapter 15.

A static automatic variable has the visibility of a local variable but the lifetime of an external variable. Thus it is visible only inside the function in which it is defined, but it remains in existence for the life of the program.

Static automatic variables are used when it's necessary for a function to remember a value when it is not being executed; that is, between calls to the function. In the next example, a function, `getavg()`, calculates a running average. It remembers the total of the numbers it has averaged before, and how many there were. Each time it receives a new number, sent as an argument from the calling program, it adds this number to the total, adds 1 to a count, and returns the new average by dividing the total by the count. Here's the listing for STATIC:

```
// static.cpp
// demonstrates static variables
#include <iostream.h>

float getavg(float);                  // prototype

void main()
    {
    float data=1, avg;

    while( data != 0 )
        {
        cout << "Enter a number: ";
        cin >> data;
        avg = getavg(data);
        cout << "New average is " << avg << endl;
        }
    }

// getavg()
// finds average of old plus new data
float getavg(float newdata)
    {
```

```
static float total = 0;   // static variables are initialized
static int count = 0;     // only once per program

count++;                  // increment count
total += newdata;         // add new data to total
return total / count;     // return the new average
}
```

Here's some sample interaction:

```
Enter a number: 10
New average is 10          ←————————total is 10, count is 1
Enter a number: 20
New average is 15          ←————————total is 30, count is 2
Enter a number: 30
New average is 20          ←————————total is 60, count is 3
```

The static variables `total` and `count` in `getavg()` retain their values after `getavg()` returns, so they're available the next time it's called.

Initialization

When static variables are initialized, as `total` and `count` are in `getavg()`, the initialization takes place only once—at the beginning of the program. They are not reinitialized each time the function is called, as ordinary automatic variables can be.

STORAGE

If you're familiar with the architecture of MS-DOS computers, you might be interested to know that automatic variables are stored in the stack segment, while external and static variables are stored in the data segment.

Table 6-2 summarizes the lifetime, visibility, and some other aspects of automatic, external, and automatic static variables:

		TABLE 6-2 Storage Types	
Storage type	automatic	static auto	external
Visibility	function	function	file
Lifetime	function	program	program
Initialized value	not initialized	0	0
Storage	stack segment	data segment	data segment
Purpose	variables used by a single function	same as auto, but must retain value when function terminates	variables used by several functions

RETURNING BY REFERENCE

Now that we know about external variables, we can examine a rather odd-looking C++ feature. It turns out that, besides passing values by reference, you can also return a value by reference. Why you would want to do this may seem obscure. The primary reason is to allow you to use a function call *on the left side of the equal sign*. This is a somewhat bizarre concept, so let's look at an example. The RETREF program shows the mechanism:

```
// retref.cpp
// returning reference values
#include <iostream.h>

int x;                      // global variable
int& setx();                // function declarations

void main()
    {                       // set x to a value, using
    setx() = 92;            // function call on left side
    cout << "\nx=" << x;    // display new value in x
    }

int& setx()
    {
    return x;               // returns the value to be modified
    }
```

In this program the function `setx()` is declared with a reference type, `int&`, as the return type:

```
int& setx();
```

This function contains the statement

```
return x;
```

where `x` has been defined as an external variable. Now—and this is what looks so strange—you can put a call to this function on the left side of the equals sign:

```
setx() = 92;
```

The result is that the variable returned by the function is assigned the value on the right side of the equals sign. That is, `x` is given the value 92. The output from the program,

```
x=92
```

verifies that this assignment has taken place.

Returning by reference may seem a baffling concept. Remember that (as we discussed earlier) passing a function argument by reference means that we are setting up an equivalence between the *variable* passed as an argument by the calling program, and the variable used as a parameter in the function. That is, we are specifying that these two variables refer to the same thing; one is an alias for the other.

Also, remember that when we return a value from a function using the normal approach, as in expressions like

```
var = func();
```

we are treating the expression `func()` as a value. In this statement `func()` is equivalent to—we could say an alias for—whatever value, such as 33, it returns. This value will be assigned to `var`. Such usage doesn't surprise us, it seems natural to treat a function call such as `func()` as a value.

Now, when we return by reference, we are establishing the same sort of equivalence, but this time between the function call (`setx()` in the RETREF example) and the *variable* being returned (`x` in RETREF), not its value. Since the function call is equivalent to a variable, and not a value, we can use it on the left side of the equal sign: We can assign it a value. The function `setx()` returns `x`, so setting `setx()` equal to 92 is the same as setting `x` equal to **92**.

Of course, the question remains why such an activity is necessary. In procedural programming there probably isn't too much use for returning by reference. As in the present example, there are easier ways to achieve the same result. However, when we cover overloaded operators in Chapter 9, we'll find that returning by reference is an indispensable technique. Until then, keep it in the back of your mind.

SUMMARY

Functions provide a way to help organize programs, and to reduce program size, by giving a block of code a name and allowing it to be executed from other parts of the program. Function declarations specify what the function looks like, function calls transfer control to the function, and function definitions contain the statements that make up the function. The function declarator is the first line of the definition.

Arguments can be sent to functions either by value, where the function works with a copy of the argument; or by reference, where the function works with the original argument in the calling program.

Functions can return only one value. Functions can return a reference, which allows the function call to be used on the left side of an assignment statement. Arguments and return values can be either simple data types or structures.

An overloaded function is actually a group of functions with the same name. Which of them is executed when the function is called depends on the type and number of arguments supplied in the call.

An inline function looks like a normal function in the source file but inserts the function's code directly into the calling program. Inline functions execute faster but may require more memory than normal functions unless they are very small.

If a function uses default arguments, calls to it need not include all the arguments shown in the declaration. Default values supplied by the function are used for the missing arguments.

Variables possess a characteristic called the storage class. The most common storage class is automatic. Variables of this class exist only while the function in which they are defined is executing, and are visible only within that function. External variables exist for the life of a program and can be visible throughout an entire file. Static automatic variables exist for the life of a program but are visible only in their own function.

In the last chapter we examined one of the two major parts of objects: structures, which are collections of data. In this chapter we explored the second part: functions. Now we're ready to put these two components together to create objects, the subject of the next chapter.

QUESTIONS

1. A function's single most important role is to
   a. give a name to a block of code
   b. reduce program size
   c. accept arguments and provide a return value
   d. help organize a program into conceptual units

2. A function itself is called the function d_____.

3. Write a function called **foo()** that displays the word *foo*.

4. A one-statement description of a function is referred to as a function d_____ or a p_____.

5. The statements that carry out the work of the function constitute the function _____.

6. A program statement that invokes a function is a function _____.

7. The first line of a function definition is referred to as the _____.

8. A function argument is
   a. a variable in the function that receives a value from the calling program.
   b. a way that functions resist accepting the calling program's values
   c. a value sent to the function by the calling program
   d. a value returned by the function to the calling program

9. True or false: When arguments are passed by value, the function works with the original arguments in the calling program.

10. What is the purpose of using argument names in a function declaration?

11. Which of the following can legitimately be passed to a function:
    a. a constant
    b. a variable
    c. a structure
    d. a header file

12. What is the significance of empty parentheses in a function declaration?

13. How many values can be returned from a function?

14. True or false: When a function returns a value, the entire function call can appear on the right side of the equals sign and be assigned to another variable.

15. Where is a function's return type specified?

16. A function that doesn't return anything has return type _____.

17. Here's a function:

```
int times2(int a)
    {
    return (a*2);
    }
```

Write a `main()` program that includes everything necessary to call this function.

18. When an argument is passed by reference,
    a. a variable is created in the function to hold the argument's value
    b. the function cannot access the argument's value
    c. a temporary variable is created in the calling program to hold the argument's value
    d. the function accesses the argument's original value in the calling program

19. What is the principle reason for passing arguments by reference?

20. Overloaded functions
    a. are a group of functions with the same name
    b. all have the same number and types of arguments
    c. make life simpler for programmers
    d. may fail unexpectedly due to stress

21. Write declarations for two overloaded functions named `bar()`. They both return type `int`. The first takes one argument of type `char`, and the second takes two arguments of type `char`. If this is impossible, say why.

22. In general, an inline function executes _____ than a normal function, but requires _____ memory.

23. Write the declarator for an inline function named `foobar()` that takes one argument of type `float` and returns type `float`.

24. A default argument has a value that
    a. may be supplied by the calling program
    b. may be supplied by the function
    c. must have a constant value
    d. must have a variable value

25. Write a declaration for a function called `blyth()` that takes two arguments and returns type `char`. The first argument is type `int`, and the second is type `float` with a default value of 3.14159.

26. Storage class is concerned with the _____ and _____ of a variable.

27. What functions can access an external variable that appears in the same file with them?

28. What functions can access an automatic variable?

29. A static automatic variable is used to
    a. make a variable visible to several functions
    b. make a variable visible to only one function
    c. conserve memory when a function is not executing
    d. retain a value when a function is not executing

30. In what unusual place can you use a function call when a function returns a value by reference?

EXERCISES

1. Refer to the CIRCAREA program of Chapter 3. Write a function called `circarea()` that finds the area of a circle in a similar way. It should take an argument of type `float` and return an argument of the same type. Write a `main()` function that gets a radius value from the user, calls `circarea()`, and displays the result.

2. Raising a number n to a power p is the same as multiplying n by itself p times. Write a function called `power()` that takes a `double` value for n and an `int` value for p, and returns the result as `double` value. Use a default argument of 2 for p, so that if this argument is omitted, the number will be squared. Write a `main()` function that gets values from the user to test this function.

3. Write a function called `zeroSmaller()` that is passed two `int` arguments by reference and then sets the smaller of the two numbers to 0. Write a `main()` program to exercise this function.

4. Write a function that takes two `Distance` values as arguments and returns the larger one. Include a `main()` program that accepts two `Distance` figures from the user, compares them, and displays the larger. (See the RETSTRC program for hints.)

OBJECTS AND CLASSES

OBJECTS AND CLASSES

MEMBER FUNCTIONS AND DATA

PRIVATE AND PUBLIC

CONSTRUCTORS AND DESTRUCTORS

OBJECTS IN THE REAL WORLD

WHEN TO USE OBJECTS

And now, the topics you've all been waiting for: objects and classes. The preliminaries are out of the way. We've learned about structures, which provide a way to group data elements. We've examined functions, which organize program actions into named entities. In this chapter we'll put these ideas together. We'll introduce several classes, starting with simple ones and working up toward more complicated examples. We'll focus first on the details of classes and objects. At the end of the chapter we'll take a wider view, discussing what is to be gained by using the OOP approach.

As you read this chapter, you may want to refer back to the concepts introduced in Chapter 1.

A SIMPLE CLASS

Our first program contains a class and two objects of that class. Although it's simple, the program demonstrates the syntax and general features of classes in C++. Here's the listing for the SMALLOBJ program:

```
// smallobj.cpp
// demonstrates a small, simple object
#include <iostream.h>

class smallobj              // specify a class
   {
   private:
      int somedata;         // class data
   public:
      void setdata(int d)   // member function to set data
         { somedata = d; }
      void showdata()       // member function to display data
         { cout << "\nData is " << somedata; }
   };

void main()
   {
   smallobj s1, s2;    // define two objects of class smallobj
```

207

```
s1.setdata(1066);    // call member function to set data
s2.setdata(1776);

s1.showdata();       // call member function to display data
s2.showdata();
}
```

The class smallobj specified in this program contains one data item and two member functions. These functions provide the only access to the data item from outside the class. The first member function sets the data item to a value, and the second displays the value. (This may sound like Greek, but we'll see what these terms mean as we go along.)

Placing data and functions together into a single entity is the central idea of object-oriented programming. This is shown in Figure 7-1.

CLASSES AND OBJECTS

Recall from Chapter 1 that an object has the same relationship to a class that a variable has to a data type. An object is said to be an *instance* of a class, in the same way my 1954 Chevrolet is an instance of a vehicle. In SMALLOBJ the class—whose name is smallobj—is specified in the first part of the program. Later, in main(), we define two objects—s1 and s2—that are instances of that class.

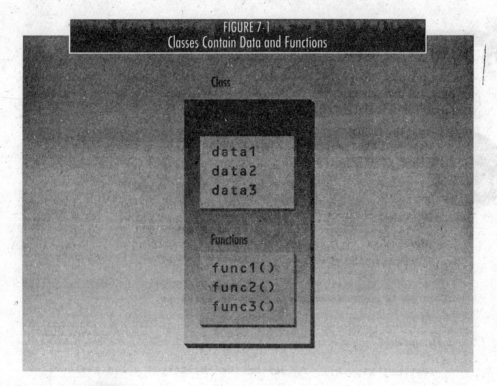

FIGURE 7-1
Classes Contain Data and Functions

Each of the two objects is given a value, and each displays its value. Here's the output of the program:

```
Data is 1066        ◄──────── object s1 displayed this
Data is 1776        ◄──────── object s2 displayed this
```

We'll begin by looking in detail at the first part of the program—the specification for the class smallobj. Later we'll focus on what main() does with objects of this class.

SPECIFYING THE CLASS

Here's the specifier for the class smallobj, copied from the SMALLOBJ listing:

```
class smallobj             // specify a class
   {
   private:
      int somedata;         // class data
   public:
      void setdata(int d)   // member function to set data
         { somedata = d; }
      void showdata()       // member function to display data
         { cout << "\nData is " << somedata; }
   };
```

The specifier starts with the keyword class, followed by the class name—smallobj in this example. Like a structure, the body of the class is delimited by braces and terminated by a semicolon. (Don't forget the semicolon. Remember, data constructs like structures and classes end with the semicolon, while control constructs like functions and loops do not.)

private and public

The body of the class contains two unfamiliar keywords: private and public. What is their purpose?

A key feature of object-oriented programming is *data hiding*. This term does not refer to the activities of particularly paranoid programmers; rather it means that data is concealed within a class, so that it cannot be accessed mistakenly by functions outside the class. The primary mechanism for hiding data is to put it in a class and make it *private*. Private data or functions can only be accessed from within the class. Public data or functions, on the other hand, are accessible from outside the class. This is shown in Figure 7-2.

Hidden from Whom?

Don't confuse data hiding with the security techniques used to protect computer databases. To provide a security measure you might, for example, require a user to supply a password before granting access to a database. The password is meant to keep unauthorized or malevolent users from altering (or often even reading) the data.

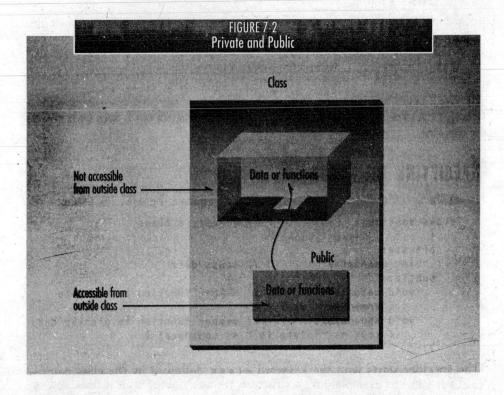

FIGURE 7-2
Private and Public

Data hiding, on the other hand, is designed to protect well-intentioned programmers from honest mistakes. Programmers who really want to can figure out a way to access **private** data, but they will find it hard to do so by accident.

Class Data

The **smallobj** class contains one data item: **somedata**, which is of type **int**. There can be any number of data items in a class, just as there can be any number of data items in a structure. The data item **somedata** follows the keyword **private**, so it can be accessed from within the class, but not from outside.

Member Functions

Member functions are functions that are included within a class. (In some object-oriented languages, such as Smalltalk, member functions are called *methods*; some writers use this term in C++ as well.) There are two member functions in **smallobj**: **setdata()** and **showdata()**. The function bodies of these functions have been written on the same line as the braces that delimit them. You could also use the more traditional format for these function definitions:

```
    void setdata(int d)
      {
      somedata = d;
      }
```

and

```
    void showdata(int d)
      {
      cout << "\nData is " << somedata;
      }
```

However, when member functions are small, it is common to compress their definitions this way to save space.

Figure 7-3 shows the syntax of a class specifier. Because `setdata()` and `showdata()` follow the keyword `public`, they can be accessed from outside the class. We'll see how this is done in a moment.

Public and Private

Usually the data within a class is private and the functions are public. This is a result of how classes are used. The data is hidden so it will be safe from accidental manipulation, while the functions that operate on the data are public so they can be accessed from outside the class. However, there is no rule that data must be

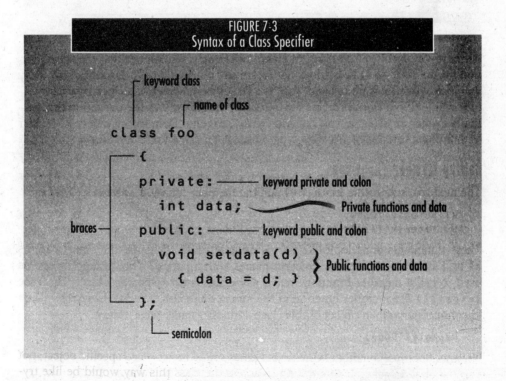

FIGURE 7-3
Syntax of a Class Specifier

private and functions public; in some circumstances you may find you'll need to use private functions and public data.

Member Functions within Class Specifier

The member functions in the `smallobj` class perform operations that are quite common in classes: setting and retrieving the data stored in the class. The `setdata()` function accepts a value as a parameter and sets the `somedata` variable to this value. The `showdata()` function displays the value stored in `somedata`.

Note that the member functions `setdata()` and `showdata()` are *definitions*: The actual code for the function is contained within the class specification. Member functions defined inside a class this way are created as *inline* functions by default. (Inline functions were discussed in the last chapter.) We'll see later that it is also possible to *declare* a function within a class but *define* it elsewhere. Functions defined outside the class are not normally inline.

USING THE CLASS

Now that the class is specified, let's see how `main()` makes use of it. We'll see how objects are defined, and, once defined, how their member functions are accessed.

Defining Objects

The first statement in `main()`,

```
smallobj s1, s2;
```

defines two objects, `s1` and `s2`, of class `smallobj`. Remember that the specification for the class `smallobj` does not create any objects. It only describes how they will look when they are created, just as a structure specifier describes how a structure will look but doesn't create any structure variables. It is the definition that actually creates objects that can be used by the program. Defining an object is similar to defining a variable of any data type: Space is set aside for it in memory.

Calling Member Functions

The next two statements in `main()` call the member function `setdata()`:

```
s1.setdata(1066);
s2.setdata(1776);
```

These statements don't look like normal function calls. Why are the object names `s1` and `s2` connected to the function names with a period? This strange syntax is used to call a member function that is associated with a specific object. Because `setdata()` is a member function of the `smallobj` class, it must always be called in connection with an object of this class. It doesn't make sense to say

```
setdata(1066);
```

by itself, because a member function is always called to act on a specific object, not on the class in general. Attempting to access the class this way would be like trying to drive the blueprint of a car. Not only does this statement not make sense, but the compiler will issue an error message if you attempt it. Member functions of a class can be accessed only by an object of that class.

To use a member function, the dot operator (the period) connects the object name and the member function. The syntax is similar to the way we refer to structure members, but the parentheses signal that we're executing a member function rather than referring to a data item. The dot operator is also called the *class member access operator*.

The first call to `setdata()`,

```
s1.setdata(1066);
```

executes the `setdata()` member function of the `s1` object. This function sets the variable `somedata` in object `s1` to the value 1066. The second call,

```
s2.setdata(1776);
```

causes the variable `somedata` in `s2` to be set to 1776. Now we have two objects whose `somedata` variables have different values, as shown in Figure 7-4.

FIGURE 7-4
Two Objects of Class `smallobj`

smallobj class specifier

Specifications for smallobj objects

Objects of class smallobj

s1

s2

somedata

1066

somedata

1776

Similarly, the following two calls to the `showdata()` function will cause the two objects to display their values:

```
s1.showdata();
s2.showdata();
```

Messages

Some object-oriented languages, such as Smalltalk, refer to calls to member functions as *messages*. Thus the call

```
s1.showdata();
```

can be thought of as sending a message to **s1** telling it to display itself. The term *message* is not a formal part of C++, but it is a useful idea to keep in mind as we discuss member functions. Talking about messages emphasizes that objects are discrete entities and that we communicate with them by calling their member functions. Referring to the analogy with company organization in Chapter 1, it's like sending a message to the secretary in the sales department to get a list of products sold in the southwest distribution area.

C++ OBJECTS AS PHYSICAL OBJECTS

The **smallobj** class in the last example had only one data item. Let's examine an example of a somewhat more ambitious class. (These are not the same ambitious classes dicussed in political science courses.) We'll create a class based on the structure for the widget parts inventory, last seen in such examples as PARTS in Chapter 5. Here's the listing for OBJPART:

```
// objpart.cpp
// widget part as an object
#include <iostream.h>

ss part                   // specify an object
   {
   private:
      int modelnumber;    // ID number of widget
      int partnumber;     // ID number of widget part
      float cost;         // cost of part
   public:
      void setpart(int mn, int pn, float c)  // set data
         {
         modelnumber = mn;
         partnumber = pn;
         cost = c;
         }
      void showpart()                             // display data
         {
```

```
        cout << "\nModel "  << modelnumber;
        cout << ", part "    << partnumber;
        cout << ", costs $"  << cost;
        }
    };

void main()
    {
    part part1;                              // define object
                                             //    of class part
    part1.setpart(6244, 373, 217.55);  // call member function
    part1.showpart();                  // call member function
    }
```

This program features the class part. Instead of one data item, as smallobj had, this class has three: modelnumber, partnumber, and cost. A single member function, setpart(), serves to supply values to all three data items at once. Another function, showpart(), displays the values stored in all three items.

In this example only one object of type part is created: part1. The member function setpart() sets the three data items in this part to the values 6244, 373, and 217.55. The member function showpart() then displays these values. Here's the output:

```
Model 6244, part 373, costs $217.55
```

This is a somewhat more realistic example than SMALLOBJ. If you were designing an inventory program you might actually want to create a class something like part. It's an example of a C++ object representing a physical object in the real world—a widget part.

C++ OBJECTS AS DATA TYPES

Here's another kind of entity C++ objects can represent: variables of a user-defined data type. We'll use objects to represent distances measured in the English system, as discussed in Chapter 5. Here's the listing for ENGLOBJ:

```
// englobj.cpp
// objects using English measurements
#include <iostream.h>

class Distance                           // English Distance class
    {
    private:
        int feet;
        float inches;
    public:
        void setdist(int ft, float in)   // set distance to args
            { feet = ft; inches = in; }
```

```
        void getdist()                    // get length from user
           {
           cout << "\nEnter feet: ";  cin >> feet;
           cout << "Enter inches: ";  cin >> inches;
           }

        void showdist()                   // display distance
           { cout << feet << "\'-" << inches << '\"'; }
     };

  void main()
     {
     Distance dist1, dist2;             // define two lengths

     dist1.setdist(11, 6.25);           // set dist1

     dist2.getdist();                   // get dist2 from user

                                        // display lengths
     cout << "\ndist1 = ";  dist1.showdist();
     cout << "\ndist2 = ";  dist2.showdist();
     }
```

In this program the class **Distance** contains two data items, **feet** and **inches**. This is similar to the **Distance** structure seen in examples in Chapter 5, but here the class **Distance** also has three member functions: **setdist()**, which uses arguments to set **feet** and **inches**; **getdist()**, which gets values for **feet** and **inches** from the user at the keyboard; and **showdist()**, which displays the distance in feet-and-inches format.

The value of an object of class **Distance** can thus be set in either of two ways. In **main()** we define two objects of class **Distance**: **dist1** and **dist2**. One is given a value using the **setdist()** member function with the arguments 11 and 6.25, and the other is given a value that is supplied by the user. Here's a sample interaction with the program:

```
Enter feet: 10
Enter inches: 4.75

dist1 = 11'-6.25"          ←———— provided by arguments
dist2 = 10'-4.75"          ←———— input by the user
```

CONSTRUCTORS

The ENGLOBJ example shows two ways to give values to the data items in an object. Sometimes, however, it's convenient if an object can initialize itself when it's first created, without the need to make a separate call to a member function. Automatic initialization is carried out using a special member function called a *constructor*. A constructor is a member function that is executed automatically whenever an object is created.

A COUNTER EXAMPLE

As an example, we'll create a class of objects that might be useful as a general-purpose programming element. A *counter* is a variable that counts things. Maybe it counts file accesses, or the number of times the user presses the (ENTER) key, or the number of customers entering a bank. Each time such an event takes place, the counter is incremented (1 is added to it). The counter can also be accessed to find the current count.

Let's assume that this counter is important in the program and must be accessed by many different functions. In procedural languages such as C, a counter would probably be implemented as an external variable. However, as we noted in Chapter 1, external variables may be modified accidentally. This example, COUNTER, provides a counter variable that can be modified only through its member functions.

```
// counter.cpp
// object represents a counter variable
#include <iostream.h>

    ss Counter
    {
    private:
        unsigned int count;                    // count
    public:
        Counter()        { count = 0; }        // constructor
        void inc_count() { count++; }          // increment count
        int get_count()  { return count; }     // return count
    };

    void main()
    {
    Counter c1, c2;                            // define and initialize

    cout << "\nc1=" << c1.get_count();         // display
    cout << "\nc2=" << c2.get_count();

    c1.inc_count();                            // increment c1
    c2.inc_count();                            // increment c2
    c2.inc_count();                            // increment c2

    cout << "\nc1=" << c1.get_count();         // display again
    cout << "\nc2=" << c2.get_count();
    }
```

The Counter class has one data item: count, of type unsigned int (since the count is always positive). It has three member functions: Counter(), which we'' look at in a moment; `inc_count`, which adds 1 to `count`; and `get_count()`, which returns the current value of `count`.

Automatic Initialization

When an object of type `Counter` is first created, we want its `count` to be initialized to 0. After all, most counts start at 0. We could provide a `set_count()` function to do this, and call it with an argument of 0, or we could provide a `zero_count()` function, which would always set `count` to 0. However, such functions would need to be executed every time we created a `Counter` object:

```
Counter c1;        // every time we do this,
c1.zero_count();   // we must do this too
```

It's more convenient, especially when there are a great many objects of a given class, to cause each object to initialize itself. In the `Counter` class the constructor `Counter()` does this. This function is called automatically whenever a new object of type `Counter` is created. Thus in `main()` the statement

```
Counter c1, c2;
```

creates two objects of type `Counter`. As each is created, its constructor, `Counter()`, is executed. This function sets the `count` variable to 0. So the effect of this single statement is to not only create two objects but to initialize their `count` variables to 0.

Same Name as the Class

There are some unusual aspects to constructor functions. First, it is no accident that they have exactly the same name (`Counter` in this example), as the class of which they are members. This is how the compiler knows they are constructors.

Second, no return type is used for constructors. Why not? Since the constructor is called automatically by the system, there's no program for it to return anything to; a return value wouldn't make sense.

Messing with the Format

Note that, in writing the functions in this example, we've compressed them so they occupy only one line each:

```
Counter()  { count = 0; }
```

This is just the same (as far as the compiler is concerned) as the normal function syntax

```
Counter()
   {
   count = 0;
   }
```

The `main()` part of this program exercises the `Counter` class by creating two counters, `c1` and `c2`. It causes the counters to display their initial values, which—

as arranged by the constructor—are 0. It then increments c1 once and c2 twice, and again causes the counters to display themselves (noncriminal behavior in this context). Here's the output:

```
c1=0
c2=0
c1=1
c2=2
```

If this isn't enough proof that the constructor is operating as advertised, we can rewrite the constructor to print a message when it executes:

```
Counter() { count = 0; cout << "I'm the constructor\n"; }
```

Now the program's output looks like this:

```
I'm the constructor
I'm the constructor
c1=0
c2=0
c1=1
c2=2
```

As you can see, the constructor is executed twice—once for c1 and once for c2—when the statement

```
Counter c1, c2;
```

is executed in main().

Do-It-Yourself Data

Constructors are pretty amazing when you think about it. Whoever writes language compilers (for C or BASIC or even for C++) must execute the equivalent of a constructor when the user defines a variable. If you define an int, for example, somewhere there's a constructor allocating 2 bytes of memory for it. If we can write our own constructors, we can start to take over some of the tasks of a compiler writer. This is one step on the path to creating our own data types, as we'll see later.

DESTRUCTORS

We've seen that a special member function—the constructor—is called automaticall when an object is first created. You might guess that another function is called al tomatically when an object is destroyed. This is indeed the case. Such a function called a *destructor*. A destructor has the same name as the constructor (which is th same as the class name) but preceded by a tilde:

```
class Foo
    {
    private:
        int data;
```

```
public:
   Foo() { data = 0; }   // constructor (same name as class)
   ~Foo() { }            // destructor (same name with tilde)
}
```

Like constructors, destructors do not have a return value. They also take no arguments (the assumption being that there's only one way to destroy an object).

The most common use of destructors is to de-allocate memory that was allocated for the object by the constructor. We'll investigate these activities in Chapter 12. Until then we won't have much use for destructors.

Objects as Function Arguments

Our next program adds some embellishments to the earlier ENGLOBJ example. It also demonstrates some new aspects of classes: constructor overloading, defining member functions outside the class, and—perhaps most important—objects as function arguments. Here's the listing for ENGLCON.CPP:

```
// englcon.cpp
// constructors, adds objects using member function
#include <iostream.h>

class Distance                     // English Distance class
   {
   private:
      int feet;
      float inches;
   public:
      Distance()                   // constructor (no args)
         { }
      Distance(int ft, float in)   // constructor (two args)
         { feet = ft; inches = in; }

      void getdist()               // get length from user
         {
         cout << "\nEnter feet: ";  cin >> feet;
         cout << "Enter inches: ";  cin >> inches;
         }

      void showdist()              // display distance
         { cout << feet << "\'-" << inches << '\"'; }

      void add_dist( Distance, Distance );    // declaration
   };
                                   // add lengths d2 and d3
void Distance::add_dist(Distance d2, Distance d3)
   {
```

```
    inches = d2.inches + d3.inches;  // add the inches
    feet = 0;                        // (for possible carry)
    if(inches >= 12.0)               // if total exceeds 12.0,
        {                            // then decrease inches
        inches -= 12.0;              // by 12.0 and
        feet++;                      // increase feet
        }                            // by 1
    feet += d2.feet + d3.feet;       // add the feet
    }

void main()
    {
    Distance dist1, dist3;           // define two lengths
    Distance dist2(11, 6.25);        // define and initialize dist2

    dist1.getdist();                 // get dist1 from user
    dist3.add_dist(dist1, dist2);    // dist3 = dist1 + dist2

                                     // display all lengths
    cout << "\ndist1 = ";  dist1.showdist();
    cout << "\ndist2 = ";  dist2.showdist();
    cout << "\ndist3 = ";  dist3.showdist();
    }
```

This program starts with a distance set to an initial value, and adds to it a distance supplied by the user, to obtain the sum of the distances. It then displays all three distances:

```
Enter feet: 17
Enter inches: 5.75

dist1 = 17'-5.75"
dist2 = 11'-6.25"
dist3 = 29'-0"
```

Let's see how the new features in this program are implemented.

OVERLOADED CONSTRUCTORS

It would be nice to be able to give variables of type Distance a value when the are first created. That is, we would like to use definitions like

```
Distance width(5, 6.25);
```

which defines an object, width, and simultaneously initializes it to a value of 5 feet and 6.25 for inches.

To do this we write a constructor like this:

```
Distance(int ft, float in)
    { feet = ft; inches = in; }
```

This sets the class data **feet** and **inches** to whatever values are passed as arguments to the constructor. So far so good.

However, we also want to define variables of type **Distance** without initializing them, as we did in ENGLOBJ:

```
Distance dist1, dist2;
```

In that program there was no constructor, but our definitions worked just fine. How could they work without a constructor? Because an implicit constructor was built into the program automatically by the compiler, and it created the objects, even though we didn't define it in the class.

Unfortunately, once we define one constructor, we must also define the implicit constructor. So we need the definition

```
Distance()
    { }           // no function body, doesn't do anything
```

in class **Distance**. The empty braces mean that the function doesn't do anything; it's just there to satisfy the compiler.

Since there are now two constructors with the same name, **Distance()**, we say the constructor is overloaded. Which of the two constructors is executed when an object is created depends on how many arguments are used in the definition:

```
Distance length;           // calls first constructor
Distance width(11, 6.0);   // calls second constructor
```

MEMBER FUNCTIONS DEFINED OUTSIDE THE CLASS

So far we've seen member functions that were defined inside the class specifier. This need not always be the case. ENGLCON shows a member function, **add_dist()**, that is not defined within the **Distance** class specifier. It is only declared inside the class, with the statement

```
void add_dist(Distance, Distance);
```

This tells the compiler that this function is a member of the class but that it will be defined outside the class specifier, someplace else in the listing.

In ENGLCON the function is defined immediately after the class specifier. It is adapted from the ENGLSTRC program of Chapter 5:

```
                        // add lengths d2 and d3
void Distance::add_dist(Distance d2, Distance d3)
    {
    inches = d2.inches + d3.inches;   // add the inches
    feet = 0;                         // (for possible carry)
    if(inches >= 12.0)                // if total exceeds 12.0,
        {                             // then decrease inches
        inches -= 12.0;               // by 12.0 and
```

```
    feet++;                      // increase feet
    }                            // by 1
feet += d2.feet + d3.feet;       // add the feet
}
```

The declarator in this definition contains some unfamiliar syntax. The function name, **add_dist()**, is preceded by the class name, **Distance**, and a new symbol—the double colon (**::**). This symbol is called the *scope resolution operator*. It is a way of specifying what class something is associated with. In this situation it means *the* **add_dist()** *member function of the* **Distance** *class*. Figure 7-5 shows its usage.

OBJECTS AS ARGUMENTS

Now we can see how ENGLCON works. The distances **dist1** and **dist3** are created using the constructor that takes no arguments; this constructor does not do any initialization. The distance **dist2** is created with the constructor that takes two arguments, and is initialized to the values passed in these arguments. A value is obtained for **dist1** by calling the member function **getdist()**, which obtains values from the user.

Now we want to add **dist1** and **dist2** to obtain **dist3**. The function call in **main()**,

```
dist3.add_dist(dist1, dist2);
```

does this. The two distances to be added, **dist1** and **dist2**, are supplied as arguments to **add_dist()**. The syntax for arguments that are objects is the same as that for arguments that are simple data types like **int**: The object name is supplied as

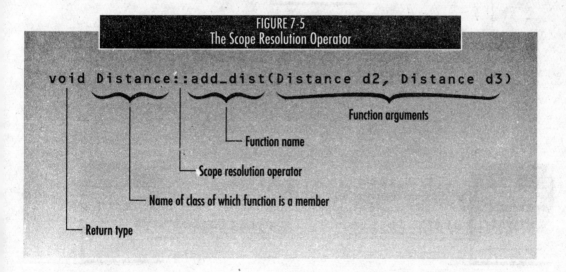

FIGURE 7-5
The Scope Resolution Operator

void Distance::add_dist(Distance d2, Distance d3)

Function arguments

Function name

Scope resolution operator

Name of class of which function is a member

Return type

the argument. Since **add_dist()** is a member function of the **Distance** class, it can access the private data in any object of class **Distance** supplied to it as an argument, using names like **dist1.inches** and **dist2.feet**.

Close examination of **add_dist()** emphasizes some important truths about member functions. When a member function is called, it is given direct access to only one object: *the object of which the function is a member*. In the following statement in ENGLCON, what objects can **add_dist()** access?

```
dist3.add_dist(dist1, dist2);
```

It can access **dist1** and **dist2**, because they are supplied as arguments. It can also access **dist3**, because it is a member function of **dist3**. You might think of **dist3** as a sort of phantom argument; the member function always has access to it, even though it is not supplied as an argument. That's what this statement means: "Execute the **add_dist()** member function of **dist3**." When the variables **feet** and **inches**

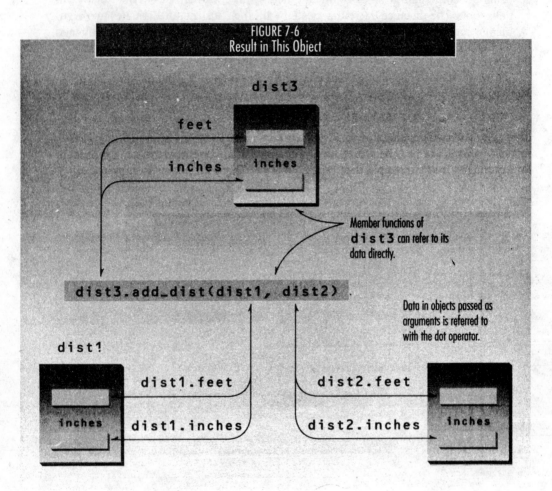

FIGURE 7-6
Result in This Object

are referred to within this function, they refer to dist3.feet and dist3.inches. Later in this book we'll see that a member function can refer to the entire object of which it is a member with the keyword this. The term this emphasizes the close relationship between a function and the object of which it is a member.

Notice that the result is not returned by the function. The return type of add_dist() is void. The result is stored automatically in the dist3 object. Figure 7-6 shows the two distances dist1 and dist2 being added together, with the result stored in dist3.

RETURNING OBJECTS FROM FUNCTIONS

In the ENGLCON example, we saw objects being passed as arguments to functions. Now we'll see an example of a function that returns an object. We'll modify the ENGLCON program to produce ENGLRET:

```
// englret.cpp
// function returns value of type Distance
#include <iostream.h>

class Distance                         //English Distance class
   {
   private:
      int feet;
      float inches;
   public:
      Distance()                       // constructor (no args)
         { feet = 0; inches = 0.0; }
      Distance(int ft, float in)  // constructor (two args)
         { feet = ft; inches = in; }

      void getdist()                   // get length from user
         {
         cout << "\nEnter feet: ";  cin >> feet;
         cout << "Enter inches: ";  cin>> inches;
         }

      void showdist()                  // display distance
         { cout << feet << "\'-" << inches << '\"'; }

      Distance add_dist( Distance );  // add
   };
                                       // add this distance to d2
Distance Distance::add_dist(Distance d2)   // return the sum
   {
   Distance temp;                      // temporary variable
   temp.inches = inches + d2.inches;   // add the inches
```

```
      if(temp.inches >= 12.0)          // if total exceeds 12.0,
         {                             // then decrease inches
         temp.inches -= 12.0;          // by 12.0 and
         temp.feet = 1;                // increase feet
         }                             // by 1
      temp.feet += feet + d2.feet;     // add the feet
      return temp;
      }

void main()
      {
      Distance dist1, dist3;           // define two lengths
      Distance dist2(11, 6.25);        // define, initialize dist2

      dist1.getdist();                 // get dist1 from user
      dist3 = dist1.add_dist(dist2);   // dist3 = dist1 + dist2

                                       // display all lengths
      cout << "\ndist1 = ";  dist1.showdist();
      cout << "\ndist2 = ";  dist2.showdist();
      cout << "\ndist3 = ";  dist3.showdist();
      }
```

From the user's viewpoint, the ENGLRET operates just the same as ENGLCON. In fact, the program is very similar to ENGLCON, but the differences reveal how functions work with objects. In ENGLCON two distances were passed to **add_dist()** as arguments, and the result was stored in the object of which **add_dist()** was a member, namely **dist3**. In ENGLRET one distance, **dist2**, is passed to **add_dist()** as an argument. It is added to the object, **dist1**, of which **add_dist()** is a member, and the result is returned from the function. In **main()** the result is assigned to **dist3**, in the statement

```
dist3 = dist1.add_dist(dist2);
```

The effect is the same as the corresponding statement in ENGLCON, but it is more natural-looking, since the assignment operator, =, is used in a natural way. In Chapter 9 we'll see how to use the arithmetic + operator to achieve the even more obvious expression

```
dist3 = dist1 + dist2;
```

ENGLCON and ENGLRET perform the same operation, but they do it differently. Here's the **add_dist()** function from ENGLRET:

```
                                       // add this distance to d2
Distance Distance::add_dist(Distance d2)   // return the sum
      {
      Distance temp;                   // temporary variable
      temp.inches = inches + d2.inches;  // add the inches
```

```
   if(temp.inches >= 12.0)          // if total exceeds 12.0,
      {                             // then decrease inches
      temp.inches -= 12.0;          // by 12.0 and
      temp.feet = 1;                // increase feet
      }                             // by 1
   temp.feet += feet + d2.feet;     // add the feet
   return temp;
   }
```

Compare this with the same function in ENGLCON. As you can see, there are some subtle differences. In this ENGLRET version, a temporary object of class Dis-tance is created. This object holds the sum until it can be returned to the calling program. The sum is calculated by adding two distances. The first is the object of

FIGURE 7-7
Result Returned from Temporary Object

temp

temp.feet

temp.inches   inches

Data in temp is assigned to dist3 using statement return temp; in add_dist() function.

dist3 = dist1.add-dist(dist2);

dist1

feet

inches   inches

dist2

d2.feet

d2.inches   inches

which `add_dist()` is a member, `dist1`. Its member data is accessed as `feet` and `inches`. The second is the object passed as an argument, `dist2`. Its member data is accessed as `d2.feet` and `d2.inches`. The result is stored in `temp` and accessed as `temp.feet` and `temp.inches`. The `temp` object is then returned by the function using the statement

```
return temp;
```

and the statement in `main()` assigns it to `dist3`. Notice that `dist1` is not modified; it simply supplies data to `add_dist()`. Figure 7-7 shows how this looks.

A CARD GAME EXAMPLE

As a larger example of objects modeling the real world, let's look at a variation of the CARDS program from Chapter 5. This program, CARDOBJ, has been rewritten to use objects. It does not introduce any new concepts, but it does use almost all the programming ideas we've discussed up to this point.

As the CARDS example did, CARDOBJ creates three cards with fixed values and switches them around in an attempt to confuse the user about their location. But in CARDOBJ each card is an object of class `card`. Here's the listing:

```
// cardobj.cpp
// cards as objects
#include <iostream.h>

enum Suit { clubs, diamonds, hearts, spades };

const int jack = 11;        // from 2 to 10 are
const int queen = 12;       // integers without names
const int king = 13;
const int ace = 14;

enum Boolean { false, true };

class card
   {
   private:
      int number;           // 2 to 10, jack, queen, king, ace
      Suit suit;            // clubs, diamonds, hearts, spades
   public:
      card ()                          // constructor 1
         { }
      card (int n, Suit s)             // constructor 2
         { suit = s; number = n; }
      void display();                  // display card
      Boolean isEqual(card);           // same as another card?
   };
```

```
void card::display()                // display the card
   {
   if( number >= 2 && number <= 10 )
      cout << number << " of ";
   else
      switch(number)
         {
         case jack:  cout << "jack of ";  break;
         case queen: cout << "queen of "; break;
         case king:  cout << "king of ";  break;
         case ace:   cout << "ace of ";   break;
         }
   switch(suit)
      {
      case clubs:    cout << "clubs"; break;
      case diamonds: cout << "diamonds"; break;
      case hearts:   cout << "hearts"; break;
      case spades:   cout << "spades"; break;
      }
   }


Boolean card::isEqual(card c2)    // return true if cards equal
   {
   return ( number==c2.number && suit==c2.suit ) ? true : false;
   }


void main()
   {
   card temp, chosen, prize;        // define various cards
   int position;

   card card1( 7, clubs );          // define & initialize card1
   cout << "\nCard 1 is the ";
   card1.display();                 // display card1

   card card2( jack, hearts );      // define & initialize card2
   cout << "\nCard 2 is the ";
   card2.display();                 // display card2

   card card3( ace, spades );       // define & initialize card3
   cout << "\nCard 3 is the ";
   card3.display();                 // display card3

   prize = card3;                   // prize is the card to guess

   cout << "\nI'm swapping card 1 and card 3";
   temp = card3; card3 = card1; card1 = temp;

   cout << "\nI'm swapping card 2 and card 3";
   temp = card3; card3 = card2; card2 = temp;
```

```
cout << "\nI'm swapping card 1 and card 2";
temp = card2; card2 = card1; card1 = temp;

cout << "\nNow, where (1, 2, or 3) is the ";
prize.display();                    // display prize card
cout << "? ";
cin >> position;                    // get user's guess of position

switch (position)
    {                               // set chosen to user's choice
    case 1: chosen = card1; break;
    case 2: chosen = card2; break;
    case 3: chosen = card3; break;
    }
if( chosen.isEqual(prize) )    // is chosen card the prize?
    cout << "That's right!  You win!";
else
    cout << "Sorry. You lose.";
cout << "  You chose the ";
chosen.display();                   // display chosen card
cout << endl;
}
```

There are two constructors in class **card**. The first, which takes no arguments, is used in **main()** to create the cards **temp**, **chosen**, and **prize**, which are not initialized. The second constructor, which takes two arguments, is used to create **card1**, **card2**, and **card3** and to initialize them to specific values. Besides the constructors, **card** has two other member functions, both defined outside the class. The **display()** function takes no arguments; it simply displays the card object of which it is a member, using the **number** and **suit** data items in the card. The **isEqual()** function checks whether the card is equal to a card supplied as an argument. The statement in **main()**

```
chosen.display();
```

displays the card chosen by the user.

The **isEqual()** member function uses the conditional operator to compare the card of which it is a member with a card supplied as an argument. This function could also have been written with an **if...else** statement:

```
if( number==c2.number && suit==c2.suit )
    return true;
else
    return false;
```

but the conditional operator is more compact.

In **isEqual()** the argument is called **c2** as a reminder that there are two cards in the comparison: The first card is the object of which **isEqual()** is a member. The expression

```
if( chosen.isEqual(prize) )
```

in main() compares the card chosen with the card prize.

Here's the output when the user guesses an incorrect card:

```
Card 1 is the 7 of clubs
Card 2 is the jack of hearts
Card 3 is the ace of spades
I'm swapping card 1 and card 3
I'm swapping card 2 and card 3
I'm swapping card 1 and card 2
Now, where (1, 2, or 3) is the ace of spaces? 1
Sorry, you lose. You chose the 7 of clubs.
```

STRUCTURES AND CLASSES

The examples so far in this book have portrayed structures as a way to group data, and classes as a way to group both data and functions. In fact, you can use structures in almost exactly the same way that you use classes. The only formal difference between class and struct is that in a class the members are private by default, while in a structure they are public by default.

Here's the format we've been using for classes:

```
class foo
    {
    private:
        int data1;
    public:
        void func();
    };
```

Since in classes private is the default, this keyword is unnecessary. You can just as well write

```
class foo
    {
        int data1;
    public:
        void func();
    };
```

and the data1 will still be private. Many programmers prefer this style. We like to include the private keyword because it offers a small increase in clarity.

If you want to use a structure to accomplish the same thing as this class, you can dispense with the keyword public, provided you put the public members before the private ones:

```
struct foo
    {
        void func();
    private:
        int data1;
    };
```

since public is the default. However, in most situations programmers use structures to group data, and classes to group data and functions.

CLASSES, OBJECTS, AND MEMORY

We've probably given you the impression that each object created from a class contains separate copies of that class's data and member functions. This is a good first approximation, since it emphasizes that objects are complete, self-contained entities, designed using the class specifier. The mental image here is of cars (objects) rolling off an assembly line, each one made according to a blueprint (the class specifier).

However, things are not quite so simple. It's true that each object has its own separate data items. (In some object-oriented languages, such as Smalltalk, a data item that is part of a class is called an *instance variable*, since there is an instance of it for each object created.)

On the other hand, contrary to what you may have been led to believe, all the objects in a given class use the same member functions. The member functions are created and placed in memory only once—when they are defined in the class specifier. This makes sense; there's really no point in duplicating all the member functions in a class every time you create another object of that class, since the functions for each object are identical. The data items, however, will hold different values, so there must be a separate instance of each data item in each object. Data is therefore placed in memory when each object is defined, so there is a set for each object. Figure 7-8 shows how this looks.

In the SMALLOBJ example there are two objects of type `smallobj`, so there are two instances of `somedata` in memory. However, there is only one instance of the functions `setdata()` and `showdata()`. These functions are shared by all the objects of the class. There is no conflict because (at least in a single-tasking system) only one function is executed at a time.

In most situations you don't need to know that there is only one member function for an entire class. It's simpler to visualize each object as containing both its own data and its own member functions. But in some situations, such as in estimating the size of an executing program, it's helpful to know what's happening behind the scenes.

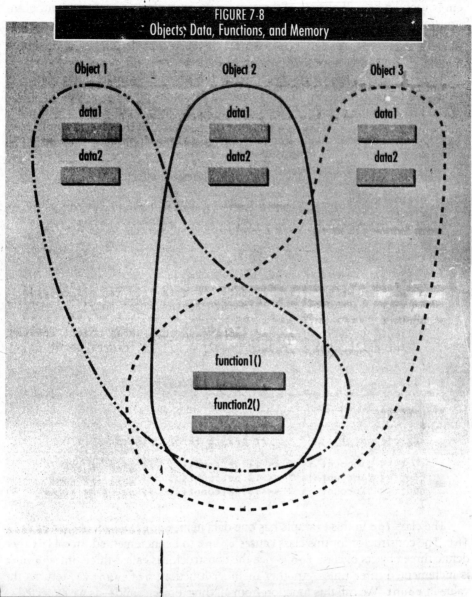

FIGURE 7-8
Objects, Data, Functions, and Memory

STATIC CLASS DATA

Having said that each object contains its own separate data, we must now amend that slightly. If a data item in a class is defined as `static`, then only one such item is created for the entire class, no matter how many objects there are. A static data item is useful when all objects of the same class must share a common item of information. A member variable defined as **static** has similar characteristics to a normal static variable: It is visible only within the class, but its lifetime is the entire program. (See Chapter 6 for a discussion of static variables.)

As an example, suppose an object needed to know how many other objects of its class were in the program. In a road-racing game, for example, a race car might want to know how many other cars were still in the race. In this case a static variable **count** could be included as a member of the class. All the objects would have access to this variable; it would be the same variable for all of them; they would all see the same count.

Here's an example, STATDATA, that demonstrates the effect:

```
// statdata.cpp
// static class data
#include <iostream.h>

class foo
    {
    private:
        static int count;      // only one data item for all objects
                               // note: *declaration* only!
    public:
        foo() { count++; }     // increments count when object created
        int getcount()  { return count; }      // returns count
    };

int foo::count;                // *definition* of count

void main()
    {
    foo f1, f2, f3;            // create three objects

    cout << "\ncount is " << f1.getcount();   // each object
    cout << "\ncount is " << f2.getcount();   // sees the same
    cout << "\ncount is " << f3.getcount();   // value of count
    }
```

The class **foo** in this example has one data item, **count**, which is type **static int**. The constructor for this class causes **count** to be incremented. In **main()** we define three objects of class **foo**. Since the constructor is called three times, **count** is incremented three times. Another member function, **getcount()**, returns the value in **count**. We call this function from all three objects, and—as we expected—each prints the same value. Here's the output:

```
count is 3             ←———————— static data
count is 3
count is 3
```

If we had used an ordinary automatic variable—as opposed to a static variable—for **count**, each constructor would have incremented its own private copy of **count** once, and the output would have been

```
count is 1          ←————— automatic data
count is 1
count is 1
```

As you can, see there's a major syntax peculiarity with static member data. A static data item such as `count` is *declared* inside the class specifier, but it must also be *defined*—so memory will be set aside for it—outside the class. This follows from the idea that static data is not part of any particular object of the class, but of the class in general. Thus it takes two lines of code to fully specify a static variable. If you declare the static variable inside the class, but forget to define it outside, the

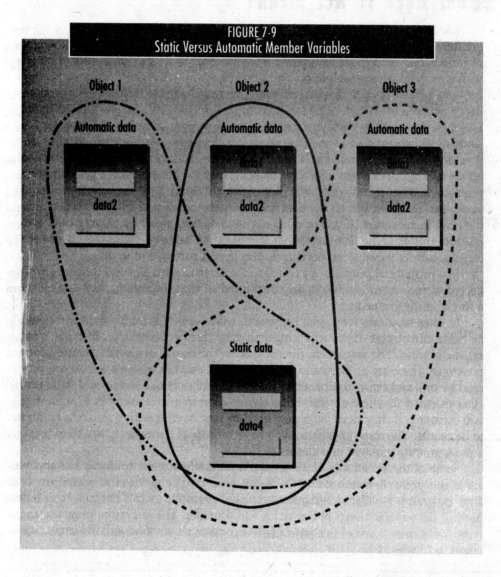

FIGURE 7-9
Static Versus Automatic Member Variables

linker will complain that it is an unresolved external. The scope resolution operator is used in the definition to specify what class `count` is a member of.

Static class variables are not used often, but they are important in special situations, and knowing about them helps to clarify how the more common automatic variables work. Figure 7-9 shows how static variables compare with automatic variables.

WHAT DOES IT ALL MEAN?

Now that you've been introduced to classes and objects, you may wonder what benefit they really offer. After all, as you can see by comparing several of the programs in this chapter with those in Chapter 5, it's possible to do the same sorts of things with a procedural approach as it is with objects.

One benefit of OOP that you may have glimpsed already is the close correspondence between the things being modeled by the program and the C++ objects in the program. A widget part object represents a widget part, a card object represents a card, and so on. In C++ everything about a widget part is included in its class description—the part number and other data items, and the functions necessary to access and operate on this data. This makes it easy to conceptualize a programming problem. You figure out what parts of the problem can be most usefully represented as objects, and then put all the data and functions connected with that object into the class specification. If you're using a C++ class to represent a playing card, you put into this class the data items that represent the value of the card, and also the functions to set its value, retrieve it, display it, compare it, and so on.

In a procedural program, by contrast, the external variables and functions connected with a real-world object are distributed all over the listing; they don't form a single, easily grasped unit.

In some situations it may not be obvious what parts of a real-life situation should be made into objects. If you're writing a program that plays chess, for instance, what are the objects? The chessmen, the squares on the board, or possibly entire board positions? There are no hard and fast rules for this sort of analysis. Often you proceed by trial and error. You break a problem into objects in one way and write trial class specifiers for these objects. If the classes seem to match reality in a useful way, you continue. If they don't, you may need to start over, selecting different entities to be classes. The more experience you have with OOP, the easier it will be to break a programming problem into classes.

Some of the benefits of object-oriented programming are probably not apparent at this point. Remember that OOP was devised to cope with the complexity of large programs. Smaller programs, such as the examples in this chapter, have less need of the organizational power that OOP provides. The larger the program, the more the benefit. Some of this power will become more obvious with the larger programs in Chapter 15.

Summary

A class is a specification for a number of objects. Objects consist of both data and functions that operate on that data. In a class specifier, the members—whether data or functions—can be `private`, meaning they can be accessed only by member functions of that class, or `public`, meaning they can be accessed by any function in the program.

A member function is a function that is a member of a class. Member functions have access to an object's private data, while nonmember functions do not.

A constructor is a member function, with the same name as its class, that is executed every time an object of the class is created. A constructor has no return type but can take arguments. It is often used to give initial values to object data members. Constructors can be overloaded, so an object can be initialized in different ways.

A destructor is a member function with the same name as its class but preceded by a tilde (~). It is called when an object is destroyed. A destructor takes no arguments and has no return value.

There is a separate copy of the data members for each object that is created from a class, but only one copy of a class's member functions. A data item can be restricted to a single instance for all objects of a class by making it `static`.

One reason to use OOP is the close correspondence between real-world objects and OOP classes. There are no rules on how to break a programming problem into classes. Often trial and error is necessary.

Questions

1. What is the purpose of a class specifier (declaration)?
2. A _____ has the same relation to an _____ that a basic data type has to a variable of that type.
3. In a class specifier, data or functions designated `private` are accessible
   a. to any function in the program
   b. only if you know the password
   c. to member functions of that class
   d. only to public members of the class
4. Write a class specifier that creates a class called `leverage` with one private data member, `crowbar`, of type `int` and one public function whose declaration is `void pry()`.
5. True or false: Data items in a class must be private.

6. Write a statement that defines an object called `lever1` of the `leverage` class described in question 4.

7. The dot operator (or class member access operator) connects the following two entities (reading from left to right):
   a. a class member and a class object
   b. a class object and a class
   c. a class and a member of that class
   d. a class object and a member of that class

8. Write a statement that executes the `pry()` function in the `lever1` object, as described in questions 4 and 6.

9. Member functions defined inside a class specifier are _____ by default.

10. Write a member function called `getcrow()` for the `leverage` class described in question 4. This function should return the value of the `crowbar` data. Assume the function is defined within the class specifier.

11. A constructor is executed automatically when an object is _____.

12. A constructor's name is the same as _____.

13. Write a constructor that initializes to 0 the `crowbar` data, a member of the `leverage` class described in question 4. Assume the constructor is defined within the class specifier.

14. True or false: In a class you can have more than one constructor with the same name.

15. A member function can always access the data
    a. in the object of which it is a member
    b. in the class of which it is a member
    c. in any object of the class of which it is a member
    d. in the public part of its class

16. Assume the member function `getcrow()` described in question 10 is defined outside the class specifier. Write the declaration that goes inside the class specifier.

17. Write a revised version of the `getcrow()` member function from question 10 that is defined outside the class specifier.

18. The only technical difference between structures and classes in C++ is that

_____

19. If three objects of a class are defined, how many copies of that class's data items are stored in memory? How many copies of its member functions?

20. *Sending a message* to an object is the same as _____.

21. Classes are useful because they
    a. are removed from memory when not in use
    b. permit data to be hidden from other classes
    c. bring together all aspects of an entity in one place
    d. can closely model objects in the real world

22. True or false: There is a precise methodology for dividing a real-world programming problem into classes.

ERCISES

1. Create a class that imitates part of the functionality of the basic data type `int`. Call the class `Int` (note different spelling). The only data in this class is an `int` varible. Include member functions to initialize an `Int` to 0, to initialize it to an `int` value, to display it (it looks just like an `int`), and to add two `Int` values.

    Write a program that exercises this class by creating two initialized and one uninitialized `Int` values, adding these two initialized values and placing the response in the uninitialized value, and then displaying this result.

2. Imagine a tollbooth at a bridge. Cars passing by the booth are expected to pay a fifty-cent toll. Mostly they do, but sometimes a car goes by without paying. The tollbooth keeps track of the number of cars that have gone by, and of the total amount of money collected.

    Model this tollbooth with a class called `tollBooth`. The two data items are a type `unsigned int` to hold the total number of cars, and a type `double` to hold the total amount of money collected. A constructor initializes both these to 0. A member function called `payingCar()` increments the car total and adds 0.50 to the cash total. Another function, called `nopayCar()`, increments the car total but adds nothing to the cash total. Finally, a member function called `display()` displays the two totals.

    Include a program to test this class. This program should allow the user to push one key to count a paying car, and another to count a nonpaying car. Pushing the (ESC) key should cause the program to print out the total cars and total cash and then exit.

3. Create a class called `time` that has separate `int` member data for hours, minutes, and seconds. One constructor should initialize this data to 0, and another should initialize it to fixed values. A member function should display it, in 11:59:59 format. The final member function should add two objects of type `time` passed as arguments.

    A `main()` program should create two initialized `time` objects, and one that isn't initialized. Then it should add the two initialized values together, leaving the result in the third `time` variable. Finally it should display the value of this third variable.

ARRAYS

ARRAY DEFINITIONS

ACCESSING ARRAY ELEMENTS

ARRAYS AS CLASS MEMBERS

ARRAYS OF OBJECTS

STRINGS

STRING INPUT/OUTPUT

In everyday life we commonly group similar objects into units. We buy peas by the can and eggs by the carton. In computer languages we also need to group together data items of the same type. The mechanism that accomplishes this in C++ is the *array*. Arrays can hold a few data items, or tens of thousands. The data items grouped in an array can be simple types like `int` or `float`, or they can be user-defined types like structures and objects.

Arrays are like structures in that they both group a number of items into a larger unit. But while a structure usually groups items of different types, an array groups items of the same type. More important, the items in a structure are accessed by name, while those in an array are accessed by an index number. Using an index number to specify an item allows easy access to a large number of items.

Arrays exist in almost every computer language, including Pascal and BASIC. Arrays in C++ are similar to those in other languages, and identical to those in C.

In this chapter we'll look first at arrays of basic data types like `int` and `char`. Then we'll examine arrays used as data members in classes, and arrays used to hold objects. Thus this chapter is intended not only to introduce arrays but to increase your understanding of object-oriented programming. We'll finish the chapter with an introduction to *strings*, which are arrays of type `char`.

ARRAY FUNDAMENTALS

A simple example program will serve to introduce arrays. This program, REPLAY, creates an array of four integers, representing the ages of four people. It then asks the user to enter four values, which it places in the array. Finally, it displays all four values.

```
// replay.cpp
// gets four ages from user, displays them
#include <iostream.h>

void main()
    {
```

```
int age[4];                        // array 'age' of 4 ints

cout << endl;
for(int j=0; j<4; j++)             // get 4 ages
   {
   cout << "Enter an age: ";
   cin >> age[j];                  // access array element
   }
for(j=0; j<4; j++)                 // display 4 ages
   cout << "\nYou entered " << age[j];
   }
```

Here's a sample interaction with the program:

```
Enter an age: 44
Enter an age: 16
Enter an age: 23
Enter an age: 68

You entered 44
You entered 16
You entered 23
You entered 68
```

The first for loop gets the ages from the user and places them in the array, while the second reads them from the array and displays them.

DEFINING ARRAYS

Like other variables in C++, an array must be defined before it can be used to store information. And, like other definitions, an array definition specifies a variable type and a name. But it includes another feature: a size. The size specifies how many data items the array will contain. It immediately follows the the name, and is surrounded by square brackets. Figure 8-1 shows the syntax of an array definition.

FIGURE 8-1
Syntax of Array Definition

In the REPLAY example the array is type `int`. The name of the array comes next, followed immediately by an opening bracket, the array size, and a closing bracket. The number in brackets must be a constant or an expression that evaluates to a constant, and should also be an integer. In the example we use the value 4.

ARRAY ELEMENTS

The items in an array are called *elements* (in contrast to the items in a structure, which are called *members*). As we noted, all the elements in an array are of the same type; only the values vary. Figure 8-2 shows the elements of the array `age`.

Following the conventional (although in some ways backward) approach, memory grows downward in the figure. That is, the first array elements are on the top of the page; later elements extend downward.

Since each element in `age` is an integer, it occupies 2 bytes. As specified in the definition, the array has exactly four elements.

Notice that the first array element has the value 0. Thus, since there are four elements, the last one is number 3. This is a potentially confusing situation; you might think the last element in a four-element array would be number 4, but it's not.

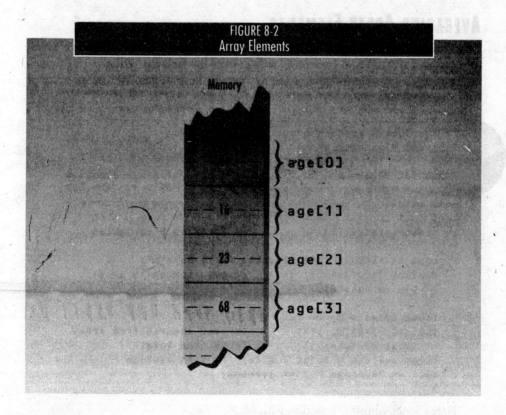

FIGURE 8-2
Array Elements

ACCESSING ARRAY ELEMENTS

In the REPLAY example, we access each array element twice. The first time, we insert a value into the array, with the line

```
cin >> age[j];
```

and the second time, we read it out with the line

```
cout << "\nYou entered " << age[j];
```

In both cases the expression for the array element is

```
age[j]
```

This consists of the name of the array, followed by brackets delimiting a variable j. Which of the four array elements is specfied by this expression depends on the value of j; age[0] refers to the first element, age[1] to the second, age[2] to the third, arid age[3] to the fourth. The variable (or constant) in the brackets is called the array *index*.

Since j is the loop variable in both for loops, it starts at 0 and is incremented until it reaches 3, thereby accessing each of the array elements in turn.

AVERAGING ARRAY ELEMENTS

Here's another example of an array at work. This one, SALES, invites the user to enter a series of six values, representing widget sales for each day of the week (including Saturday), and then calculates the average of these values. We use an array of type float so that monetary values can be entered.

```
// sales.cpp
// averages a weeks's widget sales (6 days)
#include <iostream.h>

st int SIZE = 6;              // number of array elements

void main()
   {
   float sales[SIZE];           // array of 6 variables

   cout << "\nEnter widget sales for 6 days\n";
   for(int j=0; j<SIZE; j++)   // put figures in array
      cin >> sales[j];

   float total = 0;
   for(j=0; j<SIZE; j++)        // read figures from array
      total += sales[j];        // to find total
   float average = total / SIZE;  // find average
   cout << "Average = " << average;
   }
```

Here's some sample interaction with SALES:

```
Enter widget sales for 6 days
352.64
867.70
781.32
867.35
746.21
189.45
Average = 634.11
```

A new detail in this program is the use of a `const` variable for the array size and loop limits. This variable is defined at the start of the listing:

```
const int SIZE = 6;
```

Using a variable (instead of a constant, such as the 4 used in the last example) makes it easier to change the array size: Only one program line needs to be changed to change the array size, loop limits, and anywhere else the array size appears. The all-uppercase name reminds us that the variable is a constant and cannot be modified in the program.

INITIALIZING ARRAYS

You can give values to each array element when the array is first defined. Here's an example, DAYS, that sets 12 array elements in the array `days_per_month` to the number of days in each month.

```
// days.cpp
// shows days from start of year to date specified
#include <iostream.h>

d main()
{
int month, day, total_days;
int days_per_month[12] = { 31, 28, 31, 30, 31, 30,
                           31, 31, 30, 31, 30, 31 };

cout << "\nEnter month (1 to 12): ";  // get date
cin >> month;
cout << "Enter day (1 to 31): ";
cin >> day;
total_days = day;                      // separate days
for(int j=0; j<month-1; j++)           // add days each month
   total_days += days_per_month[j];
cout << "Total days from start of year is: " << total_days;
}
```

The program calculates the number of days from the beginning of the year to a date specified by the user. (Beware: It doesn't work for leap years.) Here's some sample interaction:

```
Enter month (1 to 12): 3
Enter day (1 to 31): 11
Total days from start of year is: 70
```

Once it gets the month and day values, the program adds the number of days to the total. Then it cycles through a loop, where it adds values from the `days_per_month` array to the `total_days` variable. The number of such values to add is one less than the number of months. For instance, if the user entered month 5, the values of the first four array elements (31, 28, 31, and 30) are added to the total.

The values to which `days_per_month` is initialized are surrounded by braces and separated by commas. They are connected to the array expression by an equals sign. Figure 8-3 shows the syntax.

Actually, we don't need to use the array size when we initialize all the array elements, since the compiler can figure it out by counting the initializing variables. Thus we can write

```
int days_per_month[] = { 31, 28, 31, 30, 31, 30,
                         31, 31, 30, 31, 30, 31 };
```

What happens if you do use an explicit array size, but it doesn't agree with the number of initializers? If there are too few initializers, the missing elements will be set to 0. If there are too many, an error is signaled.

MULTIDIMENSIONAL ARRAYS

So far we've looked at arrays of one dimension: A single variable specifies each array element. But arrays can have higher dimensions. Here's a program, SALEMON, that uses a two-dimensional array to store sales figures for several districts and several months.

```
// salemon.cpp
// displays sales chart using 2-d array
#include <iostream.h>
#include <iomanip.h>                        // for setprecision, etc.

const int DISTRICTS = 4;                    // array dimensions
const int MONTHS = 3;

void main()
   {
   int d, m;
   float sales[DISTRICTS][MONTHS];   // two-dimensional array
                                     // definition
   cout << endl;
   for(d=0; d<DISTRICTS; d++)              // get array values
      for(m=0; m<MONTHS; m++)
         {
         cout << "Enter sales for district " << d+1;
         cout << ", month " << m+1 << ": ";
         cin >> sales[d][m];               // put number in array
         }

   cout << "\n\n";
   cout << "                              Month\n";
   cout << "                  1         2         3";
```

```
for(d=0; d<DISTRICTS; d++)
   {
   cout <<"\nDistrict " << d+1;
   for(m=0; m<MONTHS; m++)           // display array values
      cout << setiosflags(ios::fixed)      // not exponential
           << setiosflags(ios::showpoint)  // always use point
           << setprecision(2)              // digits to right
           << setw(10)                     // field width
           << sales[d][m];         // get number from array
   } // end for(d)
} // end main
```

This program accepts the sales figures from the user and then displays them in a table:

```
Enter sales for district 1, month 1: 3964.23
Enter sales for district 1, month 2: 4135.87
Enter sales for district 1, month 3: 4397.98
Enter sales for district 2, month 1: 867.75
Enter sales for district 2, month 2: 923.59
Enter sales for district 2, month 3: 1037.01
Enter sales for district 3, month 1: 12.77
Enter sales for district 3, month 2: 378.32
Enter sales for district 3, month 3: 798.22
Enter sales for district 4, month 1: 2983.53
Enter sales for district 4, month 2: 3983.73
Enter sales for district 4, month 3: 9494.98
```

		Month	
	1	2	3
District 1	3964.23	4135.87	4397.98
District 2	867.75	923.59	1037.01
District 3	12.77	378.32	798.22
Distruct 4	2983.53	3983.73	9494.98

FIGURE 8-3
Syntax of Array Initialization

Defining Multidimensional Arrays

The array is defined with two size specifiers, each enclosed in brackets:

```
float sales[DISTRICTS][MONTHS];
```

One way to think about this statement is that **sales** is an array of arrays. It is an array of **DISTRICTS** elements, each of which is an array of **MONTHS** elements. Figure 8-4 shows how this looks.

Of course there can be arrays of dimensions higher than two. A three-dimensional array is an array of arrays of arrays. It is accessed with three indexes:

```
elem = dimen3[i][j][k];
```

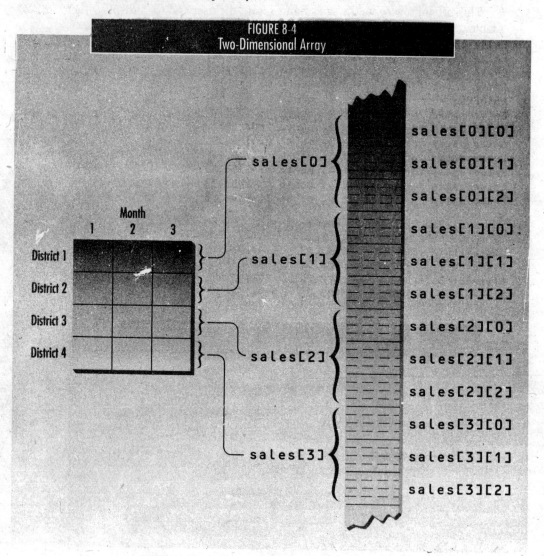

FIGURE 8-4
Two-Dimensional Array

This is entirely analogous to one- and two-dimensional arrays; it is an array of arrays of arrays.

Accessing Multidimensional Array Elements

Array elements in two-dimensional arrays require two indexes:

```
sales[d][m]
```

Notice that each index has its own set of brackets. Don't write `sales[d,m]`; this works in some languages, but not in C++.

Formatting Numbers

The SALEMON program displays a table of dollar values. It's important that such values be formatted properly, so let's digress long enough to see how this is done in C++. With dollar values you normally want to have exactly two digits to the right of the decimal point, and you want the decimal points of all the numbers in a column to line up. It's also nice if trailing zeros are displayed; you want 79.50, not 79.5.

Convincing the C++ I/O streams to do all this requires a little work. You've already seen the manipulator `setw()`, used to set the output field width. Formatting decimal numbers requires several additional manipulators.

Here's a statement that prints a floating-point number called `fpn` in a field ten characters wide, with two digits to the right of the decimal point:

```
cout << setiosflags(ios::fixed)        // fixed (not exponential)
     << setiosflags(ios::showpoint)    // always show decimal point
     << setprecision(2)                // two decimal places
     << setw(10)                       // field width 10
     << fpn;                           // finally, the number
```

A group of 1-bit flags in a `long int` in the `ios` class determines how formatting will be carried out. At this point we don't need to know what the `ios` class is, or the reasons for the exact syntax used with this class, to make the manipulators work.

We're concerned with two of the `ios` flags: `fixed` and `showpoint`. To set the flags you use the manipulator `setiosflags`, with the name of the flag as an argument. The name must be preceded by the class name, `ios`, and the scope resolution operator (`::`).

The first two lines of the `cout` statement set the `ios` flags. (If you need to unset—that is, clear—the flags at some later point in your program, you can use the `resetiosflags` manipulator.) The `fixed` flag prevents numbers from being printed in exponential format, such as 3.45e3. The `showpoint` flag specifies that there will always be a decimal point, even if the number has no fractional part: 123.00, instead of 123.

To set the precision to two digits to the right of the decimal place, you use the `setprecision` manipulator, with the number of digits as an argument. We've already seen how to set the field width by using the `setw` manipulator. Once all these manipulators have been sent to `cout`, you can send the number itself; it will be displayed in the desired format.

Initializing Multidimensional Arrays

As you might expect, you can initialize multidimensional arrays. The only prerequisite is a willingness to type a lot of braces and commas. Here's a variation of the SALEMON program that uses an initialized array instead of asking for input from the user. This program is called SALEINIT.

```
// saleinit.cpp
// displays sales chart, initializes 2-d array
#include <iostream.h>
#include <iomanip.h>              // for setprecision, etc.

const int DISTRICTS = 4;          // array dimensions
const int MONTHS = 3;

void main()
   {
   int d, m;
                                  // initialize array elements
   float sales[DISTRICTS][MONTHS]
               = { {  1432.07,    234.50,    654.01 },
                   {   322.00, 13838.32, 17589.88 },
                   {  9328.34,    934.00,   4492.30 },
                   { 12838.29,   2332.63,     32.93 } };
   cout << "\n\n";
   cout << "                          Month\n";
   cout << "               1         2         3";
   for(d=0; d<DISTRICTS; d++)
      {
      cout <<"\nDistrict " << d+1;
      for(m=0; m<MONTHS; m++)
         cout << setw(10) << setiosflags(ios::fixed)
              << setiosflags(ios::showpoint) << setprecision(2)
              << sales[d][m];  // access array element
      }
   }
```

Remember that a two-dimensional array is really an array of arrays. The format for initializing such an array is based on this fact. The initializing values for each subarray are enclosed in braces and separated by commas:

```
{ 1432.07, 234.50, 654.01 }
```

and then all four of these subarrays, each of which is an element in the main array, is likewise enclosed by braces and separated by commas, as can be seen in the listing.

PASSING ARRAYS TO FUNCTIONS

Arrays can be used as arguments to functions. Here's an example, a variation of the SALEINIT program, that passes the array of sales figures to a function whose purpose is to display the data as a table. Here's the listing for SALEFUNC:

```
// salefunc.cpp
// passes array as argument
#include <iostream.h>
#include <iomanip.h>              // for setprecision, etc.

const int DISTRICTS = 4;     // array dimensions
const int MONTHS = 3;

void display( float[DISTRICTS][MONTHS] );  // prototype

void main()
    {                           // initialize two-dimensional array
    float sales[DISTRICTS][MONTHS]
                = { {  1432.07,    234.50,    654.01 },
                    {   322.00, 13838.32, 17589.88 },
                    {  9328.34,    934.00,  4492.30 },
                    { 12838.29,  2332.63,    32.93 }  };

    display(sales);             // call function, array as argument
    }  // end main

// display()
// function to display 2-d array passed as argument
void display( float funsales[DISTRICTS][MONTHS] )
    {
    int d, m;

    cout << "\n\n";
    cout << "                        Month\n";
    cout << "          ,        1         2         3";

    for(d=0; d<DISTRICTS; d++)
        {
        cout <<"\nDistrict " << d+1;
        for(m=0; m<MONTHS; m++)
            cout << setiosflags(ios::fixed) << setw(10)
                 << setiosflags(ios::showpoint) << setprecision(2)
                 << funsales[d][m];   // array element
        }  // end for(d)
    }  // end display
```

Function Declaration with Array Argument

In a function declaration, array arguments are represented by the data type and sizes of the array. Here's the declaration of the `display()` function:

```
void display( float[DISPLAY][MONTHS] );  // declaration
```

Actually, there is one unnecessary piece of information here. The following statement works just as well:

```
void display( float[][MONTHS] );  // declaration
```

Why doesn't the function need the size of the first dimension? Again, remember that a two-dimensional array is an array of arrays. The function first thinks of the argument as an array of districts. It doesn't need to know how many districts there are, but it does need to know how big each district element is, so it can calculate where a particular element is (by multiplying the bytes per element times the index). So we must tell it the size of each element, which is MONTHS, but not how many there are, which is DISTRICTS.

It follows that if we were declaring a function that used a one-dimensional array as an argument, we would not need to use the array size:

```
void somefunc( int elem[] );  // declaration
```

Function Call with Array Argument

When the function is called, only the name of the array is used as an argument:

```
display(sales);  // function call
```

This name (`sales` in this case) actually represents the memory *address* of the array. We aren't going to explore addresses in detail until Chapter 12 on pointers, but here are a few preliminary points about them.

Using an address for an array argument is similar to using a reference argument, in that the values of the array elements are not duplicated (copied) into the function. (See the discussion of reference arguments in Chapter 6.) Instead, the function works with the original array, although it refers to it by a different name. This system is used for arrays because they can be very large; duplicating an entire array in every function that called it would be both time-consuming and wasteful of memory.

However, an address is not the same as a reference. No ampersand (&) is used with the array name in the function declaration. Until we discuss pointers, take it on faith that arrays are passed using their name alone, and that the function accesses the original array, not a duplicate.

Function Definition with Array Argument

In the function definition the declarator looks like this:

```
void display( float funsales[DISTRICTS][MONTHS] )  // declarator
```

The array argument uses the data type, a name, and the sizes of the dimensions. The array name used by the function (`funsales` in this example) can be different from the name that defines the array (**sales**), but they both refer to the same array. All the array dimensions (except, in some cases, the last one) must be specified; the function needs them to properly access the array elements.

References to array elements in the function use the function's name for the array:

```
funsales[d][m]
```

But in all other ways, the function can access array elements as if the array had been defined in the function.

ARRAYS OF STRUCTURES

Arrays can contain structures as well as simple data types. Here's an example based on the **part** structure from Chapter 5.

```
// partaray.cpp
// structure variables as array elements
#include <iostream.h>

st int SIZE = 4;                    // number of parts in array

struct part                         // specify a structure
   {
   int modelnumber;                 // ID number of widget
   int partnumber;                  // ID number of widget part
   float cost;                      // cost of part
   };

void main()
   {
   int n;
   part apart[SIZE];                // define array of structures

   for(n=0; n<SIZE; n++)            // get values for all members
      {
      cout << endl;
      cout << "Enter model number: ";
      cin >> apart[n].modelnumber;     // get model number
      cout << "Enter part number: ";
      cin >> apart[n].partnumber;      // get part number
      cout << "Enter cost: ";
      cin >> apart[n].cost;            // get cost
      }
   for(n=0; n<SIZE; n++)            // show values for all members
      {
      cout << "\nModel " << apart[n].modelnumber;
      cout << "  Part "  << apart[n].partnumber;
      cout << "  Cost "  << apart[n].cost;
      }
   }
```

The user types in the model number, part number, and cost of a part. The program records this data in a structure. However, this structure is only one element in an array of structures. The program asks for the data for four different parts, and stores it in the four elements of the **apart** array. It then displays the information. Here's some sample input:

```
Enter model number: 44
Enter part number: 4954
Enter cost: 133.45

Enter model number: 44
Enter part number: 8431
Enter cost: 97.59

Enter model number: 77
Enter part number: 9343
Enter cost: 109.99

Enter model number: 77
Enter part number: 4297
Enter cost: 3456.55

Model 44   Part 4954   Cost 133.45
Model 44   Part 8431   Cost 97.59
Model 77   Part 9343   Cost 109.99
Model 77   Part 4297   Cost 3456.55
```

The array of structures is defined in the statement

```
part apart[SIZE];
```

This has the same syntax as that of arrays of simple data types. Only the type name, **part**, shows that this is an array of a more complex type.

Accessing a data item that is a member of a structure that is itself an element of an array involves a new syntax. For example,

```
apart[n].modelnumber
```

refers to the **modelnumber** member of the structure that is element **n** of the **apart** array. Figure 8-5 shows how this looks.

Arrays of structures are a useful data type in a variety of situations. We've shown an array of parts, but we could also store an array of personnel data (name, age, salary), an array of geographical data about cities (name, population, elevation), and many other types of data.

ARRAYS AS CLASS MEMBER DATA

Arrays can be used as data items in classes. Let's look at an example that models a common computer data structure: the stack.

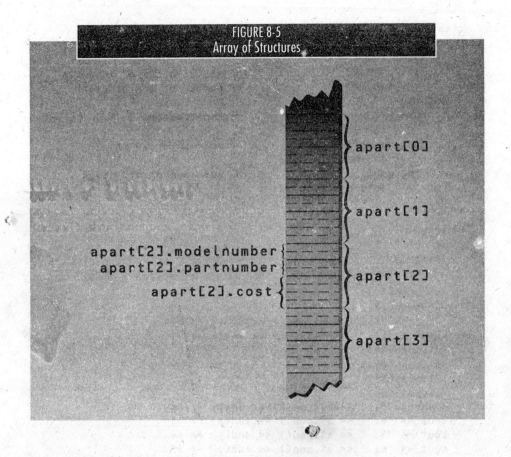

FIGURE 8-5
Array of Structures

A stack works like the spring-loaded devices that hold trays in cafeterias. When you put a tray on top, the stack sinks down a little; when you take a tray off, it pops up. The last tray placed on the stack is always the first tray removed.

Stacks are one of the cornerstones of the architecture of the 80x86 microprocessor used in MS-DOS computers. As we've mentioned earlier, functions pass their arguments and store their return address on the stack. This kind of stack is implemented partly in hardware and is most conveniently accessed in assembly language. However, stacks can also be created completely in software. Software stacks offer a useful storage device in certain programming situations, such as in parsing (analyzing) algebraic expressions.

Our example program, STAKARAY, creates a simple stack class:

```
// stakaray.cpp
// a stack as a class
#include <iostream.h>

const int MAX = 100;
```

```
class Stack
   {
   private:
      int st[MAX];              // stack: array of integers
      int top;                  // number of top of stack
   public:
      Stack()                   // constructor
         { top = 0; }
      void push(int var)        // put number on stack
         { st[++top] = var; }
      int pop()                 // take number off stack
         { return st[top--]; }
   };

void main()
   {
   Stack s1;

   s1.push(11);
   s1.push(22);
   cout << "1: " << s1.pop() << endl;   // 22
   cout << "2: " << s1.pop() << endl;   // 11
   s1.push(33);
   s1.push(44);
   s1.push(55);
   s1.push(66);
   cout << "3: " << s1.pop() << endl;   // 66
   cout << "4: " << s1.pop() << endl;   // 55
   cout << "5: " << s1.pop() << endl;   // 44
   cout << "6: " << s1.pop() << endl;   // 33
   }
```

The stack itself consists of the array st. An int variable, top, indicates the index of the last item placed on the stack; the location of this item is the top of the stack. Figure 8-6 shows the stack.

Since memory grows downward in the figure, the top of the stack is at the bottom in the figure. When an item is added to the stack, the address in top is incremented to point to the new top of the stack. When an item is removed, the value in top is decremented. (We don't need to erase the old value left in memory when an item is popped; it just becomes irrelevent.)

To place an item on the stack—a process called *pushing* the item—you call the push() member function with the value to be stored as an argument. To retrieve (or *pop*) an item from the stack, you use the pop() member function, which returns the value of the item.

The main() program in STAKARAY exercises the stack class by creating an object, s1, of the class. It pushes two items onto the stack, and pops them off and displays them. Then it pushes four more items onto the stack, and pops them off and displays them. Here's the output:

```
1: 22
2: 11
3: 66
4: 55
5: 44
6: 33
```

As you can see, items are popped off the stack in reverse order; the last thing pushed is the first thing popped.

Notice the subtle use of prefix and postfix notation in the increment and decrement operators. The statement

```
st[++top] = var;
```

in the **push()** member function first increments **top** so that it points to the next available array element—one past the last element. It then assigns **var** to this location, which becomes the new top of the stack. The statement

```
return st[top--];
```

first returns the value it finds at the top of the stack, and then decrements **top** so that it points to the preceding element.

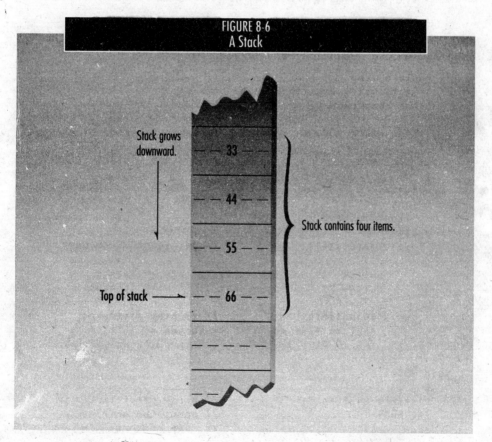

FIGURE 8-6
A Stack

Stack grows downward.

33

44

Stack contains four items.

55

Top of stack ⟶ 66

The **Stack** class is an example of an important feature of object-oriented programming: using a class to implement a certain kind of data-storage mechanism. In Chapter 16, when we discuss the Microsoft Foundation class library, we'll see that there are other class-based storage mechanisms, such as linked lists and maps. A data-storage scheme is chosen that matches the specific requirements of the program. Using a preexisting class to provide data-storage means that the programmer does not need to waste time duplicating the details of a data-storage mechanism.

ARRAYS OF OBJECTS

We've seen how an object can contain an array. We can also reverse that situation and create an array of objects. We'll look at two situations: an array of English distances and a deck of cards.

ARRAYS OF ENGLISH DISTANCES

In the last chapter, we showed several examples of an English **Distance** class that incorporated feet and inches into an object representing a new data type. The next program, ENGLARAY, demonstrates an array of such objects.

```
// englaray.cpp
// objects using English measurements
#include <iostream.h>

      st int MAX = 100;                 // maximum number of elements

   class Distance                       // English Distance class
      {
      private:
         int feet;
         float inches;
      public:
         void getdist()                 // get length from user
            {
            cout << "\n   Enter feet: ";  cin >> feet;
            cout << "   Enter inches: ";  cin >> inches;
            }
         void showdist()                // display distance
            { cout << feet << "\'-" << inches << '\"'; }
      };

   void main()
      {
      Distance dist[MAX];               // array of distances
      int n=0;                          // count the entries
      char ans;                         // user response ('y' or 'n')
```

```
    cout << endl;
    do                            // get distances from user
        {
        cout << "Enter distance number " << n+1;
        dist[n++].getdist();      // store distance in array
        cout << "Enter another (y/n)?: ";
        cin >> ans;
        }                         // quit if user types 'n'
    while( ans != 'n' );

    for(int j=0; j<n; j++)        // display all distances
        {
        cout << "\nDistance number " << j+1 << " is ";
        dist[j].showdist();
        }
    }
```

In this program the user types in as many distances as desired. After each distance is entered, the program asks if the user desires to enter another. If not, it terminates, and displays all the distances entered so far. Here's a sample interaction when the user enters three distances:

```
Enter distance number 1
   Enter feet: 5
   Enter inches: 4
Enter another (y/n)? y
Enter distance number 2
   Enter feet: 6
   Enter inches: 2.5
Enter another (y/n)? y
Enter distance number 3
   Enter feet: 5
   Enter inches: 10.75
Enter another (y/n)? n

Distance number 1 is 5'-4"
Distance number 2 is 6'-2.5"
Distance number 3 is 5'-10.75"
```

Of course, instead of simply displaying the distances already entered, the program could have averaged them, written them to disk, or operated on them in other ways. For simplicity we avoid these embellishments.

Array Bounds

This program uses a do loop to get input from the user. This way the user can input data for as many objects of class Distance as seems desirable, up to MAX, the size of the array (which is set to 100).

Although it's hard to imagine anyone having the patience, what would happen if the user entered more than 100 distances? The answer is, something unpredictable but almost certainly bad. There is no bounds-checking in C++ arrays. If the program inserts something beyond the end of the array, neither the compiler nor the run-time system will object. However, the renegade data will probably be written on top of other data or the program code itself. This may cause bizarre effects or crash the system completely.

The moral is that it is up to the programmer to deal with the array bounds-checking. If it seems possible that the user will insert too much data for an array to hold, then the array should be made larger, or some means of warning the user should be devised. For example, you could insert the following code at the beginning of the do loop in ENGLARAY:

```
if( n >= MAX )
    {
    cout << "\nThe array is full!!!";
    break;
    }
```

This causes a break out of the loop and prevents the array from overflowing.

Accessing Objects in an Array

The specification of the Distance class in this program is similar to that used in previous programs. However, in the main() program we define an array of such objects:

```
Distance dist[MAX];
```

Here the data type of the dist array is Distance, and it has MAX elements. Figure 8-7 shows what this looks like.

A class member function that is an array element is accessed similarly to a structure member that is an array element, as in the PARTARAY example. Here's how the showdist() member function of the jth element of the array dist is invoked:

```
dist[j].showdist();
```

As you can see, a member function of an object that is an array element is accessed using the dot operator: The array name followed by the index in brackets is joined, using the dot operator, to the member function name followed by parentheses. This is similar to accessing a structure (or class) data member, except that the function name and parentheses are used instead of the data name.

Notice that when we call the getdist() member function to put a distance into the array, we take the opportunity to increment the array index n:

```
dist[n++].getdist();
```

This way the next group of data obtained from the user will be placed in the structure in the next array element in dist. The n variable must be incremented manually like this because we use a do loop instead of a for loop. In the for loop, the loop variable—which is incremented automatically—can serve as the array index.

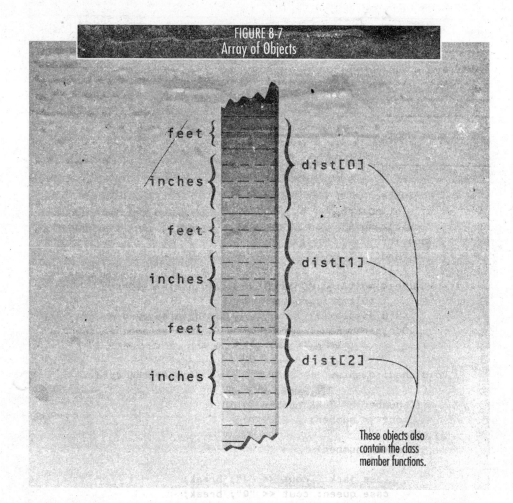

FIGURE 8-7
Array of Objects

feet { dist[0]

inches {

feet { dist[1]

inches {

feet { dist[2]

inches {

These objects also
contain the class
member functions.

ARRAYS OF CARDS

Here's another, somewhat longer, example of an array of objects. You will no doubt remember the CARDOBJ example from the last chapter. We'll borrow the card class from that example, and group an array of 52 such objects together in an array, thus creating a deck of cards. Here's the listing for CARDARAY.CPP:

```
// cardaray.cpp
// cards as objects
#include <iostream.h>
#include <stdlib.h>          // for srand(), rand()
#include <time.h>            // for time()
```

```
enum Suit { clubs, diamonds, hearts, spades };

const int jack = 11;          // from 2 to 10 are
const int queen = 12;         // integers without names
const int king = 13;
const int ace = 14;

enum Boolean { false, true };

class card
   {
   private:
      int number;             // 2 to 10, jack, queen, king, ace
      Suit suit;              // clubs, diamonds, hearts, spades
   public:
      card()                              // constructor
         { }
      void init(int n, Suit s)    // initialize card
         { suit = s; number = n; }
      void display();                 // display card
      Boolean isEqual(card);          // same as another card?
   };

void card::display()                // display the card
   {
   if( number >= 2 && number <= 10 )
      cout << number;
   else
      switch(number)
         {
         case jack:  cout << "J"; break;
         case queen: cout << "Q"; break;
         case king:  cout << "K"; break;
         case ace:   cout << "A"; break;
         }
   switch(suit)
      {
      case clubs:    cout << char(5); break;
      case diamonds: cout << char(4); break;
      case hearts:   cout << char(3); break;
      case spades:   cout << char(6); break;
      }
   }

void main()
   {
   card deck[52];
```

```
   cout << endl;
   for(int j=0; j<52; j++)
      {
      int num = (j % 13) + 2;    // cycles through 2 to 14, 4 times
      Suit su = Suit(j / 13);    // cycles through 0 to 3, 13 times
      deck[j].init(num, su);     // set card
      }

   cout << "\nOrdered deck:\n";
   for(j=0; j<52; j++)                // display ordered deck
      {
      deck[j].display();
      cout << "   ";
      if( !( (j+1) % 13) )           // newline every 13 cards
         cout << endl;
      }

   srand( unsigned(time(NULL)) );  // seed random number gen
                                   // with system time
   for(j=0; j<52; j++)             // for each card in the deck,
      {
      int k = rand() % 52;         // pick another card at random
      card temp = deck[j];         // and swap them
      deck[j] = deck[k];
      deck[k] = temp;
      }

   cout << "\nShuffled deck:\n";
   for(j=0; j<52; j++)                // display shuffled deck
      {
      deck[j].display();
      cout << "   ";
      if( !( (j+1) % 13) )           // newline every 13 cards
         cout << endl;
      }
   }  // end main
```

Once we've created a deck, it's hard to resist the temptation to shuffle it. We display the cards in the deck, shuffle it, and then display it again. To conserve space we use the IBM graphics characters for the club, diamond, heart, and spade. Figure 8-8 shows the output from the program. This program incorporates several new ideas, so let's look at them in turn.

IBM Graphics Characters

There are several special characters in the range below ASCII code 32. (See Appendix A for a list of ASCII codes.) In the display() member function of card we use

265

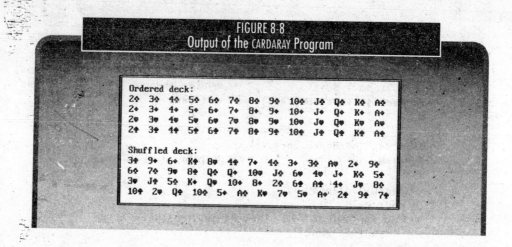

FIGURE 8-8
Output of the CARDARAY Program

codes 5, 4, 3, and 6 to create the characters for a club, a diamond, a heart, and a spade, respectively. Casting these numbers to type `char`, as in

    char(5)

causes the `<<` operator to print them as characters rather than as numbers.

The Card Deck

The array of structures that constitutes the deck of cards is defined in the statement

    card deck[52];

which creates an array called `deck`, consisting of 52 objects of type `card`. To display the jth card in the deck, we call the `display()` member function:

    deck[j].display();

Random Numbers

It's always fun and sometimes even useful to generate random numbers. In this program we use them to shuffle the deck. Two steps are necessary to obtain random numbers in Microsoft C/C++. First, the random-number generator must be *seeded* or initialized. To do this we call the `srand()` library function. This function uses the system time, obtained from the library function `time()`, as the seed. These require the header files STDLIB.H and TIME.H.

To actually generate a random number, we call the `rand()` library function, which returns a random number in the range 0 to 32.767. To obtain a number in the range 0 to 51, we use the expression

    rand() % 52

The resulting random number is then used as an index to swap two cards. We go through the `for` loop, swapping one card, whose index points to each card in

0-to-51 order, with another card, whose index is the random number. When all 52 cards have been exchanged with a random card, the deck is considered to be shuffled. This program could form the basis for a card-playing program, but we'll leave these details for the reader.

Arrays of objects are widely used in C++ programming. We'll see other examples as we go along.

STRINGS

Now that we have some familiarity with arrays, we can examine strings, which are a specialized way to use arrays of type char. As with other data types, strings can be variables or constants. We'll look at these two entities before going on to examine more complex string operations.

STRING VARIABLES

Here's an example that defines a single string variable. It asks the user to enter a string, and places this string in the string variable. Then it displays the string. Here's the listing for STRINGIN:

```
// stringin.cpp
// simple string variable
#include <iostream.h>
const int MAX = 80;                  // max characters in string

void main()
    {
    char str[MAX];                   // string variable str

    cout << "\nEnter a string: ";
    cin >> str;                      // put string in str
    cout << "You entered: " << str;  // display string from str
    }
```

The definition of the string variable str looks like (and is) the definition of any array of type char:

```
char str[MAX];
```

We use the insertion operator >> to read a string from the keyboard and place it in the string variable str. This operator knows how to deal with strings; it understands that they are arrays of characters. If the user enters the string "Amanuensis" (one employed to copy manuscripts) in this program, the array str will look something like Figure 8-9.

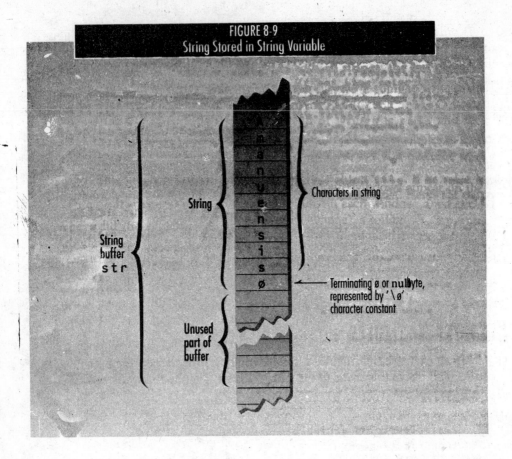

FIGURE 8-9
String Stored in String Variable

Each character occupies 1 byte of memory. An important aspect of strings in C++ is that they must terminate with a byte containing 0. This is often represented by the character constant '\0', which is a character with an ASCII value of 0. This terminating zero is called the *null* character. When the << operator displays the string, it displays characters until it encounters the null character.

AVOIDING BUFFER OVERFLOW

The STRINGIN program invites the user to type in a string. What happens if the user enters a string that is longer than the array used to hold it? As we mentioned earlier, there is no built-in mechanism in C++ to keep a program from inserting array elements outside an array. So an overly enthusiastic typist could end up crashing the system.

However, it is possible to tell the **>>** operator to limit the number of characters it places in an array. The SAFETYIN program demonstrates the approach:

```
// safetyin.cpp
// avoids buffer overflow with cin.width
#include <iostream.h>
#include <iomanip.h>                         // for setw
const int MAX = 20;                          // max characters in string

void main()
    {
    char str[MAX];                           // string variable str

    cout << "\nEnter a string: ";
    cin >> setw(MAX) >> str;                 // put string in str,
                                             // no more than MAX chars
    cout << "You entered: " << str;          // display string from str
    }
```

This program uses the **setw** manipulator to specify the maximum number of characters the input buffer can accept. The user may type more characters, but the **>>** operator won't insert them into the array. Actually, one character fewer than the number specified is inserted, so there is room in the buffer for the terminating null character. Thus in SAFETYIN, a maximum of 19 characters are inserted.

STRING CONSTANTS

You can initialize a string to a constant value when you define it. Here's an example, STRINIT, that does just that (with the first line of a Shakespearean sonnet):

```
// strinit.cpp
// initialized string
#include <iostream.h>

void main()
    {
    char str[] = "Farewell! thou art too dear for my possessing";

    cout << str;
    }
```

Here the string constant is written as a normal English phrase, delimited by quotes. This may seem surprising, since a string is an array of type **char**. In past examples you've seen arrays initialized to a series of values delimited by braces and separated by commas. Why isn't **str** intialized the same way? In fact you could use such a sequence of character constants:

```
char str[] = { 'F', 'a', 'r', 'w', 'e', 'l', 'l', ' ', 't', 'h',
```

and so on. Fortunately, the designers of C++ (and C) took pity on us and provided the shortcut approach shown in STRINIT. The effect is the same: The characters are placed one after the other in the array. As with all strings, the last character is a null (0).

READING EMBEDDED BLANKS

If you tried the STRINGIN program with strings that contained more than one word, you may have had an unpleasant surprise. Here's an example:

```
Enter a string: Law is a bottomless pit.
You entered: Law
```

Where did the rest of the phrase (a quotation from the Scottish writer John Arbuthnot, 1667–1735) go? It turns out that the insertion operator >> considers a space to be a terminating character. Thus it will read strings consisting of a single word, but anything typed after a space is thrown away.

To read text containing blanks we use another function, `cin::get()`. This syntax means a member function `get()` of the `cin` stream class. The following example, BLANKSIN, shows how it's used:

```
// blanksin.cpp
// reads string with embedded blanks
#include <iostream.h>
const int MAX = 80;                  // max characters in string

void main()
    {
    char str[MAX];                   // string variable str

    cout << "\nEnter a string: ";
    cin.get(str, MAX);               // put string in str
    cout << "You entered: " << str;  // display string from str
    }
```

The first argument to `cin::get()` is the array address where the string being input will be placed. The second argument specifies the maximum size of the array, thus automatically avoiding buffer overrun.

Using this function, the input string is now stored in its entirety:

```
Enter a string: Law is a bottomless pit.
You entered: Law is a bottomless pit.
```

READING MULTIPLE LINES

We may have solved the problem of reading strings with embedded blanks, but what about strings with multiple lines? It turns out that the `cin::get()` function can take a third argument to help out in this situation. This argument specifies the character that tells the function to stop reading. The default value for this argument is the newline ('\n') character, but if you call the function with some other character for this argument, the default will be overridden by the specified character.

In the next example, LINESIN, we call the function with a dollar sign ('$') as the third argument:

```
// linesin.cpp
// reads multiple lines, terminates on '$' character
#include <iostream.h>
const int MAX = 2000;                   // max characters in string

char str[MAX];                          // string variable str
                                        // (too large to be local)
void main()
    {
    cout << "\nEnter a string:\n";
    cin.get(str, MAX, '$');             // terminate with $
    cout << "You entered:\n" << str;    // display string from str
    }
```

Now you can type as many lines of input as you want. The function will continue to accept characters until you enter the terminating character (or until you exceed the size of the array). Remember, you must still press (ENTER) after typing the '$' character. Here's a sample interaction with a poem from Thomas Carew, 1595–1639:

```
Enter a string:
Ask me no more where Jove bestows
When June is past, the fading rose;
For in your beauty's orient deep
These flowers, as in their causes, sleep.
$
You entered:
Ask me no more where Jove bestows
When June is past, the fading rose;
For in your beauty's orient deep
These flowers, as in their causes, sleep.
```

We terminate each line with (ENTER), but the program continues to accept input until we enter '$'.

Copying a String the Hard Way

The best way to understand the true nature of strings is to deal with them character by character. The following program does this.

```
// strcopy1.cpp
// copies a string using a for loop
#include <iostream.h>
#include <string.h>              // for strlen()
const int MAX = 80;             // size of str2 buffer
void main()
```

```
{                                        // initialized string
char str1[] = "Oh, Captain, my Captain! "
             "our fearful trip is done";

char str2[MAX];                          // empty string

for(int j=0; j<strlen(str1); j++)        // copy strlen characters
   str2[j] = str1[j];                    //     from str1 to str2
str2[j] = '\0';                          // insert null character
cout << endl;
cout << str2;                            // display str2

}
```

This program creates a string constant, `str1`, and a string variable, `str2`. It then uses a `for` loop to copy the string constant to the string variable. The copying is done one character at a time, in the statement

```
str2[j] = str1[j];
```

This program also introduces string library functions. Because there are no string operators built into C++, strings must usually be manipulated using library functions. Fortunately, there are many such functions. The one we use in this program, `strlen()`, finds the length of a string (that is, how many characters are in it). We use this length as the limit in the `for` loop so that the right number of characters will be copied. When string functions are used, the header file STRING.H must be `#included` in the program.

The copied version of the string must be terminated with a null. However, the string length returned by `strlen()` does not include the null. We could copy one additional character, but it's safer to insert the null overtly. We do this with the line

```
str2[j] = '\0';
```

If you don't insert this character, you'll find that the string printed by the program includes all sorts of weird characters following the string you want. The `<<` just keeps on printing characters, whatever they are, until by chance it encounters a '\0'.

COPYING A STRING THE EASY WAY

Of course you don't need to use a `for` loop to copy a string. As you might have guessed, a library function will do it for you. Here's a revised version of the program, STRCOPY2, that uses the `strcpy()` function.

```
// strcopy2.cpp
// copies a string using strcpy() function
#include <iostream.h>
#include <string.h>        // for strcpy()
const int MAX = 80;        // size of str2 buffer
void main()
   {
```

```
static char str1[] = "Tiger, tiger, burning bright\n"
                     "In the forests of the night";

char str2[MAX];                       // empty string

strcpy(str2, str1);                   // copy str1 to str2
cout << endl;
cout << str2;                         // display str2

}
```

Note that you call this function like this:

```
strcpy(destination, source)
```

with the destination first. The right-to-left order is reminiscent of the format of normal assignment statements: The variable on the right is copied to the variable on the left.

ARRAYS OF STRINGS

If there are arrays of arrays, of course there can be arrays of strings. This is actually quite a useful construction. Here's an example, STRARAY, that puts the names of the days of the week in an array:

```
// straray.cpp
// array of strings
#include <iostream.h>
const int DAYS = 7;                // number of strings in array
const int MAX = 10;                // maximum size of each string

void main()
    {                              // array of strings
    char star[DAYS][MAX] = { "Sunday", "Monday", "Tuesday",
                             "Wednesday", "Thursday",
                             "Friday", "Saturday" };
    for(int j=0; j<DAYS; j++)    // display every string
        cout << star[j] << endl;
    }
```

The program prints out each string from the array:

```
Sunday
Monday
Tuesday
Wednesday
Thursday
Friday
Saturday
```

Since a string is an array, it must be that **star**—an array of strings—is really a two-dimensional array. The first dimension of this array, **DAYS**, tells how many strings are in the array. The second dimension, MAX, specifies the maximum length of the strings (9 characters for "Wednesday" plus the terminating null makes 10). Figure 8-10 shows how this looks.

Notice that some bytes are wasted following strings that are less than the maximum length. We'll learn how to remove this inefficiency when we talk about pointers.

The syntax for accessing a particular string may look surprising:

```
star[j];
```

If we're dealing with a two-dimensional array, where's the second index? Since a two-dimensional array is an array of arrays, we can access elements of the "outer" array, each of which is an array (in this case a string), individually. To do this we don't need the second index. So star[j] is string number j in the array of strings.

STRINGS AS CLASS MEMBERS

Strings frequently appear as members of classes. The next example, a variation of the OBJPART program of Chapter 7, uses a string to hold the name of the widget part.

```
// strpart.cpp
// string used in widget part object
#include <iostream.h>
#include <string.h>         // for strcpy()

class part
    {
    private:
        char partname[30];  // name of widget part
        int partnumber;     // ID number of widget part
        float cost;         // cost of part
    public:
        void setpart(char pname[], int pn, float c)
            {
            strcpy(partname, pname);
            partnumber = pn;
            cost = c;
            }
        void showpart()                          // display data
            {
            cout << "\nName=" << partname;
            cout << ", number=" << partnumber;
            cout << ", cost=$" << cost;
            }
    };

void main()
    {
    part part1, part2;
```

```
part1.setpart("handle bolt", 4473, 217.55);
part2.setpart("start lever", 9924, 419.25);
cout << "\nFirst part: "; part1.showpart();
cout << "\nSecond part: "; part2.showpart();
}
```

This program defines two objects of class part, and gives them values with the setpart() member function. Then it displays them with the showpart() member function. Here's the output:

```
First part:
Name=handle bolt, number=4473, cost=$217.55
Second part:
Name=start lever, number=9924, cost=$419.25
```

To reduce the size of the program, we've dropped the model number from the class members.

In the setpart() member function, we use the strcpy() string library function to copy the string from the argument pname to the class data member partname. Thus this function serves the same purpose with string variables that an assignment statement does with simple variables.

Besides those we've seen, there are library functions to add a string to another, to compare strings, to search for specific characters in strings, and to perform many other actions. Descriptions of these functions can be found in the Microsoft C/C++ documentation. (See the bibliography for other books that contain descriptions of library functions.)

FIGURE 8-10
Array of Strings

A User-Defined String Type

There are some problems with strings as normally used in C++. For one thing, you can't use the perfectly reasonable expression

```
strDest = strSrc;
```

to set one string equal to another. (In some languages, like BASIC, this is perfectly all right.) But if we define our own string type, using a C++ class, we can use just such assignment statements. (Many other string operations can be simplified as well, but we'll have to wait until we've learned about overloaded operators in the next chapter to see how this is done.)

The STROBJ program creates a class **String**. Here's the listing:

```
// strobj.cpp
// a string as a class
#include <iostream.h>
#include <string.h>         // for strcpy(), strcat()

const int SZ = 80;          // size of all Strings

class String
   {
   private:
      char str[SZ];
   public:
      String()                          // constructor, no args
         { str[0] = '\0'; }
      String( char s[] )                // constructor, one arg
         { strcpy(str, s); }
      void display()                    // display string
         { cout << str; }
      void concat(String s2)            // add arg string to
         {                              // this string
         if( strlen(str)+strlen(s2.str) < SZ )
            strcat(str, s2.str);
         else
            cout << "\nString too long";
         }
   };

void main()
   {
   String s1("Merry Christmas!  ");    // uses constructor 2
   String s2 = "Season's Greetings!";  // alternate form of 2
   String s3;                          // uses constructor 1

   cout << "\ns1="; s1.display();      // display them all
   cout << "\ns2="; s2.display();
   cout << "\ns3="; s3.display();
```

```
    s3 = s1;                               // assignment
    cout << "\ns3="; s3.display();         // display s3

    s3.concat(s2);                         // concatenation
    cout << "\ns3="; s3.display();         // display s3
    }
```

The `string` class contains a single data item: an array of type `char`. It may seem that our newly defined class is just the same as the original definition of a string: an array of type `char`. But, by making it a class, we have achieved some interesting benefits. Since an object can be assigned the value of another object of the same class, we can use statements like

```
    s3 = s1;
```

as we do in `main()`, to set one string equal to another. We can also define our own member functions to deal with Strings (objects of class `string`).

In the STROBJ program, all Strings have the same length: `SZ` characters (which we set to 80). There are two constructors. The first creates a string object and sets the first character to the null character, '\0', so the string has a length of 0. This constructor is called with statements like

```
    String s3;
```

The second constructor sets the String object to a "normal" (that is, not a String) string constant. It uses the `strcpy()` library function to copy the string constant into the object's data. It's called with statements like

```
    String s1("Merry Christmas! ");
```

An alternative format for calling this constructor, which works with any one-argument constructor, is

```
    String s1 = "Merry Christmas! ";
```

Whichever format is used, this constructor effectively converts a string to a String—that is, a normal string constant to an object of class `string`. A member function, `display()`, displays the String.

Another member function, `concat()`, concatenates (adds) one String to another. The original String is the object of which `concat()` is a member. To this String will be added the String passed as an argument. Thus the statement in `main()`,

```
    s3.concat(s2);
```

causes `s2` to be added to the existing `s3`. Since `s2` has been initialized to "Season's Greetings!" and `s3` has been assigned the value of `s1`, which was "Merry Christmas !" the resulting value of `s3` is "Merry Christmas! Season's Greetings!"

The `concat()` function uses the `strcat()` C++ library function to do the concatenation. This library function adds the string specified in the second argument to the string specified in the first argument. The output from the program is

```
    s1=Merry Christmas!
```

```
s2=Season's Greetings!
s3=                              ←——— nothing here yet
s3=Merry Christmas!             ←——— set equal to s1
s3=Merry Christmas! Season's Greetings!  ←——— s2 concatenated
```

If the two Strings given to the `concat()` function together exceed the maximum String length, then the concatenation is not carried out, and a message is sent to the user.

SUMMARY

Arrays contain a number of data items of the same type. This type can be a simple data type, a structure, or a class. The items in an array are called elements. Elements are accessed by number; this number is called an index. Elements can be initialized to specific values when the array is defined. Arrays can have multiple dimensions. A two-dimensional array is an array of arrays. The address of an array can be used as an argument to a function; the array itself is not copied. Arrays can be used as member data in classes. Care must be taken to prevent data from being placed in memory outside an array.

Strings are arrays of type `char`. The last character in a string must be the null character, '\0'. String constants take a special form so that they can be written conveniently. A variety of string library functions are used to manipulate strings. An array of strings is an array of arrays of type `char`. Strings are frequently used as class members.

QUESTIONS

1. An array element is accessed using
   a. a first-in–first-out approach
   b. the dot operator
   c. a member name
   d. an index number
2. All the elements in an array must be the _____ data type.
3. Write a statement that defines a one-dimensional array called `doubleArray` of type `double` that holds 100 elements.
4. The elements of a ten-element array are numbered from _____ to
5. Write a statement that takes element j of array `doubleArray` and writes it to `cout` with the insertion operator.

6. Element `doubleArray[7]` is which element of the array?
   a. the sixth
   b. the seventh
   c. the eighth
   d. impossible to tell

7. Write a statement that defines an array `coins` of type `int` and initializes it to the values of the penny, nickel, dime, quarter, half-dollar, and dollar.

8. When a multidimensional array is accessed, each array index is
   a. separated by commas
   b. surrounded by brackets and separated by commas
   c. separated by commas and surrounded by brackets
   d. surrounded by brackets

9. Write an expression that accesses element 4 in subarray 2 in a two-dimensional array called `twoD`.

10. True or false: In C++ there can be an array of four dimensions.

11. For a two-dimensional array of type `float`, called `flarr`, write a statement that declares the array and initializes the first subarray to 52, 27, 83; the second to 94, 73, 49; and the third to 3, 6, 1.

12. An array name, used in the source file, represents the _____ of the array.

13. When an array name is passed to a function, the function
    a. accesses exactly the same array as the calling program
    b. accesses a copy of the array passed by the program
    c. refers to the array using the same name as that used by the calling program
    d. refers to the array using a different name from that used by the calling program

14. Tell what this statement defines:

    `employee emplist[1000];`

15. Write an expression that accesses a structure member called `salary` in a structure variable that is the 17th element in an array called `emplist`.

16. In a stack, the data item placed on the stack first is
    a. not given an index number
    b. given the index number 0
    c. the first data item to be removed
    d. the last data item to be removed

17. Write a statement that defines an array called `manybirds` that holds 50 objects of type `bird`.

18. True or false: The compiler will complain if you try to access array element 14 in a ten-element array.

19. Write a statement that executes the member function `cheep()` in an object of class `bird` that is the 27th element in the array `manybirds`.

20. A string in C++ is an _____ of type _____.

21. Write a statement that defines a string variable called **city** that can hold a string of up to 20 characters (this is slightly tricky).

22. Write a statement that defines a string constant, called **dextrose**, that has the value "C6H12O6-H2O".

23. True or false: The **<<** insertion operator stops reading a string when it encounters a space.

24. You can read input that consists of multiple lines of text using
    a. the normal **cout <<** combination
    b. the **cin.get()** function with one argument
    c. the **cin.get()** function with two arguments
    d. the **cin.get()** function with three arguments

25. Write a statement that uses a string library function to copy the string **name** to the string **blank**.

26. Write the specification for a class called **dog** that contains two data members: a string called **breed** and an **int** called **age**. (Don't include any member functions.)

EXERCISES

1. Write a function called **reversit()** that reverses a string (an array of **char**). Use a **for** loop that swaps the first and last characters, then the second and next-to-last characters, and so on. The string should be passed to **reversit()** as an argument.

   Write a program to exercise **reversit()**. The program should get a string from the user, call **reversit()**, and print out the result. Use an input method that allows embedded blanks. Test the program with Napoleon's famous phrase, "Able was I ere I saw Elba."

2. Create a class called **employee** that contains a name (an array of **char**) and an employee number (type **long**). Include a member function called **getdata()** to get data from the user for insertion into the object, and another function called **putdata()** to display the data. Assume the name has no embedded blanks.

   Write a **main()** program to exercise this class. It should create an array of type **employee**, and then invite the user to input data for up to 100 employees. Finally, it should print out the data for all the employees. You may need to make the array of employees an external variable to avoid stack overflow.

3. Write a program that calculates the average of up to 100 English distances input by the user. Create an array of objects of the **Distance** class, as in the

ENGLARAY example in this chapter. To calculate the average, you can borrow the dist_add() member function from the ENGLCON example in Chapter 7. You'll also need a member function that divides a Distance value by an integer. Here's one possibility:

```
void Distance::div_dist(Distance d2, int divisor)
    {
    float fltfeet = d2.feet + d2.inches/12.0;
    fltfeet /= divisor;
    feet = int(fltfeet);
    inches = (fltfeet-feet) * 12.0;
    }
```

OPERATOR OVERLOADING

THE operator KEYWORD

OVERLOADING UNARY OPERATORS

OVERLOADING BINARY OPERATORS

CONSTRUCTORS AS CONVERSION ROUTINES

CONVERTING BETWEEN BASIC AND USER-DEFINED TYPES

THOUGHTS ON OVERLOADING

Operator overloading is one of the most exciting features of object-oriented programming. It can transform complex, obscure program listings into intuitively obvious ones. For example, a statement like

```
d3.addobjects(d1, d2);
```

can be changed to the much more readable

```
d3 = d1 + d2;
```

The rather forbidding term *operator overloading* refers to giving the normal C++ operators, such as +, *, <=, and +=, additional meanings when they are applied to user-defined data types. Normally

```
a = b + c;
```

works only with basic types like `int` and `float`, and attempting to apply it when `a`, `b`, and `c` are objects of a user-defined class will cause complaints from the compiler. However, using overloading, you can make this statement legal even when `a`, `b`, and `c` are user-defined types.

In effect, operator overloading gives you the opportunity to redefine the C++ language. If you find yourself limited by the way the C++ operators work, you can change them to do whatever you want. By using classes to create new kinds of variables, and operator overloading to create new definitions for operators, you can extend C++ to be, in many ways, a new languge of your own design.

Another kind of operation, *data type conversion*, is closely connected with operator overloading. C++ handles the conversion of simple types, like `int` and `float`, automatically; but conversions involving user-defined types require some work on the programmer's part. We'll look at data conversions in the second part of this chapter.

Overloaded operators are not all beer and skittles. We'll discuss some of the dangers in their use at the end of the chapter.

Overloading Unary Operators

Let's start off by overloading a *unary operator*. As you may recall from Chapter 2, unary operators act on only one operand. (An operand is simply a variable acted on by an operator). Examples of unary operators are the increment and decrement operators ++ and --, and the unary minus, as in -33.

In the COUNTER example in Chapter 7, we created a class `Counter` to keep track of a count. Objects of that class were incremented by calling a member function:

```
c1.inc_count();
```

That did the job, but the listing would have been more readable if we could have used the increment operator ++ instead:

```
++c1;
```

All dyed-in-the-wool C++ (and C) programmers would guess immediately that this expression increments `c1`.

Let's rewrite COUNTER to make this possible. Here's the listing for COUNTPP1:

```
// countpp1.cpp
// increment counter variable with ++ operator
#include <iostream.h>

class Counter
    {
    private:
        unsigned int count;                         // count
    public:
        Counter()          { count = 0; }           // constructor
        int get_count()    { return count; }        // return count
        void operator ++ () { ++count; }            // increment (prefix)
    };

void main()
    {
    Counter c1, c2;                                 // define and initialize

    cout << "\nc1=" << c1.get_count();  // display
    cout << "\nc2=" << c2.get_count();

    ++c1;                                           // increment c1
    ++c2;                                           // increment c2
    ++c2;                                           // increment c2

    cout << "\nc1=" << c1.get_count();  // display again
    cout << "\nc2=" << c2.get_count();
    }
```

In this program we create two objects of class `Counter`: c1 and c2. The counts in the objects are displayed; they are initially 0. Then, using the overloaded ++

operator, we increment c1 once and c2 twice, and display the resulting values. Here's the program's output:

```
c1=0        ←————————counts are initially 0
c2=0
c1=1        ←———————— incremented once
c2=2        ←———————— incremented twice
```

The statements responsible for these operations are

```
++c1;
++c2;
++c2;
```

The ++ operator is applied once to c1 and twice to c2. We use only the prefix form of ++ in this example. We'll see later how to use the postfix form.

THE operator KEYWORD

How do we teach a normal C++ operator to act on a user-defined operand? The keyword operator is used to overload the ++ operator in this declarator:

```
void operator ++ ()
```

The return type (void in this case) comes first, followed by the keyword operator, followed by the operator itself (++), and finally the argument list enclosed in parentheses (which are empty here). This declarator syntax tells the compiler to call this member function whenever the ++ operator is encountered, provided the operand (the variable operated on by the ++) is of type Counter.

We've already seen in Chapter 6 that the only way the compiler can distinguish between overloaded functions is by looking at the data type of their arguments. In the same way, the only way it can distinguish between overloaded operators is by looking at the data type of their operands. If the operand is a basic type like an int, as in

```
++intvar;
```

then the compiler will use its built-in routine to increment an int. But if the operand is a Counter variable, then the compiler will know to use our user-written operator++() instead.

OPERATOR ARGUMENTS

In main() the ++ operator is applied to a specific object, as in the expression ++c1;, yet operator++() takes no arguments. What does this operator increment? It increments the count data in the object of which it is a member function. Since member functions can always access the particular object for which they've been called, this operator requires no arguments. This is shown in Figure 9-1.

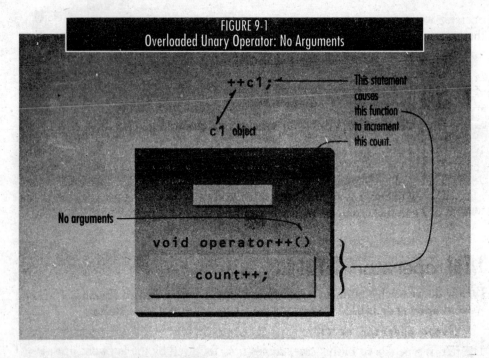

FIGURE 9-1
Overloaded Unary Operator: No Arguments

OPERATOR RETURN VALUES

The `operator++()` function in the COUNTPP1.CPP program has a subtle defect. You will discover it if you use a statement like this in `main()`:

```
c1 = ++c2;
```

The compiler will complain. Why? Because we have defined the `++` operator to have a return type of `void` in the `operator++()` function, while in the assignment statement it is being asked to return a variable of type `Counter`. That is, the compiler is being asked to return whatever value `c2` has after being operated on by the `++` operator, and assign this value to `c1`. So, as defined in COUNTPP1, we can't use `++` to increment `Counter` objects in expressions; it must always stand alone with its operand. (Of course the normal `++` operator, applied to basic data types like `int`, would not have this problem.)

To make it possible to use our homemade `operator++()` in expressions, we must provide a way for it to return a value. The next program, COUNTPP2, does just that.

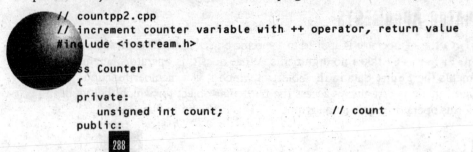

```
// countpp2.cpp
// increment counter variable with ++ operator, return value
#include <iostream.h>

class Counter
    {
private:
    unsigned int count;                          // count
public:
```

```
        Counter()           { count = 0; }    // constructor
        int get_count()   { return count; } // return count
        Counter operator ++ ()                 // increment count
        {
        ++count;             // increment count
        Counter temp;        // make a temporary Counter
        temp.count = count;  // give it same value as this obj
        return temp;         // return the copy
        }
    };

void main()
    {
    Counter c1, c2;                          // c1=0, c2=0

    cout << "\nc1=" << c1.get_count();       // display
    cout << "\nc2=" << c2.get_count();

    ++c1;                                    // c1=1
    c2 = ++c1;                               // c1=2, c2=2

    cout << "\nc1=" << c1.get_count();       // display again
    cout << "\nc2=" << c2.get_count();
    }
```

In this program the `operator++()` function creates a new object of type
`Counter`, called `temp`, to use as a return value. It increments the `count` data in its
own object as before, then creates the new `temp` object and assigns `count` in the
new object the same value as in its own object. Finally, it returns the `temp` object.
This has the desired effect: Expressions like

```
++c1
```

now return a value, so they can be used in other expressions, such as:

```
c2 = ++c1;
```

as shown in COUNTPP2. In this statement the value returned from `++c1` will be assigned to `c2`.

NAMELESS TEMPORARY OBJECTS

In COUNTPP2 we created a temporary object of type `Counter`, named `temp`, whose
sole purpose was to provide a return value for the `++` operator. This required three
statements:

```
    Counter temp;        // make a temporary Counter object
    temp.count = count;  // give it same value as this object
    return temp;         // return it
```

There are more convenient ways to return objects from functions and overloaded
operators. Let's examine another approach, as shown in the program COUNTPP3:

```
// countpp3.cpp
// increment counter variable with ++ operator
// uses unnamed temporary object
#include <iostream.h>

class Counter
    {
    private:
        unsigned int count;                    // count
    public:
        Counter()        { count = 0; }       // constructor  no args
        Counter(int c)   { count = c; }       // constructor, one arg
        int get_count()  { return count; }    // return count
        Counter operator ++ ()                // increment count
            {
            ++count;                  // increment count, then return
            return Counter(count);    // an unnamed temporary object
            }                         // initialized to this count
    };

void main()
    {
    Counter c1, c2;                            // c1=0, c2=0

    cout << "\nc1=" << c1.get_count();        // display
    cout << "\nc2=" << c2.get_count();

    ++c1;            // c1=1
    c2 = ++c1;             // c1=2, c2=2

    cout << "\nc1=" << c1.get_count();        // display again
    cout << "\nc2=" << c2.get_count();
    }
```

In this program a single statement,

```
return Counter(count);
```

does what all three statements did in COUNTPP2. This statement creates an object of type `Counter`. This object has no name; it won't be around long enough to need one. This unnamed object is initialized to the value provided by the argument `count`.

But wait: Doesn't this require a constructor that takes one argument? It does, and to make this statement work, we sneakily inserted just such a constructor into the member function list in COUNTPP3:

```
Counter(int c)  { count = c; }  // constructor, one arg
```

Once the unnamed object is initialized to the value of `count`, it can then be returned.

The approaches in both COUNTPP2 and COUNTPP3 involved making a copy of the original object (the object of which the function is a member), and returning the copy. Another approach is to return the value of the original object, using the `this` pointer, as we'll see in Chapter 11.

POSTFIX NOTATION

In the three examples we've seen so far that involve the increment operator, we have always used prefix notation, such as ++c1. Can we also use statements like c1++ in postfix notation? Yes, we can, but we need to add another member function to the Counter class, as shown in COUNTPP4.CPP:

```
// countpp4.cpp
// increment counter variable with ++ operator
// use prefix and postfix notation
#include <iostream.h>

class Counter
    {
    private:
        unsigned int count;               // count
    public:
        Counter()         { count = 0; }  // constructor  no args
        Counter(int c)    { count = c; }  // constructor, one arg
        int get_count()   { return count; } // return count
        Counter operator ++ ()            // prefix (++c1)
            { return Counter(++count); }
        Counter operator ++ (int)         // postfix (c1++)
            { return Counter(count++); }
    };

void main()
    {
    Counter c1, c2;                       // c1=0, c2=0

    cout << "\nc1=" << c1.get_count();    // display
    cout << "\nc2=" << c2.get_count();

    ++c1;                                 // prefix: c1=1
    c1++;                                 // postfix: c1=2
    c2 = c1++;                            // postfix: c1=3, c2=2

    cout << "\nc1=" << c1.get_count();    // display again
    cout << "\nc2=" << c2.get_count();
    }
```

We took the liberty of condensing the prefix version of the same operator ++() member function that we saw in the last example; it operates as it did before. The member function for postfix function is similar, except that, by convention, the declarator indicates that it takes a single argument of type int:

```
Counter operator ++ (int)
```

This int is not really an argument, but a signal to the compiler that we want to use postfix notation. Also, we increment the count variable after returning the value, rather than before. Now we can use either prefix or postfix notation with the ++ operator applied to Counter objects. In the line

```
c2 = c1++;
```

the variable c1 is incremented after value of c1 is assigned to c2. This results in the following output from COUNTPP4:

```
c1=0
c2=0
c1=3
c2=2
```

OVERLOADING BINARY OPERATORS

Binary operators can be overloaded just as easily as unary operators. We'll look at examples that overload arithmetic operators, comparison operators, and arithmetic assignment operators.

ARITHMETIC OPERATORS

In the ENGLCON program in Chapter 7, we showed how two English Distance objects could be added using a member function add_dist():

```
dist3.add_dist(dist1, dist2);
```

By overloading the + operator, we can reduce this dense-looking expression to

```
dist3 = dist1 + dist2;
```

Here's the listing for ENGLPLUS, which does just this:

```
// englplus.cpp
// overloaded '+' operator adds two Distances
#include <iostream.h>

class Distance                      // English Distance class
    {
    private:
        int feet;
        float inches;
    public:
        Distance()                  // constructor (no args)
            { feet = 0; inches = 0.0; }
        Distance(int ft, float in)  // constructor (two args)
            { feet = ft; inches = in; }

        void getdist()              // get length from user
            {
            cout << "\nEnter feet: ";  cin >> feet;
            cout << "Enter inches: ";  cin >> inches;
            }

        void showdist()             // display distance
            { cout << feet << "\'-" << inches << '\"'; }

        Distance operator + ( Distance );  // add two distances
    };
```

```
                                        // add this distance to d2
Distance Distance::operator + (Distance d2)   // return the sum
   {
   int f = feet + d2.feet;        // add the feet
   float i = inches + d2.inches;  // add the inches
   if(i >= 12.0)                  // if total exceeds 12.0,
      {                           // then decrease inches
      i -= 12.0;                  // by 12.0 and
      f++;                        // increase feet by 1
      }                           // return a temporary Distance
   return Distance(f,i);          // initialized to sum
   }

void main()
   {
   Distance dist1, dist3, dist4;   // define distances
   dist1.getdist();                // get dist1 from user

   Distance dist2(11, 6.25);       // define, initialize dist2

   dist3 = dist1 + dist2;          // single '+' operator

   dist4 = dist1 + dist2 + dist3;  // multiple '+' operators

                                   // display all lengths
   cout << "\ndist1 = ";  dist1.showdist();
   cout << "\ndist2 = ";  dist2.showdist();
   cout << "\ndist3 = ";  dist3.showdist();
   cout << "\ndist4 = ";  dist4.showdist();
   }
```

To show that the result of an addition can be used in another addition as well as in an assignment, another addition is performed in main(). We add dist1, dist2, and dist3 to obtain dist4 (which should be double the value of dist3), in the statement

```
dist4 = dist1 + dist2 + dist3;
```

Here's the output from the program:

```
Enter feet: 10
Enter inches: 6.5

dist1 = 10'-6.5"       ←──────── from user
dist2 = 11'-6.25"      ←──────── initialized in program
dist3 = 22'-0.75"      ←──────── dist1+dist2
dist4 = 44'-1.5"       ←──────── dist1+dist2+dist3
```

In class Distance the declaration for the operator+() function looks like this:

```
Distance operator + ( Distance );
```

This function has a return type of Distance, and takes one argument of type Distance.

In expressions like

```
dist3 = dist1 + dist2;
```

it's important to understand how the return value and arguments of the operator relate to the objects. When the compiler sees this expression, it looks at the argument types, and finding only type **Distance**, it realizes it must use the **Distance** member function **operator+()**. But what does this function use as its argument—**dist1**, or **dist2**? And doesn't it need two arguments, since there are two numbers to be added?

Here's the key: The argument on the *left side* of the operator (**dist1** in this case) is the object of which the operator is a member function. The object on the *right* side of the operator (**dist2**) must be furnished as an argument to the operator. The operator returns a value, which can be assigned or used in other ways; in this case it is assigned to **dist3**. Figure 9-2 shows how this looks.

In the **operator+()** function, the left operand is accessed directly—since this is the object of which the function is a member—using **feet** and **inches**. The right operand is accessed as function's argument, as **d2.feet** and **d2.inches**.

We can generalize and say that an overloaded operator always requires one less argument than its number of operands, since one operand is the object of which the operator is a member function. That's why unary operators require no arguments. (This rule does not apply to **friend** functions and operators, a C++ feature we'll discuss in Chapter 13.)

FIGURE 9-2
Overloaded Binary Operator: One Argument

```
dist3 = dist1 + dist2;        This statement
                              causes
                              this object to be added to
                              this object
    dist1 object              with this function.


Distance operator + (Distance d2)

    int f = feet + d2.feet;
    float i + inches + d2.inches;
    if (i >= 12.0)
        {i -= 12.0; f++;}
    return Distance (f,i);
```

To calculate the return value of **operator+()** in ENGLPLUS, we first add the feet and inches from the two operands (adjusting for a carry if necessary). The resulting values, **f** and **i**, are then used to initialize a nameless **Distance** object, which is returned in the statement

```
return Distance(f, i);
```

This is similar to the construction used in COUNTPP3, except that the constructor takes two arguments instead of one. The statement

```
dist3 = dist1 + dist2;
```

in **main()** then assigns the value of the nameless **Distance** object to **dist3**. Compare this intuitively obvious statement with the use of a function call to perform the same task, as in the ENGLCON example in Chapter 7.

Similar functions could be created to overload other operators in the **Distance** class, so you could subtract, multiply, and divide objects of this class in natural-looking ways.

ADDING POLAR COORDINATES

Here's another example of operator overloading. Points on a plane are commonly specified with a pair of rectangular coordinates (x, y). Thus a point (4, 3) is located where x is 4 and y is 3, as shown in Figure 9-3.

There's another way to describe a point on the plane: using polar coordinates of the form (radius, angle). In this system a line called the **radius**, drawn from the origin to the point, and the angle this line makes with the positive X axis, specify the point, as shown in Figure 9-4.

FIGURE 9-3
A Point in Rectangular Coordinates

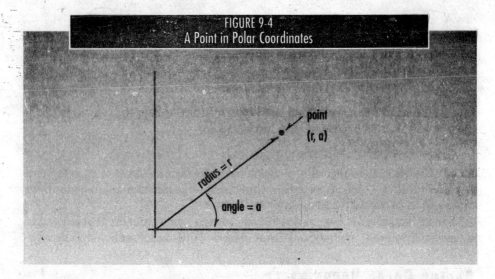

FIGURE 9-4
A Point in Polar Coordinates

Polar coordinates are handy for describing certain curves, such as spirals. They are commonly found on scientific calculators; pushing buttons performs conversions between polar and rectangular coordinates.

Our example program will show a class, **Polar**, that models polar coordinates. We'll use the overloaded + operator to add two objects of type **Polar**.

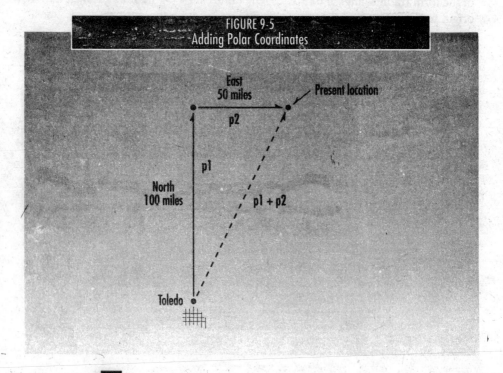

FIGURE 9-5
Adding Polar Coordinates

What does it mean to add two points on the two-dimensional plane? If the points are considered to be the end points of directed lines, they can show a distance and direction traveled, say by an airplane. If you fly north from Toledo 100 miles, and then fly east 50 miles, how far from Toledo are you, and in which direction? Adding two variables of type Polar solves this kind of problem, as shown in Figure 9-5. ·

Adding points expressed in polar coordinates requires several steps. It turns out it's easier to add points when they are expressed in rectangular coordinates. This is done by adding the X and Y coordinates separately. Say you have two points expressed in rectangular coordinates—(4,1) and (2,3)—as shown in Figure 9-6-a. To add the points, we first add their X coordinates: 4+2=6. Then we add their Y coordinates: 1+3=4. The resulting point is (6, 4), as shown in Figure 9-6-b.

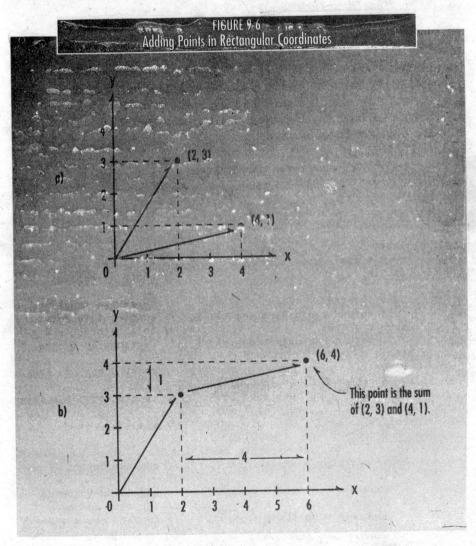

FIGURE 9-6
Adding Points in Rectangular Coordinates

Adding points in polar coordinates requires a three-step approach. First we convert the points to rectangular coordinates, then we add the points as described above, and finally we convert the result back into polar coordinates.

How do we convert between polar and rectangular coordinates? These conversions involve several trigonometric formulas. It doesn't matter if you've forgotten your trig; you need only plug values into the formulas to make them work.

To convert from polar to rectangular, use these formulas (expressed in C++ form):

```
x = radius * cos(angle);
y = radius * sin(angle);
```

The `cos()` and `sin()` (cosine and sine) functions are available as library functions (see the *Run-Time Library Reference*).

To convert back from rectangular to polar, use the formulas

```
angle = atan(x/y);
radius = sqrt(x*x + y*y);
```

The functions `atan()` (for *arctangent*) and `sqrt()` (for *square root*) are also library functions. The Pythagorean theorem is used to find the radius, and the arctangent of the X and Y sides of the triangle is the angle, as shown in Figure 9-7.

The POLAPLUS program makes use of this three-step approach to add two points in polar coordinates. Here's the listing:

```
// polaplus.cpp
// operator '+' with polar coordinates
#include <iostream.h>
#include <math.h>                    // for sin(), cos(), etc.

class Polar
    {
    private:
        double radius;                       // distance
        double angle;                        // angle in radians

        double getx()                        // these two functions
            { return radius*cos(angle); }    // convert this Polar
        double gety()                        // object into x and y
            { return radius*sin(angle); }    // rectangular coords
    public:
        Polar()                              // constructor, no args
            { radius=0.0; angle=0.0; }
        Polar(double r, double a)            // constructor, two args
            { radius=r; angle=a; }
        void display()                       // display
            { cout << "(" << radius
                << ", " << angle << ")"; }
        Polar operator + (Polar p2)          // add two Polars
            {
            double x = getx() + p2.getx();   // add x and y coords
            double y = gety() + p2.gety();   // for this and p2
            double r = sqrt(x*x + y*y);      // convert new x and y
            double a = atan(y/x);            // to Polar
```

```
        return Polar(r, a);            // return temp Polar
        }
    };
void main()
    {
    Polar p1(10.0, 0.0);               // line to the right
    Polar p2(10.0, 1.570796325);       // line straight up
    Polar p3;                          // uninitialized Polar

    p3 = p1 + p2;                      // add two Polars

    cout << "\np1="; p1.display();     // display all Polars
    cout << "\np2="; p2.display();
    cout << "\np3="; p3.display();
    }
```

The `Polar` class contains two data items: `radius` and `angle`. Since we'll be using math library functions to operate on this data, and since these functions mostly use type `double`, we'll define `radius` and `angle` to be of this type. Angles are measured in radians. (There are 2*pi, or about 6.28, radians in a circle, so a radian is about 57 degrees.)

Constructors in `Polar` initialize a variable to 0, or initialize it to specified values. Another member function displays these values.

Two other member functions, `getx()` and `gety()`, convert polar coordinates to rectangular coordinates. These functions are needed because, as we noted, adding two points in polar coordinates involves converting to rectangular coordinates before adding. The `getx()` and `gety()` functions are made private because they don't need to be accessed from outside the class; they're only used internally.

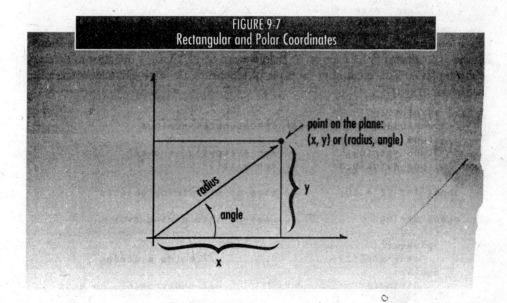

FIGURE 9-7
Rectangular and Polar Coordinates

The operator+() function adds two Polar variables. It does this by converting the Polar operands to rectangular coordinates, and adding the X coordinates to obtain x and the Y coordinates to obtain y. The x and y variables are then used to find the radius and angle of the sum, which is returned.

In the main() part of POLAPLUS, one Polar variable is initialized to (10.0, 0.0). This represents a point located 10 units horizontally along the X axis. Another variable is initialized to (10.0, 1.570796325). Since these angles are measured in radians, this represents a point 10 units straight up on the Y axis. (1.570796325 radians is 90 degrees.)

These two variables are then added, in the statement

```
p3 = p1 + p2;
```

The result should be a point at 45 degrees (half of 90), as shown in Figure 9-8. Here's the actual output:

```
p1=(10, 0)               ←————— point on X axis (0 degrees)
p2=(10, 1.5708)          ←————— point on Y axis (90 degrees)
p3=(14.1421, 0.785398)   ←————— point at 45 degree angle
```

The point (14.142136, 0.785398) is indeed at 45 degrees.

This example has shown how to overload only one operator: +. We could also overload the other arithmetic operators for the Polar type, so such coordinates could be subtracted, multiplied, divided, and so on.

CONCATENATING STRINGS

In C++ the + operator cannot normally be used to concatenate strings, as it can in some languages such as BASIC. That is, you can't say

```
str3 = str1 + str2;
```

where str1, str2, and str3 are string variables (arrays of type char), as in "cat" plus "bird" equals "catbird". However, if we use our own String class, as shown in the STROBJ program of Chapter 7, then we can overload the + operator to do such concatenation. This is another example of redefining the C++ language. Here's the listing for STRPLUS:

```
// strplus.cpp
// overloaded '+' operator concatenates strings
#include <iostream.h>
#include <string.h>        // for strcpy(), strcat()
#include <stdlib.h>        // for exit()

const int SZ = 80;         // size of all String objects

class String              // user-defined string type
   {
   private:
      char str[SZ];                    // holds a string
   public:
      String()                         // constructor, no args
```

```
        { strcpy(str, ""); }
    String( char s[] )                  // constructor, one arg
        { strcpy(str, s); }
    void display()                      // display the String
        { cout << str; }
    String operator + (String ss)       // add a String to another
        {
        String temp;                    // make a temporary String
        if( strlen(str) + strlen(ss.str) < SZ )
            {
            strcpy(temp.str, str);      // copy this string to temp
            strcat(temp.str, ss.str);   // add the argument string
            }
        else
            { cout << "\nString overflow"; exit(1); }
        return temp;                    // return temp String
        }
    };

void main()
    {
    String s1 = "\nMerry Christmas!  ";  // uses constructor 2
    String s2 = "Happy new year!";       // uses constructor 2
    String s3;                           // uses constructor 1

    s1.display();            // display strings
    s2.display();
    s3.display();

    s3 = s1 + s2;            // add s2 to s1, assign to s3

    s3.display();            // display s3
    }
```

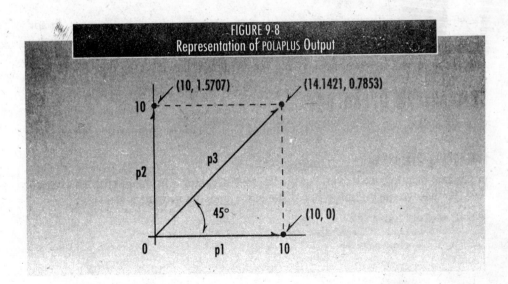

FIGURE 9-8
Representation of POLAPLUS Output

The program first displays three strings separately. (The third is empty at this point, so nothing prints when it displays itself.) Then the first two strings are concatenated and placed in the third, and the third string is displayed again. The output is:

```
Merry Christmas!  Happy new year!      ←————— s1, s2, and s3 (empty)
Merry Christmas!  Happy new year!      ←————— s3 after concatenation
```

By now the basics of overloading the + operator should be somewhat familiar. The declarator

```
String operator + (String ss)
```

shows that the + operator takes one argument of type **String** and returns an object of the same type. The concatenation process in **operator+()** involves creating a temporary object of type **String**, copying the string from our own **String** object into it, concatenating the argument string using the library function **strcat()**, and returning the resulting temporary string. Note that we can't use the

```
return String(string);
```

approach, where a nameless temporary **String** is created, because we need access to the temporary **String** not only to initialize it but to concatenate the argument string to it.

We must be careful that we don't overflow the fixed-length strings used in the **String** class. To prevent such accidents in the **operator+()** function, we check that the combined length of the two strings to be concatenated will not exceed the maximum string length. If they do, we print an error message instead of carrying out the concatenation operation. (We could handle errors in other ways, like returning a 0 if an error occurred.)

MULTIPLE OVERLOADING

We've seen three different uses of the + operator: to add English distances, to add polar coordinates, and to concatenate strings. You could put all these classes together in the same program, and C++ would still know how to interpret the + operator: It selects the correct function to carry out the "addition" based on the type of operand.

COMPARISON OPERATORS

Let's see how to overload a different kind of C++ operator: comparison operators.

Comparing Distances

In our first example we'll overload the *less than* operator < in the English **Distance** class, so that we can compare two distances. Here's the listing for ENGLESS:

```
// engless.cpp
// overloaded '<' operator compares two Distances
#include <iostream.h>

enum boolean { false, true };
```

```
class Distance                          // English Distance class
   {
   private:
      int feet;
      float inches;
   public:
      Distance()                        // constructor (no args)
         { feet = 0; inches = 0.0; }
      Distance(int ft, float in)  // constructor (two args)
         { feet = ft; inches = in; }
      void getdist()                    // get length from user
         {
         cout << "\nEnter feet: ";  cin >> feet;
         cout << "Enter inches: ";  cin >> inches;
         }
      void showdist()                   // display distance
         { cout << feet << "\'-" << inches << '\"'; }
      boolean operator < (Distance);  // compare distances
   };
                                       // compare this distance with d2
boolean Distance::operator < (Distance d2)   // return true or false
   {
   float bf1 = feet + inches/12;
   float bf2 = d2.feet + d2.inches/12;
   return (bf1 < bf2) ? true : false;
   }

void main()
   {
   Distance dist1;                    // define Distance dist1
   dist1.getdist();                   // get dist1 from user

   Distance dist2(6, 2.5);            // define and initialize dist2
                                      // display distances
   cout << "\ndist1 = ";  dist1.showdist();
   cout << "\ndist2 = ";  dist2.showdist();

   if( dist1 < dist2 )                // overloaded '<' operator
      cout << "\ndist1 is less than dist2";
   else
      cout << "\ndist1 is greater than dist2";
   }
```

This program compares a distance entered by the user with a distance, 6'-2.5", initialized by the program. Depending on the result, it then prints one of two possible sentences. Here's some typical output:

```
Enter feet: 5
Enter inches: 11.5
dist1 = 5'-11.5"
dist2 = 6'-2.5"
dist1 is less than dist2
```

The approach used in the operator<() function in ENGLESS is similar to overloading the + operator in the ENGLPLUS program, except that here the operator<()

function has a return type of **boolean** (defined in the **enum** statement at the beginning of the program). The return value is **false** or **true**, depending on the comparison of the two distances. The comparison is made by converting both distances to floating-point feet, and comparing them using the normal **<** operator. Remember that the statement

```
return (bf1 < bf2) ? true : false;
```

is the same as

```
if(bf1 < bf2)
    return true;
else
    return false;
```

Comparing Strings

Here's another example of overloading a comparison operator, this time the *equals* (==) operator. We'll use it to compare two strings, returning **true** if the strings are the same and **false** if they're different. Here's the listing for STREQUAL:

```
// strequal.cpp
// overloaded '==' operator compares strings
#include <iostream.h>
#include <string.h>        // for strcmp()

const int SZ = 80;         // size of all String objects
enum boolean { false, true };

class String                // user-defined string type
    {
    private:
        char str[SZ];                      // holds a string
    public:
        String()                           // constructor, no args
            { strcpy(str, ""); }
        String( char s[] )                 // constructor, one arg
            { strcpy(str, s); }
        void display()                     // display a String
            { cout << str; }
        void getstr()                      // read a string
            { cin.get(str, SZ); }
        boolean operator == (String ss)    // check for equality
            {
            return ( strcmp(str, ss.str)==0 ) ? true : false;
            }
    };

void main()
    {
    String s1 = "yes";
    String s2 = "no";
    String s3;
```

```
   cout << "\nEnter 'yes' or 'no': ";
   s3.getstr();                              // get String from user

   if(s3==s1)                                // compare with "yes"
      cout << "You typed yes\n";
   else if(s3==s2)                           // compare with "no"
      cout << "You typed no\n";
   else
      cout << "You didn't follow instructions\n";
   }
```

The `main()` part of this program uses the `==` operator twice, once to see if a string input by the user is "yes" and once to see if it's "no". Here's the output when the user types "yes":

```
Enter 'yes or 'no': yes
You typed yes
```

The `operator==()` function uses the library function `strcmp()` to compare the two strings. This function returns 0 if the strings are equal, a negative number if the first is less than the second, and a positive number if the first is greater than the second. Here *less than* and *greater than* are used in their lexicographical sense to indicate whether the first string appears before or after the second in an alphabetized listing.

Other comparison operators, such as `<` and `>`, could also be used to compare the lexicographical value of strings. Or, alternatively, these comparison operators could be redefined to compare string lengths. Since you're the one defining how the operators are used, you can use any definition that seems appropriate to your situation.

ARITHMETIC ASSIGNMENT OPERATORS

Let's finish up our exploration of overloaded binary operators with an arithmetic assignment operator: the `+=` operator. Recall that this operator combines assignment and addition into one step. We'll use this operator to add one English distance to a second, leaving the result in the first. This is similar to the ENGLPLUS example shown earlier, but there is a subtle difference. Here's the listing for ENGLPLEQ:

```
// englpleq.cpp
// overloaded '+=' assignment operator
#include <iostream.h>

ss Distance                                  // English Distance class
   {
   private:
      int feet;
      float inches;
   public:
      Distance()                             // constructor (no args)
         { feet = 0; inches = 0.0; }
```

```
        Distance(int ft, float in)    // constructor (two args)
          { feet = ft; inches = in; }
        void getdist()                 // get length from user
          {
          cout << "\nEnter feet: ";  cin >> feet;
          cout << "Enter inches: ";  cin >> inches;
          }
        void showdist()                // display distance
          { cout << feet << "\'-" << inches << '\"'; }
        void operator += ( Distance );
      };
                                       // add distance to this one
void Distance::operator += (Distance d2)
      {
      feet += d2.feet;                 // add the feet
      inches += d2.inches;             // add the inches
      if(inches >= 12.0)               // if total exceeds 12.0,
        {                              // then decrease inches
        inches -= 12.0;                // by 12.0 and
        feet++;                        // increase feet
        }                              // by 1
      }

void main()
      {
      Distance dist1;                  // define dist1
      dist1.getdist();                 // get dist1 from user
      cout << "\ndist1 = ";  dist1.showdist();

      Distance dist2(11, 6.25);        // define, initialize dist2
      cout << "\ndist2 = ";  dist2.showdist();

      dist1 += dist2;                  // dist1 = dist1 + dist2
      cout << "\nAfter addition,";
      cout << "\ndist1 = ";  dist1.showdist();
      }
```

In this program we obtain a distance from the user, and add to it a second distance, initialized to 11'-6.25" by the program. Here's a sample of interaction with the program:

```
Enter feet: 3
Enter inches: 5.75
dist1 = 3'-5.75"
dist2 = 11'-6.25"
After addition,
dist1 = 15'-0"
```

In this program the addition is carried out in main() with the statement

```
dist1 += dist2;
```

This causes the sum of dist1 and dist2 to be placed in dist1.

Notice the difference between the function used here, `operator+=()`, and that used in ENGLPLUS, `operator+()`. In the earlier `operator+()` function, a new object of type `Distance` had to be created and returned by the function, so it could be assigned to a third `Distance` object, as in

```
dist3 = dist1 + dist2;
```

In the `operator+=()` function in ENGLPLEQ, the object that takes on the value of the sum is the object of which the function is a member. Thus it is `feet` and `inches` that are given values, not temporary variables used only to return an object. The `operator+=()` function has no return value; it returns type `void`. A return value is not usually needed with arithmetic assignment operators like `+=`, because the result of the assignment operator is not assigned to anything. The operator is used alone, in expressions like the one in the program:

```
dist1 += dist2;
```

If you wanted to use this operator in more complex expressions, like

```
dist3 = dist1 += dist2;
```

then you would need to provide a return value. This can be done by ending the `operator+=()` function with a statement like

```
return Distance(feet, inches);
```

in which a nameless object is initialized to the same values as this object, and returned.

DATA CONVERSION

We've discussed how several kinds of operators can be overloaded, but we haven't looked at the assignment operator =. This is a rather special operator, with complex properties.

You already know that the = operator will assign a value from one variable to another, in statements like

```
intvar1 = intvar2;
```

where `intvar1` and `intvar2` are integer variables. You may also have noticed that = assigns the value of one user-defined object to another, provided they are of the same type, in statements like

```
dist3 = dist1 + dist2;
```

where the result of the addition, which is type `Distance`, is assigned to another object of type `Distance`, `dist3`. Normally, when the value of one object is assigned to another of the same type, the values of all the member data items are simply copied into the new object. The compiler doesn't need any special instructions to use = for the assignment of user-defined objects such as `Distance` objects.

Thus assignments between types, whether they are basic types or user-defined types, are handled by the compiler with no effort on our part, provided that the same data type is used on both sides of the equals sign. But what happens when the variables on different sides of the = are of different types? This is a more thorny question, one which we will devote the balance of this chapter to exploring. We'll first review how the compiler handles the conversion of basic types, which it does automatically. Then we'll explore several situations where the compiler doesn't handle things automatically and we need to tell it what to do. These include conversions between basic types and user-defined types, and conversions between different user-defined types.

You might think it represents poor programming practice to routinely convert from one type to another. After all, languages such as Pascal go to considerable trouble to keep you from doing such conversions. However, the philosophy in C++ (and in C) is that the flexibility provided by allowing conversions outweighs the dangers of making mistakes by allowing type mixing.

CONVERSIONS BETWEEN BASIC TYPES

When we write a statement like

```
intvar = floatvar;
```

where `intvar` is of type `int` and `floatvar` is of type `float`, we are assuming that the compiler will call a special routine to convert the value of `floatvar`, which is expressed in floating-point format, to an integer format so that it can be assigned to `intvar`. There are of course many such conversions: from `float` to `double`, `char` to `float`, and so on. Each such conversion has its own routine, built into the compiler and called up when the data types on different sides of the = sign so dictate. We say such conversions are *implicit*, because they aren't apparent in the listing.

Sometimes we want to force the compiler to convert one type to another. To do this we use the cast operator. For instance, to convert `float` to `int` we could say

```
intvar = int(floatvar);
```

Casting provides *explicit* conversion: It's obvious in the listing that the `int()` conversion function will convert from `float` to `int`. However, such explicit conversions use the same built-in routines as implicit conversions.

CONVERSIONS BETWEEN OBJECTS AND BASIC TYPES

When we want to convert between user-defined data types and basic types, we can't rely on built-in conversion routines, since the compiler doesn't know anything about user-defined types besides what we tell it. Instead, we must write these routines ourselves.

Our next example shows how to convert between a basic type and a user-defined type. In this example the user-defined type is (surprise!) the English `Distance` class from previous examples, and the basic type is `float`, which we use to represent meters, a unit of length in the metric measurement system.

The example shows conversion both from Distance to float, and from float to Distance. Here's the listing for ENGLCONV:

```
// englconv.cpp
// conversions: Distance to meters, meters to Distance
#include <iostream.h>

const float MTF = 3.280833;              // meters to feet

class Distance                           // English Distance class
   {
   private:
      int feet;
      float inches;
   public:
      Distance()                         // constructor (no args)
         { feet = 0; inches = 0.0; }
      Distance( float meters )           // constructor (one arg)
         {                               // convert meters to Distance
         float fltfeet = MTF * meters;   // convert to float feet
         feet = int(fltfeet);            // feet is integer part
         inches = 12*(fltfeet-feet);     // inches is what's left
         }
      Distance(int ft, float in)         // constructor (two args)
         { feet = ft; inches = in; }
      void getdist()                     // get length from user
         {
         cout << "\nEnter feet: ";  cin >> feet;
         cout << "Enter inches: ";  cin >> inches;
         }
      void showdist()                    // display distance
         { cout << feet << "\'-" << inches << '\"'; }

      operator float()                   // conversion function
         {                               // converts Distance to meters
         float fracfeet = inches/12;     // convert the inches
         fracfeet += float(feet);        // add the feet
         return fracfeet/MTF;            // convert to meters
         }
   };

void main()
   {
   Distance dist1 = 2.35;                // uses 1-arg constructor to
                                         // convert meters to Distance
   cout << "\ndist1 = "; dist1.showdist();

   dist1 = 1.00;                         // this form also uses
                                         // 1-arg constructor
   cout << "\ndist1 = ";  dist1.showdist();
```

```
Distance dist2(5, 10.25);      // uses 2-arg constructor

float mtrs = float(dist2);     // uses conversion function to
                               // convert Distance to meters
cout << "\ndist2 = " << mtrs << " meters";

mtrs = dist1;                  // this form also uses
                               // conversion function
cout << "\ndist1 = " << mtrs << " meters";
}
```

In main() the program first converts a fixed float quantity—2.35, representing meters—to feet and inches, using the one-argument constructor:

```
Distance dist1 = 2.35;
```

It converts a second quantity in meters to feet and inches in the statement

```
dist1 = 1.00;
```

Going in the other direction, it converts a Distance to meters in the statements

```
float mtrs =float(dist2);
```

and

```
mtrs = dist1;
```

Here's the output:

```
dist1 = 7'-8.519485"        ←——————this is 2.35 meters
dist1 = 3'-3.369996"        ←——————this is 1.0 meters
dist2 = 1.784354 meters     ←——————this is 5'-10.25"
dist1 = 1 meters            ←——————this is 3'-3.369996"
```

We've seen how conversions are performed using simple assignment statements in main(). Now let's see what goes on behind the scenes, in the Distance member functions.

Converting a user-defined type to a basic type requires a different approach than converting a basic type to a user-defined type. We'll see how both types of conversions are carried out in ENGLCONV.

From Basic to User-Defined

To go from a basic type—float in this case—to a user-defined type such as Distance, we use a constructor with one argument. Here's how it looks in ENGLCONV:

```
Distance(float meters)
  {
  float fltfeet = MTF * meters;
  feet = int(fltfeet);
  inches = 12 * (fltfeet-feet);
  }
```

This function is called when an object of type `Distance` is created with a single argument. The function assumes this argument represents meters. It converts the argument to feet and inches, and assigns the resulting values to the object. Thus the conversion from meters to `Distance` is carried out along with the creation of an object, in the statement

```
Distance dist1 = 2.35;
```

But there is another way to perform the same conversion. In the program, after defining dist1 and displaying its value, we then say

```
dist1 = 1.0;
```

What is the compiler to make of this? We're converting `float` to `Distance`, but we're not creating a new object. Surprisingly, the one-argument constructor will be called in this situation as well. Confronted with a statement that calls for a particular conversion, the compiler looks for any tool that might do the job. In this case it finds a constructor that converts `float` to `Distance`, so it applies it to the assignment situation, creating an unnamed temporary object with feet-and-inches values corresponding to 1.0 meters. It assigns this object to `dist1`, and voilà, `dist1` has been assigned the correct values, converted from meters.

Thus the compiler blurs the distinction between definition and assignment. If no overloaded = operator is available, it will look for a constructor to do the same job.

From User-Defined to Basic

What about going the other way, from a user-defined type to a basic type? The trick here is to overload the cast operator, creating something called a *conversion function.* Here's where we do that in ENGLCONV:

```
operator float()
   {
   float fracfeet = inches/12;
   fracfeet += float(feet);
   return fracfeet/MTF;
   }
```

This operator takes the value of the `Distance` object of which it is a member, converts this value to a `float` value representing meters, and returns this value.

This operator can be called like this:

```
mtrs = float(dist2);
```

This converts the `Distance` object `dist2` to its equivalent `float` value in meters.

Again the compiler uses the same conversion in assignment statements. You can say

```
mtrs = dist2;
```

This has exactly the same effect. When the compiler finds that you want to convert a user-defined type to a basic type, it looks for the appropriate conversion function.

Here the compiler starts by looking for an overloaded = operator. But when it doesn't find one, it doesn't give up. It finds the conversion function and uses that instead.

Conversion between Strings and String Objects

Here's another example that uses a one-argument constructor and a conversion function. It operates on the String class that we saw in such examples as STRPLUS earlier in this chapter.

```
// strconv.cpp
// convert between ordinary strings and class String
#include <iostream.h>
#include <string.h>        // for strcpy(), etc.

const int SZ = 80;         // size of all String objects

class String               // user-defined string type
   {
   private:
      char str[SZ];              // holds a string
   public:
      String()                   // constructor 0, no args
         { str[0] = '\0'; }

      String( char s[] )         // constructor 1, one arg
         { strcpy(str, s); }     // convert string to String

      void display()             // display the String
         { cout << str; }

      operator char*()           // conversion function
         { return str; }         // convert String to string
   };

void main()
   {
   String s1;                      // use constructor 0
   char xstr[] =                   // create and initialize string
            "\nJoyeux Noel! ";
   s1 = xstr;                      // use constructor 1
                                   // to convert string to String
   s1.display();                   // display String

   String s2 = "Bonne Annee!";     // uses constructor 1
                                   // to initialize String

   cout << s2;                     // use conversion function
                                   // to convert String to string
                                   // before sending to << op
   }
```

The one-argument constructor converts a normal string (an array of `char`) to an object of class `String`:

```
String(char s[])
   { strcpy(str, s); }
```

The string `s` is passed as an argument, and copied into the `str` data member in a newly created `String` object.

This conversion will be applied when a string is created, as in

```
String s2 = "Bonne Annee!";
```

or it will be applied in assignment statements, as in

```
s1 = xstr;
```

where `s1` is type `String` and `xstr` is a normal string.

A conversion function is used to convert from a `String` type to a normal string:

```
operator char*()
   { return str; }
```

The use of the asterisk in this expression means *pointer to*. We won't explore pointers until Chapter 12, but its use here is not hard to figure out. It means *pointer to* `char`, which is very similar to *array of type* `char`. Thus `char*` is similar to `char[]`. It's another way of specifying a string data type.

The conversion function is used by the compiler in the statement

```
cout << s2;
```

Here the `s2` variable is an argument supplied to the overloaded operator `<<`. Since the `<<` operator doesn't know anything about our user-defined `String` type, the compiler looks for a way to convert `s2` to a type that `<<` does know about. It finds our conversion function and uses it to generate a normal string, which is then sent on to `<<` to be displayed. (The effect is similar to calling the `String::display()` function, but given the ease and intuitive clarity of displaying with `<<`, the `display()` function is redundant and could be removed.)

Here's the output from STRCONV:

```
Joyeux Noel! Bonne Annee!
```

The STRCONV example demonstrates that conversions take place automatically not only in assignment statements but in other appropriate places, such as in arguments sent to operators (like `<<`) or functions. If you supply an operator or a function with arguments of the wrong type, they will be converted to arguments of an acceptable type, provided you have defined such a conversion.

CONVERSIONS BETWEEN OBJECTS OF DIFFERENT CLASSES

What about converting between objects of different user-defined classes? The same two methods just shown for conversion between basic types and user-defined types also apply to conversions between two user-defined types. That is, you can use a one-argument constructor, or you can use a conversion function. The choice depends on whether you want to put the conversion routine in the class specifier of the source object or of the destination object. For example, suppose you say

```
objecta = objectb;
```

where `objecta` is a member of class `A` and `objectb` is a member of class `B`. Is the conversion routine located in `A` (the destination class, since `objecta` receives the value) or `B` (the source class)? We'll look at both cases.

Routine in Source Object

The next example program shows a conversion routine located in the source class. When the conversion routine is in the source class, it is commonly implemented as a conversion function.

The two classes used in the next program are `Rec` and `Polar`. We've already seen an example of the `Polar` class, in the POLAPLUS program earlier in this chapter. The `Rec` class is similar in that its objects are points in a two-dimensional plane. However, it uses a rectangular coordinate system, where the location of each point is specified by X and Y coordinates. Its member functions are similar to those for `Polar` but are adapted to rectangular coordinates. Here's the listing for POLAREC1.CPP:

```
// polarec1.cpp
// converts from Polar to Rec using routines in Polar (source)
#include <iostream.h>
#include <math.h>                  // for sin(), cos(), etc.

class Rec
   {
   private:
      double xco;                  // x coordinate
      double yco;                  // y coordinate
   public:
      Rec()                        // constructor 0, no args
         { xco = 0.0; yco = 0.0; }
      Rec(double x, double y)      // constructor 2, two args
         { xco = x; yco = y; }
      void display()               // display
         { cout << "("  << xco
                << ", " << yco << ")"; }
   };

class Polar
   {
   private:
      double radius;
      double angle;
   public:
      Polar()                      // constructor 0, no args
```

```
                { radius=0.0; angle=0.0; }
            Polar(double r, double a)       // constructor 2, two args
                { radius=r; angle=a; }
            void display()                  // display
                { cout << "(" << radius
                       << ", " << angle << ")"; }
            operator Rec()                  // conversion function
                {                           // Polar to Rect
                double x = radius * cos(angle);  // find x and y to
                double y = radius * sin(angle);  // initialize nameless
                return Rec(x, y);                // Rec for return
                }
        };

    void main()
        {
        Rec rec;                         // Rec using constructor 0
        Polar pol(10.0, 0.785398);       // Polar using constructor 2

        rec = pol;                       // convert Polar to Rec
                                         // using conversion function
                                         // (or use  rec = Rec(pol);

        cout << "\npol="; pol.display(); // display original Polar
        cout << "\nrec="; rec.display(); // display equivalent Rect
        }
```

In the `main()` part of POLAREC1 we define an object of type `Rec`, called `rec`, which is not initialized. We also define an object of type `Polar`, called `pol`, which is initialized to a radius of 10.0 and an angle of 0.785398 radians (45 degrees).

Now we want to be able to assign the value of the `pol` object to `rec`, with the statement

```
rec = pol;
```

Since these objects are from different classes, the assignment involves a conversion, and—as we specified—in this program the conversion function is a member of the `Polar` class:

```
operator Rec()
    {
    double x = radius * cos(angle);
    double y = radius * sin(angle);
    return Rec(x, y);
    }
```

This function transforms the object of which it is a member to a `Rec` object, and returns this object, which `main()` then assigns to `rec`. Here's the output from POLAREC1:

```
pol=(10, 0.785398)
rec=(7.071069, 7.071067)
```

Routine In Destination Object

Let's see how the same conversion is carried out when the conversion routine is in the destination class. In this situation it's common to use a one-argument constructor. However, things are complicated by the fact that the constructor in the destination class must be able to access the data in the source class to perform the conversion. The data in `Polar`—the radius and angle—is private, so we must provide special functions to allow direct access to it.

Here's the listing for POLAREC2.CPP:

```
// polarec2.cpp
// converts Polar to Rec using routine in Rec (destination)
#include <iostream.h>
#include <math.h>                         // for sin(), cos(), etc.

class Polar                               // point, polar coordinates
   {
   private:
      double radius;                      // radius coord
      double angle;                       // angle coord (radians)
   public:
      Polar()                             // constructor, no args
         { radius=0.0; angle=0.0; }
      Polar(double r, double a)           // constructor, two args
         { radius=r; angle=a; }
      void display()                      // display
         { cout << "("  << radius
                << ", " << angle << ")"; }
      double getr()                       // these routines allow
         { return radius; }               // radius and angle to be
      double geta()                       // accessed from outside
         { return angle; }                // the class
   };

class Rec                                 // point, rectangular coords
   {
   private:
      double xco;                         // x coordinate
      double yco;                         // y coordinate
   public:
      Rec()                               // constructor 0, no args
         { xco = 0.0; yco = 0.0; }
      Rec(double x, double y)             // constructor 2, two args
         { xco = x; yco = y; }
      Rec(Polar p)                        // constructor 1, one arg
         {                                //     Polar to Rec
         double r = p.getr();
         double a = p.geta();             // get r and a from Polar
         xco = r * cos(a);                // using getr() and geta()
         yco = r * sin(a);                // change to our xco and yco
         }
```

```
    void display()                    // display
       { cout << "(" << xco
              << ", " << yco << ")"; }
};

void main()
   {
   Rec rec;                           // Rec using constructor 1
   Polar pol(10.0, 0.785398);         // Polar using constructor 2

   rec = pol;                         // convert Polar to Rec

   cout << "\npol="; pol.display();   // display original Polar
   cout << "\nrec="; rec.display();   // display converted Rec
   }
```

Here's the conversion routine, a one-argument constructor, from the Rec class:

```
Rec(Polar p)
   {
   double r = p.getr();
   double a = p.geta();
   xco = r * cos(a);
   yco = r * sin(a);
   }
```

This function sets the object of which it is a member to the rectangular coordinates that correspond to the polar coordinates of the object received as an argument.

To perform the conversion, this constructor must be able to access the data values of the Polar object sent as an argument. The Polar class contains the following two routines to allow this:

```
double getr()
   { return radius; }
double geta()
   { return angle; }
```

The main() part of POLAREC2 is the same as that in POLAREC1. The one-argument constructor again allows the Polar to Rec conversion to take place in the statement

```
rec = pol;
```

CONVERSIONS: WHEN TO USE WHAT

When should you use the one-argument constructor in the destination class, as opposed to the conversion function in the source class? Sometimes the choice is made for you. If you have purchased a library of classes, you may not have access to their source code. If you use an object of such a class as the source in a conversion, then you'll have access only to the destination class, and you'll need to use a one-argument constructor. Or, if the library class object is the destination, then you must use a conversion function in the source.

PITFALLS OF OPERATOR OVERLOADING AND CONVERSION

Operator overloading and type conversions give you the opportunity to create what amounts to an entirely new language. When `a`, `b`, and `c` are objects from user-defined classes, and + is overloaded, the statement

```
a = b + c;
```

means something quite different than it does when `a`, `b`, and `c` are variables of basic data types. The ability to redefine the building blocks of the language can be a blessing in that it can make your listing more intuitive and readable. It can also have the opposite effect, making it more obscure and hard to understand. Here are some guidelines.

USE SIMILAR MEANINGS

Use overloaded operators to perform operations that are as similar as possible to those performed on basic data types. You could overload the + sign to perform subtraction, for example, but that would hardly make your listings more comprehensible.

Overloading an operator assumes that it makes sense to perform a particular operation on objects of a certain class. If we're going to overload the + operator in class X, then the result of adding two objects of class X should have a meaning at least somewhat similar to addition. For example, in this chapter we showed how to overload the + operator for the English `Distance` class. Adding two distances is clearly meaningful. We also overloaded + for the `String` class. Here we interpret the addition of two strings to mean placing one string after another to form a third. This also has an intuitively satisfying interpretation. But for many classes it may not be reasonable to talk about "adding" their objects. You probably wouldn't want to add two objects of a class called `employee` that held personal data, for example.

USE SIMILAR SYNTAX

Use overloaded operators in the same way they are used for basic types. For example, if `alpha` and `beta` are basic types, the assignment operator in the statement

```
alpha += beta;
```

sets `alpha` to the sum of `alpha` and `beta`. Any overloaded version of this operator should do something analogous. It should probably do the same thing as

```
alpha = alpha + beta;
```

where the + is overloaded.

Some syntactical characteristics of operators can't be changed even if you want to. As you may have discovered, you can't overload a binary operator to be a unary operator, or vice versa.

SHOW RESTRAINT

Remember that if you have overloaded the + operator, anyone unfamiliar with your listing will need to do considerable research to find out what a statement like

```
a = b + c;
```

really means. If the number of overloaded operators grows too large, and if they are used in nonintuitive ways, then the whole point of using them is lost, and the listing becomes less readable instead of more. Use overloaded operators sparingly, and only when the usage is obvious. When in doubt, use a function instead of an overloaded operator, since a function name can state its own purpose. If you write a function to find the left side of a string, for example, you're better off calling it getleft() than trying to overload some operator like && to do the same thing.

AVOID AMBIGUITY

Suppose you use both a one-argument constructor and a conversion function to perform the same conversion (Polar to Rec, for example). How will the compiler know which conversion to use? The answer is that it won't. The compiler does not like to be placed in a situation where it doesn't know what to do, and it will signal an error. So avoid doing the same conversion in more than one way.

NOT ALL OPERATORS CAN BE OVERLOADED

The following operators cannot be overloaded: the member access or dot operator (.), the scope resolution operator (::), and the conditional operator (?:). Also, the pointer-to-member operator (.*), which we have not yet encountered, cannot be overloaded.

SUMMARY

In this chapter we've seen how the normal C++ operators can be given new meanings when applied to user-defined data types. The keyword operator is used to overload an operator, and the resulting operator will adopt the meaning supplied by the programmer.

Closely related to operator overloading is the issue of type conversion. Some conversions take place between user-defined types and basic types. Two approaches are used in such conversions: A one-argument constructor changes a basic type to a user-

TABLE 9.1 Type Conversions		
	Routine in Destination	Routine in Source
Basic to basic		(Built-in conversion functions)
Basic to class	Constructor	NA
Class to basic	NA	Conversion function
Class to class	Constructor	

defined type, and a conversion operator converts a user-defined type to a basic type. When one user-defined type is converted to another, either approach can be used.

Table 9.1 summarizes these conversions.

QUESTIONS

1. Operator overloading is
   a. making C++ operators work with objects
   b. giving C++ operators more than they can handle
   c. giving new meanings to existing C++ operators
   d. making new C++ operators

2. Assuming that class X does not use any overloaded operators, write a statement that subtracts an object of class X, x1, from another such object, x2, and places the result in x3.

3. Assuming that class X includes a routine to overload the – operator, write a statement that would perform the same task as that specified in Question 2.

4. True or false: The >= operator can be overloaded.

5. Write a complete definition for an overloaded operator for the Counter class of the COUNTPP1 example that, instead of incrementing the count, decrements it.

6. How many arguments are required in the definition of an overloaded unary operator?

7. Assume a class C with objects obj1, obj2, and obj3. For the statement obj3 = obj1 – obj2 to work correctly, the overloaded – operator must
   a. take two arguments
   b. return a value
   c. create a named temporary object
   d. use the object of which it is a member as an operand

8. Write a complete definition for an overloaded ++ operator for the Distance class from the ENGLPLUS example. It should add 1 to the feet member data, and make possible statements like:

```
dist1++;
```

9. Repeat Question 7, except statements like the following should be allowed:

```
dist2 = dist1++;
```

10. When used in prefix form, what does the overloaded ++ operator do differently from what it does in postfix form?

11. Here are two declarators that describe ways to add two String objects:

```
void add(String s1, String s2)
String operator + (String s)
```

Match the following from the first declarator with the appropriate selection from the second:

function name (add) matches _____

return value (type void) matches _____

first argument (s1) matches _____

second argument (s2) matches _____

object of which function is a member matches _____.

a. argument (s)
b. object of which operator is a member
c. operator (+)
d. return value (type String)
e. no match for this item

12. When an object of type Polar is added to itself, the result is a radius _____ as long at the _____ angle.

13. When you overload an arithmetic assignment operator, the result
a. goes in the object to the right of the operator
b. goes in the object to the left of the operator
c. goes in the object of which the operator is a member
d. must be returned

14. Write the complete definition of an overloaded ++ operator that works with the String class from the STRPLUS example and has the effect of changing its operand to uppercase. You can use the the library function toupper() (header file CTYPE.H), which takes as its only argument the character to be changed, and returns the changed character (or the same character if no change is necessary).

15. To convert from a user-defined class to a basic type, you would most likely use
a. a built-in conversion function
b. a one-argument constructor
c. an overloaded = operator
d. a conversion function that's a member of the class

16. True or false: The statement objA=objB; will cause a compiler error if the objects are of different classes.

17. To convert from a basic type to a user-defined class, you would most likely use
    a. a built-in conversion function
    b. a one-argument constructor
    c. an overloaded = operator
    d. a conversion function that's a member of the class

18. True or false: If you've defined a constructor to handle definitions like `aclass obj = intvar;` you can also make statements like `obj = intvar;`.

19. If `objA` is in class A, and `objb` is in class B, and you want to say `objA = objB;`, and you want the conversion routine to go in class A, what type of conversion routine might you use?

20. True or false: The compiler won't object if you overload the `*` operator to perform division.

EXERCISES

1. To the `Distance` class in the ENGLPLUS program in this chapter, add an overloaded – operator for the `Distance` class that subtracts two distances. It should allow statements like `dist3=dist1-dist2;`. Assume the operator will never be used to subtract a larger number from a smaller one (that is, negative distances are not allowed).

2. Write a program that substitutes an overloaded `+=` operator for the overloaded `+` operator in the STRPLUS program in this chapter. This operator should allow statements like

   ```
   s1 += s2;
   ```

   where `s2` is added (concatenated) to `s1` and the result left in `s1`. The operator should also permit the results of the operation to be used in other calculations, as in

   ```
   s3 = s1 += s2.
   ```

3. Modify the `time` class from Exercise 3 in Chapter 7 so that instead of a function `add_time()` it uses the overloaded `+` operator to add two times. Write a program to test this class.

4. Create a class `Int` based on Exercise 1 in Chapter 7. Overload all five integer arithmetic operators (`+`, `-`, `*`, `/`, and `%`) so that they operate on objects of type `Int`. If the result of any such arithmetic operation exceeds the normal range of `int`'s—from −32,768 to 32,767—have the operator print a warning and terminate the program. Such a data type might be useful where mistakes caused by arithmetic overflow are unacceptable. Hint: To facilitate checking for overflow, perform the calculations using type `long`. Write a program to test this class.

CHAPTER 100

INHERITANCE

REASONS FOR INHERITANCE

BASE AND DERIVED CLASSES

ACCESS CONTROL

CLASS HIERARCHIES

MULTIPLE INHERITANCE

INHERITANCE AND PROGRAM DEVELOPMENT

Inheritance is probably the most powerful feature of object-oriented programming, after classes themselves. Inheritance is the process of creating new classes, called *derived classes*, from existing or *base classes*. The derived class inherits all the capabilities of the base class but can add embellishments and refinements of its own. The base class is unchanged by this process. The inheritance relationship is shown in Figure 10-1.

The arrow in this figure goes in the opposite direction to what you might expect. If it pointed downward, we would label it *inheritance*. However, the more common approach is to point the arrow up, from the derived class to the base class, and think of it as a "derived from" arrow.

Inheritance has important advantages. Most important, it permits code *reusability*. Once a base class is written and debugged, it need not be touched again but can nevertheless be adapted to work in different situations. Reusing existing code saves time and money and increases a program's reliability. Inheritance can also help in the original conceptualization of a programming problem, and in the overall design of the program.

One result of reusability is the ease of distributing class libraries. A programmer can use a class created by another person or company, and, without modifying it, derive other classes from it that are suited to particular situations.

We'll examine these features of inheritance in more detail after we've seen some specific instances of inheritance at work.

DERIVED CLASS AND BASE CLASS

Remember the COUNTPP3 example from Chapter 9? This program used a class `Counter` as a general-purpose counter variable. A count could be initialized to 0 or to a specified number with constructors, incremented with the **++** operator, and read with the `get_count()` operator.

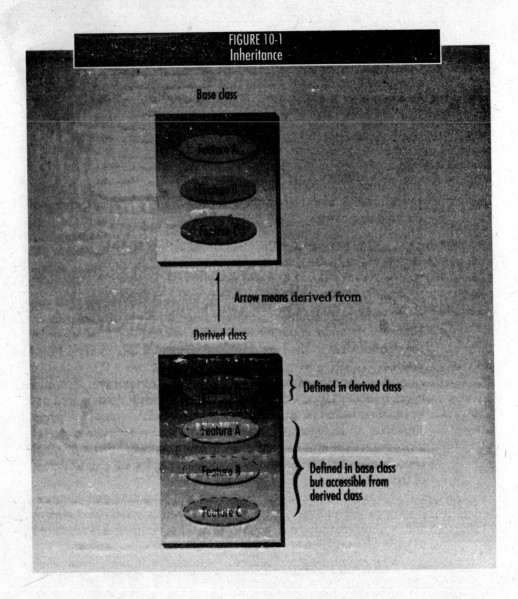

FIGURE 10-1
Inheritance

Base class

Arrow means derived from

Derived class

} Defined in derived class

} Defined in base class
but accessible from
derived class

Feature A

Feature B

Feature C

Let's suppose that we worked long and hard to make the Counter class operate just the way we want, and we're pleased with the results, except for one thing. We really need a way to decrement the count. Perhaps we're counting people entering a bank, and we want to increment the count when they come in and decrement it when they go out, so that the count represents the number of people in the bank at any moment.

We could insert a decrement routine directly into the source code of the Counter class. However, there are several reasons why we might not want to do this. First, the `Counter` class works very well and has undergone many hours of testing and debugging. (Of course that's an exaggeration in this case, but it would be true in a larger and more complex class.) If we start fooling around with the source code for `Counter`, the testing process will need to be carried out again, and of course we may foul something up and spend hours debugging code that worked fine before we modified it.

In some situations there might be another reason for not modifying the `Counter` class: We might not have access to its source code, especially if it had been distributed as part of a class library. (We'll discuss this issue further in Chapter 15.)

To avoid these problems, we can use inheritance to create a new class based on `Counter`, without modifying `Counter` itself. Here's the listing for COUNTEN, which includes a new class, `CountDn`, that adds a decrement operator to the `Counter` class:

```
// counten.cpp
// inheritance with Counter class
#include <iostream.h>

class Counter                          // base class
   {
   protected:                          // NOTE: not private
      unsigned int count;              // count
   public:
      Counter()        { count = 0; }  // constructor, no args
      Counter(int c)   { count = c; }  // constructor, one arg
      int get_count()  { return count; } // return count
      Counter operator ++ ()           // incr count (prefix)
         { return Counter(++count); }
   };

class CountDn : public Counter   // derived class
   {
   public:
      Counter operator -- ()     // decr count (prefix)
         { return Counter(--count); }
   };

void main()
   {
   CountDn c1;                            // c1 of class CountDn

   cout << "\nc1=" << c1.get_count();     // display c1

   ++c1; ++c1; ++c1;                      // increment c1
   cout << "\nc1=" << c1.get_count();     // display it

   --c1; --c1;                            // decrement c1
   cout << "\nc1=" << c1.get_count();     // display it
   }
```

The listing starts off with the `Counter` class, which is similar to that in COUNTPP3. (Only prefix forms are used in this example.)

Specifying the Derived Class

Following the `Counter` class in the listing is the specification for a new class, `CountDn`. This class incorporates a new function, `operator--()`, which decrements the count. However—and here's the key point—the new `CountDn` class inherits all the features of the `Counter` class. `CountDn` doesn't need a constructor or the `get_count()` or `operator++()` functions, because these already exist in `Counter`.

The first line of `CountDn` specifies that it is derived from `Counter`:

```
class CountDn : public Counter
```

Here we use a single colon (not the double colon used for the scope resolution operator), followed by the keyword `public` and the name of the base class `Counter`. This sets up the relationship between the classes. This line says `CountDn` is *derived from the base class* `Counter`. (We'll explore the effect of the keyword `public` later.) The relationship is shown in Figure 10-2.

Remember that the arrow in diagrams like this means *derived from*. The arrows point this way to emphasize that the derived class *refers to* functions and data in the base class, while the base class has no access to the derived class. Mathematicians call this kind of diagram a *directed acyclic graph*, or DAG (as in "DAGonnit, I drew the arrow the wrong way"). They are also called *inheritance trees*.

Accessing Base Class Members

An important topic in inheritance is knowing when a member function in the base class can be used by objects of the derived class. This is called *accessibility*. Let's see how the compiler handles the accessibility issue in the COUNTEN example.

Substituting Base Class Constructors

In the `main()` part of COUNTEN we create an object of class `CountDn`:

```
CountDn c1;
```

This causes `c1` to be created as an object of class `CountDn` and initialized to 0. But wait—how is this possible? There is no constructor in the `CountDn` class specifier, so what entity carries out the initialization? It turns out that—at least under certain circumstances—if you don't specify a constructor, the derived class will use an appropriate constructor from the base class. In COUNTEN there's no constructor in `CountDn`, so the compiler uses the no-argument constructor from `Count`.

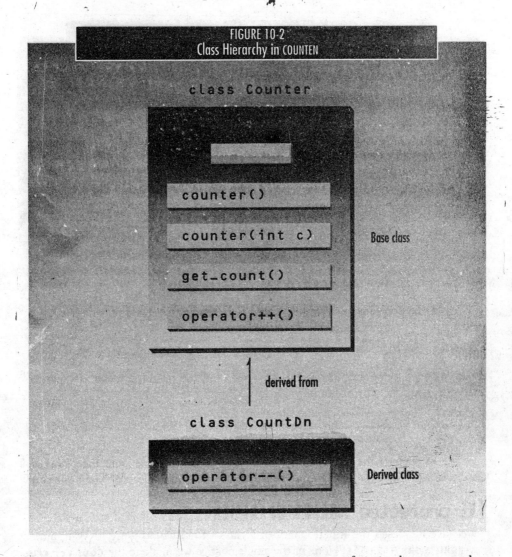

FIGURE 10-2
Class Hierarchy in COUNTEN

class Counter

counter()

counter(int c)   Base class

get_count()

operator++()

derived from

class CountDn

operator--()   Derived class

This flexibility on the part of the compiler—using one function because another isn't available—appears regularly in inheritance situations. Generally, the substitution is what you want, but sometimes it can be unnerving.

Substituting Base Class Member Functions

The object c1 of the CountDn class also uses the operator++() and get_count() functions from the Counter class. The first is used to increment c1:

```
++c1;
```

and the second is used to display the count in c1:

```
cout << "\nc1=" << c1.get_count();
```

FIGURE 10-3
Access Specifiers without Inheritance

class C

Member function of class C
can access both private and
public members.

private

public

Not
allowed

C ObjC

Object of class C can access
only public members of C.

Again the compiler, not finding these functions in the class of which **c1** is a member, uses member functions from the base class.

Output of COUNTEN

In **main()** we increment **c1** three times, print out the resulting value, decrement **c1** twice, and finally print out its value again. Here' the output:

```
c1=0          ←————————after initialization
c1=3          ←————————after ++c1, ++c1, ++c1
c1=1          ←————————after --c1, --c1
```

The **++** operator, the constructors, and the **get_count()** function in the **Counter** class, and the **--** operator in the **CountDn** class, all work with objects of type **CountDn**.

THE protected ACCESS SPECIFIER

We have increased the functionality of a class without modifying it. Well, almost without modifying it. Let's look at the single change we made to the **Counter** class.

The data in the classes we've looked at so far, including **count** in the **Counter** class in the earlier COUNTPP3 program, have used the **private** access specifier.

In the **Counter** class in COUNTEN, **count** is given a new specifier: **protected**. What does this do?

Let's first review what we know about the access specifiers **private** and **public**. Class members (which can be data or functions) can always be accessed by functions *within their own class*, whether the members are private or public. But objects of a class defined *outside the class* can access class members only if the members are public. For instance, suppose an object **objA** is an instance of class **A**, and function **funcA()** is a member function of A. Then in **main()** (or any other function that is not a member of A) the statement

```
objA.funcA();
```

will not be legal unless **funcA()** is public. The object **objA** cannot access private members of class A. Private members are, well, *private*. This is shown in Figure 10-3.

This is all we need to know if we don't use inheritance. With inheritance, however, there is a whole raft of additional possibilities. The question that concerns us at the moment is, can member functions of the derived class access members of the base class? In other words, can **operator--()** in **CountDn** access **count** in **Counter**? The answer is that member functions can access members of the base class if the members are **public**, or if they are **protected**. They can't access **private** members.

We don't want to make **count public**, since that would allow it to be accessed by any function anywhere in the program, and eliminate the advantages of data-hiding. A **protected** member, on the other hand, can be accessed by member functions in its own class or—and here's the key—in any class derived from its own class. It can't be accessed from functions outside these classes, such as **main()**. This is just what we want. The situation is shown in Figure 10-4.

FIGURE 10-4
Access Specifiers with Inheritance

The following table summarizes the situation in a different way:

Access Specifier	Accessible from own class	Accessible from derived class	Accessible from objects outside class
public	yes	yes	yes
protected	yes	yes	no
private	yes	no	no

The moral is that if you are writing a class that you suspect might be used, at any point in the future, as a base class for other classes, then any data or functions that the derived classes might need to access should be made **protected** rather than private. This ensures that the class is "inheritance ready" (to adapt a phrase from TV set advertising).

Base Class Unchanged

Remember that, even if other classes have been derived from it, the base class remains unchanged. In the **main()** part of COUNTEN, we could define objects of type **Counter**:

```
Counter c2;  ◄———————— object of base class
```

Such objects would behave just as they would if **CountDn** didn't exist.

Note also that inheritance doesn't work in reverse. The base class and its objects don't know anything about any classes derived from the base class. In this example that means that objects of class **Counter**, such as **c2** defined here, can't use the **operator--()** function in **CountDn**. If you want a counter that you can decrement, it must be of class **CountDn**, not **Counter**.

DERIVED CLASS CONSTRUCTORS

There's a potential glitch in the COUNTEN program. What happens if we want to initialize a **CountDn** object to a value? Can the one-argument constructor in **Counter** be used? The answer is no. As we saw in COUNTEN, the compiler will substitute a no-argument constructor from the base class, but it draws the line at more complex constructors. To make such a definition work we must write a new set of constructors for the derived class. This is shown in the COUNTEN2 program:

```
// counten2.cpp
// constructors in derived class
#include <iostream.h>
```

```
class Counter
   {
   protected:                            // NOTE: not private
      unsigned int count;                // count
   public:
      Counter()         { count = 0; }   // constructor, no args
      Counter(int c)    { count = c; }   // constructor, one arg
      int get_count()   { return count; } // return count
      Counter operator ++ ()             // incr count (prefix)
         { return Counter(++count); }
   };

class CountDn : public Counter
   {
   public:
      CountDn() : Counter()              // constructor, no args
         { }
      CountDn(int c) : Counter(c)        // constructor, 1 arg
         { }
      CountDn operator -- ()             // decr count (prefix)
         { return CountDn(--count); }
   };

void main()
   {
   CountDn c1;                           // class CountDn
   CountDn c2(100);

   cout << "\nc1=" << c1.get_count();    // display
   cout << "\nc2=" << c2.get_count();    // display

   ++c1; ++c1; ++c1;                     // increment c1
   cout << "\nc1=" << c1.get_count();    // display it

   --c2; --c2;                           // decrement c2
   cout << "\nc2=" << c2.get_count();    // display it

   CountDn c3 = --c2;                    // create c3 from c2
   cout << "\nc3=" << c3.get_count();    // display c3
   }
```

This program uses two new constructors in the CountDn class. Here is the one-argument constructor:

```
CountDn() : Counter()
   { }
```

This constructor has an unfamiliar feature: the colon followed by a function name. This construction causes the `CountDn()` constructor to call the `Counter()` constructor in the base class. In `main()`, when we say

```
CountDn c1;
```

the compiler will create an object of type `CountDn` and then call the `CountDn` constructor to initialize it. This constructor will in turn call the `Counter` constructor, which carries out the work. The `CountDn()` constructor could add additional statements of its own, but in this case it doesn't need to, so the function body between the braces is empty.

The statement

```
CountDn c2(100);
```

in `main()` uses the one-argument constructor in `CountDn`. This constructor also calls the corresponding constructor in the base class:

```
CountDn(int c) : Counter(c)        ←——————— argument c is passed to Counter
   { }
```

This construction causes the argument `c` to be passed from `CountDn()` to `Counter()`, where it is used to initialize the object.

In `main()`, after initializing the `c1` and `c2` objects, we increment one and decrement the other and then print the results. The one-argument constructor is also used in an assignment statement:

```
CountDn c3 = --c2;
```

OVERRIDING MEMBER FUNCTIONS

You can use member functions in a derived class that have the same name as those in the base class. You might want to do this so that calls in your program work the same way for objects of both base and derived classes.

Here's an example based on the STAKARAY program from Chapter 8. That program modeled a stack, a simple data storage device. It allowed you to push integers onto the stack and pop them off. However, STAKARAY had a potential flaw. If you tried to push too many items onto the stack, the program might bomb, since data would be placed in memory beyond the end of the `st[]` array. Or if you tried to pop too many items, the results would be meaningless, since you would be reading data from memory locations outside the array.

To cure these defects, we've created a new class, `Stack2`, derived from `Stack`. Objects of `Stack2` behave in exactly the same way as those of `Stack`, except that you will be warned if you attempt to push too many items on the stack, or if you try to pop an item from an empty stack. Here's the listing for STAKEN.CPP:

```
// staken.cpp
// overloading functions in base and derived classes
#include <iostream.h>
#include <process.h>               // for exit()

const int MAX = 100;               // maximum size of stack

class Stack
   {
   protected:                      // NOTE: can't be private
      int st[MAX];                 // stack: array of integers
      int top;                     // index to top of stack
   public:
      Stack()                      // constructor
         { top = 0; }
      void push(int var)           // put number on stack
         { st[++top] = var; }
      int pop()                    // take number off stack
         { return st[top--]; }
   };

class Stack2 : public Stack
   {
   public:
      void push(int var)           // put number on stack
         {
         if(top >= MAX)            // error if stack full
            { cout << "\nError: stack is full"; exit(1); }
         Stack::push(var);         // call push() in Stack class
         }
      int pop()                    // take number off stack
         {
         if(top <= 0)              // error if stack empty
            { cout << "\nError: stack is empty"; exit(1); }
         return Stack::pop();      // call pop() in Stack class
         }
   };

void main()
   {
   Stack2 s1;

   s1.push(11);                    // push some values onto stack
   s1.push(22);
   s1.push(33);

   cout << endl << s1.pop();       // pop some values from stack
   cout << endl << s1.pop();
```

```
        cout << endl << s1.pop();
        cout << endl << s1.pop();          // woops, pops one too many...
        }
```

In this program the `Stack` class is just the same as it was in the STAKARAY program, except that the data members have been made `protected`.

Which Function Is Used?

The `Stack2` class contains two functions, `push()` and `pop()`. These functions have the same names, and the same argument and return types, as the functions in `Stack`. When we call these functions from main, in statements like

```
        s1.push(11);
```

how does the compiler know which of the two `push()` functions to use? Here's the rule: When the same function exists in both the base class and the derived class, the function in the derived class will be executed. (This is true of objects of the derived class. Objects of base class don't know anything about the derived class and will always use the base class functions.) We say that the derived class function *overrides* the base class function. So in the statement above, since `s1` is an object of class `Stack2`, the `push()` function in `Stack2` will be executed, not the one in `Stack`.

The `push()` function in `Stack2` checks to see if the stack is full. If it is, it displays an error message and causes the program to exit. If it isn't, it calls the `push()` function in `Stack`. Similarly, the `pop()` function in `Stack2` checks to see if the stack is empty. If it is, it prints an error message and exits; otherwise, it calls the `pop()` function in `Stack`.

In `main()` we push three items onto the stack, but we try to pop four. The last pop elicits an error message:

```
33
22
11
Error: stack is empty
```

and terminates the program.

Scope Resolution with Overridden Functions

How do `push()` and `pop()` in `Stack2` access `push()` and `pop()` in `Stack`? They use the scope resolution operator, `::`, in the statements:

```
        Stack::push(var);
```

and

```
        return Stack::pop();
```

These statements specify that the `push()` and `pop()` functions in `Stack` are to be called. Without the scope resolution operator, the compiler would think the `push()`

and `pop()` functions in `Stack2` were calling themselves, which—in this case—would lead to program failure. Using the scope resolution operator allows you to specify exactly what class the function is a member of.

INHERITANCE IN THE ENGLISH Distance CLASS

Here's a somewhat more complex example of inheritance. So far in this book the various programs that used the English `Distance` class assumed that the distances to be represented would always be positive. This is usually the case in architectural drawings. However, if we were measuring, say, the water level of the Pacific Ocean as the tides varied, we might want to be able to represent negative feet-and-inches quantities. (Tide levels below mean-lower-low-water are called *minus tides*; they prompt clam diggers to take advantage of the larger area of exposed beach.)

Let's derive a new class from `Distance`. This class will add a single data item to our feet-and-inches measurements: a sign, which can be positive or negative. When we add the sign, we'll also need to modify the member functions so they can work with signed distances. Here's the listing for ENGLEN:

```
// englen.cpp
// inheritance using English Distances
#include <iostream.h>

class Distance                        // English Distance class
   {
   protected:                         // NOTE: can't be private
      int feet;
      float inches;
   public:
      Distance()                      // constructor (no args)
         { feet = 0; inches = 0.0; }
      Distance(int ft, float in)      // constructor (two args)
         { feet = ft; inches = in; }
      void getdist()                  // get length from user
         {
         cout << "\nEnter feet: ";  cin >> feet;
         cout << "Enter inches: ";  cin >> inches;
         }
      void showdist()                 // display distance
         { cout << feet << "\'-" << inches << '\"'; }
   };

enum posneg { pos, neg };  // for sign in DistSign

class DistSign : public Distance  // adds sign to Distance
   {
   private:
      posneg sign;                    // sign is pos or neg
```

```
        public:
                                        // constructor  (no args)
            DistSign() : Distance()     // call base constructor
               { sign = pos; }          // set the sign to +

                                        // constructor (2 or 3 args)
            DistSign(int ft, float in, posneg sg=pos) :
                   Distance(ft, in)     // call base constructor
               { sign = sg; }           // set the sign

            void getdist()              // get length from user
               {
               Distance::getdist();     // call base getdist()
               char ch;                 // get sign from user
               cout << "Enter sign (+ or -): ";  cin >> ch;
               sign = (ch=='+') ? pos : neg;
               }

            void showdist()             // display distance
               {
               cout << ( (sign==pos) ? "(+)" : "(-)" );  // show sign
               Distance::showdist();                     // ft and in
               }
        };

    void main()
        {
        DistSign alpha;                 // no-arg constructor
        alpha.getdist();                // get alpha from user

        DistSign beta(11, 6.25);        // 2-arg constructor

        DistSign gamma(100, 5.5, neg);  // 3-arg constructor

                                        // display all distances
        cout << "\nalpha = ";  alpha.showdist();
        cout << "\nbeta = ";   beta.showdist();
        cout << "\ngamma = ";  gamma.showdist();
        }
```

The Distance class in this program is just the same as in previous programs, except that, as usual, the data is protected. The DistSign class adds the functionality to deal with signed numbers.

OPERATION OF ENGLEN

The main() program declares three different signed distances. It gets a value for alpha from the user, initializes beta to (+)11'-6.25" and gamma to (−)100'-5.5".

We use parentheses around the sign to avoid confusion with the hyphen separating feet and inches. Here's some sample output:

```
Enter feet: 6
Enter inches: 2.5
Enter sign (+ or -): -

alpha = (-)6'-2.5"
beta = (+)11'-6.25"
gamma = (-)100'-5.5"
```

The `DistSign` class is derived from `Distance`. It adds a single variable, `sign`, which is of type `posneg`. The `sign` variable will hold the sign of the distance. The `posneg` type is defined in an `enum` statement to have two possible values: `pos` and `neg`.

CONSTRUCTORS IN DistSign

`DistSign` has two constructors, mirroring those in `Distance`. The first takes no arguments, the second takes either two or three arguments. The third, optional, argument in the second constructor is a sign, either `pos` or `neg`. Its default value is `pos`. These constructors allow us to define variables (objects) of type `DistSign` in several ways.

Both constructors in `DistSign` call the corresponding constructors in `Distance` to set the feet-and-inches values. They then set the `sign` variable. The no-argument constructor always sets it to `pos`. The second constructor sets it to `pos` if no third-argument value has been provided, or to a value (`pos` or `neg`) if the argument is specified.

The arguments `ft` and `in`, passed from `main()` to the second constructor in `DistSign`, are simply forwarded to the constructor in `Distance`.

MEMBER FUNCTIONS IN DistSign

Adding a sign to `Distance` has consequences for both its member functions. The `getdist()` function in the `DistSign` class must ask the user for the sign as well as for feet-and-inches values, and the `showdist()` function must display the sign along with the feet and inches. These functions call the corresponding functions in `Distance`, in the lines

```
Distance::getdist();
```

and

```
Distance::showdist();
```

These calls get and display the feet and inches values. The body of `getdist()` and `showdist()` in `DistSign` then go on to deal with the sign.

ABETTING INHERITANCE

C++ is designed to make it efficient to create a derived class. Where we want to use parts of the base class, it's easy to do so, whether these parts are data, constructors, or member functions. Then we add the functionality we need to create the new improved class. Notice that in ENGLEN we didn't need to duplicate any code; instead we make use of the appropriate functions in the base class.

CLASS HIERARCHIES

In the examples so far in this chapter, inheritance has been used to add functionality to an existing class. Now let's look at an example where inheritance is used for a different purpose: as part of the original design of a program.

Our example models a database of employees of a widget company. We've simplified the situation so that only three kinds of employees are represented. Managers manage, scientists perform research to develop better widgets, and laborers operate the dangerous widget-stamping presses.

The database stores a name and an employee identification number for all employees, no matter what category they are. However, for managers, it also stores their

FIGURE 10-5
Class Hierarchy in EMPLOY

titles and golf club dues. For scientists it stores the number of scholarly articles they have published. Laborers need no additional data beyond their names and numbers.

Our example program starts with a base class **employee**. This class handles the employee's last name and employee number. From this class three other classes are derived: **manager**, **scientist**, and **laborer**. The **manager** and **scientist** classes contain additional information about these categories of employee, and member functions to handle this information, as shown in Figure 10-5.

Here's the listing for EMPLOY:

```cpp
// employ.cpp
// models employee database using inheritance
#include <iostream.h>

const int LEN = 80;                    // maximum length of names

class employee                         // employee class
    {
    private:
        char name[LEN];                // employee name
        unsigned long number;          // employee number
    public:
        void getdata()
            {
            cout << "\n   Enter last name: "; cin >> name;
            cout << "   Enter number: ";       cin >> number;
            }
        void putdata()
            {
            cout << "\n   Name: " << name;
            cout << "\n   Number: " << number;
            }
    };

class manager : public employee        // management class
    {
    private:
        char title[LEN];    // "vice-president" etc.
        double dues;        // golf club dues
    public:
        void getdata()
            {
            employee::getdata();
            cout << "   Enter title: ";           cin >> title;
            cout << "   Enter golf club dues: "; cin >> dues;
            }
        void putdata()
            {
            employee::putdata();
            cout << "\n   Title: " << title;
            cout << "\n   Golf club dues: " << dues;
```

```
        }
    };
class scientist : public employee        // scientist class
    {
    private:
        int pubs;        // number of publications
    public:
        void getdata()
            {
            employee::getdata();
            cout << "   Enter number of pubs: "; cin >> pubs;
            }
        void putdata()
            {
            employee::putdata();
            cout << "\n   Number of publications: " << pubs;
            }
    };


class laborer : public employee          // laborer class
    {
    };


void main()
    {
    manager m1, m2;
    scientist s1;
    laborer l1;

    cout << endl;
    cout << "\nEnter data for manager 1";        // get data for
    m1.getdata();                                // several employees

    cout << "\nEnter data for manager 2";
    m2.getdata();

    cout << "\nEnter data for scientist 1";
    s1.getdata();

    cout << "\nEnter data for laborer 1";
    l1.getdata();

    cout << "\nData on manager 1";               // display data for
    m1.putdata();                                // several employees

    cout << "\nData on manager 2";
    m2.putdata();
```

```
    cout << "\nData on scientist 1";
    s1.putdata();

    cout << "\nData on laborer 1";
    l1.putdata();
    }
```

The `main()` part of the program declares four objects of different classes: two managers, a scientist, and a laborer. (Of course many more employees of each type could be defined, but the output would become rather large.) It then calls the `getdata()` member functions to obtain information about each employee, and the `putdata()` function to display this information. Here's a sample interaction with EMPLOY. First the user supplies the data:

```
Enter data for manager 1
    Enter last name: Wainsworth
    Enter number: 10
    Enter title: President
    Enter golf club dues: 1000000
Enter data on manager 2
    Enter last name: Bradley
    Enter number: 124
    Enter title: Vice-President
    Enter golf club dues: 500000
Enter data for scientist 1
    Enter last name: Hauptman-Frenglish
    Enter number: 234234
    Enter number of pubs: 999
Enter data for laborer 1
    Enter last name: Jones
    Enter number: 6546544
```

The program then plays it back:

```
Data on manager 1
    Name: Wainsworth
    Number: 10
    Title: President
    Golf club dues: 1000000
Data on manager 2
    Name: Bradley
    Number: 124
    Title: Vice-President
    Golf club dues: 500000
Data on scientist 1
    Name: Hauptman-Frenglish
    Number: 234234
    Number of publications: 999
```

```
Data on laborer 1
     Name: Jones
     Number: 6546544
```

A more sophisticated program would use an array or some other more complex way to arrange the data, so that a large number of employee objects could be accommodated.

"ABSTRACT" BASE CLASS

Notice that we don't define any objects of the base class `employee`. We use this as a general class whose sole purpose is to act as a base from which other classes are derived.

The `laborer` class operates identically to the `employee` class, since it contains no additional data or functions. It may seem that the `laborer` class is unnecessary, but by making it a separate class we emphasize that all classes are descended from the same source, `employee`. Also, if in the future we decided to modify the `laborer` class, we would not need to change the specifier for `employee`.

Classes used only for deriving other classes, as `employee` is in EMPLOY, can be called *abstract* classes, meaning that no actual instances (objects) of this class are created. However, the term *abstract class* has a more precise definition, connected with virtual functions, which we'll look at in Chapter 13.

CONSTRUCTORS AND MEMBER FUNCTIONS

There are no constructors in either the base or derived classes, so the compiler creates objects of the various classes automatically when it encounters definitions like

```
manager m1, m2;
```

The `getdata()` and `putdata()` functions in `employee` accept a name and number from the user, and display a name and number. Functions also called `getdata()` and `putdata()` in the `manager` and `scientist` classes use the functions in `employee`, and also do their own work. In `manager` the `getdata()` function asks the user for a title and the amount of golf club dues, and `putdata()` displays these values. In `scientist` these functions handle the number of publications.

PUBLIC AND PRIVATE INHERITANCE

C++ provides a wealth of ways to fine-tune access to class members. One such access-control mechanism is the way derived classes are declared. Our examples so far have used publicly declared classes, with specifiers like

```
class manager : public employee
```

which appeared in the EMPLOY example.

What is the effect of the `public` keyword in this statement, and what are the alternatives? Listen up: The keyword `public` specifies that objects of the derived class are able to access public member functions of the base class. The alternative is the keyword `private`. When this keyword is used, objects of the derived class cannot access public member functions of the base class. Since objects can never access `private` or `protected` members of a class, the result is that no member of the base class is accessible to objects of the derived class.

ACCESS COMBINATIONS

There are so many possibilities for access that it's instructive to look at an example program that shows what works and what doesn't. Here's the listing for PUBPRIV:

```
// pubpriv.cpp
// tests publicly- and privately-derived classes
#include <iostream.h>

class A                    // base class
    {
    private:
        int privdataA;     // (functions have the same access
    protected:             // rules as the data shown here)
        int protdataA;
    public:
        int pubdataA;
    };

class B : public A         // publicly-derived class
    {
    public:
        void funct()
            {
            int a;
            a = privdataA;     // error: not accessible
            a = protdataA;     // ok
            a = pubdataA;      // ok
            }
    };

class C : private A        // privately-derived class
    {
    public:
        void funct()
            {
            int a;
            a = privdataA;     // error: not accessible
            a = protdataA;     // ok
            a = pubdataA;      // ok
            }
    };
```

```
void main()                    // main()
{
int a;

B objB;
a = objB.privdataA;   // error: not accessible
a = objB.protdataA;   // error: not accessible
a = objB.pubdataA;    // ok                    (B is public)

C objC;
a = objC.privdataA;   // error: not accessible
a = objC.protdataA;   // error: not accessible
a = objC.pubdataA;    // error: not accessible (C is private)
}
```

The program specifies a base class, A, with private, protected, and public data items. Two classes, B and C, are derived from A. B is publicly derived, and C is privately derived.

As we've seen before, functions in the derived classes can access protected and public data in the base class. Also, objects of the derived classes cannot access private or protected members of the base class.

What's new is the difference between publicly derived and privately derived classes. Objects of the publicly derived class B can access public members of the base class A, while objects of the privately derived class C cannot. This is shown in Figure 10-6.

If you don't supply any access specifier when creating a class, private is assumed.

CLASSES AND STRUCTURES

Remember that access specifiers are the only way to distinguish structures and classes. In structures the default is public; for classes it's private.

```
class X : A          // private is assumed
   { };
struct X : A         // public is assumed
   { };
```

ACCESS SPECIFIERS: WHEN TO USE WHAT

When would you use private as opposed to public class derivation? Suppose you used a function in the base class that worked fine with objects of the base class but gave erroneous results with objects of derived classes. Further suppose that there was no function of the same name in the derived class to override the base class. How do you make sure that the function can be called only by objects of the base class? One way to handle this is to make a dummy function with the same name for the derived class and have it print an error message if called by an object of the

FIGURE 10-6
Public and Private Derivation

derived class. However, a more elegant approach is to make the derived class **private**. Now the function will simply not be accessible to objects of the derived class, although it is still accessible to objects of the base class.

LEVELS OF INHERITANCE

Classes can be derived from classes that are themselves derived. Here's a mini-program that shows the idea:

```
class A
    { };
class B : public A
    { };
class C : public B
    { };
```

FIGURE 10-7
Class Hierarchy in EMPLOY2

Here **B** is derived from **A**, and **C** is derived from **B**. The process can be extended to an arbitrary number of levels—**D** could be derived from **C**, and so on.

As a more concrete example, suppose that we decided to add a special kind of laborer called a *foreman* to the EMPLOY program. We'll create a new program, EM-PLOY2, that incorporates objects of class `foreman`.

Since foremen are a kind of laborer, the `foreman` class is derived from the `laborer` class, as shown in Figure 10-7.

Foremen oversee the widget-stamping operation, supervising groups of labor-ers. They are responsible for the widget production quota for their group. A foreman's ability is measured by the percentage of production quotas successfully met. The `quotas` data item in the `foreman` class represents this percentage. Here's the listing for EMPLOY2:

```
// employ2.cpp
// multiple levels of inheritance
#include <iostream.h>

const int LEN = 80;              // maximum length of names

class employee
    {
```

```cpp
   private:
      char name[LEN];            // employee name
      unsigned long number;      // employee number
   public:
      void getdata()
         {
         cout << "\n   Enter last name: "; cin >> name;
         cout << "   Enter number: ";       cin >> number;
         }
      void putdata()
         {
         cout << "\n   Name: " << name;
         cout << "\n   Number: " << number;
         }
   };

class manager : public employee     // management class
   {
   private:
      char title[LEN];  // "vice-president" etc.
      double dues;         // golf club dues
   public:
      void getdata()
         {
         employee::getdata();
         cout << "   Enter title: ";          cin >> title;
         cout << "   Enter golf club dues: "; cin >> dues;
         }
      void putdata()
         {
         employee::putdata();
         cout << "\n   Title: " << title;
         cout << "\n   Golf club dues: " << dues;
         }
   };
class scientist : public employee       // scientist class
   {
   private:
      int pubs;       // number of publications
   public:
      void getdata()
         {
         employee::getdata();
         cout << "   Enter number of pubs: "; cin >> pubs;
         }
      void putdata()
         {
         employee::putdata();
         cout << "\n   Number of publications: " << pubs;
         }
   };
```

```
class laborer : public employee          // laborer class
   {
   };

class foreman : public laborer           // foreman class
   {
   private:
      float quotas;        // percent of quotas met successfully
   public:
      void getdata()
         {
         laborer::getdata();
         cout << "   Enter quotas: "; cin >> quotas;
         }
      void putdata()
         {
         laborer::putdata();
         cout << "\n   Quotas: " << quotas;
         }
   };

void main()
   {
   laborer l1;
   foreman f1;

   cout << endl;
   cout << "\nEnter data for laborer 1";
   l1.getdata();
   cout << "\nEnter data for foreman 1";
   f1.getdata();

   cout << endl;
   cout << "\nData on laborer 1";
   l1.putdata();
   cout << "\nData on foreman 1";
   f1.putdata();
   }
```

Notice that a class hierarchy is not the same as an organization chart. An organization chart shows lines of command. A class hierarchy results from generalizing common characteristics. The more general the class, the higher it is on the chart. Thus a laborer is more general than a foreman, who is a specialized kind of laborer, so laborer is shown above foreman in the class hierarchy.

MULTIPLE INHERITANCE

A class can be derived from more than one base class. This is called *multiple inheritance*. Figure 10-8 shows how this looks when a class C is derived from base classes A and B.

FIGURE 10-8
Multiple Inheritance

The syntax for multiple inheritance is similar to that for single inheritance. In the situation shown in the figure, the relationship is expressed like this:

```
class A                              // base class A
   {
   };
class B                              // base class B
   {
   };
class C : public A, public B         // C is derived from A and B
   {
   };
```

The base classes from which C is derived are listed following the colon in C's specification; they are separated by commas.

MEMBER FUNCTIONS IN MULTIPLE INHERITANCE

As an example of multiple inheritance, suppose that we needed to record the educational experience of some of the employees in the EMPLOY program. Let's also suppose that, perhaps in a different project, we had already developed a class called **student** that models students with different educational backgrounds. We decide that instead of modifying the **employee** class to incorporate educational data, we will add this data by multiple inheritance from the **student** class.

The **student** class stores the name of the school or university last attended, and the highest degree received. Both these data items are stored as strings. Two member functions, **getedu()** and **putedu()**, ask the user for this information and display it.

FIGURE 10-9
Class Hierarchy in EMPMULT

Educational information is not relevant to every class of employee. Let's suppose, somewhat undemocratically, that we don't need to record the educational experience of laborers; it's only relevant for managers and scientists. We therefore modify **manager** and **scientist** so that they inherit from both the **employee** and **student** classes, as shown in Figure 10-9.

Here's a mini-program that shows these relationships (but leaves out everything else):

```
class student
    { };
class employee
    { };
class manager : private employee, private student
    { };
class scientist : private employee, private student
    { };
class laborer : public employee
    { };
```

And here, featuring considerably more detail, is the listing for EMPMULT:

```
// empmult.cpp
// multiple inheritance with employees and education
#include <iostream.h>

st int LEN = 80;              // maximum length of names

class student                 // educational background
    {
```

```
        private:
    _     char school[LEN];  // name of school or university
    _     char degree[LEN];  // highest degree earned
        public:
           void getedu()
              {
              cout << "    Enter name of school or university: ";
              cin >> school;
              cout << "    Enter highest degree earned \n";
              cout << "    (Highschool, Bachelor's, Master's, PhD): ";
              cin >> degree;
              }
           void putedu()
              {
              cout << "\n    School or university: " << school;
              cout << "\n    Highest degree earned: " << degree;
              }
        };

class employee
   {
   private:
      char name[LEN];           // employee name
      unsigned long number;     // employee number
   public:
      void getdata()
         {
         cout << "\n    Enter last name: "; cin >> name;
         cout << "    Enter number: ";        cin >> number;
         }
      void putdata()
         {
         cout << "\n    Name: " << name;
         cout << "\n    Number: " << number;
         }
   };

class manager : private employee, private student   // management
   {
   private:
      char title[LEN]; // "vice-president" etc.
      double dues;      // golf club dues
   public:
      void getdata()
         {
         employee::getdata();
         cout << "    Enter title: ";            cin >> title;
         cout << "    Enter golf club dues: "; cin >> dues;
         student::getedu();
         }
```

```
        void putdata()
            {
            employee::putdata();
            cout << "\n   Title: " << title;
            cout << "\n   Golf club dues: " << dues;
            student::putedu();
            }
    };
class scientist : private employee, private student   // scientist
    {
    private:
        int pubs;      // number of publications
    public:
        void getdata()
            {
            employee::getdata();
            cout << "   Enter number of pubs: "; cin >> pubs;
            student::getedu();
            }
        void putdata()
            {
            employee::putdata();
            cout << "\n   Number of publications: " << pubs;
            student::putedu();
            }
    };

class laborer : public  employee        // laborer
    {
    };

void main()
    {
    manager m1;
    scientist s1, s2;
    laborer l1;

    cout << endl;
    cout << "\nEnter data for manager 1";     // get data for
    m1.getdata();                             // several employees

    cout << "\nEnter data for scientist 1";
    s1.getdata();

    cout << "\nEnter data for scientist 2";
    s2.getdata();

    cout << "\nEnter data for laborer 1";
    l1.getdata();
```

```
        cout << "\nData on manager 1";        // display data for
        m1.putdata();                          // several employees

        cout << "\nData on scientist 1";
        s1.putdata();

        cout << "\nData on scientist 2";
        s2.putdata();

        cout << "\nData on laborer 1";
        l1.putdata();
        }
```

The `getdata()` and `putdata()` functions in the `manager` and `scientist` classes incorporate calls to functions in the `student` class, such as

```
        student::getedu();
```

and

```
        student::putedu();
```

These routines are accessible in `manager` and `scientist` because these classes are descended from `student`.

Here's some sample interaction with EMPMULT:

```
Enter data for manager 1
   Enter last name: Bradley
   Enter number: 12
   Enter title: Vice-President
   Enter golf club dues: 100000
   Enter name of school or university: Yale
   Enter highest degree earned
   (Highschool, Bachelor's, Master's, PhD): Bachelor's

Enter data for scientist 1
   Enter last name: Twilling
   Enter number: 764
   Enter number of pubs: 99
   Enter name of school or university: MIT
   Enter highest degree earned
   (Highschool, Bachelor's, Master's, PhD): PhD

Enter data for scientist 2
   Enter last name: Yang
   Enter number: 845
   Enter number of pubs: 101
   Enter name of school or university: Stanford
   Enter highest degree earned
   (Highschool, Bachelor's, Master's, PhD): Master's
```

```
Enter data for laborer 1
    Enter last name: Jones
    Enter number: 48323
```

As we saw in the EMPLOY and EMPLOY2 examples, the program then displays this information in roughly the same form.

private Derivation in EMPMULT

The `manager` and `scientist` classes in EMPMULT are privately derived from the `employee` and `student` classes. There is no need to use public derivation because objects of `manager` and `scientist` never call routines in the `employee` and `student` base classes. However, the `laborer` class must be publicly derived from `employer`, since it has no member functions of its own and relies on those in `employee`.

CONSTRUCTORS IN MULTIPLE INHERITANCE

EMPMULT has no constructors. Let's look at an example that does use constructors, and see how they're handled in multiple inheritance.

Imagine that we're writing a program for building contractors, and that this program models lumber-supply items. It uses a class that represents a quantity of lumber of a certain type: 100 eight-foot-long construction grade 2x4s, for example.

The class should store various kinds of data about each such lumber item. We need to know the length (3'-6" long or whatever) and we need to store the number of such pieces of lumber and their unit cost.

We also need to store a description of the lumber we're talking about. This has two parts. The first is the nominal dimensions of the cross-section of the lumber. This is given in inches. For instance, lumber two inches by four inches (for you metrickers, about 5 cm by 10 cm) is called a *two-by-four*. This is usually written 2x4. (The actual dimensions are smaller than these nominal dimensions, but that doesn't matter here.) We also need to know the grade of lumber—rough-cut, construction grade, surfaced-four-sides, and so on. We find it convenient to create a `Type` class to hold this data about the lumber. This class incorporates member data for the nominal dimensions and the grade of the lumber, both expressed as strings, such as 2x6 and *construction*. Member functions get this information from the user and display it.

We'll use the `Distance` class from previous examples to store the length. Finally we create a `Lumber` class that inherits both the `Type` and `Distance` classes. Here's the listing for ENGLMULT:

```
// englmult.cpp
// multiple inheritance with English Distances
#include <iostream.h>
#include <string.h>          // for strcpy()

const int LEN = 40;          // maximum length of strings
```

```
    class Type                    // type of lumber
       {
       private:
          char dimensions[LEN];
          char grade[LEN];
       public:
          Type()                           // constructor (no args)
             { strcpy(dimensions, "N/A"); strcpy(grade, "N/A"); }

          Type(char di[], char gr[])  // constructor (two args)
             { strcpy(dimensions, di); strcpy(grade, gr); }

          void gettype()                 // get type from user
             {
             cout << "   Enter nominal dimensions (2x4 etc.): ";
             cin >> dimensions;
             cout << "   Enter grade (rough, const, etc.): ";
             cin >> grade;
             }
          void showtype()                // display type
             {
             cout << "\n   Dimensions: " << dimensions;
             cout << "\n   Grade: " << grade;
             }
       };


    class Distance                           // English Distance class
       {
       private:
          int feet;
          float inches;
       public:
          Distance()                     // constructor (no args)
             { feet = 0; inches = 0.0; }
          Distance(int ft, float in)  // constructor (two args)
             { feet = ft; inches = in; }
          void getdist()                 // get length from user
             {
             cout << "   Enter feet: ";  cin >> feet;
             cout << "   Enter inches: ";  cin >> inches;
             }
          void showdist()                // display distance
             { cout  << feet << "\'-" << inches << '\"'; }
       };


    class Lumber : public Type, public Distance
       {
       private:
          int quantity;                         // number of pieces
          float price;                          // price of each piece
```

357

```
public:
    Lumber() : Type(), Distance()          // constructor (no args)
       { quantity = 0; price = 0.0; }

                                           // constructor (6 args)
    Lumber( char di[], char gr[],          // args for Type
            int ft, float in,              // args for Distance
            int qu, float prc ) :          // our own args
            Type(di, gr),                  // call Type constructor
            Distance(ft, in)               // call Distance constr
       {
       quantity = qu; price = prc;         // use our own args
       }
    void getlumber()
       {
       Type::gettype();
       Distance::getdist();
       cout << "    Enter quantity: "; cin >> quantity;
       cout << "    Enter price per piece: "; cin >> price;
       }
    void showlumber()
       {
       Type::showtype();
       cout << "\n    Length: ";
       Distance::showdist();
       cout << "\n    Price for " << quantity
            << " pieces: $" << price * quantity;
       }
    };

void main()
    {
    Lumber siding;                         // constructor (no args)

    cout << "\nSiding data:\n";
    siding.getlumber();                    // get siding from user

                                           // constructor (6 args)
    Lumber studs( "2x4", "const", 8, 0.0, 200, 4.45 );

                                           // display lumber data
    cout << "\nSiding"; siding.showlumber();
    cout << "\nStuds";    studs.showlumber();
    }
```

The major new feature in this program is the use of constructors in the derived class Lumber. These constructors call the appropriate constructors in Type and Distance.

No-Argument Constructor

The no-argument constructor in `Type` looks like this:

```
Type()
    { strcpy(dimensions, "N/A"); strcpy(grade, "N/A"); }
```

This constructor fills in "N/A" (not available) for the `dimensions` and `grade` variables, so the user will be made aware if an attempt is made to display data for an uninitialized lumber object.

You're already familiar with the no-argument constructor in the `Distance` class:

```
Distance()
    { feet = 0; inches = 0.0; }
```

The no-argument constructor in `Lumber` calls both these constructors:

```
Lumber() : Type(), Distance()
```

The names of the base-class constructors follow the colon and are separated by commas. These base-class constructors will be called in order when the `Lumber()` constructor is invoked.

Multi-Argument Constructor

The situation is more complex when constructors with arguments are used. Here is the two-argument constructor for `Type`:

```
Type(char di[], char gr[])
    { strcpy(dimensions, di); strcpy(grade, gr); }
```

This constructor copies string arguments to the `dimensions` and `grade` member data items.

Here's the constructor for `Distance`, which is again familiar from previous programs:

```
Distance(int ft, float in)
    { feet = ft; inches = in; }
```

The constructor for `Lumber` calls both these constructors, so it must supply values for their arguments. In addition it has two arguments of its own: the quantity of lumber and the unit price. So this constructor has six arguments. It then makes two calls to the two constructors, each of which takes two arguments. Here's what it looks like:

```
Lumber( char di[], char gr[],          ←————— args for Type class
        int ft, float in,              ←————— args for Distance class
        int qu, float prc ) :          ←————— args for this class
        Type(di, gr),                  ←————— call Type constructor
        Distance(ft, in);              ←————— call Distance constructor
```

```
    {
    quantity = qu; price = prc;    ←——————set our own data
    }
```

As before, a colon signals the start of the list of constructors to be called, with the members of the list being separated by commas. The first four arguments passed to `Lumber` are passed on to `Type()` and `Distance()`. The last two arguments are used to initialize the `quantity` and `price` members of `Lumber`, in the body of the function.

AMBIGUITY IN MULTIPLE INHERITANCE

Odd sorts of problems may surface in certain situations involving multiple inheritance. Here's a common one. Two base classes have functions with the same name, while a class derived from both base classes has no function with this name. How do objects of the derived class access the correct base class function? The name of the function alone is insufficient, since the compiler can't figure out which of the two functions is meant.

Here's an example, AMBIGU, that demonstrates the situation:

```
// ambigu.cpp
// demonstrates ambiguity in multiple inheritance
#include <iostream.h>

class A
    {
    public:
        void show()  { cout << "\nClass A"; }
    };
class B
    {
    public:
        void show()  { cout << "\nClass B"; }
    };
class C : public A, public B
    {
    };

void main()
    {
    C objC;                  // object of class C
    objC.show();             // ambiguous--will not compile
    objC.A::show();          // ok
    objC.B::show();          // ok
    }
```

The problem is resolved using the scope-resolution operator to specify the class in which the function lies. Thus

```
objC.A::show();
```

refers to the version of show() that's in the A class, while

```
objC.B::show();
```

refers to the function in the B class.

The scope-resolution operator resolves the ambiguity and keeps the compiler happy.

CONTAINERSHIP: CLASSES WITHIN CLASSES

In inheritance, if a class B is derived from a class A, we can say that "B is a kind of A." This is because B has all the characteristics of A, and in addition some of its own. It's like saying that a starling is a kind of bird: A starling has the characteristics shared by all birds (wings, feathers, and so on) but has some distinctive characteristics of its own (such as dark, iridescent plumage). For this reason inheritance is sometimes called a "kind of" relationship.

There's another kind of relationship, called a "has a" relationship, or *containership*. We say that a starling has a tail, meaning that each starling includes an instance of a tail. In object-oriented programming the "has a" relationship occurs

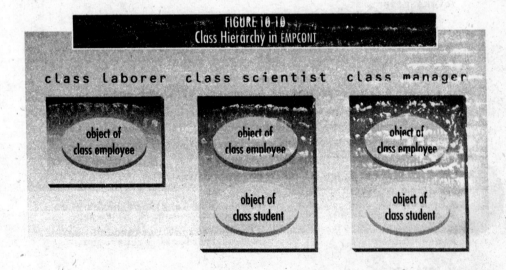

FIGURE 10-10
Class Hierarchy in EMPCONT

when one object is contained in another. Here's a case where an object of class B is contained in a class A:

```
class A
   {
   B b;    // b is an object of class B
   };
class B
   {
   };
```

In some situations inheritance and containership relationships can serve similar purposes. For example, we can rewrite the EMPMULT program to use containership instead of inheritance. In EMPMULT the **manager** and **scientist** classes are derived from the **employee** and **student** classes using the inheritance relationship. In our new program, EMPCONT, the **manager** and **scientist** classes contain instances of the **employee** and **student** classes, as shown in Figure 10-10.

The following mini-program shows these relationships in a different way:

```
class student
   {};
class employee
   {};
class manager
   {
   student stu;      // stu is an object of class student
   employee emp;     // emp is an object of class employee
   };
class scientist
   {
   student stu;      // stu is an object of class student
   employee emp;     // emp is an object of class employee
   };
class laborer
   {
   employee emp;     // emp is an object of class employee
   };
```

Here's the full-scale listing for EMPCONT:

```
// empcont.cpp
// containership with employees and education
#include <iostream.h>

const int LEN = 80;               // maximum length of names

class student                     // educational background
   {
   private:
      char school[LEN];  // name of school or university
      char degree[LEN];  // highest degree earned
```

```
   public:
      void getedu()
         {
         cout << "   Enter name of school or university: ";
         cin >> school;
         cout << "   Enter highest degree earned \n";
         cout << "   (Highschool, Bachelor's, Master's, PhD): ";
         cin >> degree;
         }
      void putedu()
         {
         cout << "\n   School or university: " << school;
         cout << "\n   Highest degree earned: " << degree;
         }
   };


class employee
   {
   private:
      char name[LEN];           // employee name
      unsigned long number;     // employee number
   public:
      void getdata()
         {
         cout << "\n   Enter last name: "; cin >> name;
         cout << "   Enter number: ";      cin >> number;
         }
      void putdata()
         {
         cout << "\n   Name: " << name;
         cout << "\n   Number: " << number;
         }
   };


class manager            // management
   {
   private:
      char title[LEN];   // "vice-president" etc.
      double dues;       // golf club dues
      employee emp;      // object of class employee
      student stu;       // object of class student
   public:
      void getdata()
         {
         emp.getdata();
         cout << "   Enter title: ";           cin >> title;
         cout << "   Enter golf club dues: "; cin >> dues;
         stu.getedu();
         }
```

```cpp
      void putdata()
         {
         emp.putdata();
         cout << "\n   Title: " << title;
         cout << "\n   Golf club dues: " << dues;
         stu.putedu();
         }
   };
class scientist         // scientist
   {
   private:
      int pubs;          // number of publications
      employee emp;      // object of class employee
      student stu;       // object of class student
   public:
      void getdata()
         {
         emp.getdata();
         cout << "   Enter number of pubs: "; cin >> pubs;
         stu.getedu();
         }
      void putdata()
         {
         emp.putdata();
         cout << "\n   Number of publications: " << pubs;
         stu.putedu();
         }
   };

class laborer          // laborer
   {
   private:
      employee emp;  // object of class employee
   public:
      void getdata()
         { emp.getdata(); }
      void putdata()
         { emp.putdata(); }
   };

void main()
   {
   manager m1;
   scientist s1, s2;
   laborer l1;

   cout << endl;
   cout << "\nEnter data for manager 1";      // get data for
   m1.getdata();                              // several employees
```

```
        cout << "\nEnter data for scientist 1";
        s1.getdata();

        cout << "\nEnter data for scientist 2";
        s2.getdata();

        cout << "\nEnter data for laborer 1";
        l1.getdata();

        cout << "\nData on manager 1";          // display data for
        m1.putdata();                            // several employees

        cout << "\nData on scientist 1";
        s1.putdata();

        cout << "\nData on scientist 2";
        s2.putdata();

        cout << "\nData on laborer 1";
        l1.putdata();
        }
```

The **student** and **employee** classes are the same in EMPCONT as they were in EMPMULT, but they are used in a different way by the **manager** and **scientist** classes.

Containership is clearly useful with classes that act like a data type, as does the **Distance** class, for example. Then an object of that type can be used in a class in almost the same way a variable would be. In other situations you will need to examine the problem carefully and perhaps try different approaches to see what makes sense. Often the inheritance relationship is simpler to implement and offers a clearer conceptual framework.

INHERITANCE AND PROGRAM DEVELOPMENT

The program-development process, as practiced for decades by programmers everywhere, is being fundamentally altered by object-oriented programming. This is due not only to the use of classes in OOP but to inheritance as well. Let's see how this comes about.

Programmer A creates a class. Perhaps it's something like the **Distance** class, with a complete set of member functions for arithmetic operations on a user-defined data type.

Programmer B likes the **Distance** class but thinks it could be improved by using signed distances. The solution is to create a new class, like **DistSign** in the

ENGLEN example, that is derived from **Distance** but incorporates the extensions necessary to implement signed distances.

Programmers C and D then write applications that use the **DistSign** class.

It may be that programmer B does not have access to the source code for the **Distance** member functions, and that programmers C and D don't have access to the source code for **DistSign**. Yet, because of the software reusability feature of C++, B can modify and extend the work of A, and C and D can make use of the work of B (and A).

Notice that the distinction between software tool developers and application writers is becoming blurred. Programmer A creates a general-purpose programming tool, the **Distance** class. Programmer B creates a specialized version of this class, the **DistSign** class. Programmers C and D create applications. A is a tool developer, and C and D are applications developers. B is somewhere in between. In any case OOP is making the programming scene more flexible and at the same time more complex.

In Chapter 15, on larger programs, we'll see how a class can be divided into a client-accessible part and a part that is distributed only in object form, so it can be used by other programmers without the distribution of source code.

SUMMARY

A class, called the derived class, can inherit the features of another class, called the base class. The derived class can add other features of its own, so it becomes a specialized version of the base class. Inheritance provides a powerful way to extend the capabilities of existing classes, and to design programs using hierarachical relationships.

Accessibility of base class members from derived classes and from objects of derived classes is an important issue. Data or functions in the base class that are prefaced by the keyword **protected** can be accessed from derived classes but not by objects of derived classes. Classes may be publicly or privately derived from base classes. Objects of a publicly derived class can access public members of the base class, while objects of a privately derived class cannot.

A class can be derived from more than one base class. This is called multiple inheritance. A class can also be contained within another class.

Inheritance permits the reusability of software: Derived classes can extend the capabilities of base classes with no need to modify—or even access the source code of—the base class. This leads to new flexibility in the software development process, and to a wider range of roles for software developers.

QUESTIONS

1. Inheritance is a way to
    a. make general classes into more specific classes
    b. pass arguments to objects of classes
    c. add features to existing classes without rewriting them
    d. improve data-hiding and encapsulation
2. A "child" class is said to be _____ from a base class.
3. Advantages of inheritance include
    a. providing class growth through natural selection
    b. facilitating class libraries
    c. avoiding the rewriting of code
    d. providing a useful conceptual framework
4. Write the first line of the specifier for a class **Bosworth** that is publicly derived from a class **Alphonso**.
5. True or false: Adding a derived class to a base class requires fundamental changes to the base class.
6. To be accessed from a member function of the derived class, data or functions in the base class must be **public** or _____.
7. If a base class contains a member function **basefunc()**, and a derived class does not contain a function with this name, can an object of the derived class access **basefunc()**?
8. Assume the classes mentioned in Question 4, and that class **Alphonso** contains a member function called **alfunc()**. Write a statement that allows object **BosworthObj** of class **Bosworth** to access **alfunc()**.
9. True or false: If no constructors are specified for a derived class, objects of the derived class will use the constructors in the base class.
10. If a base class and a derived class each include a member function with the same name, which member function will be called by an object of the derived class, assuming the scope-resolution operator is not used?
11. Write a declarator for a no-argument constructor of the derived class **Bosworth** of Question 4 that calls a no-argument constructor in the base class **Alphonso**.
12. The scope-resolution operator usually
    a. limits the visibility of variables to a certain function
    b. tells what base class a class is derived from
    c. specifies a particular class
    d. resolves ambiguities

13. True or false: It is sometimes useful to specify a class from which no objects will ever be created.

14. Assume there is a class **Derv** that is derived from a base class **Base**. Write the declarator for a derived-class constructor that takes one argument and passes this argument along to the constructor in the base class.

15. Assume a class **Derv** that is privately derived from class **Base**. An object of class **Derv** located in **main()** can access
    a. public members of **Derv**
    b. protected members of **Derv**
    c. private members of **Derv**
    d. public members of **Base**
    e. protected members of **Base**
    f. private members of **Base**

16. True or false: A class **D** can be derived from a class **C**, which is derived from a class **B**, which is derived from a class **A**.

17. A class hierarchy
    a. shows the same relationships as an organization chart
    b. describes "has a" relationships
    c. describes "is a kind of" relationships
    d. shows the same relationships as a family tree

18. Write the first line of a specifier for a class **Tire** that is derived from class **Wheel** and from class **Rubber**

19. Assume a class **Derv** derived from a base class **Base**. Both classes contain a member function **func()** that takes no arguments. Write a statement to go in a member function of **Derv** that calls **func()** in the base class.

20. True or false: It is illegal to make objects of one class members of another class.

EXERCISES

1. Imagine a publishing company that markets both book and audio-cassette versions of its works. Create a class **publication** that stores the title (a string) and price (type **float**) of a publication. From this class derive two classes: **book**, which adds a page count (type **int**); and **tape**, which adds a playing time in minutes (type **float**). Each of these three classes should have a **getdata()** function to get its data from the user at the keyboard, and a **putdata()** function to display its data.

   Write a **main()** program to test the **book** and **tape** classes by creating instances of them, asking the user to fill in their data with **getdata()**, and then displaying the data with **putdata()**.

2. Recall the STRCONV example from Chapter 9. The `string` class in this example has a flaw: It does not protect itself if its objects are initialized to have too many characters. (The SZ constant has the value 80.) For example, the definition

```
String s = "This string will surely exceed the width of the \
screen, which is what the SZ constant represents.";
```

will cause the `str` array in `s` to overflow, with unpredictable consequences, such as crashing the system. (The '\' character in this statement permits a long string to wrap over two lines in the source file, while the compiler sees an unbroken string.)

    With `String` as a base class, derive a class `Pstring` (for "protected String") that prevents buffer overflow when too long a string constant is used in a definition. A new constructor in the derived class should copy only SZ-1 characters into `str` if the string constant is longer, but copy the entire constant if it's shorter. Write a `main()` program to test different lengths of strings.

3. Start with the `publication`, `book`, and `tape` classes of Exercise 1. Add a base class `sales` that holds an array of three `floats` so that it can record the dollar sales of a particular publication for the last three months. Include a `getdata()` function to get three sales amounts from the user, and a `putdata()` function to display the sales figures. Alter the `book` and `tape` classes so they are derived from both `publication` and `sales`. An object of class `book` or `tape` should input and output sales data along with its other data. Write a `main()` function to create a `book` object and a `tape` object and exercise their input/output capabilities.

MICROSOFT C++ GRAPHICS

TEXT-MODE GRAPHICS

SETTING UP FOR GRAPHICS MODE

SHAPES, LINES, COLOR, AND PATTTERN

GRAPHICS SHAPES AS C++ OBJECTS

TEXT IN GRAPHICS MODE

Microsoft C++ includes an extensive collection of graphics-oriented library functions. These functions open up an exciting new world: With them you can place almost any sort of image on the screen. Graphics and object-oriented programming work together particularly well because specific images, such as balls or text boxes, can be represented by objects. Graphics provides a visual way to see objects in action.

Microsoft C++ graphics functions fall into two categories: those that work in text mode and those that work in graphics mode. The text mode functions, which we'll look at first, are concerned with placing text in certain areas of the screen. They work with any graphics monitor and adapter, so you can use them even if you have only a character-based system. (Of course you can also use any of the graphics characters, as shown in Appendix A, in text mode; so you can do simple graphics operations like drawing boxes around text.)

The graphics mode functions, which we look at in the second part of the chapter, require a graphics monitor and adapter card, such as CGA, EGA, or VGA. (See the description of the _setvideomode() function in the the Microsoft C++ documentation for a complete list of supported graphics adapters.) Graphics-mode functions allow you to draw dots, lines, and shapes (like circles and rectangles), add color to lines and areas, and perform many other graphics-related activities.

The emphasis in this chapter is on how graphics images can be implemented as C++ objects. No new object-oriented topics are introduced, so this chapter gives you a chance to reinforce the concepts you've learned already, including objects, classes, and inheritance. Even if your computer does not have a graphics display, you should read this chapter, as graphics provide an intuitive, visual demonstration of object-oriented programming.

We do not cover all the Microsoft C++ graphics functions. Our aim is to show the most important functions and how they work in the object-oriented environment. However, we show the general approach to a variety of situations, so you can probably figure out the remaining graphics functions on your own.

TEXT-MODE GRAPHICS FUNCTIONS

When you first boot up your computer, it's probably in text mode. In this mode the screen is divided into character positions, typically 80 columns by 25 rows (although there are also 40x25, 80x43, and other arrangements). The video output functions we've seen so far, such as `cout` and `<<`, are text-mode functions. However, Microsoft C/C++ adds additional text-mode functions to facilitate writing text to *windows*. A window in this context is a rectangular area on the screen that confines the text written to it.

Windows are useful in programs that use a Graphical User Interface (GUI) display in text mode. The Programmer's WorkBench (PWB) environment itself is an example of this kind of display. It uses windows in character mode.

We should note that, unlike most of the C++ library functions mentioned in this book, the graphics-oriented library functions described in this chapter work only in the MS-DOS environment. They are not portable to other platforms such as Unix, or even to other compilers besides Microsoft C++.

DEVELOPING GRAPHICS PROGRAMS

Graphics programs require slightly more preparation than chraracter-based programs. For text-mode graphics programs, you need to do two things: First, link an additional library file to your program, and second, include an extra header file.

The library file you need is called GRAPHICS.LIB. To combine this file with your program, you'll need to create a project file. Follow the instructions in Appendix C for creating a project file. Add the GRAPHICS.LIB file by entering

```
c:\c700\lib\graphics.lib
```

in the File Name field of the Edit Project window. Then add the name of your program's .CPP file. Finally, click on Save List. Now you can compile and link your program by selecting Build from the Project menu.

The header file you need is GRAPH.H (note the different name from the library file). This file contains the prototypes of the graphics functions, and various constant definitions. You use a normal `#include` statement at the beginning of your source file to include this file.

The first few examples in this chapter are text-mode graphics programs. Later we'll move on to graphics mode, which requires a special function to switch modes.

THE _settextwindow() FUNCTION

A key library function for text mode is `_settextwindow()`. This function (which requires the GRAPH.H header file) takes four integer arguments that determine the top, left, bottom, and right coordinates of the window. On an 80x25 display, the columns run from 1 to 80, and the rows from 1 to 25. Text written by certain functions will appear inside the window, starting at the upper-left corner. Text too long for the width of the window is automatically wrapped at the right edge. Text that goes beyond the bottom of the window causes the contents of the window to scroll upward. Note that _settextwindow() doesn't draw a border or outline around the window; it only confines text to a rectangular area. Thus you can't see where the window is until you start writing text in it.

Actually, the text window is always in effect in text mode but since its default coordinates are the entire screen, you don't notice its existence unless you've changed its coordinates with _settextwindow().

USING TEXT-MODE FUNCTIONS

Unlike graphics mode, which requires special functions to initialize the graphics system, text mode needs no preparation before use, since you're already in it when you're at the DOS prompt. You can start right in using _settextwindow() and other functions.

Here's an example that makes use of the _settextwindow() library function. This program, WINDOW, creates a class called box. This class represents a window and the text contained in it. Here's the listing for WINDOW:

```
// window.cpp
// text window as a class
#include <string.h>     // for strcpy()
#include <graph.h>      // for _settextwindow(), etc.
#include <conio.h>      // for getch()

const int LEN = 500;    // maximum length of string

class box               // text box class
    {
    private:
        int top, left, bottom, right;      // window dimensions
        char str[LEN];                     // window text
    public:
                                           // constructor (5 args)
        box(int t, int l, int b, int r, char s[])
            {
            top=t; left=l; bottom=b; right=r;
            strcpy(str, s);
            _settextwindow(top, left, bottom, right); // set window
            _outtext(str);                 // display text
            }
        void erase()                       // erase the window
            {
            _settextwindow(top, left, bottom, right); // set window
            _clearscreen(_GWINDOW);        // clear window
            }
    };
```

```
void main()
   {
   _clearscreen(_GCLEARSCREEN);  // clear entire screen

   char s1[] = "The disk drive is jammed\n\
or on fire, or the CPU\n\
is flooded.  Correct the\n\
situation and try again.\n\
Press Enter to continue: ";

   char s2[] = "This is a string that will wrap at the right \
edge of the window, probably breaking words inappropriately \
in the process.";

   box a(6, 25, 18, 55, s1);   // string 1, middle of screen
   getch();                    // wait for keypress
   a.erase();                  // erase box a

   box b(1, 1, 10, 25, s2);    // string 2, upper left corner
   getch();                    // wait for keypress
   }
```

The constructor for the **box** class takes five arguments. The first four establish the coordinates of the box (top, left, bottom, right). The fifth specifies the string that will be displayed in the box. The constructor sets a text window using the **_settextwindow()** function, and writes the text into it with the **_outtext()** library function.

Most of the Microsoft C++ graphics library functions use type **short** instead of type **int**. With current compilers and operating systems these types are the same size. Microsoft uses type **short** so that if programs are recompiled for 32-bit systems, variables will retain their 16-bit size rather than expanding to 32 bits. Unfortunately, if you set the error level of the Microsoft compiler to 3 or 4 (using the menu selection Options/Language Options/C++ Compiler/Warning Level), then, when you compile, you will see a lot of "Conversion between different integral types" warning messages. To avoid these messages you would need to cast every integer constant used as an argument to a graphics function to type **short**, as in

```
_settextwindow( short(10), short(5), short(70), short(15) );
```

This is a little cumbersome to read, so we have used type **int** instead. You can set your error level to 2, or simply ignore the warning messages.

THE _outtext() FUNCTION

The usual approach to text output, using **cout** and the **<<** operator, does not work within a text window. Most C++ functions don't recognize the existence of text windows; they assume they have the entire screen to work with. To work within a text window, you must use library functions specifically created for that purpose. One of the most useful is the function **_outtext()**, which writes a string of text to a window. We use this function to display the text from the **box** class on the screen.

Note: In this chapter we'll be talking about two kinds of functions: Microsoft C++ library functions like **_settextwindow()** and **_outtext()** on the one hand; and member functions of classes we create ourselves on the other. We will try to clarify which kind of function we mean by describing it as either a *library function* or a *member function* when it is introduced, but you should be aware of the possibility of confusion.

THE _clearscreen() FUNCTION

The **clearscreen()** library function erases the text window. It is used twice in WINDOW. The first time is in **main()**, where **_clearscreen()**, using the **_GCLEARSCREEN** constant, erases the entire screen. It's also used in the **box::erase()** member function to erase the contents of the window, using the **_GWINDOW** constant.

The **main()** part of WINDOW defines two strings and then creates two windows. The first window, in the middle of the screen, displays the first string. Then, after the user presses a key, the second window displays the second string. Figures 11-1 and 11-2 show the display at these two points.

A FANCIER box CLASS

Let's rewrite the **box** class from WINDOW so that, in addition to displaying text, it also outlines itself with a rectangle. This will give it a more "window-like" appearance. We'll do this with graphics characters that represent vertical and horizontal line

FIGURE 11-1
Output of WINDOW, Part 1

```
The disk drive is jammed
or on fire, or the CPU
is flooded.  Correct the
situation and try again.
Press Enter to continue:
```

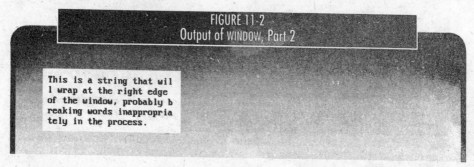

FIGURE 11-2
Output of WINDOW, Part 2

```
This is a string that wil
l wrap at the right edge
of the window, probably b
reaking words inappropria
tely in the process.
```

segments and corners. We'll also make the `box` class more flexible by giving it more member functions. Since the window created by this class is enclosed by lines, we'll refer to it as a *text box*. Here's the listing for BOXES:

```cpp
// boxes.cpp
// dialog boxes as objects
#include <string.h>      // for strcpy()
#include <graph.h>       // for _settextwindow(), etc.
#include <conio.h>       // for getch()

const int TOP = 6;         // default window dimensions
const int LEFT = 25;
const int BOTTOM = 18;
const int RIGHT = 55;
const int LEN = 500;       // maximum length of text strings

#define YELLOW 14
#define WHITE  15

class box                  // text box
   {
   private:
      int top, left, bottom, right;    // window dimensions
      char str[LEN];                   // window text
      int color;                       // text color
   public:
      box()                            // no-arg constructor
         {
         top=TOP; left=LEFT;           // set to default
         bottom=BOTTOM; right=RIGHT;   // dimensions
         color = WHITE;                // and color
         }                             // 5-arg constructor
      box(int t, int l, int b, int r, int c=WHITE)
         { top=t; left=l; bottom=b; right=r; color=c; }
      void text(char s[])              // put text in window
         { strcpy(str, s); }
      void draw();                     // display the window
      void erase()                     // erase the window
         {
         _settextwindow(top, left, bottom, right);
         _clearscreen(_GWINDOW);       // clear window
         }
   };

void box::draw()
   {
   char charbuff[2];                   // for graphics chars
   charbuff[1] = '\0';                 // terminate 1-char string

   erase();                            // erase area under window
   _settextwindow(top, left, bottom+1, right); // frame window
   int width = right - left + 1;
```

```
      int height = bottom - top + 1;
      _settextcolor(color);                      // set text color

      for(int j=1; j<=width; j++)            // draw horiz lines
         {
         charbuff[0] = char(205);
         _settextposition(1, j);         _outtext(charbuff); // top
         _settextposition(height, j);    _outtext(charbuff); // bottom
         }
      for(j=1; j<=height; j++)               // draw vertical lines
         {
         charbuff[0] = char(186);
         _settextposition(j, 1);         _outtext(charbuff);    // left
         _settextposition(j, width);     _outtext(charbuff);    // right
         }
                                           // draw corners
      _settextposition(1, 1);        charbuff[0] = char(201);
      _outtext(charbuff);                          // top left
      _settextposition(1, width);    charbuff[0] = char(187);
      _outtext(charbuff);                          // top right
      _settextposition(height, 1);   charbuff[0] = char(200);
      _outtext(charbuff);                          // bottom left
      _settextposition(height, width); charbuff[0] = char(188);
      _outtext(charbuff);                          // bottom right

      _settextwindow(top+1, left+2, bottom-3, right-2);
      _outtext(str);                               // display text

      _settextwindow(top, left, bottom+1, right); // frame window
      _settextposition(height-1, 3);               // go to last line
      _outtext("Press any key to continue: ");     // display prompt
      _settextcolor(WHITE);                        // restore color
      }

void main()
   {
   _clearscreen(_GCLEARSCREEN);                // clear screen

   box a;                          // create box, no-arg constructor
   box b(1, 1, 8, 31, YELLOW);  // create box, 5-arg constructor

                                        // text for box a
   a.text("\"The time,\" said the\n\
Duchess, \"is surely ripe;\n\
make haste, lest seconds\n\
spoil.\"");
                                        // text for box b
   b.text("Should you continue\n\
along the present path you\n\
risk investigation\n\
for felonious chicanery.");
```

```
a.draw();                      // draw box a
getch();                       // wait for keypress
a.erase();                     // erase box a
b.draw();                      // draw box b
getch();                       // wait for keypress
b.erase();                     // erase box b
b.text("Thank you");           // new text for box b
b.draw();                      // draw box b
getch();                       // wait for keypress
}
```

The box class in this program has two constructors. One uses no arguments and creates a text box with standard dimensions in the middle of the screen. The other sets the text box to dimensions chosen by the user. The text is added to the text box by a separate member function: text(). This permits changing the text inside an existing box. The draw() member function displays the text box, and the erase() member function erases it.

The draw() member function uses two new Microsoft C++ graphics functions to draw the box, and a third to set its color. Let's see what they are.

The _settextposition() Function

The _settextposition() library function positions the cursor within a text window. Since text is usually written starting at the cursor position, this allows us to position text where we want it. The _settextposition() function takes two integer parameters: the row and column coordinates where the cursor should go. The coordinate system is that of the window, not the screen, so 1,1 is the upper-left corner of the window.

The _settextcolor() Function

The fifth argument of the five-argument constructor specifies the color to be used for the box outline and for the text within the box. This color value is stored as a private member of the box class. Our member function draw() supplies this value to the library function _settextcolor(), which it executes before displaying the characters. The possible values for the argument to _settextcolor() are shown in Table 11-1. Adding 16 to these values causes the characters to blink.

Other functions, which we don't use in the program, can be used to change the appearance of text written to the screen. For instance, you can set the background color for each character with the _setbkcolor() library function.

Figures 11-3, 11-4, and 11-5 show three stages in the output of BOXES. Each new screen display is elicited when the user presses a key.

The first figure shows box a, the second shows box b with its first string, and the third shows the same box with its second string. Box a is displayed in white, while box b is yellow.

TABLE 11-1 Text-mode colors	
Color index	Color
0	BLACK
1	BLUE
2	GREEN
3	CYAN
4	RED
5	MAGENTA
6	BROWN
7	LIGHT GRAY
8	DARK GRAY
9	LIGHT BLUE
10	LIGHT GREEN
11	LIGHT CYAN
12	LIGHT RED
13	LIGHT MAGENTA
14	YELLOW
15	WHITE
add 16	BLINK

Windows within Windows

The `draw()` member function in BOXES uses the `_settextwindow()` function in several different ways. Early in `draw()` the statement

```
_settextwindow(top, left, bottom+1, right);
```

sets up what we call the *frame* window: the rectangle where the outline of the window will be drawn. The bottom of this outline is one line lower than the dimensions specified in `box` because we want to be able to display the lower-right-corner character without causing the entire window contents to scroll upward.

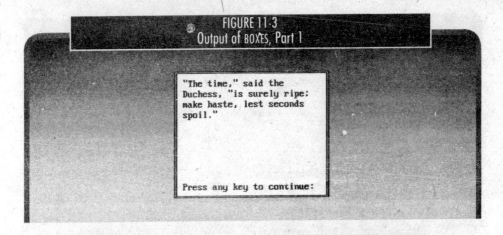

FIGURE 11-3
Output of BOXES, Part 1

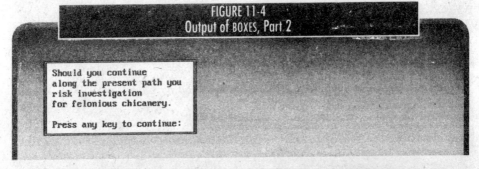

FIGURE 11-4
Output of BOXES, Part 2

FIGURE 11-5
Output of BOXES, Part 3

After the outline is drawn, the statement

```
_settextwindow(top+1, left+2, bottom-3, right-2);
```

specifies the rectangle where the text will actually be drawn. The dimensions are smaller than those in the box object because we want to keep the text inside the outline, with a one-space separation on the left and right edges. The bottom spacing allows room for the line *Press any key to continue:*, which is always placed at the bottom of the window. Remember that once a window is in effect, the `_settextposition()` library function works with the window's coordinate system. Figure 11-6 shows the relation of the various windows and dimension systems.

GRAPHICS-MODE GRAPHICS FUNCTIONS

In text mode you are restricted (as you might expect) to displaying text (or graphics characters), but in graphics mode you can display points, lines, and shapes of arbitrary complexity. In text mode you can address only 2000 locations (in an 80x25

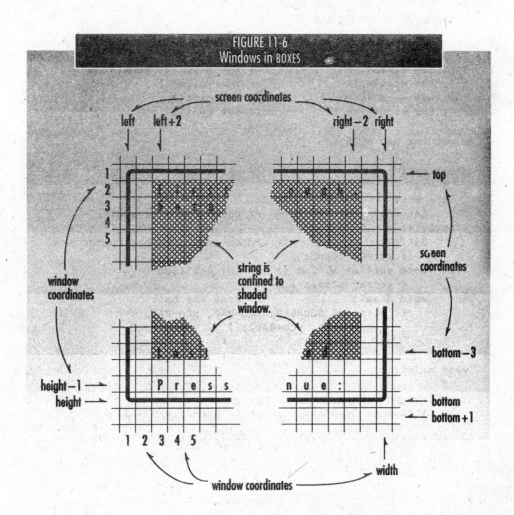

FIGURE 11-6
Windows in BOXES

display), but in graphics mode you address individual *pixels*, or dots on the screen. This gives you much finer resolution: In a 640x480 VGA mode you can address 307,200 pixels (somewhat fewer for EGA or CGA).

Graphics-mode programs use a completely different set of functions from text-mode programs to put images on the screen. A graphics-mode program must also perform some additional preliminary work to set the appropriate graphics mode. Let's look at a simple program that uses a class ball to model circles displayed on the screen.

The ball class stores the coordinates of the center of the circle. The member function set() sets these coordinates from arguments passed to it. Another member function, draw(), draws the ball. All ball objects have the same radius, as specified by the external variable RAD.

Here's the listing for EZBALL:

```
// ezball.cpp
// stationary ball class
#include <graph.h>           // for graphics functions
#include <conio.h>           // for getch()
#include <stdlib.h>          // for exit()
#include <iostream.h>        // for cout()

const int RAD = 75;

class ball                   // ball class
   {
   private:
      int xCo, yCo;          // coordinates of center
   public:
      ball()                 // no-argument constructor
         { xCo=0; yCo=0; }
      void set(int x, int y) // set position
         { xCo=x; yCo=y; }
      void draw()            // draw the ball
        { _ellipse(_GBORDER, xCo-RAD, yCo-RAD,
             xCo+RAD, yCo+RAD); }
   };

void main()
   {
   if( ! _setvideomode(_VRES16COLOR) )
      { cout << "Can't set graphics mode"; exit(1); }

   ball b1;                // create three balls
   ball b2;
   ball b3;

   b1.set(320, 150);  // position them
   b2.set(255, 150);
   b3.set(385, 150);
```

```
    b1.draw();          // draw them
    b2.draw();
    b3.draw();

    getch();            // wait for keypress
    _setvideomode(_DEFAULTMODE);  // restore original mode
    }
```

There are several new graphics functions in this program, so we'll describe the role each one plays.

THE _setvideomode() FUNCTION

Graphics-mode programs—those that deal in pixels rather than characters—must start with the `_setvideomode()` function. This function switches the display adaptor from character mode into the appropriate graphics mode. The function takes one argument: a constant that specifies the mode. Table 11-2 lists some common choices.

You can also use a constant that chooses the mode for you. The `_MAXRESMODE` constant causes the system to select the mode with the highest resolution, and `_MAXCOLORMODE` selects the mode with the most colors. The description of the `_setvideomode()` function in the *Run-Time Library Reference* gives a complete listing of these constants.

We'll use `_MAXRESMODE` for the examples in this book. If it doesn't give good results with your particular adaptor, you should try another constant. You might also need to resize the output in some of the examples, since in the interest of simplicity they make no attempt to size themselves for different graphics modes.

THE _ellipse() FUNCTION

In `main()` we use `_setvideomode()` to initialize the graphics system. Then we create three objects of class `ball`, set their locations with the `set()` member function, and display the objects with `draw()`. The `draw()` member function uses the Microsoft C++ library function `_ellipse()` to actually draw a circle.

TABLE 11-2 Common Constants for the `_setvideomode()` Function			
Constant	Display	Resolution	Colors
_MRES4COLOR	CGA	320x200	4
_ERESCOLOR	EGA	640x350	16
_VRES16COLOR	VGA	640x480	16
_MRES256COLOR	VGA	320x200	256
_VRES256COLOR	SVGA	640x480	256

The _ellipse() library function takes five parameters: a control constant, and the left, top, right, and bottom of the ellipse. The control can be either _GFILLINTERIOR to fill the ellipse, or _GBORDER to merely draw the outline. We use a fixed radius, RAD, for all objects of class ball. The X and Y coordinates are taken from the private data in ball, so the call to _ellipse() looks like this:

```
_ellipse(_GBORDER, xCo-RAD, yCo-RAD, xCo+RAD, yCo+RAD);
```

The three invocations of the ball constructor in main() establish three overlapping balls with centers on the same horizontal line. Figure 11-7 shows the output of EZBALL. (With EGA adaptors you may find that the circles look more like ellipses.)

ENDING A GRAPHICS PROGRAM

When you exit from a graphics program, you should restore the system to the video mode that was previously in use—probably a text mode. To restore the previous mode, and to release whatever memory the graphics system was using, execute the _setvideomode() function, with the _DEFAULTMODE constant, just before exiting your program.

COLORS

If you have a color display, you can draw lines, circles, and so on in different colors. You can also fill enclosed areas with color. Our next program, COLORBAL, is a variation of the EZBALL program that demonstrates the use of color. Here's the listing:

```
// colorbal.cpp
// adds colors to ball class
#include <graph.h>              // for graphics functions
#include <conio.h>              // for getch()
#include <iostream.h>           // for cout
#include <stdlib.h>             // for exit()

#define BLUE      1             // color indices
#define GREEN     2
#define RED       4
#define WHITE     7
#define YELLOW   14

const int RAD = 75;

class ball                      // ball class
   {
   private:
      int xCo, yCo;             // coordinates of center
      int linecolor;           // color of outline
      int fillcolor;           // color of interior
   public:
      ball()                   // no-arg constructor
```

```
            { xCo=0; yCo=0; linecolor=WHITE; fillcolor=WHITE; }
      void set(int x, int y, int lc, int fc)  // set data
            { xCo=x; yCo=y; linecolor=lc; fillcolor=fc; }
      void draw()                  // draw the ball
            {
            _setcolor(linecolor); // line color
            _ellipse(_GBORDER, xCo-RAD, yCo-RAD, // draw circle
                    xCo+RAD, yCo+RAD);
            _setcolor(fillcolor);                // fill color
            _floodfill(xCo, yCo, linecolor);     // fill interior
            }
      };

void main()
   {
   if( ! _setvideomode(_MAXRESMODE) )
      { cout << "Can't set graphics mode"; exit(1); }

   ball b1;                         // create three balls
   ball b2;
   ball b3;

   b1.set(100, 150, YELLOW, RED);  // set position and colors
   b2.set(200, 150, YELLOW, GREEN);
   b3.set(300, 150, YELLOW, BLUE);

   b1.draw();                       // draw them
   b2.draw();
   b3.draw();

   getch();                         // wait for keypress
   _setvideomode(_DEFAULTMODE);     // close graphics system
   }
```

The ball class in this program now features a four-argument set() function. The first two arguments are the center of the circle as before. The third argument specifies the color of the circle's outline, and the fourth specifies the color used to fill the

FIGURE 11-7
Output of EZBALL

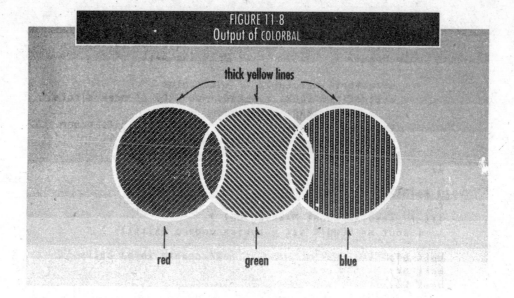

FIGURE 11-8
Output of COLORBAL

thick yellow lines

red   green   blue

interior of the circle. Figure 11-8 shows the effect. Unfortunately, we can't show the figure in color; instead different kinds of shading are used to indicate the colors.

The changes to this program lie mostly in the draw() member function. Let's examine the new Microsoft C++ graphics functions used in this function, and see how they generate colors.

THE _setcolor() FUNCTION

The _setcolor() library function sets the color used for subsequent drawing operations. In EGA and VGA modes, there are 16 colors available to _setcolor(). These are the same colors that are available for the _settextcolor() library function and are listed in Table 11-1. In the draw() member function the _setcolor() library function uses the linecolor member data as its single argument. In main() all three balls have their outlines set to YELLOW by the set() member function.

THE _floodfill() FUNCTION

The _floodfill() library function fills in the color in the interior of the circle. This function starts the fill at a particular X,Y location inside the object. This location is specified by the first two arguments. The fill, in the color specified by _setcolor(), expands outward from this point until it reaches a boundary. The color of this boundary is specified in the third parameter to _floodfill(). Remember that this argument is the boundary color, not the fill color.

Notice in the figure that, since the red ball is drawn and filled first, it is the only one completely filled with a color. The fill for the other two balls stops at the edge of the previously drawn circle. The fill will always stop at the specified boundary color.

We ccould also have used the _GFILLINTERIOR constant in the _ellipse() function to fill the cirle.

RECTANGLES AND LINES

The next program is very similar to COLORBAL, except that it models rectangles rather than circles. Each rectangle represented by the rect class is filled with color, with a diagonal line across it. Here's the listing for RECTLINE:

```
// rectline.cpp
// rectangle and line
#include <graph.h>          // for graphics functions
#include <conio.h>          //      getch()
#include <stdlib.h>         // for exit()
#include <iostream.h>       // for cout

#define BLUE     1          // color indices
#define GREEN    2
#define RED      4
#define WHITE    7
#define YELLOW   14

const int W = 75;           // 1/2 width of rectangle

class rect                  // rect class
   {
   private:
      int xCo, yCo;         // coordinates of center
      int linecolor;        // color of outline
      int fillcolor;        // color of interior
   public:
      rect()                // no-arg constructor
         { xCo=0; yCo=0; linecolor=WHITE; fillcolor=WHITE; }
      void set(int x, int y, int lc, int fc)  // set data
         { xCo=x; yCo=y; linecolor=lc; fillcolor=fc; }
      void draw()           // draw the rectangle
         {
         _setcolor(linecolor);               // line color
                                             // draw rectangle
         _rectangle(_GBORDER, xCo-W, yCo-W, xCo+W, yCo+W);
         _setcolor(fillcolor);               // fill color
         _floodfill(xCo, yCo, linecolor);    // fill rectangle
         _setcolor(linecolor);               // line color
         _moveto(xCo-W, yCo+W);              // draw diagonal
```

```
                _lineto(xCo+W, yCo-W);              //    SW to NE
                }
        };

    void main()
        {
        if( ! _setvideomode(_MAXRESMODE) )
           { cout << "Can't set graphics mode"; exit(1); }
        rect r1;                            // create three rects
        rect r2;
        rect r3;

        r1.set(80, 150, YELLOW, RED);   // set position and colors
        r2.set(250, 150, YELLOW, GREEN);
        r3.set(420, 150, YELLOW, BLUE);

        r1.draw();                          // draw them
        r2.draw();
        r3.draw();

        getch();                            // wait for keypress
        _setvideomode(_DEFAULTMODE);        // close graphics system
        }
```

Figure 11-9 shows the output of this program. The new library functions used in RECTLINE are `_rectangle()`, `_moveto()`, and `_lineto()`.

THE _rectangle() FUNCTION

The `_rectangle()` library function draws a rectangle whose edges are specified with four integers. The control argument can be set to `_GFILLINTERIOR` or `_GBORDER`.

```
    _rectangle(control, left, top, right, bottom);
```

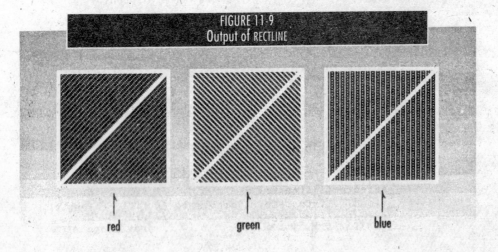

FIGURE 11-9
Output of RECTLINE

red   green   blue

THE _moveto() FUNCTION

Drawing a line in Microsoft C++ involves two different functions. First, you specify
the start of the line with the _moveto() function, then you specify the end of the
line and draw it with the _lineto() function. This may seem like twice as many
functions as necessary to draw a line, but it simplifies things when you want to draw
a whole series of connected lines.

The _moveto() function moves an invisible point called the "current position"
to the point specified by the arguments to the function:

```
_moveto(x, y);
```

This function doesn't cause anything to be drawn; it only moves the current position.

THE _lineto() FUNCTION

The _lineto() function draws a line from the current position to the point specified by its arguments.

```
_lineto(x, y);
```

At the end of the operation, the current position is set to the end of the line. Thus
a second _lineto() function will draw a line that starts at the end of the first one.
The lines are drawn in the color previously specified by _setcolor().

SHAPES AND INHERITANCE

The next example uses inheritance to tie together the circular and rectangular shapes
generated in the COLORBAL and RECTLINE examples, and a new triangle shape. This
program also introduces a new graphics library function, _polygon(), which it uses
to create the triangle. Here's the listing for MULTSHAP:

```cpp
// multshap.cpp
// balls, rects, and polygons
#include <graph.h>              // for graphics functions
#include <conio.h>              // for getch()
#include <iostream.h>           // for cout
#include <stdlib.h>             // for exit()

#define BLUE     1              // color indices
#define GREEN    2
#define RED      4
#define WHITE    7
#define YELLOW   14

const int W = 75;              // size of images

class shape                     // base class
   {
```

```
    protected:
        int xCo, yCo;                // coordinates of center
        int linecolor;              // color of outline
        int fillcolor;              // color of interior
        void init()                 // initializes line color
           { _setcolor(linecolor); }
        void fill()                 // fills interior of any shape
           {
           _setcolor(fillcolor);  // set fill color
           _floodfill(xCo, yCo, linecolor);  // fill interior
           _setcolor(linecolor);  // restore line color
           }
    public:
        shape()                      // no-arg constructor
           { xCo=0; yCo=0; linecolor=WHITE; fillcolor=WHITE; }
        void set(int x, int y, int lc, int fc)  // set data
           { xCo=x; yCo=y; linecolor=lc; fillcolor=fc; }
    };

class ball : public shape
    {
    public:
        ball() : shape()             // no-arg constr
           { }
        void set(int x, int y, int lc, int fc)  // set data
           { shape::set(x, y, lc, fc); }
        void draw()                  // draw the ball
           {
           init();                   // line color
                                     // draw circle
           _ellipse(_GBORDER, xCo-W, yCo-W, xCo+W, yCo+W);
           fill();                   // fill the shape
           }
    };

class rect : public shape
    {
    public:
        rect() : shape()             // no-arg constr
           { }
        void set(int x, int y, int lc, int fc)  // set data
           { shape::set(x, y, lc, fc); }
        void draw()                  // draw the rectangle
           {
           init();                   // line color
                                     // draw rectangle
           _rectangle(_GBORDER, xCo-W, yCo-W, xCo+W, yCo+W);
           fill();                   // fill the shape
           _moveto(xCo-W, yCo+W); // draw diagonal line
           _lineto(xCo+W, yCo-W); // SW to NE
           }
    };
```

```
class tria : public shape
   {
   public:
      tria() : shape()              // no-arg constr
         { }
      void set(int x, int y, int lc, int fc)  // set data
         { shape::set(x, y, lc, fc); }
      void draw()                   // draw the triangle
         {
         init();                    // set line color
         struct _xycoord t[3];      // set up structure
         t[0].xcoord=xCo;     t[0].ycoord=yCo-W;   // top
         t[1].xcoord=xCo-W;   t[1].ycoord=yCo+W;   // bottom left
         t[2].xcoord=xCo+W;   t[2].ycoord=yCo+W;   // bottom right
         _polygon(_GBORDER, t, 3);                 // draw polygon
         fill();                    // fill the shape
         }
   };

void main()
   {
   if( ! _setvideomode(_MAXRESMODE) )
      { cout << "Can't set graphics mode"; exit(1); }

   ball b1;                         // create ball
   rect r2;                         // create rectangle
   tria t3;                         // create triangle

   b1.set(80, 150, YELLOW, RED);    // set position and colors
   r2.set(250, 150, YELLOW, GREEN);
   t3.set(420, 150, YELLOW, BLUE);

   b1.draw();                       // draw them
   r2.draw();
   t3.draw();

   getch();                         // wait for keypress
   _setvideomode(_DEFAULTMODE);     // close graphics system
   }
```

THE shape CLASS

If you look at the ball class in the COLORBAL example, and at the rect class from
RECTLINE, you will see that they have many similarities. They both store the coordinates of the center of the shape and the colors of the shape's outline and interior.
They both have a set() member function that supplies values for these data members, and a draw() function that draws the shape, although of course the draw functions do different things.

In designing a C++ program we look for common elements of classes. Such common elements are candidates for a base class, from which the other classes will be derived. In MULTSHAP we create a base class **shape**, from which revised **ball** and **rect** classes are descended. The **shape** class contains the common elements of **ball** and **rect**, which we saw in previous examples.

We've added two new member functions to the **shape** class. The **init()** function prepares for drawing the border of the shape by setting the current color with **_setcolor()**. The **fill()** function sets the color to the fill color, and uses **_floodfill()** to fill the shape.

POLYGONS

We've added another class to MULTSHAP, the **tria** class, which models a triangle. This new class is also derived from **shape**. A triangle is the simplest example of a **polygon**—a number of straight-line segments that outline a closed shape. The triangle polygon in MULTSHAP is created using a library function called **_polygon()**. This is a somewhat more complex graphics function than those we've seen before. Before it can be used, an array must be created that contains the points that define the polygon. Each of these points is represented by a structure of type **_xycoord**. This structure is defined this way in GRAPH.H:

```
struct _xycoord
    {
    short xcoord;
    short ycoord;
    };
```

To create a polygon, we define an array of these structures, and set the various members to appropriate values. As an example, we'll define an arbitrary polygon of four points: (x0, y0), (x1, y1), (x2, y2) and (x3, y3). Figure 11-10 shows what this polygon looks like.

```
struct _xycoord rect[4];        // array of four structures of
                                // type _xycoord
rect[0].xcoord = x0;   rect[0].ycoord = y0;   // first point
rect[1].xcoord = x1;   rect[1].ycoord = y1;   // second point
rect[2].xcoord = x2;   rect[2].ycoord = y2;   // third point
rect[3].xcoord = x3;   rect[3].ycoord = y3;   // fourth point
```

Once the polygon is defined, we can draw it with the **_polygon()** function, which takes three arguments: a control constant, which is either **_GBORDER** or **_GFILLINTERIOR**, the name of the array, and the number of structures of type **_xycoord** in the array. For the array shown above, assuming we wanted to fill the interior, this would be

```
_polygon(_GFILLINTERIOR, rect, 4); // draw polygon defined by rect
```

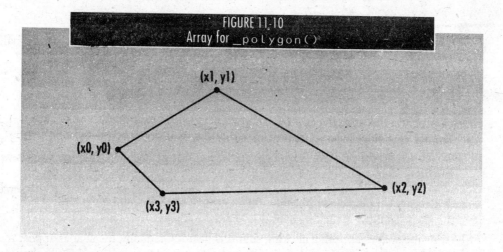

FIGURE 11-10
Array for _polygon()

PROGRAM DESIGN

We created the **shape** class by extracting the common parts of the **ball**, **rect**, and **tria** classes. However, **shape** can also be understood as a generalization of balls, rectangles, and triangles. One of the important mental processes engaged in by humans is that of creating a general category from specific cases. We do this naturally; any six-year-old could tell you that circles, squares, and triangles are all shapes. The C++ inheritance mechanism gives us a way to model this kind of abstraction in a computer language.

The **shape** class concentrates all the features of shapes into one place. As a result, the **ball**, **rect**, and **tria** classes are simpler than before. When we look at them we can see immediately what is unique about them, since the only code and data in them are what is needed to make them different from the generic **shape**. Figure 11-11 shows the class hierarchy in MULTSHAP.

FIGURE 11-11
Class Hierarchy in MULTSHAP

The `main()` part of MULTSHAP creates and displays three objects—a red ball, a green rectangle, and a blue triangle. The result is shown in Figure 11-12.

MOTION

Here's a program that uses the approach shown in previous examples to model a slot machine, where colored shapes appear in a window, as if slot-machine wheels were turning. This is shown in Figure 11-13.

When you first start the program, three square windows appear on the screen. One of four different shapes appears randomly in each window: a red circle (representing a cherry), a blue circle (representing a grape), a square, and a pyramid. Each time the shapes appear, a clicking sound is heard. Gradually, the shapes appear more and more slowly, as if the slot-machine wheels were slowing down. Finally, they stop. If three cherries are displayed, you win. Figure 11-14 shows a typical display.

Here's the listing for SLOT:

```cpp
// slot.cpp
// models a slot machine
#include <graph.h>        // for graphics functions
#include <stdlib.h>       // for srand(), rand()
#include <time.h>         // for time(), clock()
#include <conio.h>        // for getch()
#include <iostream.h>     // for cout
#include <stdlib.h>       // for exit()

#define BLUE     1        // color indices
#define GREEN    2
#define CYAN     3
```

FIGURE 11-12
Output of MULTSHAP

red   green   blue

```
#define RED        4
#define WHITE      7
#define DARKGRAY   8
#define YELLOW    14


const int W = 15;                  // 1/2 width of images
const int MAR = 10;                // margin around images

class shape                        // base class
   {
   protected:
      int xCo, yCo;                // coordinates of center
      int linecolor;              // color of outline
      int fillcolor;              // color of interior
      void init()                  // initializes line color
         { _setcolor(linecolor); }
      void fill()                  // fills interior of any shape
         {
         _setcolor(fillcolor);     // set fill color
         _floodfill(xCo, yCo, linecolor);  // fill interior
         _setcolor(linecolor);     // restore line color
         }
   public:
      shape()                      // no-arg constructor
         { xCo=0; yCo=0; linecolor=WHITE; fillcolor=WHITE; }
      void set(int x, int y, int lc, int fc)
         { xCo=x; yCo=y; linecolor=lc; fillcolor=fc; }
   };


class ball : public shape
   {
   public:
      ball() : shape()             // no-arg constructor
         { }
      void set(int x, int y, int lc, int fc)  // set data
         { shape::set(x, y, lc, fc); }
      void draw()                  // draw the ball
         {
         init();                   // set line color
         _ellipse(_GBORDER, xCo-W, yCo-W, xCo+W, yCo+W);
         fill();                   // fill the shape
         }
   };


class rect : public shape
   {
   public:
      rect() : shape()             // no-arg constructor
         { }
```

```
        void set(int x, int y, int lc, int fc)  // set data
          { shape::set(x, y, lc, fc); }
        void draw()                  // draw the rectangle
          {
          init();                    // set line color
          _rectangle(_GBORDER, xCo-W, yCo-W, xCo+W, yCo+W);
          fill();                    // fill the shape
          _moveto(xCo-W, yCo+W);     // draw diagonal line
          _lineto(xCo+W, yCo-W);     // SW to NE
          }

    };


class tria : public shape
   {
   public:
        tria() : shape()             // no-arg constructor
          { }
        void set(int x, int y, int lc, int fc)  // set data
          { shape::set(x, y, lc, fc); }
        void draw()                  // draw the triangle
          {
          init();                    // set line color
          struct _xycoord t[3];      // set up structure
          t[0].xcoord=xCo;    t[0].ycoord=yCo-W;  // top
          t[1].xcoord=xCo-W;  t[1].ycoord=yCo+W;  // bottom left
          t[2].xcoord=xCo+W;  t[2].ycoord=yCo+W;  // bottom right
          _polygon(_GBORDER, t, 3);               // draw polygon
          fill();                    // fill the shape
          }

    };


class noshape : public shape
   {
   public:
        void erase()                 // erase old shape
          {
          _setcolor(DARKGRAY);       // background color
          _rectangle(_GFILLINTERIOR, xCo-W-MAR, yCo-W-MAR,
                     xCo+W+MAR, yCo+W+MAR);
          }

    };


class Cherry : public ball, public noshape
   {
   public:
        Cherry() : ball()            // no-arg constructor
          { }
        void set(int x, int y)       // set data
          {
```

```
        ball::set(x, y, WHITE, RED);
        noshape::set(x, y, WHITE, RED);
        }
    void draw()                 // draw a cherry
        { erase(); ball::draw(); }
    };

class Grape : public ball, public noshape
    {
    public:
        Grape() : ball()            // no-arg constructor
            { }
        void set(int x, int y)      // set data
            {
            ball::set(x, y, WHITE, BLUE);
            noshape::set(x, y, WHITE, BLUE);
            }
        void draw()                 // draw a grape
            { erase(); ball::draw(); }
    };

class Square : public rect, public noshape
    {
    public:
        Square() : rect()           // no-arg constructor
            { }
        void set(int x, int y)      // set data
            {
            rect::set(x, y, WHITE, CYAN);
            noshape::set(x, y, WHITE, CYAN);
            }
        void draw()                 // draw a square
            { erase(); rect::draw(); }
    };

class Pyramid : public tria, public noshape
    {
    public:
        Pyramid() : tria()          // no-arg constructor
            { }
        void set(int x, int y)      // set data
            {
            tria::set(x, y, WHITE, GREEN);
            noshape::set(x, y, WHITE, GREEN);
            }
        void draw()                 // draw a pyramid
            { erase(); tria::draw(); }
    };

class Wheel : public shape
    {
```

```
        private:
            Cherry ch;                      // make one pip of each kind
            Grape gr;
            Square sq;
            Pyramid py;
        public:
            Wheel()                         // no-arg constructor
                { xCo=0; yCo=0; }
            void set(int x, int y)
                {
                xCo=x; yCo=y;               // set our position
                ch.set(xCo, yCo);           // set four pips to
                gr.set(xCo, yCo);           // our position
                sq.set(xCo, yCo);
                py.set(xCo, yCo);
                }
            void draw();                    // draw a random pip
        };

void Wheel::draw()                          // draw a random pip
    {
    switch( rand()%4 )                      // random number from 0 to 3
        {
        case 0 : ch.draw(); break;          // draw one of the pips
        case 1 : gr.draw(); break;          // selected randomly
        case 2 : sq.draw(); break;
        case 3 : py.draw(); break;
        }
    }

void main()
    {
    const int NUMBER = 60;                  // number of times to cycle

    if( ! _setvideomode(_MAXRESMODE) )
        { cout << "Can't set graphics mode"; exit(1); }

    srand( (unsigned)time(NULL) );          // seed random number

    Wheel w1;                               // make three wheels
    Wheel w2;
    Wheel w3;

    w1.set(100, 100);                       // position in horizontal row
    w2.set(160, 100);
    w3.set(220, 100);

    for(int j=0; j<NUMBER; j++)             // spin the wheels
        {
        w1.draw();                          // draw each wheel
        w2.draw();
        w3.draw();

                                            // cycle for j*j/10 millisecs
        clock_t end = j*j/10 + clock();     // find ending time
        while( clock() < end )              // until current time
```

```
                                   // exceeds ending time
    }
getch();                           // wait for keypress
_setvideomode(_DEFAULTMODE);       // close graphics system
}
```

FIGURE 11-13
A Slot Machine

wheels

window through which
pips are viewed

FIGURE 11-14
Output of SLOT

triangle

grape

cherry

This is a more complicated program, so we'll examine the overall organization first and then discuss some new functions.

CLASS HIERARCHY IN SLOT

The SLOT program uses the classes from previous programs in this chapter: shape, ball, rect, and tria. Our goal is to use these classes with as little modification as possible. This reflects the situation where you have purchased a library of commercial classes, or where you simply want to make use of existing code with a minimum of effort.

SLOT creates four new classes that are shapes with particular colors: Cherry, derived from ball and colored red; Grape, derived from ball and colored blue; Square, derived from rect and colored cyan (greenish blue); and Pyramid, derived from tria and colored green. The set() member functions in these new derived classes simply call the set() functions in their base classes but with these specific colors (the line color is always white).

In addition, the class noshape is introduced to erase shapes. We need to erase each shape before drawing a new one on top of it. Otherwise, the corners of the triangle would still be sticking out when you draw a circle over it. The noshape class contains a single member function, erase(), which erases the area on the screen occupied by the shape.

The classes Cherry, Grape, Square, and Pyramid are derived not only from ball and similar classes but also, through multiple inheritance, from noshape. This gives them the capability to erase themselves. Because noshape needs a place to store coordinates, just as the other shapes do, it is derived from the shape class, although it is not exactly a shape in the same sense the other classes are.

Finally, a class Wheel represents one wheel of a slot machine. Since Wheel also needs to know where it is, it is descended from shape so it can make use of its xCo and yCo data members.

Figure 11-15 shows the relationship of the different classes in SLOT.

OPERATION OF SLOT

The main() function creates three objects of type Wheel. Using the set() member function, it positions them in a row in the upper left of the screen. Then, in a for loop, it repeatedly draws and redraws the wheels.

The Wheel class contains one each of the four different kinds of pips: Cherry, Grape, Square, and Pyramid. Wheel creates these four pips as data elements in its private section; they're called ch, gr, sq, and py. (Notice that although Wheel contains instances of these other classes, this relationship is not shown in the hierarchy diagram, which deals with inheritance, not containership.) The set() member function in Wheel specifies the wheel's position and sets all the pips to the same position. A draw() member function draws a border around the pip's location and then draws one of the pips, selecting which pip to draw based on a random num-

FIGURE 11-15
Class Hierarchy in SLOT

ber. Thus the image drawn by each wheel changes randomly from one pip to another each time that wheel's `draw()` function is called.

Each time all three wheels are redrawn, the program delays for a fixed amount of time. The delay grows longer each time through the loop. This gives the illusion that the wheels are rotating—rapidly at first, and then slower and slower, until they stop.

DELAYING THE PROGRAM

To cause the program to delay for a fixed amount of time, we use the Microsoft library function `clock()`. This function returns the number of processor timer ticks that have passed since the program started. The return value is type `clock_t`, which is typedefed in the TIME.H header file to be type `long`.

We want to wait a fixed number of milliseconds; specifically, j*j/10 milliseconds. The number of timer ticks generated by the system each second is given by the constant `CLOCKS_PER_SEC`, which is #defined in TIME.H to be 1000. Thus `clock()` returns the program time in milliseconds. (Since the value of `CLOCKS_PER_SEC` might change in future versions of the compiler, it would be safer to multiply the return value of `clock()` by `CLOCKS_PER_SEC`, and then divide by 1000 to obtain milliseconds, but we avoid this nicety in the interest of brevity.)

THINKING ABOUT CLASSES

The SLOT program starts to show some of the organizational power of object-oriented programming. Starting with simple classes, we use inheritance to create more complex classes. Multiple inheritance gives even more flexibility.

The relationships among the different parts of the program are—once you get used to them, anyway—more intuitive than those in a traditional procedural program. In C++ these relationships are among classes, while in a procedural program they are among functions. Classes are often better than functions at modeling objects in the real world (or on the screen), and inheritance corresponds, more closely than functions, to something we do every day: create a more general concept from a number of specific instances.

TEXT IN GRAPHICS MODE

Creating text is far more flexibile in graphics mode than it is in character mode. You can use different fonts (character designs), change the size and proportions of the characters, print vertically as well as horizontally, and in general exercise far more control over the appearance of the finished text.

Our example program demonstrates these capabilities, and also uses objects to represent graphics strings. These strings are somewhat similar to the string objects seen in previous examples, except that they include a variety of graphics characteristics.

A GRAPHICS STRING CLASS

The example, GRAST (GRAphics STring), uses a single class of type `Gstring`. This class contains private data that specifies the graphical characteristics of the string. This includes the contents of the string, its starting point, the font in which it's displayed, its direction (vertical or horizontal), and the character size and color.

All these characteristics have default values, set by a no-argument constructor when an object of class `Gstring` is defined. The values can be modified using member functions. You modify only as many values as you need to. The simplest is to use all the defaults and specify only the string itself.

Here's the listing for GRAST:

```
// grast.cpp
// string class for graphics modes
#include <graph.h>       // for graphics functions
#include <conio.h>       // for getch()
#include <string.h>      // for strcpy()
#include <stdlib.h>      // for exit()

#define BLUE      1       // color indices
#define GREEN     2
#define CYAN      3
#define RED       4
#define MAGENTA   5
#define WHITE     7
```

```
#define DARKGRAY   8
#define YELLOW     14

#define NORM       0          // directions constants
#define UP         1
#define INVERT     2
#define DOWN       3

class Gstring                 // graphics string class
   {
   protected:
      char str[80];              // string to store text
      int xCo, yCo;              // coordinates of text
      char face[20];             // helv, courier, tms rmn, etc.
      int direction;            // NORM, UP, INVERT, DOWN
      int width;                // in pixels
      int height;               // in pixels
      int color;                // BLUE, RED, etc.
   public:
      Gstring()                            // no-arg constructor
         {                                 // set to default values
         str[0] = '\0';                    // empty string
         xCo = 0; yCo = 0;                 // top left
         strcpy(face, "courier");  // courier
         direction = NORM;                 // left to right
         width = 12;
         height = 15;
         color = WHITE;
         }
      void DrawText()                      // draw the text
         {
         _moveto(xCo, yCo);
         char string[80];            // utility string
         char options[80];           // options string
         strcpy( options, "t'" );
         strcat( options, face );  // face
         strcat( options, "'w" );
         strcat( options, itoa(width, string, 10) );  // width
         strcat( options, "h" );
         strcat( options, itoa(height, string, 10) ); // height
         if( _setfont(options) < 0 )
            {
            _outtext("Can't set font");
            getch();
            _setvideomode(_DEFAULTMODE);  // close graphics
            _unregisterfonts();           // free font memory
            exit(1);
            }
         switch(direction)
            {
```

```
         case NORM:   _setgtextvector(1, 0);    break;
         case UP:     _setgtextvector(0, 1);    break;
         case INVERT: _setgtextvector(-1, 0);   break;
         case DOWN:   _setgtextvector(0, -1);   break;
         }
      _setcolor(color);
      _outgtext(str);
      }

   void SetText(char s[])          // set text string
      { strcpy(str, s); }
   void SetPosition(int x, int y)  // set position
      { xCo=x; yCo=y; }
   void SetFont(char f[])          // set font
      { strcpy(face, f); }
   void SetDirection(int d)        // set direction
      { direction = d; }
   void SetColor(int c)            // set color
      { color = c; }
   void SetSize(int w, int h)      // set size
      { width = w; height = h; };
   };

void main()
   {
   if( ! _setvideomode(_MAXRESMODE) )
      { _outtext("Can't set graphics mode"); exit(1); }

   if( _registerfonts("C:\\C700\\LIB\\*.FON") < 0 )
      { _outtext("Can't register fonts"); exit(1); }

   Gstring s1, s2, s3, s4, s5, s6;     // make some strings

   s1.SetText("Default everything (Courier)");  // all defaults

   s2.SetText("Times Roman, 16x26");   // Times Roman
   s2.SetFont("tms rmn");
   s2.SetSize(16, 26);
   s2.SetPosition(200, 75);

   s3.SetText("Roman going up");       // vertical Roman
   s3.SetFont("roman");
   s3.SetColor(GREEN);
   s3.SetDirection(UP);
   s3.SetPosition(450, 300);

   s4.SetText("Helvetica 5x10");       // small Helvetica
   s4.SetFont("helv");
   s4.SetSize(5, 10);
   s4.SetPosition(200, 150);
```

```
        s5.SetText("Tall, narrow Modern");   // tall and narrow Modern
        s5.SetFont("modern");
        s5.SetColor(RED);
        s5.SetSize(10,50);
        s5.SetPosition(200, 225);

        s6.SetText("Script going down");     // vertical Script
        s6.SetFont("script");
        s6.SetSize(17, 37);
        s6.SetDirection(DOWN);
        s6.SetPosition(150, 50);

        s1.DrawText();                       // display all
        s2.DrawText();                       // the Gstrings
        s3.DrawText();
        s4.DrawText();
        s5.DrawText();
        s6.DrawText();

        getch();                             // wait for keypress
        _setvideomode(_DEFAULTMODE);         // close graphics system
        _unregisterfonts();                  // free font memory
        }
```

In the `main()` function, we create six objects of class `Gstring`. The first object is created using defaults for all the text characteristics (except the contents of the string). We have somewhat arbitrarily chosen Courier as the default typeface. The second `Gstring` object uses a different typeface, Times Roman. The third object is oriented vertically, running from the bottom of the page to the top, in Roman. The fourth is the smallest size of Helvetica. The fifth is a taller-than-normal version of Modern, and the sixth, in Script, runs vertically from the top to the bottom of the page.

When all the characteristics of the six `Gstring` objects have been specified, they are all displayed. Figure 11-6 shows the result.

MICROSOFT C++ TEXT GRAPHICS FUNCTIONS

The `DrawText()` member function in `Gstring` displays the text. This function uses a variety of Microsoft C/C++ library functions to change the characteristics of the text to be displayed. Let's examine these library functions.

The _registerfonts() Function

Before any of the graphics fonts can be used, they must be *registered*. This means telling the program the location of the font files. These files have the .FON extension. In the GRAST program, we assume the files are in the C:\C700\LIB directory. If your font files are in a different directory, you'll need to change the argument to this function. (Remember that you need to double the backslash in C++ strings, as a single backslash is interpreted as the escape character.)

FIGURE 11-16
Output of GRAST

The _unregisterfonts() Function

The `_registerfonts()` function loads the fonts into memory. To reclaim this memory when your program is over, you should call the `_unregisterfonts()` function.

The _outgtext() Function

To output text in using different fonts in graphics mode, you must use the `_outgtext()` function. Note that this is not the same as the `_outtext()` function, which always displays text in the system font.

The _setfont() Function

The key function for using Microsoft C++ graphics fonts is the `_setfont()` function. This function specifies what font will be used in all subsequent calls to the `_outgtext()` function. The `_setfont()` function takes a single parameter, but this parameter is somewhat complicated. You use it to specify the characteristics of the font you want. These characteristics are coded into a string. We'll be concerned with three of these characteristics: the face name, the width, and the height.

Here's how you specify the Courier font using a width of 9 pixels and a height of 12 pixels (the spaces before the w and the h are optional):

```
_setfont("t'courier' w9 h12");
```

This function will fail (return a 1) if the Courier typeface with width 9 and height 12 cannot be found. Actually, there are two kinds of fonts: vector and bitmapped. Bitmapped fonts can only be used in certain fixed sizes, while vector fonts can be scaled to any size. Table 11-3 is a list of the fonts currently available in Microsoft C++.

If you add a 'b' character to the options string in **_setfont()**, then your program will look for the font that most closely matches the font you specified. For example, the statement

```
_setfont("t'helv' w10 h20 b");
```

will cause the system to find what it considers the closest match to the Helvetica face name in a 9-by-12 size. The system first tries to match the height, then the face name, then the width, and finally whether the font is fixed-width (like Courier) or

TABLE 11-3 Fonts Available in Microsoft C++				
Face name	Fontname for _setfont()	File name	Type	Sizes
Times Roman	tms rmn	TMSRB.FON	bitmapped	16x26 12x20 9x16 8x15 6x12 5x10
Helvetica	helv	HELVB.FON	bitmapped	16x28 12x2? 9x18 8x15 7x12 5x10
Courier	courier	COURB.FON	bitmapped	12x15 9x12 8x10
Script	script	SCRIPT.FON	vector	17x37
Roman	roman	ROMAN.FON	vector	19x32
Modern	modern	MODERN.FON	vector	18x32

proportional. If you don't include the 'b' option, then _setfont() will fail for any bitmapped font for which you don't specify an existing size. You can use any size for a vector font.

The _setgtextvector() Function

The _setgtextvector() function determines the orientation of the text. It takes two parameters, X and Y. Table 11-4 shows the permissible combinations of these parameters and the resulting text orientations.

Thus the statement

```
_setgtextvector(0, 1);
```

will cause text to be printed vertically, from the bottom up.

REDEFINING A FUNCTION SET

Notice that the effect of using the Gstring class is to redefine the set of functions used to specify the text characteristics. For instance, Microsoft C++ uses a single library function, _setfont(), to specify the font size, while the Gstring class uses two separate member functions—SetFont() and SetSize(). Which approach you use is a matter of taste, but it's nice to know you can redefine an existing set of functions if you don't like their syntax.

EXTENDING THE Gstring CLASS

The Gstring class could be extended to include such features as overloading the + operator to perform concatenation (described in Chapter 9). This and similar additions could provide a powerful and versatile class for use in graphics programs.

TABLE 11-4 Constants for _setgtextvector		
X	Y	Direction
0	0	Unchanged
1	0	Horizontal (default)
0	1	Vertical, going up
−1	0	Horizontal, upside down
0	−1	Vertical, going down

SUMMARY

Microsoft C++ has two kinds of functions loosely called graphics functions. The first kind works only with text displays and is concerned with displaying text in a rectangular area of the screen called a window. The key function in this mode is _settextwindow(), which defines the rectangular area.

The second kind of graphics function requires a graphics display such as EGA or VGA. Programs that use these functions must initialize the display system to a graphics mode using the _setvideomode() function, and terminate with the same function with the _DEFAULTMODE constant.

Library functions can write lines, circles, squares, and polygons to the screen and fill shapes with color. Text in a variety of fonts can be displayed, and its size, color, aspect ratio, and positioning can be manipulated.

Graphics objects on the screen can have a close relationship with C++ objects in the program. This simplifies the conceptualization of a program and allows the generalization of common characteristics into a base class.

QUESTIONS

1. Using Microsoft C++ library functions, you can
   a. color any closed figure
   b. draw lines and circles
   c. write text in a variety of fonts and sizes
   d. make sounds of different pitches
2. The key function that confines character-mode text inside a window on the screen is _____.
3. True or false: A program that uses text-mode functions like _outtext() must start with the _setvideomode() function.
4. Write the code to initialize the graphics system to an EGA adapter in 16-color mode.
5. With a VGA adapter, in text mode, you can display up to _____ colors.
6. True or false: A graphics program must ordinarily run in the Microsoft C++ development environment, not as a standalone program.
7. Before terminating, a program that uses fonts should _____

8. Write a statement that draws a circle centered at (10,20), with a radius of 5.

9. True or false: The `_setcolor()` function determines what color will be displayed by the `_rectangle()` function.

10. Write the code necessary to draw a line from (2,7) to (5,11).

11. The `_setgtextvector()` function is used to specify
    a. the width of a line
    b. the color of a polygon
    c. the pattern of a square
    d. the orientation of text

12. Write a statement that will cause all lines to be drawn in a blue color.

13. In graphics programs C++ objects correspond nicely to
    a. relationships
    b. shapes
    c. functions
    d. programs

14. Write the code to draw a triangle with points (0,10), (5,0), (10,10). Use `_polygon()`.

15. A base class will often
    a. model more specific objects than its derived classes
    b. correspond to something in the real world
    c. behave badly when the chips are down
    d. be a generalized version of its derived classes

16. What does the `_clock()` function return?

17. The random-number generator should be seeded so that it doesn't always _____.

18. In the SLOT program, multiple inheritance is used to add to an object the ability to _____ itself.

19. To display text in the Helvetica font, you would use
    a. `outgtext()`
    b. `cputs()`
    c. `_outtext()`
    d. `cout`

20. The point on a graphics screen where the next pixel will be drawn is called the _____.

EXERCISES

1. Modify the `ball` class in the EZBALL program in this chapter so that the size of the ball is an instance variable rather than a constant. You can call this data member `rad`. Change the `set()` member function to accept a value for the

radius, and the draw() function so that it uses rad to draw a circle with any radius. Change the main() program so that each ball object is set to a different radius as well as to a different position.

2. Modify the shape class from the MULTSHAP program in this chapter so that the size of an object is variable rather than constant. Use both width and height as member data items so that the shape as well as the size of the shape can be specified.

Change the set() function to accept the width and height as arguments, along with the position. Modify the set() member function in the ball and rect classes so that it passes the width and height values along to shape::set(). (You can delete the tria class.) Modify the draw() member functions in ball and rect so that they use the width and height data (one or the other is enough for ball).

Modify the main() program to draw a car, using a rectangle for the lower part of the car, another rectangle for the windows area, and two ball objects for the wheels.

3. To the program in Exercise 2, add a class called car that models the car image that was created from four separate objects in main() in Exercise 2. The car class should make cars the same size and color but allow different positions. In main() create three car objects, set them to different positions with set() and display them with draw().

POINTERS

ADDRESS CONSTANTS AND VARIABLES

POINTERS AND ARRAYS

POINTERS AND FUNCTION ARGUMENTS

POINTERS AND STRINGS

MEMORY MANAGEMENT WITH new AND delete

POINTERS AND OBJECTS

LINKED LISTS

Pointers are the hobgoblin of C++ (and C) programming; seldom has such a simple idea inspired so much perplexity for so many. But fear not. In this chapter we will try to demystify pointers and show practical uses for them in C++ programming.

What are pointers for? Here are some common uses:

- Accessing array elements
- Passing arguments to a function when the function needs to modify the original argument
- Passing arrays and strings to functions
- Obtaining memory from the system
- Creating data structures such as linked lists

Pointers are much more commonly used in C++ (and C) than in many other languages (such as BASIC and Pascal). Is this emphasis on pointers really necessary? You can do a lot without them, as their absence from the preceding chapters demonstrates. Some operations that use pointers in C++ can be carried out in other ways. For example, array elements can be accessed with array notation rather than pointer notation (we'll see the difference soon), and a function can modify arguments passed by reference, as well as those passed by pointer.

However, in some situations pointers provide an essential tool for increasing the power of C++. A notable example is the creation of data structures such as linked lists and binary trees. In fact, several key features of C++, such as virtual functions and the **this** pointer (to be discussed in the next chapter), require the use of pointers. So, although you can do a lot of programming in C++ without using pointers, you will find them essential to obtaining the most from the language.

In this chapter we'll introduce pointers gradually, starting with fundamental concepts and working up to complex pointer applications.

If you already know C, you can probably skim over the first half of the chapter. However, you should read the sections in the second half on the **new** and **delete** operators, accessing member functions using pointers, arrays of pointers to objects, and linked-list objects.

ADDRESSES AND POINTERS

The ideas behind pointers are not complicated. Here's the first key concept: Every byte in the computer's memory has an *address*. Addresses are numbers, just as they are for houses on a street. The numbers start at 0 and go up from there—1, 2, 3, and so on. If you have 640K of memory, the highest address is 655,359; for 1 MB of memory, it is 1,048,575.

Your program, when it is loaded into memory, occupies a certain range of these addresses. That means that every variable and every function in your program starts at a particular address. Figure 12-1 shows how this looks.

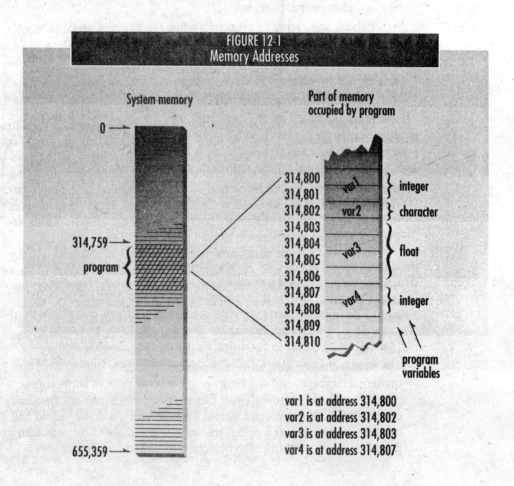

FIGURE 12-1
Memory Addresses

System memory

Part of memory occupied by program

0

314,800 — var1 } integer
314,801
314,802 — var2 } character
314,803
314,804 — var3 } float
314,805
314,759 — 314,806
program { 314,807 — var4 } integer
314,808
314,809
314,810

program variables

var1 is at address 314,800
var2 is at address 314,802
var3 is at address 314,803
var4 is at address 314,807

655,359 —

THE ADDRESS OF OPERATOR &

You can find out the address occupied by a variable by using the *address of* operator &. Here's a short program, VARADDR, that demonstrates how to do this:

```
// varaddr.cpp
// addresses of variables
#include <iostream.h>

void main()
    {
    int var1 = 11;            // define and initialize
    int var2 = 22;            // three variables
    int var3 = 33;

    cout << endl << &var1    // print out the addresses
         << endl << &var2    // of these variables
         << endl << &var3;
    }
```

This simple program defines three integer variables and initializes them to the values 11, 22, and 33. It then prints out the addresses of these variables.

The actual addresses occupied by the variables in a program depend on many factors, such as the computer the program is running on, the size of the operating system, and whether any other programs are currently in memory. For these reasons you probably won't get the same addresses we did when you run this program. Here's the output on our machine:

```
0xfff4          ←————address of var1
0xfff2          ←————address of var2
0xfff0          ←————address of var3
```

Remember that the *address* of a variable is not at all the same as its *contents*. The contents of the three variables are 11, 22, and 33. Figure 12-2 shows the three variables in memory.

The << insertion operator interprets the addresses in hexadecimal arithmetic, as indicated by the prefix 0x before each number. This is the usual way to show memory addresses. If you aren't familiar with the hexadecimal number system, don't worry. All you really need to know is that each variable starts at a unique address. However, you might note in the output above that each address differs from the next by exactly 2 bytes. That's because integers occupy 2 bytes of memory. If we had used variables of type char they would have adjacent addresses, since chars occupy 1 byte; and if we had used type double the addresses would have differed by 8 bytes.

The addresses appear in descending order (except, for some reason, the first one) because automatic variables are stored on the stack, which grows downward in memory. If we had used external variables they would have ascending addresses, since external variables are stored on the heap, which grows upward. Again, you don't need to worry too much about these considerations, since the compiler keeps track of the details for you.

FIGURE 12-2
Addresses and Contents of Variables

Don't confuse the address of operator **&**, which precedes a variable name, with the reference operator **&**, which follows the variable type. (References were discussed in Chapter 6.)

POINTER VARIABLES

Addresses by themselves are rather limited. It's nice to know that we can find out where things are in memory, as we did in VARADDR, but printing out address values is not all that useful. The potential for increasing our programming power requires an additional idea: *variables that hold address values*. We've seen variable types that store characters, integers, floating-point numbers, and so on. Addresses are stored similarly. A variable that holds an address value is called a *pointer variable*, or simply a *pointer*.

What is the data type of pointer variables? It's not the same as the variable whose address is being stored; a pointer to `int` is not type `int`. You might think a pointer data type would be called something like `pointer` or `ptr`. However, things are slightly more complicated. The next program, PTRVAR, shows the syntax for pointer variables:

```
// ptrvar.cpp
// pointers (address variables)
#include <iostream.h>

void main()
{
```

```
int var1 = 11;                 // two integer variables
int var2 = 22;

cout << endl << &var1          // print addresses of variables
     << endl << &var2;

int* ptr;                      // pointer to integers

ptr = &var1;                   // pointer points to var1
cout << endl << ptr;           // print pointer value

ptr = &var2;                   // pointer points to var2
cout << endl << ptr;           // print pointer value
}
```

This program defines two integer variables, var1 and var2, and initializes them to the values 11 and 22. It then prints out their addresses.

The program next defines a *pointer variable* in the line

```
int* ptr;
```

To the uninitiated this is a rather bizarre syntax. The asterisk means *pointer to*. Thus the statement defines the variable ptr as a *pointer to* int. This is another way of saying that this variable can hold the addresses of integer variables.

What's wrong with the idea of a general-purpose pointer type that holds pointers to any data type? If we called it type pointer, we could write declarations like

```
pointer ptr;
```

The problem is that the compiler needs to know what kind of variable the pointer points to. (We'll see why when we talk about pointers and arrays.) The syntax used in C++ allows pointers to any type to be declared

```
char* cptr;           // pointer to char
int* iptr;            // pointer to int
float* fptr;          // pointer to float
Distance* distptr;    // pointer to user-defined Distance class
```

and so on.

Syntax Quibbles

We should note that it is common to write pointer definitions with the asterisk closer to the variable name than to the type:

```
char *charptr;
```

It doesn't matter to the compiler, but placing the asterisk next to the type helps to emphasize that the asterisk is part of the variable type (pointer to char), not part of the name itself.

If you define more than one pointer of the same type on one line, you need only insert the type-pointed-to once, but you need to place an asterisk before each variable name:

```
char* ptr1, * ptr2, * ptr3;  // three variables of type char*
```

Or you can use the asterisk-next-to-the-name approach:

```
char *ptr1, *ptr2, *ptr3;  // three variables of type char*
```

Pointers Must Have a Value

An address like *0x8f4ffff4* can be thought of as a *pointer constant*. A pointer like `ptr` can be thought of as a *pointer variable*. Just as the integer variable `var1` can be assigned the constant value 11, so can the pointer variable `ptr` be assigned the constant value *0x8f4ffff4*.

When we first define a variable, it holds no value (unless we initialize it at the same time). It may hold a garbage value, but this has no meaning. In the case of pointers, a garbage value is the address of something in memory, but probably not of something that we want. So before a pointer is used, a specific address must be placed in it. In the PTRVAR program `ptr` is first assigned the address of `var1` in the line

```
ptr = &var1;        ←——————— put address of var1 in ptr
```

Following this the program prints out the value contained in `ptr`, which should be the same address printed for `&var1`. The same pointer variable `ptr` is then assigned the address of `var2`, and this value is printed out. Figure 12-3 shows the operation of the PTRVAR program. Here's the output of PTRVAR:

```
0xfff4          ←——————— address of var1
0xfff2          ←——————— address of var2
0xfff4          ←——————— ptr set to address of var1
0xfff2          ←——————— ptr set to address of var2
```

To summarize: A pointer can hold the address of any variable of the correct type; it's a receptacle awaiting an address. However, it must be given *some* value, otherwise it will point to an address we don't want it to point to, such as into our program code or the operating system. Rogue pointer values can result in system crashes and are difficult to debug, since the compiler gives no warning. The moral: Make sure you give every pointer variable a valid address value before using it.

ACCESSING THE VARIABLE POINTED TO

Suppose that we don't know the name of a variable but we do know its address. Can we access the contents of the variable? (It may seem like mismanagement to lose track of variable names, but we'll soon see that there are many variables whose names we don't know.)

The answer is that there is a special syntax to access the value of a variable using its address instead of its name. Here's an example program, PTRACC, that shows how it's done:

```
// ptracc.cpp
// accessing the variable pointed to
#include <iostream.h>

void main()
{
```

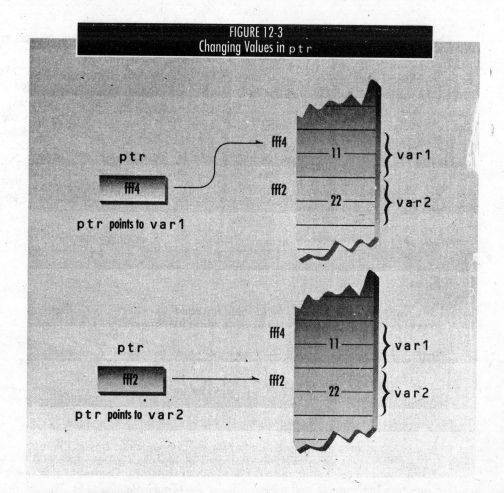

FIGURE 12-3
Changing Values in ptr

```
int var1 = 11;              // two integer variables
int var2 = 22;

int* ptr;                   // pointer to integers

ptr = &var1;                // pointer points to var1
cout << endl << *ptr;       // print contents of pointer (11)

ptr = &var2;                // pointer points to var2
cout << endl << *ptr;       // print contents of pointer (22)
}
```

This program is very similar to PTRVAR, except that instead of printing the address values in **ptr**, we print the integer value stored at the address that's stored in **ptr**. Here's the output:

```
11
22
```

The expression that accesses the variables `var1` and `var2` is `*ptr`, which occurs in each of the two `cout` statements.

When an asterisk is used in front of a variable name, as it is in the `*ptr` expression, it is called the *indirection operator*. It means *the value of the variable pointed to by*. Thus the expression `*ptr` represents the value of the variable pointed to by `ptr`. When `ptr` is set to the address of `var1`, the expression `*ptr` has the value 11, since `var1` is 11. When `ptr` is changed to the address of `var2`, the expression `*ptr` acquires the value 22, since `var1` is 22. Figure 12-4 shows how this looks.

You can use a pointer not only to display a variable's value but to perform any operation you would perform on the variable directly. Here's a program, PTRTO, that uses a pointer to assign a value to a variable, and then to assign that value to another variable:

```
// ptrto.cpp
// other access using pointers
#include <iostream.h>

d main()
{
    int var1, var2;         // two integer variables
    int* ptr;               // pointer to integers

    ptr = &var1;            // set pointer to address of var1
    *ptr = 37;              // same as var1=37
    var2 = *ptr;            // same as var2=var1

    cout << endl << var2;   // verify var2 is 37
}
```

Remember that the asterisk used as the indirection operator has a different meaning from the asterisk used to declare pointer variables. The indirection operator precedes the variable and means *value of the variable pointed to by*. The asterisk used in a declaration means *pointer to*.

```
int* ptr;     // declaration:
*ptr = 37;    // indirection:
```

Using the indirection operator to access the value stored in an address is called *indirect addressing*, or sometimes *dereferencing*, the pointer.

Here's a capsule summary of what we've learned so far:

```
int v;      // defines variable v of type int
int* p;     // defines p as a pointer to int
p = &v;     // assigns address of variable v to pointer p
v = 3;      // assigns 3 to v
*p = 3;     // also assigns 3 to v
```

The last two statements show the difference between normal or direct addressing, where we refer to a variable by name, and pointer or indirect addressing, where we refer to the same variable using its address.

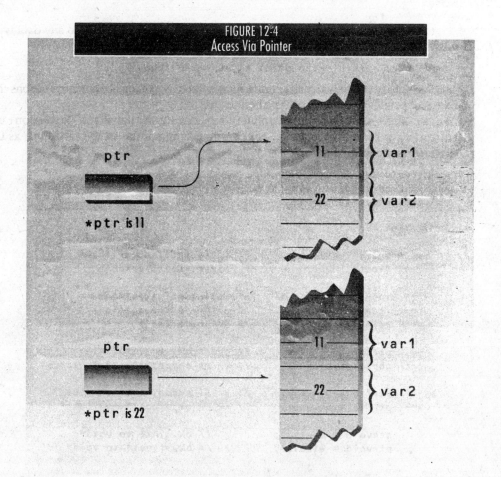

FIGURE 12-4
Access Via Pointer

These two approaches are vaguely analogous to delivering a letter to a friend. If you drive to the friend's house and stick the letter in the mailslot, that's direct addressing. You can also write the address on the envelope and put the letter in a public mailbox. The mail personnel will read the address and see that the letter gets to the right place. That's indirect addressing.

In the example programs we've shown so far in this chapter, there's really no advantage to using the pointer expression to access variables, since we can access them directly. Pointers come into their own when you can't access a variable directly, as we'll see.

POINTER TO void

Before we go on to see pointers at work, we should note one peculiarity of pointer data types. Ordinarily, the address that you put in a pointer must be the address of a variable of the same type as the pointer. You can't assign the address of a **float** variable to a pointer to **int**, for example. However, there is an exception to this. There is a sort of general-purpose pointer that can point to any data type. This is called a pointer to **void**, and is defined like this:

```
void* ptr;   // ptr can point to any data type
```

Such pointers have certain specialized uses, such as passing pointers to functions that operate independently of the data type pointed to.

The next example uses a pointer to **void** and also shows that, if you don't use **void**, you must be careful to assign pointers an address of the same type as the pointer. Here's the listing for PTRVOID:

```
// ptrvoid.cpp
// pointers to type void
#include <iostream.h>

void main()
   {
   int intvar;                 // integer variable
   float flovar;               // float variable

   int* ptrint;                // define pointer to int
   float* ptrflo;              // define pointer to float
   void* ptrvoid;              // define pointer to void

   ptrint = &intvar;           // ok, int* to int*
// ptrint = &flovar;           // error, float* to int*

// ptrflo = &intvar;           // error, int* to float*
   ptrflo = &flovar;           // ok, float* to float*

   ptrvoid = &intvar;          // ok, int* to void*
   ptrvoid = &flovar;          // ok, float* to void*
   }
```

You can assign the address of **intvar** to **ptrint** because they are both type **int***, but you can't assign the address of **flovar** to **ptrint** because the first is type **float*** and the second is type **int***. However, **ptrvoid** can be given any pointer value, such as **int***, because it is a pointer to **void**.

POINTERS AND ARRAYS

There is a close association between pointers and arrays. We saw in Chapter 8 how array elements are accessed. The following program, ARRNOTE, provides a review:

```
// arrnote.cpp
// array accessed with array notation
#include <iostream.h>

void main()
   {
```

```
    int intarray[5] = { 31, 54, 77, 52, 93 };  // array

    for(int j=0; j<5; j++)                      // for each element
       cout << endl << intarray[j];             // print value
    }
```

The `cout` statement prints each array element in turn. For instance, when `j` is 3, the expression `intarray[j]` takes on the value `intarray[3]` and accesses the fourth array element, the integer 52. Here's the output of ARRNOTE:

```
31
54
77
52
93
```

Surprisingly, array elements can be accessed using pointer notation as well as array notation. The next example, PTRNOTE, is similar to ARRNOTE except that it uses pointer notation:

```
// ptrnote.cpp
// array accessed with pointer notation
#include <iostream.h>

    d main()
      {
      int intarray[5] = { 31, 54, 77, 52, 93 };  // array

      for(int j=0; j<5; j++)                      // for each element,
         cout << endl << *(intarray+j);           // print value
      }
```

The expression `*(intarray+j)` in PTRNOTE has exactly the same effect as `intarray[j]` in ARRNOTE, and the output of the programs is identical. But how do we interpret the expression `*(intarray+j)`? Suppose `j` is 3, so the expression is equivalent to `*(intarray+3)`. We want this to represent the contents of the fourth element of the array (52). Remember that the name of an array is its address. The expression `intarray+j` is thus an address with something added to it. You might expect that `interray+3` would cause 3 bytes to be added to `intarray`. But that doesn't produce the result we want: `intarray` is an array of integers, and 3 bytes into this array is the middle of the second element, which is not very useful. We want to obtain the fourth *integer* in the array, not the fourth byte, as shown in Figure 12-5.

The C++ compiler is smart enough to take the size of the data into account when it performs arithmetic on data addresses. It knows that `intarray` is an array of type `int` because it was declared that way. So when it sees the expression `intarray+3` it interprets it as the address of the fourth *integer* in `intarray`, not the fourth byte.

But we want the *value* of this fourth array element, not the *address*. To take the value, we use the indirection operator `*`. The resulting expression, when `j` is 3, is `*(intarray+3)`, which is the contents of the fourth array element, or 52.

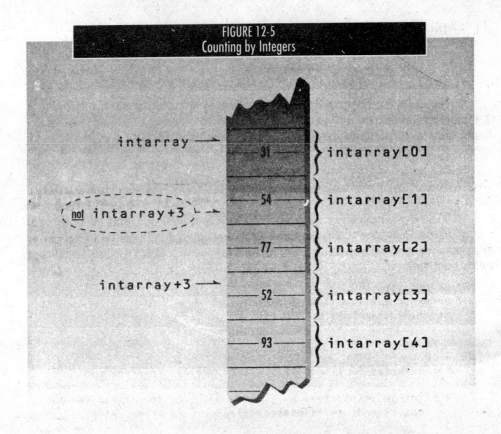

FIGURE 12-5
Counting by Integers

Now we see why a pointer declaration must include the type of the variable pointed to. The compiler needs to know whether a pointer is a pointer to `int` or a pointer to `double`, so that it can perform the correct arithmetic to access elements of the array. It multiplies the index value by 2 in the case of type `int`, but by 8 in the case of `double`.

POINTER CONSTANTS AND POINTER VARIABLES

Suppose that, instead of adding `j` to `intarray` to step through the array addresses, you wanted to use the increment operator. Could you write `*(intarray++)`?

The answer is no, and the reason is that you can't increment a constant (or indeed change it in any way). The expression `intarray` is the address where the system has chosen to place your array, and it will stay at this address until the program terminates. `intarray` is a constant. You can't say `intarray++` any more than you can say `7++`. (In a multitasking system, variable addresses may change during program execution. An active program may be swapped out to disk and then reloaded at a different memory location. However, this process is invisible to your program.)

While you can't increment an address, you can increment a pointer that holds an address. The next example, PTRINC, shows how:

```
// ptrinc.cpp
// array accessed with pointer
#include <iostream.h>

void main()
   {
   int intarray[] = { 31, 54, 77, 52, 93 }; // array
   int* ptrint;                             // pointer to int
   ptrint = intarray;                       // points to intarray

   for(int j=0; j<5; j++)                    // for each element,
      cout << endl << *(ptrint++);           // print value
   }
```

Here we define a pointer to `int`—`ptrint`—and give it the value `intarray`, the address of the array. Now we can access the contents of the array elements with the expression

```
*(ptrint++)
```

The variable `ptrint` starts off with the same address value as `intarray`, thus allowing the first array element, `intarray[0]`, which has the value 31, to be accessed as before. But, because `ptrint` is a variable and not a constant, it can be incremented. After it is incremented, it points to the second array element, `intarray[1]`. The expression `*(ptrint++)` then represents the contents of the second array element, or 54. The loop causes the expression to access each array element in turn. The output of PTRINC is the same as that for PTRNOTE.

POINTERS AND FUNCTIONS

In Chapter 6 we noted that there are three ways to pass arguments to a function: by value, by reference, and by pointer. If the function is intended to modify variables in the calling program, then these variables cannot be passed by value, since the function obtains only a copy of the variable. However, either a reference argument or a pointer can be used in this situation.

PASSING SIMPLE VARIABLES

We'll first review how arguments are passed by reference, and then compare this to passing pointer arguments. The PASSREF program shows passing by reference:

```
// passref.cpp
// arguments passed by reference
#include <iostream.h>

void main()
   {
```

```
void centimize(double&);      // prototype

double var = 10.0;            // var has value of 10 inches
cout << endl << "var=" << var << " inches";

centimize(var);              // change var to centimeters
cout << endl << "var=" << var << " centimeters";
}

void centimize(double& v)
{
v *= 2.54;                    // v is the same as var
}
```

Here we want to convert a variable `var` in `main()` from inches to centimeters. We pass the variable by reference to the function `centimize()`. (Remember that the `&` following the data type `double` in the prototype for this function indicates that the argument is passed by reference.) The `centimize()` function multiplies the original variable by 2.54. Notice how the function refers to the variable. It simply uses the argument name `v`; `v` and `var` are different names for the same thing.

Once it has converted `var` to centimeters, `main()` displays the result. Here's the output of PASSREF:

```
var=10 inches
var=25.4 centimeters
```

The next example, PASSPTR, shows an equivalent situation when pointers are used:

```
// passptr.cpp
// arguments passed by pointer
#include <iostream.h>

void main()
{
void centimize(double*);     // prototype

double var = 10.0;           // var has value of 10 inches
cout << endl << "var=" << var << " inches";

centimize(&var);             // change var to centimeters
cout << endl << "var=" << var << " centimeters";
}

void centimize(double* ptrd)
{
*ptrd *= 2.54;               // *ptrd is the same as var
}
```

The output of PASSPTR is the same as that of PASSREF.

The function `centimize()` is declared as taking an argument that is a pointer to `double`:

```
void centimize(double*)     // argument is pointer to double
```

When `main()` calls the function it supplies the address of the variable as the argument:

```
centimize(&var);
```

Remember that this argument is not the variable itself, as it is in passing by reference, but the variable's address.

Because the `centimize()` function is passed an address, it must use the indirection operator, `*ptrd`, to access the value stored at this address:

```
*ptrd *= 2.54;  // multiply the contents of ptrd by 2.54
```

Of course this is the same as

```
*ptrd = *ptrd * 2.54;  // multiply the contents of ptrd by 2.54
```

where the standalone asterisk means multiplication. (This operator really gets around.)

Since `ptrd` contains the address of `var`, anything done to `*ptrd` is actually done to `var`. Figure 12-6 shows how changing `*ptrd` in the function changes `var` in the calling program.

Passing a pointer as an argument to a function is in some ways similar to passing a reference. They both permit the variable in the calling program to be modified by the function. However, the mechanism is different. A reference is an alias for the original variable, while a pointer is the address of the variable.

FIGURE 12-6
Pointer Passed to Function

① `main()` passes address of `var` to `ptrd` in `centimize()`

② `centimize()` uses this address to access `var`

PASSING ARRAYS

We've seen numerous examples, starting in Chapter 8, of arrays passed as arguments to functions, and their elements being accessed by the function. Until this chapter, since we had not yet learned about pointers, this was done using array notation. However, it's more common to use pointer notation instead of array notation when arrays are passed to functions. The PASSARR program shows how this looks:

```
// passarr.cpp
// array passed by pointer
#include <iostream.h>

const int MAX = 5;              // number of array elements

void main()
   {
   void centimize(double*);  // prototype

   double varray[MAX] = { 10.0, 43.1, 95.9, 59.7, 87.3 };

   centimize(varray);          // change elements of varray to cm

   for(int j=0; j<MAX; j++)  // display new array values
      cout << endl << "varray[" << j << "]="
           << varray[j] << " centimeters";
   }

void centimize(double* ptrd)
   {
   for(int j=0; j<MAX; j++)
      *ptrd++ *= 2.54;         // ptrd points to elements of varray
   }
```

The prototype for the function is the same as in PASSPTR; the function's single argument is a pointer to **double**. In array notation this is written as

```
void centimize(double[]);
```

That is, **double*** is equivalent here to **double[]**, although the pointer syntax is more commonly used.

Since the name of an array is the array's address, there is no need for the address operator **&** when the function is called:

```
centimize(varray);  // pass array address
```

In **centimize()** this array address is placed in the variable **ptrd**. To point to each element of the array in turn, we need only increment **ptrd**:

```
*ptrd++ *= 2.54;
```

Figure 12-7 shows how the array is accessed. Here's the output of PASSARR:

```
varray[0]=25.4 centimeters
varray[1]=109.474 centimeters
varray[2]=243.586 centimeters
```

FIGURE 12-7
Accessing Array from Function

① main() *passes address of* **varray** *to* ptrd *in* **centimize()**

② **centimize()** *uses this address to access each array element in turn*

```
varray[3]=151.638 centimeters
varray[4]=221.742 centimeters
```

Here's a syntax question: How do we know that the expression `*ptrd++` increments the pointer and not the pointer contents? In other words, does the compiler interpret it as `*(ptrd++)`, which is what we want, or as `(*ptrd)++`? It turns out that `*` (when used as the indirection operator) and `++` have the same precedence. However, operators of the same precedence are distinguished in a second way: by **associativity**. Associativity is concerned with whether the compiler performs operations starting with an operator on the right or an operator on the left. If a group of operators have right associativity, the compiler performs the operation on the right side of the expression first, then works its way to the left. The unary operators like `*` and `++` do have right associativity, so the expression is interpreted as `*(ptrd++)`, with the pointer being incremented first and the indirection operator applied to the result.

SORTING ARRAY ELEMENTS

As a further example of using pointers to access array elements, let's see how to sort the contents of an array. We'll use two program examples—the first to lay the groundwork, and the second, an expansion of the first, to demonstrate the sorting process.

433

Ordering with Pointers

The first program is similar to the REFORDER program in Chapter 6, except that it uses pointers instead of references. It orders two numbers passed to it as arguments, exchanging them if the second is smaller than the first. Here's the listing for PTRORDER:

```
// ptrorder.cpp
// orders two arguments using pointers
#include <iostream.h>

void main()
    {
    void order(int*, int*);          // prototype

    int n1=99, n2=11;                // one pair ordered, one not
    int n3=22, n4=88;

    order(&n1, &n2);                 // order each pair of numbers
    order(&n3, &n4);

    cout << endl << "n1=" << n1;     // print out all numbers
    cout << endl << "n2=" << n2;
    cout << endl << "n3=" << n3;
    cout << endl << "n4=" << n4;
    }
void order(int* numb1, int* numb2)   // orders two numbers
    {
    if(*numb1 > *numb2)              // if 1st larger than 2nd,
        {
        int temp = *numb1;          // swap them
        *numb1 = *numb2;
        *numb2 = temp;
        }
    }
```

The function `order()` works the same as it did in REFORDER, except that it is passed the *addresses* of the numbers to be ordered, and it accesses the numbers using pointers. That is, `*numb1` accesses the number in `main()` passed as the first argument, and `*numb2` accesses the second.

Here's the output from PTRORDER:

```
n1=11        ←──────── this and
n2=99        ←──────── this are swapped, since they weren't in order
n3=22        ←──────── this
n4=88        ←──────── and this are not swapped, since they were in order
```

We'll use the `order()` function from PTRORDER in our next example program, PTRSORT, which sorts an array of integers.

```
// ptrsort.cpp
// sorts an array using pointers
#include <iostream.h>

void main()
    {
```

```
      void bsort(int*, int);          // prototype
      const int N = 10;               // array size
                                      // test array
      int arr[N] = { 37, 84, 62, 91, 11, 65, 57, 28, 19, 49 };

      bsort(arr, N);                  // sort the array

      for(int j=0; j<N; j++)          // print out sorted array
         cout << arr[j] << " ";
      }

   void bsort(int* ptr, int n)
      {
      void order(int*, int*);         // prototype
      int j, k;                       // indexes to array

      for(j=0; j<n-1; j++)            // outer loop
         for(k=j+1; k<n; k++)         // inner loop starts at outer
            order(ptr+j, ptr+k);      // order the pointer contents
      }

   void order(int* numb1, int* numb2) // orders two numbers
      {
      if(*numb1 > *numb2)             // if 1st larger than 2nd,
         {
         int temp = *numb1;           // swap them
         *numb1 = *numb2;
         *numb2 = temp;
         }
      }
```

The array **arr** of integers in **main()** is initialized to unsorted values. The address of the array, and the number of elements, are passed to the **bsort()** function. This sorts the array, and the sorted values are then printed. Here's the output of the PTRSORT:

11 19 28 37 49 57 62 65 84 91

The Bubble Sort

The **bsort()** function sorts the array using the *bubble sort*. This is a simple (although notoriously slow) approach to sorting. Here's how it works, assuming we want to arrange the numbers in the array in ascending order. First, the first element of the array (**arr[0]**) is compared in turn with each of the other elements (starting with the second). If it's greater than any of them, the two are swapped. When this is done we know that at least the first element is in order; it's now the smallest element. Next the second element is compared in turn with all the other elements, starting with the third, and again swapped if it's bigger. When we're done we know that the second element has the second-smallest value. This process is continued for all the elements until the next-to-the-last, at which time the array is assumed to be ordered. Figure 12-8 shows the bubble sort in action.

The number in the first position, 37, is compared with each element in turn, and swapped with 11. The number in the second position, which starts off being

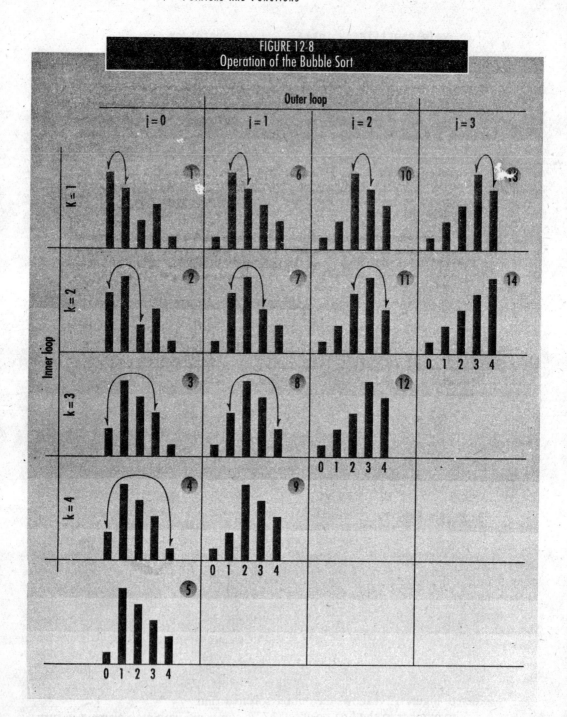

FIGURE 12-8
Operation of the Bubble Sort

84, is compared with each element. It's swapped with 62; then 62 (which is now in the second position) is swapped with 37, 37 is swapped with 28, and 28 is swapped with 19. The number in the third position, which is 84 again, is swapped with 62, 62 is swapped with 57, 57 with 37, and 37 with 28. The process continues until the array is sorted.

The `bsort()` function in PTRSORT consists of two nested loops, each of which controls a pointer. The outer loop uses the loop variable `j`, and the inner one uses `k`. The expressions `ptr+j` and `ptr+k` point to various elements of the array, as determined by the loop variables. The expression `ptr+j` moves down the array, starting at the first element (the top) and stepping down integer by integer until one short of the last element (the bottom). For each position taken by `ptr+j` in the outer loop, the expression `ptr+k` in the inner loop starts pointing one below `ptr+j` and moves down to the bottom of the array. Each time through the inner loop, the elements pointed to by `ptr+j` and `ptr+k` are compared, using the `order()` function, and if the first is greater than the second, they're swapped. Figure 12-9 shows this process.

The PTRSORT example begins to reveal the power of pointers. They provide a consistent and efficient way to operate on array elements and other variables whose names aren't known to a particular function.

POINTERS AND STRINGS

As we noted in the chapter on arrays, strings are simply arrays of type `char`. Thus pointer notation can be applied to the characters in strings, just as it can to the elements of any array.

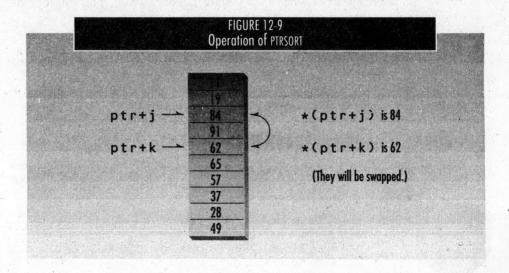

FIGURE 12-9
Operation of PTRSORT

POINTERS TO STRING CONSTANTS

Here's an example, TWOSTR, in which two strings are defined, one using array notation as we've seen in previous examples, and one using pointer notation.

```
// twostr.cpp
// strings defined using array and pointer notation
#include <iostream.h>

void main()
    {
    char str1[] = "Defined as an array";
    char* str2 = "Defined as a pointer";

    cout << endl << str1;      // display both strings
    cout << endl << str2;

// str1++;                     // can't do this; str1 is a constant
    str2++;                    // this is OK, str2 is a pointer

    cout << endl << str2;      // now str2 starts "efined..."
    }
```

In many ways these two types of definition are equivalent. You can print out both strings as the example shows, use them as function arguments, and so on. But there is a subtle difference: str1 is an address—that is, a pointer constant—while str2 is a pointer variable. So str2 can be changed, while str1 cannot, as demonstrated in the program. Figure 12-10 shows how these two kinds of strings look in memory.

We can increment str2, since it is a pointer, but once we do, it no longer points to the first character in the string. Here's the output of TWOSTR:

```
Defined as an array
Defined as a pointer
efined as a pointer        ←————— following str2++
```

A string defined as a pointer is considerably more flexible than one defined as an array. The following examples will make use of this flexibility.

STRINGS AS FUNCTION ARGUMENTS

Here's an example that shows a string used as a function argument. The function simply prints the string, by accessing each character in turn. Here's the listing for PTRSTR:

```
// ptrstr.cpp
// displays a string with pointer notation
#include <iostream.h>

void main()
    {
    void dispstr(char*);      // prototype
```

```
    char str[] = "Idle people have the least leisure ";

    dispstr(str);              // display the string
    }

void dispstr(char* ps)
    {
    cout << endl;              // start on new line
    while( *ps )               // until null character,
        cout << *ps++;         // print characters
    }
```

The array address **str** is used as the argument in the call to function **dispstr()**. This address is a constant, but since it is passed by value, a copy of it is created in **dispstr()**. This copy is a pointer, **ps**. A pointer can be changed, so the function increments **ps** to display the string. The expression ***ps++** returns the successive characters of the string. The loop cycles until it finds the null character ('\0') at the end of the string. Since this has the value 0, which represents *false*, the **while** loop terminates at that point.

FIGURE 12-10
Strings as Arrays and Pointers

String defined as array

String defined as pointer

```
char str1[] = "Def....        char* str2 = "Def....
```

COPYING A STRING USING POINTERS

We've seen examples of pointers used to obtain values from an array. Pointers can also be used to insert values into an array. The next example, COPYSTR, demonstrates a function that copies one string to another:

```
// copystr.cpp
// copies one string to another with pointers
#include <iostream.h>

d main()
{
    void copystr(char*, char*);   // prototype

    char* str1 = "Self-conquest is the greatest victory.";
    char str2[80];                 // empty string

    copystr(str2, str1);           // copy str1 to str2
    cout << endl << str2;          // display str2
}

void copystr(char* dest, char* src)
{
    while( *src )                  // until null character,
        *dest++ = *src++;          // copy chars from src to dest
    *dest = '\0';                  // terminate dest
}
```

Here the `main()` part of the program calls the function `copystr()` to copy `str1` to `str2`. In this function the expression

```
*dest++ = *src++;
```

takes the value at the address pointed to by `src` and places it in the address pointed to by `dest`. Both pointers are then incremented, so the next time through the loop the next character will be transferred. The loop terminates when a null character is found in `src`; at this point a null is inserted in `dest` and the function returns. Figure 12-11 shows how the pointers move through the strings.

LIBRARY STRING FUNCTIONS

Many of the library functions we have already used for strings have string arguments that are specified using pointer notation. As an example we can look at the description of `strcpy()` in the *Run-Time Library Reference* (or in the STRING.H header file). This function copies one string to another; we can compare it with our homemade `copystr()` function in the COPYSTR example. Here's the syntax for the `strcpy()` library function:

```
char* strcpy(char* dest, const char* src);
```

FIGURE 12-11
Operation of COPYSTR

```
*dest++ = *src++;
```

This function takes two arguments of type `char*`. What is the effect of the `const` modifier in the second argument? It indicates that `strcpy()` cannot change the characters pointed to by `src`. (It does not imply that the `src` pointer itself cannot be modified. To do that the argument declaration would be `char * const src`.)

The `strcpy()` function also returns a pointer to `char`; this is the address of the `dest` string. In other respects this function works very much like our homemade `copystr()` function.

ARRAYS OF POINTERS TO STRINGS

Just as there are arrays of variables of type `int` or type `float`, there can also be arrays of pointers. A common use for this construction is an array of pointers to strings.

In Chapter 8 the STRARAY program demonstrated an array of strings. As we noted, there is a disadvantage to using an array of strings, in that the subarrays that hold the strings must all be the same length, so that space is wasted when strings are shorter than the length of the subarrays (see Figure 8-10 in Chapter 8).

Let's see how to use pointers to solve this problem. We will modify STRARAY to create an array of pointers to strings, rather than an array of strings. Here's the listing for PTRTOSTR:

441

```
// ptrtostr.cpp
// an array of pointers to strings
#include <iostream.h>
const int DAYS = 7;                      // number of pointers in array

void main()
   {                                     // array of pointers to char
   char* arrptrs[DAYS] = { "Sunday", "Monday", "Tuesday",
                           "Wednesday", "Thursday",
                           "Friday", "Saturday"  };

   for(int j=0; j<DAYS; j++)    // display every string
      cout << arrptrs[j] << endl;
   }
```

The output of this program is the same as that for STRARAY:

```
Sunday
Monday
Tuesday
Wednesday
Thursday
Friday
Saturday
```

When strings are not part of an array, C++ places them contiguously in memory, so there is no wasted space. However, to find the strings, there must be an array that holds pointers to them. A string is itself an array of type **char**, so an array of pointers to strings is an array of pointers to **char**. That is the meaning of the definition of **arrptrs** in PTRTOSTR. Now recall that a string is always represented by a single address: the address of the first character in the string. It is these addresses that are stored in the array. Figure 12-12 shows how this looks.

MEMORY MANAGEMENT: new AND delete

We've seen many examples where arrays are used to set aside memory. The statement

```
int arr1[100];
```

reserves memory for 100 integers. Arrays are a useful approach to data storage, but they have a serious drawback: We must know at the time we write the program how big the array will be. We can't wait until the program is running to specify the array size. The following approach won't work:

```
cin >> size;       // get size from user
int arr[size];     // error; array size must be a constant
```

The compiler requires the array size to be a constant.

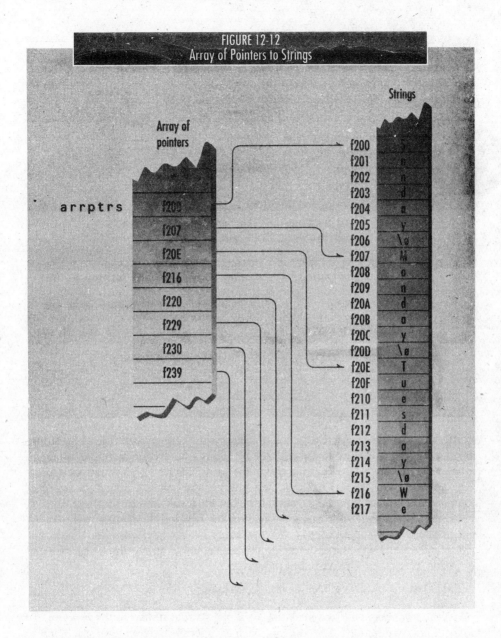

FIGURE 12-12
Array of Pointers to Strings

But in many situations we don't know how much memory we need until run time. We might want to store a string that was typed in by the user, for example. In this situation we can define an array sized to hold the largest string we expect, but this wastes memory.

443

THE new OPERATOR

C++ provides another approach to obtaining blocks of memory: the new operator. This operator obtains memory from the operating system and returns a pointer to its starting point. The NEWINTRO example shows how new is used:

```
// newintro.cpp
// introduces operator new
#include <iostream.h>
#include <string.h>        // for strcpy()

void main()
    {
    char* str = "Idle hands are the devil's workshop.";
    int len = strlen(str);      // get length of str

    char* ptr;                  // make a pointer to char
    ptr = new char[len+1];      // set aside memory: string + '\0'

    strcpy(ptr, str);           // copy str to new memory area ptr

    cout << endl << "ptr=" << ptr;  // show that str is now in ptr

    delete ptr;                 // release ptr's memory
    }
```

The expression

```
ptr = new char[len+1];
```

returns a pointer that points to a section of memory just large enough to hold the string str, whose length len we found with the strlen() library function, plus an extra byte for the null character '\0' at the end of the string. Figure 12-13 shows the syntax of a statement using the new operator. Remember to use brackets around the size; the compiler won't object if you use parentheses, but the results will be incorrect.

Figure 12-14 shows the memory obtained by new and the pointer to it.

In NEWINTRO we use strcpy() to copy string str to the newly created memory area pointed to by ptr. Since we made this area equal in size to the length of str, the string fits exactly. The output of NEWINTRO is:

```
ptr=Idle hands are the devil's workshop.
```

(C programmers will recognize that new plays a role similar to the malloc() family of library functions. The new approach is superior in that it returns a pointer to the appropriate data type, while malloc()'s pointer must be cast to the appropriate type.)

Be advised that new reserves memory on the *heap* (also called *free store*). This is a different kind of memory from that used by other program variables. Unlike local variables, heap memory is not automatically freed when a function returns, and unlike external variables it is not freed when a program terminates.

FIGURE 12-13
Syntax of new Operator

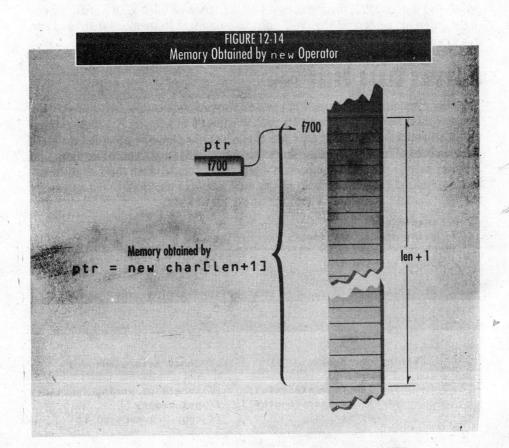

FIGURE 12-14
Memory Obtained by new Operator

THE delete OPERATOR

If your program reserves many chunks of memory using new, eventually all the available memory will be reserved and the system will crash. To ensure safe and efficient use of memory, the new operator is matched by a corresponding delete operator that returns memory to the operating system. In NEWINTRO the statement

```
delete ptr;
```

returns to the system whatever memory was pointed to by ptr.

Actually, there is no need for this operator in NEWINTRO, since memory is automatically returned when the program terminates. However, suppose you use new in a function. If the function uses a local variable as a pointer to this memory, then when the function terminates, the pointer will be destroyed but the memory will be left as an orphan, taking up space that is inaccessible to the rest of the program. Thus it is always good practice to delete memory when you're through with it.

Deleting the memory doesn't delete the pointer that points to it (ptr in NEWINTRO), and doesn't change the address value in the pointer. However, this address is no longer valid; the memory it points to may be filled with something entirely different. Be careful that you don't use pointers to memory that has been deleted.

A STRING CLASS USING new

The new operator often appears in constructors. As an example, we'll modify the String class, last seen in examples such as STRPLUS in Chapter 9. You may recall that a potential defect of that class was that all string objects occupied the same fixed amount of memory. A string shorter than this fixed length wasted memory, and a longer string—if one were mistakenly generated—could crash the system by extending beyond the end of the array. Our next example uses new to obtain exactly the right amount of memory. Here's the listing for NEWSTR:

```
// newstr.cpp
// using new to get memory for strings
#include <iostream.h>
#include <string.h>        // for strcpy(), etc

class String                // user-defined string type
    {
    private:
        char* str;                      // pointer to string
    public:
        String(char* s)                 // constructor, one arg
            {
            int length = strlen(s);     // length of string argument
            str = new char[length+1];   // get memory
            strcpy(str, s);             // copy argument to it
```

```
        }
     ~String()                          // destructor
        {
        delete str;                     // release memory
        }
     void display()                     // display the String
        {
        cout << str;
        }
     };

void main()
   {                                    // uses 1-arg constructor
   String s1 = "Who knows nothing doubts nothing.";

   cout << endl << "s1=";               // display string
   s1.display();
   }
```

The String class has only one data item: a pointer to char, called str. This pointer will point to the string held by the String object. There is no array within the object to hold the string. The string is stored elsewhere; only the pointer to it is a member of String.

Constructor in NEWSTR

The constructor in this example takes a normal string as its argument. It obtains space in memory for this string with new; str points to the newly-obtained memory. The constructor then uses strcpy() to copy the string into this new space.

Destructor in NEWSTR

We haven't seen many destructors in our examples so far, but now that we're allocating memory with new, destructors become increasingly important. If we allocate memory when we create an object, it's reasonable to deallocate the memory when the object is no longer needed. As you may recall from Chapter 7, a destructor is a routine that is called automatically when an object is destroyed. The destructor in NEWSTR looks like this:

```
~String()
   {
   delete str;
   }
```

This destructor gives back to the system the memory obtained when the object was created. Objects (like other local variables) are typically destroyed when the function in which they were defined terminates. This destructor ensures that memory obtained by the string object will be returned to the system, and not left in limbo, when the object is destroyed.

Pointers to Objects

Pointers can point to objects as well as to simple data types. We've seen many examples of objects defined and given a name, in statements like

```
Distance dist;
```

where an object called dist is defined to be of the Distance class.

Sometimes, however, we don't know, at the time that we write the program, how many objects we want to create. When this is the case, we can use new to create objects while the program is running. As we've seen, new returns a pointer to an area of memory. This memory can hold an unnamed object. Let's look at a short example program, ENGLPTR, that compares the two approaches to creating objects:

```
// englptr.cpp
// accessing member functions by pointer
#include <iostream.h>

class Distance                    // English Distance class
   {
   private:
      int feet;
      float inches;
   public:
      void getdist()              // get length from user
         {
         cout << "\nEnter feet: ";  cin >> feet;
         cout << "Enter inches: ";  cin >> inches;
         }
      void showdist()             // display distance
         { cout << feet << "\'-" << inches << '\"'; }
   };

void main()
   {
   Distance dist;           // define a named Distance object
   dist.getdist();          // access object members
   dist.showdist();         //    with dot operator

   Distance* distptr;       // pointer to Distance
   distptr = new Distance;  // points to new Distance object
   distptr->getdist();      // access object members
   distptr->showdist();     //    with -> operator
   }
```

This program uses a variation of the English Distance class seen in previous chapters. The main() function defines dist, uses the Distance member functions getdist() to get a distance from the user, and then uses showdist() to display it.

REFERRING TO MEMBERS

ENGLPTR then creates another object of type `Distance` using the `new` operator, and returns a pointer to it called `distptr`.

The question is, how do we refer to the member functions in the object pointed to by `distptr`? You might guess that we would use the dot (`.`) membership-access operator, as in

```
distptr.getdist();   // won't work; distptr is not a variable
```

but this won't work. The dot operator requires the identifier on its left to be a variable. Since `distptr` is a pointer to a variable, we need another syntax. One approach is to dereference (get the contents of the variable pointed to by) the pointer:

```
(*distptr).getdist();  // ok but inelegant
```

However, this is slightly cumbersome because of the parentheses. A more concise approach is furnished by the membership-access operator `->`, which consists of a hyphen and a greater-than sign:

```
distptr->getdist();   // better approach
```

As you can see in ENGLPTR, the `->` operator works with pointers to objects in just the same way that the `.` operator works with objects. Here's the output of the program:

```
Enter feet: 10              ←————————this object uses the dot operator
Enter inches: 6.25
10'-6.25"

Enter feet: 6               ←————————this object uses the -> operator
Enter inches: 4.75
6'-4.75"
```

ANOTHER APPROACH TO new

You may come across another—less common—approach to using `new` to obtain memory for objects.

Since `new` can return a pointer to an area of memory that holds an object, we should be able to refer to the original object by dereferencing the pointer. The ENGLREF example shows how this is done:

```
// englref.cpp
// dereferencing pointer returned by new
#include <iostream.h>

class Distance                        // English Distance class
   {
   private:
      int feet;
      float inches;
```

```
   public:
      void getdist()                 // get length from user
         {
         cout << "\nEnter feet: ";  cin >> feet;
         cout << "Enter inches: ";  cin >> inches;
         }
      void showdist()                // display distance
         { cout << feet << "\'-" << inches << '\"'; }
   };

void main()
   {
   Distance& dist = *(new Distance);   // create Distance object
                                       // alias is "dist"
   dist.getdist();                     // access object members
   dist.showdist();                    //    with dot operator
   }
```

The expression

```
new Distance
```

returns a pointer to a memory area large enough for a `Distance` object, so we can refer to the original object as

```
*(new Distance)
```

This is the object pointed to by the pointer. Using a reference, we define `dist` to be an object of type `Distance`, and we set it equal to `*(new Distance)`. Now we can refer to members of `dist` using the dot membership operator, rather than `->`.

This approach is less common than using pointers to objects obtained with `new`, or simply declaring an object, but it works in a similar way.

AN ARRAY OF POINTERS TO OBJECTS

A common programming construction is an array of pointers to objects. This arrangement allows easy access to a group of objects, and is more flexible than placing the objects themselves in an array. (For instance, in the last example in this chapter we'll see how a group of objects can be sorted by sorting an array of pointers to them, rather than sorting the objects themselves.)

Our next example, PTROBJS, creates an array of pointers to the `person` class. Here's the listing:

```
// ptrobjs.cpp
// array of pointers to objects
#include <iostream.h>

class person                          // class of persons
   {
   protected:
      char name[40];                  // person's name
```

```
    public:
        void setName()                // set the name
            {
            cout << "Enter name: ";
            cin >> name;
            }
        void printName()              // get the name
            {
            cout << "\n   Name is: "
                << name;
            }
    };

void main()
    {
    person* persPtr[100];        // array of pointers to persons
    int n = 0;                   // number of persons in array
    char choice;

    do                                       // put persons in array
        {
        persPtr[n] = new person;             // make new object
        persPtr[n]->setName();               // set person's name
        n++;                                 // count new person
        cout << "Enter another (y/n)? ";     // enter another
        cin >> choice;                       // person?
        }
    while( choice=='y' );                    // quit on 'n'

    for(int j=0; j<n; j++)                   // print names of
        {                                    // all persons
        cout << "\nPerson number " << j+1;
        persPtr[j]->printName();
        }
    } // end main()
```

The class **person** has a single data item, **name**, which holds a string representing a person's name. Two member functions, **setName()** and **printName()**, allow the name to be set and displayed.

Program Operation

The **main()** function defines an array, **persPtr**, of 100 pointers to type **person**. In a **do** loop it then asks the user to enter a name. With this name it creates a **person** object using **new**, and stores a pointer to this object in the array **persPtr**. To demonstrate how easy it is to access the objects using the pointers, it then prints out the **name** data for each **person** object.

Here's a sample interaction with program:

```
Enter name: Stroustrup    ←————— user enters names
Enter another (y/n)? y
```

```
Enter name: Ritchie
Enter another (y/n)? y
Enter name: Kernighan
Enter another (y/n)? n
Person number 1              ←———— program displays all names stored
    Name is: Stroustrup
Person number 2
    Name is: Ritchie
Person number 3
    Name is: Kernighan
```

Accessing Member Functions

We need to access the member functions `setName()` and `printName()` in the `person` objects pointed to by the pointers in the array `persPtr`. Each of the elements of the array `persPtr` is specified in array notation to be `persPtr[j]` (or equivalently by pointer notation to be `*(persPtr+j)`). The elements are pointers to objects of type `person`. To access a member of an object using a pointer, we use the `->` operator. Putting this all together, we have the following syntax for `getname()`:

```
persPtr[j]->getName()
```

This executes the `getname()` function in the `person` object pointed to by the `j`th element of the `persPtr` array. (It's a good thing we don't have to program using English syntax.)

A Linked List Example

Our next example shows a simple linked list. What is a linked list? It's another way to store data. You've seen numerous examples of data stored in arrays. Another data structure is an array of pointers to data members, as in the PTRTOSTRS and PTROBJS examples. Both the array and the array of pointers suffer from the necessity to declare a fixed-size array before running the program.

A Chain of Pointers

The linked list provides a more flexible storage system in that it doesn't use arrays at all. Instead, space for each data item is obtained as needed with `new`, and each item is connected, or *linked*, to the next data item using a pointer. The individual items don't need to be located contiguously in memory the way array elements are; they can be scattered anywhere.

In our example the entire linked list is an object of class `linklist`. The individual data items, or links, are represented by structures of type `link`. Each such structure contains an integer—representing the object's single data item—and a

FIGURE 12-15
A Linked List

pointer to the next link. The list itself stores a pointer to the link at the head of the list. This arrangement is shown in Figure 12-15.

Here's the listing for LINKLIST:

```
// linklist.cpp
// linked list
#include <iostream.h>
const int NULL = 0;                     // non-valid pointer

struct link                             // one element of list
   {
   int data;                            // data item
   link* next;                          // pointer to next link
   };

class linklist                          // a list of links
   {
   private:
      link* first;                      // pointer to first link
   public:
      linklist()                        // no-argument constructor
         { first = NULL; }              // no first link
      void additem(int d);              // add data item (one link)
      void display();                   // display all links
   };

void linklist::additem(int d)           // add data item
   {
   link* newlink = new link;            // make a new link
   newlink->data = d;                   // give it data
```

```
    newlink->next = first;              // it points to next link
    first = newlink;                    // now first points to this
    }

void linklist::display()               // display all links
    {
    link* current = first;             // set ptr to first link
    while( current != NULL )           // quit on last link
        {
        cout << endl << current->data; // print data
        current = current->next;       // move to next link
        }
    }

void main()
    {
    linklist li;          // make linked list

    li.additem(25);       // add four items to list
    li.additem(36);
    li.additem(49);
    li.additem(64);

    li.display();         // display entire list
    }
```

The linklist class has only one member data item: the pointer to the start of the list. When the list is first created, the constructor initializes this pointer, first, to NULL. The NULL constant is defined in the MEM.H header file (which is #included in the IOSTREAM.H file) to be 0. This value serves as a signal that a pointer does not hold a valid address. In our program a link whose next member has a value of NULL is assumed to be at the end of the list.

ADDING AN ITEM TO THE LIST

The additem() member function adds an item to the linked list. A new link is inserted at the beginning of the list. (We could write the additem() function to insert items at the end of the list, but that is a little more complex to program.) Let's look at the steps involved in inserting a new link.

First, a new structure of type link is created by the line

```
link* newlink = new link;
```

This creates memory for the new link structure with new and saves the pointer to it in the newlink variable.

Next we want to set the members of the newly created structure to appropriate values. A structure is just like a class in that, when it is referred to by pointer rather than by name, its members are accessed using the -> member-access operator. The following two lines set the data variable to the value passed as an argument to additem(), and the next pointer to point to whatever address was in first, which holds the pointer to the start of the list.

```
newlink->data = d;
newlink->next = first;
```

Finally, we want the `first` variable to point to the new link:

```
first = newlink;
```

The effect is to uncouple the connection between `first` and the old first link, insert the new link, and move the old first link into the second position. Figure 12-16 shows this process.

DISPLAYING THE LIST CONTENTS

Once the list is created, it's easy to step through all the members, displaying them (or performing other operations). All we need to do is follow from one `next` pointer to another until we find a `next` that is `NULL`, signaling the end of the list. In the function `display()`, the line

```
cout << endl << current->data;
```

prints the value of the data, and

```
current = current->next;
```

moves us along from one link to another, until

```
current != NULL
```

FIGURE 12-16
Adding to a Linked List

in the `while` expression becomes false. Here's the output of LINKLIST:

```
64
49
36
25
```

Linked lists are perhaps the most commonly used data storage arrangements after arrays. As we noted, they avoid the wasting of memory space engendered by arrays. The disadvantage is that finding a particular item on a linked list requires following the chain of links from the head of the list until the desired link is reached. This can be time-consuming. An array element, on the other hand, can be accessed quickly, provided its index is known in advance. We'll have more to say about linked lists and other data-storage techniques in Chapter 16.

SELF-CONTAINING CLASSES

We should note a possible pitfall in the use of self-referential classes and structures. The `link` structure in LINKLIST contained a pointer to the same kind of structure. You can do the same with classes:

```
class sampleclass
  {
  sampleclass* ptr;  // this is fine
  };
```

However, while a class can contain a *pointer* to an object of its own type, it cannot contain an *object* of its own type:

```
class sampleclass
  {
  sampleclass obj;  // can't do this
  };
```

This is true of structures as well as classes.

AUGMENTING LINKLIST

The general organization of LINKLIST can serve for a more complex situation than that shown. There could be more data in each link. Instead of an integer, a link could hold a number of data items or it could hold a pointer to a structure or object.

Additional member functions could perform such activities as adding and removing links from an arbitrary part of the chain. Another important member function is a destructor. As we mentioned, it's important to delete blocks of memory that are no longer in use. A destructor that performed this task would be a highly desirable addition to the `linklist` class. It could go through the list using `delete` to free the memory occupied by each link.

POINTERS TO POINTERS

We'll finish this chapter with an example that demonstrates an array of pointers to objects, and shows how to sort these pointers based on data in the object. This involves the idea of pointers to pointers, and may help to demonstrate why people lose sleep over pointers.

The idea in the next program is to create an array of pointers to objects of the person class. This is similar to the PTROBJS example, but we go farther and add variations of the order() and bsort() functions from the PTRSORT example so that we can sort a group of person objects based on the alphabetical order of their names. Here's the listing for PERSORT:

```cpp
// persort.cpp
// sorts person objects using array of pointers
#include <iostream.h>
#include <string.h>                  // for strcmp()

class person                         // class of persons
   {
   protected:
      char name[40];                 // person's name
   public:
      void setName()                 // set the name
         { cout << "Enter name: "; cin >> name; }
      void printName()               // display the name
         { cout << endl << name; }
      char* getName()                // return the name
         { return name; }
   };

void main()
   {
   void bsort(person**, int);        // prototype
   person* persPtr[100];             // array of pointers to persons
   int n = 0;                        // number of persons in array
   char choice;                      // input char

   do                                // put persons in array
      {
      persPtr[n] = new person;       // make new object
      persPtr[n]->setName();         // set person's name
      n++;                           // count new person
      cout << "Enter another (y/n)? "; // enter another
      cin >> choice;                 //     person?
      }
   while( choice=='y' );             // quit on 'n'
```

```
    cout << "\nUnsorted list:";
    for(int j=0; j<n; j++)              // print unsorted list
        persPtr[j]->printName();

    bsort(persPtr, n);                  // sort pointers

    cout << "\nSorted list:";
    for(j=0; j<n; j++)                  // print sorted list
        persPtr[j]->printName();
    }  // end main()

void bsort(person** pp, int n)        // sort pointers to persons
    {
    void order(person**, person**);  // prototype
    int j, k;                          // indexes to array

    for(j=0; j<n-1; j++)               // outer loop
        for(k=j+1; k<n; k++)           // inner loop starts at outer
            order(pp+j, pp+k);         // order the pointer contents
    }

void order(person** pp1, person** pp2)  // orders two pointers
    {                                      // if 1st larger than 2nd,
    if( strcmp((*pp1)->getName(), (*pp2)->getName()) > 0)
        {
        person* tempptr = *pp1;            // swap the pointers
        *pp1 = *pp2;
        *pp2 = tempptr;
        }
    }
```

When the program is first executed, it asks for a name. When the user gives it one, it creates an object of type **person** and sets the **name** data in this object to the name entered by the user. The program also stores a pointer to the object in the **persPtr** array. The user can enter up to 100 names.

When the user types n to indicate that no more names will be entered, the program calls the **bsort()** function to sort the **person** objects based on their **name** member variables. Here's some sample interaction with the program:

```
Enter name: Washington
Enter another (y/n)? y
Enter name: Adams
Enter another (y/n)? y
Enter name: Jefferson
Enter another (y/n)? y
Enter name: Madison
Enter another (y/n)? n

Unsorted list:
Washington
Adams
Jefferson
Madison
```

```
Sorted list:
Adams
Jefferson
Madison
Washington
```

SORTING POINTERS

Actually, we don't sort the objects themselves; we sort the pointers to the objects. This eliminates the need to shuffle the objects around in memory, which can be very time-consuming if the objects are large. The process is shown in Figure 12-17.

To facilitate the sorting activity, we've added a getName() member function to the person class, so we can access the names from order() to decide when to swap pointers.

THE person** DATA TYPE

You will notice that the first argument to the bsort() function, and both arguments to order(), have the type person**. What do the two asterisks mean? These arguments are used to pass the address of the array persPtr, or—in the case of order()—the addresses of elements of the array. If this were an array of type person, then the address of the array would be type person*. However, the array is of type *pointers* to person, or person*, so its address is type person**. The address of a pointer is a pointer to a pointer. Figure 12-18 shows how this looks.

Compare this program with PTRSORT, which sorted an array of type int. You'll find that the data types passed to functions in PERSORT all have one more asterisk than they did in PTRSORT, because the array is an array of pointers.

Since the persPtr array contains pointers, the construction

```
persPtr[j]->printName()
```

executes the printName() function in the object pointed to by the jth element of persPtr.

COMPARING STRINGS

The order() function in PERSORT has been modified to order two strings lexigraphically—that is, by putting them in alphabetical order. To do this it compares the strings with the C++ library function strcmp(). This function takes the two strings s1 and s2 as arguments, and returns one of the following values:

Value	Condition
<0	s1 comes before s2
0	s1 is the same as s2
>0	s1 comes after s2

FIGURE 12-17
Sorting an Array of Pointers

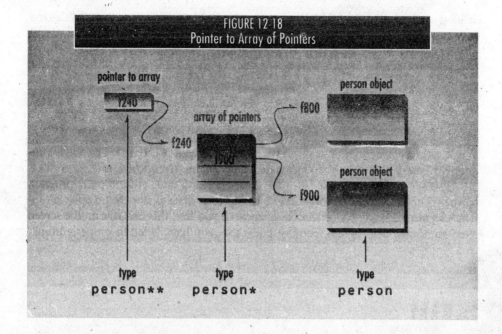

FIGURE 12-18
Pointer to Array of Pointers

pointer to array

f240

array of pointers

f240

f200

person object

f800

person object

f900

type
person**

type
person*

type
person

The strings are accessed using the syntax

```
(*pp1)->getname()
```

The argument **pp1** is a pointer to a pointer, and we want the name pointed to by the pointer it points to. The member-access operator **->** dereferences one level, but we need to dereference another level, hence the asterisk preceding **pp1**.

Just as there can be pointers to pointers, there can be pointers to pointers to pointers, and so on. Fortunately such complexities are seldom encountered.

DEBUGGING POINTERS

Pointers can be the source of mysterious and catastrophic program bugs. The most common problem is that the programmer has failed to place a valid address in a pointer variable. When this happens the pointer can end up pointing anywhere in memory. It could be pointing to the program code, or to the operating system. If the programmer then inserts a value into memory using the pointer, the value will write over the program or operating instructions, and the computer will crash or evince other uncharming behavior.

A particular version of this scenario takes place when the pointer points to address 0, which is called **NULL**. This happens, for example, if the pointer variable is defined as an external variable, since external variables are automatically initialized to 0. Instance variables in classes are considered external, so they are also initialized to 0. Here's a mini-program that demonstrates the situation:

```
int* intptr;          // external variable, initialized to 0
void main()
   {                  // failure to put valid address in intptr
   *intptr = 37;      // attempts to put 37 in address at 0
   }                  // result is "Null pointer assignment"
```

When `intptr` is defined, it is given the value 0, since it is external. The single program statement will attempt to insert the value 37 into the address at 0.

Fortunately, however, the run-time error-checking unit, built into the program by the compiler, is waiting for attempts to access address 0, and will display an infamous error message: *Null pointer assignment*. If you find this message on the screen after running your program, you can guess that you have failed to properly initialize a pointer.

SUMMARY

This has been a whirlwind tour through the land of pointers. There is far more to learn about pointers, but the topics we've covered here will provide a basis for the examples in the balance of the book, and for further study of pointers.

We've learned that everything in the computer's memory has an address, and that addresses are *pointer constants*. We can find the addresses of variables using the address operator **&**.

Pointers are variables that hold address values. Pointers are defined using an asterisk (*****) to mean *pointer to*. A data type is always included in pointer definitions, since the compiler must know what is being pointed to, so that it can perform arithmetic correctly on the pointer. We access the thing pointed to using the asterisk in a different way, as the indirection operator, meaning *contents of the variable pointed to by.*

Array elements can be accessed using either array notation, with brackets, or pointer notation, with an asterisk. Like other addresses, the address of an array is a constant, but it can be assigned to a variable, which can be incremented and changed in other ways.

When the address of a variable is passed to a function, the function can work with the original variable. (This is not true when arguments are passed by value.) In this respect passing by pointer offers the same benefits as passing by reference, although pointer arguments must be *dereferenced* or accessed using the indirection operator. However, pointers offer more flexibility in some cases.

A string constant can be defined as an array or as a pointer. The pointer approach may be more flexible, but there is a danger that the pointer value will be corrupted. Strings, being arrays of type **char**, are commonly passed to functions and accessed using pointers.

The `new` operator obtains a specified amount of memory from the system and returns a pointer to the memory. This operator is used to create variables and data structures during program execution. The `delete` operator releases memory obtained with `new`.

When a pointer points to an object, members of the object's class can be accessed using the access operator `->`. The same syntax is used to access structure members.

Classes and structures may contain data members that are pointers to their own type. This permits the creation of complex data structures like linked lists.

There can be pointers to pointers. These variables are defined using the double asterisk: `int** pptr`.

UESTIONS

1. Write a statement that displays the address of the variable `testvar`.
2. The contents of two pointers that point to adjacent variables of type `float` differ by _____.
3. A pointer is
   a. the address of a variable
   b. an indication of the variable to be accessed next
   c. a variable for storing addresses
   d. the data type of an address variable
4. Write expressions for the following:
   a. the address of `var`
   b. the contents of the variable pointed to by `var`
   c. the variable `var` used as a reference argument
   d. the data type pointer-to-`char`
5. An address is a _____, while a pointer is a _____.
6. Write a definition for a variable of type pointer to `float`.
7. One way pointers are useful is to refer to a memory address that has no _____.
8. If a pointer `testptr` points to a variable `testvar`, write a statement that represents the contents of `testvar` but does not use its name.
9. An asterisk placed after a data type means _____. An asterisk placed in front of a variable name means _____.
10. The expression `*test` can be said to
   a. be a pointer to `test`
   b. refer to the contents of `test`
   c. dereference `test`
   d. refer to the value of the variable pointed to by `test`

11. Is the following code correct?

```
int intvar = 333;
int* intptr;
cout << *intptr;
```

12. A pointer to `void` can hold pointers to _____.

13. What is the difference between `intarr[3]` and `*(intarr+3)`?

14. Write some code that uses pointer notation to display every value in the array `intarr`, which has 77 elements.

15. If `intarr` is an array of integers, why is the expression `intarr++` not legal?

16. Of the three ways to pass arguments to functions, only passing by _____ and passing by _____ allow the function to modify the argument in the calling program.

17. The type of variable a pointer points to must be part of the pointer's definition so that
    a. data types don't get mixed up when arithmetic is performed on them
    b. pointers can be added to one another to access structure members
    c. no one's religious conviction will be offended
    d. the compiler can perform arithmetic correctly to access array elements

18. Using pointer notation, write a prototype (declaration) for a function called `func()` that returns type `void` and takes a single argument that is an array of type `char`.

19. Using pointer notation, write some code that will transfer 80 characters from the string `s1` to the string `s2`.

20. The first element in a string is
    a. the name of the string
    b. the first character in the string
    c. the length of the string
    d. the name of the array holding the string

21. Using pointer notation, write the prototype for a function called `revstr()` that returns a string value and takes one argument that represents a string.

22. Write a definition for an array `numptrs` of pointers to the strings "One", "Two", and "Three".

23. The `new` operator
    a. returns a pointer to a variable
    b. creates a variable called new
    c. obtains memory for a new variable
    d. tells how much memory is available

24. Using `new` may result in less _____ memory than using an array.

25. The `delete` operator returns _____ to the operating system.

26. Given a pointer `p` that points to an object of type `upperclass`, write an expression that executes the `exclu()` member function in this object.

27. Given an object with index number 7 in array `objarr`, write an expression that executes the `exclu()` member function in this object.

28. In a linked list
    a. each link contains a pointer to the next link
    b. an array of pointers point to the links
    c. each link contains data or a pointer to data
    d. the links are stored in an array

29. Write a definition for an array `arr` of 8 pointers that point to variables of type `float`.

30. If you wanted to sort many large objects or structures, it would be most efficient to
    a. place them in an array and sort the array
    b. place pointers to them in an array and sort the array
    c. place them in a linked list and sort the linked list
    d. place references to them in an array and sort the array

EXERCISES

1. Write a program that reads a group of numbers from the user and places them in an array of type `float`. Once the numbers are stored in the array, the program should average them and print the result. Use pointer notation wherever possible.

2. Start with the `string` class from the NEWSTR example in this chapter. Add a member function called `upit()` that converts the string to all upper case. You can use the `toupper()` library function, which takes a single character as an argument and returns a character that has been converted (if necessary) to uppercase. This function uses the CTYPE.H header file. Write some code in `main()` to test this function.

3. Start with an array of pointers to strings representing the days of the week, as found in the PTRTOSTR program in this chapter. Provide functions to sort the strings into alphabetical order, using variations of the `bsort()` and `order()` functions from the PTRSORT program in this chapter. Sort the pointers to the strings, not the actual strings.

4. Add a destructor to the LINKLIST program. It should delete all the links when a `linklist` object is destroyed. It can do this by following along the chain, deleting each link as it goes. You can test the destructor by having it display a message each time it deletes a link; it should delete the same number of links that were added to the list. (A destructor is called automatically by the system for any existing objects when the program exits.)

VIRTUAL FUNCTIONS AND OTHER SUBTLETIES

VIRTUAL FUNCTIONS

FRIEND FUNCTIONS

STATIC FUNCTIONS

OVERLOADED ASSIGNMENT OPERATOR

OVERLOADED COPY CONSTRUCTOR

THE t h i s POINTER

Now that we understand something about pointers, we can delve into more advanced C++ topics. This chapter covers a rather loosely related collection of such topics: virtual functions, friend functions, static functions, the overloaded = operator, the overloaded copy constructor, and the **this** pointer. These are advanced features; they are not necessary for every C++ program. However, they are widely used, and are essential in some situations. Studying them also casts light on the inner workings of C++.

VIRTUAL FUNCTIONS

Virtual means *existing in effect but not in reality*. A virtual function, then, is one that does not really exist but nevertheless appears real to some parts of a program.

Why are virtual functions needed? Suppose you have a number of objects of different classes but you want to put them all on a list and perform a particular operation on them using the same function call. For example, suppose a graphics program includes several different shapes: a triangle, a ball, a square, and so on, as in the MULTSHAP program in Chapter 11. Each of these classes has a member function **draw()** that causes the object to be drawn on the screen.

Now suppose you plan to make a picture by grouping a number of these elements together, and you want to draw the picture in a convenient way. One approach is to create an array that holds pointers to all the different objects in the picture. The array might be defined like this:

```
shape* ptrarr[100];   // array of 100 pointers to shapes
```

If you insert pointers to all the shapes into this array, you can then draw an entire picture using a simple loop:

```
for(int j=0; j<N; j++)
    ptrarr[j]->draw();
```

This is an amazing capability: completely different functions are executed by the same function call. If the pointer in **ptrarr** points to a ball, the function that draws a ball is called; if it points to a triangle, the triangle-drawing function is called. This is an important example of *polymorphism*, or giving different meanings to the same thing.

However, for this polymorphic approach to work, several conditions must be met. First, all the different classes of shapes, such as balls and triangles, must be derived from a single base class (called **shape** in MULTSHAP). Second, the **draw()** function must be declared to be **virtual** in the base class.

This is all rather abstract, so let's start with some short programs that show parts of the situation, and put everything together later.

NORMAL MEMBER FUNCTIONS ACCESSED WITH POINTERS

Our first example shows what happens when a base class and derived classes all have functions with the same name, and you access these functions using pointers but without using virtual functions. Here's the listing for NOTVIRT:

```
// notvirt.cpp
// normal functions accessed from pointer
#include <iostream.h>

class Base                          // base class
    {
    public:
        void show()                 // normal function
            { cout << "\nBase"; }
    };
class Derv1 : public Base           // derived class 1
    {
    public:
        void show()
            { cout << "\nDerv1"; }
    };
class Derv2 : public Base           // derived class 2
    {
    public:
        void show()
            { cout << "\nDerv2"; }
    };
void main()
    {
    Derv1 dv1;              // object of derived class 1
    Derv2 dv2;              // object of derived class 2
    Base* ptr;             // pointer to base class

    ptr = &dv1;            // put address of dv1 in pointer
    ptr->show();           // execute show()

    ptr = &dv2;            // put address of dv2 in pointer
    ptr->show();           // execute show()
    }
```

The **Derv1** and **Derv2** classes are derived from class **Base**. Each of these three classes has a member function **show()**. In **main()** we create objects of class **Derv1** and **Derv2**, and a pointer to class **Base**. Then we put the address of a derived class object in the base class pointer in the line

```
ptr = &dv1;  // derived class address in base class pointer
```

But wait—how can we get away with this? Doesn't the compiler complain that we're assigning an address of one type (**Derv1**) to a pointer of another (**Base**)? On the contrary, the compiler is perfectly happy, because type checking has been relaxed in this situation, for reasons that will become apparent soon. The rule is that pointers to objects of a derived class are type-compatible with pointers to objects of the base class. (This only goes one way. You can convert pointers from derived class to base class, but not from base to derived.)

Now the question is, when you execute the line

```
ptr->show();
```

what function is called? Is it **Base::show()**, or **Derv1::show()**? Again, in the last two lines of NOTVIRT we put the address of an object of class **Derv2** in the pointer, and again execute

```
ptr->show();
```

Which of the **show()** functions is called here? The output from the program answers these questions:

```
Base
Base
```

As you can see, the function in the base class is always executed. The compiler ignores the *contents* of the pointer **ptr** and chooses the member function that matches the *type* of the pointer, as shown in Figure 13-1.

Sometimes this is what we want, but it doesn't solve the problem posed at the beginning of this section: accessing objects of different classes using the same statement.

VIRTUAL MEMBER FUNCTIONS ACCESSED WITH POINTERS

Let's make a single change in our program: We'll place the keyword **virtual** in front of the declarator for the **show()** function in the base class. Here's the listing for the resulting program, VIRT:

```
// virt.cpp
// virtual functions accessed from pointer
#include <iostream.h>

class Base                          // base class
    {
    public:
        virtual void show()         // virtual function
            { cout << "\nBase"; }
    };
class Derv1 : public Base           // derived class 1
    {
    public:
```

471

```
        void show()
           { cout << "\nDerv1"; }
     };
class Derv2 : public Base            // derived class 2
     {
     public:
        void show()
           { cout << "\nDerv2"; }
     };
void main()
     {
     Derv1 dv1;                      // object of derived class 1
     Derv2 dv2;                      // object of derived class 2
     Base* ptr;                      // pointer to base class

     ptr = &dv1;                     // put address of dv1 in pointer
     ptr->show();                    // execute show()

     ptr = &dv2;                     // put address of dv2 in pointer
     ptr->show();                    // execute show()
     }
```

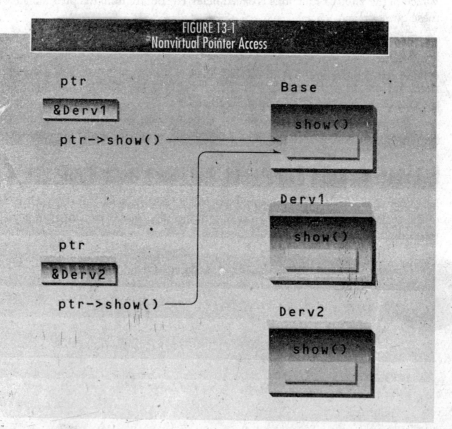

FIGURE 13-1
Nonvirtual Pointer Access

The output of this program is

```
Derv1
Derv2
```

Now, as you can see, the member functions of the derived classes, not the base class, are executed. We change the contents of `ptr` from the address of `Derv1` to that of `Derv2`, and the particular instance of `show()` that is executed also changes. So the same function call,

```
ptr->show();
```

executes different functions, depending on the contents of `ptr`. The rule is that the compiler selects the function based on the *contents* of the pointer `ptr`, not on the *type* of the pointer, as in NOTVIRT. This is shown in Figure 13-2.

LATE BINDING

The astute reader may wonder how the compiler knows what function to compile. In NOTVIRT the compiler has no problem with the expression

```
ptr->show();
```

FIGURE 13-2
Virtual Pointer Access

It always compiles a call to the **show()** function in the base class. But in VIRT the compiler doesn't know what class the contents of **ptr** may contain. It could be the address of an object of the **Derv1** class or of the **Derv2** class. Which version of **draw()** does the compiler call? In fact the compiler doesn't know what to do, so it arranges for the decision to be deferred until the program is running. At run time, when it is known what class is pointed to by **ptr**, the appropriate version of **draw** will be called. This is called *late binding* or *dynamic binding*. (Choosing functions in the normal way, during compilation, is called *early*, or *static*, binding.) Late binding requires some overhead but provides increased power and flexibility.

VIRTUAL FUNCTIONS AND THE employee CLASS

Let's put what we've learned to use. We'll modify the EMPLOY program from Chapter 10 to use virtual functions. Why do we need virtual functions in this program? In EMPLOY we created only a few fixed objects of each class: **m1**, **m2**, **s1**, and so on. This isn't very flexible. We would like to create a data structure, such as an array, to store objects representing any of the various kinds of employees in the company. This will allow the user to store data on an arbitrary number of employees and recall it later. Specifically, we would like to store objects of type **manager**, of type **scientist**, and of type **employee** in the same array. Actually, it's awkward to store the objects themselves; what we really want is to store pointers to the objects.

Note that we have dropped the **laborer** class shown in the EMPLOY example, and also the employee number, to save space. We have also allowed the inclusion of members of the **employee** class—the base class—in the array. Here's the listing for VIRTEMP:

```
// virtemp.cpp
// employee database uses virtual functions
#include <iostream.h>

class employee                            // employee class
    {
    private:
        char name[80];                    // employee name
    public:
        void getdata()
            { cout << "   Enter last name: "; cin >> name; }
        virtual void putdata()
            { cout << "\n\nName: " << name; }
    };

class manager : public employee          // management class
    {
    private:
        char title[80];                  // "vice-president" etc.
        double dues;                     // golf club dues
```

```
    public:
      void getdata()                        // get all data
        {
        employee::getdata();
        cout << "    Enter title: ";            cin >> title;
        cout << "    Enter golf club dues: "; cin >> dues;
        }
      void putdata()                        // display all data
        {
        employee::putdata();
        cout << "\n    Title: " << title;
        cout << "\n    Golf club dues: " << dues;
        }
    };
class scientist : public employee          // scientist class
    {
    private:
      int pubs;                            // number of publications
    public:
      void getdata()                        // get all data
        {
        employee::getdata();
        cout << "    Enter number of pubs: "; cin >> pubs;
        }
      void putdata()                        // display all data
        {
        employee::putdata();
        cout << "\n    Number of publications: " << pubs;
        }
    };

void main()
    {
    employee*  empArr[100];   // array of pointers to employees
    employee*  empPtr;        // pointer to employee
    manager*   manPtr;        // pointer to manager
    scientist* sciPtr;        // pointer to scientist
    int n = 0;                // number of pointers in array
    char choice;              // user's input

    do
        {
        cout << "\nEnter employee, manager or scientist (e/m/s): ";
        cin >> choice;
        if(choice == 'e')               // it's a plain employee
            {
            empPtr = new employee;    // make a new employee object
            empPtr->getdata();        // fill with data from user
            empArr[n++] = empPtr;     // put object in array
            }
```

```
else if(choice == 'm')          // it's a manager
  {
  manPtr = new manager;         // make a new manager object
  manPtr->getdata();            // fill with data from user
  empArr[n++] = manPtr;         // put object in array
  }
else                            // assume it's a scientist
  {
  sciPtr = new scientist;       // make a new scientist object
  sciPtr->getdata();            // fill with data from user
  empArr[n++] = sciPtr;         // put object in array
  }
cout << "Enter another (y/n)? ";  // get another employee?
cin >> choice;
} while( choice == 'y' );        // cycle until not 'y'

for(int j=0; j<n; j++)          // for each employee,
  empArr[j]->putdata();         // display all data
cout << endl;
}
```

The program asks the user to specify the kind of employee—manager, scientist, or plain employee—about whom data will be entered. It then prompts for data appropriate to that kind of employee: names for everyone, title and golf club dues for the managers, and number of publications for the scientists. Here's some sample interaction with the program:

```
Enter employee, manager, or scientist (e/m/s): m
  Enter last name: Wellington
  Enter title: President
  Enter golf club dues: 1000000
Enter another (y/n): y

Enter employee, manager, or scientist (e/m/s): s
  Enter last name: DuFarge
  Enter number of pubs: 99
Enter another (y/n): y

Enter employee, manager, or scientist (e/m/s): e
  Enter last name: Smith
Enter another (y/n): y

Enter employee, manager, or scientist (e/m/s): e
  Enter last name: Jones
Enter another (y/n): n

Name: Wellington
  Title: President
  Golf club dues: 1000000
```

```
Name: DuFarge
   Number of publications: 99

Name: Smith

Name: Jones
```

Array Holds All Objects

The central data structure in the program is the array empArr[], which is an array of pointers to type employee. This array can also hold pointers to manager and scientist objects, since they are derived from employee. The function putdata() is declared as a virtual function in the base employee class. This same function name is then used for functions in the derived classes manager and scientist. In each class this function displays all the data that applies to that class.

In main(), when the user specifies the type of employee, the program creates a new object of that class, and then calls the getdata() function for that object so the user can fill in the information. Notice that, although it is overloaded in all the classes, getdata() is *not* a virtual function. Thus getdata() must be used with a pointer to (or object of) a specific class, not just the base class. Once the program has obtained the data for the new object, it places a pointer to that object in the array.

The Payoff

Now, here's the payoff: when an object of any of the three classes is placed in the array, we can display it by calling the function putdata() this way:

```
empArr[j].putdata();    // display the data
```

There is nothing in the syntax of empArr[j] to specify the type of the pointer stored in this array element. However, the program nevertheless knows which version of putdata() to call: the one in manager, if the array element holds a pointer to manager, and so on. We can operate on all objects with this function, no matter what class they are, as long as they are derived from (or are members of) class employee.

Remember that for a function to have this capability it must be declared virtual. If you use an ordinary nonvirtual function on an array element, then, as we've seen, the function in the base class will always be called no matter what kind of object is pointed to. In this program, if you called getdata() (which is not virtual) with an array element, as in

```
empArr[j].getdata();    // no good -- gets base-class data only
```

the base class function would be called and query the user for the name; but no matter what was in the array element, no other data would be requested. For instance, if a pointer to scientist occupied that array location, the number of publications would not be requested. Functions must be virtual if they are to work with pointers to derived classes placed in an array of the base class.

One Virtual, One Not

A deliberate imbalance is built into the program: We obtain data with an ordinary function, `getdata()`, but we display data with a virtual function, `putdata()`. We've done this to show the difference between virtual and nonvirtual functions, and to clarify the process of putting objects into the array.

Notice how much easier it is to display data, using a virtual function, than it is to acquire it, using an ordinary function. If `getdata()` had been a virtual function, we could have simplified the programming for it as well. We'll do this in the VIRTPERS example coming up soon.

Pure Virtual Functions

A *pure* virtual function is a virtual function with no body (another OOP sentence that sounds as if it described an esoteric religious concept). You may have noticed in the VIRT program that `Base::show()` is never executed. This is a common situation. There is no need for the base-class version of the particular function; we only use the versions of the function in the derived classes. When this is true, the body of the virtual function in the base class can be removed, and the notation `=0` added to the function declaration, as shown in the VIRTPURE example:

```
// virtpure.cpp
// pure virtual function
#include <iostream.h>

class Base                            // base class
   {
   public:
      virtual void show() = 0;        // pure virtual function
   };

class Derv1 : public Base            // derived class 1
   {
   public:
      void show()
         { cout << "\nDerv1"; }
   };

class Derv2 : public Base            // derived class 2
   {
   public:
      void show()
         { cout << "\nDerv2"; }
   };

void main()
   {
   Base* list[2];          // list of pointers to base class
   Derv1 dv1;              // object of derived class 1
```

```
Derv2 dv2;               // object of derived class 2

list[0] = &dv1;          // put address of dv1 in list

list[1] = &dv2;          // put address of dv2 in list

list[0]->show();         // execute show() in both objects
list[1]->show();
}
```

Now the virtual function is declared as

```
virtual void show() = 0;  // pure virtual function
```

The equals sign here has nothing to do with assignment; the value 0 is not assigned to anything. The =0 syntax is simply how we tell the compiler that a function will be pure—that is, have no body.

You might wonder, if we can remove the body of the virtual show() function in the base class, why we can't remove the function altogether. That would be even cleaner, but it doesn't work. Without a function show() in the base class, statements like

```
list[0]->show();
```

would not be valid, because the pointers in the list[] array must point to members of class Base.

As you can see, we've made another, unrelated, change in VIRTPURE: The addresses of the member functions are stored in an array of pointers, and accessed using array elements. This works in just the same way as using a single pointer. The output of VIRTPURE is the same as VIRT:

```
Derv1
Derv2
```

VIRTUAL FUNCTIONS AND THE person CLASS

Our next example is an extension of the PTROBJ and PERSORT examples from Chapter 12, rewritten to use pure virtual functions. It uses the same person class but adds two derived classes, student and professor. These derived classes each contain a function called isOutstanding(). This function makes it easy for the school administrators to create a list of outstanding students and professors for the venerable Awards Day ceremony. Here's the listing for VIRTPERS:

```
// virtpers.cpp
// virtual functions with person class
#include <iostream.h>
enum boolean { false, true };

class person                              // person class
    {
```

```
    protected:
        char name[40];
    public:
        void getName()
            { cout << "   Enter name: "; cin >> name; }
        void putName()
            { cout << "Name is: " << name << endl; }
        virtual void getData() = 0;          // pure virtual func
        virtual boolean isOutstanding() = 0; // pure virtual func
    };

class student : public person       // student class
    {
    private:
        float gpa;                    // grade point average
    public:
        void getData()                // get student data from user
            {
            person::getName();
            cout << "   Enter student's GPA: "; cin >> gpa;
            }
        boolean isOutstanding()
            { return (gpa > 3.5) ? true : false; }
    };

class professor : public person    // professor class
    {
    private:
        int numPubs;                  // number of papers published
    public:
        void getData()                // get professor data from user
            {
            person::getName();
            cout << "   Enter number of professor's publications: ";
            cin >> numPubs;
            }
        boolean isOutstanding()
            { return (numPubs > 100) ? true : false; }
    };

void main(void)
    {
    person* persPtr[100];    // list of pointers to persons
    int n = 0;               // number of persons on list
    char choice;

    do
        {
        cout << "Enter student or professor (s/p): ";
```

```
      cin >> choice;
      if(choice=='s')                        // put new student
         persPtr[n] = new student;           // in array
      else                                   // put new professor
         persPtr[n] = new professor;         // in array
      persPtr[n++]->getData();               // get data for person
      cout << "   Enter another (y/n)? ";    // do another person?
      cin >> choice
      } while( choice=='y' );                // cycle until not 'y'

      for(int j=0; j<n; j++)                 // print names of all
         {                                   // persons, and
         persPtr[j]->putName();              // say if outstanding
         if( persPtr[j]->isOutstanding()==true )
            cout << "   This person is outstanding\n";
         }
   } // end main()
```

The student and professor Classes

The **student** and **professor** classes add new data items to the base class. The
student class contains a variable **gpa** of type **float**, which represents the student's
grade point average. The **professor** class contains a variable **numPubs** of type **int**,
which represents the number of scholarly publications the professor has published.
A student with a GPA of over 3.5, and a professor who has published more than 100
publications, are considered outstanding. (We'll refrain from comment on the desirability of these criteria for judging educational excellence.)

Virtual Functions

The **isOutstanding()** function is declared as a pure virtual function in **person**.
In the **student** class, this function returns a Boolean **true** if the student's GPA is
greater than 3.5, and **false** otherwise. In **professor** it returns **true** if the
professor's **numPubs** variable is greater than 100. The **getData()** function is also
a pure virtual function. It calls **getName()** in the **person** class, and then gets either a student's GPA or a professor's number of publications.

The main() Program

In **main()** we first let the user enter a number of student and teacher names. For
students, the program also asks for the GPA, and for professors it asks for the number
of publications. When the user is finished, the program prints out the names of all
the students and professors, noting those that are outstanding. Here's some sample
interaction:

```
Enter student or professor (s/p): s
   Enter name: Timmy
```

```
      Enter student's GPA: 1.2
      Enter another (y/n)? y
Enter student or professor (s/p): s
      Enter name: Brenda
      Enter student's GPA: 3.9
      Enter another (y/n)? y
Enter student or professor (s/p): s
      Enter name: Sandy
      Enter student's GPA: 2.4
      Enter another (y/n)? y
Enter student or professor (s/p): p
      Enter name: Shipley
      Enter number of professor's publications: 714
      Enter another (y/n)? y
Enter student or professor (s/p): p
      Enter name: Wainright
      Enter number of professor's publications: 13
      Enter another (y/n)? n

Name is: Timmy
Name is: Brenda
      This person is outstanding
Name is: Sandy
Name is: Shipley
      This person is outstanding
Name is: Wainright
```

The virtual functions in this program, isOutstanding() and getData(), can be pure because we do not create any instances (objects) of the base class person. This is a somewhat cleaner approach than that shown in the VIRTEMP example, where we allowed the creation of instances of the base class employee.

Also, unlike in the VIRTEMP example, we have made the data input function getData() a virtual function. Notice how this simplifies data acquisition. In VIRTEMP we created a separate pointer for each class, and called getData() with this pointer:

```
manPtr->getData();      // fill with data from user
empArr[n++] = manPtr;   // put object in array
```

In VIRTPERS, since getData() is a virtual function, we don't need to create a separate pointer for each class; we can use the function directly on an array element:

```
persPtr[n++]->getData();   // get data for person
```

Using pure virtual functions often allows you to simplify the conceptualization and the coding details of your program.

VIRTUAL FUNCTIONS IN A GRAPHICS EXAMPLE

If you have a graphics display, you can try out another example of virtual functions, this one derived from the MULTSHAP program of Chapter 11. As we noted at the beginning of this section, you may want to draw a number of shapes using the same statement. The VIRTSHAP program does this (don't forget to link with the GRAPHICS.LIB file):

```
// virtshap.cpp
// virtual functions with shapes
#include <graph.h>              // for graphics functions
#include <conio.h>              // for getch()
#include <iostream.h>           // for cout
#include <stdlib.h>             // for exit()

#define BLUE     1              // color indices
#define GREEN    2
#define RED      4
#define WHITE    7
#define YELLOW   14

const int W = 50;              // size of images

class shape                    // base class
   {
   protected:
      int xCo, yCo;            // coordinates of center
      int linecolor;           // color of outline
      int fillcolor;           // color of interior
      void init()              // initializes line color
         { _setcolor(linecolor); }
      void fill()                      // fills interior of any shape
         {
         _setcolor(fillcolor);              // set fill color
         _floodfill(xCo, yCo, linecolor);   // fill interior
         _setcolor(linecolor);              // restore line color
         }
   public:
      shape()                          // no-arg constructor
         { xCo=0; yCo=0; linecolor=WHITE; fillcolor=WHITE; }
      void set(int x, int y, int lc, int fc)  // set data
         { xCo=x; yCo=y; linecolor=lc; fillcolor=fc; }

      virtual void draw() = 0;   // pure virtual draw() function
   };

class ball : public shape
   {
```

```
    public:
        ball() : shape()                // no-arg constr
            { }
        void set(int x, int y, int lc, int fc)  // set data
            { shape::set(x, y, lc, fc); }
        void draw()                     // draw the ball
            {
            init();                     // line color
                                        // draw circle
            _ellipse(_GBORDER, xCo-W, yCo-W, xCo+W, yCo+W);
            fill();                     // fill the shape
            }
    };


class rect : public shape
    {
    public:
        rect() : shape()                // no-arg constr
            { }
        void set(int x, int y, int lc, int fc)  // set data
            { shape::set(x, y, lc, fc); }
        void draw()                     // draw the rectangle
            {
            init();                     // line color
                                        // draw rectangle
            _rectangle(_GBORDER, xCo-W, yCo-W, xCo+W, yCo+W);
            fill();                     // fill the shape
            _moveto(xCo-W, yCo+W);  // draw diagonal line
            _lineto(xCo+W, yCo-W);  //    SW to NE
            }
    };


class tria : public shape
    {
    public:
        tria() : shape()                // no-arg constr
            { }
        void set(int x, int y, int lc, int fc)  // set data
            { shape::set(x, y, lc, fc); }
        void draw()                     // draw the triangle
            {
            init();                     // set line color
            struct _xycoord t[3];       // set up structure
            t[0].xcoord=xCo;    t[0].ycoord=yCo-W;  // top
            t[1].xcoord=xCo-W;  t[1].ycoord=yCo+W;  // bottom left
            t[2].xcoord=xCo+W;  t[2].ycoord=yCo+W;  // bottom right
```

```
            _polygon(_GBORDER, t, 3);  // draw polygon
            fill();                    // fill the shape
            }
   };

void main()
   {
   if( ! _setvideomode(_MAXRESMODE) )
      { cout << "Can't set graphics mode"; exit(1); }

   shape* ptrarr[3];               // array of pointers to shapes

   ball b1;                        // define three shapes
   rect r1;
   tria t1;

                                   // set values in shapes
   b1.set(100, 100, WHITE, BLUE);
   r1.set(100, 225, WHITE, RED);
   t1.set(100, 350, WHITE, GREEN);

   ptrarr[0] = &b1;                // put addresses in array
   ptrarr[1] = &r1;
   ptrarr[2] = &t1;

   for(int j=0; j<3; j++)          // draw all shapes
      ptrarr[j]->draw();

   getch();                        // wait for keypress
   _setvideomode(_DEFAULTMODE);    // close graphics system
   }
```

The class specifiers in VIRTSHAP are similar to those in MULTSHAP, except that the draw() function in the shape class has been made into a pure virtual function.

In main() we set up an array, ptrarr, of pointers to shapes. Next we create three objects, one of each class, and place their addresses in an array. Now it's easy to draw all three shapes. The statement

```
   ptrarr[j]->draw();
```

does this as the loop variable j changes.

This is a powerful approach to combining graphics elements, especially when a large number of objects need to be grouped together and drawn as a unit.

ABSTRACT CLASSES

An *abstract class* is often defined as one that will not be used to create any objects, but exists only to act as a base class of other classes. Using this criteria, the shape

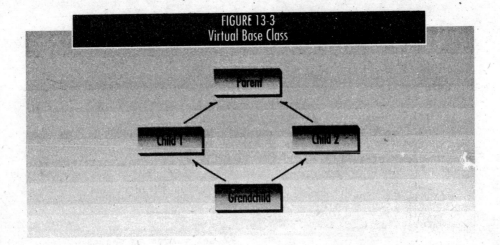

FIGURE 13-3
Virtual Base Class

class in VIRTSHAP is an abstract class. Ellis and Stroustrup (see the bibliography) tighten up this definition by requiring that, to be called abstract, a class must contain at least one pure virtual function. The **shape** class in VIRTSHAP and the **person** class in VIRTPERS meet this definition as well. A class with a pure virtual function cannot be used to create any objects—the compiler won't allow it..

VIRTUAL BASE CLASSES

Before leaving the subject of virtual programming elements, we should mention *virtual base classes*.

Consider the situation shown in Figure 13-3, with a base class, **Parent**; two derived classes, **Child1** and **Child2**; and a fourth class, **Grandchild**, derived from both **Child1** and **Child2**.

In this arrangement a problem can arise if a member function in the **Grandchild** class wants to access data or functions in the **Parent** class. The NORMBASE program shows what happens:

```
// normbase.cpp
// ambiguous reference to base class

class Parent
   {
   protected:
      int basedata;
   };
class Child1 : public Parent
   { };
```

```
class Child2 : public Parent
    { };
class Grandchild : public Child1, public Child2
    {
    public:
        int getdata()
            { return basedata; }    // ERROR: ambiguous
    };
```

A compiler error occurs when the getdata() member function in Grandchild attempts to access basedata in Parent. Why? When the Child1 and Child2 classes are derived from Parent, each inherits a copy of Parent; this copy is called a *subobject*. Each of the two subobjects contains its own copy of Parent's data, including basedata. Now, when Grandchild refers to basedata, which of the two copies will it access? The situation is ambiguous, and that's what the compiler reports.

To eliminate the ambiguity, we make Child1 and Child2 into virtual base classes, as shown by example VIRTBASE:

```
// virtbase.cpp
// virtual base classes

class Parent
    {
    protected:
        int basedata;
    };
class Child1 : virtual public Parent    // shares copy of Parent
    { };
class Child2 : virtual public Parent    // shares copy of Parent
    { };
class Grandchild : public Child1, public Child2
    {
    public:
        int getdata()
            { return basedata; }    // OK: only one copy of Parent
    };
```

The use of the keyword virtual in these two classes causes them to share a single common *subobject* of their base class Parent. Now, since there is only one copy of basedata, there is no ambiguity when it is referred to in Grandchild.

FRIEND FUNCTIONS

The concepts of encapsulation and data hiding dictate that nonmember functions should not be able to access an object's private or protected data. The policy is, if you're not a member, you can't get in. However, there are situations where such rigid discrimination leads to considerable inconvenience.

FRIENDS AS BRIDGES

Imagine that you want a function to operate on objects of two different classes. Perhaps the function will take objects of the two classes as arguments, and operate on their private data. If the two classes are inherited from the same base class, then you may be able to put the function in the base class. But what if the classes are unrelated?

In this situation there's nothing like a friend function. Here's a simple example, FRIEND, that shows how friend functions can act as a bridge between two classes:

```
// friend.cpp
// friend functions
#include <iostream.h>

class beta;                      // needed for frifunc declaration

class alpha
    {
    private:
        int data;
    public:
        alpha()  { data = 3; }             // no-arg constructor
        friend int frifunc(alpha, beta);  // friend function
    };

class beta
    {
    private:
        int data;
    public:
        beta()  { data = 7; }             // no-arg constructor
        friend int frifunc(alpha, beta);  // friend function
    };

int frifunc(alpha a, beta b)              // function definition
    {
    return( a.data + b.data );
    }

void main()
    {
    alpha aa;
    beta bb;
    cout << frifunc(aa, bb);              // call the function
    }
```

In this program the two classes are alpha and beta. The constructors in these classes initialize their single data items to fixed values (3 in alpha and 7 in beta).

We want the function frifunc() to have access to both these private data members, so we make it a friend function. It's declared with the friend keyword in both classes:

```
friend int frifunc(alpha, beta);
```

This declaration can be placed anywhere in the class; it doesn't matter if it goes in the `public` or the `private` section.

An object of each class is passed as an argument to the function `frifunc()`, and it accesses the private `data` member of both classes through these arguments. The function doesn't do much: It adds the data items and returns the sum. The `main()` program calls this function and prints the result.

A minor point: Remember that a class can't be referred to until it has been declared. Class `beta` is referred to in the declaration of the function `frifunc()` in class `alpha`, so `beta` must be declared before `alpha`. Hence the declaration

```
class beta;
```

at the beginning of the program.

BREACHING THE WALLS

We should note that `friend` functions are controversial. During the development of C++, arguments raged over the desirability of including this feature. On the one hand, it adds flexibility to the language; on the other, it is not in keeping with the philosophy that only member functions can access a class's private data.

How serious is the breach of data integrity when `friend` functions are used? A `friend` function must be declared as such within the class whose data it will access. Thus a programmer who does not have access to the source code for the class cannot make a function into a `friend`. In this respect the integrity of the class is still protected. Even so, `friend` functions are conceptually messy, and potentially lead to a spaghetti-code situation if numerous `friend`s muddy the clear boundaries between classes. For this reason `friend` functions should be used sparingly. If you find yourself using many `friend`s, it may be that you need to rethink the design of the program.

ENGLISH DISTANCE EXAMPLE

However, sometimes `friend` functions are too convenient to avoid. One example is when `friend`s are used to increase the versatility of overloaded operators. The following program shows a limitation in the use of such operators when `friend`s are not used. This example is a variation on the ENGLPLUS and ENGLCONV programs of Chapter 9. It's called NOFRI.

```
// nofri.cpp
// limitation to overloaded + operator
#include <iostream.h>

ss Distance                          // English Distance class
   {
   private:
      int feet;
      float inches;
```

```
    public:
        Distance()                    // constructor (no args)
            { feet = 0; inches = 0.0; }
        Distance( float fltfeet )     // constructor (one arg)
            {                         // convert float to Distance
            feet = int(fltfeet);          // feet is integer part
            inches = 12*(fltfeet-feet);   // inches is what's left
            }
        Distance(int ft, float in)    // constructor (two args)
            { feet = ft; inches = in; }
        void showdist()               // display distance
            { cout << feet << "\'-" << inches << '\"'; }
        Distance operator + (Distance);
    };
                                      // add this distance to d2
Distance Distance::operator + (Distance d2)    // return the sum
    {
    int f = feet + d2.feet;        // add the feet
    float i = inches + d2.inches;  // add the inches
    if(i >= 12.0)                  // if total exceeds 12.0,
        { i -= 12.0; f++; }        // less 12 inches, plus 1 foot
    return Distance(f,i);          // return new Distance with sum
    }

void main()
    {
    Distance d1 = 2.5;             // constructor converts
    Distance d2 = 1.25;            // meters to Distance
    Distance d3;
    cout << "\nd1 = "; d1.showdist();
    cout << "\nd2 = "; d2.showdist();

    d3 = d1 + 10.0;                // distance + float: ok
    cout << "\nd3 = "; d3.showdist();
//  d3 = 10.0 + d1;                // float + Distance: ERROR
//  cout << "\nd3 = "; d3.showdist();
    }.
```

In this program the + operator is overloaded to add two objects of type Distance. Also, there is a one-argument constructor that converts a value of type
float, representing feet and decimal fractions of feet, into a Distance value. (That
is, it converts 10.25' into 10'-3".)

When such a constructor exists, you can make statements like this in
main():

```
    d3 = d1 + 10.0;
```

The overloaded + is looking for objects of type Distance both on its left and on
its right, but if the argument on the right is type float, the compiler will use the
one-argument constructor to convert this float to a Distance value, and then
carry out the addition.

Here is what appears to be a subtle variation on this statement:

```
d3 = 10.0 + d1;
```

Does this work? No, because the object of which the overloaded + operator is a member must be the variable to the left of the operator. When we place a variable of a different type there, or a constant, then there is no object of which + can be a member, and so there is no constructor to convert the type float to type Distance. The compiler can't handle this situation. Here's the output from NOFRI:

```
d1 = 2'-6"
d2 = 1'-3"
d3 = 12'-6"
```

The second addition won't compile, so these statements are commented out.

How can we write statements that have nonmember data types to the left of the operator? As you may have guessed, a friend can help you out of this dilemma. The FRENGL program shows how:

```cpp
// frengl.cpp
// friend overloaded + operator
#include <iostream.h>

class Distance                          // English Distance class
   {
   private:
      int feet;
      float inches;
   public:
      Distance()                        // constructor (no args)
         { feet = 0; inches = 0.0; }
      Distance( float fltfeet )   // constructor (one arg)
         {                              // convert float to Distance
         feet = int(fltfeet);          // feet is integer part
         inches = 12*(fltfeet-feet);   // inches is what's left
         }
      Distance(int ft, float in)  // constructor (two args)
         { feet = ft; inches = in; }
      void showdist()                   // display distance
         { cout << feet << "\'-" << inches << '\"'; }
      friend Distance operator + (Distance, Distance);  // friend
   };
                                        // add D1 to d2
Distance operator + (Distance d1, Distance d2)
   {
   int f = d1.feet + d2.feet;          // add the feet
   float i = d1.inches + d2.inches;    // add the inches
   if(i >= 12.0)                       // if inches exceeds 12.0,
      { i -= 12.0; f++; }              // less 12 inches, plus 1 foot
   return Distance(f,i);               // return new Distance with sum
   }

void main()
   {
```

```
        Distance d1 = 2.5;              // constructor converts
        Distance d2 = 1.25;            // float-feet to Distance
        Distance d3;
        cout << "\nd1 = "; d1.showdist();
        cout << "\nd2 = "; d2.showdist();

        d3 = d1 + 10.0;                // distance + float: ok
        cout << "\nd3 = "; d3.showdist();
        d3 = 10.0 + d1;                // float + Distance: ok
        cout << "\nd3 = "; d3.showdist();
        }
```

The overloaded + operator is made into a friend:

```
friend Distance operator + (Distance, Distance);
```

Notice that, while the overloaded + operator took one argument as a member function, it takes two as a friend function. In a member function, one of the objects on which the + operates is the object of which it was a member, and the second is an argument. In a friend, both objects must be arguments.

The only change to the body of the overloaded + function is that the variables feet and inches, used in NOFRI for direct access to the object's data, have been replaced in FRENGL by d1.feet and d1.inches, since this object is supplied as an argument.

friends FOR FUNCTIONAL NOTATION

Sometimes a friend allows a more obvious syntax for calling a function than does a member function. For example, suppose we want a function that will return an object of the English Distance class rounded off to the nearest foot. The MROUND example shows how this might be done with a member function:

```
// mround.cpp
// member function roundoff() for Distance class
// returns Distance object rounded off to nearest whole foot
#include <iostream.h>

class Distance                          // English Distance class
    {
    private:
        int feet;
        float inches;
    public:
        Distance()                      // constructor (no args)
            { feet = 0; inches = 0.0; }
        Distance(int ft, float in)  // constructor (two args)
            { feet = ft; inches = in; }
        void showdist()                 // display distance
            { cout << feet << "\'-" << inches << '\"'; }
        Distance roundoff();            // member function
    };
```

```
Distance Distance::roundoff()    // return this Distance rounded
    {                            //    to nearest foot
    int f = int(feet);           // convert feet
    if(inches >= 6.0) ++f;       // increment feet if necessary
    float i = 0.0;               // inches always zero
    return Distance(f, i);       // return temp Distance
    }

void main()
    {
    Distance d1(3, 6.0);         // two-arg constructor
    Distance d2;                 // no-arg constructor

    d2 = d1.roundoff();          // return rounded-off d1
                                 // display both distances
    cout << "\nd1 = "; d1.showdist();
    cout << "\nd2 = "; d2.showdist();
    }
```

The `main()` part of the program creates a `Distance` value, rounds it off, and prints out the result. The output shows the original distance and the rounded-off value:

```
d1 = 3'-6"
d2 = 4'-0'
```

In `main()` we use the statement

```
d2 = d1.roundoff();
```

to find the rounded-off value of `d1` and assign it to `d2`. This works all right, but if we want to work with `Distance` objects using the same syntax that we use with typical math functions on ordinary numbers, we would probably prefer a functional notation:

```
d2 = roundoff(d1);
```

We can achieve this effect by making `roundoff()` a `friend` of the `Distance` class, as shown in FROUND:

```
// fround.cpp
// friend function roundoff() for Distance class
// returns Distance object rounded off to nearest whole foot
#include <iostream.h>

class Distance                           // English Distance class
    {
    private:
        int feet;
        float inches;
    public:
        Distance()                       // constructor (no args)
            { feet = 0; inches = 0.0; }
        Distance(int ft, float in)       // constructor (two args)
            { feet = ft; inches = in; }
```

```
        void showdist()                  // display distance
           { cout << feet << "\'-" << inches << '\"'; }
        friend Distance roundoff(Distance);  // friend function
   };

Distance roundoff(Distance d)       // return argument
   {                                // rounded to nearest foot
   int f = int(d.feet);             // convert feet
   if(d.inches >= 6.0) ++f;         // increment feet if necessary
   float i = 0.0;                   // inches always zero
   return Distance(f, i);           // return temp Distance
   }

void main()
   {
   Distance d1(3, 6.0);             // two-arg constructor
   Distance d2;                     // no-arg constructor

   d2 = roundoff(d1);               // return rounded-off d1
                                    // display both distances
   cout << "\nd1 = "; d1.showdist();
   cout << "\nd2 = "; d2.showdist();
   }
```

Where `roundoff()`, as a member function in MROUND, takes no arguments, it takes one as a **friend** in FROUND. In general, the **friend** version of a function requires one more argument than when the function is a member. The `roundoff()` function in FROUND is similar to that in MROUND, but it refers to the data in the source `Distance` object as `d.feet` and `d.inches` instead of as `feet` and `inches`.

friend CLASSES

The member functions of a class can all be made **friend**s at the same time when you make the entire class a **friend**. The program FRICLASS shows how this looks:

```
// friclass.cpp
// friend classes
#include <iostream.h>

class alpha
   {
   private:
      int data1;
   public:
      alpha() { data1 = 99; }
      friend class beta;           // beta is a friend class
   };
```

494

```
class beta
  {                               // all member functions can
  public:                         // access private alpha data
    void func1(alpha a)   { cout << "\ndata1=" << a.data1; }
    void func2(alpha a)   { cout << "\ndata1=" << a.data1; }
    void func3(alpha a)   { cout << "\ndata1=" << a.data1; }
  };

void main()
  {
  alpha a;
  beta b;

  b.func1(a);
  b.func2(a);
  b.func3(a);
  }
```

In class **alpha** the entire class **beta** is proclaimed a friend. Now all the member functions of **beta** can access the private data of **alpha** (in this program the single data item **data1**).

Note that in the **friend** declaration we specify that **beta** is a class using the **class** keyword:

```
friend class beta;
```

We could also have declared **beta** to be a class before the **alpha** class specifier, as in previous examples:

```
class beta;
```

and then, within **alpha**, referred to **beta** without the **class** keyword:

```
friend beta;
```

STATIC FUNCTIONS

In the STATDATA example in Chapter 7, we introduced **static** member data. As you may recall, a static data member is not duplicated for each object; rather a single data item is shared by all objects of a class. The STATIC example showed a class that kept track of how many objects of itself there were. Let's extend this concept by showing how functions as well as data may be **static**. Besides showing static functions, our example will model a class that provides an ID number for each of its objects. This allows you to query an object to find out which object it is—a capability that is sometimes useful in debugging a program, among other situations. The program also casts some light on the operation of destructors. Here's the listing for STATFUNC:

```
// statfunc.cpp
// static functions and ID numbers for objects
#include <iostream.h>

class gamma
    {
    private:
        static int total;          // total objects of this class
                                   // (declaration only)
        int id;                    // ID number of this object
    public:
        gamma()                    // no-argument constructor
            {
            total++;               // add another object
            id = total;            // id equals current total
            }
        ~gamma()                   // destructor
            {
            total--;
            cout << "\nDestroying ID number=" << id;
            }
        static void showtotal()    // static function
            {
            cout << "\nTotal is " << total;
            }
        void showid()              // non-static function
            {
            cout << "\nID number is " << id;
            }
    };

int gamma::total;                  // definition of total

void main()
    {
    cout << endl << endl;
    gamma g1;
    gamma::showtotal();

    gamma g2, g3;
    gamma::showtotal();

    g1.showid();
    g2.showid();
    g3.showid();
    cout << "\n----------end of program----------";
    }
```

ACCESSING static FUNCTIONS

In this program there is a static data member, total, in the class gamma. This data keeps track of how many objects of the class there are. It is incremented by the constructor and decremented by the destructor.

Suppose we want to access **total** from outside the class. We construct a function, **showtotal()**, that prints the **total**'s value. But how do we access this function?

When a data member is declared **static**, there is only one such data value for the entire class, no matter how many objects of the class are created. In fact, there may be no such objects at all, but we still want to be able to learn this fact. We could create a dummy object to use in calling a member function, as in

```
gamma dummyObj;        // make an object so we can call function
dummyObj.showtotal();  // call function
```

But this is rather inelegant. We shouldn't need to refer to a specific object when we're doing something that relates to the entire class. It's more reasonable to use the name of the class itself with the scope-resolution operator:

```
gamma::showtotal();   // more reasonable
```

However, this won't work if **showtotal()** is a normal member function; an object and the dot member-access operator is required in such cases. To access **showtotal()** using only the class name, we must declare it to be a **static** member function. This is what we do in STATFUNC. Now the function can be accessed using only the class name. Here's the output:

```
Total is 1
Total is 3
ID number is 1
ID number is 2
ID number is 3
----------end of program--------
Destroying ID number 3
Destroying ID number 2
Destroying ID number 1
```

We define one object, **g1**, and then print out the value of **total**, which is 1. Then we define two more objects, **g2** and **g3**, and again print out the total, which is now 3.

NUMBERING THE OBJECTS

We've placed another function in **gamma()** to print out the ID number of individual members. This ID number is set equal to **total** when an object is created, so each object has a unique number. The **showid()** function prints out the ID of its object. We call it three times in **main()**, in the statements

```
g1.showid();
g2.showid();
g3.showid();
```

As the output shows, each object has a unique number. The **g1** object is numbered 1, **g2** is 2, and **g3** is 3.

INVESTIGATING DESTRUCTORS

Now that we know how to number objects, we can investigate an interesting fact about destructors. STATFUNC prints an *end of program* message in its last statement, but it's not done yet, as the output shows. The three objects created in the program must be destroyed before the program terminates, so that memory is not left in an inaccessible state. The compiler takes care of this by invoking the destructor.

We can see that this happens by inserting in the destructor a statement that prints a message. Since we've numbered the objects, we can also find out the order in which the objects are destroyed. As the output shows, the last object created, g3, is destroyed first. One can infer from this last-in–first-out approach that local objects are stored on the stack.

ASSIGNMENT AND COPY-INITIALIZATION

The C++ compiler is always busy on your behalf, doing things you can't be bothered to do. If you take charge, it will defer to your judgment; otherwise it will do things its own way. Two important examples of this process are the assignment operator and the copy constructor.

You've used the assignment operator many times, probably without thinking too much about it. Suppose a1 and a2 are objects. Unless you tell the compiler otherwise, the statement

```
a2 = a1;        // set a2 to the value of a1
```

will cause the compiler to copy the data from a1, member-by-member, into a2. This is the default action of the assignment operator, =.

You are also familiar with initializing basic variable types to a value when they're defined, as in the expression

```
int a = 27;    // initialize a to 27
```

You can also initialize a variable to a value provided by another variable, as in

```
int b = a;
```

An alternative syntax to this last statement is

```
int b(a);
```

which uses functional notation but has exactly the same effect: b is created and the value of a is copied into b.

In the same way, you can create objects and initialize them to the value of other objects:

```
alpha a2 = a1;   // initialize a2 to a1
alpha a2(a1);    // initialize a2 to a1
```

These statements both cause a2 to be created and the value of a1 to be copied into it. As with assignment, the copying is normally done on a member-by-member basis.

Both these default activities are provided, free of charge, by the compiler. If member-by-member copying is what you want, you need take no further action. However, if you want assignment or initialization to do something more complex, then you can override the default functions. We'll discuss the techniques for overloading the assignment operator and the copy constructor separately, and then put them together in an example that gives a `string` class a more efficient way to manage memory.

OVERLOADING THE ASSIGNMENT OPERATOR

Let's look at a short example that demonstrates the technique of overloading the assignment operator. Here's the listing for ASSIGN:

```
// assign.cpp
// overloads assignment operator (=)
#include <iostream.h>

class alpha
    {
    private:
        int data;
    public:
        alpha()                         // no-arg constructor
            { }
        alpha(int d)                    // one-arg constructor
            { data = d; }
        void display()                  // display data
            { cout << data; }
        alpha operator = (alpha& a)     // overloaded = operator
            {
            data = a.data;              // not done automatically
            cout << "\nAssignment operator invoked";
            return alpha(data);         // return copy of this alpha
            }
    };

void main()
    {
    alpha a1(37);
    alpha a2;

    a2 = a1;                            // invoke overloaded =
    cout << "\na2="; a2.display();      // display a2

    alpha a3 = a2;                      // does NOT invoke =
    cout << "\na3="; a3.display();      // display a3
    }
```

The `alpha` class is very simple; it contains only one data member. Constructors initialize the data, and a member function can print out its value. The new aspect of ASSIGN is the function `operator=()`, which overloads the = operator.

In `main()` we define `a1` and give it the value 37, and define `a2` but give it no value. Then we use the assignment operator to set `a2` to the value of `a1`:

```
a2 = a1;   // assignment statement
```

This causes our overloaded `operator=()` function to be invoked. Here's the output from ASSIGN:

```
Assignment operator invoked
a2=37
a3=37
```

Initialization Is Not Assignment

In the last two lines of ASSIGN, we initialize the object `a3` to the value `a2`, and display it. Don't be confused by the syntax here. The equals sign in

```
alpha a3 = a2;   // copy initialization, not an assignment
```

is not an assignment but an initialization, with the same effect as

```
alpha a3(a2);    // alternative form of copy initialization
```

This is why the the assignment operator is executed only once, as shown by the single invocation of the line

```
Assignment operator invoked
```

in the output of ASSIGN.

Taking Responsibility

When you overload the = operator you assume responsibility for doing whatever the default assignment operator did. Often this involves copying the member data from one object to another. The `alpha` class in ASSIGN has only one data item, `data`, so the `operator=()` function copies its value with the statement

```
data = a.data;
```

The function also prints the *Assignment operator invoked* message so that we can tell when it executes.

Passing by Reference

Notice that the argument to `operator=()` is passed by reference. It is not absolutely necessary to do this, but it's often a good idea. Why? As you know, an argument passed by value generates a copy of itself in the function to which it is passed. The argument passed to the `operator=()` function is no exception. If such objects are large, the copies can waste a lot of memory. Values passed by reference don't generate copies, and thus help to conserve memory.

Also, there are certain situations in which you want to keep track of the number of objects (as in the STATFUNC example, where we assigned numbers to the objects). If the compiler is generating extra objects every time you use the assignment operator, you may wind up with more objects than you expected. Passing by reference helps to avoid such spurious object creation.

Returning a Value

As we've seen, a function can return information to the calling program by value or by reference. When an object is returned by value, a new object is created and returned to the calling program. In the calling program, the value of this object can be assigned to a new object, or it can be used in other ways. When an object is returned by reference, no new object is created. A reference to the original object in the function is all that's returned to the calling program.

The `operator=()` function in ASSIGN returns a value by creating a temporary `alpha` object and initializing it using the one-argument constructor in the statement

```
return alpha(data);
```

The value returned is a copy of, but not the same object as, the object of which the overloaded = operator is a member. Returning a value makes it possible to chain = operators:

```
a3 = a2 = a1;
```

However, returning by value has the same disadvantages as passing an argument by value: It creates an extra copy that wastes memory and can cause confusion. Can we return this value with a reference, using the declarator shown here for the overloaded = operator?

```
alpha& operator = (alpha& a)   // bad idea in this case
```

Unfortunately, we can't use reference returns on variables that are local to a function. Remember that local (`automatic`) variables—that is, those created within a function (and not designated `static`)—are destroyed when the function returns. A return by reference returns only the address of the data being returned, and, for local data, this address points to data within the function. When the function is terminated and this data is destroyed, the pointer is left with a meaningless value. (We'll see one way to solve this problem when we talk about the `this` pointer later in this chapter.)

Not Inherited

The assignment operator is unique among operators in that it is not inherited. If you overload the assignment operator in a base class, you can't use this same function in any derived classes.

THE COPY CONSTRUCTOR

As we discussed, you can define and at the same time initialize an object to the value of another object with two kinds of statement:

```
alpha a3(a2);     // copy initialization
alpha a3 = a2;    // copy initialization, alternate syntax
```

Both styles of definition invoke a *copy constructor*: that is, a constructor that copies its argument into a new object. The default copy constructor, which is provided automatically by the compiler for every object, performs a member-by-member copy.

This is similar to what the assignment operator does; the difference is that the copy constructor also creates a new object.

Like the assignment operator, the copy constructor can be overloaded by the user. The XOFXREF example shows how it's done:

```
// xofxref.cpp
// copy constructor: X(X&)
#include <iostream.h>

class alpha
    {
    private:
        int data;
    public:
        alpha()                    // no-arg constructor
            { }
        alpha(int d)               // one-arg constructor
            { data = d; }
        alpha(alpha& a)            // copy constructor
            {
            data = a.data;
            cout << "\nCopy constructor invoked";
            }
        void display()             // display
            { cout << data; }
        void operator = (alpha& a) // overloaded = operator
            {
            data = a.data;
            cout << "\nAssignment operator invoked";
            }
    };

void main()
    {
    alpha a1(37);
    alpha a2;

    a2 = a1;                       // invoke overloaded =
    cout << "\na2="; a2.display(); // display a2

    alpha a3(a1);                  // invoke copy constructor
//  alpha a3 = a1;                 // equivalent definition of a3
    cout << "\na3="; a3.display(); // display a3
    }
```

This program overloads both the assignment operator and the copy constructor. The overloaded assignment operator is similar to that in the ASSIGN example. The copy constructor takes one argument: an object of type `alpha`, passed by reference. Here's its declarator:

```
alpha(alpha&)
```

This declarator has the form `X(X&)` (pronounced "X of X ref"), which is often used as a shorthand name for copy constructors. Here's the output of XOFXREF:

```
Assignment operator invoked
a2=37
Copy constructor invoked
a3=37
```

The statement

```
a2 = a1;
```

invokes the assignment operator, while

```
alpha a3(a1);
```

invokes the copy constructor. The equivalent statement

```
alpha a3 = a1;
```

could also be used to invoke the copy constructor.

We've seen that the copy constructor may be invoked when an object is defined It is also invoked when arguments are passed by value to functions and when values are returned from functions. Let's mention these situations briefly.

Function Arguments

The copy constructor is invoked when an object is passed by value to a function. It creates the copy that the function operates on. Thus if the function

```
void func(alpha);
```

was declared in XOFXREF, and this function was called by the statement

```
func(a1);
```

then the copy constructor would be invoked to create a copy of the **a1** object for use by **func()**. (Of course, the copy constructor is not invoked if the argument is passed by reference or if a pointer to it is passed. In these cases no copy is created; the function operates on the original variable.)

Function Return Values

The copy constructor also creates a temporary object when a value is returned from a function. Suppose there were a function like this in XOFXREF:

```
alpha func();
```

and this function was called by the statement

```
a2 = func();
```

then the copy constructor would be invoked to create a copy of the value returned by **func()**, and this value would be assigned (invoking the assignment operator) to **a2**.

Why Not an X(X) Constructor?

Do we need to use a reference in the argument to the copy constructor? Could we pass by value instead? No, the compiler complains that it is *out of memory* if we try to compile

```
alpha(alpha a)
```

Why? Because when an argument is passed by value, a copy of it is constructed. What makes the copy? The copy constructor. But this *is* the copy constructor, so it calls itself. In fact it calls itself over and over until the compiler runs out of memory. So, in the copy constructor, the argument must be passed by reference, which creates no copies.

A Memory-Efficient String Class

The ASSIGN and XOFXREF examples don't really need to have overloaded assignment operators and copy constructors. They use straightforward classes with only one data item, so the default assignment operator and copy constructor would work just as well. Let's look at an example where it is essential for the user to overload these operators.

Defects with the String Class

We've seen various versions of the **String** class in previous chapters. However, these versions are not very sophisticated. It would be nice to overload the = operator so that we could assign the value of one **string** object to another with the statement

```
s2 = s1;
```

If we overload the = operator, the question arises how we will handle the actual string (the array of type **char**), which is the principal data item in the **String** class.

One possibilty is for each **string** object to have a place to store a string. If we assign one **string** object to another (from **s1** into **s2** in the previous statement), we simply copy the string from the source into the destination object. The problem with this is that the same string now exists in two (or more) places in memory. This is not very efficient, especially if the strings are long. Figure 13-4 shows how this looks.

Instead of having each **string** object contain its own string, we could arrange for it to contain only a *pointer* to a string. Now, if we assign one **string** object to another, we need only copy the pointer from one object to another; both pointers will point to the same string. This is efficient, since only a single copy of the string itself needs to be stored in memory. Figure 13-5 shows how this looks.

However, if we use this system we need to be careful when we destroy a **string** object. If a **string**'s destructor uses **delete** to free the memory occupied by the string, and if there are several objects with pointers pointing to the string, then these other objects will be left with pointers pointing to memory that may no longer hold the string they think it does; they become dangling pointers.

To use pointers to strings in **string** objects, we need a way to keep track of how many **string** objects point to a particular string, so that we can avoid **delete**ing the string until the last **string** that points to it is itself deleted. Our next example, STRIMEM, does just this.

FIGURE 13-4
Replicating Strings

s1

"This is a long
string in memory."

s2

"This is a long
string in memory."

FIGURE 13-5
Replicating Pointers to Strings

s1

"This is a long
string in memory."

s2

A String-Counter Class

Suppose we have several **string** objects pointing to the same string and we want to keep a count of how many **strings** point to the string. Where will we store this count?

It would be cumbersome for every **string** object to maintain a count of how many of its fellow **strings** were pointing to a particular string, so we don't want to use a member variable in **string** for the count. Could we use a static variable?

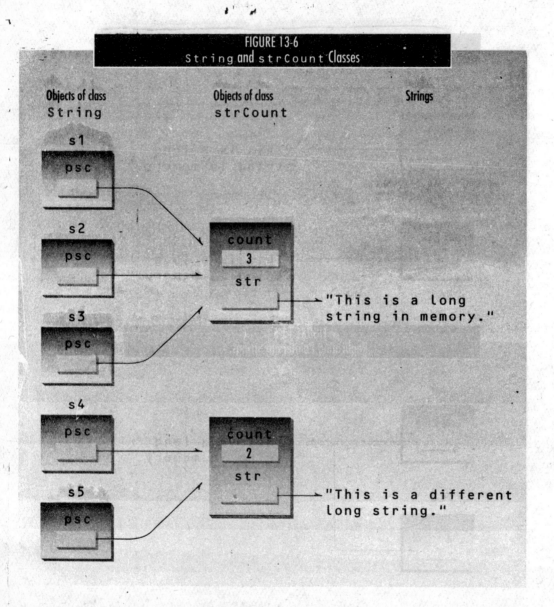

FIGURE 13-6
String and strCount Classes

Objects of class String	Objects of class strCount	Strings

s1

psc

s2

psc

count
3
str

"This is a long
string in memory."

s3

psc

s4

psc

count
2
str

"This is a different
long string."

s5

psc

This is a possibility; we could create a static array and use it to store a list of string addresses and counts. However, this requires considerable overhead. It's more efficient to create a new class to store the count. Each object of this class, which we call **strCount**, contains a count and also a pointer to the string itself. Each **string** object contains a pointer to the appropriate **strCount** object. Figure 13-6 shows how this looks.

To ensure that **string** objects have access to **strCount** objects, we make **String** a **friend** of **strCount**. Here's the listing for STRIMEM:

```
// strimem.cpp
// memory-saving String class
// overloaded assignment and copy constructor
#include <iostream.h>
#include <string.h>                    // for strcpy(), etc

class strCount                         // keep track of number
   {                                   // of unique strings
   private:
      int count;                       // number of instances
      char* str;                       // pointer to string
      friend class String;             // make ourselves available
   public:
      strCount(char* s)                // one-arg constructor
         {
         int length = strlen(s);       // length of string argument
         str = new char[length+1];     // get memory for string
         strcpy(str, s);               // copy argument to it
         count=1;                      // start count at 1
         }
      ~strCount()                      // destructor
         {
         delete str;                   // delete the string
         }
   };

class String                          // String class
   {
   private:
      strCount* psc;                   // pointer to strCount
   public:
      String()                         // no-arg constructor
         {
         psc = new strCount("NULL");
         }
      String(char* s)                  // 1-arg constructor
         {
         psc = new strCount(s);
         }
      String(String& S)                // copy constructor
         {
         psc = S.psc;
         (psc->count)++;
         }
      ~String()                        // destructor
         {
         if(psc->count==1)             // if we are its last user,
            delete psc;                // delete our strCount
         else                          // otherwise,
            (psc->count)--;            // decrement its count
         }
      void display()                   // display the String
         {
         cout << psc->str;             // print string
```

507

```
            cout << " (addr=" << psc << ")";  // print address
            }
         void operator = (String& S)      // assign the string
            {
            if(psc->count==1)              // if we are its last user,
               delete psc;                 //    delete our strCount
            else                           //    otherwise,
               (psc->count)--;             //    decrement its count
            psc = S.psc;                   // use argument's strCount
            (psc->count)++;                // increment its count
            }
      };

   void main()
      {
      String s3 = "When the fox preaches, look to your geese.";
      cout << "\ns3="; s3.display();    // display s3

      String s1;                           // define String
      s1 = s3;                             // assign it another String
      cout << "\ns1="; s1.display();    // display it

      String s2(s3);                       // initialize with String
      cout << "\ns2="; s2.display();    // display it
      }
```

In the `main()` part of STRIMEM we define a `String` object, `s3`, to contain the proverb "When the fox preaches, look to your geese." We define another `String` `s1` and set it equal to `s3`; then we define `s2` and initialize it to `s3`. Setting `s1` equal to `s3` invokes the overloaded assignment operator; initializing `s2` to `s3` invokes the overloaded copy constructor. We print out all three strings, and also the address of the `strCount` object pointed to by each object's `psc` pointer, to show that these objects are all the same. Here's the output from STRIMEM:

```
s3=When the fox preaches, look to your geese. (addr=0x0e00)
s1=When the fox preaches, look to your geese. (addr=0x0e00)
s2=When the fox preaches, look to your geese. (addr=0x0e00)
```

The other duties of the `String` class are divided between the `String` and `strCount` classes. Let's see what they do.

The strCount Class

The `strCount` class contains the pointer to the actual string and the count of how many `String` class objects point to this string. Its single constructor takes a pointer to a string as an argument and creates a new memory area for the string. It copies the string into this area and sets the count to 1, since just one `String` points to it when it is created. The destructor in `strCount` frees the memory used by the string.

The String Class

The `String` class uses three constructors. If a new string is being created, as in the one- and two-argument constructors, a new `strCount` object is created to hold the string, and the psc pointer is set to point to this object. If an existing string object is being copied, as in the copy constructor and the overloaded assignment operator, then the pointer psc is set to point to the old strCount object, and the count in this object is incremented. The overloaded assignment operator must also delete

FIGURE 13-7
Assignment Operator in STRIMEM

Before execution of s1 = s3;

After execution of s1 = s3;

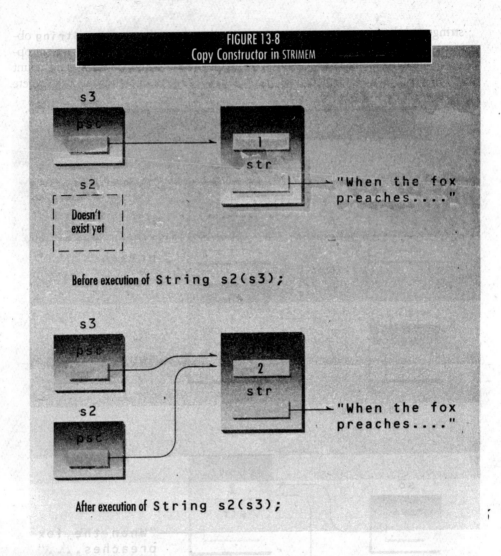

FIGURE 13-8
Copy Constructor in STRIMEM

Before execution of `String s2(s3);`

After execution of `String s2(s3);`

the old `strCount` object pointed to by `psc`. The statement `delete psc;` causes the destructor for `strCount` to be called. Figure 13-7 shows the action of the overloaded assignment operator, and Figure 13-8 shows the copy constructor.

THE this POINTER

The member functions of a particular object have access to a sort of magic pointer named `this`, which points to the object itself. Thus any member function can find out the address of the object of which it is a member. Here's a short example, WHERE, that shows the mechanism:

```
// where.cpp
// the this pointer
#include <iostream.h>

class where
    {
    private:
        char charray[10];    // occupies 10 bytes
    public:
        void reveal()
            { cout << "\nMy object's address is " << this; }
    };

void main()
    {
    where w1, w2, w3;        // make three objects
    w1.reveal();             // see where they are
    w2.reveal();
    w3.reveal();
    }
```

The `main()` program in this example creates three objects of type `where`. It then asks each object to print its address, using the `reveal()` member function. This function prints out the value of the `this` pointer. Here's the output:

```
My object's address is 0xffec
My object's address is 0xffe2
My object's address is 0xffd8
```

Since the data in each object consists of an array of 10 bytes, the objects are spaced 10 bytes apart in memory. (EC minus E2 is 10 decimal, as is E2 minus D8.)

ACCESSING MEMBER DATA WITH this

When you call a member function, it comes into existence with the value of `this` set to the address of the object for which it was called. The `this` pointer can be treated like any other pointer to an object, and can thus be used to access the data in the object it points to, as shown in the DOTHIS program:

```
// dothis.cpp
// the this pointer referring to data
#include <iostream.h>

class what
    {
    private:
        int alpha;
    public:
        void tester()
            {
            this->alpha = 11;       // same as alpha = 11;
            cout << this->alpha;    // same as cout << alpha;
            }
```

```
};
void main()
    {
    what w;
    w.tester();
    }
```

This program simply prints out the value 11. Notice that the **tester()** member function accesses the variable **alpha** as

```
this->alpha
```

This is exactly the same as referring to **alpha** directly. This syntax works, but there is no reason for it except to show that **this** does indeed point to the object.

USING **this** FOR RETURNING VALUES

A more practical use for **this** is in returning values from member functions and overloaded operators.

Recall that in the ASSIGN program, we could not return an object by reference, because the object was local to the function returning it, and thus was destroyed when the function returned. We need a more permanent object if we're going to return it by reference. The object of which a function is a member is more permanent than its individual member functions. An object's member functions are created and destroyed every time they're called, but the object itself endures until it is destroyed by some outside agency (for example, when it is **deleted**). Thus returning by reference the object of which a function is a member is a better bet than returning a temporary object created in a member function. The **this** pointer makes this easy.

Here's the listing for ASSIGN2, in which the **operator=()** function returns by reference the object (actually the contents of a pointer to the object) that invoked it:

```
// assign2.cpp
// returns contents of the this pointer
#include <iostream.h>

class alpha
    {
    private:
        int data;
    public:
        alpha()                        // no-arg constructor
            { }
        alpha(int d)                   // one-arg constructor
            { data = d; }
        void display()                 // display data
            { cout << data; }
        alpha& operator = (alpha& a)   // overloaded = operator
            {
            data = a.data;             // not done automatically
            cout << "\nAssignment operator invoked";
            return *this;              // return copy of this alpha
```

512

```
        }
    };
void main()
    {
    alpha a1(37);
    alpha a2, a3;

    a3 = a2 = a1;                   // invoke overloaded =
    cout << "\na2="; a2.display();  // display a2

    cout << "\na3="; a3.display();  // display a3
    }
```

In this program we can use the declaration

```
alpha& operator = (alpha& a)
```

which returns by reference, instead of

```
alpha operator = (alpha& a)
```

which returns by value. The last statement in this function is

```
return *this;
```

Since `this` is a pointer to the object of which the function is a member, `*this` is that object itself, and the statement returns it by reference. Here's the output of ASSIGN2:

```
Assignment operator invoked
Assignment operator invoked
a2=37
a3=37
```

Each time the equals sign is encountered in

```
a3 = a2 = a1;
```

the overloaded `operator=()` function is called, which prints the messages. The three objects all end up with the same value.

REVISED STRIMEM PROGRAM

Using the `this` pointer we can revise the `operator=()` function in STRIMEM to return a value by reference, thus making possible multiple assignment operators for `String` objects, such as

```
s1 = s2 = s3;
```

At the same time, we can avoid the creation of spurious objects such as those that are created when objects are returned by value. Here's the listing for STRIMEM2:

```
// strimem2.cpp
// memory-saving String class
// the this pointer in overloaded assignment
#include <iostream.h>
#include <string.h>                 // for strcpy(), etc
```

```
class strCount                          // keep track of number
    {                                   // of unique strings
    private:
        int count;                      // number of instances
        char* str;                      // pointer to string
        friend class String;            // make ourselves available
    public:
        strCount(char* s)               // one-arg constructor
            {
            int length = strlen(s);     // length of string argument
            str = new char[length+1];   // get memory for string
            strcpy(str, s);             // copy argument to it
            count=1;                    // start count at 1
            }
        ~strCount()                     // destructor
            {
            delete str;                 // delete the string
            }
    };

class String                            // String class
    {
    private:
        strCount* psc;                  // pointer to strCount
    public:
        String()                        // no-arg constructor
            {
            psc = new strCount("NULL");
            }
        String(char* s)                 // 1-arg constructor
            {
            psc = new strCount(s);
            }
        String(String& S)               // copy constructor
            {
            cout << "\nCOPY CONSTRUCTOR";
            psc = S.psc;
            (psc->count)++;
            }
        ~String()                       // destructor
            {
            if(psc->count==1)           // if we are its last user,
                delete psc;             //    delete our strCount
            else                        //    otherwise,
                (psc->count)--;         //    decrement its count
            }
        void display()                  // display the String
            {
            cout << psc->str;           // print string
            cout << " (addr=" << psc << ")"; // print address
            }
```

```
    String& operator = (String& S)          // assign the string
    {
    cout << "\nASSIGNMENT";
    if(psc->count==1)                        // if we are its last user,
        delete psc;                          //     delete our strCount
    else                                     //     otherwise,
        (psc->count)--;                      //     decrement its count
    psc = S.psc;                             // use argument's strCount
    (psc->count)++;                          // increment count
    return *this;                            // return this object
    }
    };

void main()
    {
    String s3 = "When the fox preaches, look to your geese.";
    cout << "\ns3="; s3.display();           // display s3

    String s1, s2;                           // define Strings
    s1 = s2 = s3;                            // assign them
    cout << "\ns1="; s1.display();           // display it
    cout << "\ns2="; s2.display();           // display it
    }
```

Now the declarator for the = operator is

```
String& operator = (String& S)   // return by reference
```

And, as in ASSIGN2, this function returns a pointer to this. Here's the output:

```
s3=When the fox preaches, look to your geese. (addr=0x0d3a)
ASSIGNMENT
ASSIGNMENT
s1=When the fox preaches, look to your geese. (addr=0x0d3a)
s2=When the fox preaches, look to your geese. (addr=0x0d3a)
```

The output shows that, following the assignment statement, all three String objects point to the same strCount object.

We should note that the this pointer is not available in static member functions, since they are not associated with a particular object.

Summary

Virtual functions provide a way for a program to decide, when it is running, what function to call. Ordinarily such decisions are made at compile time. Virtual functions make possible greater flexibility in performing the same kind of action on different kinds of objects. In particular, they allow the use of functions called from an array of type pointer-to-base, that actually holds pointers to a variety of derived types. Typically, a function is declared virtual in the base class, and other functions with the same name are declared in derived classes. A pure virtual function has no body in the base class.

A **friend** function can access a class's private data, even though it is not a member function of the class. This is useful when one function must have access to two or more unrelated classes and when an overloaded operator must use, on its left side, a value of a class other than the one of which it is a member. **friend**s are also used to facilitate functional notation.

A **static** function is one that operates on the class in general, rather than on objects of the class. In particular it can operate on static variables. It can be called with the class name and scope-resolution operator.

The assignment operator = can be overloaded. This is necessary when it must do more than merely copy one object's contents into another. Also, the copy constructor, which creates copies during initialization, and also when arguments are passed and returned by value, can be overloaded. This is necessary when the copy constructor must do more than simply copy an object.

The **this** pointer is predefined in member functions to point to the object of which the function is a member. The **this** pointer is useful in returning the object of which the function is a member.

QUESTIONS

1. Virtual functions allow you to
   a. create an array of type pointer-to-base-class that can hold pointers to derived classes
   b. create functions that have no body
   c. group objects of different classes so they can all be accessed by the same function code
   d. use the same function call to execute member functions of objects from different classes

2. True or false: A pointer to a base class can point to objects of a derived class.

3. If there is a pointer **p** to objects of a base class, and it contains the address of an object of a derived class, and both classes contain a nonvirtual member function, **ding()**, then the statement **p->ding()**, will cause the version of **ding()** in the _____ class to be executed.

4. Write a declarator for a virtual function called **dang()** that returns type **void** and takes one argument of type **int**.

5. Deciding—*after* a program starts to execute—what function will be executed by a particular function call statement, is called _____.

6. If there is a pointer, **p**, to objects of a base class, and it contains the address of an object of a derived class, and both classes contain a virtual member function, **ding()**, then the statement **p->ding();** will cause the version of **ding()** in the _____ class to be executed.

7. Write the declaration for a pure virtual function called **aragorn** that returns no value and takes no arguments.

8. A pure virtual function is a virtual function that
   a. has no body
   b. returns nothing
   c. is used in a base class
   d. takes no arguments

9. Write the definition of an array called **parr** of 10 pointers to objects of class **dong**.

10. A virtual base class is useful when
    a. different functions in base and derived classes have the same name
    b. there are multiple paths from one derived class to another
    c. the identification of a function in a base class is ambiguous
    d. it makes sense to use a base class with no body

11. True or false: A **friend** function can access a class's private data without being a member of the class.

12. A **friend** function can be used to
    a. avoid arguments between classes
    b. allow access to classes whose source code is unavailable
    c. allow one class to access an unrelated class
    d. increase the versatility of an overloaded operator

13. Write the declaration for a friend function called **harry()** that returns type **void** and takes one argument of class **george**.

14. The keyword **friend** appears in
    a. the class allowing access to another class
    b. the class desiring access to another class
    c. the private section of a class
    d. the public section of a class

15. Write a declaration that, in the class in which it appears, will make every member of the class **harry** a **friend** function.

16. A static function
    a. should be called when an object is destroyed
    b. is closely connected with an individual object of a class
    c. can be called using the class name and function name
    d. is used when a dummy object must be created

17. Explain what the default assignment operator = does when applied to objects.

18. Write a declaration for an overloaded assignment operator in class **zeta**.

19. An assignment operator might be overloaded to
    a. help keep track of the number of identical objects
    b. assign a separate ID number to each object
    c. ensure that all member data is copied exactly
    d. signal when assignment takes place

20. True or false: The user must always define the operation of the copy constructor.

21. The operation of the assignment operator and that of the copy constructor are
    a. similar, except that the copy constructor creates a new object
    b. similar, except that the assignment operator copies member data
    c. different, except that they both create a new object
    d. different, except that they both copy member data

22. Write the declaration of a copy constructor for a class called **Bertha**.

23. True or false: A copy constructor could be defined to copy only part of an object's data.

24. The lifetime of a variable that is defined as
    a. automatic in a member function coincides with the lifetime of the function
    b. external coincides with the lifetime of a class
    c. member data of an object coincides with the lifetime of the object
    d. static in a member function coincides with the lifetime of the function

25. True or false: There is no problem with returning the value of a variable defined as automatic within a member function so long as it is returned by value.

26. Explain the difference in operation between these two statements:

```
person p1(p0);
person p1 = p0;
```

27. A copy constructor is invoked when
    a. a function returns by value
    b. an argument is passed by value
    c. a function returns by reference
    d. an argument is passed by reference

28. What does the **this** pointer point to?

29. If, within a class, **da** is a member variable, will the statement **this.da=37;** assign 37 to **da**?

30. Write a statement that a member function can use to return the entire object of which it is a member, without creating any temporary objects.

EXERCISES

1. Imagine the same publishing company described in Exercise 1 of Chapter 10 that markets both book and audio-cassette versions of its works. As in that exercise, create a class called **publication** that stores the title (a string) and price

(type float) of a publication. From this class derive two classes: book, which adds a page count (type int); and tape, which adds a playing time in minutes (type float). Each of the three classes should have a getdata() function to get its data from the user at the keyboard, and a putdata() function to display the data.

Write a main() program that creates an array of pointers to publication. This is similar to the VIRTPERS example in this chapter. In a loop, ask the user for data about a particular book or tape, and use new to create an object of type book or tape to hold the data. Put the pointer to the object in the array. When the user has finished entering the data for all books and tapes, display the resulting data for all the books and tapes entered, using a for loop and a single statement such as

```
pubarr[j]->putdata();
```

to display the data from each object in the array.

2. In the Distance class, as shown in the FRENGL and FRISQ examples in this chapter, create an overloaded * operator so that two distances can be multiplied together. Make it a friend function so that you can use such expressions as

```
dist1 = 7.5 * dist2;
```

You'll need a one-argument constructor to convert floating-point values into Distance values. Write a main() program to test this operator in several ways.

3. You can make a class that acts like an array. This involves overloading the subscript operator, which consists of the pair of braces: []. The CLARRAY example shown here is a complete program that demonstrates how to create your own array class:

```
// clarray.cpp
// creates array class
#include <iostream.h>

class Array                          // models a normal C++ array
   {
   private:
      int* ptr;                      // pointer to Array contents
      int size;                      // size of Array
   public:
      Array(int s)                   // one-argument constructor
         {
         size = s;                   // argument is size of Array
         ptr = new int[s];           // make space for Array
         }
      ~Array()                       // destructor
         { delete ptr; }
      int& operator [] (int j)       // overloaded subscript operator
         { return *(ptr+j); }
   };
```

```
void main()
   {
   const int ASIZE = 10;          // size of array
   Array arr(ASIZE);              // make an array

   for(int j=0; j<ASIZE; j++)     // fill it with squares
      arr[j] = j*j;

   for(j=0; j<ASIZE; j++)         // display its contents
      cout << arr[j] << "   ";
   }
```

The output of this program is

0 1 4 9 16 25 36 49 64 81

Starting with CLARRAY, add an overloaded assignment operator and an overloaded copy constructor to the `Array` class. Then add statements such as

`Array arr2(arr1);`

and

`arr3 = arr1;`

to the `main()` program to test whether these overloaded operators work.

One of the advantages of making your own array class is that you can make it into a "safe" array by adding statements to the member functions to perform bounds-checking operations. In this way you can guarantee that the user of such an array doesn't write a subscript that's too big (or small) for the array and thereby cause the usual sort of catastrophe. You can create such an array class for extra credit, although we don't show this in the answers.

14

FILES AND STREAMS

THE STREAM CLASS HIERARCHY

READING AND WRITING OBJECTS

FILE POINTERS

REDIRECTION

COMMAND-LINE ARGUMENTS

PRINTER OUTPUT

OVERLOADING << AND >>

Most serious programs need to read and write data to disk files. In this chapter we describe how to perform these activities using C++ streams. We'll begin with a brief examination of the classes used in stream-oriented I/O operations in C++. Then we'll see how these classes are used for disk file I/O in various situations. We'll also examine several other features of C++ that are related to files, including redirection, command-line arguments, overloading the insertion and extraction operators, and sending data to the printer.

C programmers will note that the approach to disk I/O used in C++ is quite different from that in C. The old C functions, such as `fread()` and `fwrite()`, will still work in C++, but they are not so well suited to the object-oriented environment. The new C++ approach is considerably cleaner and easier to implement.

STREAMS

A *stream* is a general name given to a flow of data. Different streams are used to represent different kinds of data flow. Each stream is associated with a particular class, which contains member functions and definitions for dealing with that particular kind of data flow. For example, the `ifstream` class represents input disk files. Thus each file in C++ is an object of a particular stream class.

THE STREAM CLASS HIERARCHY

The stream classes are arranged in a rather complex hierarchy. You don't need to understand this hierarchy in detail to program basic file I/O, but a brief overview may be helpful. Figure 14-1 shows a simplified version of the arrangement of the classes used for I/O in Microsoft C++.

We've already made extensive use of some of these classes. The extraction operator `>>` is a member of the `istream` class, and the insertion operator `<<` is a member of the `ostream` class. Both of these classes are derived from the `ios` class. The `cout` object, representing the standard output stream, which is usually directed to the video display, is a predefined object of the `ostream_withassign` class, which

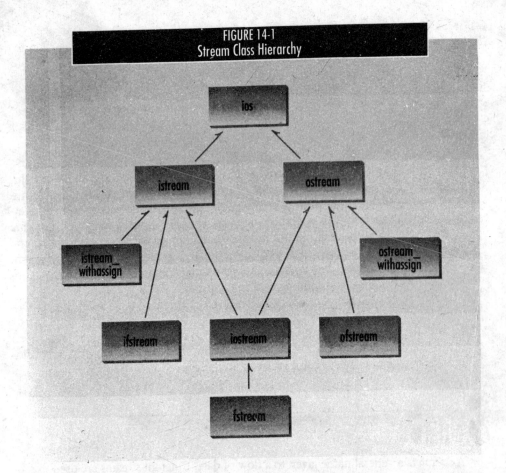

FIGURE 14-1
Stream Class Hierarchy

is derived from the `ostream` class. Similarly, `cin` is an object of the `istream_withassign` class, which is derived from `istream`.

The classes used for input and output to the video display and keyboard are declared in the header file IOSTREAM.H, which we routinely included in our examples in previous chapters, and in various files included in IOSTREAM.H. The classes used for disk file I/O are declared in the file FSTREAM.H. The figure shows which classes are in which header file. You may find it educational to print out these files and trace the relationships among the various classes. Many questions about streams can be answered by studying these class and constant declarations.

STREAM CLASSES

As you can see from Figure 14-1, the `ios` class is the base class for the hierarchy. It contains many constants and member functions common to input and output operations of all kinds. Some of these, such as the `showpoint` and `fixed` flags, we've seen already. It also supports some general error-status flags, which we'll look at later.

The `istream` and `ostream` classes are derived from `ios` and are dedicated to input and output, respectively. Their member functions perform both formatted and unformatted operations. The `istream` class contains such functions as `get()`, `getline()`, `read()`, and overloaded extraction (`>>`) operators, while `ostream` contains `put()` and `write`, and overloaded insertion (`<<`) operators.

The `iostream` class is derived from both `istream` and `ostream` by multiple inheritance, so that other classes can inherit both of these classes from it. The classes in which we are most interested for file I/O are `ifstream` for input files, `ofstream` for output files, and `fstream` for files that will be used for both input and output. These classes are derived from `istream`, `ostream`, and `iostream`, respectively. Figure 14-2 shows some of the options available with the `ifstream` and `ofstream` classes.

HEADER FILES

The `ifstream`, `ofstream`, and `fstream` classes are declared in the FSTREAM.H file. This file also includes the IOSTREAM.H header file, so there is no need to include it explicitly; FSTREAM.H takes care of all stream I/O.

FIGURE 14-2
File Input and Output

STRING I/O

Let's look at some simple programs that read and write disk files. We'll start by reading and writing character strings.

WRITING STRINGS

Our first program, OLINE, outputs some strings to a file.

```
// oline.cpp
// file output with strings
#include <fstream.h>                        // for file functions

void main()
    {
    ofstream outfile("TEST.TXT");           // create file for output
                                            // send text to file
    outfile << "I fear thee, ancient Mariner!\n";
    outfile << "I fear thy skinny hand\n";
    outfile << "And thou art long, and lank, and brown,\n";
    outfile << "As is the ribbed sea sand.\n";
    }
```

Here we define an object called outfile to be a member of the ofstream class. At the same time, we initialize it to the file name TEST.TXT. This initialization sets aside various resources for the file, and accesses the file of that name on the disk.

Since the insertion operator << is appropriately overloaded in ostream (from which ofstream is derived), we can use it to output text to the file.

When the program terminates, the outfile object goes out of scope. This calls the destructor, which closes the file, so we don't need to close the file explicitly.

When you run the program, the lines of text (from Samuel Taylor Coleridge's *The Rime of the Ancient Mariner*) are written to the file. There is no output to the screen. To see that the text is in the TEST.TXT file, you can display it with the DOS *TYPE* command.

READING STRINGS

To read the same file we must create an object of class ifstream. We do this in the ILINE example:

```
// iline.cpp
// file input with strings
#include <fstream.h>                        // for file functions
```

```
void main()
    {
    const int MAX = 80;                 // size of buffer
    char buffer[MAX];                   // character buffer
    ifstream infile("TEST.TXT");        // create file for input
    while( infile )                     // until end-of-file
        {
        infile.getline(buffer, MAX);    // read a line of text
        cout << buffer << endl;         // display it
        }
    }
```

Here the insertion operator does not work. Instead, we read the text from the file one line at a time using the getline() function, which is a member of istream (from which ifstream is derived). This function reads characters until it encounters the '\n' character, and places the resulting string in the buffer supplied as an argument. The maximum size of the buffer is given as the second argument. The contents of the buffer is displayed after each line.

The output of ILINE will be the same data written to the TEST.TXT file by OLINE: the four-line Coleridge stanza.

DETECTING END-OF-FILE

An ifstream object, such as infile in this program, has a value that can be tested for various error conditions. If a condition is true, the object returns a 0 value; otherwise it's non-0. One of these conditions is the end of file (EOF). The EOF is a signal sent to the program from the hardware when a read or write operation has reached the end of the file. The program checks for the EOF in the while loop so that it can stop reading after the last string. (We'll see other error conditions later.) The value returned by a stream object is actually a pointer, but the "address" returned has no significance except to be tested for a 0 or non-0 value.

CHARACTER I/O

The put and get() functions, which are members of ostream and istream, respectively, are used to output and input a single character at a time. Here's a program, OCHAR, that outputs a string, one character at a time:

```
// ochar.cpp
// file output with characters
#include <fstream.h>        // for file functions
#include <string.h>         // for strlen()
```

```
void main()
   {
   char str[] = "Time is a great teacher, \
but unfortunately it kills all its pupils.  Berlioz";

   ofstream outfile("TEST.TXT");      // create file for output
   for(int j=0; j<strlen(str); j++)   // for each character,
      outfile.put(str[j]);            // write it to file
   }
```

In this program an **ofstream** object is created as it was in OLINE. The length
of the string is found using the **strlen()** function, and the characters are output
using **put()** in a **for** loop. The aphorism by Hector Berlioz (a nineteenth-century
composer of operas and program music) is written to the file TEST.TXT. We can read
this file back in and display it using the ICHAR program:

```
// ichar.cpp
// file input with characters
#include <fstream.h>              // for file functions

void main()
   {
   char ch;                       // character to read
   ifstream infile("TEST.TXT");   // create file for input
   while( infile )                // read until EOF
      {
      infile.get(ch);             // read character
      cout << ch;                 // display it
      }
   }
```

This program uses the **get()** function and continues reading until the EOF is
reached. Each character read from the file is displayed using **cout**, so the entire
aphorism is displayed on the screen.

OBJECT I/O

Since C++ is an object-oriented language, it's reasonable to wonder how objects can
be written to and read from disk. The next examples show the process. The **person** class, used in several previous examples, supplies the objects.

WRITING AN OBJECT TO DISK

Here's the listing for OPERS, which asks the user for information about an object of
class **person**, and then writes this object to the disk file PERSON.DAT:

```
// opers.cpp
// saves person object to disk
#include <fstream.h>                    // for file streams

class person                           // class of persons
    {
    protected:
        char name[40];                 // person's name
        int age;                       // person's age
    public:
        void getData(void)             // get person's data
            {
            cout << "Enter name: "; cin >> name;
            cout << "Enter age: "; cin >> age;
            }
    };

void main(void)
    {
    person pers;                       // create a person
    pers.getData();                    // get data for person

    ofstream outfile("PERSON.DAT");    // create ofstream object
    outfile.write( (char *)&pers, sizeof(pers) );  // write to it
    }
```

The `getData()` member function of `person` is called to prompt the user for information, which it places in the `pers` object. Here's some sample interaction:

```
Enter name: Coleridge
Enter age: 62
```

The contents of the `pers` object are then written to disk, using the `write()` function. This function, like the other output functions we've seen, is a member of `ostream`. It takes two arguments: the address of the object to be written, and the length of the object in bytes. We use the `sizeof` operator to find the length of the `pers` object. The address of the object must be cast to type pointer to `char`.

BINARY VERSUS TEXT FILES

Notice that `write()`, unlike the functions we've used before, such as `<<`, `>>`, `get()`, and `put()`—operates on binary values, not on characters. That is, it treats the data stored in the object as a sequence of bytes, and makes no assumptions about how these bytes should be handled. By contrast, the text-based functions take some liberties with the data. For example, they expand the '\n' character into 2 bytes—a carriage-return and a linefeed—before storing it to disk. This makes the file more readable by DOS-based utilities like TYPE, but it would cause confusion if it were applied to binary file data.

READING AN OBJECT FROM DISK

Reading an object back from the PERSON.DAT file requires the **read()** member function. Here's the listing for IPERS:

```
// ipers.cpp
// reads person object from disk
#include <fstream.h>                  // for file streams

class person                         // class of persons
    {
    protected:
        char name[40];               // person's name
        int age;                     // person's age
    public:
        void showData(void)          // display person's data
            {
            cout << "\n   Name: " << name;
            cout << "\n   Age: " << age;
            }
    };

void main(void)
    {
    person pers;                                      // create person
    ifstream infile("PERSON.DAT");                    // create file
    infile.read( (char*)&pers, sizeof(pers) );        // read file
    pers.showData();                                  // display person
    }
```

The output from IPERS reflects whatever data the OPERS program placed in the PERSON.DAT file:

```
Name: Coleridge
Age: 62
```

COMPATIBLE DATA STRUCTURES

To work correctly, programs that read and write objects to files, as do OPERS and IPERS, must be talking about the same class of objects. Objects of class **person** in these programs are exactly 42 bytes long, with the first 40 being occupied with a string representing the person's name, and the last two containing an `int` representing the person's age. If two programs thought the name field was a different length, for example, neither could accurately read a file generated by the other.

Notice, however, that while the `person` classes in OPERS and IPERS have the same data, they have different member functions. The first includes the single function `getData()`, while the second has only `showData()`. It doesn't matter what member functions you use, since they are not written to disk along with the object's data. The data must have the same format, but inconsistencies in the member functions have no effect. (Of course, in a more serious programming situation, it would be desirable for all `person` objects to be derived from the exact same class.)

I/O WITH MULTIPLE OBJECTS

The OPERS and IPERS programs wrote and read only one object at a time. Our next example opens a file and writes as many objects as the user wants. Then it reads and displays the entire contents of the file. Here's the listing for DISKFUN.CPP:

```
// diskfun.cpp
// reads and writes several objects to disk
#include <fstream.h>                    // for file streams

class person                           // class of persons
    {
    protected:
        char name[40];                 // person's name
        int age;                       // person's age
    public:
        void getData(void)             // get person's data
            {
            cout << "\n   Enter name: "; cin >> name;
            cout << "   Enter age: "; cin >> age;
            }
        void showData(void)            // display person's data
            {
            cout << "\n   Name: " << name;
            cout << "\n   Age: " << age;
            }
    };

void main(void)
    {
    char ch;
```

```
    person pers;                    // create person object
    fstream file;                   // create input/output file
                                    // open for append
    file.open("PERSON.DAT", ios::app | ios::out | ios::in );

    do                              // data from user to file
        {
        cout << "\nEnter person's data:";
        pers.getData();             // get one person's data
                                    // write to file
        file.write( (char*)&pers, sizeof(pers) );
        cout << "Enter another person (y/n)? ";
        cin >> ch;
        }
    while(ch=='y');                 // quit on 'n'

    file.seekg(0);                  // reset to start of file
                                    // read first person
    file.read( (char*)&pers, sizeof(pers) );
    while( !file.eof() )            // quit on EOF
        {
        cout << "\nPerson:";        // display person
        pers.showData();
        file.read( (char*)&pers, sizeof(pers) );  // read another
        }                                         // person
    }
```

Here's some sample interaction with DISKFUN. The output shown assumes that the program has been run before and that two **person** objects have already been written to the file.

```
Enter person's data:
    Enter name: McKinley
    Enter age: 22
Enter another person (y/n)? n

Person:
    Name: Whitney
    Age: 20
Person:
    Name: Rainier
    Age 21
Person:
    Name: McKinley
    Age: 22
```

Here one additional object is added to the file, and the entire contents, consisting of three objects, are then displayed.

THE fstream CLASS

So far in this chapter, the file objects we created were for either input or output. In DISKFUN we want to create a file that can be used for both input and output. This requires an object of the fstream class.

THE open() FUNCTION

In previous examples we created a file object and initialized it in the same statement:

```
ofstream outfile("TEST.TXT");
```

In DISKFUN we use a different approach: We create the file in one statement and open it in another, using the open() function, which is a member of the fstream class.

In the open() function we include several *mode bits* to specify certain aspects of the file object we are opening. Table 14-1 shows the possibilities.

We use app because we want to preserve whatever was in the file before. That is, we can write to the file, terminate the program, and start up the program again, and whatever we write to the file will be appended to the existing contents. We use in and out because we want to perform both input and output on the file. The vertical bars between the flags cause the bits representing these flags to be logically ORed together, so that several flags can apply simultaneously.

We write one person object at a time to the file, using the write() function. When we've finished writing we want to read the entire file. Before doing this we must reset the file's current position. We do this with the seekg() function, which we'll examine in the next section, on file pointers. Then, in a while loop, we repeatedly read a person object from the file and display it on the screen.

	TABLE 14-1
	Mode Bits for open() Function
Mode bit	**Result**
in	open for reading (default for *ifstream*)
out	open for writing (default for *ofstream*)
app	start reading or writing at end of file (*APPend*)
ate	erase file before reading or writing (*truncATE*)
nocreate	error when opening if file does not already exist
noreplace	error when opening for output if file already exists, unless *ate* or *app* is set
binary	open file in binary (not text) mode

This continues until we've read all the **person** objects—a state that we discover using **eof()**, a member function of the **ios** class. This is an alternative approach to simply checking the value of the file object itself. The **eof()** function returns a nonzero value if the EOF is encountered, and a zero otherwise. It's one of a number of stream-state functions, which we'll look at in the section on stream errors later in this chapter.

FILE POINTERS

Each file object has associated with it two integer values called the *get pointer* and the *put pointer*. These are also called the *current get position* and the *current put position*, or—if it's clear which one is meant—simply the *current position*. These values specify the byte number in the file where writing or reading will take place. (The term *pointer* in this context should not be confused with normal C++ pointers used as address variables.)

Often you want to start reading an existing file at the beginning, and continue until the end. When writing, you may want to start at the beginning, deleting any existing contents, or at the end, in which case you can open the file with the **ios::app** mode specifier. These are the default actions, so no manipulation of the file pointers are necessary. However, there are times when you must take control of the file pointers yourself so that you can read from and write to an arbitrary location in the file. The **seekg()** and **tellg()** functions allow you to set and examine the get pointer, and the **seekp()** and **tellp()** functions perform these same actions on the put pointer.

SPECIFYING THE POSITION

We saw an example of positioning the get pointer in the DISKFUN program, where the **seekg()** function set it to the beginning of the file so that reading would start there. This form of **seekg()** takes one argument, which represents the absolute position in the file. The start of the file is byte 0, so that's what we used in DISKFUN. Figure 14-3 shows how this looks.

SPECIFYING THE OFFSET

The **seekg()** function can be used in two ways. We've seen the first, where the single argument represents the position. You can also use it with two arguments, where the first argument represents an offset from a particular location in the file, and the second specifies the location from which the offset is measured. There are three possibilities for the second argument: **beg** is the beginning of the file, **cur** is the current pointer position, and **end** is the end of the file. The statement

```
seekp(-10, ios::end);
```

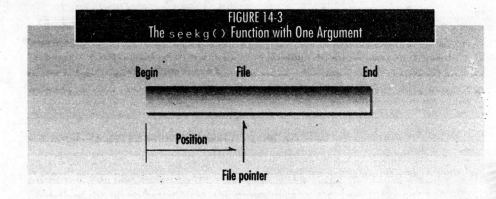

FIGURE 14-3
The seekg() Function with One Argument

Begin   File   End

Position

File pointer

for example, will set the put pointer to 10 bytes before the end of the file. Figure 14-4 shows how this looks.

Here's an example that uses the two-argument version of **seekg()** to find a particular **person** object in the PERSON.DAT file already created with DISKFUN, and to display the data for that particular person. Here's the listing for SEEKG:

```cpp
// seekg.cpp
// seeks particular person in file
#include <fstream.h>              // for file streams

class person                      // class of persons
  {
  protected:
     char name[40];               // person's name
     int age;                     // person's age
  public:
     void showData(void)          // display person's data
        {
        cout << "\n   Name: " << name;
        cout << "\n   Age: " << age;
        }
  };

void main(void)
   {
   person pers;                      // create person object
   ifstream infile;                  // create input file
   infile.open("PERSON.DAT");        // open file

   infile.seekg(0, ios::end);        // go to 0 bytes from end
   int endposition = infile.tellg();        // find where we are
   int n = endposition / sizeof(person);    // number of persons
   cout << "\nThere are " << n << " persons in file";
```

```
cout << "\nEnter person number: ";
cin >> n;
int position = (n-1) * sizeof(person);  // number times size
infile.seekg(position);                 // bytes from begin
                                        // read one person
infile.read( (char*)&pers, sizeof(pers) );
pers.showData();                        // display the person
}
```

Here's the output from the program, assuming that the PERSON.DAT file is the same as that just accessed in the DISKFUN example:

```
There are 3 persons in file
Enter person number: 2

Name: Rainier
Age: 21
```

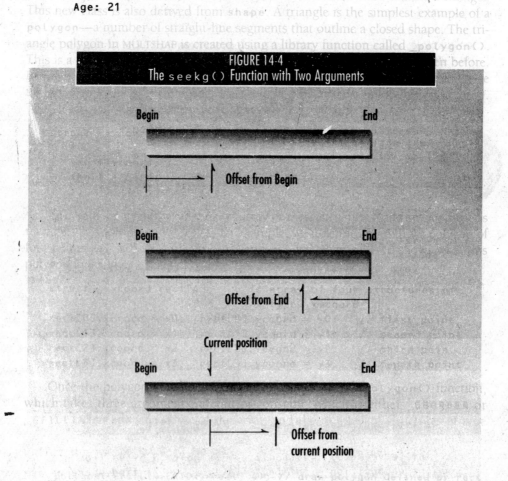

FIGURE 14-4
The seekg() Function with Two Arguments

Begin — End

Offset from Begin

Begin — End

Offset from End

Current position

Begin — End

Offset from
current position

For the user we number the items starting at 1, although the program starts numbering at 0; so person 2 is the second person of the three in the file.

THE tellg() FUNCTION

The first thing the program does is figure out how many persons are in the file. It does this by positioning the get pointer at the end of the file with the statement

```
infile.seekg(0, ios::end);
```

The tellg() function returns the current position of the get pointer. The program uses this function to return the pointer position at the end of the file; this is the length of the file in bytes. Next, the program calculates how many person objects there are in the file, by dividing by the size of a person; it then displays the result.

In the output shown, the user specifies the second object in the file, and the program calculates how many bytes into the file this is, using seekg(). It then uses read() to read one person's worth of data starting from that point. Finally, it displays the data with showData().

DISK I/O WITH MEMBER FUNCTIONS

So far we've let the main() function handle the details of stream I/O. When you use more sophisticated classes, it's natural to include stream I/O operations as member functions of the class. Our next example shows how this might be done. The class consists of an array, called parr, of structures of type person. These structures hold a name and age as the person class did in previous examples, but the class group is now responsible for input and output. Here's the listing for DAROBJ:

```
// darobj.cpp
// person array object does disk I/O
#include <fstream.h>              // for file streams

struct person                     // one person
    {
    char name[40];                // person's name
    int age;                      // person's age
    };

class group                       // group of persons, in array
    {
    private:
        int count;                // number of persons in array
        person parr[20];          // array of persons
    public:
        group()                   // no-arg constructor
            { count = 0; }
        void addData();
        void showData();
```

```
        void diskIn();
        void diskOut();
    };
void group::addData()              // get one person's data
    {
    cout << "\n   Enter name: ";
    cin >> parr[count].name;
    cout << "   Enter age: ";
    cin >> parr[count++].age;
    }
void group::showData()             // display all persons in group
    {
    for(int j=0; j<count; j++)
        {
        cout << "\nPerson #" << j+1;
        cout << "\n   Name: " << parr[j].name;
        cout << "\n   Age: " << parr[j].age;
        }
    }
void group::diskIn()               // read array from file
    {
    ifstream infile;                           // make file
    infile.open("GROUP.DAT", ios::nocreate);   // open it
    if( infile )                               // if it exists,
        infile.read( (char*)this, sizeof(*this) ); // read it
    }
void group::diskOut()              // write array to file
    {
    ofstream outfile;                          // make file
    outfile.open("GROUP.DAT");                 // open it
    outfile.write( (char*)this, sizeof(*this) ); // write to it
    }

void main(void)
    {
    group grp;               // make a group
    grp.diskIn();            // fill it with disk data (if any)
    grp.showData();          // display data for group

    char ch;
    do                       // get new persons for group
        {
        cout << "\nEnter data for person:";
        grp.addData();
        cout << "Enter another (y/n)? ";
        cin >> ch;
        }
    while(ch=='y');
    grp.showData();          // display augmented group
    grp.diskOut();           // write augmented group to disk
    }
```

The `main()` program creates a `group` object called `grp`. Such an object holds the data for 20 `person` structures. The program then displays all the `persons` in the group, and asks the user to enter data for an additional `person`. The user can enter as many `persons` as desired. Before terminating, the program again displays the data for all `persons`.

Here's some sample interaction with DAROBJ. This interaction assumes that two `persons` were placed in the GROUP.DAT file by a previous invocation of the program.

```
Person #1
    Name: Stimson
    Age: 45
Person #2
    Name: Hull
    Age: 58
Enter data for person:
    Enter name: Acheson
    Enter age: 63
Enter another (y/n)? y

Enter data for person:
    Enter name: Dulles
    Enter age: 72
Enter another (y/n)? n

Person #1
    Name: Stimson
    Age: 45
Person #2
    Name: Hull
    Age: 58
Person #3
    Name: Acheson
    Age: 63
Person #4
    Name: Dulles
    Age: 72
```

Besides the array of `persons`, `group` contains four member functions and a count of how many of the object spaces are actually in use.

The first function, `addData()`, is the only one that acts on a single `person` structure. It prompts the user for data, and adds a `person` object to the end of the array.

The other member functions act on the array as a whole. The `showData()` function displays the data for each of the `count` structures stored in the array in memory.

The `diskIn()` function checks to see that the GROUP.DAT file exists. If so, it opens the file and reads its entire contents into the array `parr` in a single statement. The `infile` object will return a 0 value if the GROUP.DAT file does not exist, so that the statement

```
if( infile )
```

can be used to determine whether an attempt should be made to read the file. The `diskOut()` function writes the entire array `parr` from memory to the disk file GROUP.DAT.

Notice how we refer to the `group` object that we're going to write to disk with `diskOut()` and read in with `diskIn()`. In the `read()` and `write()` stream functions the address of the object to be read or written is `this` and its size is `sizeof(*this)`. The `this` pointer holds the address of the object of which `diskOut()` and `diskIn()` are members, so we can use it to read or write the entire object.

CLOSING FILES

There is no need for `diskIn()` or `diskOut()` to explicitly close the file objects `infile` or `outfile`, since they are closed automatically when the functions terminate. If it were necessary to close a file explicitly, the `close()` member function could be used:

```
file.close();
```

OTHER DATA STRUCTURES

Of course, the objects stored on disk need not be arranged as an array in memory, as they are in the DAROBJ program. They could also be read from the disk and stored in some other data structure, such as a linked list.

ERROR HANDLING

In our examples so far, we have not concerned ourselves with error situations. In particular, we have assumed that the files we opened for reading already existed, and that those opened for writing could be created. In a real program it is important to verify such assumptions and take appropriate action if they turn out to be incorrect. A file that you think exists may not, or a filename that you assume you can use for a new file may already apply to an existing file. Or, perhaps there is no more room on the disk.

In previous examples we examined the error state of a stream object to find out whether we had reached the end of file. We demonstrated two approaches to finding this piece of information. First, we checked the value of the file object itself, in situations such as

```
while( infile )
    // read the next part of file
```

Here `infile` becomes zero when the EOF is reached. We also used the `eof()` member function of the `ios` class. This function returned a non-0 value when an EOF was encountered.

FIGURE 14-5
Stream Status Bits

unused

eofbit 0x01

failbit 0x02

badbit 0x04

Bit	Meaning
	TABLE 14-2
	Stream Status Bits
0x00	No bit set, no errors
0x01	At EOF
0x02	Error, can continue
0x04	Fatal error, cannot continue

Both these methods report the state of a status byte that contains several bits other than the one that reports the EOF. Figure 14-5 shows the other bits. Table 14-2 shows the meaning of these bits.

The status word can be read with **rdstate()**, a member function of **ios**. Several other member functions, including **eof()**, return the status of individual bits. Our next example demonstrates these functions.

```
// ferrors.cpp
// checks for errors opening file
#include <fstream.h>              // for file functions

void main()
    {
    ifstream file;
    file.open("GROUP.DAT", ios::nocreate);

    if( !file )
        cout << "\nCan't open GROUP.DAT";
```

```
else
    cout << "\nFile opened successfully.";
cout << "\nfile = " << file;
cout << "\nError state = " << file.rdstate();
cout << "\ngood() = " << file.good();
cout << "\neof() = " << file.eof();
cout << "\nfail() = " << file.fail();
cout << "\nbad() = " << file.bad();
file.close();
}
```

This program first checks the value of the object file. If its value is 0, then probably the file could not be opened because it didn't exist. Here's the output from FERRORS when that's the case:

```
Can't open GROUP.DAT
file = 0x0000
Error state = 2
good() = 0
eof() = 0
fail() = 2
bad() = 0
```

The error state returned by rdstate() is 2. In this case this bit indicates that the file doesn't exist; it's set to 1. The other bits are all set to 0. The good() function returns 1 (true) only when no bits are set, so it returns 0 (false). We're not at EOF, so eof() returns 0. The fail() function returns non-0, since an error occurred; but bad() returns 0, since the error was not fatal.

In a serious program some or all of these functions should be used after every I/O operation to ensure that things went as expected.

REDIRECTION

You can read and write to files using only the objects cout and cin. These predefined objects normally represent the display and the keyboard, but they can be redirected by the user to represent disk files. Redirection is a technique, originally imported from Unix into DOS, that allows the user considerable flexibility in the way programs are used. Redirection is supplied by DOS, not by C++; but C++ supports it, so it's interesting to see how to use it. As an example, consider the program REDIR:

```
// redir.cpp
// demonstrates redirection
// syntax: redir <source >destination
#include <iostream.h>
#include <iomanip.h>                        // for resetiosflags()

void main()
    {
```

```
    char ch;
    while( !cin.eof() )                    // quit on EOF
        {
        cin >> resetiosflags(ios::skipws)  // keep whitespace
            >> ch;                         // read from std input
        cout << ch;                        // send to std output
        }
    }
```

ios FLAGS

Before exploring how this program can be used for redirection, we should note a peculiarity in the programming: We must reset the `skipws` flag when getting input from `cin` in REDIR. This is necessary because `cin` normally skips over white space, which includes spaces, newlines, and EOFs. We want to read all these characters, and fortunately `cin` has a formatting flag that allows us to disable white space skipping.

We've used a variety of other `ios` flags in previous chapters. For reference, Table 14-3 shows the complete list.

USING REDIR

When invoked in the usual way at the command line, REDIR simply echoes whatever the user types, each time E   is pressed. Here's some sample interaction (from a poem by the sixteenth-century poet Ben Jonson):

```
C>redir
Truth is the trial of itself,        ←————————entered by user
Truth is the trial of itself,        ←————————echoed by program
And needs no other touch;
And needs no other touch;
And purer than the purest gold,
And purer than the purest gold,
Refine it ne'er so much.
Refine it ne'er so much.
^Z
```

The user enters the Q   -»Z combination to terminate the program. This character is interpreted as an EOF.

When the program is used for redirection, it can take input from the keyboard and write it to a disk file, display text from a disk file on the screen, or copy one text file to another.

REDIRECTING OUTPUT

To redirect a program's output from the screen to a file, you use the > operator. This is a DOS operator; it has nothing to do with C++ overloading. Here's how to invoke REDIR to take keyboard input and redirect it to a file called SAMPLE.TXT:

```
C>redir >sample.txt
If you would avoid suspicion,                    ←──────── entered by user
don't lace your shoes in a melon field.  ←──────── entered by user
^Z                                                ←──────── entered by user
```

You can check SAMPLE.TXT with *TYPE* to be sure it contains this text.

REDIRECTING INPUT

To redirect a program's input so that it comes from a file and not the keyboard, you use the < operator. Here's how to invoke REDIR to take data from the file SAMPLE.TXT and use it as input to the program, which then displays it:

```
C>redir <sample.txt
If you would avoid suspicion,            ←──────── displayed by program
don't lace your shoes in a melon field.  ←──────── displayed by program
```

TABLE 14-3 ios Flags	
Flag	**Purpose**
skipws	Skip whitespace on input
left	Left-justify output
right	Right-justify output
internal	Use padding after sign or base indicator
dec	Decimal conversion
oct	Octal conversion
hex	Hexadecimal conversion
showbase	Use base indicator on output
showpoint	Use decimal point in floating-point output
uppercase	Uppercase hex output
showpos	Preface positive integers with '+'
scientific	Floating-point notation with E (5.4321E3)
fixed	Fixed floating-point notation (5432.1)
unitbuf	Flush all streams after insertion
stdio	Flush stdout and stderr after insertion

REDIRECTING INPUT AND OUTPUT

Both input and output can be redirected at the same time. As an example, here's how to use REDIR to copy one file to another:

```
C>redir <src.txt >dest.txt
```

Nothing is displayed, but you will find that SRC.TXT has been copied to DEST.TXT.

THE cerr AND clog OBJECTS

If you want to display a particular message even when the output of your program has been redirected to a file, you can use the `cerr` object. Insert this line into the `while` loop in REDIR:

```
cerr << ch;
```

Now try copying one file to another. Each character `ch` will be sent to the screen by `cerr`, even though the output to `cout` is going to a file. The `cerr` object is normally used to display error messages; hence the name. Another object, `clog`, is similar to `cerr` except that its output is buffered while `cerr`'s is not.

COMMAND-LINE ARGUMENTS

You are no doubt familiar with command-line arguments, used when invoking a program from DOS. They are typically used to pass the name of a data file to an application. For example, you can invoke the Programmer's WorkBench and a .CPP file at the same time:

```
C>pwb afile.cpp
```

Here `afile.cpp` is a command-line argument. How can we get a C++ program to read the command-line arguments? Here's an example, COMLINE, that reads and displays as many command-line arguments as you care to type:

```
// comline.cpp
// demonstrates command-line arguments
#include <iostream.h>

void main(int argc, char* argv[] )
   {
   cout << "\nargc = " << argc;

   for(int j=0; j<argc; j++)
      cout << "\nArgument " << j << " = " << argv[j];
   }
```

And here's a sample interaction with the program:

```
C>comline uno dos tres

argc = 4
Argument 0 = C:\CPP\CHAP14\COMLINE.EXE
Argument 1 = uno
Argument 2 = dos
Argument 3 = tres
```

We're shown the arguments entered at the DOS prompt, but you can also use the Program Arguments item in the Run menu.

To read command-line arguments, the `main()` function (don't forget it's a function!) must itself be given two arguments. The first, `argc` (for *argument count*), represents the total number of command-line arguments. The first command-line argument is always the pathname of the current program. The remaining command-line arguments are those typed by the user; they are delimited by the space character. In the example above, they are *uno*, *dos* and *tres*.

The system stores the command-line arguments as strings in memory, and creates an array of pointers to these strings. In the example the array is called `argv` (for *argument values*). Individual strings are accessed through the appropriate pointer, so the first string (the pathname) is `argv[0]`, the second (*uno* in this example) is `argv[1]`, and so on. COMLINE accesses the arguments in turn and prints them out in a `for` loop that uses `argc`, the number of command-line arguments, as its upper limit.

You don't need to use the particular names `argc` and `argv` as arguments to `main()`, but they are so common that any other names would cause consternation to everyone but the compiler.

Here's a program that uses a command-line argument for something useful. It displays the contents of a text file whose name is supplied by the user on the command line. Thus it imitates the DOS command *TYPE*. Here's the listing for OTYPE:

```
// otype.cpp
// imitates TYPE command
#include <fstream.h>              // for file functions
#include <process.h>             // for exit()

void main(int argc, char* argv[] )
   {
   if( argc != 2 )
      {
      cerr << "\nFormat: otype filename";
      exit(-1);
      }
   char ch;                        // character to read
   ifstream infile;                // create file for input
   infile.open( argv[1], ios::nocreate );  // open file
   if( !infile )                   // check for errors
      {
      cerr << "\nCan't open " << argv[1];
      exit(-1);
      }
```

```
   while( infile.get(ch) != 0 )    // read a character
      cout << ch;                   // display the character
   }
```

This program first checks to see if the user has entered the correct number of command-line arguments. Remember that the pathname of OTYPE.EXE itself is always the first command-line argument. The second argument is the name of the file to be displayed, which the user should have entered when invoking the program:

```
C>otype ichar.cpp
```

Thus the total number of command-line arguments should equal 2. If it doesn't, the user probably doesn't understand how to use the program, and the program sends an error message via cerr to clarify matters.

If the number of arguments is correct, the program tries to open the file whose name is the second command-line argument (argv[1]). Again, if the file can't be opened, the program signals an error. Finally, in a while loop, the program reads the file character by character and writes it to the screen.

A value of 0 for the result of the character input operation signals an EOF. This is another way to check for EOF. You can also use the value of the file object itself, as we've done before:

```
   while( infile )
      {
      infile.get(ch);
      cout << ch;
      }
```

PRINTER OUTPUT

Sending data to the printer is similar to sending data to a disk file. DOS predefines a number of special filenames for hardware devices. Here they are:

Name	Device
CON	Console (keyboard and screen)
AUX or COM1	First serial port
COM2	Second serial port
PRN or LPT1	First parallel printer
LPT2	Second parallel printer
LPT3	Third parallel printer
NUL	Dummy (nonexistent) device

In most systems the printer is connected to the first parallel port, so the filename for the printer should be PRN or LPT1. (You can substitute the appropriate name if your system is configured differently.) The following program, OPRINT, prints the contents of a disk file, specified on the command line, to the printer.

```
// oprint.cpp
// imitates print command
#include <fstream.h>                    // for file functions
#include <process.h>                    // for exit()

void main(int argc, char* argv[] )
{
    if( argc != 2 )
    {
        cerr << "\nFormat: oprint filename";
        exit(-1);
    }
    char ch;                            // character to read
    ifstream infile;                    // create file for input
    infile.open( argv[1], ios::nocreate );  // open file
    if( !infile )                       // check for errors
    {
        cerr << "\nCan't open " << argv[1];
        exit(-1);
    }
    ofstream outfile;                   // make file
    outfile.open("PRN");                // open it for printer
    while( infile.get(ch) != 0 )        // read a character
        outfile.put(ch);                // write character to printer
}
```

You can use this program to print any text file, such as any of your .CPP source files. It acts much the same as the DOS *PRINT* command.

Like the OTYPE example, this program checks for the correct number of command-line arguments, and for a successful opening of the specified file. Then it opens PRN and writes the file to it, character by character.

OVERLOADING THE EXTRACTION AND INSERTION OPERATORS

We'll finish this chapter by showing how to overload the extraction and insertion operators. This is a powerful feature of C++. It lets you treat I/O for user-defined data types in the same way as basic types like **int** and **double**. For example, if you have an object of class **crawdad** called **cd1**, you can display it with the statement

```
cout << "\ncd1=" << cd1;
```

just as if it were a basic data type.

Here's an example, ENGLIO, that overloads the insertion and extraction operators for the **Distance** class.

```
// englio.cpp
// overloaded << and >> operators
#include <iostream.h>

class Distance                          // English Distance class
   {
   private:
      int feet;
      float inches;
   public:
      Distance()                        // constructor (no args)
         { feet = 0; inches = 0.0; }
      Distance(int ft, float in)        // constructor (two args)
         { feet = ft; inches = in; }
      friend istream& operator >> (istream& s, Distance& d);
      friend ostream& operator << (ostream& s, Distance& d);
   };

istream& operator >> (istream& s, Distance& d)   // get Distance
   {                                             // from user
   cout << "\nEnter feet: ";  s >> d.feet;       // using
   cout << "Enter inches: ";  s >> d.inches;     // overloaded
   return s;                                     // >> operator
   }

ostream& operator << (ostream& s, Distance& d)   // display
   {                                             // Distance
   s << d.feet << "\'-" << d.inches << '\"';     // using
   return s;                                     // overloaded
   }                                             // << operator

void main()
   {
   Distance dist1, dist2;          // define Distances
   cout << "\nEnter two Distance values:";
   cin >> dist1 >> dist2;          // get values from user

   Distance dist3(11, 6.25);       // define, initialize dist3

                                   // display distances
   cout << "\ndist1 = " << dist1 << "\ndist2 = " << dist2;
   cout << "\ndist3 = " << dist3;
   }
```

This program asks for two distance values from the user, and then prints out these values and another value that was initialized in the program. Here's a sample interaction:

```
Enter feet: 10
Enter inches: 3.5
```

```
Enter feet: 12
Enter inches: 6

dist1 = 10'-3.5"
dist2 = 12'-6"
dist3 = 11'-6.25"
```

Notice how convenient and natural it is to treat `Distance` objects like any other data type, using statements like

```
cin >> dist1 >> dist2;
```
and
```
cout << "\ndist1 = " dist1 << "\ndist2 = " << dist2;
```

As you can see, the `<<` and `>>` operators can be chained, permitting the input or output of multiple data items in a single statement.

The `operator<<()` and `operator>>()` functions must be **friends** of the `Distance` class, since the `istream` and `ostream` objects appear on the left side of the operator. (See the discussion of **friend** functions in Chapter 13.) The `operator>>()` function takes an `istream` object, which will usually be `cin`, as its first argument, and an object of the `Distance` class as its second. It returns an `istream` so that the operator can be chained. The `operator<<()` function is constructed similarly but uses `ostream` instead of `istream`.

SUMMARY

In this chapter we briefly examined the hierarchy of stream classes. Then we saw how to perform disk I/O in a variety of ways. Files in C++ are objects of various classes, typically `ofstream` for output, `ifstream` for input, and `fstream` for both input and output. Member functions of these or base classes are used to perform I/O operations. Such functions as `put()` and `write()` are used for output, while `get()` and `read()` are used for input.

The `read()` and `write()` functions work in binary mode, so that entire objects can be saved to disk no matter what sort of data they contain. Single objects can be stored, as can arrays or other data structures of many objects.

A check for error conditions should be made after each file operation. The file object itself takes on a value of 0 if an error occurred, or non-0 otherwise. Also, several member functions can be used to determine specific kinds of errors.

Redirection provides an easily programmed (although not entirely user-friendly) approach to file I/O, using input and output to `cin` and `cout`. Sending output to the printer involves outputting to a file usually called PRN. The extraction operator `>>` and the insertion operator `<<` can be overloaded so that they work with programmer-defined data types.

STIONS

1. A C++ stream is
   a. the flow of control through a function
   b. a flow of data from one place to another
   c. associated with a particular class
   d. a file

2. The base class for most stream classes is the _____ class.

3. Name three stream classes commonly used for disk I/O.

4. Write a statement that will create an object called **satefile** of the **ofstream** class and associate it with a file called SALES.JUN.

5. True or false: Some streams work with input, and some with output.

6. Write an **if** statement that checks if an **ifstream** object called **foobar** has reached the end of file or has encountered an error.

7. We can output text to an object of class **ofstream** using the insertion operator **<<** because
   a. the **ofstream** class is a stream
   b. the insertion operator works with all classes
   c. we are actually outputting to **cout**
   d. the insertion operator is overloaded in **ofstream**

8. Write a statement that writes a single character to an object called **fileOut**, which is of class **ofstream**.

9. To write data that contains variables of type **float**, to an object of type **ofstream**, you should use
   a. the insertion operator
   b. **seekg()**
   c. **write()**
   d. **put()**

10. Write a statement that will read the contents of an **ifstream** object called **ifile** into an array called **buff**.

11. Mode bits such as **app** and **ate**
    a. are defined in the **ios** class
    b. can specify if a file is open for reading or writing
    c. work with the **put()** and **get()** functions
    d. specify ways of opening a file

12. Define what *current position* means when applied to files.

13. True or false: A file pointer always contains the address of the file.

14. Write a statement that moves the current position 13 bytes backward in a stream object called **f1**.

15. The statement

    ```
    f1.write( (char*)&obj1, sizeof(obj1) );
    ```

    a. writes the member functions of `obj1` to `f1`
    b. writes the data in `obj1` to `f1`
    c. writes the member functions and the data of `obj1` to `f1`
    d. writes the address of `obj1` to `f1`

16. Redirection redirects
    a. a stream from a file to the screen
    b. a file from a device to a stream
    c. a device from the screen to a file
    d. the screen from a device to a stream

17. Used with `cin`, what does the `skipws` flag accomplish?

18. Write a declarator for `main()` that will enable command-line arguments.

19. The printer can be accessed using the predefined filename _____.

20. Write the declarator for the overloaded `>>` operator that takes output from an object of class `istream` and displays it as the contents of an object of class `Sample`.

EXERCISES

1. Start with the `Distance` class from the ENGLCON example in Chapter 7. Using a loop similar to that in the DISKFUN example in this chapter, get a number of `Distance` values from the user and write them to a disk file. Append them to existing values in the file, if any. When the user signals that no more values will be input, read the file and display all the values.

2. Write a program that emulates the DOS *COPY* command. That is, it should copy the contents of a character file (such as any .CPP file) to another file. Invoke the program with two command-line arguments—the source file and the destination file—like this:

    ```
    C>ocopy srcfile.ext destfile.ext
    ```

    In the program, check that the user has typed the correct number of command-line arguments, and that the files specified can be opened. Improve on the DOS *TYPE* command by having the program signal an error if the destination file already exists. This will prevent inadvertently writing over a valuable file. (Hint: Use the `noreplace` flag.)

3. Write a program that returns the size in bytes of a file entered on the command line:

    ```
    C>filesize program.ext
    ```

LARGER PROGRAMS

REASONS FOR MULTI-FILE PROGRAMS

PUBLIC AND PRIVATE COMPONENTS

SCREEN WINDOWS AS OBJECTS

A CLASS OF VERY LARGE NUMBERS

MODELING A WATER SYSTEM

In previous chapters we've seen how the various parts of a C++ program—such as class declarations, member functions, and a `main()` function—are combined. However, the programs in these chapters all consisted of a single file. Now let's look at program organization from a more global perspective, involving multiple files.

Besides demonstrating multi-file programs, this chapter will introduce some longer and more ambitious applications. Our aim in these programs is not that you necessarily understand every detail of their operation, but that you acquire a general understanding of how the elements of larger programs relate to one another. These programs also show how classes can be used in more realistic applications than the short examples we've seen so far. On the other hand, they are not so long that it takes all spring to wade through them.

REASONS FOR MULTI-FILE PROGRAMS

There are several reasons for using multi-file programs. These include the use of class libraries, the organization of programmers working on a project, and the conceptual design of a program.

CLASS LIBRARIES

In traditional procedure-oriented languages it has long been customary for software vendors to furnish **libraries** of functions. Other programmers then combine these libaries with their own custom-written routines to create an application for the end-user.

Libraries provide ready-made functions for a wide variety of fields. For instance, a vendor might supply a library of functions for handling statistics calculations, or for advanced memory management. Libraries that provide the functions necessary to create a graphics user interface for DOS programs are popular.

Since C++ is organized around classes rather than functions, it's not surprising that libraries for C++ programs consist of classes. What may be surprising is how superior a class library is to an old-fashioned function library. Because classes encapsulate both data and functions, and because they more closely model real life, the interface between a class library and the application that makes use of it can be much cleaner than that provided by a function library.

For these reasons class libraries assume a more important role in C++ programming than function libraries do in traditional programming. A class library can take over a greater portion of the programming burden. An applications programmer, if the right class library is available, may find that only a minimal amount of programming is necessary to create a final product. Also, as more and more class libraries are created, the chances of finding one that solves your particular programming problem continues to increase.

COMPONENTS OF A CLASS LIBRARY

A class library often furnishes two components: public and private. Let's see what the difference is.

Public Components

To use a class library, the applications programmer needs to access various declarations, including class declarations. These declarations can be thought of as the public part of the library and are furnished in source-code form as a header file, with the .H extension. This file is typically combined with the client's source code using an `#include` statement. The declarations in such a header file need to be public for several reasons. First, it's a convenience to the client to see the actual definitions rather than to read a description of them. More important, the client's program will need to declare objects based on these classes, and call on member functions from these objects. Only by declaring the classes in the source file is this possible.

Private Components

On the other hand, the inner workings of the member functions of the various classes don't need to be known by the client. The developers of the class library, like any other software developer, don't want to release source code if they can help it, since it might be illegally modified or pirated. Member functions—except for short inline functions—are therefore usually distributed in object form, as .OBJ files or as library (.LIB) files.

Figure 15-1 shows how the various files are related in a multi-file system.

In this chapter we'll show several larger programs organized according to these principles. The first provides a set of classes of visual screen elements, such as buttons and output windows. An application then uses these classes to create a four-function pocket calculator. The second program introduces a class of very large numbers. By *very large*, we mean numbers with an almost unlimited number of digits. Such numbers are important in various kinds of mathematics, such as calculating *pi* to thousands of digits. The third example provides classes that allow you to create your own water-distribution system. You can connect valves, tanks, pipes, and

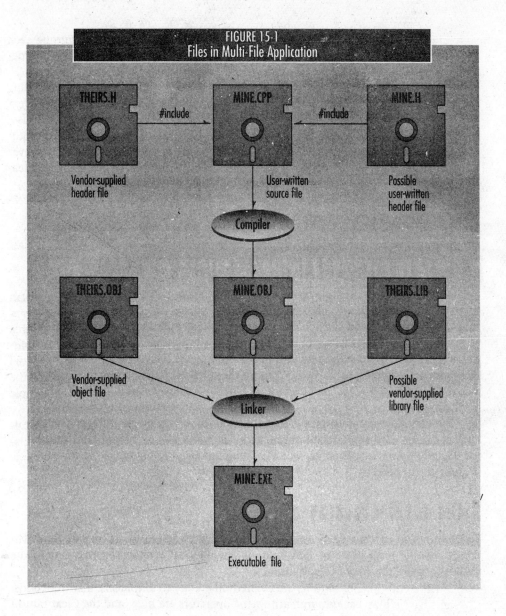

FIGURE 15-1
Files in Multi-File Application

THEIRS.H — #include → MINE.CPP ← #include — MINE.H

Vendor-supplied header file

User-written source file

Possible user-written header file

Compiler

THEIRS.OBJ — MINE.OBJ — THEIRS.LIB

Vendor-supplied object file

Possible vendor-supplied library file

Linker

MINE.EXE

Executable file

similar components to model systems such as the cooling water system in a nuclear reactor.

OTHER REASONS FOR MULTI-FILE PROGRAMS

Programs may be broken down into multiple files for reasons other than the accommodation of class libraries. As in other programming languages, such as C, a common situation involves a project with several programmers. Confining each programmer's responsibility to a separate file helps to organize the project and define more cleanly the interface among different parts of the program.

It is also often the case that a program is divided into separate files according to functionality: One file can handle the code involved in a graphics display, for example, while another file handles mathematical analysis, and a third disk I/O. Also, in large programs, a single file may simply become too large to handle conveniently.

The techniques used for working with multi-file programs are similar, whatever the reasons for dividing the program. Appendix C shows how to use the Project feature in the PWB to combine several files into one executable program.

A POCKET CALCULATOR: THE CALC PROGRAM

Let's look at our first example based on the multi-file approach. Suppose you plan to write a program that models a four-function pocket calculator, placing a picture of the calculator on the screen. However, you don't want to go to the trouble of programming the visual elements, such as pushbuttons and output display windows. Fortunately, you know where to obtain a set of classes designed to model the elements of screen calculators. You use these ready-made classes to model the visual elements, and write the interface and math routines yourself. In this example we'll show these two major parts of the program, and how they fit together.

The complete program puts a four-function calculator on the screen. The calculator can be used to perform arithmetic in the same way as a hand-held calculator. The program requires an EGA or VGA graphics adapter. Figure 15-2 shows how it looks on the screen.

USING THE CALCULATOR

The buttons on the calculator appear to push in when activated, as they do in Microsoft Windows applications. This is an optical illusion, achieved by changing the shading around the edge of the button.

Different kinds of buttons are colored differently to emphasize their functions. Digits have a gray background, arithmetic operators are blue, and the Clear button is red.

To use the calculator, the user types the digits of the first number, then an arithmetic operator (/, *, −, or +), then a second number, and then the equals sign (=). The answer is displayed. You can chain to another calculation: The answer automatically becomes the first operand, so you can press another arithmetic operator and key in another number to get the next answer. You can use a decimal point in the numbers you input, but not exponential notation or negative signs. The output has

FIGURE 15-2
Output of CALC Program

a fixed decimal place with two digits on its right. The equals sign and the plus sign are on the same button on the screen, and you can use either the ⊜ key or the ⊙ keyboard key (actually the same key shifted) for either operation; the program distinguishes them by context, as on many pocket calculators.

To exit the program, press the (ESC) key.

Ideally a calculator screen-display would have its buttons activated by a mouse. However, Microsoft C++ does not provide library functions for the mouse, and writing our own would make the program excessively complex. Also, not everyone has a mouse. We simulate the action of a mouse using the keyboard keys: When you type a digit, for instance, the corresponding button on the screen appears to push in.

FILES IN THE CALC PROGRAM

The CALC program consists of three files. First there is the header file, CALC.H, containing the class declarations. Next is CALC.CPP, which contains the member functions. We present this file in source form so you can read it; but if you had actually purchased it from a class library vendor, it would probably be in object form, as a .LIB or .OBJ file. Finally, there is CALC_APP.CPP, the file that we write ourselves.

To build this program, make sure these three files are in the same directory. Create a project called CALC_APP.PRJ, as described in Appendix C. Add the files CALC.CPP and CALC_APP.CPP to the project file. When you're finished, you can compile and run the program.

Let's look first at CALC.H and CALC.CPP, the programs supplied by our mythical class vendor.

```
// calc.h
// header file for calc.cpp
#include <iostream.h>      // for cout, etc.
#include <string.h>        // for strcpy()
#include <graph.h>         // for graphics functions
#include <conio.h>         // for getch()
#include <stdio.h>         // for sprintf()
#include <math.h>          // for atof()
#include <stdlib.h>        // for exit()
#include <time.h>          // for clock()

#define BLACK      0       // color indices
#define BLUE       1
#define RED        4
#define LIGHTGRAY  7
#define DARKGRAY   8
#define WHITE      15

class Window;                          // (needed for SCREEN)
Window* const SCREEN = (Window*)0;  // ultimate owner

enum buttonstatus { unpushed, pushed };
enum boolean { false, true };

class Window                // parent class
   {
   protected:
      Window* ptrOwner;         // address of owner of this window
      int left, top, right, bot; // outside edges of rectangle
      int delta;                // distance between borders
      int deltacolor;           // color between borders
      int centercolor;          // color within inside border

   public:                      // constructor: initialize window
      Window(Window* ptro, int l, int t, int r, int b,
             int dc, int cc);
      void Display(void);       // display the window
   };

class Border : public Window    // border
   {
   public:
      Border(Window* ptro, int l, int t, int r, int b,
             int dc=BLUE, int cc=DARKGRAY)
            : Window(ptro, l, t, r, b, dc, cc)
         { }
   };

class Button : public Window         // push button
   {
```

```
    private:
        char text[20];              // characters on button
        buttonstatus bstatus;       // pushed or unpushed
    public:
        Button(Window* ptro, int l, int t, int r, int b,
               int cc=BLACK, char* tx="")
              : Window(ptro, l, t, r, b, BLACK, cc)
           { strcpy(text, tx);  bstatus = unpushed; }
        void Click(void);           // click the button
        void Display(void);         // display the button
    };

class Output : public Window       // output window
    {
    public:
        Output(Window* ptro, int l, int t, int r, int b,
               int dc=BLUE, int cc=WHITE)
              : Window(ptro, l, t, r, b, dc, cc)
           { }
        void Text(char *);     // display text sent as string
        void Number(double);   // display number
    };


// calc.cpp
// member functions for calc
#include "calc.h"                   // calc header file

                                    // constructor: initialize window
Window::Window(Window* ptro, int l, int t, int r, int b,
       int dc, int cc)
    {                               // set private data
    ptrOwner=ptro; left=l; top=t; right=r; bot=b;
    deltacolor=dc; centercolor=cc;
                                    // calculate delta
    delta = ((right-left)+(bot-top))/150 + 3;
    if( ptrOwner != SCREEN )        // if there is an owner,
        {                           // our coordinates
        left  += ptrOwner->left;    // start at owner's
        right += ptrOwner->left;    // upper left corner
        top   += ptrOwner->top;
        bot   += ptrOwner->top;
        }
    }


void Window::Display(void)  // display the window
    {
    _setcolor(deltacolor);    // draw and fill outer rectangle
    _rectangle(_GFILLINTERIOR, left, top, right, bot);
    _setcolor(centercolor);   // draw and fill inner rectangle
    _rectangle(_GFILLINTERIOR, left+delta+1, top+delta,
               right-delta-1, bot-delta);
    }
```

```
void Button::Click(void)            // click the button
    {
    bstatus = pushed;               // push it
    Button::Display();              // display it
                                    // cycle 200 millisecs
    clock_t end = 200 + clock();    // find ending time
    while( clock() < end )          // until current time
        ;                           // exceeds ending time
    bstatus = unpushed;             // unpush it
    Button::Display();              // display it
    }

void Button::Display(void)          // display the button
    {
    Window::Display();              // display basic button
                                    // character on button
    _moveto(left+delta*4, top+delta*2);
    _setcolor(WHITE);               // always white text
    _outgtext(text);                // write the character

    _setcolor(LIGHTGRAY);           // brighter edge color
    struct _xycoord t[6];           // shade L-shaped area
    if(bstatus==unpushed)
        {                           // top left
        t[0].xcoord = left;         t[0].ycoord = top;
        t[1].xcoord = right;        t[1].ycoord = top;
        t[2].xcoord = right-delta;  t[2].ycoord = top+delta;
        t[3].xcoord = left+delta;   t[3].ycoord = top+delta;
        t[4].xcoord = left+delta;   t[4].ycoord = bot-delta;
        t[5].xcoord = left;         t[5].ycoord = bot;
        }
    else                            // pushed
        {                           // bottom right
        t[0].xcoord = right;        t[0].ycoord = top;
        t[1].xcoord = right;        t[1].ycoord = bot;
        t[2].xcoord = left;         t[2].ycoord = bot;
        t[3].xcoord = left+delta;   t[3].ycoord = bot-delta;
        t[4].xcoord = right-delta;  t[4].ycoord = bot-delta;
        t[5].xcoord = right-delta;  t[5].ycoord = top+delta;
        }
    _polygon(_GFILLINTERIOR, t, 6); // fill L-shaped area
    }

void Output::Text(char *ptrstring)  // display text
    {
    Display();                      // clear output window
    _moveto(left+delta*2, top+delta*2);
    _setcolor(BLACK);               // black text
    _outgtext(ptrstring);           // insert the text
    }

void Output::Number(double d)       // display number
    {
    char buffer[80];                // set up text buffer
```

562

```
    sprintf(buffer, "%16.2lf", d);    // convert number to string
    Output::Text(buffer);             // display string
}
```

CLASS DECLARATIONS

The CALC.H file contains the declarations of the member functions. CALC.CPP contains the member functions themselves. Note that CALC.CPP #includes CALC.H. Every file that works with the classes declared in CALC.H must #include this file.

' The image of the calculator has a border, an output window to display the results, and 16 buttons. These three kinds of visual objects—border, output window, and buttons—have common features. They all occupy a certain position on the screen, and they all have a certain size. We make the further assumption that all these objects are created from two rectangles: an outer edge and an inner edge close to it. The space between these edges can be colored differently from the space within the inner rectangle, thus creating a picture-frame effect.

Since the image elements have common features, it's natural to put these features into a base class, and use derived classes for borders, output windows, and buttons.

THE BASE CLASS Window

In CALC.H we first declare a base class called Window that has the characteristics described above. Its private data includes the left, top, right, and bottom coordinates of the outside edge of the window. A variable, delta, specifies the distance in pixels between the inside and outside edges. The variables deltacolor and centercolor hold the color of the space between the edges and the color of the inner rectangle, respectively.

Window Owners

In a visual image like a calculator, the graphics elements have a fixed visual relationship to one another; the "1" button is next to the "2" button, and so forth. Ordinarily we want to position one graphics element at a particular location on the screen, and then position other graphics elements *relative to the first*. This makes it easy to move an entire image, consisting of many elements, by changing only one set of coordinates. In our calculator we want to position the border relative to the screen, and then position the buttons and the output window relative to this border. However, we might want to position a second border relative to the first (to provide visual separation for a group of buttons, for instance). Thus when we create a window—whether it is a border, a button, or an output window—we want to tell it what other window it should position itself relative to. We'll call this other window its owner. (We could have used the term *parent*, as is done in Microsoft Windows and OS/2 Presentation Manager programming, but this could be confused with the C++ concept of inheritance.)

When we create a window we'll send it a pointer to its owner so it can access the owner's coordinates and position itself relative to them. This is the variable ptrOwner in the declaration of the Window class.

Windows can own windows that own other windows. But the ultimate owner—the root of the ownership tree—is assumed to be the screen itself. In CALC.H we define the variable SCREEN to be a null (0) pointer. When a window detects that the pointer to its parent has a null value, it assumes that it should position itself relative to the screen, not to another window, so it treats the coordinates passed to it as absolute coordinates. Figure 15-3 shows the ownership relationship.

Window Member Functions

The member functions for the **Window** class are declared in CALC.H, but are defined in CALC.CPP. There are only two of these functions. The first is the constructor **Window()**. This function calculates the coordinates of the window, using the coordinates of the

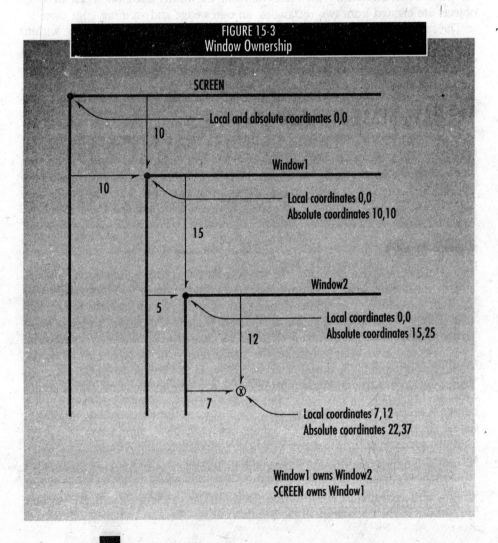

FIGURE 15-3
Window Ownership

SCREEN

Local and absolute coordinates 0,0

10

10

Window1

Local coordinates 0,0
Absolute coordinates 10,10

15

Window2

5

Local coordinates 0,0
Absolute coordinates 15,25

12

7

Local coordinates 7,12
Absolute coordinates 22,37

Window1 owns Window2
SCREEN owns Window1

owner and the relative coordinates passed from the window definition, and then copies them into the window's protected data space. The constructor also copies the color arguments from the definition, and calculates `delta`, the distance between the inner and outer rectangles, based on the size of the window. The relationship of `delta` to the window is shown in Figure 15-4.

The value of `delta` is larger for larger windows but never smaller than 3 pixels. (The constant 150 in its definition was chosen by trial and error.)

The second member function, `Display()`, displays the window. This involves drawing and filling two rectangles, for which we use the `fillpoly()` library function.

THE Border CLASS

The `Border` class is very simple, being almost identical to the `Window` class. It simply adds some optional colors, so you can declare a standard border without worrying about what colors to use. We could have dispensed with the Border class entirely, but it's conceptually cleaner to avoid creating objects of the base class and instead use it as an abstract class from which usable (or *instance*) classes are derived.

FIGURE 15-4
Window and delta

THE Button CLASS

The **Button** class adds two items of data to a window: the status of the button (whether it is pushed in or not) and the text that will appear in the center of the button. We use an **enum** to specify two possible values for the type **buttonstatus**: **unpushed** and **pushed**. A button's text is printed in the center of the button, and is usually very short, although you could specify larger buttons that accommodated longer text.

The **Button** class adds three member functions, declared in CALC.H and defined in CALC.CPP. They are **Click()**, **Display()**, and the constructor **Button()**, which is similar to that in **Border**.

The **Click()** function depresses the button for one-fifth of a second. (This is a little long if you're a fast typist, but it gives you time to see the button sink in and pop out.) It does this by changing the button status to **pushed**, displaying it, then changing the status back to **unpushed** and displaying it again.

The **Display()** function in the **Button** class first calls the **Display()** function in **Window** to draw the underlying rectangles. Note that the scope-resolution operator (**::**) must be used to distinguish which **Display()** we want. Next **Display()** draws the button's text. Finally, it shades the button's edges—the space between the button's inner and outer rectangles.

To shade the button's edges, two inverted L-shaped areas are defined: the upper-left border and the lower-right border.

What happens next depends on the status of the button. If it is not pushed, the upper and left sections are colored light gray, and the right and lower sections remain black. If it is pushed, the coloring is reversed: The upper and left sections remain black, and the lower and right sections are colored light gray. The eye assumes that light falls from the upper left, so this scheme provides the illusion that the button protrudes from the screen when unpushed, and sinks below the screen when pushed. Figure 15-5 shows a button.

FIGURE 15-5
A Push Button

Unpushed   Pushed

THE OUTPUT WINDOW

The `Output` class creates the window in which the numerical results of calculations are displayed. This class adds one additional data item to `Window`: the text to be displayed in the output window. There are two member functions. `Text()` displays output provided by a string argument to the function, and `Number()` displays output taken from a numerical argument. `Number()` converts the floating-point number to a string using the `sprintf()` library function, and then calls `Text()` to display the string.

THE CALC_APP.CPP FILE

The CALC_APP.CPP file contains the code that uses the various classes to create the calculator. This code also interacts with the keyboard and performs the arithmetic requested by the user of the program. This is all handled in one function—`main()`. As written, the program specifies maximum resolution mode, but you can change it to specify another mode if you wish.

```
// calc_app.cpp
// four-function calculator with 15 digits
// uses calc.cpp

#include "calc.h"                          // header file for calc.app

void main()
    {
    char options[] = "t'helv'w12h22";  // helvetica 12x22
    if( ! _setvideomode(_MAXRESMODE) )
        { cout << "Can't set graphics mode"; exit(1); }
    if( _registerfonts("C:\\C700\\LIB\\*.FON") < 0 )
        { _outtext("Can't register fonts"); goto exit; }
    if( _setfont(options) < 0 )
        {
        _outtext("Can't set font");
        _unregisterfonts();                // free font memory
exit: getch();
        _setvideomode(_DEFAULTMODE);       // close graphics
        exit(1);
        }

    // this section defines the various objects
                                    // border and output windows
    Border border1(SCREEN,  240, 30, 480, 330);
    Output output1(&border1, 20, 20, 220,  60, BLUE, WHITE);
                                    // buttons
    Button button0(&border1, 30, 230, 65, 265, DARKGRAY, "0");
    Button button1(&border1, 30, 180, 65, 215, DARKGRAY, "1");
    Button button2(&border1, 78, 180, 113, 215, DARKGRAY, "2");
    Button button3(&border1, 127, 180, 162, 215, DARKGRAY, "3");
```

```
Button button4(&border1, 30, 130, 65, 165, DARKGRAY, "4");
Button button5(&border1, 78, 130, 113, 165, DARKGRAY, "5");
Button button6(&border1, 127, 130, 162, 165, DARKGRAY, "6");
Button button7(&border1, 30, 80, 65, 115, DARKGRAY, "7");
Button button8(&border1, 78, 80, 113, 115, DARKGRAY, "8");
Button button9(&border1, 127, 80, 162, 115, DARKGRAY, "9");
Button buttonDiv(&border1, 175, 80, 210, 115, BLUE, "/");
Button buttonMul(&border1, 175, 130, 210, 165, BLUE, "*");
Button buttonSub(&border1, 175, 180, 210, 215, BLUE, "-");
Button buttonDot(&border1, 78, 230, 113, 265, DARKGRAY, " _ ");
Button buttonClr(&border1, 127, 230, 162, 265, RED, "c");
Button buttonAdd(&border1, 175, 230, 225, 265, BLUE, "+=");

// this section displays the various objects
border1.Display();              // border and output windows
output1.Display();

                         // buttons
button7.Display();      button8.Display();      button9.Display();
button4.Display();      button5.Display();      button6.Display();
button1.Display();      button2.Display();      button3.Display();
buttonSub.Display();    buttonDiv.Display();
buttonMul.Display();    buttonAdd.Display();
button0.Display();      buttonDot.Display();    buttonClr.Display();

output1.Number(0.0);            // display 0.0

// this section handles the keyboard and activates display
const char ESC=27;              // Escape key
char dstring[80];               // string for display
char tempbuf[80];               // temp string holder
int numchars = 0;               // number of chars in dstring
char ch;                        // character read from keyboard
char oper;                      // operator: /, *, -, +
boolean isfirst = true;         // first (not second) operator
boolean chain = false;          // chaining to next number
double number1, number2;        // first and second numbers
double answer;                  // answer to arithmetic

while( (ch=getch()) != ESC )    // quit program on Escape key
   {                            // is it a digit (or dot)
   if( (ch>='0' && ch<='9') || ch=='.' )
      {
      switch(ch)
         {                      // click the button
         case '0': button0.Click(); break;
         case '1': button1.Click(); break;
         case '2': button2.Click(); break;
         case '3': button3.Click(); break;
         case '4': button4.Click(); break;
         case '5': button5.Click(); break;
         case '6': button6.Click(); break;
```

```
   case '7': button7.Click(); break;
   case '8': button8.Click(); break;
   case '9': button9.Click(); break;
   case '.': buttonDot.Click(); break;
   }  // end switch
  dstring[numchars++] = ch;   // put char in buffer
  dstring[numchars] = '\0';   // put 0 at end of string
  if( atof( dstring) > 99999999999.99 ||  // if too big
      numchars > 11 )              // or too long
    dstring[--numchars] = '\0';  // delete last char
  output1.Text(dstring);      // send it to output window
  }                           // end if (it's a digit)

                              // if it's a valid math operator
else if( ch=='/' || ch=='*' || ch=='-' || ch=='+' ||
        ch=='=')
  {
  strcpy(tempbuf,dstring);  // save the input string
  numchars = 0;             // empty input buffer
  dstring[numchars] = '\0';
  output1.Text(dstring);    // display empty buf
  if( isfirst )               // if first operator
    {                         // 1st time, n1 = answer
    number1 = (chain) ? answer : atof(tempbuf);
    isfirst = false;          // next op will be second
    switch(ch)                // store the operator
      {
      case '/': buttonDiv.Click();  oper='/';  break;
      case '*': buttonMul.Click();  oper='*';  break;
      case '-': buttonSub.Click();  oper='-';  break;
      case '+':
      case '=': buttonAdd.Click();  oper='+';  break;
      }                       // end switch (ch)
    }                         // end if (first number)
  else                        // second operator
    {                         //    (should be '=')
    buttonAdd.Click();        // assume it was '='
    number2 = atof(tempbuf);  // get second number
    switch(oper)              // do the action
      {
      case '/': answer = number1 / number2;  break;
      case '*': answer = number1 * number2;  break;
      case '-': answer = number1 - number2;  break;
      case '+': answer = number1 + number2;  break;
      }
    if(answer > 99999999999.99)  // if answer too big
      output1.Text("Overflow"); // to display
    else                         // otherwise
      {                          // answer ok
      output1.Number(answer);    // display the answer
      number1 = answer;
```

```
                     }                    // set up to chain to
              isfirst = true;            // another 2nd operator
              chain = true;              // and another 2nd number
              }                          // end else (second operator)
        }                                // end else if (operator)

      else if( ch=='C' || ch=='c' )      // if it's Clear
         {
         buttonClr.Click();              // click the button
         isfirst = true;                 // next number is first
         chain = false;                  // not chaining
         numchars = 0;                   // empty input buffer
         dstring[numchars] = '\0';
         output1.Number(0.0);            // display 0.0
         } // end else if (clear)
      } // end while
   _unregisterfonts();                   // free font memory
   _setvideomode(_DEFAULTMODE);          // close graphics system
   } // end main()
```

Note that CALC_APP.CPP, like CALC.CPP, must #include the header file CALC.H, so that it can access the various class declarations.

In main() we first define all the visual elements of the calculator, then display them using each one's Display() function. (We could have made these display routines into a family of virtual functions, but in this particular application there was no need to do so. In a more general situation, virtual functions would provide added flexibility.)

The complicated part of main() involves handling the keyboard input. This is done in a large while loop. At the top of the loop, the character is read by the getche() function. Pressing (ESC) terminates the loop and the program. The body of the loop is a series of if and else if constructions that decipher the character typed.

Digits

If the character is a digit or the decimal point, the appropriate button is clicked and the digit is added to the end of a character buffer called dstring. The '\0' character is then added in the position following the character to terminate the string. If the buffer is too full or the number too big, the offending digit is removed from the buffer (by writing over it with '\0'). The resulting buffer contents are displayed using the Output.Text() function.

Operators

If the character is an arithmetic operator, the string in dstring is saved temporarily, and dstring is emptied and the empty buffer displayed.

What we do next depends on whether this is the first arithmetic operator or the second. A Boolean flag variable, isfirst, keeps track of this state. If this flag is true, we know we are dealing with the first operator, which should be \, *, - or +. We save the number from dstring in number1, then click the button corresponding to the operator and save the operator for later use. (We'll ignore the possibility of chaining for the moment.)

If we've just read the second operator, it must be the = operator, so we click the += button, store the number in `number2`, and—using the previously stored operator—perform the corresponding arithmetic operation on `number1` and `number2`. The result is stored in `answer`. If it isn't too big, we display it; otherwise we display the word *Overflow*.

Clear Button

If the character is 'C' or 'c', we click the `clr` button and clear the `dstring` buffer in preparation for starting over. We respond to any other keyboard character with an error beep but no other change.

Chaining

Often the user wants to retain the result of an operation and use it as the first operand of a second operation. This is mediated by a `chain` flag variable, which is set to `true` if we've already completed one operation. When this is the case the value to be inserted in `number1` is taken from `answer` rather than from the user, before the indicated arithmetic is carried out.

NOT A STANDALONE FILE

Note that, as written, CALC.EXE is not a standalone program; the \C700\LIB directory specified in the `_registerfonts()` function must be available to the program. This directory contains the file HELV.FON (the font file for the helvetica font).

NOT THE WINDOWS APPROACH

In Windows and the OS/2 Presentation Manager, window-type objects like buttons are supplied with the operating system. The operating system also informs your program when the mouse is clicked on certain objects. For these reasons, writing a program like CALC is easier, in some ways, using Windows or PM than writing your own visual interface, as we've shown here.

A VERY LONG NUMBER CLASS

Sometimes even the basic data type `unsigned long` does not provide enough precision for certain integer arithmetic operations. `unsigned long` is the largest integer type in Microsoft C++, holding integers up to 4,294,967,295, or about ten digits. This is about the same number of digits a pocket calculator can handle. But if you need to work with numbers containing more significant digits than this, you have a problem.

FIGURE 15-6
A verylong Number

Our next example shows a way to solve this problem. It provides a class that holds numbers up to 200 digits long. If you want to make even longer numbers, you can change a single constant in the program.

Numbers as Strings

The **verylong** class stores numbers as strings of digits. This explains its large capacity; the basic types in C++ can handle long strings, since they are simply arrays. By representing numbers as strings, we can make them as long as we want. There are two data members in **verylong**: a **char** array to hold the string of digits, and an **int** to tell how long the string is. (This length data isn't strictly necessary, but it saves using **strlen()** to find the string length over and over.) The digits in the string are stored in reverse order, with the least significant digit stored first, at **vlstr[0]**. This simplifies various operations on the string. Figure 15-6 shows a number stored as a string.

We've provided user-accessible routines for addition and multiplication of **verylong** numbers. (We leave it as an exercise for the reader to write subtraction and division routines.)

The Class Specifier

Here's the header file for VERYLONG. It shows the specifiers for the **verylong** class:

```
// verylong.h
// class specifier for very long integer type
#include <iostream.h>
#include <string.h>          // for strlen(), etc.
#include <stdlib.h>          // for ltoa()
```

```
const int SZ = 200;              // maximum digits in verylongs

class verylong
    {
    private:
        char vlstr[SZ];          // verylong number as a string
        int vlen;                // length of verylong string
        verylong multdigit(int); // prototypes for
        verylong mult10(verylong); // private functions
    public:
        verylong()               // no-arg constructor
            { vlstr[0]='\0'; vlen=0; }
        verylong(char s[SZ])     // one-arg constructor
            { strcpy(vlstr, s); vlen=strlen(s); }   // for string
        verylong(unsigned long n) // one-arg constructor
            {                     // for long int
            ltoa(n, vlstr, 10);  // convert to string
            strrev(vlstr);       // reverse it
            vlen=strlen(vlstr);  // find length
            }
        void putvl();            // display verylong
        void getvl();            // get verylong from user
        verylong operator + (verylong);  // add verylongs
        verylong operator * (verylong);  // multiply verylongs
    };
```

In addition to the data members, there are two private-member functions in class **verylong**. One multiplies a **verylong** number by a single digit, and one multiplies a **verylong** number by 10. These routines are used internally by the multiplication routine.

There are three constructors. One sets the **verylong** to 0, by inserting a terminating null at the beginning of the array and setting the length to 0. The second initializes it to a string (which is in reverse order), and the third initializes it to a **long int** value.

The **putvl()** member function displays a **verylong**, and the **getvl** gets a **verylong** value from the user. You can type as many digits as you like, up to 200. Note that there is no error checking in this routine; if you type a nondigit the results will be inaccurate.

Two overloaded operators, **+** and *****, perform addition and multiplication. You can use expressions like

```
alpha = beta * gamma + delta;
```

to do **verylong** arithmetic.

THE MEMBER FUNCTIONS

Here's VERYLONG.CPP, the file that holds the member function definitions:

```cpp
// verylong.cpp
// implements very long integer type
#include "verylong.h"          // header file for verylong

void verylong::putvl()                 // display verylong
    {
    char temp[SZ];
    strcpy(temp,vlstr);                 // make copy
    cout << strrev(temp);               // reverse the copy
    }                                   // and display it

void verylong::getvl()                 // get verylong from user
    {
    cin >> vlstr;                       // get string from user
    vlen = strlen(vlstr);               // find its length
    strrev(vlstr);                      // reverse it
    }

verylong verylong::operator + (verylong v)  // add verylongs
    {
    char temp[SZ];
                                        // find longest number
    int maxlen = (vlen > v.vlen) ? vlen : v.vlen;
    int carry = 0;                      // set to 1 if sum >= 10
    for(int j = 0; j<maxlen; j++)       // for each position
        {
        int d1 = (j > vlen-1)   ? 0 : vlstr[j]-'0';   // get digit
        int d2 = (j > v.vlen-1) ? 0 : v.vlstr[j]-'0'; // get digit
        int digitsum = d1 + d2 + carry;               // add digits
        if( digitsum >= 10 )            // if there's a carry,
            { digitsum -= 10; carry=1; } // decrease sum by 10,
        else                            // set carry to 1
            carry = 0;                  // otherwise carry is 0
        temp[j] = digitsum+'0';         // insert char in string
        }
    if(carry==1)                        // if carry at end,
        temp[j++] = '1';                // last digit is 1
    temp[j] = '\0';                     // terminate string
    return verylong(temp);              // return temp verylong
    }

verylong verylong::operator * (verylong v)  // multiply verylongs
    {
    verylong pprod;                     // product of one digit
    verylong tempsum;                   // running total
    for(int j=0; j<v.vlen; j++)         // for each digit in arg
        {
        int digit = v.vlstr[j]-'0';     // get the digit
        pprod = multdigit(digit);       // multiply this by digit
```

```
      for(int k=0; k<j; k++)                // multiply result by
         pprod = mult10(pprod);             //    power of 10
      tempsum = tempsum + pprod;            // add product to total
      }
   return tempsum;                          // return total of prods
   }


verylong verylong::mult10(verylong v)       // multiply argument by 10
   {
   char temp[SZ];
   for(int j=v.vlen-1; j>=0; j--)           // move digits one
      temp[j+1] = v.vlstr[j];               //    position higher
   temp[0] = '0';                           // put zero on low end
   temp[v.vlen+1] = '\0';                   // terminate string
   return verylong(temp);                   // return result
   }


verylong verylong::multdigit(int d2)        // multiply this verylong
   {                                        // by digit in argument
   char temp[SZ];
   int carry = 0;
   for(int j = 0; j<vlen; j++)              // for each position
      {                                     // in this verylong
      int d1 = vlstr[j]-'0';                // get digit from this
      int digitprod = d1 * d2;              // multiply by that digit
      digitprod += carry;                   // add old carry
      if( digitprod >= 10 )                 // if there's a new carry,
         {
         carry = digitprod/10;              // carry is high digit
         digitprod -= carry*10;             // result is low digit
         }
      else
         carry = 0;                         // otherwise carry is 0
      temp[j] = digitprod+'0';              // insert char in string
      }
   if(carry != 0)                           // if carry at end,
      temp[j++] = carry+'0';                // it's last digit
   temp[j] = '\0';                          // terminate string
   return verylong(temp);                   // return verylong
   }
```

The putvl() and getvl() functions are fairly straightforward. They use the strrev() library function to reverse the string, so it is stored in reverse order but input is displayed normally.

The operator+() function adds two verylongs and leaves the result in a third verylong. It does this by considering their digits one at a time. It adds digit 0 from both numbers, storing a carry if necessary. Then it adds the digits in position 1, adding the carry if necessary. It continues until it has added all the digits in the larger of the two numbers. If the numbers are different lengths, the nonexistent digits in the shorter number are set to 0 before being added. Figure 15-7 shows the process.

Multiplication uses the `operator*()` function. This function performs multiplication by multiplying the multiplicand (the top number when you write it by hand) by each separate digit in the multiplier (the bottom number). It calls the `multdigit()` routine to this. The results are then multiplied by 10 an appropriate number of times to shift the result to match the position of the digit, using the `mult10()` function. The results of these separate calculations are then added together using the `operator+()` function.

FIGURE 15-7
Adding veryLong Numbers

THE APPLICATION PROGRAM

To test the `verylong` class we use a variation of the FACTOR program from Chapter 4 to calculate the factorial of a number entered by the user. Here's the listing for VL_APP.CPP:

```
// vl_app.cpp
// calculates factorials of larger numbers using verylong class
#include "verylong.h"                      // verylong header file
void main()
   {
   unsigned long numb, j;
   verylong fact=1;                        // initialize verylong

   cout << "\n\nEnter number: ";
   cin >> numb;                            // input a long int

   for(j=numb; j>0; j--)                   // factorial is numb *
      fact = fact * j;                     //    numb-1 * numb-2 *
   cout << "Factoral is ";                 //    numb-3 and so on
   fact.putvl();                           // display factorial
   }
```

In this program `fact` is a `verylong` variable. The other variables, `numb` and `j`, don't need to be `verylong`s because they don't get so big. To calculate the factorial of 100, for example, `numb` and `j` require only three digits, while `fact` requires 158. Notice how, in the expression

```
fact = fact * j;
```

the `long` variable `j` is automatically converted to `verylong`, using the one-argument constructor, before the multiplication is carried out.

Here's the output when we ask the program to find the factorial of 100:

```
Enter number: 100
Factoral is 93326215443944152681699238856266700490071596826438162
146859296389521759999322991560894146397615651828625369792082722375825118521091686400000000000000000000000000
```

Try *that* using type `long` variables! Surprisingly, the routines are fairly fast; this program executes in a fraction of a second. (If you want to calculate the factorial of numbers greater than about 120, you'll need to increase the size of SZ.)

A WATER-DISTRIBUTION SYSTEM

Have you ever wondered how your house is supplied with water? Or how the cooling system in a nuclear reactor operates? Or how the Alaska Pipeline was designed? The next application can help you answer these questions. It models a liquid-distribution system, consisting of pipes, valves, tanks, and other components. This example shows how easy it is to create a set of classes for a specialized situation. A similar approach could be used in other process-control applications, such as the hydraulic systems used to operate aircraft. The general approach is even applicable to electrical distribution systems, or economic systems that track the flow of money.

Figure 15-8 shows a water-distribution system for a small community built on a hillside. This water system will be modeled in the PIPES program.

As in the previous program, we'll break this program into three files. PIPES.H will contain the class declarations, and PIPES.CPP will contain the definitions of the

FIGURE 15-8
A Typical Water System

member functions. These files can be assumed to be provided by a vendor of class libraries. The PIPE_APP.CPP file is the one we write ourselves to specify a water system with a particular arrangement of tanks, valves, and pipes.

COMPONENTS OF A WATER SYSTEM

In this application we find that physcal objects in the real world—objects we can see and touch—correspond closely with objects in the program. Let's see what these objects are.

- A *source* supplies water to the system. In the real world, it might correspond to a spring, well, or reservoir. The water from the source is assumed to be always available but cannot be supplied faster than a certain fixed rate.

- A *sink* is a user of water. It represents a house, factory, or farm, or a group of such water consumers. A sink absorbs water from the system at a fixed rate.

- A *pipe* carries water over a distance. A pipe has a characteristic resistance that limits the amount of water that can flow through it. The water flowing into a pipe equals the water flowing out.

- A *tank* stores water. It also decouples the input/output flows: The rate at which water flows into the tank can be different from the rate at which it flows out. For example, if the input flow is greater than the output, the contents of the tank increases. A tank has a characteristic maximum output flow rate, determined (in this model, at least) by the size of the outlet in the tank.

- To keep a tank from overflowing, and to make sure it doesn't run out of water, we can associate *switches* with the tank. A switch turns on when the amount of water in the tank reaches a certain quantity. Switches are usually used to actuate a valve, which in turn controls the level of water in the tank.

- A *valve* regulates the flow of water. It can be on, causing no resistance to the flow, or off, which stops the flow entirely. A valve is assumed to be operated by some sort of servo-mechanism, and is typically controlled by switches associated with a tank.

FLOW, PRESSURE, AND BACK PRESSURE

Every component in the system has three important aspects: flow, pressure, and back pressure. When we connect one component to another, we're connecting these three aspects.

Flow

The bottom-line characteristic of components in the water system is *flow*. This is the amount of water passing through the component per unit time. It's usually what we're interested in measuring when we model a system.

Often the flow into a component is the same as the flow out. This is true of pipes and of valves. However, as noted above, it is not true of tanks.

Pressure

Flow isn't the whole story. For example, when a valve is turned off, the flow both into it and out of it stops, but water may still be *trying* to flow through the valve. This potential for flow is *pressure*. A source or a tank provides water at a certain pressure. If the rest of the system permits, this pressure will cause a proportional flow: The greater the pressure, the greater the flow. But if a valve is turned off, the flow will stop, regardless of what the pressure is. Pressure, like flow, is transmitted downstream from one component to another.

A tank decouples pressure as well as flow. The pressure downstream from a tank is determined by the tank, not by the upstream pressure.

Back Pressure

In opposition to pressure is *back pressure*. This is caused by the resistance to flow of some components. A small-diameter pipe, for instance, will slow the flow of water, so that no matter how much pressure is supplied, the flow will still be small. This back pressure will slow the flow not only into the component causing the back pressure but into all components upstream.

Back pressure goes the opposite way from flow and pressure. It's transmitted from the downstream component to the upstream component. Tanks decouple back pressure as they do pressure and flow.

COMPONENT INPUT AND OUTPUT

Sometimes the flow, pressure, or back pressure are the same on both ends of a component. The flow into one end of a pipe, for example, is the same as the flow out the other end (we assume no leaks). However, these characteristics can also be different on the upstream and downstream sides. When a valve is turned off, the pressure on its downstream side becomes 0, no matter what the pressure on the upstream side is. The flow into a tank may be different from the flow out; the difference between input and output flow is reflected in changes to the contents of the tank. The output pressure of a pipe may be less than the input pressure because of the pipe's resistance.

Thus each component, at any given instant, can be characterized by six values. There are three inputs: pressure (from the upstream component), back pressure (from downstream), and flow (from upstream). There are also three outputs: pressure (on the downstream component), back pressure (on the upstream component), and flow (to the downstream component). This situation is shown in Figure 15-9.

The outputs of a component are calculated from its inputs, and also from the internal characteristics and state of the component, such as the resistance of a pipe, or whether a valve is open or closed. A member function of each component, called Tick() because it occurs at fixed time intervals, is used to calculate the components'

FIGURE 15-9
A Component's Characteristics

output based on its input and internal characteristics. If the input pressure to a pipe is increased, for example, the flow will increase correspondingly (unless the back pressure caused by the pipe's resistance and other components beyond it in the line is too high).

MAKING CONNECTIONS

To create a water system, we need to connect the various components together. It should be possible to connect any component to any other component so that water flows from one to another. (Switches are not connected in this way, since they don't carry water.) Besides flow, both pressure and back pressure must be connected, since they are also transmitted from component to component.

Thus making a connection means setting the output pressure and output flow from the upstream object to the input pressure and input flow of the downstream object, and setting the output back pressure from the downstream object to the input back pressure of the upstream object. This is shown in Figure 15-10.

SIMPLIFYING ASSUMPTIONS

To avoid complex mathematics, we've made some simplifying assumptions.

What we call back pressure in the program should probably be called something like *ease of flow*. The values we use for this characteristic are *proportional* to the resulting flow, being small if only a small amount can flow, and large when the flow can be large. Real back pressure would be the reciprocal of the resulting flow, but this would complicate the program unduly.

Both pressure and back pressure are assumed to be measured in the same units as flow. To calculate the flow, we examine the pressure pushing water into the system, and the back pressure resisting its flow. The resulting flow is the smallest of these two numbers. Thus if a source provides 100 gallons/minute, and a pipe has

FIGURE 15-10
Connection Between Components

flows into
connection

c1   c2

c2.inpress = c1.outpress
c1.inbackp = c2.outbackp
c2.inflow = c1.outflow

a resistance of 60 gallons/minute, which causes a back pressure of 60 gallons/minute, the flow will be 60 gallons/minute.

These assumptions don't model exactly the real world of hydraulic flow, in which flow is determined by complex formulas relating pressure and back pressure, but they do provide a good first approximation.

We assume the output pressure of a tank is a constant. In reality it would depend on the contents of the tank. However, for tanks considerably higher in elevation than the sink, this is a reasonable approximation.

There is also an unavoidable built-in kind of imperfection in our approach to this problem. The physical system we are modeling is an analog system that changes continuously with time. But our model is "digital": it samples the state of the components at discrete "ticks," or time intervals. Thus when something changes, like a valve opening, it may take several loop cycles for the resulting pressure and flow changes to propagate throughout the system. These transients can be ignored in analyzing the system's behavior.

PROGRAM DESIGN

Our goal in this program is to create a family of classes that make it easy to model different water-distribution systems. In this application it's easy to see what the classes should represent. We create a class for each kind of component—a valve class, a tank class, a pipe class, and so on. Once these classes are established, the programmer can then connect components as necessary to model a specific system.

Here are the listings for the PIPES.H and PIPES.CPP files. We assume these files are supplied by a class software vendor.

```
// pipes.h
// header file for pipes

const int infinity = 32767;    // infinite back pressure
enum offon { off, on };        // status of valves and switches
class Tank;                     // for using Tank in Switch

class Component                 // components (Pipe, Valve, etc.)
    {
    protected:
        int inpress, outpress;   // pressures in and out
        int inbackp, outbackp;   // back pressures in and out
        int inflow, outflow;     // flow in and out
    public:
        Component(void)
            { inpress = outpress = inbackp = outbackp =
              inflow = outflow = 0; }
        int Flow(void)
            { return inflow; }
        friend void operator >= (Component&, Component&);
        friend void Tee(Component&, Component&, Component&);
    };


class Source : public Component       // flow begins here
    {
    public:
        Source(int outp)
            { outpress = inpress = outp; }
        void Tick(void)                // update
            {                          // output pressure fixed
            outbackp = inbackp;
            outflow = (outpress < outbackp) ? outpress : outbackp;
            inflow = outflow;
            }
    };


class Sink : public Component         // flow ends here
    {
    public:
        Sink(int obp)                  // initialize backpressure
            { outbackp = inbackp = obp; }
        void Tick(void)                // update
            {                          // output back pressure fixed
            outpress = inpress;
            outflow = (outbackp < outpress) ? outbackp : outpress;
            inflow = outflow;
            }
    };
```

```
class Pipe : public Component        // connects other components,
   {                                 // has resistance to flow
   private:
      int resist;
   public:
      Pipe(int r)          // initialize
         { inbackp = resist = r; }
      void Tick(void);  // update
   };

class Valve : public Component       // turns flow on or off
   {
   private:
      offon status;                  // on (open) or off (closed)
   public:
      Valve(offon s)
         { status = s; }
      offon& Status(void)
         { return status; }
      void Tick(void);
   };

class Tank : public Component        // stores water
   {
   private:
      int contents;                  // water in tank (gals)
      int maxoutpress;               // max output pressure
   public:
      Tank(int mop)                  // initialize to empty tank
         { maxoutpress = mop; contents = 0; }
      int Contents(void)             // get contents
         { return(contents); }
      void Tick(void);
   };

class Switch                         // activated by tank level
   {                                 // can operate valves
   private:
      offon status;     // 'on' if contents > triggercap
      int cap;          // capacity where switch turns on
      Tank* tankptr;    // pointer to owner tank
   public:
      Switch(Tank *tptr, int tcap)   // initialize
         { tankptr = tptr; cap = tcap; status = off; }
      int Status(void)               // get status
         { return(status); }
      void Tick(void)                // update status
         { status = (tankptr->Contents() > cap) ? on : off; }
   };
```

```cpp
// pipes.cpp
// function definitions for pipes

#include "pipes.h"                    // needed for class definitions

                                      // "flows into" operator: c1 >= c2
void operator >= (Component& c1, Component& c2)
    {
    c2.inpress = c1.outpress;
    c1.inbackp = c2.outbackp;
    c2.inflow =  c1.outflow;
    }
                                 // "tee" divides flow into two
void Tee(Component& src, Component& c1, Component& c2)
    {
                            // avoid division by 0
    if( (c1.outbackp==0 && c2.outbackp==0) ||
        (c1.outbackp==0 && c2.outbackp==0) )
        {
        c1.inpress = c2.inpress = 0;
        src.inbackp = 0;
        c1.inflow = c2.inflow = 0;
        return;
        }                       // proportion for each output
    float f1 = (float)c1.outbackp / (c1.outbackp + c2.outbackp);
    float f2 = (float)c2.outbackp / (c1.outbackp + c2.outbackp);
                                // pressures for two outputs
    c1.inpress = src.outpress * f1;
    c2.inpress = src.outpress * f2;
                                // back pressure for single input
    src.inbackp = c1.outbackp + c2.outbackp;
                                // flow for two outputs
    c1.inflow = src.outflow * f1;
    c2.inflow = src.outflow * f2;
    }


void Pipe::Tick(void)               // update pipes
    {
    outpress = (inpress < resist) ? inpress : resist;
    outbackp = (inbackp < resist) ? inbackp : resist;

    // outflow is the lesser of outpress, outbackp, and resist
    if(outpress < outbackp && outpress < resist)
        outflow = outpress;
    else if(outbackp < outpress && outbackp < resist)
        outflow = outbackp;
    else
        outflow = resist;
    }
```

```
void Valve::Tick(void)              // update valves
   {
   if(status==on)                   // if valve open
      {
      outpress = inpress;
      outbackp = inbackp;
      outflow = (outpress < outbackp) ? outpress : outbackp;
      }
   else                             // if valve closed
      {
      outpress = 0;
      outbackp = 0;
      outflow = 0;
      }
   }


void Tank::Tick(void)               // update tanks
   {
   outbackp = infinity;             // will take all the flow
                                    // you can give it
   if( contents > 0 )               // if not empty
      {
      outpress = (maxoutpress<inbackp) ? maxoutpress : inbackp;
      outflow = outpress;
      }
   else                             // if empty
      {
      outpress = 0;                 // no out pressure,
      outflow = 0;                  // no flow
      }
   contents += inflow - outflow;    // always true
   }
```

Programming the Connections

A key part of program usability is a simple, intuitive way of describing connections in the program. We could use a function, such as

```
Connect(valve1, tank1);
```

However, this can be confusing: Is the upstream component the right argument or the left?

A better approach is to overload an operator to represent connections between components. We'll choose the greater-than-or-equal-to operator, >=, which provides a visual indication of flow direction from left to right. We can call it the *flows into* operator. A program statement establishing a connection would look like this:

```
valve1 >= tank1;
```

meaning that water from valve1 *flows into* tank1.

BASE AND DERIVED CLASSES

When designing our program, we look first for similarities among the various objects. The common attributes can be placed in a base class, while the individual features that distinguish the components can be placed in derived classes.

THE Component BASE CLASS

In this application we note that all the objects (except switches) have water flowing through them and can be connected to each other. We will therefore create a base class that permits connections. We'll call it `Component`.

```
class Component                     // components (Pipe, Valve, etc.)
   {
   protected:
      int inpress, outpress;    // pressures in and out
      int inbackp, outbackp;    // back pressures in and out
      int inflow, outflow;      // flow in and out
   public:
      Component(void)
         { inpress = outpress = inbackp = outbackp =
           inflow = outflow = 0; }
      int Flow(void)
         { return inflow; }
      friend void operator >= (Component&, Component&);
      friend void Tee(Component&, Component&, Component&);
   };
```

A component has pressure, back pressure, and flow. These all have two values: input to the component, and output from it. For input we have the flow into the object from upstream, the pressure exerted by objects on its upstream side, and the back pressure exerted by objects on the downstream side. For output there is the flow out of the object, the pressure it transmits to the downstream object, and the back pressure it transmits to the upstream object. These values are all stored in objects of the Component class. A constructor for this class initializes all the data items to 0, and another member function returns the flow, which is, for most components, what we want to measure to see how the system is working.

THE *FLOWS INTO* OPERATOR

The *flows into* operator, `>=`, connects an upstream component with a downstream component. Three inputs (the downstream object's pressure and flow and the upstream object's back pressure) are set equal to three outputs (the upstream object's pressure and flow and the downstream object's back pressure).

```
// "flows into" operator: c1 >= c2
void operator >= (Component& c1, Component& c2)
    {
    c2.inpress = c1.outpress;
    c1.inbackp = c2.outbackp;
    c2.inflow  = c1.outflow;
    }
```

The >= operator is defined as a **friend** of the **Component** class. It could also be defined as a member class, but another kind of connection, the **Tee()** function, must be a **friend**, so we'll make >= a **friend** for consistency. Both arguments to >= are passed by reference, since the original arguments must both be modified.

Since the >= operator applies to objects of the base class **Component**, it works on objects of the derived classes, such as tanks, valves, and pipes. This saves you from having to write a separate function to handle each kind of connection, such as

```
friend void operator >= (Pipe&, Valve&);
friend void operator >= (Valve&, Tank&);
friend void operator >= (Tank&, Sink&);
```

and so on *ad infinitum*.

DERIVED CLASSES

The classes that model the physical objects in the system are derived from the base class **Component**. These are **Source**, **Sink**, **Pipe**, **Valve**, and **Tank**. Each has specific characteristics. A source has a fixed input pressure. A sink has a fixed back pressure. A pipe has a fixed internal resistance; its output back pressure can never be greater than a fixed value. A valve has a status of type **offon**, **off**, or **on** (defined in an **enum** statement). A tank has contents—how full it is. A valve's status and a tank's contents change as the program runs.

Variables that will be constant throughout the program, such as the resistance of a pipe, or the output pressure of a tank, are initialized when the object is first created.

As we noted, all these derived classes, and the **switch** class as well, include member functions called **Tick()**. This function is called for each object in the system—once each time period—to update the internal state of the object and to calculate the three outputs (pressure, back pressure, and flow) from the three inputs.

The Tee() Function

The **Tee()** function divides a single input flow into two output flows. The proportion of flow going into each downstream component is proportional to the back pressure of each component. A pipe with a lot of resistance will get a smaller proportion of the flow than one with low resistance. (See the listing for this function.)

Tee() is called with three arguments: the source component and the two downstream components, in order:

```
Tee(input, output1, output2);
```

It would be nice to use a more intuitive operator than a function with three parameters to connect three components. For instance,

```
input >= output1 + output2;
```

Unfortunately there is no ternary operator (one that takes three arguments) that can be overloaded in C++.

The Switch Class

The Switch class has a special relationship to the Tank class. Each tank is typically associated with two switches. One switch is set to turn on when the tank level is above a certain minimum value (when the tank is almost empty). The other turns on when the level is above a certain maximum value (when the tank is full). This maximum determines the capacity of the tank.

Let's define the relationship between switches and tanks by saying that a switch is "owned" by a tank. When a switch is defined, it's given two values. One is the address of the tank that owns it. The other is the contents level at which it will turn on. The Tick() member function in Switch uses the address of its owner tank to directly access the tank contents. This is how it figures out whether to turn itself on or off.

Switches are typically used to control a valve that regulates the flow of water into a tank. When the tank is full, the valve turns off; when it's nearing empty, the valve turns on again.

THE PIPE_APP.CPP FILE

The main() part of the program would be written by an application programmer to model a specific water system. Here's the listing for PIPE_APP.CPP. This file contains only one function: main().

```
// pipe_app.cpp
// models a water supply system

#include "pipes.h"              // for pipes header file
#include <iostream.h>           // for cout, etc.
#include <iomanip.h>            // for setw
#include <conio.h>              // for kbhit()

main()
    {
    Source src(100);            // source(maximum capacity)
    Pipe pipe1(80);             // pipe(resistance)
    Valve valve1(on);           // valve(initially on)

    Tank tank1(60);             // tank1(maximum outflow)
    Switch switch1(&tank1, 300); // tank1 high switch
    Switch switch2(&tank1, 50);  // tank1 low switch
```

```
Pipe pipe2(80);                    // pipe
Sink sink1(30);                    // sink(maximum capacity)
Pipe pipe3(40);                    // pipe
Valve valve2(on);                  // valve

Tank tank2(80);                    // tank2
Switch switch3(&tank2, 250);       // tank2 high switch
Switch switch4(&tank2, 50);        // tank2 low switch

Sink sink2(20);                    // sink

while( !kbhit() )                  // quit on keypress
   {                               // make connections
   src >= pipe1;                   //    source flows into pipe
   pipe1 >= valve1;                //    pipe1 flows into valve'
   valve1 >= tank1;                //    valve1 flows into tank1
   Tee(tank1, pipe2, pipe3);       //    output of tank1 splits
   pipe2 >= sink1;                 //    pipe2 flows into sink1
   pipe3 >= valve2;                //    pipe3 flows into valve2
   valve2 >= tank2;                //    valve2 flows into tank2
   tank2 >= sink2;                 //    tank2 flows into sink2

   src.Tick();                     // update all components
   pipe1.Tick();                   //    and switches
   valve1.Tick();
   tank1.Tick();
   switch1.Tick();
   switch2.Tick();
   pipe2.Tick();
   sink1.Tick();
   pipe3.Tick();
   valve2.Tick();
   tank2.Tick();
   switch3.Tick();
   switch4.Tick();
   sink2.Tick();
                              // if tank1 gets too high
   if( valve1.Status()==on && switch1.Status()==on )
      valve1.Status() = off;
                              // if tank1 gets too low
   if( valve1.Status()==off && switch2.Status()==off )
      valve1.Status() = on;
                              // if tank2 gets too high
   if( valve2.Status()==on && switch3.Status()==on )
      valve2.Status() = off;
                              // if tank2 gets too low
   if( valve2.Status()==off && switch4.Status()==off )
      valve2.Status() = on;
                              // output
   cout << "  Src=" << setw(2) << src.Flow();
```

590

```
      cout << "  P1=" << setw(2) << pipe1.Flow();
      if( valve1.Status()==off )
         cout << "  V1=off";
      else
         cout << "  V1=on ";
      cout << "  T1=" << setw(3) << tank1.Contents();
      cout << "  P2=" << setw(2) << pipe2.Flow();
      cout << "  Snk1=" << setw(2) << sink1.Flow();
      cout << "  P3=" << setw(2) << pipe3.Flow();
      if( valve2.Status()==off )
         cout << "  V2=off";
      else
         cout << "  V2=on ";
      cout << "  T2=" << setw(3) << tank2.Contents();
      cout << "  Snk2=" << setw(2) << sink2.Flow();
      cout << "\n";
      }
   }
```

Declaring the Components

In main() the various components—pipes, valves, tanks, and so on, are first declared. At this time their fixed characteristics are initialized: A pipe is given a fixed resistance, and a tank's contents are initialized to empty.

Connecting and Updating

The bulk of the work in main() is carried out in a loop. Each time through the loop represents one time period, or tick of the clock. Pressing any key causes an exit from the loop and terminates the program.

The first business in the loop is to connect the various components. The source src is connected to pipe1, pipe1 is connected to valve1, and so on. The resulting system was shown in Figure 15-8.

Once the connections are made, the internal states of all the components are updated by calling their Tick() functions.

Valves are opened and closed in if statements, based on the previous state of the valves and on switches. The goal is to keep the contents of the tank between the upper switch and the lower switch by opening and closing the valve as appropriate. When the tank contents reach the high switch, this switch is turned on, and the if statement causes the valve to close. When the contents drop below the bottom switch, turning it off, the valve is opened.

Output

To see what's happening in the system, we use cout statements to print out the flow of various components, the capacity of the tanks, and the status of the valves as they change with time. Figure 15-11 shows some sample output.

FIGURE 15-11
Output of PIPES Program

```
Src=80  P1=80  V1=on   T1=300  P2=30  Snk1=30  P3= 0  V2=off  T2=172  Snk2=20
Src=80  P1=80  V1=off  T1=350  P2=30  Snk1=30  P3= 0  V2=off  T2=152  Snk2=20
Src=80  P1=80  V1=off  T1=400  P2=30  Snk1=30  P3= 0  V2=off  T2=132  Snk2=20
Src=80  P1=80  V1=off  T1=370  P2=30  Snk1=30  P3= 0  V2=off  T2=112  Snk2=20
Src= 0  P1=80  V1=off  T1=340  P2=30  Snk1=30  P3= 0  V2=off  T2= 92  Snk2=20
Src= 0  P1= 0  V1=off  T1=310  P2=30  Snk1=30  P3= 0  V2=off  T2= 72  Snk2=20
Src= 0  P1= 0  V1=off  T1=280  P2=30  Snk1=30  P3= 0  V2=off  T2= 52  Snk2=20
Src= 0  P1= 0  V1=off  T1=250  P2=30  Snk1=30  P3= 0  V2=on   T2= 32  Snk2=20
Src= 0  P1= 0  V1=off  T1=220  P2=30  Snk1=30  P3= 0  V2=on   T2= 12  Snk2=20
Src= 0  P1= 0  V1=off  T1=190  P2=30  Snk1=30  P3= 0  V2=on   T2= -8  Snk2=20
Src= 0  P1= 0  V1=off  T1=130  P2=12  Snk1=30  P3=17  V2=on   T2= -8  Snk2=20
Src= 0  P1= 0  V1=off  T1= 70  P2=25  Snk1=12  P3=34  V2=on   T2= -8  Snk2= 0
Src= 0  P1= 0  V1=on   T1= 10  P2=25  Snk1=25  P3=34  V2=on   T2=  9  Snk2= 0
Src= 0  P1= 0  V1=on   T1=-50  P2=25  Snk1=25  P3=34  V2=on   T2= 23  Snk2= 0
Src= 0  P1= 0  V1=on   T1= 30  P2=25  Snk1=25  P3=34  V2=on   T2= 37  Snk2=20
Src=80  P1= 0  V1=on   T1= 50  P2= 0  Snk1=25  P3= 0  V2=on   T2= 51  Snk2=20
Src=80  P1=80  V1=on   T1= 70  P2=25  Snk1= 0  P3=34  V2=on   T2= 65  Snk2=20
Src=80  P1=80  V1=on   T1= 90  P2=25  Snk1=25  P3=34  V2=on   T2= 45  Snk2=20
Src=80  P1=80  V1=on   T1=110  P2=25  Snk1=25  P3=34  V2=on   T2= 59  Snk2=20
Src=80  P1=80  V1=on   T1=130  P2=25  Snk1=25  P3=34  V2=on   T2= 73  Snk2=20
Src=80  P1=80  V1=on   T1=150  P2=25  Snk1=25  P3=34  V2=on   T2= 87  Snk2=20
Src=80  P1=80  V1=on   T1=170  P2=25  Snk1=25  P3=34  V2=on   T2=101  Snk2=20
Src=80  P1=80  V1=on   T1=190  P2=25  Snk1=25  P3=34  V2=on   T2=115  Snk2=20

C:\WORK\PIPES>
```

Notice in this figure that some values occasionally fall below zero. This is due to the digital nature of the simulation, mentioned earlier. Such transients can be ignored.

The goal of most water systems is to supply a continuous flow of water to the various sinks. The output of PIPES shows that there are some problems in the system modeled. The flow to **sink1** alternates between 25 and 30 gallons/minute, depending on whether **tank2** is filling or not. The water-system client would probably prefer that the supply was constant. Even worse, **sink2** experiences periods of no flow at all. It would seem that some components of the system need to be resized to eliminate these defects.

Of course **cout** provides a very unsophisticated output system. It would be easy to provide a graphic output, where pictures of the components appear on the screen. A **Display()** function built into each component would draw a picture of that component. Pictures would be connected as they are in the program—valve to tank, tank to pipe, and so on. The user could watch tanks fill and empty and valves open and close. Numbers beside pipes could display the flow within. This would make it easier to interpret the system's operation. It would also make the program larger and more complicated, which is why it is not implemented here.

Summary

Vendor-provided object libraries are often distributed as a public component containing class declarations in a .H header file, and a private component containing member function definitions in a .OBJ object file or .LIB library file.

The Microsoft C++ project feature can be used to combine several source or object files into a single executable file. This permits files provided by one vendor to be combined with user-written files to create a final application.

Questions

1. Breaking a program into several files is desirable because
   a. some files don't need to be recompiled each time
   b. a program can be divided functionally
   c. files can be marketed in object form
   d. each programmer can work on a separate file
2. A .H file is attached to a .CPP file using the _____.
3. A .OBJ file is attached to a .CPP file using _____.
4. A *project* file
   a. examines the contents of the files in the project
   b. examines the dates of the files in the project
   c. contains instructions for compiling and linking
   d. contains definitions for C++ variables
5. A group of related classes, supplied as a separate product, is often called a

   _____.

6. True or false: A header file may need to be accessed by more than one source file in a project.
7. The so-called private files of a class library
   a. require a password
   b. can be accessed by **friend** functions
   c. help prevent code from being pirated
   d. contain object code
8. True or false: Class libraries can be more powerful than function libraries.

9. To create a project file, you must
   a. close all other project files in your directory
   b. put all the relevent filenames into a project file
   c. put the dates of the relevant files into a project file
   d. start by selecting *Open Project* from the Project menu
10. The public files in a class library usually contain
   a. constant definitions
   b. member function definitions
   c. class declarations
   d. variable definitions

PROJECTS

Unfortunately, we don't have room in this book for exercises that involve the kind of larger programs discussed in this chapter. However, here are some suggestions for projects you may wish to pursue on your own.

1. Using the **Window** and related classes from the CALC example, write a new **main()** program that models a hexadecimal calculator. Or, create a scientific calculator with trigonometric (sine, cosine, and tangent), exponential, and similar function keys.

2. Create member functions to perform subtraction and division for the **verylong** class in the VERYLONG example. These should overload the – and **/** operators. Warning: There's some work involved here. When you include subtraction, you must assume that any **verylong** can be negative as well as positive. This complicates the addition and multiplication routines, which must do different things depending on the signs of the numbers.

   To see one way to perform division, do a long-division example by hand and write down every step. Then incorporate these steps into a division member function. You'll find that you need some comparisons, so you'll need to write a comparison routine, among other things.

3. Add a pump class to the PIPES example, so you can model water systems that don't rely on gravity. Create a water system that incorporates such a class. (Hint: A pump should derive its input from a tank.)

4. Create a class library that models something you're interested in. Create a **main()** or "client" program to test it. Market your class library and become rich and famous.

CHAPTER 160

MICROSOFT FOUNDATION CLASSES

TIME, DATE, AND STRING CLASSES

FILE CLASSES

DATA-STRUCTURE CLASSES: ARRAYS, LISTS, AND MAPS

EXCEPTION CLASSES

SERIALIZING OBJECTS TO DISK

DEBUGGING AIDS

Microsoft C/C++ comes with a powerful library of pre-written C++ classes called the *Microsoft Foundation Classes* (MFC). These classes serve a variety of purposes. There is a string class similar to (but more complete than) the ones we developed in previous chapters, and time and date classes to simplify operations on these quantities. There are classes to help with debugging, and classes that allow you to easily store objects to disk. Perhaps most interestingly for our discussion, there is a set of *data-structure* classes—arrays, lists, and maps—that simplify the creation of common data structures in your program.

Besides being useful in their own right, you will find that examining the Foundation classes will increase your understanding of classes in general, and demonstrate how you can use class libraries written by other vendors in your own programs.

Our intention in this chapter is not to present a complete description of every class in the Foundation class library, but to cover a representative sample, so that you will get an idea of how they work and what they're used for. The majority of the classes discussed in the MFC documentation are related to Microsoft Windows. Windows programming is beyond the scope of this book, but the classes we do discuss can be used in both DOS and Windows environments.

PROGRAMMING ENVIRONMENT

Before you can use the Microsoft Foundation classes, you need to make some minor changes in your programming environment. These are the use of a new library file, and the addition of two new directives to your source file.

LIBRARY FILE

The Microsoft Foundation classes all require the use of a separate library file that contains the member functions. If you told the installation program to include the Foundation classes when you first installed Microsoft C/C++, then the appropriate files should be available. If you didn't, you will need to run the installation program again, asking it specifically to install the MFC library files.

There are potentially quite a number of these files, usually stored in a directory with a name like \C700\MFC\LIB. These files all have the letters AFX in the middle of their names. In the C/C++ compiler, this is followed by a C, so we have AFXC. These four letters are preceded by a letter indicating the memory model, and followed by either R, indicating a real-mode DOS program, or W, indicating a Windows program. A letter D appended to all this means a DEBUG version of the library file. Thus MAFXCR.LIB is the Medium model Foundation class library for DOS development, and SAFXCWD.LIB is the debugging version of the Small model library for Windows programs.

Since we are discussing DOS programs in this book, and since our example programs require only the Small memory model, most of the example programs in this chapter can be developed using SAFXCR.LIB. When we get to the section on debugging at the end of this chapter, you'll need the SAFXCRD.LIB library file.

We describe in Appendix C how to use the Project feature in the Programmer's WorkBench to create a program using nonstandard library files. Simply include the SAFXCR.LIB (or SAFXCRD.LIB) file in your project, along with your .CPP source file, and you're ready to go. If you fail to place the library file in the project, you'll receive a lot of "unresolved external" messages from the linker when you build your program.

Microsoft provides the source code for the Foundation class libraries, in the form of .CPP files. If you're curious, you can examine these files in the \C700\MFC\SRC directory. Many .CPP source files are combined into a single .LIB file; that is what the installation program does when you request the building of a Foundation class library.

Header Files

All programs that use the Microsoft Foundation Class Library must **#include** a header file to provide specifications, prototypes, and constants for these classes. The general-purpose workhorse of these files (for non-Windows programs) is AFX.H. This file works with all the Foundation classes except the data-structure classes, which require the AFXCOLL.H file.

The AFX.H and AFXCOLL.H files must be preceded by a define statement indicating whether you are developing a DOS program or a Windows program. These constants are **_DOS** and **_WINDOWS**. Since we're developing DOS programs, a source file that uses the Foundation classes must include the lines

```
#define _dos
#include <afx.h>
```

Notice that the order is important: **_DOS** must be defined before AFX.H is included. (If you're using the command-line compiler, **_DOS** is usually defined with the **/D** compiler flag rather than in the listing.)

STRINGS

We've already experimented with various versions of a string class. The goal of such a class is to simplify programming the rather cumbersome C++ style string, which is treated in most ways as an array of type `char`. By defining a new string class, we can overload operators like the equal sign (=) to permit string assignment, and add various other useful functions.

The Microsoft implementation of a string class is called `CString`. (All the classes in the Foundation class library start with the letter C.)

Our example program, CSTRING.CPP, creates several objects of class `CString`, and exercises them using a variety of `CString` member functions. Note that in this book the word "string" in program listings and elsewhere often means a normal C/C++ string: that is, an array of type `char` terminated with a 0, as opposed to a `CString`, as in comments like "convert `CString` to string."

```cpp
// cstring.cpp
// demonstrates CString class
#define _DOS                    // must use before #include <afx.h>
#include <afx.h>                // for foundation classes
#include <iostream.h>           // for cout

void main()
    {
    CString cs1, cs2;           // create two CStrings

    cs1 = "Happy ";             // convert string to CString
    cs2 = "New Year!!";
    cs1 += cs2;                 // overloaded += for concatenation
    cout << cs1;                // convert CString to string

    cout << "\nLength="
         << cs1.GetLength();                    // like strlen()
    cout << "\nLeftmost 10 chars: "
         << cs1.Left(10);                       // like BASIC Left$
    cout << "\nRightmost 10 char: "
         << cs1.Right(10);                      // like BASIC Right$
    cout << "\nMiddle 10 chars: "
         << cs1.Mid(3, 10);                     // like BASIC Mid$
    cout << "\nFound \"New\" at "
         << cs1.Find("New");                    // like strstr()
    cout << "\nFirst match of y or w at "
         << cs1.FindOneOf("yw");                // like strcspn()
    cout << "\ncs1[4] = "
         << cs1[4];                             // get char
    cs1.SetAt(10, 'B');                         // insert char
    cout << endl << cs1;
    cs1.Empty();                               // zero length
    cout << "\nLength=" << cs1.GetLength();
    }
```

Here's the result of running CSTRING:

```
Happy New Year!!
Length=16
Leftmost 10 chars: Happy New
Rightmost 10 char: New Year!!
Middle 10 chars: py New Yea
Found "New" at 6
First match of y or w at 4
cs1[4] = y
Happy New Bear!!
Length=0
```

We create two CString objects, and then set them equal to ordinary C++ strings. That is, the line

```
cs1 = "Happy ";
```

causes the overloaded assignment operator in the CString object cs1 to copy the string "Happy " into itself. We could have achieved the same effect by initializing cs1 to the string when it was created, using the overloaded copy constructor, with a statement like

```
CString cs1 = "Happy ";
```

Next, the overloaded assignment operator += is used to concatenate cs2 to cs1. The result is a CString object with the value "Happy New Year!!". When we say

```
cout << cs1;
```

the cs1 object converts itself to a normal C++ string, so it can be displayed by cout. Note how easy it is to convert back and forth between CString objects and normal strings.

A member function GetLength() is used to return the length of the resulting CString object cs2.

We exercise three member functions whose format has been borrowed from the BASIC programming language. These member functions, Left(), Right(), and Mid(), return a CString object whose value is a specified number of characters on the left, on the right, or in the middle, of the original CString.

We use the Find() member function to look for the first occurrence of a particular string, in this case "New", and we use the FindOneOf() function to find the first occurrence of either 'y' or 'w'.

The overloaded [] operator can be used to extract a single character from a CString, just as it can from an ordinary string. In the example, the character at index 4 turns out to be 'y'. We use the SetAt() member function to change the 'Y' in "Year" to a 'B'. Finally, we empty the CString object cs1 with the member function Empty(), and print out its length to show that it's empty.

We have not demonstrated all the member functions for CStrings, but we've shown enough to give the flavor of this class. You can also perform comparisons (to arrange CStrings in alphabetical order), convert CStrings to uppercase, and perform many other actions.

You can use `CString` practically anyplace you could use an ordinary string, but you can do more things, and do them more conveniently, with `CStrings`. One thing the `CString` class does not do is to economize on memory when more than one object has the same value. We demonstrated a string class in the STRIMEM program in Chapter 13 that uses a single string when one `String` object is set equal to another, but `CString` objects don't attempt this nicety.

TIME AND DATE

The `CTime` class is a Foundation class that stores both a time and a date value. You can set the time and date in various ways, retrieve the year, month, day, hour, minute, and second, and display the date and time in different formats. A companion class, `CTimeSpan`, stores the difference between two `CTime` values. It is far more convenient to use these two classes for operations on time and date values than doing it "by hand" or trying to create your own classes.

Our demonstration program, CTIME, creates several `CTime` objects and a `CTimeSpan` object, and applies various member functions to them.

```
// ctime.cpp
// demonstrates CTime class
#define _DOS                    // must use before #include <afx.h>
#include <afx.h>                // for foundation classes
#include <iostream.h>           // for cout

void main()
    {
    CTime t1(1990, 3, 11, 10, 30, 0); // 10:30 am, March 11, 1990

    cout << "\nt1 date is "
         << t1.GetMonth() << "/"       // functions get
         << t1.GetDay()   << "/"       // individual
         << t1.GetYear();              // values
    cout << "\nt1 time is "
         << t1.GetHour() << ":"
         << t1.GetMinute() << ":"
         << t1.GetSecond();

    CTime t2 = CTime::GetCurrentTime();  // set to system clock

    CString cstr = t2.Format("%c");    // display time and date
    cout << "\nt2 date and time are " << cstr;

    if(t1 < t2)                        // comparison
        cout << "\nt1 is earlier than t2";

    CTimeSpan span;                    // define a time span
    span = t2 - t1;                    // difference of two times
```

```
cout << "\nSpan in days = "     << span.GetDays()
     << "\nSpan in hours = "    << span.GetTotalHours()
     << "\nSpan in minutes = " << span.GetTotalMinutes();
```

Here's the output from the CTIME program. (The numbers will be different when you run the program, since some of the data is the current time and date from your computer's system clock.)

```
t1 date is 3/11/1990
t1 time is 10:30:0
t2 date and time are 03/19/92 11:13:11
t1 is earlier than t2
Span in days = 739
Span in hours = 17736
Span in minutes = 1064203
```

The program creates a `CTime` object and initializes it to a fixed date and time: 10:30 a.m., March 11, 1990. Because `CTime` objects are stored in only 4 bytes, you are limited to years in the range 1900 to 2036. Months run from 1 to 12, days from 1 to 31, hours (in 24-hour time) from 0 to 23, minutes and seconds from 0 to 59. In the program we use `GetMonth()` and similar member functions to print out the various values of the time and date. These functions simply return the appropriate value.

We use the `GetCurrentTime()` member function to get the current date and time from the system clock, which we use to initialize another `CTime` value, `t2`. We display this new date and time using another member function, `Format()`. This is a two-step process. First, `Format()` returns a `CString` object that includes the date and/or time in various formats. You specify the format using an argument to the function. There are quite a number of these arguments, which can all be seen in the description of the function `strftime()` in the Microsoft *Run-Time Library Reference*. The most useful of these arguments is probably `%c`, which gives the local date and time; but you can also specify the year, day, and so on separately, so you can print the date and time information in any format you like. Once we have a `CString` object that contains the time and date info, we then display it with `cout`.

We use a comparison operator to compare two `CTime` values, and then we create a `CTimeSpan` object, `span`, which we set equal to the difference between the two `CTime` values, using overloaded assignment and subtraction operators. Finally, we print out the value of the `CTimeSpan` object. Note that the `CTimeSpan` member functions don't print out absolute times, but the difference between times. Thus the number of hours can greatly exceed 24.

FILES

The Foundation class library contains several classes that model disk files. The `CFile` base class supports low-level (binary) file operations that treat data as a buffer full of bytes. A derived class, `CStdioFile`, handles formatted data such as text files. We'll look at both these classes. A third class, CMemFile, allows you to treat memory as a disk file. This is useful for specialized situations like transferring data from one application to another on the Windows clipboard, but we won't be concerned with it here.

THE CFile CLASS

The CFile class provides a set of member functions for handling low-level unbuffered binary-only disk I/O, where data is treated as an unformatted group of bytes. (C programmers will find it analogous to the low-level C library file functions like _open(), _read(), and so on.) But the real usefulness of CFile lies in its integration with the rest of the MFC library. We'll find out more about this when we discuss serialization (saving objects to disk) and exceptions, later in this chapter.

Our example program creates a CFile object, writes some data to it, and then reads it back. The data is eight arbitrary integers. Here's the listing for CFILE.CPP:

```
// cfile.cpp
// demonstrates CFile class
#define _DOS                         // must use before #include <afx.h>
#include <afx.h>                     // for foundation classes
#include <iostream.h>                // for cout

void main()
   {
   const int number = 8;            // number of data items
   const int size = number * 2;     // size of file (bytes)
   int arr1[number] =               // array of data items
      { 12, 23, 34, 45, 56, 67, 78, 89 };
   int arr2[number];                // empty array

   CFile cf;                        // create CFile object
   cf.Open("integers.dat",          // open for writing
           CFile::modeCreate | CFile::modeWrite);
   cf.Write(arr1, size);            // write arr1 to file
   cf.Close();                      // close file

   if( !cf.Open("integers.dat",     // open for reading
                CFile::modeRead) )
      cout << "\nCould not open file";
   else                             // open successful
      {
      cf.Read(arr2, size);          // read into arr2
      for(int j=0; j<number; j++)   // display arr2
         cout << arr2[j] << " ";
      cf.Close();                   // close file
      }
   }
```

If all goes well, the data read back from the file is the same as that written. The program displays the data it has read, so the output should look like this:

```
12 23 34 45 56 67 78 89
```

The program uses a single **CFile** object, **cf**, for both reading and writing (although not at the same time). The **Open()** member function opens the file, using a variety of *style flags* to specify the characteristics of the file. These are are shown in Table 16-1.

You can combine style flags with the bitwise OR operator (**|**), as shown in the listing. The **Open()** member function needs at least one style flag. As with most systems of file functions, you can open the file in read-only, write-only, or read-write modes. The *sharing modes* govern the access of other processes to your file. This is important in a multitasking system such as Windows, or if you're running the SHARE utility to control access to your file system.

You may want to derive a class of your own from the **CFile** class. With this in mind, **CFile** contains various features not intended to be used in the class itself, but to be helpful for classes derived from it. One of these is the ability to specify binary or text files. (**CFiles** themselves are binary.) Style flags provide this option.

The **Open()** function returns false (0) if the open was not successful. We make use of this when we open the file for reading; if it doesn't exist, or some other problem arises, we print an error message and exit. We didn't check the return value when we opened the file for writing, since you can almost always create a file, but a serious program should check the return values of all file-related programs.

	TABLE 16-1
	Style Flags for CFile::Open()
Style flag	**Action**
CFile::modeCreate	Create new file, or truncate existing file to 0 length
CFile::modeRead	Open file in read-only mode
CFile::modeReadWrite	Open file in read-write mode
CFile::modeWrite	Open file in write-only mode
CFile::modeNoInherit	File can't be inherited by child process
CFile::shareDenyNone	Other processes can read or write to file
CFile::share DenyRead	Other processes cannot read from file
CFile::shareDenyWrite	Other processes cannot write to file
CFile::shareExclusive	Other processes can neither read nor write to file
CFile::shareCompat	Other processes can open file any number of times
CFile::typeText	Text mode (used in derived classes only)
CFile::typeBinary	Binary mode (used in derived classes only)

The Write() and Read() member functions each take two arguments: the address of the data buffer, and the size of the buffer in bytes.

The CFile class has other member functions we don't show in the example. You can duplicate, remove, and rename files, move the file pointer around in the file, lock all or part of the file to prevent access by other processes, and take various other actions.

THE CStdioFile CLASS

The CStdioFile class is derived from the CFile class, and inherits much of its behavior. However, it operates on buffered files, and can read and write text files, while CFile is designed for binary files. CStdioFile plays a role similar to the stream classes we've been using all along (such as the insertion and extraction operators << and >>), but it can make use of exceptions. (Remember that in text files a '\n' character in memory is stored on disk as two characters, a carriage-return and linefeed; in binary files this expansion does not take place.)

Most of the member functions for CStdioFile are the same as those in CFile. A few functions exist in CFile but not in CStdioFile; and several, including ReadString() and WriteString(), exist in CStdioFile but not in CFile. Our next example program demonstrates these two string-oriented functions. Here's the listing for CSTDIO.CPP:

```
// cstdio.cpp
// demonstrates CStdioFile class
#define _DOS                    // must use before #include <afx.h>
#include <afx.h>                // for foundation classes
#include <iostream.h>           // for cout

void main()
   {
   const int number = 6;        // number of data items
   const int size = 20;         // size of input array
   char *arr1[number] = { "aardvark\n", "baboon\n", "capybara\n",
                          "dingo\n", "earwig\n", "flamingo\n" };
   char arr2[size];             // empty string array

   CStdioFile cf;               // create CStdioFile object
   cf.Open("names.dat",         // open it for writing
      CFile::modeCreate | CFile::modeWrite);
   for(int j=0; j<number; j++)  // for each string,
      cf.WriteString( arr1[j] ); // write string to file
   cf.Close();                  // close file
                                // open file for reading
   if( !cf.Open("names.dat", CFile::modeRead) )
      { cout << "\nCould not open file for reading"; exit(1); }
                                // read into arr2
   while( cf.ReadString(arr2, size-1) != NULL )  // until EOF
      cout << arr2;             // display arr2
   cf.Close();                  // close file
   }
```

This program writes six strings consisting of animal names to a disk file, and then reads them back and displays them. Here's the output for CSTDIO:

```
aardvark
baboon
capybara
dingo
earwig
flamingo
```

As you can with CFile objects, you can perform the usual file-related operations on CStdioFile objects, such as reading and writing numerical data, and using Seek() and related functions to manipulate the file pointer.

THE DATA-STRUCTURE CLASSES

Most programs involve the storage of a number of similar data items—such as numbers, structures, strings, or objects—in some kind of data structure. Creating a suitable storage structure is often an important part of a programming effort. In C++ the difficulty of creating such structures can be significantly reduced by using pre-written classes that incorporate the functionality for the storage structure you need. The *data-structure* Foundation classes are Microsoft's approach to this problem. They constitute one of the most useful and interesting groups of classes in the Microsoft Foundation library. (They are sometimes called "collection" classes, since they hold collections of objects.)

There are three basic types of data-structure classes: arrays, lists, and maps. You already know something about arrays because they're one of the fundamental aspects of the C++ language. We touched on the subject of lists—also called "linked lists"—in Chapter 12. A list uses a chain of pointers to connect one data element to the next. Maps are another kind of storage structure. They provide a way to look up a data item, given a short key, in the same way you look up a definition in a dictionary using a word.

Each of these kinds of storage structure has advantages and disadvantages. It is easy to access an element in an array if you know its index number, but it's difficult to insert a new element into the middle of the array (since you need to move all the elements above it). It's easy to insert a new element into a list, but not so easy to access a particular element, since you need to chain along the list, examining each element in turn to see if it's the one you want. And neither an array nor a list is very efficient if you want to quickly access a particular data element using a key value. In this case the map is the storage structure of choice.

Microsoft provides several variations for each of these three kinds of data-structure. In this section we'll look at some representative data-structure classes.

HEADER FILE

Previous programs that used the Foundation class library required the header file AFX.H. For the data-structure classes, you need a different file: AFXCOLL.H. This file includes AFX.H, so you don't need to include both of them. Like AFX.H, AFXCOLL.H must be preceded by a statment that defines _DOS. You use the same libary file as with the other classes in the MFC library, probably SAFXCR.LIB.

ARRAY CLASSES

Arrays are such a versitile kind of data structure that they are built into most languages. Using an index value, they provide very fast access to any element in the array.

However, normal arrays in C++ suffer from a major disadvantage: you must know, before you create an array, how many data items will be placed in it. This can lead to inefficient use of memory, since an array must be sized to hold the largest number of items that will ever be placed in it. Most of the time the array will be partially empty. This means there is less room for the rest of your program. In an operating environment like Windows, where more than one program can reside in memory at once, it means there is less room for other programs as well.

The Microsoft Foundation classes solve this problem by providing classes of "growable" arrays—arrays that can be expanded or contracted at any time after they have been created. Such an array uses memory more efficiently because it need never be much larger than the amount of data in it.

Each array class in the Foundation class library is capable of holding a different kind of data. These classes are shown in Table 16-2.

TABLE 16-2
Array Classes in the MFC Library

Class	Data type
CByteArray	bytes
CWordArray	words
CDWordArray	double words
CStringArray	CString objects
CObArray	pointers to CObject
CPtrArray	pointers to void

The array classes are all quite similar in operation. They use the same set of member functions, and operate in the same way. Thus an example for one array class shows how all the classes work.

Our first example program is very simple. It creates an array of class `CWordArray`, puts three data items in the array, and then retrieves the items and displays them. The data items are type `Word`, which is, in the present version of the compiler, a 16-bit unsigned value (`WORD` is defined to be type `unsigned short` in AFX.H.) Here's the listing for WDARRAY.CPP:

```
// wdarray.cpp
// demonstrates CWordArray class

#define _DOS               // for afxcoll.h
#include <afxcoll.h>       // for data-structure classes
#include <iostream.h>      // for cout

void main()
   {
   CWordArray cwa;                  // define a CWordArray object

   cwa.Add(16);                     // add three elements to array
   cwa.Add(25);
   cwa.Add(36);

   cout << endl << cwa.GetAt(0);    // access numbers in array
   cout << endl << cwa.GetAt(1);
   cout << endl << cwa.GetAt(2);
   }
```

Notice that we don't need to specify the size of the array when we create it. It starts out with 0 length, and expands as you add elements using the `Add()` member function. This function inserts each element at the end of the array, as shown in Figure 16-1. The `GetAt()` member function reads it back, using an index value as a parameter. The output of WDARRAY is

```
16
25
36
```

You can also use the traditional bracket syntax to access the elements. The next example, WDARRAY2, shows how this looks:

```
// wdarray2.cpp
// CWordArray class using bracket notation

#define _DOS               // for afxcoll.h
#include <afxcoll.h>       // for data-structure classes
#include <iostream.h>      // for cout

void main()
   {
```

```
CWordArray cwa;                 // define a CWordArray object
cwa.SetSize(3);                 // size the array

cwa[0] = 16;                    // insert three elements
cwa[1] = 25;
cwa[2] = 36;

cout << endl << cwa[0];         // access numbers in array
cout << endl << cwa[1];
cout << endl << cwa[2];
}
```

Notice that the bracket operator will not expand an array as **Add()** will; it will only access an exisiting element. Thus if we use brackets on the left of the equal sign to insert data into the array, we must insert data into an already existing element. This is more analogous to the traditional array syntax, where the array size is fixed when it is created. However, we can set the size of the array to a new value at any time with the **SetSize()** member function.

When you use the **Add()** member function, you add an element in the next available location. If the last element in an existing array is at 4, for example, **Add()** will put the next element at 5. What do you do if you want to add an element at 20? You can add elements beyond the end of an existing array using the **SetAtGrow()** member function. The next example, WDARRAY3, demonstrates this as well as several other functions.

FIGURE 16-1
Operation of the Add() Function

```cpp
// wdarray3.cpp
// demonstrates SetAtGrow(), etc. in CWprdArray class

#define _DOS                    // for afxcoll.h
#include <afxcoll.h>            // for data-structure classes
#include <iostream.h>           // for cout

void main()
  {
  CWordArray cwa;              // define a CWordArray object  // 0

  cwa.Add(900);                // add numbers to array        // 1
  cwa.Add(901);                                               // 2
                               // access numbers in array
  cout << endl << "cwa[0]=" << cwa[0];
  cout << endl << "cwa[1]=" << cwa[1];
  cwa[1] = 911;                // overwrite existing element  // 2
  cout << endl << "cwa[1]=" << cwa[1];

// cwa[3] = 903;               // don't do this: beyond end

  cwa.SetAtGrow(3, 913);       // add element beyond end       // 4
  cout << endl << "cwa[3]=" << cwa[3];

  cout << endl << "\nsize of cwa is " << cwa.GetSize();        // 4
  for(int j=0; j<cwa.GetSize(); j++)
    cout << endl << "cwa[" << j << "]=" << cwa[j];

  cwa.InsertAt(2, 912);        // insert in the middle

  cout << endl << "\nsize of cwa is " << cwa.GetSize();        // 5
  for(j=0; j<cwa.GetSize(); j++)
    cout << endl << "cwa[" << j << "]=" << cwa[j];

  cwa.RemoveAll();             // give back the memory
  cout << endl << "\nsize of cwa is " << cwa.GetSize();        // 0
  }
```

We can use array notation to overwrite existing elements, just as we can with a normal array. In the program we do this after putting elements in the array with **Add()**, as we've seen before. However, as the commented-out statement shows, you can't use the bracket operator to insert an element into the array beyond its end. To do this, we use the **SetAtGrow()** function, which takes both an index and a data value as parameters. This function expands the array to the size specified, and inserts the data element at that point. If there are unfilled positions in between, they are filled with 0s. This is shown in Figure 16-2.

We use the **GetSize()** member function to report the size of the array, and then again in a **for** loop to print out the array contents.

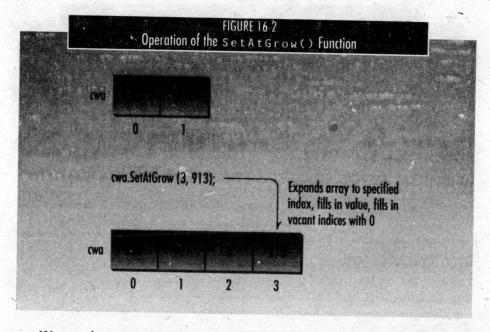

FIGURE 16-2
Operation of the SetAtGrow() Function

cwa

0   1

cwa.SetAtGrow (3, 913);

Expands array to specified
index, fills in value, fills in
vacant indices with 0

cwa

0   1   2   3

We can also insert data in the middle of the array, causing the data in higher positions to be moved upward, and the array expanded accordingly to make room. This is done with the **InsertAt()** member function.

Finally, the **RemoveAll()** member function removes all the elements from an array and reduces it to 0 size.

LISTS

An array works very well if you don't need to insert new elements in the middle of the array. Such insertions require moving all the elements beyond the insertion point. This is possible, as we saw in the example above, but it can be quite time-consuming for large arrays. The linked list, on the other hand, handles insertions very quickly. As we saw in the LINKLIST example in Chapter 12, inserting a new element involves only changing the pointer in the preceding element to point to the newly inserted element. When such insertions must be made frequently, the linked list (also called simply a "list") is far more efficient than an array.

The Microsoft list classes are doubly-linked lists, meaning that both the beginning (the "head") and end (the "tail") of the list are accessible, and you can chain along the list in either the forward or backward direction. Thus each item on the list has a pointer not only to the next item but to the preceding one, as shown in Figure 16-3.

Microsoft also assigns each list element a *position value*. This is used for chaining through the list, and also as a way to remember particular elements and reference them quickly. The position value gives the list some of the flexibility of an array, although—if you don't know the position value for a particular element—it is still a slow process to chain through the list looking for a particular element.

FIGURE 16-3
A Doubly-Linked List

There are list classes for three different kinds of data, as shown in Table 16-3.

Iterating through Lists

The member functions for all three list classes are similar and behave in the same way. To demonstrate their use, we'll show how to create a `CStringList` list and use it for `CString` storage. Here's the listing for STRLST:

```
// strlst.cpp
// demonstrates CStringList

#define _DOS                     // for afxcoll.h
#include <afxcoll.h>             // for data-structure classes
#include <iostream.h>            // for cout

void main()
    {
    CStringList csl;             // define a CStringList object

    CString s1("ants");          // define some CString objects
    CString s2("birds");
    CString s3("cats");
    CString s4("dogs");

    csl.AddHead(s1);             // put strings on head of list
    csl.AddHead(s2);
    csl.AddTail(s3);             // put strings on tail of list
    csl.AddTail(s4);

    POSITION pos;                // pointer to list elements
    CString s;                   // empty string

    pos = csl.GetHeadPosition(); // set pointer to list head
    while( pos != NULL )         // iterate through the list
        {
        s = csl.GetNext(pos);    // get next list element
        cout << endl << s;       // display it
        }
```

```
    cout << "\nNumber of elements = " << csl.GetCount();
    pos = csl.GetTailPosition();  // set pointer to list tail
    while( pos != NULL )          // iterate through the list
       {
       s = csl.GetPrev(pos);      // get previous list element
       cout << endl << s;         // display it
       }
    }
```

This program creates a CStringList object called cs1, and four CString objects to put on the list. It adds two CStrings to the head of the list, and two to the tail, using the member functions AddHead() and AddTail(). Figure 16-4 shows how this looks.

Next the program iterates through the list, examining each element in turn and printing out its value. It does this twice, once in the forward direction, and once going backward. In the forward direction we start with the GetHeadPosition() function, which returns a POSITION value, pos. We use this value to iterate through the list with the GetNext() member function. Each time this function is called, the value of pos is advanced to the next list element. When pos becomes NULL, the end of the list has been reached.

The process is similar in the reverse direction, except that the GetTailPosition() and GetPrev() member functions are used. The GetCount() function returns the number of elements in the list. Here's the output from STRLST:

```
birds
ants
cats
dogs
Number of elements = 4
dogs
cats
ants
birds
```

The list is displayed from head to tail, then the size is displayed, and then the list is displayed again from tail to head. Notice that lists use a last-in-first-out protocol: We put "ants" on the list before "birds", but "birds" is printed out first (at least

| TABLE 16-3 | |
| List Classes in the MFC Library | |
Class	Data type
CStringList	CStrings
CObList	pointers to CObject
CPtrList	pointers to void

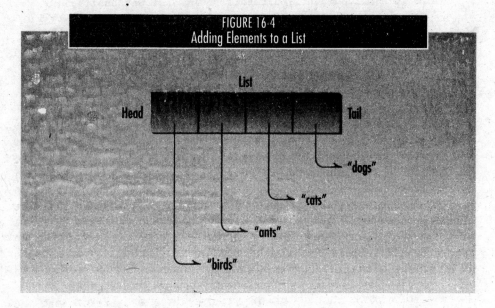

FIGURE 16-4
Adding Elements to a List

when we start from the head of the list) because **AddHead()** inserts each new element *before* those already on the list. (Similarly **AddTail()** inserts each new element at the end of the list.)

Before we leave the subject of iterating through lists, we should note that it is dangerous to change anything in the list while the iteration process is going on. Finish the iteration before altering the list.

Finding List Elements

It's also possible to chain through the list looking for a specific element. In fact, this is the only way to find a specific element, unless its position value is already known. The next example program shows how to find a particular element on the list, and also how to insert a new element. Here's the listing for STRLST2:

```
// strlst2.cpp
// demonstrates CStringList Find() function

#define _DOS                    // for afxcoll.h
#include <afxcoll.h>            // for data-structure classes
#include <iostream.h>           // for cout

void main()
    {
    CStringList csl;            // define a CStringList object

    CString s1("ants");         // define CString objects
    CString s2("birds");
    CString s3("cats");
    CString s4("dogs");
```

```
   csl.AddTail(s1);              // put strings on tail of list
   csl.AddTail(s2);
   csl.AddTail(s4);

   POSITION pos, pos2;           // pointers to list elements

   pos = csl.GetHeadPosition();  // set pointer to list head
   while( pos != NULL )          // iterate through the list
      cout << endl << csl.GetNext(pos);  // display items

   pos = csl.GetHeadPosition();  // look for "dogs"
   if( (pos2=csl.Find("dogs", pos) ) != NULL )
      cout << "\nFound " << csl.GetAt(pos2);   // (pos2 remembers
   else                                        //      "dogs")
      cout << "\nNot found.";

   csl.InsertBefore(pos2, s3);   // insert "cats" before "dogs"

   pos = csl.GetHeadPosition();  // set pointer to list head
   while( pos != NULL )          // iterate through the list
      cout << endl << csl.GetNext(pos);  // display item
   }
```

This program starts out much as STRLST did, by iterating through the list to display all the items (although here we've combined the two statements in the `while` loop into one). However, in STRLST2 we next search for the list element "dogs", using the `Find()` member function. This function returns the `POSITION` value of the desired element if it is found, and `NULL` otherwise.

Once the "dogs" element is found, the program uses its `POSITION` value, stored in `pos2`, to insert another element, "cats", into the list just before "dogs". Here's the output for STRLST2:

```
ants
birds
dogs
Found dogs
ants
birds
cats
dogs
```

Putting Persons on Lists

So far we've shown data-structure classes used as storage for simple data types such as `WORD`s and `CString`s. `CString`s are objects, of course, but they are already part of the Foundation classes, and there are specific data-structure objects, such as `CStringList`, to hold them. Is it also possible to store objects from classes that we have defined ourselves? As it turns out, it is. The capability to handle user-defined classes is one of the important strengths of the data-structure classes.

There is only one small catch. If you are going to store objects of your own class in a data-structure, this class must be derived from the Foundation class **CObject**. The **CObject** class is actually the base class for almost all the Foundation classes. As we'll see later, this makes possible the serialization (disk storage) of entire data structures, among other benefits. For the moment, however, think back to the discussion of virtual functions in Chapter 13. A key point there was that pointers to a derived class were type-compatible with pointers to the base class. This made it possible to put pointers to objects of different classes in the same array, and operate on them with the same member function, provided they were all descended from the same base class. For this same reason, all the objects stored in the data-structure classes must be derived from **CObject**.

Our next example uses the **Person** class that we've seen before in previous chapters, and a list of type **CObList**. Here's the listing for PERSLST:

```
// perslst.cpp
// CObList and user-defined Person class

#define _DOS                        // for afxcoll.h
#include <afxcoll.h>                // for data-structure classes
#include <iostream.h>               // for cout
#include <string.h>                 // for strlen(), strcpy()

class Person : public CObject       // user-defined class
   {                                // derived from CObject
   private:
      char* name;
      int age;
   public:
      Person()                                // 0-arg constructor
         {
         name = new char;                     // make a zero-length
         name[0] = '\0';                      // string
         age = 0;
         }
      Person(const char* str, const int a)    // 2-arg constructor
         {
         name = new char[ strlen(str)+1 ];    // use name and age
         strcpy(name, str);                   // passed as
         age = a;                             // arguments
         }
      ~Person()                               // destructor
         { delete name; }
      void DisplayPerson()                    // display
         { cout << "\nname=" << name << ", age=" << age; }
      char* GetName()
         { return name; }
   };
```

```
void main()
   {
   CObList csl;          // define a list

   Person* p1 = new Person("Bart", 23);    // create
   Person* p2 = new Person("Casey", 25);   // Persons
   Person* p3 = new Person("Red", 32);
   Person* p4 = new Person("Slade", 27);

   csl.AddTail(p1);              // put Persons (except "Red")
   csl.AddTail(p2);              // on tail of list
   csl.AddTail(p4);

   POSITION pos, pos2;           // pointers to list elements
   Person* p;                    // pointer to Person

   cout << "\n\nList has " << csl.GetCount() << " members";

   // display the list elements
   pos = csl.GetHeadPosition();  // set pointer to list head
   while( pos != NULL )          // iterate through the list
      {
      p = (Person*)csl.GetNext(pos);  // get the next object
      p->DisplayPerson();             // display it
      }

   // search for known member and insert member before it
   pos = csl.GetHeadPosition();  // set pointer to list head
   pos2 = csl.Find(p4, pos);     // find "Slade" member
   csl.InsertBefore(pos2, p3);   // insert "Red" before "Slade"

   cout << "\n\nList has " << csl.GetCount() << " members";

   pos = csl.GetHeadPosition();  // display list
   while( pos != NULL )
      {
      p = (Person*)csl.GetNext(pos);
      p->DisplayPerson();
      }

   // search for member whose pointer is not known
   pos = csl.GetHeadPosition();
   while(pos != NULL)
      {                              // look for name "Casey"
      p = (Person*)csl.GetNext(pos);
      if( _stricmp( p->GetName(), "Casey") == 0 )
         {
         cout << "\n\nFound: ";
         p->DisplayPerson();
         }
      }
   }  // end main
```

This program creates four objects of the `Person` class, and puts pointers to three of them on the tail of the list (note that the third person, "Red", is left out). Then it displays all the list elements, using the same approach as in the last two examples. We've already seen how to search for a particular list element if its value is known. In this program we know the value of the pointer to the "Slade" object, so we use this pointer value to find the `POSITION` value of this object on the list. Then, using the `POSITION` value and the `InsertBefore()` function, we insert the "Red" object just before "Slade". The operation of the program is shown in Figure 16-5.

Suppose we want to search for an object that has a particular characteristic, but whose pointer value is not known. In this case we must iterate through the list, checking to see if each element has the desired characteristic. In the last section of

FIGURE 16-5
List in the PERSLST Program

PERSLST we look for the object with the name "Casey". This involves iterating through the list the same way we did when displaying the list elements, except that we use the `GetName()` member function of the `Person` class, rather than `DisplayPerson()`. We can then compare the returned name with the name we're looking for. Here's the output for PERSLST:

```
List has 3 members
name=Bart, age=23
name=Casey, age=25
name=Slade, age=27

List has 4 members
name=Bart, age=23
name=Casey, age=25
name=Red, age=32
name=Slade, age=27

Found:
name=Casey, age=25
```

MAPS

The third kind of storage system in the Microsoft data-structure classes is the *map*. Maps, often called "dictionaries," are useful when it's natural to access data elements using a *key*. That is, you know the key, and you want to access data related to the key. Typically, the key is a string (like "aardvark") but it can also be a numerical value or a pointer.

A map is implemented using a *hash table*. Hash tables use an algorithm to transform a key into the address where the corresponding data is stored. Since the hashing algorithm can be executed quickly, looking up a partcular data element—assuming you know the key—is very fast. It's also easy to insert a new element in a map, since the other data elements don't need to be rearranged. On the other hand, maps aren't efficient if you want to iterate through all the elements in order; in this case you'll need an array or linked list. Figure 16-6 shows a map.

There are map classes for three different kinds of keys: pointers, `CStrings`, and integers (type `WORD`); and four different kinds of data: pointers to `void`, `WORDs`, `CStrings`, and `CObjects` (including classes derived from `CObjects`). However, not all possible combinations are implemented. Table 16-4 shows the available map classes.

We're going to show two examples of of the `CMapStringToOb` class. This is probably the most often-used class. For data, we'll use objects of the `Person` class, which we've seen before in various incarnations. We arrange for this class to be derived from `CObject` so its objects can be stored in the map.

The first example program is quite simple. It creates a map and three objects of type `Person`. Then it puts pointers to these objects on the map, along with a key

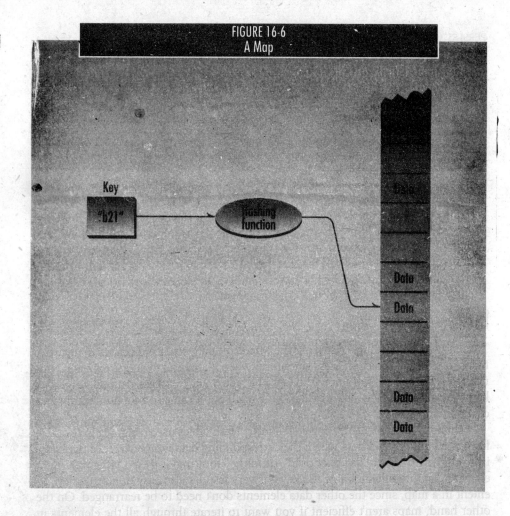

FIGURE 16-6
A Map

to each object. Finally, it looks up one of the objects, using its key, and displays it. This is a common operation in a map. Here's the listing for MAPTOB:

```
// maptob.cpp
// demonstrate CMapStringToOb class

#define _DOS                    // for afxcoll.h
#include <afxcoll.h>            // for collection classes
#include <iostream.h>           // for cout
#include <string.h>             // for strlen(), strcpy()

class Person : public CObject   // user-defined class
{                               // derived from CObject
    private:
        char* name;
        int age;
```

```
public:
    Person()                              // constructor
        { name = new char; name[0] = '\0'; age = 0; }
    Person(const char* str, const int a) // constructor
        {
        name = new char[ strlen(str)+1 ];
        strcpy(name, str);
        age = a;
        }
    ~Person()                             // destructor
        { delete name; }
    void DisplayPerson()                  // display
        { cout << "name=" << name << ", age=" << age; }
};

void main()
    {
    CMapStringToOb map;          // define a string-to-object map

    Person* p1 = new Person("Bart", 23);    // create
    Person* p2 = new Person("Casey", 25);   // Person
    Person* p3 = new Person("Red", 32);     // objects

    map.SetAt("b23", p1);                   // put entries (keys
    map.SetAt("c25", p2);                   // and persons) on
    map.SetAt("r32", p3);                   // the map

    CObject* pObj;                          // pointer to CObject
    if( map.Lookup("c25", pObj) )           // look up key "c25"
        {
        cout << "\nFound key c25: ";
        ((Person*)pObj)->DisplayPerson();   // display Person
        }
    } // end main
```

TABLE 16-4 Map Classes in the MFC Library	
class	Map from key to data
CMapPtrToPtr	pointers to pointers
CMapPtrToWord	pointers to words
CMapStringToOb	CStrings to CObjects (and derived classes)
CMapStringToPtr	CStrings to pointers
CMapStringToString	CStrings to CStrings
CMapWordToOb	WORDs to CObjects (and derived classes)
CMapWordToPtr	WORDs to pointers

Notice that the the `SetAt()` function works with pointers to objects, not with objects themselves.

The keys could be any string but we somewhat arbitrarily made them reflect some of the data they refer to. Thus the key for "Bart", age 25, is b25. This is reminiscent of the codes found on some magazine address labels, which are made up of the subscriber's name and zipcode. Here's the output from MAPTOB:

```
found key c25: name=Casey, age=25
```

Another thing to note is the syntax necessary for the pointer `pObj` when calling the `DisplayPerson()` function. The outer parentheses ensure that the cast is applied to the pointer before the `->` operator.

The next example demonstrates several other techniques for use with maps. Here's the listing for MAPTOB2:

```cpp
// maptob2.cpp
// demonstrate CMapStringToOb class

#define _DOS                    // for afxcoll.h
#include <afxcoll.h>            // for collection classes
#include <iostream.h>           // for cout
#include <string.h>             // for strlen(), strcpy()
void dispmap();                 // prototype

class Person : public CObject           // user-defined class
   {                                     // derived from CObject
   private:
     char* name;
     int age;
   public:
     Person()                                  // constructor
        { name = new char; name[0] = '\0'; age = 0; }
     Person(const char* str, const int a) // constructor
        {
        name = new char[ strlen(str)+1 ];
        strcpy(name, str);
        age = a;
        }
     ~Person()                                 // destructor
        { delete name; }
     void DisplayPerson()                      // display
        { cout << "name=" << name << ", age=" << age; }
   };

CMapStringToOb map;             // define a string-to-object map

void main()
   {
   POSITION pos;                // position in map
   CObject* pObj;               // for data returned from map
   CString key;
```

```
Person* p1 = new Person("Bart", 23);       // create
Person* p2 = new Person("Casey", 25);      // Person
Person* p3 = new Person("Red", 32);        // objects
Person* p4 = new Person("Slade", 27);
Person* p5 = new Person("Rover", 32);

map.SetAt("b23", p1);                      // put entries (keys
map.SetAt("c25", p2);                      // and persons) on
map.SetAt("r32", p3);                      // the map
dispmap();                                 // display the map

map.SetAt("s27", p4);                      // add another Person
dispmap();                                 // display the map

// insert new object with the same key
if( map.Lookup("r32", pObj) )              // if key already used,
    delete pObj;                           // delete old object
map.SetAt("r32", p5);                      // insert new object
dispmap();                                 // display the map

// delete all map entries (objects first, then entries in map)
pos = map.GetStartPosition();              // start at beginning
while(pos != NULL)                         // iterate thru map
    {
    map.GetNextAssoc(pos, key, pObj);      // get next entry
    delete pObj;                           // delete obj
    }
map.RemoveAll();                           // remove map entries
dispmap();                                 // display the map
}  // end main

// dispmap()
// function to display all map entries
void dispmap()
    {
    CObject* pObj;                         // for data from map
    CString key;
                                           // display # of entries
    cout << "\n\nMap has " << map.GetCount() << " entries";
    POSITION pos = map.GetStartPosition(); // start at beginning
    while(pos != NULL)                     // iterate thru map
        {
        map.GetNextAssoc(pos, key, pObj);  // get next entry
        cout << "\nkey="<< key << ": ";    // display key
        ((Person*)pObj)->DisplayPerson();  // display Person
        }
    }  // end dispmap
```

This program creates a map and five **Person** objects, stores three objects on the map, and then displays the map by iterating through the elements using **POSITION** values and the **GetNextAssoc()** member function. (For convenience we've made the display routine into a function.) The program then adds another object, and displays the map again. The moral here is that the items aren't ordered like those of arrays and lists. When we insert an item on a map, it may show up anyplace when we iterate through the elements. Here's the output from MAPTOB2:

```
Map has 3 entries
key=r32: name=Red, age=32
key=b23: name=Bart, age=23
key=c25: name=Casey, age=25

Map has 4 entries
key=s27: name=Slade, age=27
key=r32: name=Red, age=32
key=b23: name=Bart, age=23
key=c25: name=Casey, age=25

Map has 4 entries
key=s27: name=Slade, age=27
key=r32: name=Rover, age=32
key=b23: name=Bart, age=23
key=c25: name=Casey, age=25

Map has 0 entries
```

One thing to know about maps is that distinct objects must have different keys, otherwise they could not both be referenced. MAPTOB2 demonstrates this by looking up the element with the key "r32", deleting the object it finds there ("Red", age 32) and inserting a new object ("Rover", age 32). Displaying the entire map finds this new object. Finally, the program deletes the map by first deleting the individual objects contained in the map, and then deleting the map itself with the RemoveAll() member function. You shouldn't try to delete a data structure without first removing the data items from it.

Once you get used to the Microsoft container classes, you'll find that using them is far easier than writing (or rewriting) your own custom array, linked list, and map routines every time you need to create a data structure. You get an already debugged system you can plug right into your program.

EXCEPTIONS

An *exception* is an unusual event that happens in a program as a result of circumstances beyond the program's control. Exceptions typically occur in memory and file operations. For example, an exception occurs if your program requests memory, but other programs have used all the available memory and the request fails. An exception also occurs if your program attempts to write to a file that was opened for reading, perhaps by some other program; or if your program attempts to create a file but the disk is full.

Traditionally, this kind of event has been handled in ad hoc fashion by obtaining the return value of any function likely to cause an exception, using an if statement to check the result, and taking appropriate action if an exception occurred. However, this approach has some weaknesses. For example, suppose you perform several file operations in sequence, such as opening a file, reading from the file, writing to the file, and closing the file. Each of these functions must have its own check-and-respond code. This code can take a lot of room, since it must be duplicated for each file-handling function.

The exception mechanism solves this problem by allowing a single error-handling routine to handle a number of different functions. The exception mechanism also takes care of the actual check to see if an error occurred, so you don't need to worry about function return values or if statements. You need only write the code to respond to an entire group of exceptions.

An exception-handling mechanism has been proposed as an integral part of the C++ language (see Chapter 15 of Ellis and Stroustrup, listed in the bibliography), but it has not yet been officially implemented; the specifications are still evolving. However, Microsoft provides an interim solution using the Foundation classes. The syntax of the Microsoft approach is close to that proposed by Ellis and Stroustrup.

EXCEPTION SYNTAX

In the Microsoft approach, exceptions are generated only by certain object-oriented operations. To use exceptions you must use classes that contain an exception-handling mechanism. This means using new for file allocation, or CFile member functions for file operations.

Here's the basic format for handling exceptions:

```
TRY
    {
    // statement that might throw an exception
    // another statement that might throw an exception
    }
CATCH
    {
    // statements to catch these exceptions
    }
END_CATCH
```

The word "throw" is used as a synonym for *causing* an exception, and "catch" means to handle the exception. The CATCH block (the section of code between the braces following CATCH) is called the *exception handler*. The exception mechanism is actually a set of macros that create a complex if...else statement. (A macro is a kind of #define statement. You don't need to know how macros work to use exceptions, but if you're curious the tutorials on C-language programming listed in the bibliography explain macros in more detail.) Figure 16-7 shows the exception mechanism.

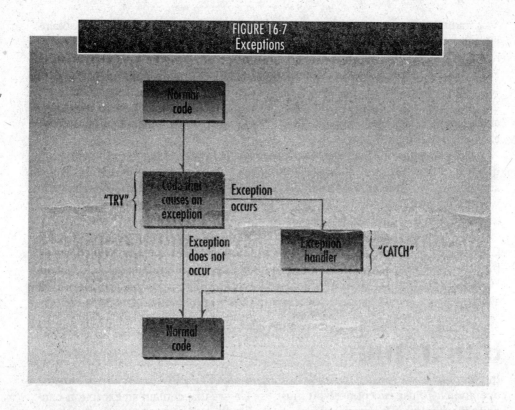

FIGURE 16-7
Exceptions

There are different kinds of exceptions, each represented by a class. These classes are all derived from the CException class. Table 16-5 shows the exception classes. We'll look at the two most common categories: memory and file exceptions.

TABLE 16-5
Exception Classes

Class	Responds to
CMemoryException	insufficient memory
CNotSupportedException	request for unsupported operation
CArchiveException	archive operation exceptions
CFileException	file operation exceptions
CResourceException	windows resource exceptions

MEMORY EXCEPTIONS

Our first example is a simple one that catches a memory exception. The program guarantees that an exception will occur by first finding how much memory is available with the `_memmax()` run-time library function, and then requesting 1 byte more than this with the `new` operator. Here's the listing for XCPTMEM:

```
// xcptmem.cpp
// tests memory exceptions

#define _DOS              // for afx.h
#include <afx.h>          // for exceptions
#include <iostream.h>     // for cout
#include <malloc.h>       // for _memmax()

void main()
   {
   char *p;
   size_t maxsize;              // for _memmax() (unsigned int)
   maxsize = _memmax();         // maximum size we can get

   TRY
      {
      p = new char[maxsize+1];  // can't get this size
      // Never reaches here if exception occurs
      delete p;
      }
   // don't put any code here
   CATCH(CMemoryException, ex)
      {
      cout << "\nCaught a memory exception";
      }
   END_CATCH
   // Always reaches here
   }
```

When we run the program, it always prints the line

```
Caught a memory exception
```

Since it is located in the TRY block, the `new` operator throws an exception when it can't find the amount of memory requested. The exception is caught by the exception handler (the CATCH block), which prints the output line. In a real program, of course, the exception handler would be more complex, perhaps asking the user what to do next, or terminating the program.

Note that in the TRY block, the statements that follow the statement that caused the exception won't be executed if an exception occurs; control immediately goes to the exception handler. Also, don't put any code between the end of the TRY block and the CATCH macro (any more than you would put code between the **if** and **else** parts of an **if...else** statement).

Remember that there are different kinds of exceptions. The argument to the CATCH macro is CMemoryException, so only memory exceptions will be caught here.

FILE EXCEPTIONS

For our next death-defying act, let's look at a somewhat more complex example that handles file exceptions. In this example we not only catch the exceptions, we also investigate the cause of the exception and take different actions (printing different messages) depending on the cause. Here's the listing for XCPTFILE:

```
// xcptfile.cpp
// demonstrates file exceptions

#define _DOS                      // for afx.h
#include <afx.h>                  // for exceptions
#include <iostream.h>             // for cout

void main()
   {
   char Buffer[100];
   CFile* pFile = new CFile;      // make a CFile object
   BOOL result;
                                  // this causes normal error
   result = pFile->Open("no_exist.dat", CFile::modeRead);
   if( !result )
      cout << "\nUser error -- can't open file";

   TRY
      {
      pFile->Write(Buffer, 100);  // this causes exception
      }
   CATCH(CFileException, ex)
      {
      cout << "\nCaught a file exception";

                  // not thrown, even if file doesn't exist
      if( ex->m_cause == CFileException::fileNotFound )
         cout << " -- file not found";

                  // tried to write to file opened for reading
      if( ex->m_cause == CFileException::accessDenied )
         cout << " -- access denied";

                  // file doesn't exist
      if( ex->m_cause == CFileException::invalidFile )
         cout << " -- invalid file handle";
```

```
        }
    END_CATCH

    pFile->Close();              // close the file
    delete pFile;                // delete the CFile object
    }
```

Assuming the file NO_EXIST.DAT does not exist, this program will generate the following output:

```
User error -- can't open file
Caught a file exception -- invalid file handle
```

The first output line is caused by the the `Open()` function, which generates a "normal" error return, which is trapped by the program with an `if` statement. A subtle distinction can be made between exceptions and normal error returns from file-handling functions. If you attempt to open a file for reading but the file doesn't exist, this is not considered an exception by `CFile::Open()` but a normal error, since this is something that can be expected to happen quite often. This function should thus be queried by the program to see if a normal error occurred, as we show in XCPTFILE.

The second output line is caused by the exception that occurs when the `Write()` function attempts to write to a file using an invalid file handle. (The handle it uses is invalid since the file couldn't be opened.)

In the exception handler, the program figures out what the exception was by investigating the `m_cause` member of the `ex` structure that is given to the `CATCH` macro. The possible values of `m_cause`, which are declared in an `enum` statement in AFX.H, are shown in Table 16-6.

To cause another kind of exception to occur in the XCPTFILE example, you must create a file called NO_EXIST.DAT in the same directory as the XCPTFILE program, and run the program again. Since the file exists this time, the `Open()` function is successful. However, the file is opened as read-only, so the `Write()` function generates an exception when it attempts to write to it. This time the output from the program is

```
Caught a file exception -- access denied
```

Don't forget to close the file and delete the `CFile` object when you're done.

Using this mechanism your program can take whatever action is appropriate for different kinds of errors.

THROWING YOUR OWN EXCEPTIONS

Our third exception example demonstrates that your program can throw an exception itself, rather than waiting for an outside agency to throw it. Suppose you want to handle the error generated in the last program—where the `Open()` command

TABLE 16-6
Values of `CFileException::m_cause`

Identifier	Cause
none	no error
generic	unspecified error
fileNotFound	could not find file
badPath	invalid path
tooManyOpenFiles	more than specified in CONFIG.SYS
accessDenied	can't write to read-only, etc.
invalidFile	invalid file handle
removeCurrentDir	can't remove current directory
directoryFull	too many directory entries
badSeek	can't set file pointer
hardIO	hardware error
sharingViolation	SHARE.EXE not loaded, or file locked
lockViolation	can't lock region
diskFull	disk is full
endOfFile	reached the end of file

failed to open a nonexistent file—using the exception mechanism instead of printing your own error message. You can cause an exception to be thrown using the THROW macro, as shown in XCPTFIL2:

```
// xcptfil2.cpp
// tests file exceptions generated by THROW macro

#define _DOS              // for afx.h
#include <afx.h>          // for exceptions
#include <iostream.h>     // for cout

void main()
    {
    char Buffer[100];     // for file info

    TRY
        {
        CFile* pFile = new CFile;
```

```
    CFileException* theException = new CFileException;
                              // open non-existent file
    BOOL result = pFile->Open("no_exist.dat", CFile::modeRead);
    if( !result )                // if we can't open it,
        THROW(theException);     // throw exception
    delete theException;         // open was OK

    pFile->Write(Buffer, 100);  // opened OK, now try writing
                              //    (may throw exception)
    }

CATCH(CFileException, theException)
{
cout << "\nCaught a file exception";

                // tried to write to file opened for reading
    if( theException->m_cause == CFileException::accessDenied )
        cout << " -- access denied";

    else        // non-specific catch, probably from THROW
        cout << " -- can't open file";
    }
END_CATCH

    pFile->Close();              // close the file
    delete pFile;                // delete the CFile object
    }
```

Assuming you have erased the file NO_EXIST.DAT, which you created for the last example, the output of this program will be

```
Caught a file exception -- can't open file
```

When the Open() statement can't find the file, the if statement checks the result and calls the THROW macro. This triggers the exception, just as an exception produced internally by a file-handling function does. (If the file does exist, you'll get the same "access denied" message as in the XCPTFILE example.)

The THROW macro lets you use the exception mechanism with any code you write.

THROWING SPECIFIC EXCEPTIONS

You can also cause an exception to be generated by executing the function AfxThrowFileException() (which takes the Golden Overrun award as the longest function name in this book). This approach has the advantage that you can specify the kind of exception as an argument to the function. The exception handler can then take different actions, depending on the type of exception. Here's the listing for XCPTFIL3:

```
// xcptfil3.cpp
// tests application-defined file exceptions

#define _DOS                    // for afx.h
#include <afx.h>                // for exceptions
#include <iostream.h>           // for cout

void main()
  {
  char Buffer[100];             // for file info
  CFile* pFile = new CFile;     // make a CFile object

  TRY
    {
    BOOL result;
                                // open non-existent file
    result = pFile->Open("no_exist.dat", CFile::modeRead);
    if( !result )               // on error, throw exception
      AfxThrowFileException(CFileException::fileNotFound);
    pFile->Write(Buffer, 100);
    }

  CATCH(CFileException, theException)
    {
    cout << "\nCaught a file exception";

            // caused by AfxThrowException()
    if( theException->m_cause == CFileException::fileNotFound )
      cout << " -- file not found";

            // tried to write to file opened for reading
    if( theException->m_cause == CFileException::accessDenied )
      cout << " -- access denied";

            // file doesn't exist
    if( theException->m_cause == CFileException::invalidFile )
      cout << " -- invalid file handle";
    }
  END_CATCH

  pFile->Close();       // close the file
  delete pFile;         // delete the CFile object
  }
```

The output of XCPTFIL3 when it tries to open a nonexistent file is:

```
Caught a file exception -- file not found
```

If the Open() fails, then AfxThrowFileException() is called with an argument of NOTFOUND (which has the value 2). This is the value of m_cause when a file is not found, so the function causes this part of the CATCH block to be executed, just as if an exception with this cause had really taken place. The "invalid file handle" message is never printed, because (if the file does not exist) the exception occurs before **Write()** is executed.

Exception Note

The exception mechanism works even if the exception occurs in a function called from within a TRY block. That is, the statement that generates the exception can be in a function anywhere in the program, so long as this function is called from within the TRY block.

Serialization

When you create an object in your program, it is stored in your computer's memory (RAM). When you exit from your program (or the power fails!), the object is destroyed. Suppose you want an object to persist between programs? The process of *serialization* allows an object (or a data structure containing many objects) to be stored to a peristent, nonvolatile medium, such as a disk file.

Of course, as we saw in Chapter 14, you can write the data from an object quite readily to disk using the normal I/O streams (or, as we saw in this chapter, **CFile** objects). However, serialization gives you a convenient and systematic way to write complex objects using the insertion (**<<**) and extraction (**>>**) operators.

Serialization is a generalized approach that can be applied to media other than disk files. To make this generalization possible, objects are saved, not to a disk file, but to an object of type **CArchive**. To store an object on disk, the **CArchive** object is connected to an object of type **CFile**, but it could be connected to objects of other classes, representing other physical storage devices, as well. Figure 16-8 shows the role of the archive in serialization.

Our example shows how an object can be serialized. The object is a list containing objects of the well-known **Person** class. However, this class has been modified somewhat. The **name** data item that was formerly of type **char*** has been changed to type **CString**, and the **age** data that was type **int** has been changed to type **WORD**.

There are five steps involved in modifying a class so it can be serialized:

1. The class must be derived from **CObject**.
2. The **DECLARE_SERIAL** macro must appear in the class specification.
3. There must be a no-argument constructor.
4. The class must override the **CObject::Serialize()** member function.
5. The **IMPLEMENT_SERIAL** macro must appear before any executable functions.

FIGURE 16-8
Serialization

If you break your program into a header (.H) file and a source (.CPP) file, as described in Chapter 15, then the first four steps go in the class specification in the .H file, and the fifth goes at the beginning of the .CPP file. For simplicity, our example program consists of a single file. Here's the listing for SERIAL.CPP:

```cpp
// serial.cpp
// demonstrates serialization of collection class

#define _DOS                        // for afxcoll.h
#include <afxcoll.h>                // for collection classes
#include <iostream.h>               // for cout

class Person : public CObject       // user-defined class
   {                                // derived from CObject
   DECLARE_SERIAL( Person )
   private:
      CString name;
      WORD age;
   public:
      Person()                                   // 0-arg constructor
         { name = '\0'; age = 0; }
      Person(const CString cs, const WORD a) // 2-arg constructor
         { name = cs; age = a; }
      void DisplayPerson()
         { cout << "\nname=" << name << ", age=" << age; }
      CString GetName()
         { return name; }
      virtual void Serialize( CArchive& archive );
   };

IMPLEMENT_SERIAL( Person, CObject, 0 )
```

```
void Person::Serialize( CArchive& archive )
    {
    CObject::Serialize(archive);   // call base class
    if( archive.IsStoring() )
        archive << name << age;    // store on disk
    else
        archive >> name >> age;    // load from disk
    }

void main()
    {
    CObList list;
    CObList* pcsl = &list;            // make a list
                                      // and a pointer to it

    Person* p1 = new Person("Bart", 23);    // create
    Person* p2 = new Person("Casey", 25);   // Persons
    Person* p3 = new Person("Red", 32);
    Person* p4 = new Person("Slade", 27);

    pcsl->AddTail(p1);
    pcsl->AddTail(p2);                // put Persons on list
    pcsl->AddTail(p3);
    pcsl->AddTail(p4);


    // serialize list to archive
    CFile cfile;                      // make a CFile object
    CFile* pFile = &cfile;            // and a pointer to it
    pFile->Open("perslst.dat",        // open it
        CFile::modeCreate | CFile::modeWrite);
    CArchive carch(pFile, CArchive::store);  // connect to archive
    carch << pcsl;                    // write to archive (very easy!)
    carch.Close();                    // close archive (do 1st)
    pFile->Close();                   // close file (do 2nd)
//////////////////////////////////////////////////////////////////////
    // read list back from archive, into different list
    CObList* pcslb;                   // new uninitialized pointer
    pFile->Open("perslst.dat", CFile::modeRead); // open file
    CArchive carch2(pFile, CArchive::load);  // connect to archive
    carch2 >> pcslb;                  // read from archive -- creates
                                      //   new list of objects
    carch2.Close();                   // close archive
    pFile->Close();                   // close file

    // display new list elements
    POSITION pos = pcslb->GetHeadPosition();   // start at head
    Person* p;
    while( pos != NULL )              // iterate through the list
        {                            // get the next object
        p = (Person*)pcslb->GetNext(pos);
        p->DisplayPerson();          // display it
        }
    } // end main
```

The `Person` class has been modified to include the five items mentioned above: It's derived from `CObject`, it starts with `DECLARE_SERIAL`, it has a no-argument constructor, and it overrides the `Serialize()` function in `CObject`. Finally, the `IMPLEMENT_SERIAL` macro precedes any function definitions.

The program first creates a list of type `CObList`, the pointer to which is `pcsl`. It then creates four `Person` objects and puts pointers to them on the list.

Now we serialize this list, with all its embedded objects, to disk. This also involves several steps. First we create a `CFile` object, pointed to by `pFile`, and open it for writing. Next we create a `CArchive` object and connect it to the file, using the statement

```
CArchive carch(pFile, CArchive::store);
```

The `CArchive::store` constant opens the archive for storing (writing) data, as opposed to loading (reading) it.

Finally, we're ready for the payoff. The single statement

```
carch << pcsl;
```

saves the list and all the objects on it to the archive, which in this case is the disk file PERSLST.DAT. As you can see, this is a lot easier than writing individual data objects.

The slashed line in the listing at this point separates two parts of the program that might in a real situation be separate functions or even separate programs. Above the line the list is serialized, below the line it is *deserialized* or read back from permanent storage (the disk file) into memory. Note that we need create only a pointer to the item to be deserialized. The statement

```
charch2 >> pcslb;
```

then creates a new list, complete with objects, in memory, and connects the pointer `poslb` to it. Now subsequent references to the pointer will reference the list contents, as shown when we display the list. Here's the output from SERIAL:

```
name=Bart, age=23
name=Casey, age=25
name=Red, age=32
name=Slade, age=27
```

DEBUGGING

The Microsoft Foundation Class Library includes a number of routines that are used in the debugging phase of program development. Many of these routines can be used in non-object-oriented programs. They constitute a powerful approach to speeding the debugging process, so we'll mention a few of the most common ones here.

These diagnostic routines require variations in the way you build (compile and link) your program. When you build with these variations, the diagnostic routines in the resulting .EXE file print diagnostic messages and perform other checks. When you build the normal way, the diagnostic routines are deactivated. Thus you can generate two versions of the .EXE file from the same source code: a debug version and a release version. In the release version, the diagnostic routines are ignored by the compiler.

PREPARATION

Three steps are necessary to build a debug version of your program (in addition to including the AFX.H file, which is common to all Foundation classes). You need a different library file, you need to select the debug option when you build your program (as we described briefly in Chapter 2), and you need to define the constant _DEBUG at the beginning of your source file. Here's how to carry out these three steps. (They can be performed with arguments to the command-line versions of the compiler and linker, but we'll assume you're working in the PWB.)

Special Library File

The debugging version of the library file has the same file name you normally use, but with a letter 'D' appended. For example, if you're using SAFXCR.LIB for normal building, then you'll use SAFXCRD.LIB for the debugging version.

You'll need two separate project files with different names: one for the release version of your program and one for the debugging version (perhaps MYPROG.MAK and MYPROGD.MAK). Use the Edit Project item on the Project menu to install the appropriate version of the library file in each project file. The source file is the same in both projects. (See Appendix C for how to use the Project feature.)

Use Debug Options

This one is easy, at least in the PWB. Select Build Options from the Options menu, and click on the Use Debug Options button. Then click on OK.

Define _DEBUG Constant

You need to #define the constant _DEBUG at the beginning of your source file. You can actually insert such a statement in your source file, but it's more convenient to tell the compiler you want it defined; that way you don't need to change your source file at all to switch between the debug and release versions. In the Programmer's WorkBench (PWB), select Additional Debug Options from the C++ Compiler Options submenu of the Language Options submenu in the Options menu. Then fill in _DEBUG in the Defines field. (This is equivalent to the argument /D_DEBUG in the command-line version of the compiler.)

TRACE AND ASSERT

Our first example program will demonstrate two of the most commonly used diagnostic routines, TRACE and ASSERT. We have commented out some of the statements in the program. By deleting the comment symbols and rebuilding, you can cause individual lines to execute while keeping others deactivated, thus experimenting with various kinds of program errors. Here's the listing for DEBUG.CPP:

```
// debug.cpp
// demonstrates diagnostic/debugging features
// requires _DEBUG to activate diagnostics

...ine _DOS                              // for afx.h
...nclude <afx.h>                        // for diagnostics
#include <iostream.h>                     // for cout

char* p;                                 // global pointer

void main()
   {
   TRACE("Starting arithmetic section\n");
   int answer = 2 - 3;
// ASSERT(answer > 0);                   // check for negative answer

   TRACE("Starting file section\n");
   CFile afile;                          // make a file
   CFile* pFile = &afile;                // and a pointer to it
   BOOL result = pFile->Open("no_exist.dat", CFile::modeRead);
// ASSERT(result);                       // check for unsuccessful open
// pFile->Close();                       // close the file

   TRACE("Starting memory section\n");
// ASSERT(p);                            // check for invalid pointer
// p = new char[65535];                  // can't get this size
   }
```

The TRACE Macro

If you build this DEBUG program in the normal way, with the release version of the library file and build options, it will generate no output at all when you run it. That makes sense; there are no normal output statements (like cout) in it.

However, when you build a debug version of this program, using the steps outlined above, it will print the following output:

```
Starting arithmetic section
Starting file section
Starting memory section
```

This output comes from the three TRACE macros. In the debug version of a program, all the TRACE macros are activated, and print out the strings given them as arguments. (You can also cause TRACE to print out the value of variables. See the description of the run-time library function printf() for a description of the format for doing this.) Using TRACE lets you know where you are in the program, and can tell you the value of variables at particular places. You could achieve the same effect by inserting cout statements in the source file, but then you would need to edit out these statements when you were ready to generate the release version of the program.

The ASSERT Macro

The ASSERT macro checks that a particular condition is true. If the condition is false, the macro prints out a message and terminates the program. If the condition is true, no action is taken. ASSERT is useful for checking the validity of variables. Most variables can only assume certain values; if they stray outside the allowed range, something is wrong.

To see how ASSERT works in the DEBUG program, you'll need to remove the comments in front of various statements, one at a time, starting at the beginning of the listing.

When you remove the comments from the line

```
ASSERT(answer > 0);
```

you'll get the following output:

```
Starting arithmetic section
Assertion Failed: file debug.cpp, line 15
AfxAbort called
abnormal program termination
```

The answer variable is not greater than 0 when the ASSERT is executed, so it fails, generating the output shown. You can use a similar approach to ensure that the value of any variable in your program is in the proper range.

If you restore the comment symbol in front of line 15, and delete the comment in front of the line

```
ASSERT(result);
```

you'll get a similar output, except that the line number is different:

```
Starting arithmetic section
Starting file section
Assertion Failed: file debug.cpp, line 21
AfxAbort called
abnormal program termination
```

The CFile::Open() function returns NULL if it can't open the file. The ASSERT macro checks the return value from this function, and if it's false (0) it prints its message and terminates the program.

The debugging mechanism is at work in files other than your source file. There are ASSERT statements in the source files that generated the debugging library file (SAFXCRD.LIB) you're using. If these fail, you'll get an error message just as you would if an ASSERT failed in your own source file. You can demonstrate this by restoring the comment symbol to line 21, and removing the one before the line

```
pFile->Close();
```

This will generate the output

```
Starting arithmetic section
Starting file section
Assertion Failed: file file.cpp, line 343
AfxAbort called
abnormal program termination
```

The line that failed is in the file FILE.CPP, which is one of the source files for the SAFXCRD.LIB (or similar) debugging file. You can find FILE.CPP in the \C700\MFC\SRC directory. Here an ASSERT checks for a valid file handle. Since our program did not open the file successfully, the file handle isn't valid and the assertion fails.

Now restore the comment symbol to the pFile->Close() line and remove it from the line

```
ASSERT(p);
```

This statement checks to be sure the pointer p is not NULL. But the p is NULL. Why? That's right, we forgot to initialize it, and since it's a global variable, it's initialized to 0 (NULL). The output is

```
Starting arithmetic section
Starting file section
Starting memory section
Assertion Failed: file debug.cpp, line 25
AfxAbort called
abnormal program termination
```

Finally, restore the comments in line 25 and remove them in front of the line

```
p = new char[65535];
```

This generates another kind of diagnostic situation. Here's the output:

```
Starting arithmetic section
Starting file section
Starting memory section
Error: memory allocation: tried to allocate 65535 bytes
    object too large or negative size
Warning: Throwing an Exception of type CMemoryException
Error: Un-caught Exception (CMemoryException)
AfxTerminate called
AfxAbort called
abnormal program termination
```

This diatribe is instigated by a memory allocation routine, the source code for which is in MEMORY.CPP. This routine prints the first message seen above, and then throws an exception using the AfxThrowMemoryException() function. This causes the next warning message. There is no exception handler, so another message informs us of this fact. Finally the program is terminated in the usual way.

The ASSERT_VALID Macro

Let's look at a macro that helps to diagnose bugs in objects. This is ASSERT_VALID, which takes an object as an argument and checks the valididty of all the object's data.

We need to do a little work for this one, by installing a new member function, called AssertValid(), in our class. This function can use ASSERT statements to check the validity of the object's data. Also (as usual) the class must be derived from CObject. Here's the listing for DEBUGOB.CPP:

```
// debugob.cpp
// demonstrates ASSERT_VALID macro for objects
// requires _DEBUG to activate diagnostics

#define _DOS                          // for afx.h
#include <afx.h>                      // for diagnostics
#include <iostream.h>                 // for cout

class Person : public CObject         // user-defined class
    {                                 // derived from CObject
    private:
        char* name;
        int age;
    public:
        Person()                                    // constructor
            { name = new char; name[0] = '\0'; age = 0; }
        Person(const char* str, const int a) // constructor
            {
            name = new char[ strlen(str)+1 ];
            strcpy(name, str);
            age = a;
            }
        ~Person()                                   // destructor
            { delete name; }
        void DisplayPerson()                        // display
            { cout << "\nname=" << name << ", age=" << age; }
        virtual void AssertValid() const     // validate Person
            {
            CObject::AssertValid();          // check base class
            ASSERT( age>0 && age<120 );  // reasonable age range
            ASSERT( name );                  // name not NULL
            ASSERT( strlen(name)<15 );       // name not too long
            }
    };

Person* ppers;                                // global pointer

void main()
    {                                         // make three Persons
```

```
Person* ppers1 = new Person("George", 29);
Person* ppers2 = new Person("Alice", -40);
Person* ppers3 = new Person("excessivelylongname", 21);

   ASSERT_VALID(ppers1);        // ok
// ASSERT_VALID(ppers2);        // fails; age too small
// ASSERT_VALID(ppers3);        // fails; name too long
// ASSERT_VALID(ppers);         // fails; uninitialized pointer
   }
```

Again, we use comment symbols to generate different errors. When you run the program as shown above, it generates no output. But if you remove the comment symbol from the line

```
ASSERT_VALID(ppers2);
```

the following output is generated:

```
Assertion Failed: file debugob.cpp, line 30
AfxAbort called
abnormal program termination
```

In this case, the age in ppers2 is invalid, so when the ASSERT_VALID macro causes the AssertValid() member function to be called, the appropriate ASSERT statement is triggered, checking the object's age data.

Similarly, if we replace the comment symbol for the ppers2 line and remove it in front of the line

```
ASSERT_VALID(ppers3);
```

we'll get the output

```
Assertion Failed: file debugob.cpp, line 32
AfxAbort called
abnormal program termination
```

This fails because the length of the name data in ppers3 is too long. Finally, restore the comment for the ppers3 line, and remove it from the line

```
ASSERT_VALID(ppers);
```

This generates the output

```
ASSERT_VALID fails with NULL pointer
Assertion Failed: file object.cpp, line 77
AfxAbort called
abnormal program termination
```

Here the AssertValid() routine for the base class CObject (in the OBJECT.CPP source file) detected the fact that the pointer ppers was uninitialized.

A common use for the ASSERT_VALID macro is in a class's own member functions, where it's applied to the this pointer:

```
ASSERT_VALID(this);
```

There are many other diagnostic routines we don't have space to explore here. If you're writing serious programs, you will want to explore this topic further. The larger and more complex an application, the more useful the diagnostic routines will be.

SUMMARY

We've looked at some of the wide variety of services provided by the Microsoft Foundation class library. There are useful standalone classes for strings (**CString**), data-and-time data (**CTime**), and files (**CFile**). Data-structure Classes provide a handy way to add sophisticated data storage capabilities to your program, including enhanced arrays, linked lists, and maps (which are also called dictionaries or hash tables). We discussed which of these storage structures is useful in different situations, and saw how to implement them. You can consider using one of these classes in your own program the next time you need to store data, instead of using normal C++ arrays or building your own data structure.

We looked at exceptions, which provide a systematic way to deal with unexpected events outside the program. We saw how objects can be made persistent—that is, lasting after the program stops—by saving them to disk through the archive process. Finally, we explored some of the diagnostic services the Foundation classes provide.

QUESTIONS

1. The Microsoft Foundation Class Library (MFC)
   a. is useful only in highly specialized situations
   b. contains a variety of useful classes
   c. is useful only for Windows programmers
   d. provides classes primarily used in the construction industry
2. True or false: You compile and link programs using Foundation classes just as you do any other C++ program.
3. You must include the _____ header file when using many Foundation classes (except the data-structure classes).
4. The library file for the Medium memory model real-mode nondebugging version of the Foundation classes is _____.
5. Assuming **s1** and **s2** are members of the **CString** class, which of the following statements are valid?
   a. `s1 = s2;`
   b. `s1 += s2;`
   c. `ch = s1[3];`
   d. `s1[3] = ch;`

6. Objects of the `CTime` class store

    a. times

    b. differences between two times

    c. date and time

    d. differences between dates and times

7. True or false: `CFile` objects operate on binary-mode files only, while `CStdioFile` objects operate on either binary- or text-mode files.

8. Write a statement that opens for writing an object called `file1` of class `CFile` and file name WHO.DAT, truncating the file to 0 length if it already exists.

9. A data-structure class is

    a. an unstructured group of other classes

    b. a storage structure for objects or data

    c. a hierarchical class structure

    d. night school for repo men

10. Programs that use the data-structure classes must `#include` the _____ header file.

11. To be stored in a data-structure class, objects must be instances of a class derived from the _____ class.

12. Write two statements that, in different ways, set the contents of element 5 of a `CPtrArray`, called `arr1`, to `ptr`.

13. True or false: It is fast to insert a new element between two others in an array, but slow to iterate through the array.

14. A major advantage of the Foundation class arrays, over a normal C++ array, is that they

    a. access data faster

    b. can hold a mixture of objects, numerical quantities, and pointers in the same array

    c. can hold objects of any class

    d. can expand to hold more data as the program runs

15. In a list it's fast and easy to

    a. find a particular element whose position is unknown

    b. insert a new element into the list

    c. find a particular element whose position is known

    d. find the end of the list

    e. none of the above

16. Write a statement that will place a new object of class `class1` on the tail of the list `list1`.

17. A map uses a _____ to look up a data value.

18. Which of the following would normally cause an exception?
    a. Division by 0
    b. Overwriting memory in another program
    c. Attempting to open a nonexistent file for reading
    d. Requesting too much memory
    e. Attempting to write to a file with an invalid file pointer

19. Serialization is the act of _____ an object to _____.

20. Which of the following must you do to create a diagnostic version of your program?
    a. Use a modified version of the Foundation Class Libary.
    b. Change the WIN.INI file to mark your program.
    c. Put the equivalent of a `#define _DEBUG` statement at the start of the program.
    d. Include the file DEBUG.H in your program.

EXERCISES

1. Use `CString` objects to write an anagram program, in which the user enters a word, say "cat," and the program prints all the variations of these letters: "cat," "cta," "atc," "act," "tca," "tac." Use `Right()` and similar functions to manipulate parts of the `CString` objects. Hint: you can use a recursive function, called originally with the whole word as an argument. This function then calls itself repeatedly with an argument that is the word it was given, less the leftmost character. Then it rotates the entire word it was given and calls itself again. If this exercise drives you crazy, you can forget about it.

2. Create pointers to five `Person` objects (use the `Person` class from the PERSLST program in this chapter). Make an array, using the appropriate Microsoft Foundation class, and put three of these pointers in the array. Display all the members of the array. Now overwrite the first element with the fourth `Person`, and insert the fifth `Person` between the fourth and fifth elements. Again, display the contents of the entire array.

3. Create an application that models a natural-language dictionary. The user should be able to insert new words and definitions in the dictionary, and look up any previously inserted word to find its definition. The data should exist only in memory; in this exercise there is no need to save it to disk.

4. Extend the application of Exercise 2 so that the dictionary is stored on disk. Do this by serializing the data using a `CArchive` object. One strategy is always to read the data from the disk file into memory when the program starts, and write the current data back to disk when the program ends.

6. Objects of the `aTime` class store

    a. times

    b. differences between two times

    c. date and time

    d. differences between date and times

7. Time objects _____ a Time object operate on him and made of files only while

8. Write a statement that is needed to perform an object that stores data next to

    and if he came into another, demoting the file to fettingful if there are prints.

9. A data-structure class is

    a. an unstructured group of other classes

    b. a storage structure for objects or data

    c. a hierarchical class structure

    d. night school for repo men

10. Programs that use the data-structure classes must _____ outside the header files.

11. In order to insert a data-structure class object into or remove a class object

    read from the _____?

12. Name the statement that in different ways set the structure of elements of a

    _____

13. _____

14. _____

    a. _____ pieces the length and find the _____ item. A _____

    the _____ are there ever

    c. find a new item and an item whose position is unknown

    d. _____ are prominent to the list _____

    b. find a new _____ element whose position is known

    d. find the ordinal position _____

16. Write a statement that will place a new object of class `aTuss` at the tail of the _____

17. A map uses a _____

JUST FOR FUN

FRACTAL FLOWERS

GAME OF LIFE

TIC-TAC-TOE GAME

This chapter contains several programs that are more complex or idiosyncratic than those we've seen earlier in this book. Nevertheless, they demonstrate some interesting ways that classes can be used in C++ programming. (These programs are also fun to use, even for people who don't know anything about C++.)

There are three programs. The first uses fractals to generate flowers, the second is an OOP version of Conway's game of Life, and the third is a program that will probably beat (or at least tie) you in tic-tac-toe. The fractal program requires a graphics display, but the other two programs require only a character display, and so will run on any MS-DOS computer.

FRACTAL FLOWERS

Fractals are mathematical graphics constructions with the property of self-similarity. This means that a part has the same appearance as the whole, a part of a part has the same appearance as a part, and so on. The best way to understand fractals is to see an example. Our program, TENDRILS, uses fractals to create a flowering plant. Figure 17-1 shows the output of the program.

Every time you run TENDRILS, the output is different. Some plants look fairly regular; others are weird and distorted. You can create an entire jungle of plants, each completely unique.

FRACTAL FUNDAMENTALS

Fractals start with a simple graphics element and duplicate this element at various scales to build up the final image. In TENDRILS the fundamental graphics element is a series of short line segments that form a curved line. Each segment is connected to the next at a slight angle, so the result is a line with a curving shape and a fixed length, which we'll call a *tendril*. This is shown in Figure 17-2.

When fractals are used to imitate natural phenomena such as flowers (or mountains or clouds or similar forms), an element of randomness is commonly introduced into the creation of the fundamental graphics elements so that the image will display natural-looking variations. We introduce randomness by deciding, in a random

FIGURE 17-1
Output of TENDRILS Program

way, whether the angle that joins any two segments in a tendril will bend to the left or to the right. We also arrange things so that the angle is more likely to turn to the left than to the right. This generates tendrils that tend to curve leftward but do so in an irregular way.

A number of tendrils are grouped together to form a cluster. The tendrils in a cluster all start at the same point and radiate from this point at equally spaced angles. However, their random bending soon destroys this initial symmetry.

Here's the listing for TENDRILS:

```
// tendrils.cpp
// draws "biological" forms
#include <graph.h>              // for graphics functions
#include <stdlib.h>             // for srand(), rand()
#include <time.h>               // for randomize()
#include <math.h>               // for sin(), cos()
#include <conio.h>              // for getch()
#include <iostream.h>           // for cout

#define GREEN 2                 // color indices
#define RED 4
#define LIGHTGREEN 10
#define YELLOW 14
```

```
const int    X0=320;          // center of screen
const int    Y0=240;
const float  PI=3.14159;      // pi
const int    NUME=30;         // numerator of probability
const int    DENOM=100;       // denomenator of probability
const int    NUMBER = 7;      // number of tendrils per cluster
const float  RAD = 3.0;       // length of straight line segments
const float  DELTHETA = 0.1;  // change in theta (radians)
const int    SEGS = 60;       // max line segments per tendril
const int    REDUX = 3;       // how much to divide # of segments
const int    MIN = 1;         // minimum number of line segments

class cluster
   {
   public:
     void display(int size, int x, int y);
   };

class tendril
   {
   public:
     void display(int size, float theta, int x, int y);
   };

void cluster::display(int size, int x, int y)
   {
   if( kbhit() )
      exit(0);
   for(int i=0; i<NUMBER; i++)          // for each tendril
      {
      float theta = i * 2*PI/NUMBER;
      _moveto(x, y);
      tendril t;                         // make a tendril
      t.display(size, theta, x, y);  // display it
      }
   }

void tendril::display(int size, float theta, int x, int y)
   {
   for(int j=0; j<size; j++)
      {                      // get random number, range 0 to DENOM
      int randy = rand() % DENOM;
      int chng = ( randy<NUME ) ? -1 : 1;  // left or right?
      theta = theta + chng*DELTHETA;       // new angle
      x = x + RAD*sin(theta);              // x and y of
      y = y + RAD*cos(theta);              //     next point
      if(size < 4)        _setcolor(RED);
      else if(size < 13) _setcolor(GREEN);
      else if(size < 40) _setcolor(LIGHTGREEN);
      else                _setcolor(YELLOW);
      _lineto(x, y);                             // draw line
      }
   if( size > MIN )
      {                                   // if tendril long enough
```

651

```
        cluster c;                  // make a new cluster
        int newsize = size / REDUX;  // but smaller than before
        c.display(newsize, x, y);    // display it
        }
   }

void main()
   {
   if( ! _setvideomode(_VRES16COLOR) )  // set VGA 16 color mode
      { cout << "Can't set graphics mode"; exit(1); }
   srand( (unsigned)time(NULL) );         // seed random number

   int x=X0, y=Y0;                    // set origin of cluster
   int size = SEGS;
   cluster c;                         // define a cluster
   c.display(size, x, y);             // display the cluster
   getch();                           // hold image until keypress
   _setvideomode(_DEFAULTMODE);       // restore previous mode
   }
```

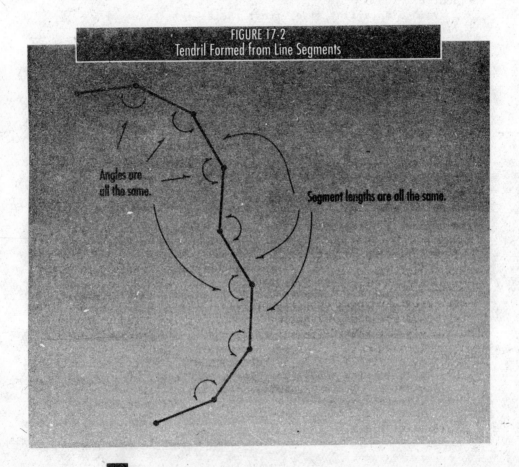

FIGURE 17-2
Tendril Formed from Line Segments

Angles are all the same.

Segment lengths are all the same.

There are two classes in TENDRILS. The class `cluster` models a group or cluster of tendrils, and the class `tendril` models a single tendril. Each class has only one member function: `display`. After a `tendril` or `cluster` object draws itself, it is not used again in the program. Since it doesn't need to remember anything, it has no need of any data items; thus there is no private data in either class.

The main program creates a single object of class `cluster` and displays it. This cluster object in turn creates a series of tendril objects, all starting at the same place but at different angles. The cluster object displays each one. Each of these tendril objects, in the course of displaying itself, draws the series of line segments that form its body, and then—at the end of the tendril—it creates an object of type cluster but with a smaller size. It then tells this cluster to display itself. Figure 17-3 shows how this looks.

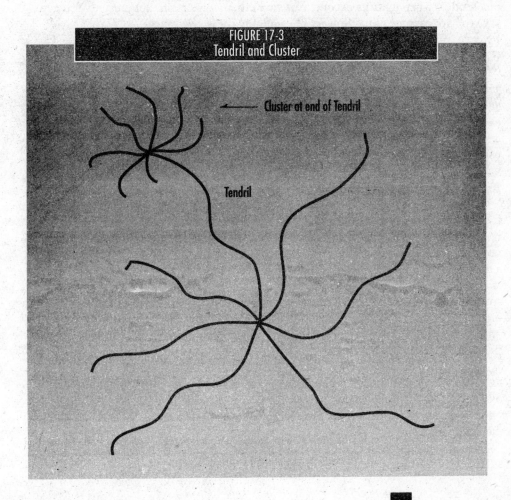

FIGURE 17-3
Tendril and Cluster

Cluster at end of Tendril

Tendril

Tendrils create clusters; and clusters create tendrils, until the tendrils are too short to be usefully displayed. At this point each tendril creates itself but no cluster, and the program ends. The result is a screen display that looks like some sort of exotic flowering plant.

CONSTANTS

The program starts with a series of constant definitions. These constants are used to control the appearance of the flowers generated by the program. NUME divided by DENUM specifies the probability that a segment will bend to the right. NUMBER is the number of tendrils in a cluster. RAD is the length of a straight line segment. DELTHETA is the change in angle between one line segment of a tendril and the next. SEGS is the number of line segments per tendril. REDUX is the scale factor; each set of clusters is REDUX times as small as the previous one. MIN is the minimum length of a tendril; when tendrils become this small their clusters are not created. You can vary the appearance of the flowers by changing these constants.

CLUSTERS

The cluster::display() function uses a for loop to create NUMBER tendrils. It calculates the angle of each tendril (theta), creates a tendril, and calls tendril::display() to display the tendril—sending it arguments to specify its size, angle, and starting point. The size parameter determines the number of line segments used to create a tendril.

POLAR COORDINATES

It turns out to be convenient to use polar coordinates to draw the line segments. As noted in Chapter 9, polar coordinates specify a radius and an angle from a central point. This system is useful in TENDRILS because each of the line segments that form a tendril is drawn at an angle from the previous segment.

In the tendril::display() function each tendril starts from a point that is specified by the arguments x and y. Another argument, theta, specifies the starting angle of the tendril. The function first calculates a variable, chng, which is given one of two values, 1 or −1, depending on whether a random number selected from the range 0 to DENUM is less than NUME.

The chng variable is then multiplied by the amount the angle will change, DELTHETA, to create an angle change that is sometimes positive and sometimes negative (to the left or to the right). The angle change is added to the original angle to find the new angle, theta. This process tends to generate a few more lefthand turns than righthand turns.

To find the endpoint of each line segment we go a fixed distance, RAD, from the current point, at angle theta, as shown in Figure 17-4.

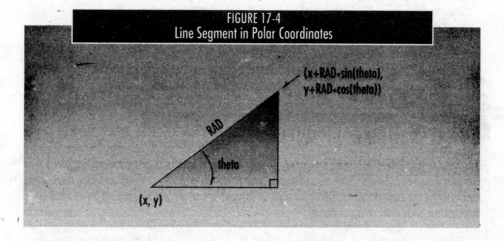

FIGURE 17-4
Line Segment in Polar Coordinates

To draw the line segment, we use the graphics function `lineto()`, which requires rectangular (x,y) coordinates. These can be calculated from the formulas

```
x = x + RAD*sin(theta);
y = y + RAD*cos(theta);
```

Depending on the size of the tendril, the function then selects an appropriate color and draws the segment.

RECURSION

When all the line segments that constitute the tendril have been drawn, `tendril::display()` then creates a cluster, using a size `REDUX` times as small as its own size.

Since a `tendril` object is created by a `cluster` object, and a `cluster` object is created by a `tendril` object, the program is *recursive*. This nesting of one object within another, like Chinese boxes, must terminate at some point, or the program will run forever, generating ever more microscopic tendrils. This terminating point is determined by the `if` statement in `tendril::display()`, which decides whether to create a cluster, based on the current tendril size. If the size is smaller than the `MIN` constant, the recursion stops.

The TENDRILS program could easily be written without classes, as a series of nested `for` loops. Using classes, however, makes clearer the association between the parts of the program (class `tendril` and class `cluster`) and the specific graphics elements they display.

You can cause radical alterations in the appearance of the flowers generated by the TENDRILS program by altering the constants at the start of the program. For example, by causing all the tendrils to branch upward in each cluster, you can create shapes that look like trees rather than flowers. Fine tuning of the constants will reveal different kinds of trees, from poplars to evergreens.

For more on fractals, read *Computers, Pattern, Chaos and Beauty*, by Clifford A. Pickover (listed in the bibliography), which sowed the seeds of the TENDRILS program.

CONWAY'S GAME OF LIFE

The game of Life is an old favorite, invented by Cambridge mathematician John Conway in the 1970s. Life simulates a microbe colony. The cells are displayed on the computer screen as squares in a two-dimensional array. Each cell lives and dies according to a few simple rules.

Our C++ program LIFE models this game. This program (unlike most versions of Life) runs on a character display; you don't need a graphics monitor. The display routine in this program uses a somewhat unusual approach to displaying the cells. To make the cells square instead of oblong, and to increase the number of cells, we put two cells in each character position, one over the other, as shown in Figure 17-5. An 80x25-character screen can thus display an array of 80x50 cells—enough for most Life demonstrations.

RULES OF LIFE

A cell can be either alive (displayed as a white square) or dead (a dark or empty square). Each cell has eight potential neighbors: those cells above and below it, those to its left and right, and the four diagonal cells. If an empty (dead) cell has exactly

FIGURE 17-5
Two Cells in Each Character

character position

top cell

bottom cell

screen

three neighbors, it becomes alive (is born). If a living cell has either two or three neighbors, it continues to live. But if a living cell has fewer than two neighbors, it dies (presumably from loneliness), and if it has more than three neighbors it also dies (from overcrowding).

The program calculates the fate of all the cells and then changes the cells to their new states and displays them. Some cells are born, others die, others continue to live. Each calculation-display sequence is called a `generation`.

The fascinating thing about Life is that these simple rules can give rise to very complex displays of pattern growth and change from generation to generation. Some simple patterns behave in predictable ways. For example, a four-by-four block of living cells is stable; since every cell has three living neighbors, they all continue to live. However, a line of three cells (called a *semaphore*) will flip back and forth between vertical and horizontal; the cell in the middle lives, the ones at the ends die, and new cells are born next to the middle. Other fairly simple patterns, such as the

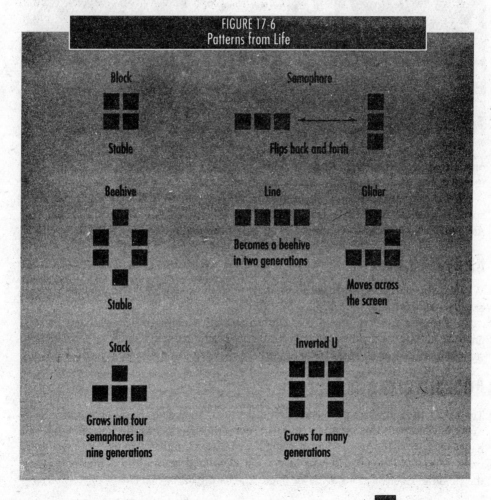

FIGURE 17-6
Patterns from Life

Block
Stable

Semaphore
Flips back and forth

Beehive
Stable

Line
Becomes a beehive
in two generations

Glider
Moves across
the screen

Stack
Grows into four
semaphores in
nine generations

Inverted U
Grows for many
generations

FIGURE 17-7
Initial Position in LIFE Program

FIGURE 17-8
Intermediate Position in LIFE Program

one used in the program, can grow into patterns of hundreds of cells, shifting and moving in fantastic kaleidoscopic animation. Figure 17-6 shows some possibilities.

Considerable research has been done on Life, which is far richer than we have space to discuss here. To learn more, read *Wheels, Life, and Other Mathematical Amusements*, by Martin Gardner (listed in the bibliography).

Running LIFE

When you start LIFE, you'll see a simple pattern: an inverted "U" shape made of seven cells, as shown in Figure 17-7.

Pressing any key causes this pattern to start evolving. This particular pattern grows for several hundred generations before reaching a stable state. An intermediate state in its evolution is shown in Figure 17-8. To stop the program, press any key.

Architecture of LIFE

The LIFE program uses only one class, called **cell**. We define a two-dimensional array of objects of this class, each object representing a cell on the screen. Each cell has four items of private data: its X and Y coordinates, and two variables representing the **state** of the cell. The **state** variable is defined in an **enum** definition to have the possible values **alive** or **dead**. Here' the listing for LIFE.CPP:

```cpp
// life.cpp
// recreates Conway's "Game of Life"
#include <conio.h>                      // for kbhit(), getch(), etc.
#include <graph.h>                      // for _settextposition(), etc.

const unsigned char top  = '\xDF';  // square in upper half
const unsigned char bot  = '\xDC';  // square in lower half
const unsigned char both = '\xDB';  // square in both halves
const int maxCols = 80;             // screen width
const int maxRows = 50;             // two cells per character
const int maxRealRows = 25;         // really only 25 rows

enum state { dead, alive };

class Cell
   {
   private:
      int xCo, yCo;                 // coordinates of cell
      state oldState, newState;     // dead or alive
   public:
      void InitCell(int, int);      // initialize cell
      void SetLive(void);           // to set initial pattern
      state GetOldState(void);      // used to find new states
      state GetNewState(void);      // used for display
      void Calc(void);              // calculate new state
      void Display(void);           // display the cell
   };

Cell c[maxCols][maxRows];           // define array of cells

void Cell::InitCell(int x, int y)   // initialize cell
   {
   xCo = x;                         // set coordinates
   yCo = y;
   oldState = newState = dead;      // set to dead
   }

void Cell::SetLive()                // set cell to alive
   {
   newState = alive;
   }

state Cell::GetOldState(void)       // get old state of cell
   {
   return(oldState);
   }

state Cell::GetNewState(void)       // get new state of cell
   {
   return(newState);
   }

void Cell::Calc()                   // calculate new state
   {                    // find number of neighbors alive
   int neighbors =  c[xCo-1][yCo-1].GetOldState() +  // nw
```

```
                    c[xCo  ][yCo-1].GetOldState() +    // n
                    c[xCo+1][yCo-1].GetOldState() +    // ne
                    c[xCo-1][yCo ].GetOldState() +     // w
                    c[xCo+1][yCo ].GetOldState() +     // e
                    c[xCo-1][yCo+1].GetOldState() +    // sw
                    c[xCo  ][yCo+1].GetOldState() +    // s
                    c[xCo+1][yCo+1].GetOldState();     // se

        newState = dead;        // cell is dead unless
                                // it's alive and has 2 or 3 neighbors
        if( oldState==alive && (neighbors==2 || neighbors==3) )
            newState = alive;
                                // or it's dead and has 3 neighbors
        else if( oldState==dead && neighbors==3 )
            newState = alive;
        }


// display the cell
// ( yCo goes from 0 to 49, screenRow from 0 to 24 )
void Cell::Display(void)
    {
    unsigned char ch;           // char to be inserted on screen

    oldState = newState;        // update oldState

    if( !(yCo%2) )              // if we're on an even row
        {                       // display this cell and one below
        int tophalf = newState; // this cell
        int bothalf = c[xCo][yCo+1].GetNewState(); // cell below
        if(tophalf || bothalf)  // if either is alive,
            {                   //      display them
            if(tophalf)                     // select correct
                ch = (bothalf) ? both : top; //   char based on
            else                            //   this cell and
                ch = bot;                   //   the one below
            _settextposition(yCo/2, xCo);   // move cursor
            putch(ch);                      // insert character
            }
        }
    }

void main()
    {
    int x, y;

    _clearscreen(_GCLEARSCREEN);                    // erase screen
    short oldcursor = _settextcursor(0x2000); // turn off cursor

    for(x=0; x<maxCols; x++)            // initialize to dead
        for(y=0; y<maxRows; y++)
            c[x][y].InitCell(x, y);
```

```
c[39][25].SetLive();                 // set inverted U pattern
c[40][25].SetLive();
c[41][25].SetLive();
c[39][26].SetLive();
c[41][26].SetLive();
c[39][27].SetLive();
c[41][27].SetLive();

for(x=0; x<maxCols; x++)             // display initial cells
    for(y=0; y<maxRows; y++)
        c[x][y].Display();
getch();                             // wait for keypress

while( !kbhit() )                    // continue until keypress
    {
    for(x=1; x<maxCols-1; x++)       // find new states
        for(y=1; y<maxRows-1; y++)
            c[x][y].Calc();

    _clearscreen(_GCLEARSCREEN);     // erase screen

    for(x=0; x<maxCols; x++)         // display cells
        for(y=0; y<maxRows; y++)
            c[x][y].Display();

    }  // end while
_settextcursor(oldcursor);           // restore cursor
}  // end main()
```

Two states, represented by oldState and newState, are necessary for each cell, because calculating the new state of all the cells is a two-step process. First the new state of each cell is calculated, based on the old state of its neighbors. Until this is carried out for all cells, no cell may change its old state. Then the old state is set to the value of the new state, and all the old states are displayed.

Initializing the Cells

Each cell must know where it is so that it knows what neighbors to query to find out if it lives or dies. A member function, InitCell(), executed once for each cell at the beginning of the program, tells each cell its coordinates and sets its states to *dead*. (A constructor can't be used because you can't pass arguments when initializing array members in a constructor.)

Getting and Setting the State

The two member functions GetOldState() and GetNewState() return the state, alive or dead, of a cell. They are used to help calculate the number of living neighbors and to display the pattern. The SetAlive() function sets the new state of the cell to *alive*, and is used in main() to set the initial cell pattern.

Calculating the New State

The member function `Calc()` determines whether the cell will live or die. This function finds the state of all eight neighboring cells and adds them together to obtain the number of living neighbors. A living cell will die unless it has two or three living neighbors, and a dead cell will be born if it has three neighbors. This function changes the cell's `newState` variable accordingly. The `Calc` member function is unusual in that it assumes the existence of objects of its own class, namely `c[x][y]`.

Displaying the Cell

Before displaying the cell, the `Display()` function first sets the `oldState` variable equal to `newState`. It can do this because it knows that `Calc()` has finished calculating the new state for all the variables. `Display()` uses the library function `_settextposition()` to cause a cell to display itself at the correct position.

Because the screen is erased just before all the cells display themselves, they need do nothing if they are dead. If a cell is alive, it must figure out what character on the screen to modify. Since each character has two cell positions, some logic is devoted to figuring out the correct graphics character to insert. There are three possibilities: a character with a cell on the bottom but not on the top, a character with a cell on the top but not on the bottom, and a character with cells on both the top and the bottom. Figure 17-9 shows the possibilities.

THE main() FUNCTION

The `main()` function erases the screen, using the `_clearscreen()` function. Then it initializes all the cells to *dead*, and sets some of them back to *alive* to form the initial pattern. It displays this initial pattern and waits for a keypress.

Following this keypress, the program enters a loop (which can be terminated with a second keypress). Three actions take place in the loop. First the new state of all the cells is found, using `Calc()`. Notice that the cells on the outer edges of the array are not calculated (the index variables go from 1 to the maximum-1). This avoids out-of-bounds array references when a cell examines its neighbors. Next the screen is erased, and finally all cells are displayed using `Calc()`.

The present version of LIFE requires you to rewrite the calls to `SetLive()` in `main()` if you want to change to a new initial pattern. This simplifies the program but makes it rather inflexible. It would be easy to modify this program so the user could type in initial patterns using cell coordinates. This would give it much more flexibility. Even better would be a routine that allowed the user to input cell positions using the cursor keys.

FIGURE 17-9
Combining a Cell with a Character

tophalf
no   yes

bothalf
no

yes   bot   both

A TIC-TAC-TOE PROGRAM

Tic-tac-toe is a classic pencil-and-paper game in which each of two opponents tries to get three marks, usually represented by O and X, in a row. Figure 17-10 shows such a game, where X (due to an unfortunate lapse in concentration by O) wins.

The next program, TICTAC, enables the computer to play tic-tac-toe against a human opponent. This program actually demonstrates a minor form of artificial intelligence. In terms of OOP, it provides another example of recursion. A member function in one object creates another object of the same type, the same member function in the second object creates a third object, and so on.

You may think that tic-tac-toe is too simple a game to merit serious analysis. However, the approach used in TICTAC is fundamentally the same as that of programs that play other, more challenging, games, such as checkers, chess, go, and bridge.

FIGURE 17-10
Moves in a Typical Tic-Tac-Toe Game

X wins

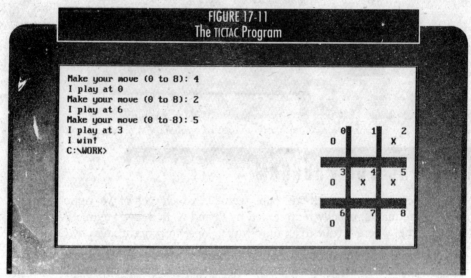

FIGURE 17-11
The TICTAC Program

```
Make your move (0 to 8): 4
I play at 0
Make your move (0 to 8): 2
I play at 6
Make your move (0 to 8): 5
I play at 3
I win!
C:\WORK>
```

It uses the same strategy of recursively evaluating positions on a game tree, following the tree from a few initial branches to hundreds or thousands of subbranches.

TICTAC "thinks ahead" all the way to the end of the game, so it plays as well as, or better than, many humans. Figure 17-11 shows the screen display after several moves.

Here's the listing for TICTAC.CPP:

```
// tictac.cpp
// tic-tac-toe game
#include <graph.h>      // for _settextposition(), etc.
#include <conio.h>      // for putch(), etc.
#include <process.h>    // for exit()

enum whoplays { human, machine };
enum cell { empty, full };
enum boolean { false, true };

int deep = 0;           // recursion depth

class Position          // represents one board position
   {
   private:
      cell mcell[9];    // cells marked with machine moves
      cell hcell[9];    // cells marked with human moves
      whoplays player;  // human or machine to play next
   public:
      Position();                  // constructor
      boolean IsWin();             // win in this position?
      boolean IsLegal(int);        // move is legal?
      void MakeMove(int);          // make move
      void SetPlayer(whoplays);    // swap player and machine
      static void InitDisplay();   // displays lines & numbers
      void Display();              // display board position
      int Evaluate(int&);          // score this position
   };

// Position()
// constructor: reset all cells to empty
Position::Position()
   {
   for( int j=0; j<9; j++ )
      mcell[j] = hcell[j] = empty;
   }

// IsWin()
// see if the current position is a win for player
boolean Position::IsWin()
   {
   cell *ptr;           // pointer to cells
   if( player==human )  // point to appropriate array
      ptr = hcell;
   else
      ptr = mcell;
                        // check for a 3-in-a-row
   if( (ptr[0] && ptr[1] && ptr[2]) ||  // horizontal
       (ptr[3] && ptr[4] && ptr[5]) ||
       (ptr[6] && ptr[7] && ptr[8]) ||
```

```
        (ptr[0] && ptr[3] && ptr[6]) ||   // vertical
        (ptr[1] && ptr[4] && ptr[7]) ||
        (ptr[2] && ptr[5] && ptr[8]) ||
        (ptr[0] && ptr[4] && ptr[8]) ||   // diagonal
        (ptr[2] && ptr[4] && ptr[6]) )
      return(true);
   else
      return(false);
   }


// IsLegal()
// find if move is legal in this position
boolean Position::IsLegal(int move)
   {
   if( move>=0 && move<=8 &&
                 mcell[move]==empty && hcell[move]==empty )
      return(true);
   else
      return(false);
   }


// MakeMove()
// make move in current position with current player
void Position::MakeMove(int move)
   {
   if( player==human )         // player is human
      hcell[move] = full;
   else                        // player is machine
      mcell[move] = full;
   }


// SetPlayer()
// set player to human or machine
void Position::SetPlayer(whoplays p)
   {
   player = p;
   }


// InitDisplay()
// Draws lines, numbers squares
void Position::InitDisplay()
   {
   const unsigned char block = '\xB2';      // gray block

   void Insert(unsigned char, int, int);  // prototype
   int row, col;

   _clearscreen(_GCLEARSCREEN); // clear screen
   for(row=0; row<11; row++)    // vertical lines
      {
```

```
        Insert( block,  5, row);
        Insert( block, 11, row);
        }
    for(col=0; col<17; col++)          // horizontal lines
        {
        Insert( block, col, 3);
        Insert( block, col, 7);
        }
    for(int j=0; j<9; j++)             // number squares
        Insert( (char)(j+'0'), (j%3)*6+4, (j/3)*4 );
    } // end InitDisplay()

// Display()
// displays board
void Position::Display()
    {
    void Insert(unsigned char, int, int);  // prototype
    int row, col;

    for(int j=0; j<9; j++)                        // for each square
        {
        if( hcell[j] )                            // human move
            Insert('X', (j%3)*6+2, (j/3)*4+1);
        else if( mcell[j] )                       // machine move
            Insert('0', (j%3)*6+2, (j/3)*4+1);
        else                                      // no move
            Insert(' ', (j%3)*6+2, (j/3)*4+1);
        }
    _settextposition(23, 1);                      // restore cursor pos
    } // end Display()

// Insert()
// inserts character ch at col, row
void Insert(unsigned char ch, int col, int row)
    {
    // start 5 lines down, 50 cols over
    _settextposition(row+5+1, col+50+1);   // insert the char
    putch(ch);
    }

// Evaluate()
// set score to chance of win (0-100), return the best move
int Position::Evaluate( int& score )
    {
    int const winscore = 100;        // score for a win (lose=0)
    int const drawscore = 50;        // score for a draw
    int returnmove;                  // move to be returned
    Position *posptr;                // pointer to new position
    int legalmoves = 0;              // count legal moves
    int totalscore = 0;              // cumulative score
```

```
int highscore = 0;              // highest score to date
int avgscore;                   // average score
int score2;                     // score from recursive call
boolean waswin = false;         // true if at least one win
boolean wasother = false;       // if at least one non-win

++deep;                         // down one recursion level
for(int move=0; move<9; move++) // for each of 9 moves
   {                            // 'player' can make
   if( IsLegal(move) )          // if no one played there yet
      {
      if( legalmoves==0 )       // set returnmove to first
         returnmove = move;     //   legal move
      ++legalmoves;             // count a legal move
      posptr = new Position;    // make new position
                                //    for this move
      *posptr = *this;          // transfer this pos to posptr
      posptr->MakeMove(move);   // make the move
      if (deep < 3)             // display, if in first two
         posptr->Display();     // levels of recursion
      if( posptr->IsWin() )     // check if it's a win
         {
         waswin = true;         // there was a win
         highscore = winscore;  // win is highest score
         totalscore += winscore; // update total
         returnmove = move;     // return this move
         }
      else                      // no win, so check deeper
         {
                                // swap human/machine
         whoplays newp = (player==machine) ? human : machine;
         posptr->SetPlayer(newp); // in new position

                                // recursive call
         posptr->Evaluate(score2); // to new position

         if(score2==winscore)   // if wining score,
            waswin = true;      // remember there was a win
         else
            wasother = true;    // remember non-win
         totalscore += score2;  // add new score to total
         if( score2 > highscore ) // remember the move that
            {                   // produced the
            highscore = score2; // highest score, and
            returnmove = move;  // the score
            }
         }                      // end else (no win)
      delete posptr;            // delete the position
      }                         // end if IsLegal
   }                            // end for
                                // summarize results of all
```

```
moves
    if( legalmoves==0 )       // if there are no legal moves
        {
        score = drawscore;    // it must be a draw
        --deep;               // go up one recursion level
        return(99);           // return nonsense move
        }
    else                      // there were some legal moves
        {
        avgscore = totalscore / legalmoves; // find average
        if( waswin && wasother )      // if wins and non-wins,
            score = winscore - (winscore-avgscore)/5;  // favor wins
        else
            score = avgscore;  // otherwise, use the average score
        score = 100 - score;  // invert: bad for them, good for us
        --deep;               // go up one recursion level
        return(returnmove);   // return best move
        } // end else (legal moves)
    } // end Evaluate()

// main()
// get human move, get machine move, etc.
void main(void)
    {
    int move;                     // store moves
    int sc;                       // for Evaluate()
    int movecount = 0;            // number of move-pairs
    Position current;             // create current position
    int cursrow = 0;              // cursor row for text

    Position::InitDisplay();      // display the board
    while(1)                      // cycle until game over
        {
        current.SetPlayer(human); // set player to human
        current.Display();        // display the position
        _settextposition(++cursrow, 1);
        _outtext("Make your move (0 to 8): ");  // get human move
        move = getche() - '0';    // convert char to move
        if( ! current.IsLegal(move) )
            {
            _settextposition(++cursrow, 1);
            _outtext("Illegal move.");
            continue;             // return to top of loop
            }
        current.MakeMove(move);   // make human move
        current.Display();
        if( current.IsWin() )     // check for human win
            {
            _settextposition(++cursrow, 1);
            _outtext("You win!");
            exit(0);
```

```
            }
    if( ++movecount==5 )          // if human move was
       {                          // the last possible move
    _settextposition(++cursrow, 1);
    _outtext("It's a draw");
    exit(0);
       }                          // now machine can play
    current.SetPlayer(machine);   // set player to machine
    move = current.Evaluate(sc);  // get machine move
    _settextposition(++cursrow, 1);
    _outtext("I play at ");
    putch( char(move+'0') );      // (convert move to char)
    current.MakeMove(move);       // make machine move
    current.Display();
    if( current.IsWin() )         // check for machine win
       {
    _settextposition(++cursrow, 1);
    _outtext("I win!");
    exit(0);
       }
    }  // end while
 }  // end main()
```

THE Position CLASS

TICTAC uses objects of the class **Position**. Each object of this class represents a board position—that is, some arrangement of Xs and Os on the 3-by-3 matrix of squares. Besides recording the X and O moves made to date, a **Position** object also includes a variable that specifies the player with the next turn.

The **main()** program creates a single object of class **Position** called **current**. This position records the current state of the game, and is displayed so the user can see what's happening.

MEMBER FUNCTIONS OF Position

Let's look at each member function of **Position** in turn. This will serve to explain how TICTAC works.

The Position() Constructor

The constructor for **Position** initializes all the cells in a given position to **empty**. A single array could be used to represent the board, but it turns out to be simpler to use two arrays: one for human moves (**hcell**) and one for machine moves (**mcell**). The elements of these arrays are of type **cell**, which is declared in an **enum** statement to have two possible values: **empty** and **full**.

The cells are numbered from 0 in the upper-left corner down to 8 in the lower-right corner.

The IsWin() Function

The `isWin()` function figures out if a particular position represents a win. If the human is playing, a win is three `hcell` (for *human cell*) elements in a row; if the player is the machine, it's three `mcell` elements. `IsWin()` sets a pointer to the appropriate array, and then checks each of the eight possible three-in-a-rows to see if its cells are occupied. It returns the Boolean value of `true` if it finds a win, or `false` if it doesn't.

The IsLegal() Function

The `IsLegal()` function checks to see if a move, sent to it as an argument, is legal. A move is legal if it is a number between 0 and 8 and if neither human nor machine has already played in the specified cell.

The MakeMove() Function

The `MakeMove()` function changes the contents of the specified cell from `empty` to `full`. This happens in `mcell` or in `hcell`, depending on whether the player in the position is the machine or the human.

The SetPlayer() Function

The `SetPlayer()` function changes the player in a particular position. The `main()` program uses it to switch back and forth between the human—who always plays first—and the machine, as they alternate moves in the `current` position.

The InitDisplay() Function

When the program is first executed, it calls `InitDisplay()` to draw the crossed lines that form the tic-tac-toe game board, and to number each of the resulting nine squares, so the human knows what they are. The squares are numbered from 0 to 8, as shown in the program output. `InitDisplay()` starts by clearing the screen with `clrscr()`. It uses the `Insert()` function to actually place characters on the screen.

The Display() Function

The `main()` program displays the moves made on the board by calling `Display()` as a member function of the `current` position. This function translates the contents of `hcell` and `mcell` into the X and O display. `Display()` is also used by the `Evaluate()` function to show—very briefly—the positions it's thinking about as it looks ahead. `Display()` places characters on the screen by calling the `Insert()` function.

The Insert() Function

The `Insert()` function inserts a character at a fixed column-row position on the screen, using the `gotoxy()` and `putch()` library functions. `Insert()` uses a coordinate system that starts 5 lines down and 50 columns over from the upper-left corner of the screen; that's where the game board is drawn.

The Evaluate() Function

We now come to the "brains" of the program. The Evaluate() function evaluates a particular position to see how likely it is to lead to a win for a particular player. It also returns the best move in a particular position.

The main() function calls Evaluate to determine the best machine move, and makes the machine's move based on the recommendations of this function. How does Evaluate() figure out the best move? Its overall strategy is to create a new Position object (using new) for each move that can be legally made from its position. Each of these positions is then evaluated. For instance, the human has the first move and selects one of the nine choices. Thus on its first move the machine is faced with eight possible moves. Which is the best? To decide, it evaluates each of the eight moves. For each of the eight moves it creates a new Position. From this position it then calculates a score, based on how likely the move is to lead to a win. When all possible moves have been evaluated, it returns the move with the highest score, and main() then executes this move.

How is each of the eight possible moves evaluated? For the position corresponding to each move, Evaluate() calls itself again. For each of the eight moves the machine can make, the human has seven possible responses. When Evaluate() is called for one of the machine's eight moves, it generates a position for each of the seven possible human responses. Each of these seven positions then uses Evaluate again to determine the best move. This involves creating six positions for each possible machine move, and calling Evaluate() for each of the six moves. The resulting branching of nine initial moves, each with eight responses, and so on, is partially shown in Figure 17-12. Since there are 9! (9 factorial, or 9*8*7*6*5*4*3*2*1, or more than 300,000) possible move combinations, we can't show them all. We show the first few, and several toward the end of the tree.

Eventually, as the Evaluate() function works its way down lower and lower into the move tree, one of several things happens. The first possibility is that somebody wins—that is, they get three-in-a-row. This is the end of that branch of the move tree, since the game ends at that point. (Thus there are actually somewhat fewer possible positions than 9!, since the tree stops branching when there's a win, although this does not reduce the size of the tree substantially.) The Evaluate() function assigns a number, called a *score*, to each possible outcome so that the various moves can be compared. A win results in a score of 100; this is the highest score. A score of 0 represents a loss.

The other possibility when the move tree is followed to the end is that no more moves can be made; all the squares have been filled by Xs or Os, and the game is a draw. A draw results in a score of 50.

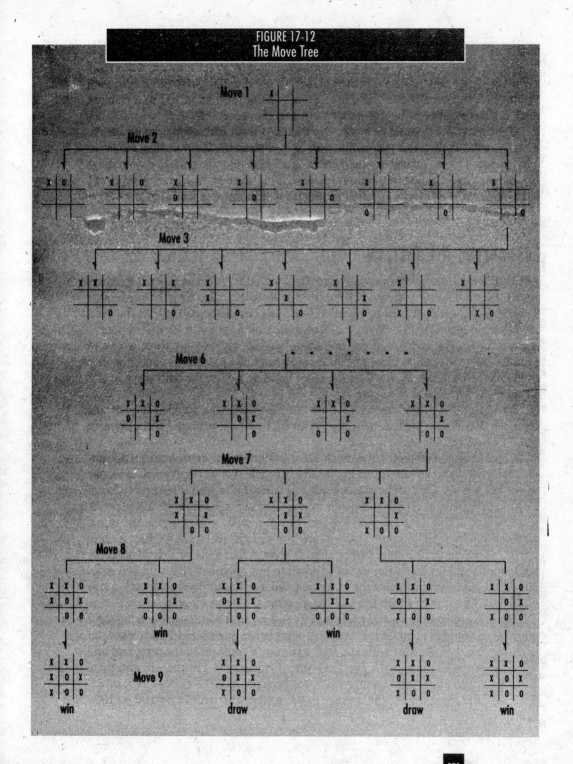

FIGURE 17-12
The Move Tree

The `Evaluate()` function is set up in the form of a loop that cycles through nine possible moves. In each cycle through the loop, it checks to see if the move is legal. If so, it creates a new position, transfers the current position into it, and makes the move in the new position. It then checks to see if making this move results in a win. If so, it places 100 in the `highscore` variable, and adds 100 to a running total. It also remembers the move that generated the score.

If the move didn't generate a win, `Evaluate()` must look deeper, so it calls the `Evaluate()` function that is a member of the new position. This function will eventually return a score, either because there's a win or because the game ends in a draw. This score is again added to the running total. If the score is the highest seen so far, it is placed in the `highscore` variable, and the return move is set to this new high-scoring move.

EVALUATING A POSITION

When all the moves have been evaluated, the loop ends, and `Evaluate()` figures out a total score for its position. You can approximate this calculation by saying that it averages the scores of the opponent's moves. `Evaluate()` then inverts the average to obtain the score. The inversion is necessary because a win for our opponent is a loss for us. For instance, if our opponent has four moves—say three wins and a draw—the total score is close to 100 for him, but close to 0 for us, since there's a good chance we'll lose. A draw, on the other hand, is a draw for both players, and 50 subtracted from 100 is still 50.

This inversion of the score each time the player changes is called the *minmax* approach. We assume we'll do what's good for us, but we also assume our opponent will do what's bad for us.

Combining several scores into one is actually a little more complicated than simply averaging them. To see the reason for this, imagine that our opponent can make one of four moves. One of the moves leads to a win for him, and three lead to losses for him. What's the score for these four moves? The average would be 100+0+0+0, or 25, which is less than a draw. However, our opponent won't choose one of the moves at random; he'll choose the best one for him. So the score for him is close to 100. It's not quite 100, since it's not quite as good as four wins (which would score 100), but it's still up there. For us (as opposed to our opponent) the situation is reversed. We don't want to make the move that will lead to our opponent having four possible moves, one of which is a win, so we score the move close to 0.

These considerations—and trial and error—lead to the following scoring algorithm: If our opponent has some wins and some other outcomes (draws, losses, or other scores), then we start with 100 (the `winscore` constant in the program) and subtract from it 100 minus the average score, divided by 5. For the win and three losses described above, the average is 25, so the score is 100 – (100–25)/5, or 85. For a win and three draws, the average is 62, so the score would be 100 – (100–62)/5, or 92.

If there are no wins, or all wins, the average can be used without modification. Four draws is 50, two losses and two draws is 25 (75 for us), four wins is 100 (0 for us), and so on.

THE main() FUNCTION

The main() function cycles around a loop. It asks the user for his move, and makes it on the current position. It then displays this position, calls Evaluate() to find the best response, makes this move, displays it, and returns to the top of the loop to ask for the next human move. After either a human or a machine move, the current position is checked for a win. If the human has made his or her fifth move, the game is a draw. Messages are printed for these three outcomes.

FURTHER THOUGHTS

You may have noticed how long it takes the program to make its first move (actually the second move of the game) when it has 8 choices, and how much more quickly it figures out its next move (the fourth move of the game) when it has only 6 choices. Not only is 8 larger than 6, but the branches of the move tree that start at the second move are far larger than those starting at the fourth move. There are about 8! choices for the second move, but only 6!, or 56 times fewer, for the fourth. If we changed the program to let the machine play first, its first move would take nine times as long as the current first move.

Thus you can see that if the tic-tac-toe game were even slightly more complicated than it is, we could not use the approach of following the move tree to the end. For more complex games a different strategy must be used. One approach is to follow the move tree downward only a fixed number of moves. At an appropriate depth no more positions are created. Instead, the position is evaluated in other ways. In a chess game, for example, an evaluation is based on such factors as the number of pawns occupying center squares and the total value of the pieces on the board. Also, branches that lead to unlikely situations are not explored; this is called "pruning" the tree. Such topics are beyond the scope of this book.

SUMMARY

This chapter has explored some diverse applications of C++ programming. If nothing else, these examples should demonstrate that the uses to which you can put C++ are limited only by your imagination (or perhaps the spur of necessity). The object-oriented approach can be applied to most programming problems. Now that you understand how to use this new approach, as embodied in C++, you have at your disposal one of the most powerful programming tools yet created. We hope you enjoyed this introduction to OOP and C++, and that your use of these tools is amusing as well as profitable.

QUESTIONS AND EXERCISES

Because this chapter is just for fun, there are no questions or exercises.

APPENDICES

A: ASCII TABLE

B: MICROSOFT C++ KEYWORDS

C: USING THE PROJECT FEATURE

D: ANSWERS TO QUESTIONS AND EXERCISES

E: BIBLIOGRAPHY

ASCII TABLE

IBM Character Codes					IBM Character Codes			
DEC	HEX	Symbol	Key		DEC	HEX	Symbol	Key
0	00	(NULL)	CTRL 2		27	1B	←	ESC
1	01	☺	CTRL A		28	1C	∞	CTRL \
2	02	●	CTRL B		29	1D	↔	CTRL]
3	03	♥	CTRL C		30	1E	▲	CTRL 6
4	04	♦	CTRL D		31	1F	▼	CTRL -
5	05	♣	CTRL E		32	20		SPACEBAR
6	06	♠	CTRL F		33	21	!	!
7	07	•	Beep		34	22	"	"
8	08	◘	BACKSPACE		35	23	#	#
9	09		TAB		36	24	$	$
10	0A	■	Newline (linefeed)		37	25	%	%
					38	26	&	&
11	0B	♂	CTRL K		39	27	'	'
12	0C	♀	CTRL L		40	28	(	(
13	0D	♪	ENTER (carriage return)		41	29	)	)
					42	2A	*	*
14	0E	♫	CTRL N		43	2B	+	+
15	0F	☼	CTRL O		44	2C	,	,
16	10	►	CTRL P		45	2D	-	-
17	11	◄	CTRL Q		46	2E	.	.
18	12	↕	CTRL R		47	2F	/	/
19	13	‼	CTRL S		48	30	0	0
20	14	¶	CTRL T		49	31	1	1
21	15	§	CTRL U		50	32	2	2
22	16	▬	CTRL V		51	33	3	3
23	17	↨	CTRL W		52	34	4	4
24	18	↑	CTRL X		53	35	5	5
25	19	↓	CTRL Y		54	36	6	6
26	1A	→	CTRL Z		55	37	7	7

IBM Character Codes				IBM Character Codes			
DEC	HEX	Symbol	Key	DEC	HEX	Symbol	Key
56	38	8	⑧	95	5F	_	⬚
57	39	9	⑨	96	60	`	`
58	3A	:	:	97	61	a	ⓐ
59	3B	;	;	98	62	b	ⓑ
60	3C	<	<	99	63	c	ⓒ
61	3D	=	=	100	64	d	ⓓ
62	3E	>	>	101	65	e	ⓔ
63	3F	?	?	102	66	f	ⓕ
64	40	@	@	103	67	g	ⓖ
65	41	A	Ⓐ	104	68	h	ⓗ
66	42	B	Ⓑ	105	69	i	ⓘ
67	43	C	Ⓒ	106	6A	j	ⓙ
68	44	D	Ⓓ	107	6B	k	ⓚ
69	45	E	Ⓔ	108	6C	l	ⓛ
70	46	F	Ⓕ	109	6D	m	ⓜ
71	47	G	Ⓖ	110	6E	n	ⓝ
72	48	H	Ⓗ	111	6F	o	ⓞ
73	49	I	Ⓘ	112	70	p	ⓟ
74	4A	J	Ⓙ	113	71	q	ⓠ
75	4B	K	Ⓚ	114	72	r	ⓡ
76	4C	L	Ⓛ	115	73	s	ⓢ
77	4D	M	Ⓜ	116	74	t	ⓣ
78	4E	N	Ⓝ	117	75	u	ⓤ
79	4F	0	Ⓞ	118	76	v	ⓥ
80	50	P	Ⓟ	119	77	w	ⓦ
81	51	Q	Ⓠ	120	78	x	ⓧ
82	52	R	Ⓡ	121	79	y	ⓨ
83	53	S	Ⓢ	122	7A	z	ⓩ
84	54	T	Ⓣ	123	7B	{	{
85	55	U	Ⓤ	124	7C	¦	¦
86	56	V	Ⓥ	125	7D	}	}
87	57	W	Ⓦ	126	7E	~	~
88	58	X	Ⓧ	127	7F	Δ	CTRL ←
89	59	Y	Ⓨ	128	80	Ç	ALT 128
90	5A	Z	Ⓩ	129	81	ü	ALT 129
91	5B	[	[	130	82	é	ALT 130
92	5C	\	\	131	83	â	ALT 131
93	5D	]	]	132	84	ä	ALT 132
94	5E	^	^	133	85	à	ALT 133

IBM Character Codes

DEC	HEX	Symbol	Key		DEC	HEX	Symbol	Key
134	86	å	(ALT) 134		173	AD	¡	(ALT) 173
135	87	ç	(ALT) 135		174	AE	«	(ALT) 174
136	88	ê	(ALT) 136		175	AF	»	(ALT) 175
137	89	ë	(ALT) 137		176	B0	▒	(ALT) 176
138	8A	è	(ALT) 138		177	B1	▓	(ALT) 177
139	8B	ï	(ALT) 139		178	B2	�	(ALT) 178
140	8C	î	(ALT) 140		179	B3	│	(ALT) 179
141	8D	ì	(ALT) 141		180	B4	┤	(ALT) 180
142	8E	Ä	(ALT) 142		181	B5	╡	(ALT) 181
143	8F	Å	(ALT) 143		182	B6	╢	(ALT) 182
144	90	É	(ALT) 144		183	B7	╖	(ALT) 183
145	91	æ	(ALT) 145		184	B8	╕	(ALT) 184
146	92	Æ	(ALT) 146		185	B9	╣	(ALT) 185
147	93	ô	(ALT) 147		186	BA	║	(ALT) 186
148	94	ö	(ALT) 148		187	BB	╗	(ALT) 187
149	95	ò	(ALT) 149		188	BC	╝	(ALT) 188
150	96	û	(ALT) 150		189	BD	╜	(ALT) 189
151	97	ù	(ALT) 151		190	BE	╛	(ALT) 190
152	98	ÿ	(ALT) 152		191	BF	┐	(ALT) 191
153	99	Ö	(ALT) 153		192	C0	└	(ALT) 192
154	9A	Ü	(ALT) 154		193	C1	┴	(ALT) 193
155	9B	¢	(ALT) 155		194	C2	┬	(ALT) 194
156	9C	£	(ALT) 156		195	C3	├	(ALT) 195
157	9D	¥	(ALT) 157		196	C4	─	(ALT) 196
158	9E	₧	(ALT) 158		197	C5	┼	(ALT) 197
159	9F	ƒ	(ALT) 159		198	C6	╞	(ALT) 198
160	A0	á	(ALT) 160		199	C7	╟	(ALT) 199
161	A1	í	(ALT) 161		200	C8	╚	(ALT) 200
162	A2	ó	(ALT) 162		201	C9	╔	(ALT) 201
163	A3	ú	(ALT) 163		202	CA	╩	(ALT) 202
164	A4	ñ	(ALT) 164		203	CB	╦	(ALT) 203
165	A5	Ñ	(ALT) 165		204	CC	╠	(ALT) 204
166	A6	ª	(ALT) 166		205	CD	═	(ALT) 205
167	A7	º	(ALT) 167		206	CE	╬	(ALT) 206
168	A8	¿	(ALT) 168		207	CF	╧	(ALT) 207
169	A9	⌐	(ALT) 169		208	D0	╨	(ALT) 208
170	AA	¬	(ALT) 170		209	D1	╤	(ALT) 209
171	AB	½	(ALT) 171		210	D2	╥	(ALT) 210
172	AC	¼	(ALT) 172		211	D3	╙	(ALT) 211

IBM Character Codes					IBM Character Codes			
DEC	HEX	Symbol	Key		DEC	HEX	Symbol	Key
212	D4	T	(ALT) 212		234	EA	Ω	(ALT) 234
213	D5	U	(ALT) 213		235	EB	δ	(ALT) 235
214	D6	V	(ALT) 214		236	EC	∞	(ALT) 236
215	D7	W	(ALT) 215		237	ED	φ	(ALT) 237
216	D8	X	(ALT) 216		238	EE	ε	(ALT) 238
217	D9	⌐	(ALT) 217		239	EF	∩	(ALT) 239
218	DA	⌐	(ALT) 218		240	F0	≡	(ALT) 240
219	DB	▪	(ALT) 219		241	F1	±	(ALT) 241
220	DC	▪	(ALT) 220		242	F2	≥	(ALT) 242
221	DD	▪	(ALT) 221		243	F3	≤	(ALT) 243
222	DE		(ALT) 222		244	F4	⌠	(ALT) 244
223	DF		(ALT) 223		245	F5	⌡	(ALT) 245
224	E0	α	(ALT) 224		246	F6	÷	(ALT) 246
225	E1	β	(ALT) 225		247	F7	≈	(ALT) 247
226	E2	Γ	(ALT) 226		248	F8	°	(ALT) 248
227	E3	π	(ALT) 227		249	F9	•	(ALT) 249
228	E4	Σ	(ALT) 228		250	FA	·	(ALT) 250
229	E5	σ	(ALT) 229		251	FB	√	(ALT) 251
230	E6	μ	(ALT) 230		252	FC	η	(ALT) 252
231	E7	τ	(ALT) 231		253	FD	^{2}	(ALT) 253
232	E8	Φ	(ALT) 232		254	FE	▪	(ALT) 254
233	E9	Θ	(ALT) 233		255	FF	(blank)	(ALT) 255

Note that IBM Extended ASCII characters can be displayed by pressing the (ALT) key and then typing the decimal code of the character on the keypad.

MICROSOFT C++ KEYWORDS

Keywords implement specific C++ language features. They cannot be used as names for variables or other user-defined program elements. Most of the keywords are common to both C and C++, but some are specific to C++. A few are specific to MS-DOS computers and are not found in other C++ implementations, such as Unix. Some keywords are spcific to Microsoft compilers.

__asm	float	return
auto	for	__saveregs
__based	__fortran	__segment
break	friend	short
case	goto	signed
catch	__huge	sizeof
__cdecl	if	static
char	__inline	__stdcall
class	int	struct
const	__interrupt	switch
continue	__loadds	__syscall
default	long	template
delete	__near	this
do	new	typedef
double	operator	union
else	__pascal	unsigned
enum	private	virtual
__export	protected	void
extern	public	volatile
__far	register	while

USING
THE PROJECT
FEATURE

The Programmer's WorkBench automatically creates a project to handle "normal" programs, that is, those with a single source file and no special requirements for library files. If you want to go beyond this simple scenario, you must take control of the project yourself. In this appendix we describe how to create your own project file using the Programmer's WorkBench.

A GROUP OF FILES

A project is a group of related files. These files, their relationship to each other, and details of how they are to be compiled, linked, and otherwise operated on, are stored in a file called a make file, with the .MAK extension. In the PWB, creating a project consists of adding appropriate file names to a list. The names on this list are then combined with other information that the PWB already knows to create the .MAK file.

In this book there are three occasions for using the project feature. The first is the graphics programs described in Chapter 11, which needs a special library file called GRAPHICS.LIB. The second is programs that consist of more than one source file, which are described in Chapter 15. The third is programs that use the Microsoft Foundation classes, described in Chapter 16, which need the library file SAFXCR.LIB (or something similar). If you attempt to build any of these programs without creating a project, the linker will not be able to find functions you call in your source file, and you will get "unresolved external" error messages.

We'll examine a program that has multiple source files as well as a nonstandard library file. This covers both reasons for using the project feature. Let's say that you want to create a project for a program called MYPROG, which has two source files, MYPROG1.CPP and MYPROG2.CPP. This program also requires an unusual library file, NONSTAND.LIB.

Adding Files

Start the PWB in the directory where you want to develop your program. Create the source files if they don't already exist. Select New Project from the Project menu. Fill in the name MYPROG (with no file extension) in the Project Name field. In programs with a single source file, you often use the source file name as the project name (although this isn't necessary). Whatever name you give the project will be given to the final executable file. In our example you will end up with an executable called MYPROG.EXE. When you've filled in the project name, click on OK.

Now a dialog box appears called Edit Project. This box contains a list of the files in the current directory, and also an empty list called Project. You need to put the names of all your source files and the names of any nonstandard library file on this empty list. You can either type the file names into the File Name field (along with complete pathnames, if they are not in the current directory), or you can select them from the list of files. It's probably easiest to select your source files from the list and type in the library files, which are typically in a different directory.

In our example you would could double-click on MYPROG1.CPP and MYPROG2.CPP (or select each one and then click on the Add/Delete button). This will cause them to be added to the Project list.

For the library file, enter the full pathname of the library file into the File Name field. For example, if the NONSTAND.LIB file is in the C:\C700\LIB directory, you would enter C:\C700\LIB\NONSTAND.LIB. Then press (ENTER), or click on the Add/Delete button. The library file will appear on the list.

Environmental Variables

The PWB needs to know not only what files you need to operate on, but also where to find standard library and include files. These are normally set when you install the Microsoft C/C++ system. However, sometimes you may need to modify some of these environmental values to let your compiler know where things are.

You can examine the environmental variables, and change them if necessary, by selecting the Environmental Variables item from the Options menu. Selecting a line in the Variables List window then displays that line in the Variable field, where you can edit it.

For example, suppose you're trying to create programs that use the Microsoft foundation classes. These classes require that the directory \C700\MFC\INCLUDE be part of the INCLUDE variable. If for some reason this has not already been done, you might need to edit this variable to look something lke this:

```
INCLUDE=C:\C700\INCLUDE;C:\C700\MFC\INCLUDE
```

Similarly, you might need to modify the LIB variable to look this:

```
LIB=C:\C700\LIB;C:\C700\MFC\LIB
```

Once you have the environmental variables set correctly in your system you won't ordinarily need to worry about them again.

SAVING THE PROJECT LIST

When you have added all the necessary files to the project list, click on the Save List button. This saves the project file to disk in the form of a .MAK file, in this case MYPROG.MAK. You can examine it with the DOS TYPE command if you like; but it is much harder to read this file than it is to create it with the PWB.

Now you can compile and link your program by selecting Build from the Project menu. The process generates MYPROG1.OBJ and MYPROG2.OBJ, and links them with NONSTAND.LIB to create MYPROG.EXE. You can run this file in the usual way.

When you're finished with a project, select Close from the Project menu. Otherwise, if you load some other source file and attempt to compile it, you'll find that selecting Build from the Project menu compiles the open project, rather than the open file.

You can open an existing project by selecting Open from the Project menu, and modify it by selecting Edit Project from the Project menu. The Add/Delete button in the Edit Project box will delete files selected in the Project list box, so you can delete and add files until you've got it right.

AUTOMATIC VERSION CONTROL

The Project feature avoids unnecessary operations by keeping track of the time and date when all the files in a project were last changed. By knowing this it can figure out whether a particular file needs to be recompiled when a build operation is taking place, and whether relinking is necessary. That is, if a source file was last compiled before the executable was created, there's no need to compile it again before relinking. If it has been changed since the last relinking, then the Project feature will cause it to be recompiled before relinking takes place. Thus only those source files that have been changed since the last build will be recompiled. This saves a lot of compile time, and frees the programmer from having to remember what needs compiling and what doesn't.

ANSWERS TO QUESTIONS AND EXERCISES

Chapter 1

Answers to Questions

1. procedural, object-oriented
2. b
3. data, act on that data
4. a
5. data hiding
6. a, d
7. objects
8. false; the organizational principles are different
9. encapsulation
10. d
11. false; most lines of code are the same in C and C++
12. polymorphism
13. d
14. b

Chapter 3

Answers to Questions

1. b, c
2. parentheses
3. braces { }
4. It's the first function executed when the program starts
5. statement

6. ```
   // this is a comment
   /* this is a comment */
   ```

7. a, d

8. a. 2
   b. 10
   c. 4
   d. 4

9. false

10. a. integer constant
    b. character constant
    c. floating-point constant
    d. variable name (could also be something else)
    e. function name

11. a. `cout << 'x';`
    b. `cout << "Jim";`
    c. `cout << 509;`

12. false; they're not equal until the statement is executed

13. `cout << setw(10) << george;`

14. IOSTREAM.H

15. `cin >> temp;`

16. IOMANIP.H

17. string constants, preprocessor directives, comments

18. true

19. 2

20. assignment (=) and arithmetic (like + and *)

21. ```
    temp += 23;
    temp = temp + 23;
    ```

22. 1

23. 2020

24. to provide declarations and other data for library functions, overloaded operators, and objects

25. CS.LIB

Solutions to Exercises

1. ```
   // ex3_1.cpp
   // converts gallons to cubic feet
   #include <iostream.h>

   void main()
      {
      float gallons, cufeet;
   ```
   ```

```
    cout << "\nEnter quantity in gallons: ";
    cin >> gallons;
    cufeet = gallons / 7.481;
    cout << "Equivalent in cublic feet is " << cufeet;
    }
```

2.
```
// ex3_2.cpp
// generates table
#include <iostream.h>
#include <iomanip.h>

main()
    {
    cout << endl << 1990 << setw(8) << 135
         << endl << 1991 << setw(8) << 7290
         << endl << 1992 << setw(8) << 11300
         << endl << 1993 << setw(8) << 16200;
    }
```

3.
```
// ex3_3.cpp
// exercises arithmetic assignment and decrement
#include <iostream.h>

void main()
    {
    int var = 10;
    cout << endl << var;        // var is 10
    var *= 2;                   // var becomes 20
    cout << endl << var--;      // displays var, then decrements it
    cout << endl << var;        // var is 19
    }
```

Chapter 4

Answers to Questions

1. b, c

2. `george != sally`

3. -1 is true; only 0 is false.

4. The initialize expression initializes the loop variable, the test expression tests the loop variable, and the increment expression changes the loop variable.

5. c, d

6. true

7.
```
for(int j=100; j<=110; j++)
    cout << endl << j;
```

8. braces (curly brackets)

9. c

10.
```
int j = 100;
while( j <= 110 )
    cout << endl << j++;
```

11. false

12. at least once

13.
```
int j = 100;
do
    cout << endl << j++;
while( j <= 110 );
```

14.
```
if(age > 21)
    cout << "Yes";
```

15. d

16.
```
if( age > 21 )
    cout << "Yes";
else
    cout << "No";
```

17. a, c

18. '\r'

19. preceding, surrounded by braces

20. reformatting

21.
```
switch(ch)
    {
    case 'y':
        cout << "Yes";
        break;
    case 'n':
        cout << "No";
        break;
    default:
        cout << "Unknown response";
    }
```

22. `ticket = (speed > 55) ? 1 : 0;`

23. d

24. `limit == 55 && speed > 55`

25. unary, arithmetic, relational, logical, conditional, assignment

26. d

27. the top of the loop

28. b

Solutions to Exercises

1.
```
// ex4_1.cpp
// displays multiples of a number
#include <iostream.h>
#include <iomanip.h>                          // for setw()
```

```cpp
    void main()
       {
       unsigned long n;                        // number

       cout << "\nEnter a number: ";
       cin >> n;                               // get number
       for(int j=1; j<=200; j++)               // loop from 1 to 200
          {
          cout << setw(5) << j*n << "  ";      // print multiple of n
          if( j%10 == 0 )                      // every 10 numbers,
             cout << endl;                     // start new line
          }
       }
```

2.
```cpp
// ex4_2.cpp
// converts fahrenheit to centigrad, or
// centigrad to fahrenheit
#include <iostream.h>

void main()
   {
   int response;
   double temper;

   cout << "\nType 1 to convert fahrenheit to celsius,"
        << "\n     2 to convert celsius to fahrenheit: ";
   cin >> response;
   if( response == 1 )
      {
      cout << "Enter temperature in fahrenheit: ";
      cin >> temper;
      cout << "In celsius that's " << 5.0/9.0*(temper-32.0);
      }
   else
      {
      cout << "Enter temperature in celsius: ";
      cin >> temper;
      cout << "In fahrenheit that's " << 9.0/5.0*temper + 32.0;
      }
   }
```

3.
```cpp
// ex4_3.cpp
// makes a number out of digits
#include <iostream.h>
#include <conio.h>                            // for getche()

void main()
   {
   char ch = 'a';                             // ensure it isn't '\r'
   unsigned long total = 0;                   // this holds the number

   cout << "\nEnter a number: " << flush;
   while( (ch=getche()) != '\r' )             // quit on Enter
```

```
            total = total*10 + ch-'0';        // add digit to total*10
         cout << "\nNumber is: " << total;
         }

4.  // ex4_4.cpp
    // models four-function calculator
    #include <iostream.h>
    #include <conio.h>                      // for getche()

    void main()
       {
       double n1, n2, ans;
       char oper, ch;
       do
          {
          cout << "\nEnter first number, operator, second number: ";
          cin >> n1 >> oper >> n2;
          switch(oper)
             {
             case '+':   ans = n1 + n2;  break;
             case '-':   ans = n1 - n2;  break;
             case '*':   ans = n1 * n2;  break;
             case '/':   ans = n1 / n2;  break;
             default:    ans = 0;
             }
          cout << "Answer = " << ans;
          cout << "\nDo another (y/n)?" << flush;
          ch = getche();
          } while( ch != 'n' );
       }
```

Chapter 5

Answers to Questions

1. b, d
2. true
3. semicolon
4. ```
   struct time
      {
      int hrs;
      int mins;
      int secs;
      };
   ```
5. false; only a variable definition creates space in memory
6. c
7. `time2.hrs = 11;`
8. 18 (3 structures times 3 integers times 2 bytes)

694
   ```

9. `time time1 = { 11, 10, 59 };`

10. true

11. `temp = fido.dog.paw;`

12. c, d

13. `enum players { B1, B2, SS, B3, RF, CF, LF, C, P };`

14. ```
players joe, tom;
    joe = LF;
    tom = P;
```

15. a. no

    b. yes

    c. no

    d. yes

16. 0, 1, 2

17. `enum speeds { obsolete=78, single=45, album=33 };`

18. Because `false` should be represented by 0.


## Solutions to Exercises

1.
```cpp
// ex5_1.cpp
// uses structure to store phone number
#include <iostream.h>

struct phone
    {
    int area;          // area code (3 digits)
    int exchange;      // exchange (3 digits)
    int number;        // number (4 digits)
    };

void main()
    {
    phone ph1 = { 212, 767, 8900 };  // initialize phone number
    phone ph2;                        // define phone number
                                      // get phone no from user
    cout << "\nEnter your area code, exchange, and number: ";
    cin >> ph2.area >> ph2.exchange >> ph2.number;

    cout << "\nMy number is "         // display numbers
         << '(' << ph1.area << ") "
         << ph1.exchange << '-' << ph1.number;

    cout << "\nYour number is "
         << '(' << ph2.area << ") "
         << ph2.exchange << '-' << ph2.number;
    }
```
```

```
2. // ex5_2.cpp
   // structure models point on the plane
   #include <iostream.h>

   struct point
      {
      int xCo;        // X coordinate
      int yCo;        // Y coordinate
      };

   void main()
      {
      point p1, p2, p3;                            // define 3 points

      cout << "\nEnter coordinates for p1:  ;      // get 2 points
      cin >> p1.xCo >> p1.yCo;                     // from user
      cout << "Enter coordinates for p2: ";
      cin >> p2.xCo >> p2.yCo;

      p3.xCo = p1.xCo + p2.xCo;                    // find sum of
      p3.yCo = p1.yCo + p2.yCo;                    // p1 and p2

      cout << "Coordinates of p1+p2 are: "         // display the sum
           << p3.xCo << ", " << p3.yCo;
      }
3. // ex5_3.cpp
   // uses structure to model volume of room
   #include <iostream.h>

   struct Distance
      {
      int feet;
      float inches;
      };

   struct Volume
      {
      Distance length;
      Distance width;
      Distance height;
      };

   void main()
      {
      float l, w, h;
      Volume room1 = { { 16, 3.5 }, { 12, 6.25 }, { 8, 1.75 } };

      l = room1.length.feet + room1.length.inches / 12.0;
      w = room1.width.feet  + room1.width.inches  / 12.0;
      h = room1.height.feet + room1.height.inches / 12.0;

      cout << "\nVolume = " << l*w*h << " cubic feet";
      }
```

Chapter 8

Answers to Questions

1. d (half credit for b)
2. definition
3. ```
   void foo()
       {
       cout << "foo";
       }
   ```
4. declaration, prototype
5. body
6. call
7. declarator
8. c
9. false
10. to clarify the purpose of the arguments
11. a, b, and c
12. empty parentheses mean the function takes no arguments
13. one
14. true
15. at the beginning of the declaration and declarator
16. `void`
17. ```
    main()
        {
        int times2(int);        // prototype
        int alpha = times2(37);  // function call
        }
    ```
18. a
19. to modify the original argument
20. a, c
21. ```
    int bar(char);
    int bar(char, char);
    ```
22. faster, more
23. `inline float foobar(float)`
24. a, b
25. `char blyth(int, float=3.14159);`
26. visibility, lifetime
27. those functions defined following the variable definition
28. the function in which it is defined
29. b, d
30. on the left side of the equals sign
    ```

Solutions to Exercises

```
1. // ex6_1.cpp
   // function finds area of circle
   #include <iostream.h>

   float circarea(float radius);

   void main()
      {
      double rad;
      cout << "\nEnter radius of circle: ";
      cin >> rad;
      cout << "Area is " << circarea(rad);
      }

   float circarea(float r)
      {
      const float PI = 3.14159;
      return r * r * PI;
      }

2. // ex6_2.cpp
   // function raises number to a power
   #include <iostream.h>

   double power( float n, int p=2);     // p has default value 2

   void main()
      {
      double number, answer;
      int pow;
      char yeserno;

      cout << "\nEnter number: ";         // get number
      cin >> number;
      cout << "Want to enter a power (y/n)? ";
      cin >> yeserno;
      if( yeserno == 'y' )                // user wants a non-2 power?
         {
         cout << "Enter power: ";
         cin >> pow;
         answer = power(number, pow);  // raise number to pow
         }
      else
         answer = power(number);         // square the number
      cout << "Answer is " << answer;
      }

   // power()
   // returns number n raised to a power p
   double power( float n, int p )
```

```
   {
   double result = 1.0;              // start with 1
   for(int j=0; j<p; j++)            // multiply by n
      result *= n;                   // p times
   return result;
   }
```

3. ```
   // ex6_3.cpp
   // function sets larger of two numbers to 0
   #include <iostream.h>

   void main()
      {
      void zeroSmaller(int&, int&);
      int a=4, b=7, c=11, d=9;

      zeroSmaller(a, b);
      zeroSmaller(c, d);
      cout << "\na=" << a << " b=" << b
           << " c=" << c << " d=" << d;
      }

   // zeroSmaller()
   // sets the smaller of two numbers to 0
   void zeroSmaller(int& first, int& second)
      {
      if( first < second )
         first = 0;
      else
         second = 0;
      }
```

4. ```
   // ex6_4.cpp
   // function returns larger of two distances
   #include <iostream.h>

   struct Distance                    // English distance
      {
      int feet;
      float inches;
      };
                                      // declarations
   Distance bigengl(Distance, Distance);
   void engldisp(Distance);

   void main()
      {
      Distance d1, d2, d3;           // define three lengths
                                     // get length d1 from user
      cout << "\nEnter feet: ";  cin >> d1.feet;
      cout << "Enter inches: ";  cin >> d1.inches;
                                     // get length d2 from user
```

```
   cout << "\nEnter feet: ";   cin >> d2.feet;
   cout << "Enter inches: ";   cin >> d2.inches;

   d3 = bigengl(d1, d2);          // d3 is larger of d1 and d2
                                  // display all lengths
   cout << "\nd1="; engldisp(d1);
   cout << "\nd2="; engldisp(d2);
   cout << "\nlargest is "; engldisp(d3);
   }

// bigengl()
// compares two structures of type Distance, returns the larger
Distance bigengl( Distance dd1, Distance dd2 )
   {
   if(dd1.feet > dd2.feet)        // if feet are different, return
      return dd1;                 // the one with the largest feet
   if(dd1.feet < dd2.feet)
      return dd2;
   if(dd1.inches > dd2.inches)    // if inches are different,
      return dd1;                 // return one with largest
   else                           // inches, or dd2 if equal
      return dd2;
   }

// engldisp()
// display structure of type Distance in feet and inches
void engldisp( Distance dd )
   {
   cout << dd.feet << "\'-" << dd.inches << "\"";
   }
```

Chapter 7

Answers to Questions

1. A class specifier describes how objects of a class will look when they are created.

2. class, object

3. c

4.
```
class leverage
   {
   private:
      int crowbar;
   public:
      void pry();
   };
```

5. false; both data and functions can be private or public

6. `leverage lever1;`

7. d

8. `lever1.pry();`

9. `inline` (also `private`)

10. `int getcrow()`
    `{ return crowbar; }`

11. defined (created)

12. the class of which it is a member

13. `leverage()`
    `{ crowbar = 0; }`

14. true

15. a

16. `int getcrow();`

17. `int leverage::getcrow()`
    `{ return crowbar; }`

18. Member functions and data are, by default, public in structures but private in classes.

19. three, one

20. calling one of its member functions

21. b, c, d

22. false; trial and error may be necessary

Solutions to Exercises

```
1. // ex7_1.cpp
   // uses a class to model an integer data type
   #include <iostream.h>

   class Int                        // (not the same as int)
      {
      private:
         int i;
      public:
         Int()                      // create an Int
            { i = 0; }
         Int(int ii)                // create and initialize an Int
            { i = ii; }
         void add(Int i2, Int i3)   // add two Ints
            { i = i2.i + i3.i; }
         void display()             // display an Int
            { cout << i; }
      };

   void main()
      {
```

```
      Int Int1(7);                  // create and initialize an Int
      Int Int2(11);                 // create and initialize an Int
      Int Int3;                     // create an Int

      Int3.add(Int1, Int2);                 // add two Ints
      cout << "\nInt3 = "; Int3.display();  // display result
      }
```

2.
```
   // ex7_2.cpp
   // uses class to model toll booth
   #include <iostream.h>
   #include <conio.h>

   const char ESC = 27;        // escape key ASCII code
   const double TOLL = 0.5;    // toll is 50 cents

   class tollBooth
      {
      private:
        unsigned int totalCars;   // total cars passed today
        double totalCash;         // total money collected today
      public:
        tollBooth()                           // constructor
           { totalCars = 0; totalCash = 0.0; }
        void payingCar()                      // a car paid
           { totalCars++; totalCash += TOLL; }
        void nopayCar()                       // a car didn't pay
           { totalCars++; }
        void display()                        // display totals
           { cout << "\nCars=" << totalCars
                  << ", cash=" << totalCash; }
      };

   void main()
      {
      tollBooth booth1;           // create a toll booth
      char ch;

      cout << "\nPress 0 for each non-paying car,"
           << "\n      1 for each paying car,"
           << "\n      Esc to exit the program.\n" << flush;
      do
         {
         ch = getche();          // get character
         if( ch == '0' )         // if it's 0, car didn't pay
            booth1.nopayCar();
         if( ch == '1' )         // if it's 1, car paid
            booth1.payingCar();
         } while( ch != ESC );   // exit loop on Esc key
      booth1.display();          // display totals
      }
```

```
3. // ex7_3.cpp
   /-/ uses class to model a time data type
   #include <iostream.h>

   class time
      {
      private:
         int hrs, mins, secs;
      public:
         time()                               // no-arg constructor
            { hrs = mins = secs = 0; }

         time(int h, int m, int s)            // 3-arg constructor
            { hrs=h; mins=m; secs=s; }

         void display()                       // format 11:59:59
            { cout << hrs << ":" << mins << ":" << secs; }

         void add_time(time t1, time t2)      // add two times
            {
            secs = t1.secs + t2.secs;         // add seconds
            if( secs > 59 )                   // if overflow,
               { secs -= 60; mins++; }        //    carry a minute
            mins += t1.mins + t2.mins;        // add minutes
            if( mins > 59 )                   // if overflow,
               { mins -= 60; hrs++; }         //    carry an hour
            hrs += t1.hrs + t2.hrs;           // add hours
            }
      };

   void main()
      {
      time time1(5, 59, 59);                  // creates and initialze
      time time2(4, 30, 30);                  //    two times
      time time3;                             // create another time

      time3.add_time(time1, time2);           // add two times
      cout << "\ntime3 = "; time3.display();  // display result
      }
```

Chapter 8

Answers to Questions

1. d
2. same
3. `double doubleArray[100];`
4. 0, 9
5. `cout << doubleArray[j];`

6. c

7. `int coins[] = { 1, 5, 10, 25, 50, 100 };`

8. d

9. `twoD[2][4]`

10. true

11. `float flarr[3][3] = { {52,27,83}, {94,73,49}, {3,6,1}, };`

12. memory address

13. a, d

14. an array with 1000 elements of structure or class `employee`.

15. `emplist[17].salary`

16. c

17. `bird manybirds[50];`

18. false

19. `manybirds[27].cheep();`

20. array, `char`

21. `char city[21]` (An extra byte is needed for the null character.)

22. `char dextrose[] = "C6H1206-H20";`

23. true

24. d

25. `strcpy(blank, name);`

26.
```
class dog
    {
    private:
        char breed[80];
        int age;
    }
```

Solutions to Exercises

1.
```
// ex8_1.cpp
// reverses a string
#include <iostream.h>
#include <string.h>              // for strlen()

const int MAX = 80;

void main()
    {
    void reversit( char[] );     // prototype
    char str[MAX];               // string

    cout << "\nEnter a string: ";   // get string from user
    cin.get(str, MAX);
```

```
    reversit(str);                          // reverse the string

    cout << "Reversed string is: ";  // display it
    cout << str;
    }

// reversit()
// function to reverse a string passed to it as an argument
void reversit( char s[] )
    {
    int len = strlen(s);                    // find length of string
    for(int j = 0; j < len/2; j++)  // swap each character
        {                           //      in first half
        char temp = s[j];           //      with character
        s[j] = s[len-j-1];          //      in second half
        s[len-j-1] = temp;
        }
    }
```

2.
```
// ex8_2.cpp
// employee object uses a string as data
#include <iostream.h>

const int LEN = 80;

class employee
    {
    private:
        char name[LEN];
        long number;
    public:
        void getdata()                          // get data from user
            {
            cout << "\nEnter name: ";  cin >> name;
            cout << "Enter number: "; cin >> number;
            }
        void putdata()                          // display data
            {
            cout << "\n   Name: " << name;
            cout << "\n   Number: " << number;
            }
    };

employee emparr[100];           // an array of employees

void main()
    {
    int n = 0;                  // how many employees
    char ch;                    // user response

    do                          // get data from user
        {
        cout << "\nEnter data for employee number " << n+1;
```

```
            emparr[n++].getdata();
            cout << "Enter another (y/n)? "; cin >> ch;
            }
        while( ch != 'n' );

        for(int j=0; j<n; j++)        // display data in array
            {
            cout << "\nEmployee number " << j+1;
            emparr[j].putdata();
            }
        }
```

3. // ex8_3.cpp
   // averages an array of Distance objects input by user
   #include <iostream.h>

```
    class Distance                        // English Distance class
        {
        private:
            int feet;
            float inches;
        public:
            Distance()                        // constructor (no args)
                { feet = 0; inches = 0; }
            Distance(int ft, float in)  // constructor (two args)
                { feet = ft; inches = in; }

            void getdist()                    // get length from user
                {
                cout << "\nEnter feet: ";  cin >> feet;
                cout << "Enter inches: ";  cin >> inches;
                }

            void showdist()                   // display distance
                { cout << feet << "\'-" << inches << '\"'; }

            void add_dist( Distance, Distance );    // declarations
            void div_dist( Distance, int );
        };
                                              // add Distances d2 and d3
    void Distance::add_dist(Distance d2, Distance d3)
        {
        inches = d2.inches + d3.inches;   // add the inches
        feet = 0;                         // (for possible carry)
        if(inches >= 12.0)                // if total exceeds 12.0,
            {                             // then decrease inches
            inches -= 12.0;               // by 12.0 and
            feet++;                       // increase feet
            }                             // by 1
        feet += d2.feet + d3.feet;        // add the feet
        }

                                          // divide Distance by int
```

```
void Distance::div_dist(Distance d2, int divisor)
   {
   float fltfeet = d2.feet + d2.inches/12.0;   // convert to float
   fltfeet /= divisor;                         // do division
   feet = int(fltfeet);                        // get feet part
   inches = (fltfeet-feet) * 12.0;             // get inches part
   }

void main()
   {
   Distance distarr[100];        // array of 100 Distances
   Distance total, average;      // other Distances
   int count = 0;                // counts Distances input
   char ch;                      // user response character
   do
      {
      cout << "\nEnter a Distance";        // get Distances
      distarr[count++].getdist();          // from user, put
      cout << "\nDo another (y/n)? ";      // in array
      cin >> ch;
      }
   while( ch != 'n' );

   for(int j=0; j<count; j++)               // add all Distances
      total.add_dist( total, distarr[j] );  // to total
   average.div_dist( total, count );        // divide by number

   cout << "\nThe average is: ";            // display average
   average.showdist();
   }
```

Chapter 9

Answers to Questions

1. a, c

2. `x3.subtract(x2, x1);`

3. `x3 = x2 - x1;`

4. true

5. `void operator -- ()   { counter--; }`

6. none

7. b, d

8. ```
   void Distance::operator ++ ()
      {
      ++feet;
      }
   ```

9. ```
   Distance Distance::operator ++ ()
      {
      int f = ++feet;
   ```

```
        float i = inches;
        return Distance(f, i);
        }
```

10. There is no difference (at least in current versions of Turbo C++ and Borland C++)

11. c, e, b, a, d

12. twice, same

13. b

14.
```
String String::operator ++ ()
        {
        int len = strlen(str);
        for(int j=0; j<len; j++)
            str[j] = toupper( str[j] )
        return String(str);
        }
```

15. d

16. false if there is a conversion routine; true otherwise

17. b

18. true

19. constructor

20. true, but it will be hard for humans to understand

Solutions to Exercises

1.
```
// ex9_1.cpp
// overloaded '-' operator subtracts two Distances
#include <iostream.h>

class Distance                      // English Distance class
    {
    private:
        int feet;
        float inches;
    public:
        Distance()                      // constructor (no args)
            { feet = 0; inches = 0.0; }
        Distance(int ft, float in)  // constructor (two args)
            { feet = ft; inches = in; }

        void getdist()                  // get length from user
            {
            cout << "\nEnter feet: "; cin >> feet;
            cout << "Enter inches: ";  cin >> inches;
            }

        void showdist()                 // display distance
            { cout << feet << "\'-" << inches << '\"'; }
```

```
        Distance operator + ( Distance );  // add two distances
        Distance operator - ( Distance );  // subtract two distances
    };
                                    // add d2 to this distance
Distance Distance::operator + (Distance d2)  // return the sum
    {
    int f = feet + d2.feet;          // add the feet
    float i = inches + d2.inches;    // add the inches
    if(i >= 12.0)                    // if total exceeds 12.0,
        {                            // then decrease inches
        i -= 12.0;                   // by 12.0 and
        f++;                         // increase feet by 1
        }                            // return a temporary Distance
    return Distance(f,i);            // initialized to sum
    }

                                    // subtract d2 from this dist
Distance Distance::operator - (Distance d2)  // return the diff
    {
    int f = feet - d2.feet;          // subtract the feet
    float i = inches - d2.inches;    // subtract the inches
    if(i < 0)                        // if inches less than 0,
        {                            // then increase inches
        i += 12.0;                   // by 12.0 and
        f--;                         // decrease feet by 1
        }                            // return a temporary Distance
    return Distance(f,i);            // initialized to difference
    }

void main()
    {
    Distance dist1, dist3;           // define distances
    dist1.getdist();                 // get dist1 from user

    Distance dist2(3, 6.25);         // define, initialize dist2

    dist3 = dist1 - dist2;           // subtract

                                    // display all lengths
    cout << "\ndist1 = ";  dist1.showdist();
    cout << "\ndist2 = ";  dist2.showdist();
    cout << "\ndist3 = ";  dist3.showdist();
    }
2. // ex9_2.cpp
// overloaded '+=' operator concatenates strings
#include <iostream.h>
#include <string.h>      // for strcpy(), strcat()
#include <stdlib.h>      // for exit()

const int SZ = 80;       // size of all String objects

class String             // user-defined string type
    {
```

```
    private:
       char str[SZ];                      // holds a string
    public:
       String()                           // constructor, no args
          { strcpy(str, ""); }
       String( char s[] )                 // constructor, one arg
          { strcpy(str, s); }
       void display()                     // display the String
          { cout << str; }
       String operator += (String ss)     // add a String to this one
          {                               // result stays in this one
          if( strlen(str) + strlen(ss.str) >= SZ )
             { cout << "\nString overflow"; exit(1); }
          strcat(str, ss.str);            // add the argument string
          return String(str);             // return temp String
          }
    };

void main()
    {
    String s1 = "\nMerry Christmas!  ";   // uses constructor 2
    String s2 = "Happy new year!";        // uses constructor 2
    String s3;                            // uses constructor 1

    s3 = s1 += s2;           // add s2 to s1, assign to s3

    cout << "\ns1="; s1.display();        // display s1
    cout << "\ns2="; s2.display();        // display s2
    cout << "\ns3="; s3.display();        // display s3
    }
```

3. // ex9_3.cpp
```
// overloaded '+' operator adds two times
#include <iostream.h>

class time
    {
    private:
       int hrs, mins, secs;
    public:
       time()                                     // no-arg constructor
          { hrs = mins = secs = 0; }

       time(int h, int m, int s)                  // 3-arg constructor
          { hrs=h; mins=m; secs=s; }

       void display()                             // format 11:59:59
          { cout << hrs << ":" << mins << ":" << secs; }
```

```cpp
       time operator + (time t2)          // add two times
          {
          secs += t2.secs;                // add seconds
          if( secs > 59 )                 // if overflow,
             { secs -= 60; mins++; }      //    carry a minute
          mins += t2.mins;                // add minutes
          if( mins > 59 )                 // if overflow,
             { mins -= 60; hrs++; }       //    carry an hour
          hrs += t2.hrs;                  // add hours
          return time(hrs, mins, secs);   // return this value
          }
    };

  void main()
     {
     time time1(5, 59, 59);               // create and initialze
     time time2(4, 30, 30);               //    two times
     time time3;                          // create another time

     time3 = time1 + time2;               // add two times
     cout << "\ntime3 = "; time3.display(); // display result
     }
```

4. ```cpp
   // ex9_4.cpp
   // overloaded arithmetic operators work with type Int
   #include <iostream.h>
   #include <process.h>       // for exit()

   class Int
      {
      private:
         int i;
      public:
         Int()                            // no-arg constructor
            { i = 0; }
         Int(int ii)                      // 1-arg constructor
            { i = ii; }                   //    (int to Int)
         void putInt()                    // display Int
            { cout << i; }
         void getInt()                    // read Int from kbd
            { cin >> i; }
         operator int()                   // conversion function
            { return i; }                 //    (Int to int)
         Int operator + (Int i2)          // addition
            { return checkit( long(int(i))+long(int(i2)) ); }
         Int operator - (Int i2)          // subtraction
            { return checkit( long(int(i))-long(int(i2)) ); }
         Int operator * (Int i2)          // multiplication
            { return checkit( long(int(i))*long(int(i2)) ); }
```
```

```
      Int operator / (Int i2)              // division
         { return checkit( long(int(i))/long(int(i2)) ); }
      Int operator % (Int i2)              // remainder
         { return checkit( long(int(i))%long(int(i2)) ); }

      Int checkit(long answer)             // check results
         {
         if( answer > 32767 || answer < -32768 )
            { cout << "\nError: overflow"; exit(1); }
         return Int(int(answer));
         }
   };

void main()
   {
   Int alpha = 20;
   Int beta = 7;
   Int gamma;

   gamma = alpha + beta;
   cout << "\ngamma="; gamma.putInt();
   gamma = alpha - beta;
   cout << "\ngamma="; gamma.putInt();
   gamma = alpha * beta;
   cout << "\ngamma="; gamma.putInt();
   gamma = alpha / beta;
   cout << "\ngamma="; gamma.putInt();
   gamma = alpha % beta;
   cout << "\ngamma="; gamma.putInt();
   }
```

Chapter 10

Answers to Questions

1. a, c
2. derived
3. b, c, d
4. class Bosworth : public Alphonso
5. false
6. `protected`
7. yes
8. `BosworthObj.alfunc();`
9. true
10. the one in the derived class
11. `Bosworth() : Alphonso()  { }`
12. c, d

13. true
14. `Derv(int arg) : Base(arg)`
15. d
16. true
17. c
18. `class Tire : public Wheel, public Rubber`
19. `Base::func();`
20. false

Solutions to Exercises

1.
```cpp
// ex10_1.cpp
// publication class and derived classes
#include <iostream.h>

const int LEN = 80;

class publication                    // base class
   {
   private:
      char title[LEN];
      float price;
   public:
      void getdata()
         {
         cout << "\nEnter title: "; cin >> title;
         cout << "Enter price: "; cin >> price;
         }
      void putdata()
         {
         cout << "\nTitle: " << title;
         cout << "\nPrice: " << price;
         }
   };

class book : private publication     // derived class
   {
   private:
      int pages;
   public:
      void getdata()
         {
         publication::getdata();
         cout << "Enter number of pages: "; cin >> pages;
         }
      void putdata()
         {
         publication::putdata();
```

```
                    cout << "\nPages: " << pages;
                    }
            };

        class tape : private publication      // derived class
            {
            private:
                float time;
            public:
                void getdata()
                    {
                    publication::getdata();
                    cout << "Enter playing time: "; cin >> time;
                    }
                void putdata()
                    {
                    publication::putdata();
                    cout << "\nPlaying time: " << time;
                    }
            };

        void main()
            {
            book book1;                        // define publications
            tape tape1;

            book1.getdata();                   // get data for them
            tape1.getdata();

            book1.putdata();                   // display their data
            tape1.putdata();
            }

2.  // ex10_2.cpp
    // inheritance from String class
    #include <iostream.h>
    #include <string.h>        // for strcpy(), etc.

    const int SZ = 80;         // size of all String objects

    class String                        // base class
        {
        protected:                      // Note: can't be private
            char str[SZ];               // holds a string
        public:
            String()                    // constructor 0, no args
                { str[0] = '\0'; }
            String( char s[] )          // constructor 1, one arg
                { strcpy(str, s); }     //    convert string to String
            void display()              // display the String
                { cout << str; }
```

```
        operator char*()           // conversion function
           { return str; }         //    convert String to string
    };

  class Pstring : public String     // derived class
     {
     public:
        Pstring( char s[] );        // constructor
     };

  Pstring::Pstring( char s[] )       // constructor for Pstring
     {
     int len = strlen(s);            // check length of argument
     if(len > SZ-1)                  // if too long,
        {
        for(int j=0; j<SZ-1; j++)    // copy the first SZ-1
           str[j] = s[j];            // characters "by hand"
        str[j] = '\0';               // add the null character
        }
     else                           // not too long,
        strcpy(str, s);             // so copy entire string
     }

  void main()
     {                                         // define String
     Pstring s1 = "This is a very long string which is probably--\
  no, certainly--going to exceed the limit set in SZ.";
     cout << "\ns1="; s1.display();            // display String

     Pstring s2 = "This is a short string.";  // define String
     cout << "\ns2="; s2.display();            // display String
     }

3. // ex10_3.cpp
   // multiple inheritance with publication class
   #include <iostream.h>

   const int LEN = 80;
   const int MONTHS = 3;

   class publication
      {
      private:
         char title[LEN];
         float price;
      public:
         void getdata()
            {
            cout << "\nEnter title: "; cin >> title;
            cout << "   Enter price: "; cin >> price;
            }
```

```
        void putdata()
           {
           cout << "\nTitle: " << title;
           cout << "\n   Price: " << price;
           }
      };

class sales
   {
   private:
      float sdata[MONTHS];
   public:
      void getdata();
      void putdata();
   };

void sales::getdata()
   {
   cout << "   Enter sales for 3 months\n";
   for(int j=0; j<MONTHS; j++)
      {
      cout << "      Month " << j+1 << ": ";
      cin >> sdata[j];
      }
   }
void sales::putdata()
   {
   for(int j=0; j<MONTHS; j++)
      {
      cout << "\n   Sales for month " << j+1 << ": ";
      cout << sdata[j];
      }
   }

class book : private publication, private sales
   {
   private:
      int pages;
   public:
      void getdata()
         {
         publication::getdata();
         cout << "   Enter number of pages: "; cin >> pages;
         sales::getdata();
         }
      void putdata()
         {
         publication::putdata();
         cout << "\n   Pages: " << pages;
         sales::putdata();
         }
      };
```

```
class tape : private publication, private sales
    {
    private:
        float time;
    public:
        void getdata()
            {
            publication::getdata();
            cout << "    Enter playing time: "; cin >> time;
            sales::getdata();
            }
        void putdata()
            {
            publication::putdata();
            cout << "\n    Playing time: " << time;
            sales::putdata();
            }
    };

void main()
    {
    book book1;              // define publications
    tape tape1;

    book1.getdata();         // get data for publications
    tape1.getdata();

    book1.putdata();         // display data for publications
    tape1.putdata();
    }
```

Chapter 11

Answers to Questions

1. a, b, c
2. `_settextwindow()`
3. false
4. `_setvideomode (_MRES4COLOR);`
5. 16
6. false, except when a font file is needed
7. execute the `_unregisterfonts()` function
8. `_ellipse(_GBORDER, 5, 15, 15, 25);`
9. true
10. `_moveto(2, 7);`
    `_lineto(5, 11);`
11. d
12. `_setcolor(BLUE);`

13. b

14.
```
struct _xycoord +[3];
+[0].xcoord=0;  +[0].ycoord=10;
+[1].xcoord=5;  +[1].ycoord=0;
+[2].xcoord=10; +[2].ycoord=10;
_polygon(_GBORDER, +, 3);
```

15. b, d

16. the time in milliseconds since the program started

17. produce the same sequence of random numbers

18. erase

19. a

20. current position

Solutions to Exercises

```cpp
1. // ex11_1.cpp
   // adds size to ball
   #include <graph.h>          // for graphics functions
   #include <conio.h>          // for getch()
   #include <stdlib.h>         // for exit()
   #include <iostream.h>       // for cout

   class ball                  // ball class
      {
      private:
         int xCo, yCo;         // coordinates of center
         int rad;
      public:
         ball()                     // no-argument constructor
            { xCo=0; yCo=0; rad=0; }
         void set(int x, int y, int r)  // set position
            { xCo=x; yCo=y; rad=r; }
         void draw()                // draw the ball
            { _ellipse(_GBORDER, xCo-rad, yCo-rad,
                       xCo+rad, yCo+rad); }
      };

   void main()
      {
      if( ! _setvideomode(_VRES16COLOR) )
         { cout << "Can't set graphics mode"; exit(1); }

      ball b1;                          // create three balls
      ball b2;
      ball b3;

      b1.set(250, 150, 50);            // position and size them
      b2.set(300, 150, 75);
      b3.set(350, 150, 100);
```

```
    b1.draw();                       // draw them
    b2.draw();
    b3.draw();

    getch();                         // wait for keypress
    _setvideomode(_DEFAULTMODE);     // restore original mode
    }
```

2.
```
// ex11_2.cpp
// adds size data to shap class
#include <graph.h>              // for graphics functions
#include <conio.h>              // for getch()
#include <iostream.h>           // for cout
#include <stdlib.h>             // for exit

#define BLUE      1             // color indices
#define GREEN     2
#define RED       4
#define BROWN     6
#define WHITE     7
#define YELLOW   14

class shape                     // base class
    {
    protected:
        int xCo, yCo;           // coordinates of center
        int width, height;      // width and height
        int linecolor;          // color of outline
        int fillcolor;          // color of interior
        void init()             // initialize line color
            { _setcolor(linecolor); }
        void fill()             // fills interior of any shape
            {
            _setcolor(fillcolor);              // set fill color
            _floodfill(xCo, yCo, linecolor);   // fill interior
            _setcolor(linecolor);              // set line color
            }
    public:
        shape()                 // no-arg constructor
            {
            xCo=0; yCo=0; width=0; height=0;
            linecolor=WHITE; fillcolor=WHITE;
            }                    // set data
        void set(int x, int y, int w, int h, int lc, int fc)
            {
            xCo=x; yCo=y; width=w; height=h;
            linecolor=lc; fillcolor=fc;
            }
    };

class ball : public shape
    {
    public:
        ball() : shape()        // no-arg constr
            { }
```

719

```cpp
        void set(int x, int y, int r, int lc, int fc)  // set data
           { shape::set(x, y, r, r, lc, fc); }
        void draw()                  // draw the ball
           {
           init();                   // set colors
                                     // draw circle
           _ellipse(_GBORDER, xCo-width/2, yCo-height/2,
                    xCo+width/2, yCo+height/2);
           fill();                   // fill circle
           }
     };

class rect : public shape
     {
   public:
        rect() : shape()             // no-arg constr
           { }                       // set data
        void set(int x, int y, int w, int h, int lc, int fc)
           { shape::set(x, y, w, h, lc, fc); }
        void draw()                  // draw the rectangle
           {
           init();                   // line color
                                     // draw rectangle
           _rectangle(_GBORDER, xCo-width/2, yCo-height/2,
                      xCo+width/2, yCo+height/2);
           fill();                   // fill the shape
           }
     };

void main()
     {
     if( ! _setvideomode(_MAXRESMODE) )
        { cout << "Can't set graphics mode"; exit(1); }

     rect windowbox;               // create top part of car
     rect bodybox;                 // create bottom part of car
     ball wheel1, wheel2;          // create wheels

     windowbox.set(300, 75, 40, 20, YELLOW, BLUE);  // set size,
     bodybox.set(320, 100, 100, 30, YELLOW, BLUE);  // position,
     wheel1.set(290, 117, 27, YELLOW, BROWN);       // and colors
     wheel2.set(350, 117, 27, YELLOW, BROWN);

     windowbox.draw();              // draw the car parts
     bodybox.draw();
     wheel1.draw();
     wheel2.draw();

     getch();                       // wait for keypress
     _setvideomode(_DEFAULTMODE);   // close graphics system
     }

3. // ex11_3.cpp
   // makes a car class out of various shapes
   #include <graph.h>               // for graphics functions
```

```
#include <conio.h>          // for getch()
#include <iostream.h>       // for cout
#include <stdlib.h>         // for exit()

#define BLUE    1           // color indices
#define GREEN   2
#define RED     4
#define BROWN   6
#define WHITE   7
#define YELLOW  14

class shape                 // base class
   {
   protected:
      int xCo, yCo;         // coordinates of center
      int width, height;    // width and height
      int linecolor;        // color of outline
      int fillcolor;        // color of interior
      void init()           // initialize line color
         { _setcolor(linecolor); }
      void fill()           // fills interior of any shape
         {
         _setcolor(fillcolor);            // set fill color
         _floodfill(xCo, yCo, linecolor); // fill interior
         _setcolor(linecolor);            // set line color
         }
   public:
      shape()               // no-arg constructor
         {
         xCo=0; yCo=0; width=0; height=0;
         linecolor=WHITE; fillcolor=WHITE;
         }                  // set data
      void set(int x, int y, int w, int h, int lc, int fc)
         {
         xCo=x; yCo=y; width=w; height=h;
         linecolor=lc; fillcolor=fc;
         }
   };

class ball : public shape
   {
   public:
      ball() : shape()      // no-arg constr
         { }
      void set(int x, int y, int r, int lc, int fc)  // set data
         { shape::set(x, y, r, r, lc, fc); }
      void draw()           // draw the ball
         {
         init();            // set colors
                            // draw circle
         _ellipse(_GBORDER, xCo-width/2, yCo-height/2,
                  xCo+width/2, yCo+height/2);
         fill();            // fill circle
         }
   };
```

721

```
    class rect : public shape
       {
       public:
          rect() : shape()        // no-arg constr
             { }                   // set data
          void set(int x, int y, int w, int h, int lc, int fc)
             { shape::set(x, y, w, h, lc, fc); }
          void draw()             // draw the rectangle
             {
             init();              // line color
                                  // draw rectangle
             _rectangle(_GBORDER, xCo-width/2, yCo-height/2,
                        xCo+width/2, yCo+height/2);
             fill();              // fill the shape
             }
       };

    class car
       {
       private:
          rect windowbox;         // create top part of car
          rect bodybox;           // create bottom part of car
          ball wheel1, wheel2;    // create wheels
       public:
          void set(int x, int y)
             {                    // set size, position, and colors
             windowbox.set(x+10, y, 40, 20, YELLOW, BLUE);
             bodybox.set(x+30, y+25, 100, 30, YELLOW, BLUE);
             wheel1.set(x, y+42, 27, YELLOW, BROWN);
             wheel2.set(x+60, y+42, 27, YELLOW, BROWN);
             }
          void draw()
             {
             windowbox.draw();    // draw the car parts
             bodybox.draw();
             wheel1.draw();
             wheel2.draw();
             }
       };

    void main()
       {
       if( ! _setvideomode(_MAXRESMODE) )
          { cout << "Can't set graphics mode"; exit(1); }

       car car1, car2, car3;      // create three cars
       car1.set(100, 100);        // position them
       car2.set(200, 200);
       car3.set(300, 300);
       car1.draw();               // draw them
       car2.draw();
       car3.draw();

       getch();                   // wait for keypress
       _setvideomode(_DEFAULTMODE); // close graphics system
       }
```

Chapter 12

Answers to Questions

1. `cout << &testvar;`
2. four bytes
3. c
4. `&var, *var, var&, char*`
5. constant; variable
6. `float* ptrtofloat;`
7. name
8. `*testptr`
9. pointer to; contents of the variable pointed to by
10. b, c, d
11. No. The address `&intvar` must be placed in the pointer `intptr` before it can be accessed.
12. any data type
13. They both do the same thing.
14. `for(int j=0; j<77; j++)`
    `    cout << endl << *(intarr+j);`
15. Because array names represent the address of the array, which is a constant and can't be changed.
16. reference; pointer
17. a, d
18. `void func(char*);`
19. `for(int j=0; j<77; j++)`
    `    *s2++ = *s1++;`
20. b
21. `char* revstr(char*);`
22. `char* numptrs[] = { "One", "Two", "Three" };`
23. a, c
24. wasted
25. memory that is no longer needed
26. `p->exclu();`
27. `objarr[7].exclu();`
28. a, c
29. `float* p[8];`
30. b

Solutions to Exercises

1.
```cpp
// ex12_1.cpp
// finds average of numbers typed by user
#include <iostream.h>

void main()
    {
    float flarr[100];                   // array for numbers
    char ch;                            // user decision
    int num = 0;                        // counts numbers input
    do
        {
        cout << "Enter number: ";       // get numbers from user
        cin >> *(flarr+num++);          // until user answers 'n'
        cout << "   Enter another (y/n)? ";
        cin >> ch;
        }
    while(ch != 'n');

    float total = 0.0;                  // total starts at 0
    for(int k=0; k<num; k++)            // add numbers to total
        total += *(flarr+k);
    float average = total / num;        // find and display average
    cout << "Average is " << average;
    }
```

2.
```cpp
// ex12_2.cpp
// member function converts String objects to upper case
#include <iostream.h>
#include <string.h>        // for strcpy(), etc
#include <ctype.h>         // for toupper()

class String               // user-defined string type
    {
    private:
        char* str;                      // pointer to string
    public:
        String(char* s)                 // constructor, one arg
            {
            int length = strlen(s);     // length of string argumen'
            str = new char[length+1];   // get memory
            strcpy(str, s);             // copy argument to it
            }
        ~String()                       // destructor
            { delete str; }
        void display()                  // display the String
            { cout << str; }
        void upit();                    // uppercase the String
    };
```

```
void String::upit()                 // uppercase each character
   {
   char* ptrch = str;               // pointer to this string
   while( *ptrch )                  // until null,
      {
      *ptrch = toupper(*ptrch);     // uppercase each character
      ptrch++;                      // move to next character
      }
   }

void main()
   {
   String s1 = "He who laughs last laughs best.";

   cout << "\ns1=";                 // display string
   s1.display();
   s1.upit();                       // uppercase string
   cout << "\ns1=";                 // display string
   s1.display();
   }
```

3.
```
// ex12_3.cpp
// sort an array of pointers to strings
#include <iostream.h>
#include <string.h>                 // for strcmp(), etc.
const int DAYS = 7;                 // number of pointers in array

void main()
   {
   void bsort(char**, int);         // prototype
                                    // array of pointers to char
   char* arrptrs[DAYS] = { "Sunday", "Monday", "Tuesday",
                           "Wednesday", "Thursday",
                           "Friday", "Saturday"  };

   cout << "\nUnsorted:\n";
   for(int j=0; j<DAYS; j++)        // display unsorted strings
      cout << *(arrptrs+j) << endl;

   bsort(arrptrs, DAYS);            // sort the strings

   cout << "\nSorted:\n";
   for(j=0; j<DAYS; j++)            // display sorted strings
      cout << *(arrptrs+j) << endl;
   }

void bsort(char** pp, int n)        // sort pointers to strings
   {
   void order(char**, char**);      // prototype
   int j, k;                        // indexes to array

   for(j=0; j<n-1; j++)             // outer loop
      for(k=j+1; k<n; k++)          // inner loop starts at outer
```

```
            order(pp+j, pp+k);        // order the pointer contents
    }

void order(char** pp1, char** pp2)   // orders two pointers
    {                                 // if string in 1st is
    if( strcmp(*pp1, *pp2) > 0)       // larger than in 2nd,
        {
        char* tempptr = *pp1;         // swap the pointers
        *pp1 = *pp2;
        *pp2 = tempptr;
        }
    }
```

4.
```
// ex12_4.cpp
// linked list includes destructor
#include <iostream.h>
#define NULL 0

struct link                          // one element of list
    {
    int data;                        // data item
    link* next;                      // pointer to next link
    };

class linklist                       // a list of links
    {
    private:
        link* first;                 // pointer to first link
    public:
        linklist()                   // no-argument constructor
            { first = NULL; }        // no first link
        ~linklist();                 // destructor
        void additem(int d);         // add data item (one link)
        void display();              // display all links
    };

void linklist::additem(int d)        // add data item
    {
    link* newlink = new link;        // make a new link
    newlink->data = d;               // give it data
    newlink->next = first;           // it points to next link
    first = newlink;                 // now first points to this
    }

void linklist::display()             // display all links
    {
    link* current = first;           // set ptr to first link
    while( current != NULL )         // quit on last link
        {
        cout << endl << current->data; // print data
        current = current->next;     // move to next link
        }
    }
```

```
linklist::~linklist()                    // destructor
   {
   link* current = first;                // set ptr to first link
   while( current != NULL )              // quit on last link
      {
      cout << "\nDeleting link " << current->data;
      link* temp = current;              // save ptr to this link
      current = current->next;           // get ptr to next link
      delete temp;                       // delete this link
      }
   }

void main()
   {
   linklist li;            // make linked list

   li.additem(25);         // add four items to list
   li.additem(36);
   li.additem(49);
   li.additem(64);
   li.display();           // display entire list
   cout << "\n----------program ends----------";
   }
```

Chapter 13

Answers to Questions

1. d
2. true
3. base
4. `virtual void dang(int);` or `void virtual dang(int);`
5. late binding or dynamic binding
6. derived
7. `virtual void aragorn()=0;` or `void virtual aragorn()=0;`
8. a, c
9. `dong* parr[10];`
10. c
11. true
12. c, d
13. `friend void harry(george);`
14. a, c, d
15. `friend class harry;` or `friend harry;`
16. c
17. It performs a member-by-member copy.
18. `zeta& operator = (zeta&);`

19. a, b, d
20. false; the compiler provides a default copy constructor
21. a, d
22. `Bertha(Bertha&);`
23. true, if there was a reason to do so
24. a, c
25. true; trouble occurs if it's returned by reference
26. They operate identically.
27. a, b
28. the object of which the function using it is a member
29. no; since `this` is a pointer, use `this->da=37;`
30. `return *this;`

Solutions to Exercises

1.
```cpp
// ex13_1.cpp
// publication class and derived classes
#include <iostream.h>

const int LEN = 80;

class publication
    {
    private:
        char title[LEN];
        float price;
    public:
        virtual void getdata()
            {
            cout << "\nEnter title: "; cin >> title;
            cout << "Enter price: "; cin >> price;
            }
        virtual void putdata()
            {
            cout << "\n\nTitle: " << title;
            cout << "\nPrice: " << price;
            }
    };

class book : public publication
    {
    private:
        int pages;
```

```
    public:
        void getdata()
            {
            publication::getdata();
            cout << "Enter number of pages: "; cin >> pages;
            }
        void putdata()
            {
            publication::putdata();
            cout << "\nPages: " << pages;
            }
    };

class tape : public publication
    {
    private:
        float time;
    public:
        void getdata()
            {
            publication::getdata();
            cout << "Enter playing time: "; cin >> time;
            }
        void putdata()
            {
            publication::putdata();
            cout << "\nPlaying time: " << time;
            }
    };

void main()
    {
    publication* pubarr[100];           // array of ptrs to pubs
    int n = 0;                          // number of pubs in array
    char choice;                        // user's choice

    do
        {
        cout << "\nEnter data for book or tape (b/t)? ";
        cin >> choice;
        if( choice=='b' )                    // make book object
            pubarr[n] = new book;            //     put in array
        else                                 // make tape object
            pubarr[n] = new tape;            //     put in array
            pubarr[n++]->getdata();          // get data for object
            cout << "   Enter another (y/n)? ";  // another pub?
```

```
                cin >> choice;
         }
    while( choice =='y');                    // cycle until not 'y'

    for(int j=0; j<n; j++)                   // cycle thru all pubs
        pubarr[j]->putdata();                // print data for pub
    }
```

2.
```
// ex13_2.cpp
// overloaded multiply operator for Distance
#include <iostream.h>

class Distance                      // English Distance class
   {
   private:
      int feet;
      float inches;
   public:
      Distance()                    // constructor (no args)
         { feet = 0; inches = 0.0; }
      Distance(float fltfeet)       // constructor (one arg)
         {
         feet = int(fltfeet);            // feet is integer part
         inches = 12*(fltfeet-feet);  // inches is what's left
         }
      Distance(int ft, float in)  // constructor (two args)
         { feet = ft; inches = in; }
      void showdist()                  // display distance
         { cout << feet << "\'-" << inches << '\"'; }

      friend Distance operator * (Distance, Distance); // friend
   };
                                         // multiply d1 by d2
Distance operator * (Distance d1, Distance d2)
   {                                     // argument
   float fltfeet1 = d1.feet + d1.inches/12;  // convert to float
   float fltfeet2 = d2.feet + d2.inches/12;
   float multfeet = fltfeet1 * fltfeet2;      // find the product
   return Distance(multfeet);          // return temp Distance
   }

void main()
   {
   Distance dist1(3, 6.0);             // make some distances
   Distance dist2(2, 3.0);
   Distance dist3;

   dist3 = dist1 * dist2;              // multiplication

   dist3 = 10.0 * dist3;              // mult and conversion
                                       // display all distances
```

```
        cout << "\ndist1 = "; dist1.showdist();
        cout << "\ndist2 = "; dist2.showdist();
        cout << "\ndist3 = "; dist3.showdist();
        }
3.  // ex13_3.cpp
    // creates array class
    // overloads assignment operator and copy constructor
    #include <iostream.h>

    class Array
        {
        private:
            int* ptr;                   // pointer to "array" contents
            int size;                   // size of array
        public:
            Array()                     // no-argument constructor
                { }
            Array(int s)                // one-argument constructor
                {
                size = s;
                ptr = new int[s];
                }
            Array(Array&);              // copy constructor
            ~Array()                    // destructor
                { delete ptr; }
            int& operator [] (int j)    // overloaded subscript op
                { return *(ptr+j); }
            Array& operator = (Array&); // overloaded = operator
        };

    Array::Array(Array& a)              // copy constructor
        {
        size = a.size;                  // new one is same size
        ptr = new int[size];            // get space for contents
        for(int j=0; j<size; j++)       // copy contents to new one
            *(ptr+j) = *(a.ptr+j);
        }

    Array& Array::operator = (Array& a)  // overloaded = operator
        {
        size = a.size;                  // new one is same size
        ptr = new int[size];
        for(int j=0; j<size; j++)       // copy contents to new one
            *(ptr+j) = *(a.ptr+j);
        return *this;                   // return this object
        }

    void main()
        {
        const int ASIZE = 10;           // size of array
        Array arr1(ASIZE);              // make an array
```

```
    for(int j=0; j<ASIZE; j++)    // fill it with squares
        arr1[j] = j*j;

    Array arr2(arr1);             // use the copy constructor
    cout << endl;
    for(j=0; j<ASIZE; j++)        // check that it worked
        cout << arr2[j] << "   ";

    Array arr3;                   // make an empty Array
    arr3 = arr1;                  // use the assignment operator
    cout << endl;
    for(j=0; j<ASIZE; j++)        // check that it worked
        cout << arr3[j] << "   ";
    }
```

Chapter 14

Answers to Questions

1. b, c

2. ios

3. ifstream, ofstream, and Fstream

4. ofstream salefile ("SALES.JUN");

5. true

6. if(foobar)

7. d

8. fileOut.put(ch);

9. c

10. ifile.read((char*)buff, sizeof(buff));

11. a, b, d

12. the byte location at which the next read or write operation will take place

13. false; *file pointer* can be a synonym for *current position*

14. f1.seekg(-13, ios:cur);

15. b

16. a

17. skipws causes white space characters to be ignored on input so that cin will not assume the input has terminated.

18. void main(argc, *argv[])

19. PRN, LPT1, etc.

20. istream& operator >> (istream&, Sample&)

Solutions to Exercises

1.
```cpp
// ex14_1.cpp
// write array
#include <iostream.h>
#include <fstream.h>                    // for file streams

class Distance                          // English Distance class
   {
   private:
      int feet;
      float inches;
   public:
      Distance()                        // constructor (no args)
         { feet = 0; inches = 0.0; }
      Distance(int ft, float in)  // constructor (two args)
         { feet = ft; inches = in; }
      void getdist()                    // get length from user
         {
         cout << "\n   Enter feet: ";  cin >> feet;
         cout << "   Enter inches: ";  cin >> inches;
         }
      void showdist()                   // display distance
         { cout << feet << "\'-" << inches << '\"'; }
   };

void main()
   {
   char ch;
   Distance dist;                       // create a Distance object
   fstream file;                        // create input/output file
                                        // open it for append
   file.open("DIST.DAT", ios::app | ios::out | ios::in );

   do                                   // data from user to file
      {
      cout << "\nDistance";
      dist.getdist();                   // get a distance
                                        // write to file
      file.write( (char*)&dist, sizeof(dist) );
      cout << "Enter another distance (y/n)? ";
      cin >> ch;
      }
   while(ch=='y');                      // quit on 'n'

   file.seekg(0);                       // reset to start of file
                                        // read first distance
   file.read( (char*)&dist, sizeof(dist) );
   int count = 0;
```

```
        while( !file.eof() )                    // quit on EOF
            {
            cout << "\nDistance " << ++count << ": "; // display dist
            dist.showdist();
            file.read( (char*)&dist, sizeof(dist) );  // read another
            }                                          // distance
        }
 2. // ex14_2.cpp
    // imitates COPY command
    #include <fstream.h>               // for file functions
    #include <process.h>               // for exit()

    void main(int argc, char* argv[] )
        {
        if( argc != 3 )
            { cerr << "\nFormat: ocopy srcfile destfile"; exit(-1); }
        char ch;                        // character to read

        ifstream infile;                // create file for input
        infile.open( argv[1] );         // open file
        if( !infile )                   // check for errors
            { cerr << "\nCan't open " << argv[1]; exit(-1); }

        ofstream outfile;                       // create file for output
        outfile.open( argv[2], ios::noreplace );  // open file
        if( !outfile )                  // check for errors
            { cerr << "\nCan't open " << argv[2]; exit(-1); }

        while( infile )                 // until EOF
            {
            infile.get(ch);             // read a character
            outfile.put(ch);            // write the character
            }
        }
 3. // ex14_3.cpp
    // displays size of file
    #include <fstream.h>               // for file functions
    #include <process.h>               // for exit()

    void main(int argc, char* argv[] )
        {
        if( argc != 2 )
            { cerr << "\nFormat: filesize filename"; exit(-1); }
        ifstream infile;                // create file for input
        infile.open( argv[1] );         // open file
        if( !infile )                   // check for errors
            { cerr << "\nCan't open " << argv[1]; exit(-1); }
        infile.seekg(0, ios::end);              // go to end of file
                                                // report byte number
        cout << "Size of " << argv[1] << " is " << infile.tellg();
        }
```

Chapter 15
Answers to Questions

1. a, b, c, d
2. #include directive
3. the project feature to compile the .CPP file and link the resulting .OBJ files
4. b, c
5. class library
6. true
7. c, d
8. true
9. b, d
10. a, c

Chapter 16
Answers to Questions

1. b
2. false; a different library file, and other changes, are necessary
3. AFX.H
4. MAFXCR.H
5. a, b, c
6. c
7. true
8. `file1.Open("who.dat", CFile::modeCreate | CFile::modeWrite);`
9. b
10. AFXCOLL.H
11. `CObject`
12. `arr1[5] = ptr;`
    and
    `arr1.SetAt(5, ptr);`
13. false; it's slow to insert a new element, but fast to iterate through an array
14. d
15. b, c, d
16. `list1.AddTail(new class1);`
17. key
18. d, e
19. saving or writing
20. a, c

Solutions to Exercises

1.
```cpp
// ex16_1.cpp
// anagram program -- exercises CString class

#define _DOS                       // for afx2.h
#include <afx2.h>                  // for collection classes
#include <iostream.h>              // for cout
#include <string.h>                // for strlen(), strcpy()

void permute(UINT);               // prototype
char buffer[20];                  // for cin input

CString wd;                       // full-length word
UINT tlen;                        // total lenth of dw

void main()
   {
   cout << "\nEnter a word: ";    // get the word to permute
   cin >> buffer;
   wd = buffer;                   // make it a Cstring
   tlen = wd.GetLength();         // get its length
   permute(tlen);                 // permute and display it
   }

void permute(UINT len)            // re-arrange word
   {
   if(len < 2)                    // if one char left, we're done
      return;
   for(UINT j=0; j<len; j++)      // for every char in word
      {
      permute(len-1);            // permute all but first char
      if( len == 2 )             // display innermost perms
         cout << wd << " ";
      wd = wd.Left(tlen-len)     // rotate rightmost
         + wd.Right(len-1)       //    len characters
         + wd.Mid(tlen-len, 1);  //    one char left
      } // end for
   cout << endl;                 // new line
   } // end permute
```

2.
```cpp
// ex16_2.cpp
// CObList and user-defined Person class

#define _DOS                       // for afxcoll.h
#include <afxcoll.h>               // for collection classes
#include <iostream.h>              // for cout
#include <string.h>                // for strlen(), strcpy()

class Person : public CObject     // user-defined class
   {                              // derived from CObject
```

```
    private:
       char* name;
       int age;
    public:
       Person()                             // 0-arg constructor
          {
          name = new char;                  // make a zero-length
          name[0] = '\0';                   // string
          age = 0;
          }
       Person(const char* str, const int a) // 2-arg constructor
          {
          name = new char[ strlen(str)+1 ]; // use name and age
          strcpy(name, str);                // passed as
          age = a;                          // arguments
          }
       ~Person()                            // destructor
          { delete name; }
       void DisplayPerson()                 // display
          { cout << "name=" << name << ", age=" << age; }
       char* GetName()
          { return name; }
    };

void main()
   {
   CObArray persArr;           // define a CObArray array
   Person* pp;                 // pointer to Person

   Person* p1 = new Person("Bart", 23);    // create
   Person* p2 = new Person("Casey", 25);   // Persons
   Person* p3 = new Person("Red", 32);
   Person* p4 = new Person("Slade", 27);
   Person* p5 = new Person("Rich", 19);

   persArr.Add(p1);                 // put three Persons
   persArr.Add(p2);                 // in array
   persArr.Add(p3);

   cout << "\n\nArray has " << persArr.GetSize() << " members";

   // display the array elements
   for(int j=0; j<persArr.GetSize(); j++)
      {
      cout << "\nElement " << j << ": ";
      pp = (Person*)persArr[j];
      pp->DisplayPerson();
      }

   persArr[0] = p4;       // overwrite first element with "Slade"
   persArr.InsertAt(2, p5);    // insert "Rich" at index 2
```

737

```
        cout << "\n\nArray has " << persArr.GetSize() << " members";

        // display the array elements
        for(j=0; j<persArr.GetSize(); j++)
            {
            cout << "\nElement " << j << ": ";
            pp = (Person*)persArr[j];
            pp->DisplayPerson();
            }
    }  // end main
```

3. ```
   // ex16_3.cpp
   // imitates natural-language dictionary
   // demonstrate CMapStringToString class

   #define _DOS                    // for afxcoll.h
   #include <afxcoll.h>            // for collection classes
   #include <iostream.h>           // for cout

   const int MAXINP = 30;          // maximum length of keys, responses
   char key[MAXINP];               // buffer for keys
   char response[MAXINP];          // buffer for responses
   const int MAXDEF = 1000;        // maximum length of definitions
   char definition[MAXDEF];        // buffer for definitions

   void main()
       {
       CMapStringToString map;     // string-to-string map
       CString Cdefinition;
       while( response[0] != 'Q' && response[0] != 'q' )
           {
           cout << "\nI to insert an entry,"
                << "\nL to look up an entry,"
                << "\nQ to quit."
                << "\nEnter action to take: ";
           cin.getline(response, MAXINP);
           if( response[0]=='I' || response[0]=='i' )
               {
               cout << "\nEnter word to define: ";
               cin.getline(key, MAXINP);
               cout << "Enter definition ('$' to end): ";
               cin.getline(definition, MAXDEF, '$');
                                          // store key and definition
               map.SetAt((CString)key, (CString)definition);
               cin.getline(definition, MAXDEF);  // kill leftover chars
               }
           else if( response[0]=='L' || response[0]=='l' )
               {
               cout << "\nEnter word to look up: ";
               cin.getline(key, MAXINP);
                                          // look up the item
```
```

```
            map.Lookup((CString)key, Cdefinition);
            cout << "Definition of " << key << " is:\n"
                << Cdefinition << "\n";
            }
        }  // end while
    }  // end main

4. // ex16_4.cpp
   // imitates natural-language dictionary; archives to disk

   #define _DOS              // for afxcoll.h
   #include <afxcoll.h>      // for collection classes
   #include <iostream.h>     // for cout

   const int MAXINP = 30;    // maximum length of keys, responses
   char key[MAXINP];         // buffer for keys
   char response[MAXINP];    // buffer for responses
   const int MAXDEF = 1000;  // maximum length of definitions
   char definition[MAXDEF];  // buffer for definitions

   void main()
       {                                // string-to-string map
       CMapStringToString* pmap = new CMapStringToString;
       CString Cdefinition;
                                        // get dictionary from archive
       CFile* pFile = new CFile;
       if( pFile->Open("diction.dat", CFile::modeRead) )
          {
          CArchive carch(pFile, CArchive::load);
          carch >> pmap;
          carch.Close();
          pFile->Close();
          }
                                        // get selection from user
       while( response[0] != 'Q' && response[0] != 'q' )   // quit
          {
          cout << "\nI to insert an entry,"
               << "\nL to look up an entry,"
               << "\nQ to quit."
               << "\n" << pmap->GetCount() << " entries."
               << " Enter action to take: ";
          cin.getline(response, MAXINP);
          if( response[0]=='I' || response[0]=='i' )  // insert
             {                                        // entry
             cout << "\nEnter word to define: ";
             cin.getline(key, MAXINP);
             cout << "Enter definition ('$' to end): ";
             cin.getline(definition, MAXDEF, '$');
                                        // store key and definition
             pmap->SetAt((CString)key, (CString)definition);
             cin.getline(definition, MAXDEF);  // kill leftover chars
             }
```

```
         else if( response[0]=='L' || response[0]=='l' ) // look up
           {                                              // entry
           if( pmap->IsEmpty() )
              cout << "\nDictionary is empty\n";
           else
              {
              cout << "\nEnter word to look up: ";
              cin.getline(key, MAXINP);
                             // look up the item
              if( pmap->Lookup((CString)key, Cdefinition) )
                 cout << "Definition of " << key << " is:\n"
                      << Cdefinition << "\n";
              else
                 cout << "\nWord " << key << " not found\n";
              }
           } // end elseif
      } // end while
                          // store dictionary in archive
   pFile->Open("diction.dat",
              CFile::modeCreate | CFile::modeWrite);
   CArchive carch(pFile, CArchive::store);
   carch << pmap;
   carch.Close();
   pFile->Close();
}  // end main
```

BIBLIOGRAPHY

Here are some books that might prove interesting to students of object-oriented programming who are using Microsoft C++.

The ultimate reference to the C++ language is *The Annotated C++ Reference Manual*, by Margaret Ellis and Bjarne Strousstrup (Addison Wesley, Reading, MA, 1990). This is not a book for beginners, but as you become more proficient in C++ you will find yourself turning to it to resolve subtle points that other books don't mention. Eventually you will find it indispensable.

If you want to learn more about the C language, try *The Waite Group's C Programming Using Microsoft C*, by Robert Lafore (Howard W. Sams & Co., Carmel, IN, 1990). This book explains many details of how to program in the MS-DOS environment, including details of keyboard use and the process of speeding up the screen display with direct memory access. It also describes hardware-oriented language features that are common to both C and C++ but do not appear in the present book, such as bitwise operators and bitfields.

The Waite Group's Microsoft C Bible, by Naba Barkakati, 2nd Edition (Howard W. Sams & Co., Carmel, IN, 1990) provides a complete list and descriptions, with examples, of Microsoft C library functions.

No one book, including the present one, can cover every detail of C++. Here are several tutorial books that approach C++ from slightly different angles: *C++ for C Programmers*, by Ira Pohl (Benjamin/Cummings, Redwood City, CA, 1989) and *Teach Yourself C++*, by Al Stevens (MIS Press, Portland, OR, 1990). Both of these books assume you already know C, but the present book also gives you all the background you need to understand them.

For more on data structures such as linked lists and hash tables, not to mention all sorts of other topics such as searching and sorting, read *Algorithms*, by Robert Sedgewick (Addison Wesley, Reading, MA, 1988).

Computers, Pattern, Chaos and Beauty, by Clifford A. Pickover (St. Martin's Press, New York, 1990) is filled with fascinating material, not only on fractals, but on using computer graphics to show chaos, the Mandelbrot set, and other mathematical ideas. The illustrations make it fun to read, and program listings make it easy to reproduce the results on your computer.

If you're interested in fractals, try *The Waite Group's Fractal Creations*, by Tim Wegner and Mark Peterson (Waite Group Press, Mill Valley, CA, 1991). This is an addicting software product that demonstrates fractals and the Mandelbrot set. It's accompanied by a sizable book that explores many byways of the fractal world, while also explaining the operation of the program.

You can read about Conway's game of Life, among other topics (many of which are related in some way to computer programming), in *Wheels, Life, and Other Mathematical Amusements*, by Martin Gardner (W. H. Freeman Co., New York, 1983).

INDEX

! logical NOT, 117–118
!= not equal to, 79–80
" " header delimiters, 72
header prefix, 41–42
% remainder operator, 64–65
%= remainder-assignment, 65–66
& address of, 419–420
& reference to, 180–181
&& logical AND, 115–116
* indirection operator, 424
   vs. pointer to, 424
* pointer to, 421
   vs. indirection operator, 424
*= multiplication-assignment, 65–66
+ addition, 67
   overloading, 292–302
+= addition–assignment, 65–67
   overloading, 305–307
++ increment, 67
–– decrement, 69
–= subtraction-assignment, 65–66
–> membership access operator, 449
. class member access operator, 213
. dot operator, 135–137
/= division-assignment, 65–66
:: scope resolution operator, 222–223
   example of use, 335–337
; statement terminator, 39
< less than, 79–80
   overloading, 320–304
<< insertion operator
   cascading, 51, 56–57
   defined, 40
   vs. bitwise left shift, 40
<= less than or equal to, 79–80
< > header delimiters, 72
== equal to, 79–80
   overloading, 304–305
= assignment operator
   defined, 46
   overloading, 499–500

> greater than, 79–80
>= greater than or equal to, 79–80
>> extraction operator
   cascading, 51
   defined, 50
   overloading, 548–549
? *expression* : conditional, 112–115
\' single quote, 49
\" double quote, 49
\\ backslash, 49
\0 null denotation, 268
\a bell (beep), 49
\b backspace, 49
\f formfeed, 49
\n newline, 49
\r return, 49
\t tab, 49
\xdd hexadecimal, 49
|| logical OR, 117
~ destructor prefix, 219–220

Accessibility, 328–332
Addition-assignment operator (+=), 65–67
Addition operator (+), 67
   overloading, 292–302
Address of operator (&), 419–420
ADELSEIF.CPP, 107
ADIFELSE.CPP, 103–104
ADSWITCH.CPP, 110–111
ADVENAND.CPP, 115–116
ADVENOR.CPP, 117
AMBIGU.CPP, 360–361
Answers to questions and exercises
   Chapter 1, 689
   Chapter 3, 689–691
   Chapter 4, 691–694
   Chapter 5, 694–696
   Chapter 6, 697–700
   Chapter 7, 700–703
   Chapter 8, 703–707
   Chapter 9, 707–712

Answers to questions and exercises (Cont.)
Chapter 10, 712–717
Chapter 11, 717–722
Chapter 12, 723–727
Chapter 13, 727–732
Chapter 14, 732–734
Chapter 15, 735
Chapter 16, 735–740

Arguments
command-line, 545–547
default, 191–193
defined, 38, 69, 167
naming, 173
objects as function, 220–221
parameters vs., 168
reference, 178–184
strings as function, 438–439
Arrays
accessing elements
using array notation, 246
using pointer notation, 432–437
accessing objects in, 262–263
arrays of, 250–251
averaging **float** elements, 246–247
basics, 243–244
bounds of, 261–262
class member data, as, 256–260
defining, 244–245
elements defined, 245
index defined, 246
initializing, 247–249
inserting strings into, 440
multidimensional, 248–252
accessing elements, 251
defining, 250
initializing, 252
objects, of, 260–267
passing to functions
using array notation, 253–255
using pointer notation, 432–433
pointers, and, 426–428
pointers to objects, of, 450–452, 457–461
pointers to strings, of, 441–442
sorting elements, 433–437
string pointers, of, 441–442
strings, of, 273–275
structures, of, 255–256

ARRNOTE.CPP, 426–427
ASCII character set, 47
table with IBM characters, 679–682
ASSIGN.CPP, 65–66
ASSIGN.CPP, 499–501
ASSIGN2.CPP, 512–513
Assignment statements
defined, 46
overloading the operator, 499–500
reviewed, 498
Associativity, 433
auto, 193
Automatic variables, 193–195

Backslash (\\), 49
Backspace (\b), 49
BASIC, 3
Bell (or beep) (\ a), 49
BLANKSIN.CPP, 270
Boolean
types, 151–152
values, 115
BOXES.CPP, 377–383
Braces ({}), 38
break statement
within loops, 119–121
within **switch** statements, 109–110
Browser basics, 31–32
Bubble sort, 435–437
Buffer overflow, avoiding, 268–269
Build process
basics, 26–27
with debug options, 30

C, 3
vs. C++, 14–16
CALC.CPP, 561–567
CALC.H, 560–561, 563–567
CALC_APP.CPP, 567–570
CARDARAY.CPP, 263–267
CARDENUM.CPP, 152–154
CARDOBJ.CPP, 228–231
CARDS.CPP, 145–147
case, 108–109
CAST.CPP, 62–63
Casts, basics of, 62–64, 308
cerr object, 545

CFILE.CPP, 603–605
.C file suffix, 24
Characters
  constants, 47
  variables, 47
CHARVARS.CPP, 47–49
CHCOUNT.CPP, 102–103
cin, 50, 543
  getche() vs., 101
cin::get(), 270
CIRCAREA.CPP, 52–54
Classes
  abstract
    defined, 344
    example, 483–486
  access specifiers, 330–332, 346–347
  arrays as member data in, 256–260
  base
    accessing members of, 328–330
    defined, 12–13, 325
  basics of, 11–12
  classes within, 361–365
  derived
    constructors for, 332–334
    creating, 325–334
    defined, 12–13, 325
    privately, 345–347
    publicly, 345–347
    specifying, 328
  examples of, 207, 212–213, 217–219
  friend, 494–495
  hierarchies of, 340–344
  member functions, overriding, 334–337
  Microsoft Foundation, 597–643
  self-referencing, 456
  specifiers
    defined, 209
    member functions within, 212
    syntax illustrated, 211
  stack, 257–260
  static data in, 233–236
  stream, 524–525
  string, memory efficient, 504–510
  string, using new, 446–447
  strings as members of, 274–275
  strings in graphics, 404–410

Classes (Cont.)
  structures, vs., 131, 147, 231–232
  very long number, 571–577
  virtual base, 486–487
  See also Microsoft Foundation Class Library
_clearscreen(), 377
clock(), 403
clog object, 545
CodeView basics, 30–31
Coercion, 64
COLORBAL.CPP, 386–389
Colors
  _setcolor() function, 387–388
  table of text-mode, 381
COMLINE.CPP, 545–546
Command-line arguments, 545–547
Comments
  alternative syntax for, 43
  basics of, 42–43
Compiling, 24–27
CONDI.CPP, 114–115
Conditional operator, 112–115
Constants
  character
    basics, 47–48
  floating-point
    basics, 53
  integer
    basics, 46
  pointer, 428–429
  string, 40–41, 269–270
const defined, 54
Constructors
  base class, substituting, 328–329
  basics, 216–219
  copy, 501–505
  derived class, 332–334, 356–360
  implicit, 222
  multi-argument, 359
  multiple inheritance, in, 356–360
  new operator in, 446–447
  overloaded, 221–222
  syntax, 218
Containership, 361–365
continue statement, 122–123
Control statement defined, 79

Conversions
  automatic type, 61–62
  by casting, 62–64, 308
  implicit vs. explicit, 308
  objects and basic types, between, 308–310
  objects of different classes, between, 313–317
  pitfalls involved, 318–319
  strings and string objects, between, 312–313
  table summary, 320
  type, 61–64
  user-defined and basic types, between, 310–312
  user-defined type, 140–141
  when to use what, 317
CONVERT.CPP, 173–175
CONVERT2.CPP, 176
COPYSTR.CPP, 440–441
COUNTEN.CPP, 327–332
COUNTEN2.CPP, 332–334
COUNTER.CPP, 217–219
COUNTPP1.CPP, 286–288
COUNTPP2.CPP, 288–289
COUNTPP3.CPP, 290
COUNTPP4.CPP, 291–292
cout basics, 40
  formatted numbers, 251–252
.CPP file suffix, 24
CSTDIO.CPP, 605–606
CSTRING.CPP, 599–601
CTIME.CPP, 601–602
CUBELIST.CPP, 84–85
Cursor commands in editor, 25

DAROBJ.CPP, 537–540
Data hiding, 209–210
Data types
  enumerated, 148–155
  objects as user-defined, 215–216
  string, user-defined, 276–278
  unsigned, 59–61
DAYENUM.CPP, 148–151
DAYS.CPP, 247–248
DEBUG.CPP, 638–640
Debugging
  basics, 30–31

Debugging (Cont.)
  library classes for, 636–643
  pointers, 461–462
  with class ID numbers, 495
DEBUGOB.CPP, 641–642
Decision basics, 94
Declarations
  defined, 45
  function, 162–163
  vs. definitions, 45
Declarator defined, 164, 166
Decrement operator (--), 69
default, 111
#define, 54
Definitions
  blocks, within, 85
  defined, 44–45
  multiple, 57
  vs. declarations, 45
delete, 446–447
Dereferencing, 424
Design case studies
  four-function calculator, 558–571
  very long number class, 571–577
  water distribution system, 577–592
Destructors
  debugging statements, containing, 498
  defined, 219–220
  delete in, 447
Directed acyclic graph, 328–329
DISKFUN.CPP, 531–534
DIVDO.CPP, 92–93
DIVDO2.CPP, 122
Division-assignment (/=), 65–66
DOS special file names, 547
DOTHIS.CPP, 511–512
double defined, 58–59
Dynamic binding, 473–474

Early binding, 474
_ellipse(), 384–386
else...if construction, 107
EMPCONT.CPP, 362–365
EMPLOY.CPP, 341–344
EMPLOY2.CPP, 348–350
EMPMULT.CPP, 352–356
endl, 54–55

End-of-file (EOF), detecting, 527
ENDON0.CPP, 88
ENGLARAY.CPP, 260–261
ENGLCON.CPP, 220–225
ENGLCONV.CPP, 309–310
ENGLDISP.CPP, 170–173
ENGLEN.CPP, 337–340
ENGLESS.CPP, 302–304
ENGLIO.CPP, 549–550
ENGLMULT.CPP, 356–360
ENGLOBJ.CPP, 215–216
ENGLPLEQ.CPP, 305–307
ENGLPLUS.CPP, 292–295
ENGLPTR.CPP, 448–449
ENGLREF.CPP, 449–450
ENGLRET.CPP, 225–228
ENGLSTRC.CPP, 139–141
Enumerated data types, 148–155
Error handling, file I/O, 540–542
Errors
    assignment/equality operator confusion, 80
    compiler, 28–29, 32
    conceptual, 30
    linker, 29–30
    run-time
        defined, 30
        integer divide by 0, 122
        null pointer assignment, 462
Escape sequences
    basics, 48–49
    table of, 49
Exceptions
    generating, 629–633
    handling, 624–629
exit(), 98–99
Expressions
    assignment, 102–103
    defined, 51
    true/false without relational operators, 118
External variables, 195–197
EXTERN.CPP, 195–196
Extraction operator (>>)
    cascading, 51
    defined, 50
    overloading, 548–549
EZBALL.CPP, 384–386

FACTOR.CPP, 86
Factorials, 86–87
FAHREN.CPP, 50–51
FERRORS.CPP, 541–542
FIBO.CPP, 91–92
Fibonacci series, 91
File pointers, 534–537
Files, copying, 545
FIRST.CPP, 23–30
float
    basics, 52–53
    precision, 52
    range, 52
Floating-point
    basics, 52–53
    constants, 53
    variables, types of, 52
_floodfill(), 387–388
Fonts available, Microsoft C++, 409
FORDEMO.CPP, 81
Formatting numbers, 251–252
Formfeed (\f), 49
Fortran, 3
Fractals, 649–656
Frame window, 381
FRENGL.CPP, 491–492
FRICLASS.CPP, 494–495
FRIEND.CPP, 488–489
friend functions
    basics, 487–489
    examples, 489–492
    functional notation, for, 492–494
fstream class, 524, 533
Functions
    basics, 37–38, 161–162
    calling, 163
        with array arguments, 254
    declarations
        array arguments, with, 254
        basics, 162–163
        naming arguments in, 173
        omitting, 164–166
    default arguments for, 191–193
    definitions of, 164–165
        declarator portion, 164, 166
        with array arguments, 254–255

Functions (Cont.)
  friend, 487–495
  inline, 189–191
  library functions, vs., 164
  overloaded
    different kinds of arguments, 187–189
    different numbers of arguments,
      185–187
  passing arguments to
    by pointer, 430–431
    by reference
      illustration of, 181
      simple data types, 179–183, 429–430
      structures, 183–184
    by value, 169–171
    constants, 167–168
    structure variables, 170–173
    variables, 168–169
  prototypes, 162–163
  returning objects from, 225–228
  returning values from, 173–175
  static, 495–498
  syntax illustrated, 165
  virtual, 469–486
    non-virtual functions, difference
      between, 474–478

getche(), 100–102
  cin vs., 101
  getch() vs., 102
Get from operator
  See Extraction operator
Global variables
  See External variables
Golden ratio, 91
goto statement, 123
Graphics functions
  graphics mode
    _ellipse(), 384–386
    _floodfill(), 387–388
    hardware requirements, 373
    _lineto(), 390–391
    _moveto(), 389, 391
    _polygon(), 393–394
    _rectangle(), 389–390
    _setcolor(), 387–388

Graphics functions (Cont.)
    _setvideomode(), 384–385
  text functions
    _outgtext(), 408
    _registerfonts(), 407
    _setfont(), 408
    _setgtextvector(), 410
    _unregisterfonts(), 408
  text mode
    basics of, 373–374
    _clearscreen(), 377
    _outtext(), 376–377
    _settextcolor(), 379–381
    _settextposition(), 379–380,
      382–383
    _settextwindow(), 374–376,
      381–382
Graphics programs
  developing, 374
  ending, 386
  text in, 404–410
GRAST.CPP, 404–408

Hardware dependencies
  integer sizes, 61
Header files
  defined, 42
  I/O stream, 524–525
  library files vs., 70–72
  library functions, for, 70
Header prefix (#), 41–42
Hexadecimal (xdd), 49

IBM extended character set, 121
  illustrated in table, 679–682
IBM graphics characters, 265–266
IF2.CPP, 96–97
IFDEMO.CPP, 95
IFELSE.CPP, 99
if...else statements
  basics, 99–102
  nested, 103–107
  vs. switch, 112
if statements
  basics, 95–97
  inside loops, 97–98

ILINE.CPP, 526–527
Include files. *See* Header files
#include. *See* Preprocessor
INCREM.CPP, 67–69
Increment operator (++), 67
Indirect addressing, 424
Indirection operator (*), 424
    vs. pointer to, 424
Inheritance
    accessibility, 328–332
    basics of, 12–13, 325
    examples of
        complex, 337–340
        graphics, 391–395
        motion, 396–404
    levels of, 347–350
    multiple
        ambiguity in, 360–361
        constructors in, 356–360
        defined, 350
        example of, 396–404
        member functions in, 351–356
    trees, 328–329
Initializing
    objects, 498–499, 501–504
    variables
        automatic, 48, 195
        external, 196
        static, 198
        structure, 139
INLINE.CPP, 190–191
Inline functions, 189–191
Input
    cin basics, 50
    getche() library function, 100–102
    getche() vs. cin, 101
    redirecting, 544–545
    See also I/O
Insertion operator (<<)
    cascading, 51, 56–57
    defined, 40
    vs. bitwise left shift, 40
Instance defined, 208
Instance variable, 232
Integer divide by 0 error, 122
Integers
    basics, 43–45

Integers (Cont.)
    char, 47
    defining variables, 44
    long, 56–57
    sorting array of, 434–437
I/O
    character, 527–528
    error handling, 540–542
    file
        closing files, 540
        detecting end-of-file, 527
        member functions, using, 537–540
        reading strings, 526–527
        writing strings, 526
    multiple object, 531–532
    object
        binary vs. text files, 529–530
        fstream class, using, 533–534
        reading an object, 530
        writing an object, 528–529
    redirection, 542–545
IOMANIP.H, 57
ios flags, table of, 544
IOSTREAM.H, 42, 524–525
IPERS.CPP, 530–531

Keywords defined, 46

Languages
    object-oriented, 7–14
    procedural, 3–6
Late binding, 473–474
Library files
    defined, 70
    header files vs., 70–72
    vendor-supplied, using, 555–557
    See also Microsoft Foundation Class Library
Library functions
    basics, 69–70
    non-library functions, vs., 164
    redefining, 410
    screen
        graphics mode, 383–391, 407–410
        text mode, 375–383
    string, 272–273, 277, 440–441
Life, 656–663
LIFE.CPP, 659–662

Lifetime of variables
   automatic, 193–194
   external, 197
   static automatic, 197
Line drawing, 389–391
LINESIN.CPP, 271
_lineto(), 390–391
Linked lists
   adding to, 454–455
   basics, 452–454
   displaying contents of, 455–456
Linking, 24–27
LINKLIST.CPP, 453–456
Local variables. *See* Automatic variables
Logical operators, 115–118
long, 56–57
long double defined, 58–59
Loops
   body of, 82
   continue statements within, 122–123
   do
      basics, 92–93
      operation illustrated, 95
      syntax illustrated, 94
      while loop vs., 92
   for
      basics, 81–86
      operation illustrated, 84
      syntax illustrated, 82
      variations, 86–87
      while loop vs., 87
   loop variable defined, 82
   when to use which, 93
   while
      basics, 87–88
      do loop vs., 92
      for loop vs., 87
      multiple statements in, 88–90
      operation illustrated, 90
      syntax illustrated, 89

main() defined, 38
Manipulators
   declarations header file, 57
   endl, 54–55
   setw, 54–56

MAPTOB.CPP, 620–622
MAPTOB2.CPP, 622–624
MATH.H, 70–71
Member functions
   accessing, in object pointers, 449, 452,
      470–471
   base class, substituting, 329–330
   calling, 212–214
   constructors, 216–219
   defined, 210
   defined outside the class, 222–223
   defining vs. declaring, 212
   destructors, 219–220
   overriding, 334–337
   virtual, accessing with pointers, 471–474
Membership access operator (–>), 449
Memory management, 442–447
Messages defined, 214
Methods defined, 210
Microsoft C/C++
   installing
      without Windows installed, 22
      with Windows installed, 21–22
   manual list, annotated, 32–33
Microsoft C++ keywords list, 683
Microsoft Foundation Class Library
   data structures
      arrays, 607–611
      lists, 611–619
      maps, 619–624
      overview, 606–607
   date and time, 601–602
   debugging, 636–643
   exceptions
      basics of handling, 624–626
      file, 628–629
      generating, 629–633
      memory, 627–628
   files
      buffered text, 605–606
      unbuffered binary, 603–605
   preparing your system to use, 597–598
   serializing objects, 633–636
   strings, 599–601
   time and date, 601–602
MISSARG.CPP, 191–192

MIXED.CPP, 61–62
_moveto(), 389, 391
MROUND.CPP, 492–494
Multi-file programs
    examples of, 558–571, 571–577, 577–592
    purposes of, 555–558
Multiplication-assignment (*=), 65–66
MULTSHAP.CPP, 391–394

Naming variables, 45–46
new, 444–447, 449–450
NEWINTRO.CPP, 444
Newline (\n), 49
NEWSTR.CPP, 446–447
NOFRI.CPP, 489–491
NORMBASE.CPP, 486–487
Not equal to (!=), 79–80
NOTVIRT.CPP, 470–471
Null character (\n), 268
Numbers
    formatting, 251–252
    random, obtaining, 266–267
    strings, as, 572

Object-oriented programming, overview of,
        7–14
Objects
    arrays of, 260–267
    basics of, 9–11
    defining, 212
    functions arguments, as, 220–221
    nameless temporary, 289–290
    pointers to, 448–452
        array of, 450–452, 457–461
    return results from functions, as, 225–228
    serializing, 633–636
    user-defined data types, as, 215–216
.OBJ file suffix, 25
OBJPART.CPP, 214–215
OCHAR.CPP, 527–528
OLINE.CPP, 526
open function, 533–534
Operand defined, 286
operator
    arguments, 287–288
    defined, 287
    return values, 288–290

Operators
    address of (&), 419–420
    arithmetic
        addition (+), 67
            overloading, 292–302
        assignment, 65–67
        overloading, 292–302
        remainder (%), 64
    assignment (=)
        defined, 46
        overloading, 499–500
    class member access (.), 213
    conditional, 112–115
    decrement (––), 69
    delete, 446–447
    dot (.), 135–137
    extraction (>>), 50
        overloading, 548–549
    increment (++), 67
    indirection (*), 424
        vs. pointer to, 424
    insertion (<<)
        cascading, 51, 56–57
        defined, 40
        vs. bitwise left shift, 40
    logical
        AND (&&), 115–116
        NOT (!), 117–118
        OR (||), 117
    manipulators
        endl, 54–55
        setw, 54–56
    membership access (–>), 449
    new, 444–447, 449–450
    overloaded
        arguments of, 294
        defined, 40
    overloading
        arithmetic, 292–302
        arithmetic-assignment, 305–307
        binary, 292–307
        comparison, 302–305
        pitfalls involved, 318–319
        unary, 286–292
    precedence summary, 118–119
    Reference to (&), 180–181
    relational, 79–81

Operators (Cont.)
  scope resolution (::), 222–223
    example of use, 335–337
  uninheritable, 501
  unoverloadable, 319
OPERS.CPP, 529–531
OPRINT.CPP, 548
OTYPE.CPP, 546–547
_outgtext(), 408
Output
  field widths, 55–56
  printer, 547–548
  redirecting, 543–544, 545
  See also I/O; cout
_outtext(), 376–377
OVERENGL.CPP, 187–189
OVERLOAD.CPP, 185–187
Overloaded functions, 185–189
Overloaded operators, 40
Overloading
  arithmetic operators, 292–302
  binary operators, 292–307
  comparison operators, 302–305
  multiple, defined, 302
  pitfalls involved, 318–319
  unary operators, 286–292

Paradigm, 3
Parameters
  arguments vs., 168
  defined, 168
Parentheses after function names, 38
  when empty, 162
PARTARAY.CPP, 255–256
PARTINIT.CPP, 138
PARTSCOM.CPP, 137–138
PARTS.CPP, 132
Pascal, 3
PASSARR.CPP, 432–433
PASSPTR.CPP, 430–431
PASSREF.CPP, 429–430
PERSLST.CPP, 616–619
PERSORT.CPP, 457–461
PIPES.CPP, 585–592
PIPES.H, 583–585
PIPE_APP.CPP, 589

PLATTERS.CPP, 108–110
Pointers
  array of pointers, to, 461
  arrays, and, 426–428
  basics of, 417–418
  constants, 428–429
  debugging, 461–462
  file, 534–537
  objects, to, 448–452
  passing to functions, 430–431
  pointers to, 457–461
  string constants, to, 438
  string copying using, 440
  string variables, to, 438
  syntax of, 421–422
  this, 225, 510–515
  variables, 420–426, 428–429
  void, to, 425–426
POLAPLUS.CPP, 298–300
Polar coordinates, 295–300
POLAREC1.CPP, 314–315
POLAREC2.CPP, 316–317
_polygon(), 393–394
Polymorphism basics, 14, 469–470
Popping from stack, 258–259
Postfix notation, 67–69
  in objects, 291–292
Precedence
  defined, 52
  illustrated, 91–92, 102–103
  operators with the same, 433
  summary of operators, 118–119
Prefix notation, 67–69
Preprocessor
  #define, 54
  defined, 41
  directives defined, 41
  #include
    defined, 41
    delimiters for, 72
PRIME.CPP, 98–99
Printer output, 547–548
private
  basics, 209–210, 330–331
  derivation, 356
  inheritance, 344–347

Procedural languages, 3–6
Programmer's WorkBench (PWB)
    compiling, 24–27
    editor basics, 23, 25
    linking, 24–27
    project feature, 685–687
    starting up, 22–23
Programming guidelines, C++
    base class design, 332
    data conversion, 318–319
    expressions in **return** statements, 176
    function declaration return types, 175
    function placement in source code
        inline, 191
        non-inline, 164–166
    operator overloading, 318–319
    pointer initializing, 422
    variable type size, 59
Programming style
    brace placement, 86
    indentation, loop body, 85–86
    loop variable definition placement, 87
    member function layout, 210–211
    naming conventions, 46
    parentheses in expressions, 176
    white space, use of, 39–40
Programs
    basic design of, 37–40
    design case studies
        four-function calculator, 558–571
        very long number class, 571–577
        water distribution system, 577–592
    naming of source code, 24
    running, 27
    saving, 24
protected, 330–332, 366
PTRACC.CPP, 422–424
PTRINC.CPP, 429
PTRNOTE.CPP, 427–428
PTROBJS.CPP, 450–452
PTRORDER.CPP, 434
PTRSORT.CPP, 434–437
PTRSTR.CPP, 438–439
PTRTO.CPP, 424
PTRTOSTR.CPP, 442
PTRVAR.CPP, 420–421

PTRVOID.CPP, 426
public
    basics, 209–210, 330
    inheritance, 344–347
    vs. **protected**, 331
PUBPRIV.CPP, 345–346
Pushing onto stack, 258
Put to operator. *See* Insertion operator
PWB. *See* Programmer's WorkBench

Quotes (\\') and (\\"), 49

rand(), 266
_rectangle(), 389–390
Rectangles, drawing, 389–391
RECTLINE.CPP, 389–391
Recursion, 655
REDIR.CPP, 542–545
Redirection, I/O, 542–545
REF.CPP, 179–181
Reference arguments, 178–184
Reference to operator (&), 180–181
REFERST.CPP, 183–184
REFORDER.CPP, 182–183
_registerfonts(), 407
RELAT.CPP, 79–80
Relational operators, 79–81
REMAIND.CPP, 64–65
Remainder operator (%), 64–65
Remainder-assignment (%=), 65–66
REPLAY.CPP, 243–244
RETSTRC.CPP, 177–178
Return character (\\r), 49
Returning values
    arithmetic-assignment operators, with, 307
    basics, 69–70
    Boolean values, 304
    by reference, 199–200
    illustrated, 175
    return statement basics, 174–175
    structure variables, 177–178
    using **this**, 512–513
Running programs, 27

SAFETYIN.CPP, 269
SALEFUNC.CPP, 253–255

SALEINIT.CPP, 252
SALEMON.CPP, 248–251
SALES.CPP, 246–247
Saving programs, 24
Scope resolution operator (::), 222–223
   example of use, 335–337
seekg() function, 534–537
SEEKG.CPP, 535–537
Semicolon (;) as statement terminator, 39
SERIAL.CPP, 634–636
_setcolor(), 387–388
_setfont(), 408
_setgtextvector(), 410
_settextcolor(), 379–381
_settextposition(), 379–380,
   382–383
_settextwindow(), 374–376, 381–382
_setvideomode(), 384–385
   common constants for, table of, 385
setw, 54–56, 269
short defined, 58
SHOWPRIM.CPP, 119–120
SIGNTEST.CPP, 60–61
SLIBCE.LIB, 70–71
SLOT.CPP, 396–404
SMALLOBJ.CPP, 207–214
Sorting
   bubble, 435–437
   integer arrays, 434–437
   pointers, 459
Source files
   defined, 25
   loading existing, 27–28
Specifiers
   class, 209
sqrt()
   as library function, 69–70
   header needed for, 70
SQRT.CPP, 69–70
srand(), 266
Stacks
   basics, 256–259
   class. 257–260
     derived, 334–337
STAKARAY.CPP, 257–259
STAKEN.CPP, 334–337
Standard output stream. *See* **cout**

STATDATA.CPP, 234–235
Statements defined, 38–39
STATFUNC.CPP, 496–498
Static binding, 474
Static class data, 233–236
STATIC.CPP, 197–198
Static functions, 495–498
Static variables, 197–198
STRARAY.CPP, 273–274
strcat(), 277
strcmp(), 305, 459
STRCONV.CPP, 312–313
STRCOPY1.CPP, 271–272
STRCOPY2.CPP, 272–273
strcpy(), 272–273
Streams
   classes, 524–525
   class hierarchy, 523–524
   defined, 40, 523
   flushing, 104–105
Stream status bits, 541
STREQUAL.CPP, 304–305
STRIMEM2.CPP, 513–515
STRIMEM.CPP, 504–510
STRING.H, 272
STRINGIN.CPP, 267
Strings
   arrays of, 273–275
   classes
     memory efficient, 504–510
     using **new**, 446–447
     See also Microsoft Foundation Class
      Library
   class members, as, 274–275
   comparing, 304–305, 459
   concatenating, 300–302
   constants, 40–41, 269–270
     pointers to, 438
   copying, 272–273
     using pointers, 440
   function arguments, as, 438–439
   graphics class for, 404–410
   library functions, 440–441
   reading from keyboard, 267–271
     multiple lines, 270–271
     with embedded spaces, 270
   user-defined type for, 276–278

Strings (Cont.)
  variables, 267–268
    pointers to 438
STRINIT.CPP, 269–270
strlen(), 272
STRLST2, 614–615
STRLST.CPP, 612–614
STROBJ.CPP, 276–278
STRPART.CPP, 274–275
STRPLUS.CPP, 300–302
struct defined, 133
Structured programming, 4, 195
Structures
  arrays of, 255–256
  basics, 131–132
  classes, vs., 131, 147, 231–232
  declarations, 133
  defining variables, 134–135
    while specifying, 137–138
  dot operator (.), 135–137
  example program, 139–141, 145–147
  members
    accessing, 135–137
    initializing, 138
  nested
    accessing members, 142–143
    basics, 141–142
    depth of, 144
    initializing, 144
  self-referencing, 456
  specifier syntax, 133
  specifying, 132–134
    while defining, 137–138
  struct, 133
  variables
    assignments, in, 139
    defining, 134–135
      while specifying, 137–138
    initializing, 139
    returning, 177–178
Style. See Programming style
Subobject defined, 487
Subtraction-assignment operator (–=), 65–66
switch statement, 108–112
  operation illustrated, 111
  syntax illustrated, 109

switch statement (Cont.)
  vs. if...else, 112
  with char variables, 110

TABLE.CPP, 161–162
TABLE2.CPP, 165–166
TABLEARG.CPP, 167–168
Tab (\t), 49
tellg() function, 537
TENDRILS.CPP, 650–656
this, 225, 510–515
TICTAC.CPP, 665–675
Tic-Tac-Toe, 663–675
TWOSTR.CPP, 438
Type conversion
  automatic, 61–62
  defined, 61

_unregisterfonts(), 408
unsigned defined, 59–61

VARADDR.CPP, 419
VARARG.CPP, 168–169
Variables
  automatic, 193–195
  defining at point of use, 50–51
  eliminating unnecessary, 176
  expressions in place of, 176
  external, 195–197
  initializing
    automatic, 48, 195
    external, 196
    static, 198
  loop, 82, 87
  memory locations of, under MS-DOS, 198
  pointer, 420–426, 428–429
  scope re blocks, 85
  static, 197–198
  static automatic, 197
  static class vs. automatic member, 235
  storage classes and, 193–198
  string, 267–268
  summary of types, 58
  See also Characters; Floating-point; Integers
VERYLONG.CPP, 571–577
VERYLONG.H, 572–573

VIRTBASE, 487
VIRT.CPP, 471–473
VIRTEMP.CPP, 474–478
VIRTPERS.CPP, 479–482
VIRTPURE.CPP, 478–479
VIRTSHAP.CPP, 483–486
virtual, 470–487
Virtual functions
  basics, 469–474
  examples of, 474–482
  non-virtual functions, difference between,
    474–478
  pure, 478–479
Visibility of variables
  automatic, 195
  basics, 194–195
  external, 197
  static automatic, 197
VL_APP.CPP, 577
void
  defined, 38
  in function declarations, 162, 175

WDARRAY2, 608–609
WDARRAY3, 610–611
WDARRAY.CPP, 608
WDCOUNT.CPP, 151–152
WHERE.CPP, 511
WHILE4.CPP, 89–90
White space characters
  compiler's treatment of, 39–40
  defined, 39
WIDTH1.CPP, 55–56
WIDTH2.CPP, 55–56
WINDOW.CPP, 375–377
Windows
  text-mode
    frame window, 381
    windows within, 381–383
write(), 529

XCPTFILE.CPP, 628–629
XCPTFIL2.CPP, 630–631
XCPTFIL3.CPP, 632–633
XCPTMEM.CPP, 627–628
XOFXREF.CPP, 502–504

ing Books from Waite Group Press

The Waite Group's
FLIGHTS OF FANTASY
Programming 3-D Video Games in Borland C++
by Chris Lampton
Describes and teaches in detail how commercial quality three-dimensional animation is achieved in the latest video games. The book is written for intermediate level programmers who want to create 3-D effects using the latest techniques for polygon-fill graphics, joystick control, and digitized sound effects using the Sound Blaster board and compatibles. Besides the step-by-step instruction, **Flights of Fantasy** includes a complete flight simulator program. The complete source code for the simulator is provided so the reader can expand and customize it.
Available October 1992, $39.95, ISBN 1-878739-29-8, 500 pp, 7 × 9, One 5.25 inch disk included

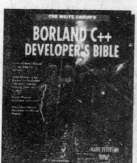

The Waite Group's
BORLAND C++ DEVELOPER'S BIBLE
by Mark Peterson
Completely covers the compilers, linkers, debuggers, assemblers, projects, and utilities needed to develop object-oriented C++ programs in both DOS and Windows environments. Covers Borland C++ 3.0, Turbo C++ for Windows, and Applications Framework including ObjectWindows.

Available August 1992, Rs 250/-

Qty	Book	Price	Total
____	OOP In Turbo C++	$29.95	_____
____	Turbo C++ For Windows How-To	$26.95	_____
____	Flights Of Fantasy	$39.95	_____
____	Master C	$44.95	_____
____	Master C++	$39.95	_____
____	Workout C	$39.95	_____
____	Windows API Bible	$39.95	_____
____	C++ Primer Plus	$26.95	_____
____	Fractal Creations	$34.95	_____
____	Visual Basic How-To	$34.95	_____
____	Visual Basic Super Bible	$39.95	_____

Calif. residents add 7.25% Sales Tax _____

Shipping
PS ($5 first book/$1 each add'l) _____
Two Day ($10/$2) _____

TOTAL _____

Ship to

Name _____

Company _____

Address _____

City, State, Zip _____

Phone _____

Payment Method

☐ Check Enclosed ☐ VISA ☐ MasterCard

Card# _____ Exp. Date _____

Signature _____

(783)

Related Object-Oriented Programm

The Waite Group's
OBJECT-ORIENTED PROGRAMMING IN TURBO C++
by Robert Lafore

Suitable for students, hackers, and enthusiasts, Lafore's step-by-step lessons teach the basics of object-oriented programming, focusing on C++ as a separate language, distinct from C, and assumes no prior experience with C. Specifically covers Turbo C++, Borland C++, and Borland BGI Graphics on the IBM PC family of computers. Includes objects, classes, overloading, constructors, inheritance, and virtual functions. End of chapter quizzes and exercises.

Available now, Trade paper, ISBN 1-878739-06-9, 776 pp., 7X9, Rs 250/-

The Waite Group's
TURBO C++ FOR WINDOWS HOW-TO
by Gary Syck

The easy-access question and answer problem-solving guide to Borland's ObjectWindows Library. Get up to speed on OWL and harness the power of object-oriented programming to easily add buttons, scroll bars, floating menus, dialog boxes, and other Windows elements to programs. The book is designed for the programmer with some C experience but little or no experience with C++ or Windows programming.

Available November 1992, 700 pp., 7X9, Rs 250/-

Write or call us for a unique catalog with more information about these and other Waite Group Press titles like:

Master C: Let the PC Teach You C, and **Master C++:** Let the PC Teach you Object-Oriented Programming. Both are book/disk software packages that turn your computer into an infinitely patient C professor.

Workout C: Learn C through Exercises. Hundreds of C projects and exercises and a full-featured C compiler make this an unbeatable training program and value.

Windows API Bible: The only comprehensive guide to the 800 functions and messages in the Windows Application Programming Interface.

C++ Primer Plus: Teach yourself Object-Oriented Programming. Written by Steven Prata in the same style as his C Primer Plus, which won the coveted Computer Press Association's "Best How-To Computer Book Award" and sold over 400,000 copies.

Fractal Creations: Explore the Magic of Fractals on your PC. The bestselling book/software package that made the complexity of fractals understandable and available for fascination and fun on any PC.

Visual Basic How-To and **Visual Basic Super Bible:** Both books cover the unique Microsoft language that makes Windows programming much more accessible. **How-To** covers tricks, tips, and traps of VB programming. **Super Bible** is the ultimate compendium of reference information on VB.

And check our catalog for more exciting and informative forthcoming Waite Group Press titles like **Virtual Reality Playhouse, Image Lab, Windows Programming Primer Plus, Object Oriented Programming In Microsoft C++, Multimedia Creations, Fractals Fo Windows, Ray Tracing Creations,** and **Falcon 3: Complete Handbook.**

Waite Group Press Publishes Books and Software That Take You From How? To